"Distinguished Oklahomans"

Victoria Lee

Preassigned LCCN: 2001-129315
ISBN 1-888225-23-8

A Touch of Heart Publishing
P.O. Box 470212
Tulsa, Oklahoma 74147-0212

Table of Contents

In order to rightly identify the people profiled, I think it is imperative to define the word "Distinguished" that so wonderfully describes each participant. It is very important you do not link the word "Distinguished" to the amount of monetary gain a person might have obtained, but simply the expression of who they are inside that has created their "Distinguished" attributes. In doing so, you will find individuals from every walk of life that are worthy of the title "Distinguished Oklahoman."

Distinguished

Characterized by excellence or distinction, eminent, renowned, dignified in conduct or appearance.

Excellence - The state, quality or condition of excelling, superiority, pre-eminence. Something in which a person or thing excels, a surpassing feature or virtue.

Distinction - The condition or fact of making a difference. A distinguishing factor, attribute or characteristic. Excellence or eminence as of performance, character or reputation. Recognition of achievement or superiority and honor.

Eminent - Towering above others - outstanding in performance or character - noteworthy - esteemed for his great
achievements - to stand out or project.

Renowned - The quality of being widely honored and acclaimed.

Dignified - Having or expressing dignity - The presence of poise and self-respect to the degree that inspires respect. Inherent nobility and worth.
The respect and honor associated with an important position - worthy.

Special Thanks

I want to thank the many individuals who gave of their time to interview with me. I know they must have thought I was never going to finish this book especially when none of us expected the project to take such a long time to accomplish. It certainly has been the most time consuming and yet rewarding project I have ever completed. My prayer is that in honoring the people profiled others will be able to grab onto the brass ring of wisdom that will take them also to heights they never knew were attainable.

Christy Wheeland has been extremely valuable to me during this whole 3 and a half year long pursuit. As the editor she has not only spent numerous hours editing, but her smile, her upbeat personality, her "you can do it girl" words of encouragement as well as her many notes and cards helped me tremendously.

Thanks Christy.

My daughter, Kimberlee Clark is a hair stylist and has always had the ability to transform a bad hair day into a glamour shot pose. Thanks to her make-up techniques and styling abilities I was able to include a picture of myself in the conclusion that I was proud of.

Thanks Kimberlee

Last, but certainly not least, thanks to Dale Dobbins for his steadfast friendship and longlasting belief in my writing talent. He stood by me protecting me from others who couldn't entirely appreciate my dedication to the project. He made sure life was made a little easier while my hands were glued to the keys of my computer. On many occasions he rewarded my efforts by escorting me to some of Tulsa's finest eating establishments. All in all, he helped make this project become a reality for which I will forever be grateful.

Thanks Dale

Ray Ackerman

Advertising

The Ackerman McQueen Advertising Agency has become the biggest agency headquartered in Oklahoma. How interesting that a man from Pittsburgh, Pennsylvania would choose the state of Oklahoma as the foundation for his success.

From the instant I sat down in Ray Ackerman's office to begin our interview I felt amazingly at home. Some people have a knack at being a friend to all and I think Mr. Ackerman is one of those people.

Like a lot of individuals, after graduating from high school Ray didn't know what he wanted to do with his life. What seemed appropriate was to follow in his father's footsteps and become an accountant. He went to work for Mellon Bank in Pittsburgh and began taking courses at night studying accounting and business law.

However, that came to an end a couple of years later when he enlisted in the Navy shortly after Pearl Harbor and became a fighter pilot. After almost 5 years of active duty in the Navy he was discharged in 1947, once again he found himself seeking the next career direction for his life while flying in the Navy Reserve as a weekend warrior.

His older sister had been working as a publicist for the Ice Capades, being one of the first women to enter the man's field of sports publicity. While visiting his sister in Los Angeles she introduced him to some of her friends in the advertising agency business who fanned a spark of interest in Ray for the advertising business which began while serving in the Pacific.

On his way home to Pennsylvania he decided to make a short stop in Oklahoma City to visit an uncle who lived there, never knowing that this visit was getting ready to change the course of his life. When his uncle found out Ray was interested in advertising he secured an interview for him with the advertising manager of the Daily Oklahoman.

At the time, Ray had never considered living in Oklahoma. However, he decided to go to the interview since his uncle had gone to so much trouble. Not long after Ray's return to Pennsylvania he received a wire saying if he wanted the job, to report to the newspaper on June 12, 1947. Ray had seen enough of Oklahoma City on his visit to get excited about living there so he took the job and a new direction for his life began. His duties were to call on retail merchants and sell them advertising space in both the Daily Oklahoman and The Oklahoma City Times.

For the next five years Ray continued to work for the newspapers, received a degree from night school at Oklahoma City University and flew one weekend a month and two weeks in the summer out of the Naval Air Station in Dallas. Upon graduating from college he asked his employer on many occasions what his future was at the newspaper. After never getting a satisfactory answer he decided it was time to join an advertising agency.

George W. Knox had established an agency on January 1, 1939 and had the reputation of having one of the best agencies in Oklahoma City. Mr. Knox wanted to move to Colorado and needed someone to take over his business. Ray seemed to be just the right man capable of building on Mr. Knox's success, so Ray was hired in 1952.

Ray was indeed a natural and in two years he was able to purchase the company from Mr. Knox. It was renamed the Knox Ackerman Agency and two years later it became Ackerman Associates. From 1952 to 1972 the agency grew from $250 thousand in billings to $5 million in billings. Mr. Ackerman said the success of an advertising agency is based on its creativity, so he tried successfully to maintain the creative reputation established by Mr. Knox. In 1967, he opened an office in Tulsa.

He had always dreamed of building an agency big enough to handle the biggest account headquartered in Oklahoma, so he merged with a company in New York which at the time was the 12th largest agency in the world. He sold 80% of his company to the New York agency, thinking this action would help make his dream come true. Two years later Mr. Ackerman and the agency's employees bought the company back from the New York agency when it got into financial difficulties.

During this New York upheaval Ray met Marvin McQueen, a senior vice-president with the New York office of the Darcy Agency who was interested in moving to Tulsa where his only daughter lived. He joined the Ackerman Agency in 1972 and a year later his son, Angus came aboard as well. This resulted in success for all. In 1980 the company name was changed to Ackerman McQueen; in the 80's offices were added in Dallas and Washington, D.C.

Mr. Ackerman retired from active participation in the company in 1992 when billings reached $92 million. In 2000, billings had grown to $250 million. His military career spanned 35 years, most of which were in the active Reserve and he retired with the rank of Rear Admiral. Mr. Ackerman has had such a successful and fun life. His 52 year marriage to Lucille has rewarded them with six children, (another child passed away at infancy) and nine grandchildren.

As my interview with Mr. Ackerman concluded, he handed me a book he had written in 1964 titled *Tomorrow Belongs To Oklahoma*, which I have added to my own home library. Mr. Ackerman may have been born and raised in Pennsylvania, but he is definitely a loyal and successful Oklahoman. Along with many awards in his career, Mr. Ackerman was inducted into the Oklahoma Hall of Fame in 1993.

Troy Aikman – Athlete

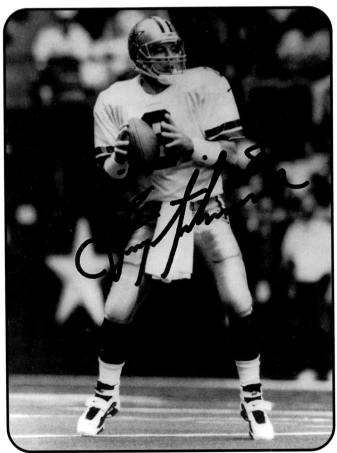

I don't know where a person could have possibly been all their life if they didn't recognize the name Troy Aikman.

Troy was born in West Covina, California on November 21, 1966 to Kenneth and Charlyn Aikman. As an infant Troy had a mild case of club feet. When he was 8 months old casts were put on both legs to straighten them and every two weeks for 6 months the casts had to be changed. Then until he was 3 years old he was forced to wear special shoes so his feet would continue to grow normally. Well, as we can all attest to, a shaky start certainly didn't hamper one of the nation's best football players.

Troy grew up in Cerritos, California, near Long Beach along with his two older sisters Terri and Tammy. Even at a young age he was extremely motivated to play sports. At one time he dreamed of becoming a pro baseball player and practiced signing his name on blank sheets of paper so he would be ready when the time came and someone asked for his autograph.

At age 12 Troy's parents decided to move from the suburbs of sunny California to a small town of 6,000 people in Henryetta, Oklahoma. The move was a total culture shock to Troy. Not only did they leave behind suburban life in California, but they traded it for farm life on a 172 acre plot of land which included chores that Troy was not accustomed to.

He enrolled in the eighth grade, that fall and immediately made friends, so country living didn't seem quite as bad after all. He signed up for junior high football and quickly realized that people in Oklahoma are crazy about football.

His first varsity game he was a sophomore for the Henryetta High School Fighting Hens. The school had been tagged as being a losing team and was ridiculed quite a bit for their Fighting Hens nickname. Even though they didn't win a title Troy did throw a touchdown pass for the victory against Checotah in his first varsity game.

His junior year the team lost their first eight games, yet they still made the state playoffs. It was the school's first playoff team in 25 years.

In Troy's senior year the team didn't make the playoffs, but they did finish 6-4, which caused Troy to be sought after by college football coaches.

Coach Jimmy Johnson was doing a pretty good job convincing Troy to play for Oklahoma State University, but Coach Barry Switzer finally won out and Troy signed up for the Sooners at the University of Oklahoma.

Troy's first season they played the University of Kansas and were ranked No.2 in the country, but lost 22-11.

Oklahoma University entered the 1985 season rated No. 1 in the country and won their first three games. On the fourth game playing against Miami, Troy was tackled which painfully resulted in a broken ankle.

The next season Troy transferred to UCLA and finished his UCLA career as the third-highest rated passer in NCAA history. His last college game was played in Dallas at the Cotton Bowl, where they beat Arkansas 17-3. In 1989 he returned to Dallas and signed an $11 million contract with the Dallas Cowboys playing for their newly appointed coach Jimmy Johnson. He was rated as the number one overall draft pick for the NFL even though his first year in the NFL was a disaster. In the fourth game of the season he broke a finger on his left hand. Then his first game back he was knocked out and lay unconscious for 8 minutes. He finished his rookie season with the worst rating of all starting NFL quarterbacks. Yet defeat was not to reign in Troy's life. He became one of only three players to lead a team to three Super Bowl victories.

Troy of course has received many awards and recognitions throughout his career. He was given the Jim Thorpe Performance of the Year Award in 1992. He was the National Quarterback Association Pro Quarterback of the Year in 1993 as well as ESPN's Insider Quarterback and NFL Alumni Quarterback that same year.

In 1990 the town of Henryetta was extremely proud of Troy's accomplishments and acknowledged him by placing his name along with rodeo legend Jim Shoulders on a sign as you enter the town. Jim Shoulders told me about that event and said Troy would only agree to accepting the recognition if Jim Shoulders received top billing.

In addition Troy was named in Sports Illustrated as one of the 50 Greatest Sports Figures of the Century and Sporting News ranked him in the top 100 Players of the Century in 1999. Of course the list of awards and acknowledgements Troy has received is far too lengthy to list them all. He even had a cameo appearance in the movie "Jerry Maguire" starring Tom Cruise.

Troy has appeared on the "Tonight Show," the "Dave Letterman Show" and the "Regis & Kathy Lee Show," among others as well as several radio programs. He has two books to his credit - *Things Change* (a children's book released in 1995) and *Aikman: Mind, Body & Soul* -a pictorial autobiography released in 1998.

In 1992 Troy established the Troy Aikman Foundation. In 1995 his foundation made a donation to Children's Medical Center in Dallas for the funding of "Aikman's End Zone," an interactive playroom and education center for children staying at the hospital.

In 1997, Aikman's End Zone was opened at Cook Children's Medical Center in Fort Worth, and in 1998 one was opened in Oklahoma City followed by one in Houston in 2002.

After retirement in 2001 he began a broadcasting career with Fox Sports broadcasting NFL football games. In 2002 he was promoted to the #1 team as color analyst.

Of course swooning women all over the nation had to focus their energies elsewhere after Troy tied the knot and married Rhonda. Then the icing on the cake came when little Jordan Ashley was born and made Troy a father for the first time.

Carl Albert - Congressman

Carl Albert was the son of an Oklahoma coal miner and farmer, Ernest Homer Albert. His mother, Leona Ann Scott had originally come from Texas.

Carl was born on May 10, 1908 and two years later along came his brother Noal. Carl's father was working in the Bolen-Darnell mining camp near McAlester. The family lived in a four room house in the mining camp.

After a mining accident Carl's mother pleaded with her husband to quit the mining business. The only other thing he knew to do was farm so they moved to an area 10 miles northeast of McAlester called Bug Tussle. Bug Tussle was a rural school district which housed a couple of schools used also as community centers. The name Bug Tussle came about when a local resident complained about the swarm of bugs that always surrounded the kerosene lamps when they were holding functions at the community school house.

Ernest began farming a piece of bottomland he had rented along with his father and brother. The farmhouse was a double log cabin: two rooms separated by a breezeway. It was there that Carl's sister, Kathryn was born two weeks before his fifth birthday.

In 1917 they moved to another rental house a mile west and as times got better they were able to buy the house. There the last two brothers were born, Homer and Earl.

As a young boy, Carl had plenty of daily chores to perform on the farm before and after school. He learned at an early age the meaning of hard work and perseverance.

He started school in Bug Tussle in 1914 when he was 6 years old. That year he remembers Congressman Charles D. Carter coming to his class and remarking that someday someone in their class may grow up to be a congressman. It was something Carl never forgot. From that point on he had an insatiable thirst for learning. He had several teachers growing up and he talked very highly of them. Interestedly he remembered them all, something I wish I could do. It certainly links him to the love he had for education and his own ability to progress successfully in life.

When Carl graduated from Bug Tussle in 1922 the next step was to go to high school in McAlester a few miles away. But for a year he had no means of transportation to get him there. The next year was spent working on the farm until eventually his family moved to McAlester and moved into a house two miles from the school.

Carl first learned about public speaking from his teacher Perrill Munch. Every year in high school he entered the oratory contests that newspaper publishers were giving which offered winners a trip to Washington and a summer in Europe.

In 1927, his senior year, he won the contest. What would have made the experience much more rewarding would have been to share the excitement with his mother, but she passed away a year earlier at age forty after suffering the last few years with tuberculosis.

In the fall of 1927 he entered the University of Oklahoma where he continued his oratory skills and was determined he would work for the highest grades. There was a collegiate-level contest for oratory on the U.S. Constitution, and he was going to compete for it. He won. The money he earned, well over $4,000, lasted for the rest of his college years.

In hearing Carl Albert's story, I thought about how mapped out his life seemed to be. At the age of 6 he knew he wanted to be a congressman and through hard work and perseverance he met his goals. Why, I thought, doesn't everyone do the same thing? I think a lot of times it boils down to belief in yourself. Carl wanted to become a congressman and prepared himself. Others stand back and only wish they could.

His OU professor Dr. Cortez Ewing was instrumental in encouraging Carl to apply for the coveted Rhodes Scholarship during his junior year. Carl received three years of Oxford University schooling and an annual stipend of $2,000. His first money would come only when he arrived in Oxford, England. He had no money to get there so Lew Wentz, Oklahoma's richest man and chief Republican, lent him $500.

After his third year he earned his graduate degree in law an returned to Oklahoma where he passed his bar exam in 1934. He was somewhat concerned at first about the job possibilities because the country was still in the midst of the Great

Depression. However, he landed a job as a legal assistant for the Federal Housing Administration in Oklahoma City. His salary was $150 a month.

He purchased his first car, a Model A, for $475. He used the car to cover the countryside explaining the government's rules concerning the FHA. It was at that time and the devastation he saw during the Dust Bowl era that he realized even more his desire to be a part of Congress and help the people of Oklahoma.

By the spring of 1937 he had spent nearly two years with the FHA. He then spent six years in the practice of oil law in Oklahoma, Illinois and Ohio. In 1941 he entered the Armed Forces as a private, serving briefly in the Third Armored Division.

While in the Army he married Mary Harmon, a pretty girl which stood just under five feet with a unique accent that revealed her South Carolina upbringing.

He left the service as a Lieutenant Colonel in February 1946 and he and Mary returned to McAlester with his dreams still intact to become a congressman. For a while he thought it wasn't going to happen and then because of the sudden illness of Paul Stewart he was given the opportunity. He won against Bill Steger and was on his way to Washington as the U.S. Representative from the Third Congressional District of Oklahoma, something he had waited for all of his life.

January 3, 1947 was his first official day as a congressman. On February 2, 1947 he wrote himself a letter stating what he wanted to accomplish as a congressman. This was the same technique he had used earlier in life when he had dreamed of winning oratorical contests, traveling to Europe, capturing a Rhodes scholarship, or going to Congress.

He was a freshman congressman of the minority party, the lowest-ranking member of the most obscure committee in the entire Congress. Never again would he find time to write out his dreams. He was too busy making them come true. First elected with him to the House side of Congress were two future presidents, John F. Kennedy and Richard M. Nixon.

The Third District of Oklahoma has always been called "Little Dixie" because its settlers came from nearby Arkansas, Louisiana, and Texas. Carl, because his work outweighed his small stature, became "the little giant from Little Dixie."

His career in the House of Representatives, 1947-1976 was distinguished. He served on numerous committees. In 1955 he was chosen as Majority Whip and began his ascent of the House leadership ladder. He succeeded John McCormach as Majority Leader in 1962 and as Speaker of the House in 1971. His term officially ended on January 3, 1977. He served in Congress longer and held more power than any other Oklahoman.

After retirement he returned to McAlester where he lived until his death on February 4, 2000. Mary suffering from chronic illness, lived only a couple of months longer. Their son David lives in Oklahoma City and daughter Mary Frances resides in Norman.

Sam Allton - Horticulturist

Part of the perks of writing your own book is getting to pick the characters you want to include. One of my earliest childhood memories was the excitement of gathering around my Uncle Sam to hear him tell the same poetic story *Little Boy Blue* I had heard hundreds of times before. It didn't matter how many times I heard it, I loved it just as much every time.

I know now it was because I loved Uncle Sam so much. I don't think it would have mattered what story he told, because the chuckle in his voice and the twinkle in his eye told me he loved telling it as much as I loved hearing it.

I'm not sure if I ever saw Uncle Sam in any other apparel besides his work clothes. When my parents took me to visit it was usually at the greenhouse where Uncle Sam's world revolved. I was well familiar with the quick left hand turn that needed to be made onto Sixth Street as we crossed the Arkansas River Bridge into Jenks. As the car came to a stop on the gravel parking area I always looked up at the familiar sign painted on the pane glass window that read ALLTON'S GREENHOUSE.

As a small child I was extremely shy, so words didn't flow freely from my lips, but I'm sure my eyes must have lit up when I glanced over to the potting beds and saw Uncle Sam's inviting smile. Even though he was usually at a customer's side helping him or her make choices on the beautiful plants he had grown, he always made time to greet us there.

If it was anywhere close to lunch time a quick walk through the glass covered greenhouse to the living quarters at the end of the walkway was where we would find another familiar face. Aunt Tessie, even though not quite as jubilant as Uncle Sam, pulled her fair share of work on the plant farm. If she wasn't out potting plants or greeting customers she was preparing a meal fit for a king in their back room facilities.

Three children completed the Allton home with Carol, Patty and Sam David Jr. I believe Aunt Tessie was quite outnumbered when they all got together. Unlike Uncle Sam and the three children who were always clowning around about something, Aunt Tessie normally remained more rigid and businesslike with her soft side only emerging on occasion.

WORK was spelled out in capital letters for Aunt Tessie and she set her mind like flint to accomplish each task. A lot of work went into building a successful plant farm and Aunt Tessie took her work very seriously.

It all started on March 21, 1909 when Samuel David Allton was born in Oologah, Oklahoma to parents Bertha Mae and Samuel Billingsly Allton. When a flood demolished their crops the family decided to take refuge for a short while in Jenks, but as it turned out the little town across the Arkansas River became their home and they never returned to Oologah.

Sam David was only 6 years old when the family loaded all of its belongings along with a few pigs in a covered wagon and made their way down old dirt roads headed for Jenks. Before long, three other children were added to the Allton family, making a total of nine energetic siblings who were eager to make a mighty impression on the small town that lay quietly on the outskirts of Tulsa.

For a couple of years the elder Allton found work on the oil field pipelines. By 1917 the townspeople had recruited him as their town marshall. It is said that Jenks certainly didn't rate the reputation of Dodge City, needing a Marshal Dillon to corral its feisty brawlers, but there was a time or two when a little overseeing was needed by the gun toting Marshall Allton.

I'm sure with nine children to raise there was always a need lurking around the corner somewhere, but knowing Uncle Sam I feel safe in saying he probably never noticed how poor they really were.

Uncle Sam graduated from Jenks High School and then enrolled at Oklahoma A&M which is now called Oklahoma State University. He intended to be an agriculture teacher, because even as a young man he loved the soil and the beauty that could come forth from the land.

Unfortunately his father died before he had a chance to finish college. Since he was the oldest son he returned home to help his mother support the other siblings.

On October 23, 1937 he married Tessie Rust and the two of them began to build their lives in Jenks, America. Before the greenhouse was ever established Uncle Sam was known as a truck farmer until the war broke out and partially sidetracked him for a while. He went to work for McDonnell Douglas Aircraft in Tulsa, but his love for planting and watching the ground produce for him never ceased it just slowed down for a while.

In a tax sale in the late 1930's he purchased a portion of the property that steadily grew into what has been known for 56 years as ALLTON'S GREENHOUSE. As time went on he acquired more land and the business continued to grow. At first he only planted vegetables, but to increase his business and stretch out the growing seasons he added plants.

Uncle Sam's greenhouse became widely known for its homegrown tomatoes and the beauty of its colorful pansies. It wasn't long before friends and acquaintances began spreading the word about the plant farm and soon a mailing list had to be established. There was a time when 800,000 pansies were mailed out in a single season. Sam and Tessie Allton were building a life together that encouraged a world of blooming beauties.

The greenhouse and its surroundings eventually grew to 35 city lots. Back across the river on South Delaware Uncle Sam and Aunt Tessie bought eight city lots which included a small house. It was there that they raised their three children. I seriously doubt if you could find one single person who didn't love and admire Sam Allton. He loved life, cherished his family and friends and welcomed the new birth of nature.

On February 15, 1994 just shy of his 85th birthday, Uncle Sam left this earthly world for a place in the heavenlies. Alzheimer's had taken over his mind a few years earlier and he could no longer perform duties at the greenhouse. Aunt Tessie held on for a year and eight months, but died on October 27, 1995 at the age of 74.

Sam David Jr. took over the business in 1984 and has given the farm a new facelift so to speak with technology and appearance. I grew up calling him David, but he has since chosen to be called Sam. Rightly so, since he seems to be somewhat walking in his father's footsteps.

I'll always look back fondly on those days when Uncle Sam recited *Little Boy Blue* and remember what an incredible human being he really was. I'm thankful for the way he touched my life. There is only one thing I regret in knowing him, I don't think I ever told him how he made me feel. I certainly *Samuel Allton* hope he knew.

French Anderson

Physician

It is reported there are over 4,000 diseases caused by faulty genes and every person carries at least seven potentially lethal genes. (Brownlee, US News & World Report).

Dr. French Anderson, who was born and raised in Tulsa, Oklahoma, took on the tasks of helping destroy those lethal genes. In doing so he has respectfully been given the title "Father of Gene Therapy."

If most diseases can be traced to an alteration in a gene, then gene therapy represents the ultimate medical cure. It attempts to eradicate disease by treating the gene itself. Gene therapy does this by inserting a functioning copy of the gene into DNA and augmenting the cell's production of the lacking protein.

There are two main categories of gene therapy, somatic and germ-line. Germ-line gene therapy has the potential to alter one's offsprings characteristics. However, it can sometimes become vital in the treatment of childhood diseases where current drugs and treatment are ineffective. Somatic gene therapy does not involve the alteration of eggs or sperm and therefore is more widely studied.

Dr. Anderson single-mindedly campaigned for the first approved test of the technology in 1990. After 27 years with the National Institutes of Health where he advanced the art of using genes to treat disease, he departed in 1992 to join the University of Southern California. There, while serving as a professor of biochemistry and pediatrics and director of the Gene Therapy Laboratories, he helped produce a new generation of delivery systems, or vectors, that enable doctors to give patients therapeutic genes much as they administer drugs.

Dr. Anderson states that he personally inherited a remarkable collection of genes. As a child prodigy in Tulsa, he could read, write, add and subtract before kindergarten and was devouring college science books when he was eight - skills, he says, that "did not endear him to the other school children of Oklahoma." He was also a stutterer, which made him a target of taunts. To overcome his stammer, he talked with pebbles in his mouth (like Demosthenes") and joined his high school debating team. Also a track star, he won a scholarship to Harvard.

At Harvard he audited a chemistry course taught by John Edsall, an expert in proteins. Edsall soon took Anderson under his wing, as author Larry Thompson recounts in Correcting the Code, a book about the pioneers of gene therapy. At one of Edsall's seminars, Anderson became intrigued by a visiting British scientist's talk about the hemoglobin molecule, which transports oxygen in the bloodstream. A thought occurred to Anderson, and he blurted it out. "If you could determine its structure," he reasoned out loud, "then you could do the same with sickle hemoglobin and determine what the defect is." And because that structure is determined by genes, he went on excitedly, "you could actually change the genes and correct sickle-cell anemia."

At the time the British scientist didn't take well to Anderson's observation, but encouragement from Edsall kept the idea alive in Anderson's mind. He decided to figure out how to cure sickle-cell anemia by changing genes.

After graduating from Harvard Medical School, he landed a job at the NIH, excelled and soon had his own laboratory. As early as 1968 he predicted in a speech that "the first attempts to correct genetic defects will take place within the next few years."

But Anderson's optimism was not matched by the state of the art. In 1981, discouraged by the lack of reliable technique for inserting genes into the nuclei of mammalian cells, he temporarily abandoned gene therapy and turned to other research. As balm for his disappointment, he relentlessly practiced the Korean martial art Tae Kwon Do, won a fourth-degree black belt and was eventually appointed team physician for the U.S. Tae Kwon Do squad at the Seoul Olympics.

During Anderson's gene-therapy hiatus, M.I.T. researcher Richard Mulligan, showed that genetically engineered mouse-leukemia retroviruses were effective vectors for inserting human genes into mouse DNA. To Anderson, this meant one thing: gene therapy was now possible and he was back in business.

Knowing he needed help, he began collaborating with retrovirus researcher Eli Bilboa and Dr. Michael Blaese, an NIH pediatrician and expert in immunology. Over the next few years, Anderson submitted proposals for human gene-therapy trials to the NIH Recombinant DNA Advisory Committee which must approve such tests.

Turned down time and again, Anderson persisted, diplomatically adding to and revising his telephone-book-size protocols to meet RAC demands. In 1989 he finally won approval for a nontherapeutic test that would transfer bacterial genes into immune cells of terminal cancer patients to serve as markers in trials conducted by Dr. Steven Rosenberg of the National Cancer Institute. Those experiments established the safety of using retroviral vectors.

Having put his foot in the door, Anderson doggedly went on to win approval in 1990 for the historic and eventually successful gene-therapy trials on two girls with ADA deficiency. The final committee vote was 16 to 1. The only opposition came from Mulligan, who has been Anderson's most vociferous critic, and who called the proposal "bad science."

In 1986 while Anderson was still at NIH, he and venture capitalist Wallace Steinberg established Genetic Therapy Inc., a biotech company in Gaithersburg, Maryland dedicated to producing retroviral vectors. Under an arrangement with the NIH - the first of its kind - GTI would have the initial rights to technology developed in Anderson's lab in return for NIH receiving payments and royalties from sales of GTI products.

Since arriving at U.S.C., Anderson has assumed the post of director of GTI's scientific advisory board. While he still draws no GTI salary, he is eligible for stock options.

W. French Anderson

C.R. Anthony – Proprietor

It still amazes me when I learn about individuals who have accomplished so much in life and yet created their success through necessity. It tends to solidify the belief that hard work, initiative and elbow grease can turn any poverty stricken person into a well-spring of achievements.

Charles Ross Anthony's birth date is assumed to be around 1884 in West Tennessee. His parents Zachery and Elvira moved the family to Cooter, Missouri when C.R. was about six years old. Unfortunately, Elvira died by the time C.R. was 12.

Zachery remarried, but C.R. was never able to adjust to the marriage and his new stepmother.

With very minimal schooling C.R. was left with a deficit in book learning but an astute desire to succeed in life.

He left Cooter hoping to find a better way of life and stayed for a while with other relatives in middle Tennessee. Knowing that his older brother Will had settled in Indian territory near Holdenville, Oklahoma he decided to make his way there and examine Will's way of life.

It wasn't long before the laborious work on what was then the Autry Ranch led C.R. once again to look for another way to make his fortune. He was introduced to a lady whose husband had died and left her with the responsibility of running a mercantile store as well as the family ranch.

C.R. was only 17 years old at the time, but soon he convinced the widow that age had nothing to do with his ability. He eventually received two more years of schooling which qualified him for a 6th grade education. He then enrolled in business courses which proved to be helpful as well.

Over the six years he worked for the widow he learned a great deal about merchandising. At the same time he was making contacts with suppliers that would help him in the future.

The widow eventually sold the mercantile store to C.R. and he thought his troubles were over. For a while life was good, but C.R. became accustomed to giving credit to many of his customers. That worked out well until the drought came, crops didn't yield and farmers couldn't pay. C.R. had to sell out or lose his good name. But truly successful people never give up - like Paul Harvey once told me "We all fall from time to time, but those who deserve even a modicum of what the world calls success, get up again and sometimes again and again and dust themselves off."

At the end of 1908 C.R. took a job as a bookkeeper at the Wewoka Trading Company. It was one of the largest trading posts in Indian Territory. It was another start for C.R. and an opportunity that would soon open another type of door. One day a young lady named Lutie Mauldin came into the trading post and a year later wedding bells were heard.

Still wanting to seek his own fortune C.R. and Lutie decided to leave the trading post and move to Muskogee. One position led to another and stepping stones were being laid for C.R. to create his own niche in the merchandising industry.

Their first child Helen was born in 1911 followed by Ray in 1913 and Guy in 1915 all during the time C.R. was making great strides in his career.

A few years later C.R. had been introduced to J.C. Penney, who on several occasions tried to convince C.R. to come to work for him. At the time Penney's stores were named the Golden Rule chain. C.R. had observed J.C.Penney and was eager to learn from his successes, so in 1916 he left his current job at the J.P. Martin Company in Cleveland, Oklahoma to take Penney up on his offer. The new position consisted of a move to Idaho which was a startling climate change from what C.R. had been use to.

For almost two years C.R.'s talents were honed as he learned tricks of the trade from one of the master merchandising gurus. A second daughter, Betty, was also born during this time. Then the opportunity was presented for him to move back to Cleveland and align himself once again with the J.P. Martin stores. The agreement was that C.R. would own interest in the store he was able to open and get functional. Of course that was an offer he couldn't refuse.

Their fifth child Dana was born in Cleveland, followed by Charles Ross Anthony, Jr., who died at age three.

For the next four years C.R. was busy accumulating more stores for the Martin company all over parts of Oklahoma. In 1922 he was preparing to take over a lease in Cushing, Oklahoma when Martin decided to put a halt on the expansions. That decision created a turning point for C.R. He decided to end his ties with Martin and open up what would be the beginning of his own chain of stores.

The first establishment located in Cushing was called The Dixie Store. Then came stores in Pawhuska, Hominy and Barnsdall before the name changed to the C.R. Anthony Company with the opening of the Chickasha store. Over 300 stores in 21 western states would eventually be established, which reached far beyond the first store in Cushing.

C.R. surprised his goal of creating success in his life. He had lived The American Dream. He had built an empire that signified a lifetime of dedication and perseverance. He made friends across the nation and far reaching. He finished the course. He died at St. Anthony Hospital in Oklahoma City on June 16, 1976 at age 91.

C.R.'s grandson Bob Anthony was kind enough to send me a picture of his grandfather along with a signature. His grandfather served as president of C.R. Anthony Company from 1922-1972. His son Guy M. Anthony served as president from 1972-1980 and Bob Anthony served as president from 1980-1987 after which time control of the company was sold to an investor group arranged by Citicorp. Bob at the present time is serving as Chairman for the Oklahoma Corporation Commission.

I asked Bob to add a quote about his grandfather and this is what he said. "My grandfather displayed a small wooden box on his desk. The lid reads, "The Secret of Success," and inside the box is a one-word answer..."WORK!" When people asked him why he worked all the time, he proudly explained, *It's not work unless you would rather be doing something else."* His determination and example gave me and thousands of store employees our Secret of Success."

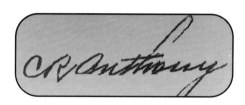

Gene Autry

Actor

Orvon Gene Autry was born in a little town in Texas called Tioga on September 29, 1907. His father, Delbert Autry, was a tenant farmer at the time of Gene's birth.

His family moved to Achille, Oklahoma when he was an infant and later moved to Ravia, Oklahoma, located about 20 miles east of the present town of Gene Autry where he finished school.

At the age of 5, Gene's grandfather, a Baptist preacher, taught him to sing in order to help in the choir. At age 12 he purchased his first guitar for $8 cash from Sears Roebuck. He saved the money while working on his Uncle Calvin's farm.

At age 16 he went to work as a baggage hauler at the depot. In return for his services, he received instruction in telegraphy from the station master, Mr. Arthur Mayberry. As a vacation relief telegrapher on the Frisco Railroad, Gene filled in for regular operators from St. Louis to southern Oklahoma.

Late one night in Chelsea, Oklahoma with few messages to handle, he was singing to himself strumming on a guitar when the cowboy philosopher, Will Rogers came into his office to dispatch his daily syndicated newspaper column of humorous comment. Will was impressed by the singing.

In 1929 Gene went to New York to try to get an audition with the Victor Recording Company. They listened to him and told him to go back to Oklahoma for some experience. He went back to Tulsa and started singing on KVOO. They called him "Oklahoma's Yodeling Cowboy."

A year later he returned to New York and recorded *That Silver Haired Daddy of Mine* for the Columbia Recording Company. Art Satherley, vice-president of Columbia then sent him over to WLS in Chicago for a tryout and he wound up staying for four years. He was singing on the "Sears Roebuck" program, the "Farm and Home Hour," the "National Barn Dance" and several other programs.

In 1934 Mr. Herbert Yates, who owned Republic Studios, was looking for a singing cowboy to put in pictures. He chose Gene Autry. Gene went to Hollywood that year and began making pictures. He played in a couple of short musical scenes in Ken Maynard westerns, which led to his first feature film. By 1937 he was the "King of the Cowboys," and his popularity led a parade of singing cowboys to the movie screens.

After WWII service in the Army Air Corps, he resumed his career and also became a television star. He also resumed touring with the Gene Autry Rodeo and organized Gene Autry Enterprises, which he built into a multi-million dollar empire. His TV production unit was responsible for numerous television shows including "Annie Oakley," "Death Valley Days," and many others. In 1940 Mr. Wrigley put him on the air for Doublemint Gum.

In 1950 he became the first major movie star to enter the television medium, and for the next five years he produced and starred in 91 half hour episodes of "The Gene Autry Show." He also produced the popular TV series.

Gene Autry appeared in 94 feature films and made 635 musical recordings, over 200 of which he wrote or co-wrote. Some of his best known movies are based on his hit records, including "South of the Border," "The Last Round-up," "Mexicali Rose," "Goldmine in the Sky," "Sierra Sue," "Riders in the Sky" and "Call of the Canyon."

His records sold over 50 million copies and he had more than a dozen gold records. His Christmas and children's records like "Here Comes Santa Claus" and "Peter Cottontail" went platinum and the all-time best selling single "Rudolph the Red-Nosed Reindeer" sold over 25 million.

Gene's great love for baseball prompted him to acquire the American League California Angels.

In 1960 Gene Autry retired to Melody Ranch with his wife, the former Ina Mae Spivey, whom he married in 1932.

Gene's career spanned over 60 years in the entertainment industry. He was the only performer in Hollywood's Walk of Fame to rate five stars...one each for radio, records, movies, television and live theatrical, including rodeo.

At the age of 73, Gene married for the second time, bank vice president Jackie Ellam, 39, in Burbank, California.

In the late 1980s Gene and his movie sidekick Pat Buttram hosted 93 episodes of the 90 minute "Melody Ranch Theatre" show on the Nashville Network. The show spotlighted the telecasting of his old Republic and Columbia movies. The show was one of the highest rated programs on TNN and films were shown several times a week and repeated over a dozen times each year.

A long cherished dream came true with the November 1988 opening of the Gene Autry Western Heritage Museum. The museum has been acclaimed as one of the finest museums for its depiction of the history of the American West, its displays of authentic historical artifacts and collections of paintings, bronzes, costumes and coverage of all aspects of frontier life from conquistadors to the cowboy of today.

In his lifetime Gene Autry was inducted into the Nashville Country Music Hall of Fame, Nashville Songwriters Hall of Fame, National Cowboy Hall of Fame, Hollywood Westerners' Hall of Fame and the Oklahoma Hall of Fame. He owned four radio stations, two in Los Angeles (KMPC & KLIT) and two in Seattle KVI & KPLZ) He also owned the Gene Autry Hotel in Palm Springs, California as well as a music publishing company.

At a town meeting in the spring of 1990 the citizens of Gene Autry, Oklahoma voted to revive the Gene Autry School that closed in 1989. They transformed the school into the Gene Autry Oklahoma Museum. A retired teacher, basketball coach Elvin Sweeten, became the project's ramrod. Much time and effort has gone into this project to make it a quality tourist attraction in southern Oklahoma.

The museum is dedicated to the Singing Cowboys of the movies, and from a rather modest beginning, it has acquired a formidable collection of Singing Cowboy memorabilia as well as artifacts from the town's past. Elvin did some more thinking and decided the museum was a logical place for Cowboy music, so he organized the first Film and Music Festival in 1991.

Festivals have taken place every year since 1993. People from across the country come to see Singing Cowboy movies and Western singers, musicians and movie performers.

Rex Allen, Jr., Dale Berry, Randy Boone, Ancel Cook, Carolina Cotton, Les Gilliam, Bill Hale, Tex Hill, Whitey Hughes, Dick Jones, Donna Martel, Dale Robertson, Johnny Western and many others have appeared.. The annual event takes place each year on the last weekend in September in honor of Gene Autry's birthday, September 29.

Gene Autry's legacy will always live on in the minds of all Americans as the legendary "Singing Cowboy." I wanted to personally interview Gene Autry for this book but he passed away on October 2, 1998 at the age of 91.

Hoyt Axton - Singer

Mae and Hoyt

I had the distinct privilege of having a conference call phone interview with two former wives of the late Hoyt Axton.

Deborah and Hoyt had been together for 10 years when he passed away. Donna, one of his previous wives, shared 14 years with Hoyt. Donna and Hoyt shared a son together, Matthew, who even Deborah hails as "an angel" to all.

I was so amazed to hear the tone of gratitude, love, respect and admiration they had for Hoyt. I believe it is a rare event when you hear two women concur about a man whom they both have shared a life with. As I listened to them it was more like hearing the conversations of two close sisters rather than wives.

I commented on what an amazing man Hoyt must have been in order to leave memories that so transcend the norm that he was able to bring two women together in such unity. They both agreed that Hoyt was by far a "one of a kind" human being. Not only did his presence affect their lives greatly while he was here on earth, but the memory of his character and upbeat demeanor has carried them through the trying times as well as the jubilant times of the present.

Hoyt was one of two sons born to John T. and Mae Boren Axton on March 25, 1938 in Duncan, Oklahoma. Mae Axton was the aunt of former U.S. Senator and present Oklahoma University President, David Boren.

In earlier years John T. and Mae were both teachers with John T. also serving as a coach. Mae, however, found another niche when she was recognized for her outstanding ability as a songwriter. Among other titles, Mae co-wrote Elvis Presley's smash hit *Heartbreak Hotel* along with Tommy Durden.

Hoyt grew up with the influences of his mother's creative songwriting and his father's incredible baritone singing voice that were displayed for his own enjoyment and never on a professional scale.

Because of his coaching abilities the family on occasion moved to other cities and states so John could coach at other schools. It was while his father was coaching in Jacksonville, Florida that Hoyt graduated from Robert E. Lee High School, playing both offense and defense. His athletic ability awarded him the prestigious All State award and won him a scholarship to Oklahoma State University.

However, with an incomplete college degree, Hoyt decided continuing his education in that manner wasn't for him, so he joined the Navy instead. It was during that time he began thinking more seriously about the music business and what he would do with his own singing talents when he left the Navy. He also married his first wife, Mary Lou, while he was still part of the Navy personnel.

After his departure from military life in 1961 Hoyt's musical desires began to take on a more active role in his life. He began his career singing folk songs in California coffee houses but as Deborah and Donna informed me, Hoyt's definition of his music was country western boogie woogie gospel rock.

In 1963, The Kingston Trio had a top hit on the charts with *Greenback Dollar,* which Hoyt co-wrote with fellow songwriter Ken Ramsey. That was of course the beginning of Hoyt's career and he knew very little about the music business and how ruthless it can be. Hoyt never saw the financial gain he should have with that song, yet he took his optimistic attitude and planned a new strategy that would bring him musical success.

In the late 1960's his songs *The Pusher* and *Snowblind Friend* brought him great success when the band Steppenwolf recognized his talents and recorded his songs. *The Pusher* was then used in the hit movie "Easy Rider," which allowed Hoyt on many occasions when he frequented his mailbox to retrieve thousands of dollars in royalty fees.

In 1971 the group Three Dog Night recorded at the same time Hoyt did what has become Hoyt's signature song *Joy To The World.* It's hard to hear that title without carrying through with the rest of the line - *Joy to the world - all the boys and girls - joy to the fishes in the deep blue sea, joy to you and me.*

It made sense that Hoyt would pen a song like that, I thought, as I was reminded of the comments Deborah and Donna made about Hoyt's love for animals, children, his family and the great outdoors. In fact, Deborah said she still has nine dogs at home that vividly remind her of Hoyt.

Animals were so loved by Hoyt that he made up songs for each one of his dogs. I'm sure somehow those lyrics must have been translated into doggie language before they hit those furry, canine ears.

Success followed Hoyt at a mighty speed through the 1970's and 80's and the name Hoyt Axton became familiar to everyone. He made over 30 albums in his lifetime and was known for being a great storyteller. I'm told an instrument wasn't necessarily needed to accompany him because his acappella singing was music at its best.

As talented as Hoyt was in the music arena he was not void of other talents as well. He once published a book of his original line drawings. He was also a talented actor who in 1965 had a part in the familiar television series "Bonanza." He appeared in numerous television shows and played parts in a dozen movies. He loved playing the part of Alec's father in "The Black Stallion" (for which he wrote his own lines). He performed alongside some well-known actors and contributed his talents to numerous television commercials over the years.

Unfortunately Hoyt's life came to an end way too soon. He suffered a stroke in 1995 and even though he knew he had some physical problems he was appearing to recover. However, October 16,1999 would be the end of life for Hoyt on this earthly plain. Even though like Deborah said, "Hoyt had a Superman mentality," his natural body needed a celestial rest.

I wish I could have met Hoyt in person, although with the vivid description Deborah and Donna gave me I almost feel like I have. Hoyt was married a total of four times and besides Donna's son Matthew, he had three other children. He adopted his former wife Kathryn's son Mark, and together he and Kathryn had two children, Michael and April.

I know as a whole society sometimes frowns at a person who has multiple marriages. Yet we all know the statement to be true "Don't judge a man, until you have walked a mile in his shoes." Donna was quick to defend Hoyt and the breakup of their marriage, placing blame on the pressures of the road and performing. I guess I would have to say to the critics,with fame comes a price.

In order for the multitude to experience the magnificence of Hoyt's talents, his family at times had to suffer. But through it all, the people whose lives he touched, whether on stage or behind closed doors, will forever remember the man with the heart as big as the whole outdoors. A man who made a difference and truly brought "Joy to the World."

In closing, Deborah said Hoyt was always optimistic and would never sweat the small stuff in life. As she put it, "He never held the world hostage." If things didn't turn out the way he expected them to be, he never pointed a finger. But Deborah's funniest quote of Hoyt's was when he told her "If there is any truth to reincarnation, this must be my first time around because I don't remember a thing."

Hoyt Axton

Jimmie Baker

Producer

Rosie Greer-Jimmie Baker
Child Actor

When I sat down to write this vignette it was almost too overwhelming. I knew I had to figure out how to put an over abundance of information and thoughts into a very short profile.

Jimmie Baker is a man I have great respect for and whom I consider a friend. I met Jimmie for the first time during our interview for this book. The first thing I noticed about him was his sincere, inviting smile and his ability to immediately make you feel like you had known him for years. I've always highly admired a person that didn't feel the need to "think of himself more highly than he ought." In fact, I believe it shows how truly confident they really are with themselves.

Jimmie graciously answered all my questions and then turned to me and said, "now you tell me about yourself." I felt like he was sincerely interested, so I politely obliged. From that day on, Jimmie Baker has consistently presented himself as the same loyal friend I categorized him as on our first meeting. I wish all individuals of his stature could experience the freedom he must feel in being a non ego driven, pure to the core, Oklahoman.

Now that I have voiced my admiration for this man, I'd like to tell you how success found its way to Jimmie Baker.

At a very early age his parents paid 50 cents an hour twice a week for his after school tap dancing lessons which led into ballet as well. By the time he entered Tulsa Central High School he had perfected his tap dancing.

It doesn't take much imagination when you first meet Jimmie to visualize him going through his dance routine. While still in high school he went to New York City and won a spot on Major Edward Bowes' CBS Amateur Hour. From there, they sent him on tour making $25 dollars a week plus expenses. The summer before college a second New York visit landed him two stage shows as a chorus boy. That settled it for him, he was focused on his future. However, he thought it would be Broadway, when in fact, it was Hollywood.

His college years at Tulsa University, The University of Arkansas, and Oklahoma A &M only solidified his celebrity status as he formed the "Hurricane Swingsters" at Tulsa University. At the University of Arkansas he renamed the band Jimmie

Baker and The Collegians. The remainder of his college days were spent at Oklahoma A&M, now known as Oklahoma State University. Jimmie was known throughout his college days as one of the most colorful and dramatic drum majors to ever lead a marching band. During half time you could catch him atop a giant drum, tap dancing to the band's syncopated rhythm, which filled the stadium with excitement. When July, 1942 approached, a halt came to Jimmie's college life when he was drafted into the military. However, that didn't stop his showmanship as he was assigned to the 11th Army Air Corps Band where he continued to entertain the troops.

Three years later he found himself back at Oklahoma A&M where he completed his degree in the School of Education. The Collegians once again performed together until 1948 when Jimmie decided to disband the group and pursue his interest as a producer and director.

Since his years in the band had afforded him a great deal of experience with which to draw from, he decided to make his way to Hollywood. While in Los Angeles he was reunited with his Oklahoma City sweetheart, Sue Carlton, and they were married on June 20, 1948. Sue has continued to be the love of Jimmie's life for over 50 years.

I had the privilege of meeting Sue and she is definitely a sophisticated Hollywood beauty who has had her own success as an actress and model throughout their married life.

Jimmie thought being a big band leader with all the experience he had encountered over the years would catapult him right into Hollywood celebrity status. But he found out quickly that Hollywood expected him to pay his dues as well. Six months later he landed a job at the ABC Studios as a mail boy on the way to the top, and the rest is "creative history."

Jimmie Baker has over 50 years of television success in which he has won five Emmy awards, one Ace award, 11 Silver Angel awards and one Gold Angel award. His total accomplishments, including being inducted into the Oklahoma Hall of Fame, are too numerous to name.

Jimmie continues to keep a busy lifestyle. He is currently in pre-production on a theatrical film, "From Oklahoma to Eternity - The Life of Wiley Post and the Winnie Mae." Yet he still finds time to run five or six miles a day. He is disciplined about his choice of foods, and you'll probably never catch him without his upbeat, positive outlook on life, which obviously is his key to longevity.

If Tinseltown is made up of the quality you readily see in Jimmie Baker, we could all easily say, "Hooray for Hollywood".

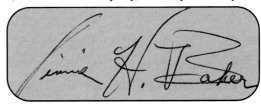

Merrill S. Bartlett - Physician

The day of our interview, Mr. Bartlett handed me a folder full of notes on an autobiography of himself he had been writing. The notes are incomplete during the later years, but the parts I received were so good I had to share them with my readers exactly as Mr. Bartlett had written them. I hope some day he finishes the whole book.

In reviewing my life and the lives of my brothers, I realize that without the profound influence of my mother and father, both of heroic stature, none of us would have known the importance of helping our fellow man, nor would we have been so inspired to overcome obstacles in order to secure an education and live up to the ideals they instilled in us.

We boys may not have always been able to live up to our parents' ideals, but their teachings were always with us and continued to help us correct our errors, "get back on track" and conduct ourselves as men of honor and integrity.

Our father, Harry U. Bartlett and mother, Eva Maud (Whitehead) Bartlett were of great influence in the lives of all of their sons. Papa, by his example, taught us the value of hard work and honesty in dealing with others. Mama devoted her life to the care of her family and to her children's instruction, both academic and religious.

Together, they provided the discipline necessary to keep lively, enterprising and mischievous sons within the bounds of acceptable behavior. My brothers and I adored them and we have tried to honor their memory in establishing charitable foundations, which have provided a hospital and medical clinics for our community.

I was born on September 11, 1906 at my Aunt Della Bartlett Gilman's home in the town of Mannford, Oklahoma, Indian Territory.

Papa was, of necessity, gone from home much of the time constructing store buildings, schools, banks, houses and barns in the newly opened Oklahoma territory, mainly in Creek, Osage and Pawnee counties. He acquired much land in the process, since he would build homes and barns for Indians in return for parcels of land.

Later on, he did much "wildcat" drilling for oil on the lands thus acquired, and proceeds from those ventures afforded the capital for his later excursions into the business of glass manufacturing and other enterprises.,

Schools had not yet been established in Mannford at the time our parents moved into the area. Our mother was faced with the necessity of teaching her eldest son, as well as other townspeople's children, from their primary lessons through what would be the equivalent of four years of high school work.

Although our parents took good care of our health, I was sickly from the age of one and a half until I was five years of age, at times having boils all over my body and frequent bouts with tonsillitis. Mama finally took me to Claremore, Oklahoma for treatment in the hot sulfur water baths there and the boils finally cleared up. The tonsils eventually had to be removed.

I survived but the trouble with my tonsils and rheumatic fever left me with mitral and aortic ring and valve damage which has had to be reckoned with throughout my life.

Our family moved to Sapulpa some time during 1912 and our first home was on the east edge of town at 1302 E. Fairview. At that time, Sapulpa was the home of several glass factories, a Frisco Railway roundhouse and machine shops, and the Harvey House, which was a favorite eating place of the people of Sapulpa, Tulsa and the surrounding area.

One memorable sight in Sapulpa was the electric sign that read "Sapulpa, The Oil City of the Southwest" and had flickering lights that looked like oil burning.

After moving to Sapulpa, Papa expanded his efforts in drilling for oil and gas in housing and farming developments. With scant formal education Papa was nevertheless endowed with many attributes which enabled him, in later years, to become a highly successful businessman, builder, farmer, rancher, oil prospector, trader with Indians, entrepreneur, and above all, a man of honor. On occasion he finalized "deals" with a handshake and his "word was as good as his bond."

Papa owned 80 acres of and near the south boundary of Sapulpa. In 1914 he joined with George F. Collins, a pioneer in the glass manufacturing business in Sapulpa, and together they built the Bartlett Collins Glass Plant. Although the glass plant is no longer owned by Bartlett family members, it is still one of the major employers in Sapulpa and has been a great asset to the city for many years.

Martin, my younger brother, and I loved the outdoors, Papa, therefore, decided to invest in ranching property in the Colorado mountains and purchased hundreds of acres of land in that area, as well as a home for the family on Pine Grove Ranch near Rye, Colorado.

My first four years in school were spent at Woodlawn Grade School in Sapulpa. At the age of 10 years, I moved to Rye, and attended public school there for a few years. I returned to Sapulpa and entered Sapulpa High School during the mid-term of my eleventh grade.

In the fall of 1924 I entered Oklahoma City University, resolved to become a minister, knowing that was Mama's cherished dream for me. Soon after graduation, I made an attempt to go into the ministry, preached three sermons and became convinced in my own mind that I could not do justice to that profession.

In 1929 the stock market crashed and bankrupted Papa. However, my brother Edward was able to hang on to the Bartlett Collins Glass Company through the depression, and went on to make a great deal of money in the business.

I eventually enrolled at Kirksville College of Osteopathy to become a medical doctor. From 1934 to 1938 I practiced medicine in Ada, Oklahoma and Alamogordo, New Mexico. Then I returned to Oklahoma City University and entered pre-med school. From there I went to school at the University of Oklahoma.

I returned to Sapulpa in 1955 after spending many years in other states practicing medicine. I joined with my brother, Edward Bartlett in providing a charity clinic in Sapulpa that would offer free medical services to citizens of the area who were unable to pay for their own medical care. Edward's wish was for this clinic to stand as a memorial to our parents, Harry U. and Eva Maud Bartlett, and at the same time to benefit the citizens of the City of Sapulpa and Creek County.

We founded the H.U. and Eva Maud Bartlett Foundation, which was to provide funds to carry out our dream. We were able to purchase Sapulpa's City Hospital. Remodeling and renovation began immediately and the doors of Bartlett Memorial Hospital were opened to the public in June, 1957. It has remained my life work from then to the present time.

The short time I spent with Dr. Bartlett was certainly memorable. Even in the sunset of his life, his caring thoughts toward others remain his primary focus. Bartlett Memorial Hospital will always be a reminder to me of a loving family whose pioneering spirit brought hope, health and restoration into the lives of many in the surrounding community.

MS Bartlett m. 19

Johnny Bench - Athlete

I was very impressed with a legend in his own time, baseball great Johnny Bench, as he talked openly with me during a February 2001 phone interview. I'm not an athlete myself, and I'm sure no team would pick me if they were choosing up sides to prepare for a game. But Johnny has proven to be one of the best in a sport that is as American as, like they say, "Mom's Apple Pie."

Johnny said he was 3 years old when he first saw Mickey Mantle playing baseball on television. As he sat on the couch next to his father Ted in their home in Erin Springs, Oklahoma he heard the sportscaster introduce the New York Yankees' next switch-hitting superstar from Oklahoma. Johnny turned to his father and said, "You mean you can be from Oklahoma and play in the major leagues? Then that is what I want to do when I grow up."

Johnny was born in Oklahoma City, Oklahoma on December 7, 1947. Except for a short time in Erin Springs, his childhood days were spent in the town of Binger.

His father had been a catcher when he played high school baseball and dreamed of playing in the major leagues, but two stints in the Army kept him from pursuing his dream. In some ways Johnny feels like he stepped in where his father's dream had ended.

In Binger Johnny's father drove a truck delivering propane gas, but almost every spare moment was spent playing ball with his three sons Ted, William and Johnny. Ted Sr. started a little league baseball team in Binger and for a while they had to knock on doors to round up enough boys to play the game. Eventually the town began showing interest in Ted's efforts and started backing the league up with sponsorship wherever needed.

Johnny's mother Katy was always supportive in whatever he did in life. She was an excellent homemaker who kept Johnny's baseball uniform cleaned, pressed and ready to go at all times. But it was his Dad who taught him how to play the game of baseball, took him fishing and hunting and taught him how to be a good man and father.

When Johnny was in the second grade he told his teacher he wanted to be a major league baseball player. Everyone in the class laughed. But Johnny knew in his heart his dream would come true, it was just a matter of time. His father had informed him of how badly teams need good baseball catchers and encouraged him to seek that position. Not only was there a great need for catchers, his father said but it would be the quickest way for Johnny to make it into the big leagues.

Life wasn't all fun and baseball games though. Johnny was taught the meaning of hard work. During his childhood he had a paper route, mowed lawns, pulled cotton, hoed cotton, chopped peanuts and worked in the fields. Even though Johnny's father was eager to play games with his boys, he also required them to abide by the rules he set up for them as productive individuals.

Johnny recalls fond memories of his childhood and admits he never thought of doing anything else other than playing baseball, even though he was academically qualified to have probably done many other things with his life. He was elected valedictorian in junior high as well as senior high, but to Johnny nothing else but baseball really mattered.

In 1965 Johnny graduated from high school. When some of his classmates were going off to various colleges he was trying to see which baseball league he was going to align himself with. He was 17 years old and 1965 was the year of the first free agent draft. Several teams were interested in Johnny's abilities, but it was the Cincinnati Reds that drafted him in their Class A minor league in Tampa, Florida.

After two seasons in the minors the Reds offered him a major league contract for the 1968 season. He surprised everyone but himself when he became the 1968 "Rookie of the Year" by catching in 154 games (a rookie record) and won the first of 10 straight Gold Gloves. The Oklahoma boy from the small town of Binger was on his way to a successful career that would eventually escalate him to celebrity status.

When 1970 rolled around Johnny hit 45 homers and was chosen "Most Valuable Player," a title he also secured in the 1972 World Series. Then Johnny suffered a setback when a medical examination verified a spot on one of his lungs. He was forced to have surgery where doctors removed part of the diseased lung. Johnny felt like he never played with his full potential after that. However, the Cincinnati Reds had not yet won a World Series until 1976 when Johnny got two hits in each of the first three games and hit two home runs in game four, making him once again the series "Most Valuable Player."

To his credit, Johnny went on to play a total of four World Series, winning two of them back to back. He set a major league record for home runs by a catcher (327 plus 62-playing elsewhere).

Johnny explained that catchers are always given single digits on their jerseys. He had wanted to be number "7" like his childhood hero, but was given number "5" which quickly satisfied him, since Joe Dimaggio had proudly worn that number.

Johnny was named to the National League All-Star team 14 times and played in every game from 1968 to 1975. Johnny retired from baseball in 1983 when he realized his elbows were going bad, his back wasn't the greatest and he didn't feel up to catching every day.

Johnny has appeared on every talk show in America. He spent nine years with CBS Radio broadcasting the National Game of the Week, the All-Star Game, the League Championship Series and the World Series. He has also sung with the Symphony Orchestra and has become a very sought after motivational speaker.

In his presentation he highlights successful people and their contributions as role models. He also informs listeners of what he calls "The Vowels of Success." "A" is the Attitude you have to have. "E" is the Effort and the Energy you have to put forth. "I" is for the you as an individual. "O" is for Opportunities that will come your way. "U" is for You. You are very special and you always have to treat yourself that way.

In 1984 Oklahoma honored Johnny by inducting him into the Oklahoma Hall of Fame. Then in 1989 the National Baseball Hall of Fame honored him with induction as well. In July 2001 Johnny was once again honored when a life size statue was placed in Red Hawk Ball Park in Oklahoma City.

As we came to the end of our interview, I asked Johnny about his family. Even though he is a single man once again he proudly talked about his 11 year old son Bobby who he described as a "wonderful kid." Johnny believes he hung on to the strong values that his parents instilled in him as a child and hopes he has successfully transferred those beliefs to Bobby.

One of his constant reminders to his son is to *encourage him to strive to be the best in everything he does. Not only will that bring you great success, but it will give you pride in yourself as well.*

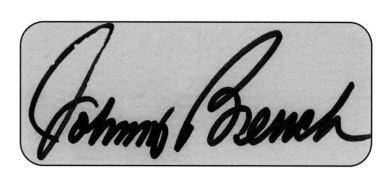

Byron Berline - Musician

It is hard to tell in a photograph, but in person Byron sure had a resemblance to actor Lloyd Bridges who played on the long running television show "Seahunt" years ago. Even though Byron was born in Kansas his growing up years took place on a farm in Oklahoma with his father Lue, mother Elizabeth and four older brothers and sisters.

I wasn't at all surprised when Byron told me he loved sports and went to Oklahoma University on a football scholarship. After all, sports and Oklahoma are synonymous, aren't they? Byron majored in physical education in college and intended coaching to be his lifelong career. But as it so often happens, what we have planned isn't necessarily how the winding road leads. Oklahoma University was the college of his choice.

Since he had grown up in a musical family playing fiddle with his dad in concerts and state fairs, he naturally involved himself in music while at college as well. There was a weekly event on campus called "Friday at 4" and on one occasion "The Dillards," a professional music group, made a guest appearance to promote their night club in Oklahoma City. They heard Byron perform that afternoon and invited him to join them in a musical jam session. They had such good repertoire and were so impressed with Byron's talent that they invited him to record with them the following summer of 1964 in California before Byron's classes resumed in the Fall.

One musical stepping stone after the other began to occur in Byron's life. He was part of a band in college called "The Cleveland Ramblers" and for a while was performing on a weekly television show put on by Garrett's Household Furniture. That is where he became involved with Wiley and Gene Walker who wrote the songs *Live and Let Live* and *When My Blue Moon Turns To Gold Again*. It was a huge thrill for Byron to perform with these two men because he had been watching them on television for years.

After graduation Byron's musical talents as a fiddler quickly began to over shadow any other activities. He became acquainted with the legendary Bill Monroe at the 1965 Newport Folk Festival and was invited to join Monroe and his band, "The Blue Grass Boys." Once again Byron was thrilled with the opportunity to perform with a group he had admired for so long.

He was given the opportunity to record three songs with Bill Monroe and the Blue Grass Boys before he was drafted into the Army seven months later. The Army only proved to be another training ground for Byron as he continued to hone his talent while being assigned to Special Services in Fort Polk, Louisiana for two years.

As fate would have it the day before he was discharged from the Army, Doug Dillard requested once again that Byron come to California and record another album with Dillard & Clark. So with his new bride by his side, he took them up on their offer. What was intended to be a short stay in California ended up accumulating into 26 years. Numerous doors continued to open for Byron as his fiddle playing became sought after by many musical artists who wanted to display his talents on their own albums.

In 1970 Byron's fiddle playing could be heard on the television movie, "Run Simon Run," the first of many films he would be privileged to be a part of.

Along with many other ventures Byron formed the band "Country Gazette" and later a group called "Sundance," which gave the well loved country star Vince Gill another stepping stone into the music business before his departure for Nashville in 1982.

Byron has toured the United States as well as abroad and his fiddle playing has put audiences in awe for many years. Byron has worked with many talented and well known musicians over the years and his work has continued to find its way on numerous artists' albums as well as on his own solo releases.

In 1995 Byron and his wife Bette returned to Oklahoma to the beautiful city of Guthrie. Byron opened a fiddle shop on Oklahoma Street. As you walk into the shop you see fiddles hanging all over the walls. There is a definite feeling of nostalgia that fills the room even if you weren't a part of the history making process and success of Byron Berline.

Byron is still a part of a band, which he calls the "Byron Berline Band." They hold mini concerts in the upstairs portion of the fiddle shop. Byron took us on a tour of the upstairs facilities and it was a treat to see how he has decorated the walls with memorabilia of past and present musical history. To top it off in 1997, Byron started the Annual Oklahoma International Bluegrass Festival to be held every year in Guthrie.

Byron Berline's talents and endeavors far exceed what I could reveal to you in a short profile. I left his fiddle shop that evening and realized how very fortunate he had been over the years, I felt very honored and privileged to hear his story.

William Bernhardt – Author

Anyone who loves reading courtroom novels has most likely read at least one book written by Bill Bernhardt.

When I met him he had that youthful, boy next door look that made it hard to believe he had actually been a lawyer for several years. Not that lawyers can't be boyish and youthful, but they can sometimes put forth an image that appears rather harsh.

Bill's parents, William and Theta Juan, raised him in Midwest City, Oklahoma, along with his three sisters Michel, Valerie and Karis. Bill was the book reader in the family so one of his first tasks was to find where the neighborhood library was located in conjunction to his house.

He was about eight years old when he first started thinking how cool it would be to become a writer. His fascination was even more enhanced when he saw the author's picture and realized someone actually sat down and wrote the book. The book didn't just happen, it was someone's job.

By the time Bill was 11 he was already receiving rejection letters from different publishers from whom he sent his work. But he never let that squelch his desire to keep trying. He did, however, think he should get some training in another field that would support him financially until he was able to write his first best seller. Such a feat obviously wasn't going to happen before he graduated from high school.

Being an attorney sounded like a good idea because it involved reading, writing and some talking. What he didn't anticipate was that he would be writing on legal subjects most of the time, which in the long run turned out to be a blessing.

He attended the University of Oklahoma and graduated with a law degree in 1986.

He was hired in Tulsa by a large law firm where he acted as a trial lawyer practicing civil cases for nine years. After six years he became a valued partner.

All during his undergraduate work he continued to write stories. He won a contest and put a couple of articles in magazines and newspapers, but nothing of any great significance. However, he wasn't giving up his desire to someday become an author like the people pictured in the many books he had been reading since childhood.

After he had been with the law firm for about a year he began to write his first novel. He knew it wouldn't be easy but he was willing to do whatever it took to make his dream become a reality. He read and learned things all the time that helped him in his pursuit. He knew if he was ever going to become a published author it wouldn't just happen. He would have to take the necessary steps to make it happen.

Primary Justice was the title of his first book which he wrote and rewrote for two years until he thought he had it polished to perfection. Another two years was spent trying to find an agent. He knew it would be hard to find someone who would want to spend their time working with an unknown writer.

He began sending out letters one after another until finally Esther Perkins in Childs, Maryland, decided to give him a try. Fortunately, she sold the book along with his next creation *The Code of Buddyhood* and thirdly *Blind Justice.*

To date his character, attorney Ben Kincaid, has come alive in a series of 10 best-selling courtroom books, which inspired Library Journal to name Bernhardt the "master of the courtroom drama."

Bill has also edited a best-selling anthology of original short fiction, *Legal Briefs.* He has appeared on CNN, CNBC, The Today Show, Nightline and a host of other national and regional television programs. His books have been translated and published in more than a dozen countries.

For his fifth novel, *Perfect Justice,* Bill received the Oklahoma Book Award for Best Fiction. In 2000 he was again awarded the Oklahoma Book Award for Best Fiction with his novel *Dark Justice* as well as Oklahoma State University's, H. Louise Cobb' Award for outstanding contributions to American literature. He has also been inducted into the Oklahoma Writers Hall of Fame, the youngest author ever so honored.

In 1995 Bill served as president of Novelists Inc., a national coalition of professional writers. He also serves on the board of directors of the Tulsa Arts and Humanities Council, the board of directors of the Oklahoma Center for the Book, the Writers Advisory Panel of the Oklahoma Arts Institute, and the Peggy V. Helmerich Literary Award Selection Committee.

In his spare time Bill plays the piano, writes songs, helps direct two children's choirs, creates board games and constructs crossword puzzles which have been published in "The New York Times" and other national publications. He is also the publisher and president of HAWK Publishing Group, which publishes a wide variety of new and classic fiction and nonfiction.

He lives in Tulsa with his wife, Kirsten, and their children, Harry, Alice and Ralph.

Elvin Bishop - Musician

I can't believe this, but after listening to the C.D.'s that were sent to me by Elvin's management company I have a whole new appreciation for the sound of blues. Regretfully, I've never really taken the time to engage myself in that type of music only because it was unfamiliar to me. Elvin certainly has a way of making it entertaining, while at the same time adding a few wisdom tips which is right up my alley.

Since Elvin is enjoying sunny California our interview was conducted from his home via telephone. Marc Lipkin from Alligator Records sent a terrific picture and bio he had written on Elvin that was so well done, with his permission I decided to use part of it for my profile.

Elvin Sr. and Mylda Bishop had no idea when their son Elvin was born on October 21, 1942 that he would some day help introduce the rock and roll generation to a new sound of blues. There had never been any musicians in the Bishop family. Since they had just managed to struggle through the evils of the

Depression, the most important family goal set for their son and daughter, Kate was to get a good education. Elvin Sr. was an employee at Douglas Aircraft in Tulsa, Oklahoma, while Mylda kept a steady hand on the affairs at home.

Elvin first got hooked on the blues listening to late night R&B radio as a teenager and collecting blues records. He used a National Merit Scholarship in 1959 as a way to get closer to his blues heroes by enrolling in the University of Chicago, with its campus tucked in the middle of the South Side ghetto.

"The first thing I did when I got there," Elvin recalls, "was make friends with the guys working in the cafeteria. Within 15 minutes I was into the blues scene."

Leaving his physics studies behind, Elvin turned to blues music full time. He befriended Hound Dog Taylor and Little Smokey Smothers, a legendary guitarist who played with Howlin' Wolf and who took Elvin under his wing. After crossing paths a few times with fellow University of California student and harmonica player Paul Butterfield, the two began sitting in at black blues clubs, often jamming with Buddy Guy and Otis Rush. Paul and Elvin soon recruited Michael Bloomfield as second lead guitarist, and a groundbreaking, all-star band began to take shape.

The Paul Butterfield Blues Band, formed in 1963 (along with Mark Naftalin on keyboards, Jerome Arnold on bass and Sam Lay on drums), introduced electric Chicago blues to the rock audience for the first time. By 1967 the band's popularity hit an all-time high as their straight Chicago blues sounds drifted even further into rock and roll. Their highly influential albums set the stage for the dual lead guitar attack that the Allman Brothers and Derek and the Dominos (among others) adopted.

Critic Kit Rachlis, writing in the Rolling Stones Record Guide, stated that Elvin, along with Bloomfield, recorded "brilliant guitar passages that did as much as anything to establish the mystique and heroism of modern rock guitarists." Elvin recorded three albums with the Paul Butterfield Band before deciding to move on.

Towards the end of the 1960's, Elvin headed to the San Francisco area. He became a regular at the famed Fillmore jam sessions, playing alongside Jimi Hendrix, Eric Clapton, B.B. King and many others before embarking on a solo career. He recorded first for Fillmore Records, then Epic and then for Capricorn, where his career took off to new heights. He charted with *Traveling Shoes* before scoring big with *Fooled Around and Fell In Love* (the song, with vocals supplied by pre-Jefferson Starship singer Mickey Thomas, reached number three on the pop charts).

With hits under his belt and his fan base growing, Elvin's party-starting abilities kept his tour schedule full even after the demise of Capricorn in the late 1970's.

After a seven-year recording hiatus, Elvin returned to his blues roots, signing with Alligator Records and releasing, *Big Fun* to critical and popular acclaim in 1988. He followed in 1991 with *Don't Let The Bossman Get You Down.* The album received four stars in a Rolling Stone review and earned him an appearance on Late Night with David Letterman.

Living Blues declared Elvin's guitar playing "as full of fresh licks and unbounded energy as the day he and Mike Bloomfield set the blues/rock world on its ear."

In 1992 Elvin joined Koko Taylor, Lonnie Brooks, Lil' Ed and the Blues Imperials and Katie Webster on a cross-country tour celebrating Alligator's 20th anniversary. Elvin can be heard on the Grammy-nominated Alligator Records 20th Anniversary Tour Album and seen in the Robert Mugge documentary, Pride and Joy: The Story of Alligator Records. Elvin can also be heard on Alligator's Hound Dog Taylor - A Tribute playing a greasy version of the legendary bluesman's Let's Get *Funky.*

I've never seen Elvin in a live performance, but I'm sure I'll attend the next time he appears in the Tulsa area. My favorite song of his so far is *The Skin They're In* which speaks truth in the varied and complicated world of relationships.

Sixteen years ago Elvin married Cara and together they enjoy raising their daughter Emily who has entered her teen years. No doubt, she has experienced a childhood full of musical wonder.

David Boren

University President

I met David Boren's mother several months before my interview with him. I was privileged to have lunch with her one afternoon along with our mutual friend, Jimmie Baker. I thought if her son is anything like his mother then I am in for quite a treat.

I wasn't disappointed. Oklahoma University President David Boren was definitely his mother's son. He was born in Washington, D.C. when his father, the late Congressman Lyle H. Boren, was still in office. He speaks very highly of his father and of course knows it was he who planted the seeds of political life inside of him when he was a small boy.

He made his first speech on the radio promoting his father when he was five years old. From then on David knew he wanted to be in politics. He wanted to be a congressman like his Dad. Along the way, his father had many opportunities to groom him with the knowledge of what it took to be successful in the political arena. David was eager to learn.

By his father's side, David witnessed examples of how to deal with the public. His father told him he could learn something worthwhile from everyone if he would take the time to listen. His father taught him to respect other people and their ideas even if they were different from his own.

Congressman Lyle Boren was part of Congress for 10 years. When they moved back to Seminole, Oklahoma David was six years old and entering the first grade. One of his mentors who remained part of his life until she died was his first grade teacher. At least once a month while he was serving in the Senate he would call her to get her opinion on how she thought he was doing.

Her thoughts of him always meant a great deal to him. When he said that it reminded me of how important it is for all of us to have people we admire and look up to. Some how that has a tendency to keep us headed in a positive direction.

David is a 1963 graduate of Yale University where he majored in American history. He graduated in the top one percent of his class and was elected Phi Beta Kappa. He was also selected as a Rhodes Scholar and earned a master's degree in politics, philosophy and economics from Oxford University, England in 1965.

From there he went to the University of Oklahoma College of Law. He still had his sights set on politics but wanted to be prepared if the elections didn't go his way. He knew he would either be applying the law or writing the law. Even his choice of majoring in American history was all part of his quest to be in politics. He felt if he was going to make a contribution as an office holder or a public official he needed to know about the country he was going to serve.

He did practice law for a short while, but would have gone broke if that remained his mainstay. He couldn't bring himself to charge people for certain services that he performed. He ran for the legislature the first year he was in law school and remained in the legislature through the remainder of his schooling and upon graduating he taught at Oklahoma Baptist University and was a captain in the Oklahoma National Guard. For a few years he must have been one busy guy.

During eight years in the state legislature, David co-authored a bill that established the statewide system of area vocational technical schools. He never set out to be governor but got so involved in state government that he began to be an outspoken reformer.

In 1975 he was elected as Governor of Oklahoma. At that time he was the youngest governor in the country. During his tenure he established the Oklahoma Summer Arts Institute and the Scholar-Leadership Enrichment Program. Also, the first state funding for Gifted and Talented K-12 students. During his term, he instituted many progressive programs, including conflict-of-interest rules, campaign financing disclosure, stronger open meeting laws for public bodies and more competitive bidding on state government contracts.

He served in office for four years and contemplated either running for another term as governor or running for the Senate. At the time Senator Bartlett was up for re-election. Even though they were with different parties, David highly respected Senator Bartlett and told him he refused to run against him. As it turned out Senator Bartlett decided not to run, which left the door wide open for David.

As a Senator, among other things, David served on the Senate Finance and Agriculture Committees and was the longest-serving chairman of the Senate Select Committee on Intelligence.

A Senator can be re-elected every six years. David was re-elected for three consecutive terms. Being part of the Senate was a very awesome task for David. He said every time he walked into the U.S. Capitol he felt a part of something that was so much bigger than himself. The excitement of being in Washington and the responsibility of being a spokesperson for the State of Oklahoma was a privilege he didn't take lightly.

After 16 years in the Senate the opportunity came for him to become president of the University of Oklahoma. He said he spent a few sleepless nights trying to decide what to do. He loved being in the Senate but he also loved Oklahoma. He knew that no state could become great without having a great university with which to train leaders of the future. Oklahoma had given so much to him and his family, and he wanted his decision to be what was right for Oklahoma.

In November of 1994 David stepped into the position as 13th president of the University of Oklahoma. That made him the only person in Oklahoma's history to have served as governor, senator and college president.

As well as running the university David teaches freshman political science every semester. It thrills him to know he is investing his life in the next generation. He certainly has the means to live off campus and away from university life after the day comes to an end. Yet President Boren and his wife Molly have chosen to live in the restored President's House on the campus grounds. Most days, he walks to work and makes himself available if by chance a student walking along the way feels the need to engage in conversation.

President Boren feels like we are all here on this earth for a purpose. *He believes service to others gives purpose to your life because what matters the most is what you give-not what you receive. Ironically, in giving of yourself, you really find the purpose for your life.*

He told me *the most insecure people he knows are the ones who seem to be focused intently on themselves. On the other hand, the ones who find a cause more important than themselves to invest in find that the ultimate happens.*

President Boren candidly told me he is never under the illusion that the Senate could not go on with out him or that the University of Oklahoma will not be able to function properly without him at the helm. However, he feels privileged to have been given opportunities in life that not only challenged him, but gave him a sense of purpose. *"Being part of something which is far more important than ourselves is what gives meaning to our lives."* he said.

Clarence Boyd – Musician

As you enter the small, quaint town of Kellyville, Oklahoma you will see a sign that reads, "Welcome to Kellyville - Home of Clarence Boyd." Truthfully, I had never heard of Clarence until someone else mentioned his name as a possible inclusion in my book. After interviewing him, I was ashamed of myself for not knowing who he was, because his talent as a musician and songwriter go way back.

Clarence, a native Oklahoman, was born in Vinita and raised on a farm in Kellyville. When he was just a small child barely reaching the age of five his father, Mack Boyd brought home a piano he had come across during a trip to the cattle market.

Clarence had never seen a piano before, so he walked over to it and with one finger began to pound out a tune.

Within a week, to the astonishment of his parents, he was playing with two fingers. By the end of the month, he was playing beautifully by ear using both hands. During this time, Clarence's father, along with some other folks, were building a country church. So at five years of age Clarence became the church pianist because there was no one else in the congregation who could play the piano like he could. Until he got older he had to stand up to play as beautiful music poured from the ivory keys.

Before long, Clarence began getting offers to play in musical bands and realized he could make money doing it. Clarence said one of his lifelong regrets was in 1943 at age 10 he turned down an offer to go to work for Lawrence Welk. At the time, not knowing how to read sheet music was very intimidating to Clarence, but as it turns out he became an extremely successful musician.

To this date, he still has never learned to read sheet music and believes people are better off if they just learn the mathematics of music. As he pointed out, the cords represent a number and just knowing the numbering system can put you on the road to success in music.

In 1953 Clarence co-wrote the song, *Release Me*, which became a number one hit for stars like Patsy Cline and Jim Reeves. He has had the opportunity to play for Billy Parker, Moe Bandy, Ray Price, Hank Thompson, Leon McAuliffe, Bob Wills and Johnny Lee Wills, Marilyn Monroe and many others.

He told me he performed with Ronnie Dunn up until he moved to Nashville and was strongly encouraged by Ronnie to come along with him. Clarence refused because he wanted to remain in Oklahoma.

For nine years beginning in the early 1980's he and his son Dewayne owned and operated the Silver Dollar Ballroom on Highway 66 where they brought in top stars like Reba Entire. Clarence has been inducted into the Western Swing Society Hall of Fame in Sacramento, California, as well as, the Pioneer Western Hall of Fame in Seattle, Washington for being in the business at least 50 years.

Clarence still plays in a few bands around Oklahoma such as the Texas Playboys and the revised Johnny Lee Wills band.

On a more endearing note, Clarence talked about his love for his family. I felt it as he thought back about the good times he had spent with his brother Delbert, who passed away in 1993. He then told me about his mother Nina who he watched suffer with crippling arthritis. It kept her bedfast for fifteen years. Even though his mother passed away quite some time ago he still recalls the last conversation he had with her when she made him promise he would never stop playing music.

Clarence, of course, kept his promise to his mother. In fact, he said that promise sustained him many times over the years.

Of course I couldn't end the interview without having my own mini concert starring the legendary Clarence Boyd. He played *Release Me*, the song he had co-written almost 50 years ago, as well as *Last Date*, one of my all-time favorites written by another songwriter but at one time recorded by Clarence. The piano keys seemed to play by themselves as his fingers flew across the keys.

I always wished I could play the piano, but as my pastor said in his sermon last week, *"A dreamer only wishes he could do something, but a visionary not only wishes, he does something to make it come to pass."* I was so impressed with Clarence Boyd and the gentleness of character that seemed to be a genuine part of this "Distinguished Oklahoman."

With his wife Wilma by his side and his two grown children living just a few blocks away, Clarence seems at peace with the world. I know I was blessed meeting him that day and I doubt if I'll ever hear the song *Release Me* or *Last Date* without thinking about Clarence Boyd and Kellyville, Oklahoma.

William Boyd

Actor

Remember the guys in the cowboy hats who were always meant to portray goodness?

On Saturday mornings in the 1950s when parents were trying to recuperate from the previous work week their children were all lined up on the couch watching one of their favorite cowboy heroes. Hopalong Cassidy was known throughout the world as one of America's most beloved characters.

William Lawrence Boyd born on June 5, 1895 in Belmont County, Ohio was one of four sons born to Lydia and Charles Boyd. The family moved to Cambridge in early 1900 and William attended school at East Side.

After a trip with his brother Clarence to visit his grandmother Mrs. Albert Baker in Tulsa, Oklahoma he convinced his parents to move to Oklahoma in 1912. His father took a job with the water department. Unfortunately, after working for only a year, Charles Boyd was killed when a pressure cap from a water line blew up.

Before William turned 20 he had already been married once to a lady named Laura Maynard, but the marriage was not to be. William struck out on his own, traveling from town to town working at several odd jobs such as grocery clerk, miner, auto salesman, lumberjack and truck driver. He ended up in Akron, Ohio working in a rubber factory.

When World War I broke out he tried to enlist in the Army, but they rejected him because of an injury he incurred while being a lumberjack. Still not sure of what direction his life was headed, he ventured off to Arizona and took a job as a hotel manager and met and married an heiress named Ruth Miller. They soon divorced and William took to the road again, this time headed for California. It was 1919 and he stumbled upon a job as an extra on a Hollywood movie. The film was called "Why Change Your Wife?" It was then that he became acquainted with Cecil B. DeMille at Paramount Studios. His relationship with DeMille proved to be satisfying for both of them and carried William to stardom.

In 1926 William's portrayal in "The Volga Boatman" established him as a leading screen performer. It wasn't long before he married his leading lady, Elinor Fair. However, that marriage was also doomed to fail and ended shortly after it began.

William's career was soaring and he appeared in first rate movies such as "Jim the Conqueror," "Yankee Clipper" and "The Leatherneck." When the era of silent movies ended William quickly adapted to the talkies.

In 1931 a major scandal erupted in Hollywood when an actor carrying the same name was arrested for gambling and drinking during a prohibition-era party. The newspaper headlines almost ruined William's career and definitely set it temporarily aside for nearly four years. Producer Harry Sherman at Paramount decided to begin a series of Westerns based on the stories of Clarence E. Mulford. Harry thought William would be the perfect person to play the role of "Hopalong Cassidy." William was somewhat leery about taking the role because he was still fearful about his name being tarnished. Fortunately, the first feature "Hopalong Cassidy Enters" became a huge success and jump-started William's career in 1935.

In 1936 William was named as one of the top 10 western movie actors, a position he would hold comfortably for 10 years.

Wedding bells rang two more times before William finally met Grace Bradley, the woman he was meant to spend the rest of his life with. Grace was an accomplished dancer and singer and in 1937 they married and spent 35 years together.

After a successful ride Harry Sherman decided to cancel the series in 1945. William, however, felt there was still a great deal of audience approval and he wanted to continue the series. By borrowing substantial money and investing everything he had he was able to buy the rights to the series and resume production in 1946.

After starring in 66 "Hopalong Cassidy" films William finally ended his screen career in 1951 when he noticed his audiences were switching their interest to television. Once again William adapted to change when television producers approached him about airing his movie series on home screens.

Television became more profitable for William than films ever had been. William returned to production and began airing an entirely new series for television viewers. He was reaping the benefits of success which quickly included product endorsements for the increasingly popular series.

For those lucky enough to see the Hopalong Cassidy series I'm sure they also remember Hoppy's wonderful horse "Topper" who he had for 19 years.

In 1954 William went on a nation-wide personal appearance tour with the Cole Brothers Circus before finally retiring in Palm Springs with his wife Grace.

In 1968, William developed a cancerous tumor on a lymph gland and underwent surgery. The whole ordeal robbed him of a great deal of energy and seemed to squelch his spirit. It is said he stayed pretty much in seclusion following his surgery and died four years later in 1972.

Hoppy, as his fans called him, was always glad to sign autographs and take time to shake a hand or two. The signature included in this profile was donated by my mother, P.J. In 1957 when she was waitressing at The 1800 Restaurant - which at the time was one of the elite - establishments in Utica Square - Hoppy came in with six other people. He wasn't seated in her station, but she wasn't going to let him get away without asking him to sign his menu.

The 1957 menu displaying the price of a lobster tail with baked potato and green salad for $2.75 is amazingly still in tack. I laughed when I saw Coca Cola for 15 cents and apple pie for 25 cents. The most fascinating inclusion was the telephone number at the bottom of the menu which read Telephone 7-7503. I don't know how she managed to hold on to such a priceless piece of memorabilia for over 40 years, but I'm glad she did.

A fan club, festival and newsletter honoring William began in 1991 in Cambridge. The festival is always held the first weekend in May and many Hollywood stars who worked with Hoppy usually attend. I was hoping to make the trip this year and have the opportunity to meet Grace Boyd, but I was unable to clear my schedule to do so.

Laura Bates is the founder of the Hopalong Cassidy Fan Club and it was she who was gracious in sending the incredible picture I have included. The fan club, Hoppy Talk, has a growing membership of over 500 members worldwide. If anyone would like to become a member they can contact Laura at Hoppy Talk - 6310 Friendship Drive - New Concord, Ohio 43762.

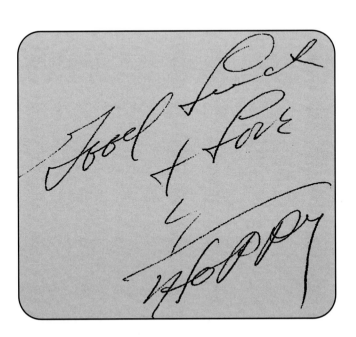

Edward Brandt - Physician

Ed Brandt's office is in the same University of Oklahoma building where he took classes as a medical student and began his career over thirty years ago.

Growing up in Oklahoma City he had never given a health career a thought until he was married and in college at Oklahoma University. He hadn't even considered college until the Korean War heated up. He enrolled at OU in 1950 as a journalism major. His father, Ed senior had worked for the local newspaper, but after he and his wife were divorced when Ed was 9, the senior Brandt moved to Dallas. So Ed and his younger brother and sister were raised by their mother, Myrtle Frances.

Ed took an immediate liking to college and soon switched his major to mathematics, an excellent choice for a young man with an analytical bent. He also took an immediate liking to Patricia Lawson, whom he escorted on a blind date to the Air Force ROTC ball. Six weeks later, they were engaged and in August 1953 were married.

Later that year, Ed's father-in-law, a Marietta physician, suffered a heart attack. While he was recuperating, Ed and Pat spent several weekends with him, and it was during this time that Ed first thought about a medical career. Nevertheless, after Ed received a B.S. in math from OU in 1954, he and Pat moved to Stillwater where at Oklahoma A&M he spent a year earning a master's degree in math. The wheels, however, were still turning and Ed decided to go to medical school and go into practice with his father-in-law in Marietta.

By his third year, Ed's idea of going into practice with his father-in-law was proving to be impractical. His clinical rotation in obstetrics and gynecology convinced him he wanted nothing to do with it, while in pediatrics he had emotional difficulties dealing with sick children.

Simultaneously Ed was being influenced in a new direction by two mentors, Dr. Stewart Wolf, chairman of the OU medicine department, and Dr. Bill Schottistaedt, who would become dean of OU's School of Public Health. After Ed received his M.D. in 1960, Dr. Wolf arranged things so that Ed could participate in an internal medicine residency as well as pursue a Ph.D. in biostatistics and epidemiology. In 1962, Ed dropped out of the medicine residency and a year later received his doctorate. He was thereupon appointed chairman of the department.

A turning point in Ed's career occurred in 1967-68, when Dr. James Dennis, OU's vice president for medical affairs asked Ed to be his assistant. "I had no interest in administration, but being a good team player I accepted the job." Later he was named associate dean of the medical school. He might have been running the entire medical center within a few years, but he decided to take a position as the dean of the graduate school at the University of Texas Medical Branch in Galveston, Texas. But he never forgot the debt he owed to his mentors at OU. He moved his family of five to Texas in 1970. Patrick, Ed III, and Rex. In 1974 he became dean of the medical school. In 1977 he was appointed vice chancellor for health affairs, administering all six of the state's health science centers.

By the time Ronald Reagan assumed the presidency in January 1981, Ed had been so successful in coordinating the institutions into a coherent state system that friends and admirers in high places, such as the American Medical Assoc., figured he could handle the big federal health agencies of the Public Health Service just as well. On a "Friday the Thirteenth" in February, Brandt was sitting in a regents" meeting when he was told, "the White House is on the line." President Reagan told Brandt he had heard good things about him from the Secretary of Health and Human Services, Richard Schweiker and wanted to offer him the job of assistant secretary for health. His nomination sailed through the Senate on April 29 and he was unanimously confirmed five days later. By 1982, AIDS cases were being reported to the CDC from more cities on the east and west coasts. Though the number was still small, a few non-gay drug abusers had contracted the disease, which implicated the bloodstream as another means of transmitting AIDS. Although some public health officials suspected the AIDS agent was a virus, no one could be sure. Three of the most popular causes people would report were a) God's punishment for sinners, b) a conspiracy to rid the world of gays and drug abusers, c) a virus developed for germ warfare that had "escaped." As 1982 wore on, it became clear that AIDS would not be a flash-in-the-pan disease, and all PHS agencies were involved. In 1982, Brandt formed a PHS committee to report within thirty days on what to do about blood collection and distribution since it was possible that some of the collected blood may have been contaminated. By July 1982, 471 cases of AIDS and almost 200 deaths had been reported. By early 1983, there were almost 1000 cases and nearly 400 deaths. Ed created the Public Health Service Executive Task Force on AIDS in 1983. He reported that of the 2,400 AIDS cases, only about twenty-four may have originated from transfused blood. He also noted that although the AIDS agent was still unknown, "It is likely transmitted by blood and semen." Ed testified on AIDS and other subjects more than one hundred times before congressional committees, serving as a dispenser of useful information or a whipping boy, depending on the attitude of the members. *He said he learned the hard way that losing your temper in public a) doesn't work, b) compels you to say something you will later regret, and c) makes you look like an idiot. It was much better for him to handle confrontations and personal attacks by going off alone to mutter to himself.* In April 1984 he was singled out along with other doctors as being able to substantially reduce the incidence of fear and panic over the disease. Effective Jan. 1, 1985 Ed took on the position of Chancellor of the university's Baltimore campus, University of Maryland. He felt he needed a rest from the PHS.

He was there for four years. After saying that Maryland had not faced AIDS issues in a serious way, Ed was named chairman of the Governor's Task Force on AIDS. In 1988, opportunity knocked. Ed was contacted to become the executive dean in May 1989 for the OU College of Medicine. Then in August 1992 he became the first director of the Center for Health Policy. He would not only teach classes which allowed him after thirty years to return to his first love, but also develop the courses. Ed has no intentions of retiring. He wants to continue doing what he is doing for as long as he can.

Food for thought:

Time is limited but the problems aren't. Set priorities and don't let the urgent crowd out the important.

Your friends make more demands on your time than your enemies and it's hard to turn down requests on the basis of friendship.

Don't let criticism get to you. Otherwise, you start avoiding making hard decisions.

Dr. Brandt's profile in part was taken from the Journal Magazine of the Oklahoma State Medical Assoc. written by Richard Green.

Bill Bright *Evangelist / Author*

Prince Phillip-Dr. Bright-Sir John Templeton-Vonette Bright

I used to work for the Christian Broadcasting Network, so I had heard about Campus Crusade and Dr. Bill Bright years ago. Although I never met him before the day of our interview, my remembrance of quality comments that had been made concerning him were still very vivid. However, the comments fell short in describing this man of God who has spent over 50 years spreading the Gospel of Jesus Christ around the world.

The day we met, I knew he was pressed for time. The state of Oklahoma was honoring their native son, Bill, by the unveiling of a new sign declaring Highway 51 between Coweta and Broken Arrow as "Dr. William R. Bright Bypass." I'm sure over the years he has had the opportunity to stand before many great men and has been awarded high honors. However, nothing could have been more important to him than the presentation of a landmark bearing his name.

As a young boy growing up on a ranch five miles

south of Coweta, he fondly remembers walking Highway 51 from the ranch to school and back on many occasions. His emotional roots still remain there as he recalls his childhood days and the many memories of his saintly mother constantly praying and in communion with God. How fitting that Dr. Bright would grow up to take on the challenges of founding and directing an organization like Campus Crusade for Christ.

Dr. Bright's life wasn't always 100% focused on God. There was a time when as a young man he had his heart set on making a lot of money and having a prestigious title before his name that noted significance. Even though as a young man he was known for his oratative abilities in academic circles, Bill was somewhat disenchanted with what he viewed as the Christian world.

Because of a bad church experience with an immoral pastor he was blinded for a while into thinking his mother was the only true Christian he could trust. Of course, he found out later his perceptions were wrong.

In 1943 Bill graduated from Northeastern State University in Tahlequah, Oklahoma as an outstanding student, having served as student body president, editor of the University Year Book, who's who and outstanding graduate. After spending a year as part of the faculty of Oklahoma State University Extension, he moved to Los Angeles, California in pursuit of a career that would bring him fortune. He started a business called Bright's California Confections and was soon supplying specialty foods to leading department stores and specialty shops across America.

In addition, he began Bright Oil, an oil leasing, drilling and producing company in Kansas and Oklahoma. Dr. Bright was determined to make it big in the financial world. All the while, his mother continued to stand firm in the prayer she prayed over him while she was still carrying him in her womb. On several occasions she had complications that threatened her life during pregnancy, but she prayed and made a vow to God. If He would spare her life, she would dedicate her child to God and teach him spiritual ways.

I know there is a scripture that says, "Train your child up in the way he should go, and when he is old he won't depart from it." Obviously Dr. Bright's mother, Mary Lee, believed those words and because of it, she not only lived to be 93 years old, but she had the privilege of watching her son become a leader of one of the largest Christian organizations in the world. God does answer prayer.

God orchestrated Dr. Bright's life in such a way that while he was in California, he was put in the path of Christian laymen and clergy at the First Presbyterian Church of Hollywood who were able to turn his focus back to God and the direction in which his life was ultimately to follow. His mother's prayers were prevailing.

From 1946 to 1951, Dr. Bright pursued graduate studies at Princeton and Fuller Theological Seminaries. During a brief break in his studies he returned to Coweta where he married his beautiful wife, Vonette Zachary on December 30, 1948. I say beautiful, because I had the opportunity of having lunch with Vonette and she is beautiful inside and out. She has the grace and poise of a woman truly marked by the presence of God in her life. She stands heart to heart with her husband and the ministry to which God has called them.

Dr. Bright enthusiastically shares how Vonette has always played a vital part in the building and sustaining of Campus Crusade for Christ. It is evident, as she stands beside her husband, that she was hand-picked to be his wife, as well as his confidant, advisor and best friend.

Soon after their wedding, Dr. Bright and Vonette returned to California to care for his business interests. A couple of years went by and the company was doing well, but there was a restlessness in Dr. Bright that just couldn't be quieted.

After spending much time in prayer they both felt compelled to make some radical changes in their lives. They made a commitment to Christ in written form pledging to go anywhere and do anything that was required of them. A couple of nights later, God gave Dr. Bright a vision of what we know now as Campus Crusade for Christ. At the time, they didn't know how it was all going to come together, but they were willing to take one step at a time and trust God for the results. They sold their businesses and moved to the nearby University of California campus.

In 1951, the organization began with Dr. Bright and Vonette, two obedient people who felt a desire and a leading to win other people to Jesus Christ around the world. The organization grew from the two of them to 22,000 full time and almost 500,000 trained volunteer staff in all the major countries of the world.

In 1996, Dr. Bright received the prestigious Templeton Prize for Progress in Religion, and was inducted into the Oklahoma Hall of Fame. He has authored over 60 books and pamphlets and received six honorary doctorate degrees. In, 1979, he sponsored a film production entitled "Jesus," which is a full length movie on the life of Christ that has been viewed by over 4 billion 500 million people in 615 languages.

It was a very special day when he was able to lead his father, Forest Dale, to Christ after he and Dr. Bright's mother had been married 35 years. They celebrated their 70th wedding anniversary before they both died at the age of 93.

Dr. Bright has certainly been an example of the power of God working in a person's life. He said he starts each day on his knees with Vonette asking for God's guidance. A lot has happened over his 50 plus years in the ministry. I'm sure the number of lives that have been changed and helped are far greater than what he even realizes. Space doesn't allow for all the many projects that Dr. Bright has been responsible for implementing. Without a doubt, he has honored God with the contract he made many years ago to spread the Gospel around the world. He is a man that is greatly admired and respected and I call it a privilege to have met him.

Bill Bright

Garth Brooks - Singer

There are some exceptions, but normally speaking most Oklahomans are known for their down-to-earth, genuine, home-spun personalities. That's why it's no surprise to us that Garth Brooks has won hearts worldwide with his Oklahoma charm.

I had been trying to make contact with Garth for three and a half years to no avail, until I was down to the wire on my time schedule for the release of this book. Since I knew Garth had moved back to Oklahoma, I decided to take a little drive to the location of his property hoping to drop off some information at the gate. After explaining my project to the gatekeeper he felt compelled to give me some needed advice. He informed me Garth had left the premises a couple of hours earlier and if I would wait patiently for a while I would most likely get to talk to him. Well, as you can imagine, after a three and a half year pursuit, wild horses couldn't have pulled me away from my appointed location.

In consideration of Garth I parked my car a reasonable distance from the gate so I wouldn't appear as a crouching tiger and settled down for my wait. To my surprise a mere 15 minutes passed and there he was pulling up to the gate. I have never been one for intrusion which may be a detriment to my interviewing techniques, but I wanted so much to speak with him. Before I could get myself out of the car he was making his way toward me with a smile that lit up the outdoors. Immediately, I was impressed. Instead of having to run a sprint to get to him before he drove off he graciously came to meet me.

Garth was dressed in a sleeveless gray t-shirt, camouflaged pants, tennis shoes and a ball cap. I'd say that is typical Oklahoma laid back style. I've been to an energy-charged Garth Brooks concert and seen him many times on television, but no appearance did him justice as did an up close and personal view of this gentle man. He always looks adorable, but he is much better looking in person. I'm quite sure he is a wise businessman, but he is still very much the boy next door, the guy who helps the little ole lady across the street and the man whose heart melts at the sound of his child's voice.

Garth was born on February 7, 1962, in Tulsa, Oklahoma and raised in Yukon, Oklahoma. His parents are Troyal Raymond Brooks and the late Colleen Carroll Brooks. Colleen Carroll recorded for Capitol Records in the 1950s and performed with Red Foley on the Ozark Jubilee. As they say "an apple doesn't fall far from the tree. Garth is the youngest of six children. His siblings are Jim, Jerry, Mike, Betsy and Kelly.

After high school Garth attended Oklahoma State University in Stillwater on a track and field scholarship. He studied advertising by day and at night he was busy with odd jobs as well as trying to hone his talents as a singer. I'm sure there are a lot of Stillwater residents who fondly remember Garth's attempts to show Oklahoma his talents. The day finally came when he was willing to make his way to the "big time" (Nashville) or at least take a chance at it.

An acquaintance of mine remembers working at Baker's Shoe store in Tulsa when Garth came in to purchase a pair of shoes. He was rather excited and preparing to leave town for his first attempt in Nashville. I bet my friend wishes now he would have bought the shoes for Garth or at least had him sign his name somewhere with indelible ink. Of course how many times have many of us seen or heard young people talking about making their way to the bright lights just to find out their beam was focused in the wrong direction?

Garth made that first trip to Nashville at the age of 24, but soon returned home feeling somewhat like a fish out of water. After observing numerous other wannabe country stars roaming the streets of Music Row in Nashville, he felt somewhat overwhelmed. However he knew what he wanted and knew he had the talent, but the key was how to convince Nashville. Forgetting about his dream really wasn't an option, nor was revisiting Nashville.

A year or so later he returned to Nashville and for 10 months worked at a boot store while struggling to make contacts to get his songs heard. One night while performing at a charity benefit his talents were finally recognized by an executive at Capitol Records, and he was signed to a recording contract. His first single *Much Too Young (To Feel This Damn Old)*, debuted in 1989. It was followed by his first #1 single, *If Tomorrow Never Comes*, a ballad reminding all of us to show our feelings for loved ones while there is still time. His third single *Not Counting You,* came out in 1990, followed by *The Dance, Friends in Low Places* and *Unanswered Prayers.* All of his songs either keep you swaying with the beat of the music or propel you into reminiscing about your own personal relationships.

In 1991 he amazed the world with *Two of a Kind, Workin' on a Full House, The Thunder Rolls* and *Rodeo*. The hits have continued to flow from Garth and he was named the top-selling solo artist of the century. He took country music to heights they had never yet soared and changed the way many people viewed country music.

If you listen to his music it would be impossible to walk away without finding at least a few songs that touch your heart and remind you of some unique situation. Garth has taken 25 singles to the #1 position on the country charts with sales of over 101 million albums. Those numbers are staggering and yet Garth remains the same humble individual that set out over a decade ago to follow his dream.

In 1993 Garth performed The National Anthem during pre-game festivities at the Super Bowl to a television audience of over 1 billion people. His award-winning music video *We Shall Be Free* premiered during the telecast.

On June 30, 1995, Garth received a star on the legendary Hollywood Walk of Fame. The master of *The Hits*, a limited edition collection of 18 singles spanning Garth's career from 1989 to 1994, was buried under Garth's star.

He also has acting credits which include guest performances on NBC's "Empty Nest" and ABC's "Muppets Tonight" and a cameo appearance on NBC's "Mad About You." Of course many of us saw him during his skits as the host of "Saturday Night Live" in February 1998. He earned a Golden Globe nomination for Best Original Song - Motion Picture for *When You Come Back To Me Again* from the feature film "Frequency."

He has received every honor the recording industry can present to an artist including 2 Grammys, 16 American Music Awards, 11 Country Music Association Awards, 18 Academy of Country Music Awards, 5 World Music Awards, 12 People's Choice Awards and 24 Billboard Music Awards. Need I say more?

Garth has his own film production company, Red Strokes Entertainment based in Los Angeles and has several television movies and feature films in development. Space keeps me from revealing in detail everything this man has accomplished in such a short time. He certainly makes the statement ring true, "good things come to good people." I've never had the opportunity to meet Garth's parents, but I'm of the belief that good people don't just happen. Their lives are in some way guided by individuals who care a great deal about them and to some extent instill values that are pathways to success.

Garth has chosen to take time away from the music business in order to spend time with his three daughters, Taylor Mayne Pearl, August Anna and Allie Colleen. Wisely, he realizes how quickly they grow up and how crucial it is for them to have his physical presence in their lives.

Oklahoma is certainly proud of Garth, not only for his many talents as a performer, but as a man with warmth, charm and a sincere love for mankind.

Bob Brown – *Television Journalist*

I remember several years ago watching Bob on the KOTV Channel 6 News and then one day I looked up and he was reporting on ABC NEWS 20/20. How does a young man born in the mid-western city of Tulsa, Oklahoma in 1944 wind up reporting on human interest stories for one of the top rated prime time television shows in the country?

When Bob was growing up his father, Frank Brown owned the Republic Exploration Company in Tulsa. Bob recalls he loved going to his father's office on South Boulder and watching him work, but he never had a desire to be in the oil business.

His mother Mary Lois, on the other hand, was a wife and homemaker and endearing mother to Bob and his brothers, Frank Eugene, Jr. and Don.

At an early age Bob began performing for the Tulsa Little Theatre as well as the Junior Little Theatre. By the time he turned 13 he was performing juvenile roles in adult productions.

It amazes me how careers develop for people. One would think Bob's life would have continued to unfold into a theatrical career. However, as it turns out acting was just part of the stepping stones that led him in the right direction. In performing a role in the play "The Caine Mutiny Court Martial" he shared the stage with Doug Humphrey's, a gentleman who was in sales for KRMG radio. Doug was so impressed with Bob's performance he asked him to audition for a weekend announcing position for KRMG. Bob took the job and began working weekends and then week days after school.

A year or so later he transferred to KAKC which was known then by Tulsa teenagers as one of the hottest rock and roll stations in town. Bob remained at KAKC for only a few months before he decided to enroll at Carnegie Tech in Pittsburgh, Pennsylvania to further examine his acting talents. After two semesters he decided he was really more suited for the field of broadcasting than the theatrical world so he headed back to Tulsa to resume his position at KAKC.

It seems most of the time he spent at Carnegie was bombarded with thoughts of broadcasting, *but his trip to Pittsburgh helped him sort out his thoughts and help him identify what he really wanted to do with his career* .

In 1964 KOTV Channel 6 hired him and he enrolled in journalism at The University of Tulsa where he graduated.

In 1968 he wore a different kind of hat when the United States Army drafted him for two years of uninterrupted service in Ft. Polk, Louisiana. When he returned KOTV had his job waiting for him.

I asked Bob if he started at the bottom rung with KOTV. He said, "Yes, but in those days the bottom rung wasn't too far down since there were only eight or nine people in the newsroom. Everyone covered their own stories, shot their own film and edited and processed it as well."

Bob stayed at KOTV until 1973 when he left to anchor at KHOU in Houston. From there he was hired by WFAA in Dallas in 1975 where he worked until 1977.

By then he was 33 years old and the opportunity came for him to step into a position on the national level with the ABC network. Mike Shapiro, general manager of WFAA in Dallas, understood Bob's desire to further himself and encouraged him to give it a try. Bob said it was a risky decision to leave a secure job at WFAA in order to step into unfamiliar territory. But he felt he had to pursue it or he would always wonder "what if."

With the job at ABC came a sizable pay cut, but at the time money was not the motivating factor. His first position was a general assignment correspondent working out of the New York Bureau where he stayed for three years. The executive producer of "ABC News," which was later called "World News Tonight," was assigned to the newly formed "20/20" program and decided to take Bob along with him to work as a correspondent. He started full time with "20/20" in 1980 and has been with them ever since reporting on mainly human interest stories.

What an interesting life he has obviously experienced with all the travel and reporting on such a variety of topics. I asked Bob to comment on a couple of stories he had reported on that stood out vividly in his mind.

He told about the episode of 20/20 when he interviewed an emergency room doctor who had been a physician in Vietnam.

Apparently for 15 years he had agonized over saving a soldier's life who probably wouldn't have what he perceived as a "life worth living." The soldier lost his sight, part of his brain and the limbs of his body. Most of the time in Vietnam the infirmary was so overcrowded with casualties that soldiers who were viewed as being hopeless were set aside so attention could be given to others.

On this particular day the infirmary had a light load and the physician, for some unknown reason, decided to try and save this dying soldier. Miraculously the soldier lived, but left the doctor wondering for years if he had made the right decision. He finally went in search for the soldier and to his amazement found him living a quite remarkable life. He was married with two children and living a very happy and productive life. The story was given the Dupont Award.

Bob is quite pleased with the opportunities life has afforded him. He has been privileged to travel the world and meet an extraordinary range of people in all professions and walks of life. He has also learned to respect people and cultures on a level he never would have imaged.

Bob and I talked about "defining moments" in a person's life and "risks" people take in order to acquire what they view as success. His opinion, and I agree, is "*nothing truly great happens unless there is some kind of risk involved." The question then becomes are you willing to take the risk?* So many people are fearful when faced with unknown territory. Often they let those fears keep them from some of the greatest rewards in life.

Bob also pointed out when a person's self esteem is lowest they tend to let opportunities pass them by for fear of failing once again. That statement reminded me of the words Paul Harvey said during our interview. "We all fall from time to time, but those who deserve even a modicum of what the world calls success get up again and sometimes again and again and dust themselves off."

On a spiritual note Bob said he tries to approach everything he does in an ethical manner (a trait he learned from his parents). He said it is very easy in his line of work to become very self-centered. But he realizes the important issue is the project and the interest of the people he is dealing with.

Bob and his wife Nancy have been married 19 years. He has a son Kevin, from a previous marriage, who is a professional musician. Obviously creativity is genetic.

Charles P. Brown

U.S. Army General

Charles was born January 11, 1918 in McAlester, Oklahoma as one of four children. His parents named him Charles Pershing Brown, as a patriotic gesture, since World War I was being fought at the time under the leadership of the great General Charles Pershing Brown. Of course it wasn't expected that young Charles P. Brown would some day himself carry the title of General as well.

Growing up, Charles' father had been the county judge for Pittsburgh County, where his hometown of McAlester was located. His mother had been a teacher, so Charles knew how important education was if he was going to create a good life for himself. His parents set a good example, so Charles set out early in life to chart out the path he would go down in order to become successful.

By the Fall of 1936, Charles had enrolled at the University of Oklahoma in Norman. In those days ROTC was mandatory for fresh-

man and sophomores. Charles had never given any thought to making a career out of the Army. Since his father was a judge, he pretty much assumed he would enter the law profession as well. His first semester he brought home 17 hours of A's, which over the years remained a source of pride for him.

When he entered his junior year of college he was given the opportunity to join the advanced ROTC program. He still wasn't planning on making a career out of the Army, but he felt since he had already spent two years, he might as well go two more years and obtain a Reserve Commission.

Upon graduation in 1940 he was commissioned as a second lieutenant in the Field Artillery Reserve. Soon after, it was obvious the U.S. was probably going to go into war, so Charles as a new lieutenant had another decision to make. He could get a two year scholarship to Harvard University to study for his MBA degree or he could accept a commission into the regular Army. He chose the Army and became one of 42 ROTC graduates who received regular Army commission that year.

Charles was assigned to the 2nd Battalion of the 18th Field Artillery Regiment and within two years he was promoted to Captain. By this time, Charles was beginning to see that an Army career was apparently going to be his present, as well as his future. His goal of getting his MBA degree was still of importance, but for the time being it would have to wait.

Since his military career seemed to be intact, he decided to add another dimension to his life. He married a graduate of his alma mater. Evelyn graduated from the University of Oklahoma a year after Charles. They were both excited to see what the world had to offer them as a couple.

It wasn't long before Charles was promoted to major and became Executive Officer of the 193rd Field Artillery Battalion. Charles was only 26 years old with only three and a half years of service under his belt, and already he was showing a tremendous amount of leadership ability.

In 1945, another promotion came and he held the rank of Lieutenant Colonel. A short time later, he began preparing for his first tour overseas.

When Charles began telling me about his experiences overseas in New Guinea, it sounded more like a war movie than a real life story. He told how intense the fighting would get and the danger that seemed to lurk around every corner. It was rough land where the Malayan people lived. Some of them were head hunters.

The men and women were relatively short and stocky. The men wore G-strings with a head hunter's ax attached to their waist. They carried a metal headed spear and wore a beenie-type head covering made of reed. Hanging around the beenie were dog teeth because they were known for eating dogs as well as people. The women would carry heavy loads held inside a cloth carrying device strapped to their forehead that hung down their backs. They wore burlap wrap around dresses with nothing on from the waist up. It sounds like something we would see in National Geographic magazines.

Shortly after the bombing of Hiroshima, Charles' command position changed and eventually he was sent back to the states. In August of 1947 he was assigned to the First Headquarters at Governor's Island New York for a tour as a student in graduate school. He went to New York University where he received his MBA degree in 1948 after only a year's work. Then orders were given to him to report to the Department of the Army Staff, specifically to the office of the Comptroller of the Army.

For the next four years until 1952, his attention was devoted to the organization of the Army. In 1955 he was promoted to a full Colonel and the progression of promotions never stopped until he was promoted to Two Star General in 1964. In 1967 he was living in Fort Myers, Virginia when he received a phone call saying he was to report to Fort Sill, Oklahoma as the Commanding General. That was a highlight of his life to come back to Fort Sill as the head man. Three years later he spent 15 months in Vietnam and then his last military assignment was at the Test Evaluation Command in Maryland.

General Charles Pershing Brown's advice to young officers is "never pass up a command. There isn't anything more enjoyable than commanding an artillery battalion, helping to train it, develop it, take it to war or anything else that is required of you."

After 35 years in the Army, General Brown retired, taking a wealth of experience and memories along with him. He believes he served with some of the finest soldiers the Army has ever had.

I enjoyed visiting General Brown in his home during our interview. It wasn't hard to visualize him as a general in command. It was so ingrained in him that the spirit of the position seemed to ooze from him with every word. There was only one time I saw a different side of the General and that was when he was talking to his current wife, Juanita. There had to be a beautiful love story contained in that relationship, because he only had eyes for her. His whole countenance changed when she began to talk to him and his arms reached lovingly out when she entered the room.

I'm thankful that I had the opportunity to meet General Brown. He passed away not long after our interview. I wish he would have had the opportunity to see the completion of this book, but hopefully his children, Michael and Patricia will see it as yet another honor bestowed on their very distinguished father.

Freckles Brown

Bull Rider

Freckles was born Warren Granger Brown in Wheatland, Wyoming on January 18, 1921. His family and friends remember him as a soft-spoken man. He only stood 5' 7" but his height didn't stop him from becoming a legend in his own time.

Freckles grew up as the youngest of 10 children, on a homesteaded farm in Lingle, Wyoming. He always wanted to be a cowboy. As a young man he didn't know about rodeo cowboys, only ranch cowboys. He rode all of the draft horses on his parents farm. By age 5 he began riding a mustang. This horse was caught running wild and broke by his oldest brother.

The nickname "Freckles" was given to him by a dairyman he worked for in Tucson, Arizona when he was 14.

In 1937 Freckles, at the age of 16, entered his first rodeo in Willcox, Arizona. His rodeo career would span 37 years, from age 16 at that first rodeo in 1937 to age 53 when he entered his last rodeo in Tulsa in 1974.

But it wasn't until 1941 after riding a bronc 50 miles to town that he won his first all-around trophy. After his win he rode the bronc back to the Cody Rodeo Ranch where he worked. Through his rodeo career he competed in bareback riding, calf roping, saddle bronc riding, steer wrestling (or bull dogging), team roping or wild horse race and bull riding.

During the first part of World War II Freckles was stationed at Lawton, Oklahoma. There he rode mules, boxed, rode jumping horses, shod mules and entered all the rodeos he could. It was during that time that he met and married Edith. Later he was sent to Ft. Riley, Kansas to horse shoeing school. After he became a licensed Farrier he never shod horses for the Army, instead he was trained for the O.S.S. He learned to speak fluent Mandarin Chinese, then trained Chinese Paratroopers for the Invasion of Japan.

Freckles' wife Edith was by his side through it all, when he was stationed at Fort Sill in World War II, when he rode in rodeos in Europe and when he returned to Oklahoma to raise cattle and hay.

Freckles was an All-Around cowboy, entering the Bareback Riding, Saddle Bronc Riding, Bulldogging, Bull Riding and the Wild Horse Race. He won his first saddle in New York in 1950 in the Wild Horse Race.

In 1959 he qualified for the first NFR in Dallas, Texas. The Army had taught Freckles to be physically fit and nutritionally minded. On a normal day Freckles ran 3 miles a day, did at least 50 clapping push-ups, then 50 one-arm push-ups on the left and right.

In 1962 Freckles won the title "World Champion Bull Rider" at the National Finals Rodeo while sitting on the sidelines. In October of that year he had been badly injured at a rodeo in Portland, Oregon. After riding a bull named "Black Smoke" for the required eight seconds, Freckles was going to use his head to break the fall, but Black Smoke ducked his head. The end result was neck surgery and traction. However he had won enough money so that he was qualified as the 'World Champion Bull Rider" for that year.

Freckles resumed riding in 1964 at Killeen, Texas. He made a classic buck-off on his Saddle Bronc and landed hard on his neck and shoulders. Freckles stated, "If I can take this kind of a fall, then I'm healthy!"

In 1967 at the National Finals in Oklahoma City, Freckles wasn't in the running for the championship, but perhaps he is remembered better than the bull rider that did win the championship that year. That year Freckles rode the "unridable" bull called Tornado. Tornado, owned by Jim Shoulders, was the first bull Freckles drew on the opening night of the Finals, December 1, 1967.

That night there was a conspicuous deficient crowd that showed up to cheer for the rodeo cowboys. Tornado in his rodeo career had scared his share of bull riders off. Some preferred to turn him out rather than try to ride him. But Freckles was tickled when he drew him. He had watched that bull for years. Tornado went high and far on his first jump out, something he was known to do. He spun three or four times. He changed his pattern on Freckles, jumping straight ahead and then back to the right, but nothing he did could throw the determined man. Freckles never heard the whistle. People that knew Freckles knew he had a hearing problem. The crowd went wild and the bullfighters moved in. That's how he knew he had him rode.

Tornado had gone unridden for 220 professional rides. He died in 1972 and is buried at the Cowboy Hall of Fame in Oklahoma City.

After Freckles' incredible first ride on Tornado, the struggling National Finals became a huge success with packed out crowds at every performance.

A tribute to Freckles became a tradition at some of the yearly Finals. Red Steagall would sing his "Ballad of Freckles Brown." Clem McSpadden would introduce Freckles to the crowd and give a little background on his memorable ride on Tornado. Clem would also later give the eulogy at Freckle's funeral.

At the December 1982 Finals, Clem announced that Freckles had prostate cancer. When the cancer was found in November, Freckles was advised to go to Houston for six weeks of radiation treatment. However, Freckles wanted to go to the Finals in December before starting treatments. Friends threw a fund raiser-dance at the end of the Finals for Freckles to help with medical expenses. Red Steagall, Reba McEntire and Moe Bandy performed.

In March 1983 Freckles was back home and giving interviews. But early in 1987 Freckles, now age 66, was back in the hospital in Houston. Clem McSpadden put together a fund-raiser auction to help pay for Freckles' medical expenses. It was to be held March 22, 1987. Sadly, Freckles died on Friday, March 20, 1987 at his ranch in Oklahoma. The fund-raiser still took place that Sunday at the Holidome in McAlester, Oklahoma.

During Freckles' rodeo career, in addition to being World Champion in 1962, he also was given the "Wrangler Award" from the "Western Heritage Awards" at Oklahoma City's Cowboy Hall of Fame and the 1983-Trophy in Denver for his "life-long contribution to the sport of rodeo."

I spoke with Freckles' daughter and only child, Donna Harrison. Her admiration for her father is undeniable and she assured me their relationship was an extremely close one. She also unashamedly pointed out what a good Christian her father was and how he lived his Christianity on a daily basis as evidenced by his warmth and compassion for his fellowman.

Donna with her husband Wiley have two children, Cody and John. Freckles considered Wiley as the son he would like to have had. His grandson Cody roped during high school and won his first buckle at the MRCA Finals at age 13. He was also put in the Pro Baseball draft at age 18. The youngest grandson, John is a PRCA Roman Rider, Trick Rider and Trick Roper. He is becoming a legend in his own way. He Roman Rode for one of the openings at the 2001 NFR in Las Vegas.

Anyone who knows the incredible work of Charles Banks Wilson will recognize his handiwork in the picture of Freckles Brown. Thank you Charles for allowing us to use your work.

Mark Bryan - *Musician*

I met an incredible man on Monday, June 3, 2002. I went to his home so he could help me on a project, not thinking of including him in this book, yet remembering the thought had briefly crossed my mind. My son, Jackson Ray had solicited his services on many occasions to record songs on C.D. He had mentioned Mark in passing but had never gone into any great depth except to say he was a talented blind guy. I remember when he said that thinking to myself, "Oh really," but two years passed before I had the opportunity to meet him. I thought our meeting would be comprised of his expertise in my narrating this book on C.D. but instead our time was spent in a very informative heartfelt conversation. The result was a knowing that I had to include Mark as one of the Distinguished Oklahomans.

Mark was born on February 14, 1961 in Port Angeles, Washington to Robert and Marla Kueber. His life began in turmoil and by the time he was 9 months old the effects of that turmoil was becoming quite evident in his young life. Infants by God's design hunger for the nurturing and cuddling of the two people they rely on most in the world -their Mom and Dad. But for Mark and his two sisters only their mom would be able to instill in them the emotional security their hearts craved. A rage of fury permeated through his father that seemed to be ignited when the needs of young Mark were made known. As an infant Mark's father shook him so hard it resulted in a cerebral hemorrhage which by the time he was 4 years old led to total blindness.

Of course I was gasping as Mark revealed these painful truths about his childhood and yet the whole time he was saying to me "wait, wait, you don't understand." From that moment on I knew exactly why Mark deserved the title of Distinguished Oklahoman. The wisdom that flowed from this faith-filled man could only have come from revelation knowledge he had received from God. I'm expecting that someday everyone will be able to learn more about Mark's incredible journey in a book that will come out in the future. Until then, I will leave you wondering, yet hopefully knowing that "what the enemy of his soul meant for evil God was turning it around for Mark's good." Mark was hesitant about speaking of what the world views as his misfortune knowing that the normal response is for the reader to be filled with rage and disgust for his father which is a reaction that Mark battles with every time the story is told. If the transactions of the past only ignite fury from the hearer then the flames of the past still continue to burn. But if the flames are put to rest with forgiveness and hope then Mark's life can bring restoration rather than defeat and hope rather than hopelessness and a knowing that all is well.

When Mark was 4 years old his family was living on an Indian reservation in Port Angeles. He recalls the young Indian children were always riding horses and hunting for game, but because of his disability he couldn't participate. Even at such a young age he knew he had to find some kind of an outlet for himself he just didn't know what that would be. Then one day his grandmother sent him a small electric organ and right away his destiny began falling into place. He recalls hiding out in his bedroom hour after hour making up youthful little songs and matching them up with tunes he was able to compose on his organ. Somehow music made total sense to Mark and the intensity of his desire to create was beginning to be cultivated through the ebony and ivorys of the keyboard.

At the age of 6 his mother decided to enroll him in the Vancouver Washington School for the Blind where he lived as a resident for a year until the family moved to Missouri. The St. Louis School for the Blind was to be Mark's home for the next several years. I asked Mark if that was a "good thing," and he said, "yes, for the time being." It was there that his shop teacher, Tom Culiton revealed to him the goodness that really can lie within a man. Tom showed Mark the caring and patient side of himself. Probably without realizing it Tom was creating in Mark's mind an image that men could be trusted and relied on. It was during those school years that Mark's musical talents began to be recognized. He had never had any formal musical training and yet people were soliciting his services to accompany them while they sang. During those years along with honing his musical talent he was also coming to the realization that he was more than just a young blind man. His life was not defined by his disabilities but what he was able to create within himself.

His mother eventually divorced his father and married Harvey Bryan who Mark grew to love deeply. Once again God had placed in his life a man that was able to leave a lasting impression on Mark of the way a good man should be. The family then moved to Stillwater, Oklahoma and Mark became a resident of the Oklahoma State School for the Blind in Muskogee, Oklahoma. However, after a year Mark decided he wanted to move to Stillwater with the rest of the family and attend Stillwater High School and acclimate himself to the rituals of the seeing world. He knew if he was ever going to live like the majority of the rest of the world lived then he had to quit being sheltered under the guise of "the disabled."

Stillwater became a great outlet for Mark's music and before long he teamed up with some other musicians in a western swing band. He fondly remembers those days when the other band members willingly carted his piano from one venue to the other in order to have him as part of the gang. Mark was learning about life and meeting an incredible array of people that would continue to produce within him a talent that couldn't be stopped.

In 1980 Mark was introduced to Audrey Alan a college student who was given a class assignment to interview a disabled person for her recreational therapy project. The interview was enlightening, but the greatest success from the interview came 10 years later when Audrey became Mark's wife. They married in 1990 and moved to Tulsa where Audrey is employed as a social worker.

Mark's talent as a musician has led him from one venue to the other and has continued to open doors for him to share his expertise with other musicians as well. Even though his musical and lyrical talents are very important to him he knows they are just the pathway being used in his spiritual journey. During our first meeting I was privileged to have Mark sit at his beautiful grand piano and play a couple of songs for me that he had written. Talent seems to flow rather easily from him and his songs leave you hungering for more. I remember a few days ago hearing about the gentleman who had written the song *It Is Well With My Soul* during a tragic time in his life. When you hear the words of that great spiritual classic you know the author has experienced the words he sang. Only from the depths of ones inner being can you truly say *It Is Well With My Soul* when tragedy occurs. Mark's singing and the revelation of his life's journey thusfar also reveals those truths that his soul cries out.

Mark is in the midst of creating his first album titled *The Sculptor and the Stone* which no doubt in my opinion will leave his audience with a sense of awe. Mark is keenly aware that we are all on a journey toward "greatness." I asked Mark what makes him different from the other sight impaired people that he grew up around. He said, "I don't see myself as impaired, I see myself as evolving and being created into the person I was meant to be."

All of us have the opportunity to make choices every day. We can choose to be bitter or better. We can choose to be overcomers or to be overcome and we can create or disintegrate. The choice is ours. For Mark, I have no doubt that life will continue to unfold as it should. *His desire is that others would understand how truly linked together and dependent we are on each other. In doing so, that understanding will bring about the real meaning of " love."*

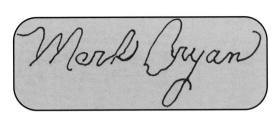

Jim Buratti and Shawntel Smith

It's true Jim still has a little bit of that Northeastern twang in his voice. Yet he has the friendliness and down home charm of what I attribute to being an Oklahoman.

Coming from Dover, N.J., a town 38 miles west of New York City, Jim never in a thousand years thought he would spend his college days, let alone his career life in the mid west state of Oklahoma. As we all know, there is definitely a cultural difference between the two states. However, one of Jim's older brothers had chosen Oklahoma State University to get his Restaurant Management Degree. He loved Oklahoma. Two years later when it was time for little brother Jim to make a college choice in the field of radio and television, OSU seemed to be the most likely choice, at least to Jim's brother and his somewhat protective parents.

Jim reluctantly enrolled at OSU after arriving during the suffering heat wave of an August afternoon. Six months later, Jim was ready to pull up stakes and transfer to California. Once again, parental reality struck when his parents gave him the option of family paid tuition at OSU verses "work to pay" tuition. It wasn't a choice he wanted to make but he opted for OSU. Now, 30 plus years later, he is still glad he did.

At the time, since most OSU students were from within the state, the majority would go home on the weekends. Jim, however, was too far from home so that gave him the opportunity to experience several more hours of radio time than the average student. When he graduated he was named "Outstanding Journalism Student" at OSU by Sigma Delta Chi the journalism fraternity. He had also been awarded a few scholarships which gave him the opportunity to learn a lot about radio.

So often students zero in on one area of their chosen field. With tunnel vision they don't allow themselves the possibilities that may be waiting right around the corner. Jim covered the gamut which gave him quite an edge over some of the other students. After graduating from OSU he took the summer off to tour Europe, never realizing what an incredible wealth of information he was gathering that would be useful to him in the future.

In the fall he took a job at a small radio station in New Jersey and shortly after became engaged to Barbara Kurtz one of his high school classmates. After a year and a half they packed their bags and moved to Atlanta where they remained for the next nine years as Jim continued to hone his talent in radio. In 1981 his brother coaxed him back to Oklahoma to get him involved in the oil business, a venture that lasted only a few years before Jim once again took over the airwaves.

Jim became the news director of the Oklahoma News Network for the next 10 years. Since his program was broadcast over 40 or 50 stations throughout the state it gave Jim a lot of name recognition which prepared him for the position he has now as host of the successful television program "Discover Oklahoma."

The state tourism department had a program called the Governor's Tourism Tour where by, they invite people to travel by bus, around the state, in an attempt to interest them on the beauty of Oklahoma. They invited Jim, as a media person, to travel on one of the chartered buses. The bus makes puddle stops along the way just long enough for a person to take in a few of the sights. Jim's intentions were to air a three-part radio broadcast on "Traveling in Oklahoma."

Jim was so enamored with what he saw on the 2 day trip that what started out as a three-part radio broadcast to promote tourism turned into a 20-part radio series. The bug had bitten him. The young man who came to Oklahoma Territory in 1968 kicking and screaming had come to realize what a beautiful state he was living in. In fact he had truly become "an Oklahoman."

Jim won the top media award in 1990 for his 20-part radio series and the following January he was recruited full-time at the Tourism Department. He suggested media coverage be done by way of television. So in April 1991 the inception of "Discover Oklahoma" began.

As of this date, over 517 shows have been produced telling about all the wonderful things there are to see and do in Oklahoma. Jim still insists most people don't realize just how beautiful Oklahoma really is. He says our finest asset is our friendly people and I tend to agree. We have numerous museums, over 150 Bed and Breakfast locations and countless outdoor recreational sites for hunting, fishing and boating.. We have beautiful state parks and resorts as well as areas of the state that are simply breathtaking parts of nature.

Since writing my last book I had already come to appreciate the people of Oklahoma better. Now, after listening to Jim, it gave me greater insight into the beauty of the state itself. I even pay more attention now when I drive past a lake or see a rolling hill lined with plush green trees. Thanks, Jim.

Dennis Byrd - Athlete

When you think of Dennis Byrd, your first thought might be, "what a great football player." But as I left Dennis's office after our interview I thought, "what a great husband, father and friend."

Several years ago I remember watching a television movie on the life of Dennis Byrd, never realizing that a few years later I would be sitting before him. I can't begin to tell you all the amazing aspects of Dennis Byrd's life. You need to read his book, *Rise and Walk,* to appreciate the degree in which he triumphed over adversity.

I was especially inspired by Dennis when I saw how strong his faith is. So often we hear people "talk the talk," but they don't know how to "walk the walk." Apparently Dennis has been groomed for this walk all of his life. As he describes it, he came from a strong, spiritual family that taught him at a very young age how to rely on God for his guidance and strength.

The ultimate test of his faith was brought to fruition in 1992 as he lay motionless on the cold hard ground at Giant Stadium in New York City. Within a split second his career as a professional football player had changed forever. He collided with a teammate, shattering his neck and paralyzing his body. After seven hours of surgery he was told he might never walk again. Yet two months later he was taking steps and on February 12, 1993 he returned to his home in Owasso, Oklahoma.

It seems like the start of recovery was so quick and easy. However, a lot transpired in those weeks and months that followed. Dennis realized the true meaning of "walking out his faith." He found out what it meant to "hold on" in spite of what he saw or how he felt. With his wife, Angela who was carrying their unborn child, Haley and his two-year old daughter Ashtin, by his side, Dennis was determined to recover from his ordeal and live life once again to its fullest. Now, several years later, Dennis has recovered with only a limited amount of disability, which he believes will continue to correct itself in time.

He has formed the Dennis Byrd Foundation to help children with disabilities. Eventually Dennis plans to have a camp located 10 miles east of Guthrie, Oklahoma. The 478 acres of land has been purchased by the Feed the Children Organization. It will be a place where children with disabilities and life threatening illnesses can come to get away from the clinical setting and receive hope and encouragement. The camp has been named Eagle Springs. The name in part comes from the scripture in Isaiah 40:31 which says: "They that wait upon the Lord will renew their strength. They will mount up with wings as eagles. They will run and not grow weary. They will walk and not faint." A natural spring also runs through the property.

Dennis said volunteers at the camp are always needed. He is heavily involved in fund raising ideas to help finance the camp. Of course any financial help from individuals would ensure the camps completion.

I asked Dennis what sets him apart from others who have gone through great trials. He said, *"It is my indomitable spirit, a spirit everyone has at their disposal, but few grab hold of."*

It was obvious to me that Dennis is a great motivational speaker. In our short conversation he quickly motivated me to be a better person. He gave me a few wisdom tips that I would like to share.

Don't allow limitations that are either put upon you by someone or physical limitations to stop you from a dream you have. Don't focus on the things you can't do. Focus on what you can do with such intensity that it becomes an unstoppable force. Be thankful for the little things.

Time exposes a person's true intentions. Time exposes a good heart and a bad heart. If you are patient enough to be observant over a long period of time, you will learn about the people you are around. Time reveals everything and people's actions reveal themselves. You need time to see a person's actions so you will know the intent of his heart.

Dennis may have gone through some tremendous trials in his life but they appear to have made him stronger. Only when you have been "tried by fire" can you come through an ordeal with the wisdom Dennis has obtained.

Ed Calhoon - Physician

Dr. Calhoon was born on December 9, 1922 in Beaver, Oklahoma a town he still considers his home. Except for a brief break from 1942-1944 where he was a private in the U.S. Army his loyalties have remained with Oklahoma. He was educated at North Western University in Alva and at the University of Oklahoma Medical Center. His internship and general surgical residency were taken at Hillcrest hospital in Tulsa. He chose to return to his home town in the panhandle to practice medicine and become a leader in that community while serving in numerous capacities on the state and national levels.

Dr. Calhoon is a small town general practitioner who epitomizes what a physician is...a man who is dedicated to the medical care of his community. He cares about what happens in this country...at the same time caring for a new born child he has just delivered or a long time neighbor he has treated professionally and worked beside as a friend. He still makes house calls and everyone in Beaver knows him. He has traveled by helicopter to rescue snow bound travelers when blizzards have struck the area. He's a leader in his home community. He says he is a surgeon by vocation, but a rancher by avocation. His office is filled with memorabilia from the old west...

Winchester rifles, antique spurs and saddles. He has a collection of 60 saddles.

Dr. Calhoon is a teacher, too. He has been a preceptor professor for Oklahoma University Health Science Center since 1954 and a visiting lecturer to Oklahoma University Medical Center many occasions over the years. He served as President of the Oklahoma Medical School Alumni Association, was given honored Medical Alumni Status by that group in 1980 and was named Oklahoma Physician of the Year in 1984 by the Oklahoma University Health Sciences Center.

He has made his influence in medicine felt around the world. From serving as President of the Oklahoma State Medical Association, he went on to serve on many committees in the American Medical Association and continues to be the Oklahoma State Medical Association delegate to the national body. The AMA saw his service on the Council on Rural Health for four years and he also served the AMA Council on Legislation.

The National Health Care Advisory Board of Bethesda, Maryland, appointed him to study health care systems in the United Kingdom in 1973. He has been a member of the International College of Surgeons since 1960. By Presidential appointment he serves on the National Cancer Advisory Board of the National Cancer Institute. He has also served on the National Advisory Council for Health Care Systems of the National Institute of Health.

He is typical of the Panhandle resident in his political stance...a friendly, warm, intelligent, down to earth conservative, with roots deeply imbedded in Western culture. Dr. Calhoon says the Panhandle is very conservative...he claims it is the most enterprising part of the state, and the most conservative. That penchant for conservatism, independence and self-reliance made him a member of the Republican Party... and not just a member, but a very active leader of that political group. He has been a delegate to the Republican National Convention and has served as State Chairman or Co-Chairman for Republican candidates for President...including Presidents Nixon, Ford and Reagan.

He has been a member of the Oklahoma State Republican Executive Committee and was Chairman of the Oklahoma Medical Political Action Committee, as well as serving on the Oklahoma State Republican Finance Committee.

Because of his dedication to causes in which he believes, he has earned many honors...among them the A.H. Robins Community Service Award given yearly to the Outstanding Oklahoma Medical Practitioner as well as the Award of Special Merit presented by the Oklahoma State Medical Association.

Dr. Ed Latta Calhoon epitomizes the spirit and image of Oklahoma...modern and productive, with a strong flavor of frontier spirit and self-reliance. His friendliness...hard work...ambition...self-sacrifice...love of family, honesty and team work are in the finest tradition of rural Oklahoma.

Dr. Calhoon's dedication to medicine...whether in practice serving a neighbor in his hometown...or in fighting for a cause to help all humanity worldwide...has earned him a place in the Oklahoma Hall of Fame. Profile written by Dr. James Davis who introduced Dr. Calhoon during his induction into the Oklahoma Hall of Fame.

Debbie Campbell - Singer

Debbie Campbell may not be a name everyone recognizes, but she has been in the music scene for quite some time. I heard a lot about her as I interviewed people around Tulsa. I was very pleased when I finally had the opportunity to meet her.

Originally a Texan, Debbie visited Tulsa, Oklahoma briefly in 1966 while touring in an all girl band called "The Kandy Kanes."

It all started when her parents bought her a guitar when she was 14 years old. She always loved music, and was part of choirs and performed in talent shows whenever there was an opportunity. When she became a part of the girl's band, it was quite a chore at their young age to find someone willing to manage their careers. Luckily they were introduced to a young man that put everything in motion.

By the summer of 1968 after finishing the ninth grade, the girls packed up their belongings and headed for Hollywood in search of an agent. Correspondence courses then became Debbie's avenue for education. She began devoting tremendous time and effort in the pursuit of her dream. From 1968 to 1974, Debbie honed her talent in California before making her final move to Tulsa. Her music went through different changes as the decades changed. The 60's brought rock and roll. The 70's ushered in rhythm and blues and her tour with the legendary J.J. Cale. In the 80's, Emily, a friend of Debbie's, opened a club on 15th Street in Tulsa called "Cherry's." That is where Debbie began her jazz format.

Emily was a good friend of Leon Russell. In fact, she was the inspiration for his song *Sweet Emily.* It was Emily who introduced Debbie to what was called "torch singing," a rendition of old songs, the older the better. Debbie's range of music went from the early 1920's to the present day music.

It hasn't always been an easy road that Debbie has traveled on. She readily admits she had to make some changes in her life in order to function as a better human being. However, the hard times made her see life more clearly. *She views all people as individuals on their own personal journeys to wholeness.*

As most of us can testify, we want to be successful in our chosen careers. Debbie had the opportunity to meet many well known people along the way and quickly recognized that success comes in different forms. Fame is fleeting, but *success is knowing who you are and feeling comfortable in your own skin doing what makes you happy.*

Debbie found out that fame comes with a price, and she wasn't willing to get that fame at "any cost." Instead, after releasing a few albums and contemplating a move to Nashville, she decided to settle into a career based solely in Tulsa. She knows she is not setting the world on fire. Yet she is happy with her life and what she has accomplished.

As I sat there and listened to Debbie, I felt her contentment and was eager to hear how she viewed everyday life that sometimes throws us so many curves. *Debbie feels like life is a process, not a destination and each day is a unique gift. To make any other day more special than the one we are living at the time is to lose sight of that day.* She tries simply to enjoy breathing in and out knowing it is a gift to wake up every morning. *You don't have to fear the day and self-pity is a bad place to be.*

I could relate to what Debbie was saying and was thankful that even though it took me a while to get there, I, too, had begun to feel some of that contentment that seems to appear with the wisdom of time.

Debbie says she will continue her singing and let life unfold as it should. In November of 1999 she was the featured entertainer for a banquet at the Betty Ford Center. Some of the past entertainers had been Elizabeth Taylor and Liza Minnelli.

I haven't had the opportunity to hear Debbie sing, but with her exuberant personality and her love of music, I'm sure it would be a night to remember.

Debbie Campbell

Vida Chenoweth

Musician / Missionary

Vida's father, Louis Chenoweth, was the founder of the Chenoweth and Green Music Company which served the Southwest for 75 years with five stores in Oklahoma. Vida's childhood was entrenched with the knowledge of musical instruments as far back as she can remember. Saturday, Sundays, and anytime her father's store was closed, she and her siblings had full run of the instruments and learned to play several of them. But, after learning to play the Marimba at the age of thirteen, nothing else seemed quite as interesting. The Marimba is a large wooden instrument, a type of Xylophone that makes unusually mellow, resonant tones. Even though the Marimba's origin dates back many centuries in Indonesia, Africa and Central America, it was uncommon in European countries and so an instructor was hard to find. Consequently,

Vida had to apply her knowledge of piano technique to develop her own method of playing 4-part harmonies and counterpoint on the Marimba.

On November 18, 1956 the very gifted Vida Chenoweth stepped onto the stage of New York's Town Hall as an unknown performer playing an unusual instrument that was totally unknown to symphony audiences. When the evening was over, Vida had shown New York that she was a gifted artist and the Marimba had been introduced to the 20th Century world of concert music.

From then on, with 3 double degrees all in different areas of music, Vida began to tour the world as the foremost concert Marimbist. The New York Times and other papers praised Vida for her mastery of the Marimba; she played with 4 mallets often independent of one another and was capable of using 5 and 6 mallets when the music made those demands.

Jorge Sarmientos, Guatemala's foremost composer, dedicated his Concerto for Marimba and Orchestra to Vida. Robert Kurka, noted as a composer and also as a performer (San Diego Symphony), wrote Concerto for Marimba and Orchestra especially for her to perform. The demands of the piece were so strenuous that Vida found it necessary to take fencing lessons to strengthen her legs in order to have balance of movement. Ultimately, the wide leaps and agile artistic movements became a hallmark of her performance.

She eventually went to Guatemala to research the history of the Marimba and authored Marimbas of Guatemala, her first book; it was published by the University of Kentucky Press in 1962.

Vida was in the midst of a great career when she began attending the Calvary Baptist Church where Rev. Stephen Olford was teaching. Her heart was deeply moved as he began challenging people to examine their commitments to Christ. Two nights later, while lighting a gas oven, an explosion severely injured her right hand. Gangrene eventually set in and there was a real possibility that the fingers of her right hand would have to be amputated. If not amputated the doctors felt her hand would be permanently stiff. She returned to Oklahoma to recuperate. During her months of recovery Vida had to rethink where her life was headed. A new spiritual vision was beginning to form in her mind. Her hand miraculously was restored to complete wholeness, yet Vida had found a new path to follow. That summer she attended the Summer Institute of Linguistics sponsored by the Wycliffe Bible Translators on the University of Oklahoma campus. Vida decided to turn from the concert stage to the needy people of the jungle even though her hand was no longer a threat to her career. She wanted to devote her life to translating the Bible into their unknown language, in a part of the world few knew. This, like being a Marimbist previously, was breaking new ground. On a 7,000 ft. ridge in the middle of New Guinea the Usarufa people were just emerging from the Stone Age. Like many other tribes there, they still ate their dead and practiced mutilation in some of their rites. Her teammate Dr. Darlene Bee was a distinguished linguist who cracked the code of their grammar and made communication possible.

Their surroundings were primitive to say the least. Vida had gone from extravagant concert halls to the vast jungles of New Guinea.

Immediately Vida and Darlene began deciphering the New Guinea language and started to produce an alphabet. Deciphering the New Guinea language was quite a task since the Usarufas language was tonal and its grammar unrelated to other languages of the world. After many months of listening Vida and Darlene became proficient in Usarufa and ceased to speak English in the village. At that point they were ready to develop a written language that would become the basis for translating the Bible.

During the next fourteen years Vida lived and worked with these people as one of their own. Her daily food consisted of white sweet potatoes and a type of greens. Every three months she would travel to the base of operations where she would indulge in some type of meat and fruit. After a five year stay Vida took a brief trip back to the states and was amazed at all the changes that had taken place since she had left. She had never seen a drive-in bank or push buttons on telephones. Before the mission was completed Dr. Darlene Bee tragically died in a plane crash over the jungle. They had worked together for seven years. That left Vida alone in a world where she was still virtually a stranger. Not only had she lost a partner, but she had lost her best friend.

The Usarafas loved to sing about everything that happened, even stubbing their toe. Vida knew that music was a universal language. While language conveys fact, music tells us of the emotional life of a culture. We've all seen church congregations raise their voices together in Praise to God, that is what Vida wanted to see accomplished with the Usarafas. However the Usarafas had no way of developing hymns or songs. They had no techniques to help them learn. So a new pioneering work in the field of ethnomusicology was beginning to emerge through Vida. She felt if she could teach other translators her discoveries they could give many tribes the ability to sing. After fourteen years the work of translating the Bible was done. Vida had analyzed tribal music from 26 New Guinea tribes. The Dean at the Wheaton College Conservatory in Illinois paved the way for Vida to become Professor of Ethomusicology. Vida spent 14 years at Wheaton College and because of her work, her students are going out to jungles, deserts, and across oceans helping primitive people sing the praises of God with understanding.

I've heard people in church services talk about mission work all of my life, but I had never realized the degree of dedication that it must take until I met Dr. Vida Chenoweth. I told her I was glad it was she and not me because I don't think I could have endured the lack of comforts. Her reply was, " You really missed out." *Vida assured me that God became her "all sufficient one." There was no one else to put her trust in.. She felt that once she was committed it wasn't a sacrifice, it was a privilege. She experienced with God that the more she trusted Him, the greater things He did for her, if she was patient and waited on His timing.*

Ernest Childers
U.S. Army Colonel

Exactly what is a Congressional Medal of Honor? Webster's dictionary defines it as a U.S. military decoration awarded in the name of Congress for conspicuous gallantry and intrepidity (fearlessness) at the risk of life above and beyond the call of duty in action with an enemy.

This well deserved award was given to 26-year-old Second Lieutenant Ernest Childers when he risked his own life to save those who had been placed under his leadership. The year was 1943 and the place was Oliveto, Italy. Under German attack, Childers and his enlisted men began making their way steadily around the Saline River. They were exchanging artillery fire with the Germans, but there had not been much direct contact. Childers had dispatched his men, and orders were to advance at 3 a.m. that morning while darkness still pervaded the area.

While crossing a bridge that had been bombed during the night, Childers fell forward after stepping into a hole and broke his instep. He said it was very painful but it was a blessing it happened. The Germans heard Childers fall and opened up machine gun fire on him. But Childers' quick response allowed him to overtake the enemy who was only 20 feet from him.

He was then ordered to report to the aid station to get medical care. While he was there a bomb hit the building and killed the doctor Childers had come to see. With his survival instinct as well as a desire to eliminate the enemy, Childers ordered his men to direct a line of fire at the Germans while he made his way to their machine gun nests. Once he reached them he ordered his men to lift their fire, giving him ample time to make an attack on the enemy.

Childers said he expected to die but at that point he didn't care. He just wanted to do whatever he could to help his troops before it was too late. It turned out Childers was faster and more accurate than the enemy. As he approached the last machine gun nest, he threw a rock into the hole, just as he had often done on his father's farm to flush birds. Thinking it was a grenade the Germans fled, and Childers and a fellow soldier shot them as they stood. The battle ended at 11:45 a.m.

The following year on April 12, 1944 at a replacement center in Italy, nine companies stood at attention while General Jacob L. Devers, Allied deputy commander of the Mediterranean Theater, placed a blue ribbon of the nation's highest military honor around the neck of Ernest Childers. This honor marked Childers as being the 13th U.S. Citizen to ever receive the award and the first American Indian.

On September 25, 1945 Ernest Childers married Yolanda Le Dema (Chadwell). The couple had three children together, Ernest Sherman, Yolanda Elaine and Donna Lynn.

Childers continued serving in the U.S. Army for over 28 years until retiring as a Lt. Colonel at Fort Sill in 1965. After retiring from the active military service, Colonel Childers worked nine years for the U.S. Department of the Interior as a Job Corps Coordinator.

Colonel Childers has been honored also by receiving the Bronze Star, Purple Heart, Italian Cross of Valor, the Combat Infantryman's Badge and several theater ribbons. He also received the first Oklahoma Distinguished Service Medal ever awarded.

He has received many other honors including the Key to the City of Broken Arrow. Broken Arrow also honored him by naming one of their middle schools after him as well as having a nine-foot statue sculpted by famed Indian artist Allan Houser.

Childers, a three-quarter blood Creek Indian, learned at an early age the meaning of hard work. He attended the city's public schools and earned spending money by throwing a newspaper route that covered half of his surrounding community.

Following his father's death in 1930 Childers enrolled in the Chilocco Indian School near Ponca City. This was a military-type facility and had been since the end of World War I. Male students were known as cadets and they had military classes as part of the regular curriculum. They also had their own guard unit which was made up entirely of Indians.

When World War II began the Chilocco guard was activated and Childers, along with most of his male classmates, went on active duty. He first wore the distinctive Thunderbird insignia of Oklahoma's famed 45th Division at Fort Sill during basic training. It was a mark he would honor throughout a long and distinguished military career.

By 1939 Childers' mother, Tennie Starks had also passed away, leaving him orphaned but nevertheless equipped with lessons both she and his dad had successfully taught him.

In our interview Mrs. Yolanda Childers remarked how well trained Indians become just by learning the skills passed down through their Indian culture. Interestingly she pointed out that American Indians can see further into the night sky because they have been instructed to guide themselves by the stars. They know that certain stars are in certain places and focused in certain directions, and if you located a particular star you will know which direction you are going. It is like a sixth sense to the Indians.

I was surprised with the amount of knowledge Mrs. Childers had concerning her husband's military exploits. You could tell she hadn't just set idly by, but she had been in full support of her active husband. If they gave out medals (which they should) for military career wives, she would certainly merit receiving one.

Colonel Childers said one of his proudest moments involved working with former President Dwight David Eisenhower to establish the Medal of Honor Society. There are 400 charter members and three of them are from Oklahoma.

"I guess that shows you how seriously we Sooners take the concept of honor, duty and country" he remarked.

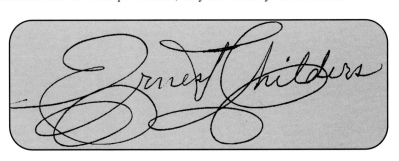

Stan Clark
Business Executive

On the day of my interview with Stan, I drove to Stillwater expecting to meet the typical business owner dressed in a blue suit and tie. I was pleasantly surprised when I walked into the beautiful old home on Elm Street which was built in 1906 and had been converted into offices for Eskimo Joe's.

I was greeted first by a bubbly receptionist who began to set the stage for the down-home interview I was about to engage in. Before long, in walked Stan clad in jeans and an Eskimo Joe's T-shirt. I guess being so close to the college campus and around students all the time just automatically causes you to look and act like one of them.

Stan was definitely "Mr. Personality" with the most hospitable presence about him. He ushered me into his conference room that was like no other I had ever been in, arrayed with a long, massive solid wood table and stately high back chairs. I felt like I was sitting in the midst of an era from the past. As Stan began to tell his story it was so easy to see how success found its way to him. First, he was raised in an emotionally successful family. His father Emerson had always encouraged Stan to go into business for himself. So while Stan was in college at Oklahoma State University getting a business degree, he always kept in mind that the knowledge he was gaining was preparing him for his own business. He just didn't know at the time what that business would be.

The inception of Eskimo Joe's began with a simple conversation between Stan and his friend, Steve File. They had just graduated from OSU two weeks earlier and Stan was making plans to enter graduate school in the fall. Just off the cuff, Steve said, "Let's open a bar here in Stillwater." As Stan describes it, "It was just a nutz-o, spur of the moment, wild hair idea." But within the hour they had rented the building where Eskimo Joe's proudly stands today.

Opening day began July 21, 1975 with a turn table stereo, a few rock and roll records, a pool table, a pinball machine, some snacks, beer and soda pop and the place began jumping. Hence came the by-line "Stillwater's Jumpin' Little Juke Joint." Stan played records, poured beer and entertained his customers. It was like a huge party every night with all of his friends showing up to party with him.

As an advertising gimmick Stan ordered 72 t-shirts to sell and sold them all during his first week in business. Steve was the one who came up with the name of Eskimo Joe's and an OSU commercial art student designed the logo while sitting at one of the front windows scribbling on an art pad with a magic marker. As it turns out, T-shirts and clothing were not just an advertising gimmick, they were and have become the heart of Eskimo Joe's.

For the next 10 years Stan put his heart and soul into Eskimo Joe's. For his 10 year celebration he recorded two songs that played on local radio stations. One was *Last Night At Joes*, and the other was *The Juke Joint Shuffle.* He recalled how cool it was to drive down 15th Street in Tulsa, Oklahoma and hear Jim Jones on KMOD play his songs. On his 20th year anniversary Stan put out a whole C.D. titled, *Twenty Years Later*, which is sold through the Eskimo Joe's product line.

In 1978, two and a half years after the opening of Eskimo Joe's, Stan bought out Steve's interest in the company so Steve could pursue other avenues, probably not realizing at the time that Eskimo Joe's would turn into such a phenomenon.

In 1983 Stan expanded his outlook and changed Eskimo Joe's from a basic beer hangout to an eating establishment. From there, he opened up Stillwater Bay Restaurant, Mexico Joe's and Joseppi's Italian Kitchen all located in Stillwater.

Eskimo Joe's has become a household name over the past 25 plus years. I doubt if you can stand in a crowd of people in Oklahoma without seeing someone wearing an Eskimo Joe shirt. They have several retail locations, an active web site and a thriving catalog business with a mailing list of over 300,000. Eskimo Joe's has customers/friends who not only live in the area, but there are hundreds that stop by each year while vacationing in the area. Stan considers all of his customers his friends. You can't doubt that because Stan is just too friendly for it to be any other way.

Stan went from bachelorhood to married life a few years ago when he married the love of his life, Shannon. Children are, of course, in the plans for their future. I asked Stan what his parents think of his success. Stan said, "If the fact that my father always has an Eskimo Joe shirt on means anything, then I would say they are my greatest fans."

Xernona Clayton

Corporate Executive

I first heard of Xernona from another Distinguished Oklahoman, Ernestine Dillard who had a lot of nice things to say about her friend. When I contacted Xernona at her CNN office she very kindly offered to send me a copy of her autobiography titled *I've Been Marching All The Time*. I have chosen to use the autobiography in profiling this really unique and brilliant woman.

Xernona lived directly across the street from a white school while growing up in Muskogee, Oklahoma and yet she, her sister Xenobia, and her brother James had to walk several miles each day to get to a black school. Even though she was aware of segregation it was just part of life and she took it in stride. She had a wonderful time meeting her friends along the way, talking and joking and living the life given to her.

Xernona's father was a Baptist minister and was known and respected in the white community as well as the black. Her father had three children Fred, Mary and Selena by a first marriage. Following his first wife's death he married Xernona's mother and they had four children, Vera, James, and twins Xenobia and Xernona. Xernona's mother was one-quarter Cherokee Indian who was very contemplative in nature. Her father was just the opposite being very gregarious.

Xernona feels very blessed to have been raised in a good home with good parents that counseled and loved her as they fed and took care of her and her other siblings. Her father always reminded her that she couldn't control the superficial things, but she could control how she thought and felt about herself and other people. She believes her father was an amazing influence in her life and to this day remembers many of the wise words he conveyed that have helped her along in life.

He taught her if she gives her word on something it has to have meaning. *If you say you are going to be somewhere at an appointed time then be there. If you are late or you don't show up you are showing disregard and total disrespect for everybody else. Even if your reason for being there was unimportant you still have to keep your word because it is a reflection on your character.*

Xernona graduated from Tennessee State University in June 1952. She and her sister Xenobia headed to Chicago for their first real jobs as undercover agents for the Urban League. Their jobs were to try and break down racial barriers in the work place. They went to work for a company named Sunset. In the beginning white folks didn't invite them to lunch but as time went on things changed. They became the first black people to eat at Ricardo's, a fine restaurant in town.

After working for the Urban League Xernona began teaching at Tilden Tech, an all boys high school. It was during this time she met her husband Ed Clayton at a gathering with some of her friends. Ed was the executive editor of Jet Magazine, a popular publication in black communities all over the U.S.

In 1960 she and Ed moved to California at the request of his boss at Jet Magazine who wanted him to run the west coast office of Jet. When they finally left California in 1963 it was to go to work for Dr. Martin Luther King, Jr. in the Southern Christian Leadership Conference. Dr. King had been told that Ed was the best, experienced journalist who could help his public relations in the media with speech writing and press releases.

Ed eventually resigned his position at Jet Magazine because of the significance of Dr. King's work even though his salary could never compare with what he was receiving from Jet Magazine. Xernona eventually started traveling with Coretta King because of her organizational skills. They never regretted their decision to leave their other jobs but Ed died unexpectedly in 1966. His last three years of life with Dr. King were a part of history.

In July 1968 Xernona became the first black person in the south to host a television program which lasted until 1975. It started out being called Themes and Variations and after its first anniversary was changed to the " Xernona Clayton Show." She eventually gave up the show so she could spend more time with her new husband, Judge Paul L. Brady whom she married in 1974.

In 1979 Xernona went to work for what later became known as Ted Turner's super station WTBS. It was then only a low powered station that ran mostly old movies. She first worked for the station helping produce documentaries and then for a time in the early 1980's hosting its weekly public affairs show. Then in sequence she became coordinator of Minority Affairs for Turner Broadcasting, director of public affairs for WTBS, vice president for public affairs for WTBS and in 1988 became the assistant corporate vice president for Urban Affairs for the Turner Broadcasting Systems. That last title translates into acting as liaison for Turner with civic and minority groups in Atlanta and around the country. As a practical matter, it means getting involved in any aspects of special projects of programming.

With over 20 years at Turner Broadcasting, Xernona has a stronghold on who she is and what God has called her to do. She has been recognized worldwide for her diverse skills and for her plight to bring forth the accomplishments of African Americans. "When I look at my life retrospectively, so many things that I have done were just not planned by me. I feel like my life has had a very strong direction from the Lord."

In her efforts to herald the achievements of African Americans in 1993 she created TBS's Trumpet Awards, an annual black-tie awards ceremony where recognition is given to a few who have succeeded in their profession or overcome great odds of racism and poverty in their endeavors.

In addition to the creation of the Trumpet Awards she has created several other historical projects for Turner Broadcasting. These include the award-winning "Black History Minutes", a daily broadcast that airs each year during Black History Month. Xernona was the first black female corporate executive at Turner Broadcasting. She feels blessed to be able to work with Ted Turner, who has given her the opportunity to present newsworthy information in a positive fashion.

Xernona has sought a spiritual path since childhood. She said she is grateful to God and appreciates His guidance. She believes very strongly that her connection to Him is the key to her survival.

Xernona gives motivational speeches for businesses, universities and organizations and she always encourages others to never give up on their aspirations. "Just because the door is shut in your face doesn't mean the world is shut out to you."

I would like to meet Xernona in person some day. Her outstanding contributions say a lot for a young woman who worked her way out of the grasp of a prejudiced society and into a world where opportunities are just an echo away.

Sherri Coale

Basketball Coach

They don't come any cuter or more personable than Sherri Coale. If I had not seen her on television when she took her team to the Final Four and then on to compete in the NCAA championship game, I wouldn't have believed it was her when I saw her in person. Here was this petite, delicate featured, 5'5" female wearing a gray Oklahoma Sooners t-shirt and a pair of jogging pants. She looked like one of the students. But don't let her feminine qualities fool you. As she has proven, there's no lack of quality leadership and athletic ability in her.

Sherri grew up in the small town of Healdton, Oklahoma. Her parents, Beverly Stash and Joe Buben, divorced when she was a year old. But Sherri said she never felt like she was from a typical divorced home. Her parents remained friends and equally supported her in her childhood endeavors.

Her father worked for an oil company as a chemist and her mother for the last 37 years has worked for the Noble family as an executive secretary. Her parents always made her feel like she could accomplish anything she wanted. In a silent sort of way, her mother taught by example that she could accomplish great things as a single female. Her grandparents, Estella and Shorty Claxton, played a major role in her childhood which added tremendous stability to her life.

She remembers playing ball in the third grade at school during recess and it felt like such a natural thing for her. She was always very coordinated and admits she was ridiculously competitive. Fortunately, that trait never ceased.

The summer before the fifth grade she went to basketball camp and loved it. She was so good at basketball that some of her brother's female classmates who were four years older than Sherri would come and get her so she could practice basketball with them. To this day it's still hard for Sherri to believe they let an 11-year-old into their group.

Sherri believes in the saying, "it takes a village to raise a child." She commented in a respectful way that Healdton is a great place to be from. It was there that she learned character lessons that would last a lifetime. She remembers people in her town that played such an important part of influencing her future. One teacher in particular taught her the meaning of integrity. She told the class that *integrity is when you approach a stop sign at two o'clock in the morning and you actually come to a stop. You know no one is looking and you could drive on through, but you don't because integrity says you do the right thing even when no one is watching.*

Sherri had a basketball goal in front of her house and it was used on a constant basis. Since she could make jump shots without a partner she spent a lot of time practicing. She knew if she wanted to be good she would have to do what it took to get there. She also used jump shots as a source of therapy when things didn't quite go her way during the course of a day. She said she would go shoot a hundred jump shots and all of a sudden the world seemed to be all right again.

Her brother Jack played some sports also, but never felt as committed to it as Sherri did. Yet Jack was and still is Sherri's greatest fan. It was refreshing to hear her speak about her brother in such a loving way. It is obvious there are very close ties between them.

By the time Sherri entered Oklahoma Christian College with a full scholarship she knew she wanted to be a coach. She played basketball at Oklahoma Christian for four years and graduated summa cum laude with degrees in English and Physical Education.

After graduation she was hired as Junior varsity coach at Edmond Memorial High School where she stayed for two years. Then she was recruited as head coach for Norman High School where she remained for the next seven years. While there she directed Norman to two Class 6A state championships and amassed a 147-40 career record. She was honored as the regional, All-State and Big All-City High School Coach of the Year in 1993.

Right before the fall of her seventh year at Norman Sherri met Coach Geno Auriemma from the University of Connecticut when he came to recruit one of her best players, Stacy Hansmeyer. In spite of their tremendously different backgrounds Sherri and Coach Auriemma suddenly became what she calls "fast friends." He was so impressed with Sherri's coaching abilities that they even discussed the possibility of her becoming one of his assistants. However, Sherri just didn't think the timing was right. She was expecting a child and really didn't want to leave Oklahoma.

The following April after Stacy went to Connecticut the head coach's position became available at the University of Oklahoma and Sherri really wanted the job. She called Geno and asked if he would call the interview committee and put in a good word for her. She knew if someone of his caliber vouched for her abilities, she would have a better chance of being considered.

Of course, he did and the rest is history. Sherri said she will always be grateful for his timely phone call. But what she is most grateful for is the belief he had in her abilities. It was Coach Auriemma that made her believe in herself and gave her the courage to face the committee knowing in her heart she had what it took to lead the Sooners.

Well of course the whole nation knows now that Coach Sherri Coale has what it takes to be a great leader. She's been named Coach of the Year by numerous publications and organizations. Sherri teaches her players the importance of a good work ethic that includes a combination of weight lifting and cardiovascular workouts. She also directs them to be conscientious about watching films, reading and studying the game. She learned early in life if you practice, practice and practice you can be anything you want to be.

With her husband of 15 years, Coach Dane Coale, and her two children, Colton and Chandler, life is beautiful. Sherri has a contagious enthusiasm and a born ability to be a winner. No doubt there are many honors and trophies yet to be won for the Oklahoma Sooners with Coach Sherri Coale at the helm. After meeting and talking with her for a short while I can't think of anyone more deserving.

Jerrie Cobb - Pilot

Jerrie was born March 5, 1931 in Norman, Oklahoma to William Harvey and Helena Stone Cobb. Their first daughter Carolyn loved tea parties and dolls, but Geraldyn, called Jerrie, ran through fields, played soldier, rode horses and climbed in trees. Jerrie's father, a captain in Oklahoma's 45th Division, sparked her imagination when he purchased a Waco bi-plane. He needed air hours to qualify for a pilot's license so he could serve overseas during World War II.

She was 12 years-old before her parents finally consented for her to begin flying, seated behind her father in the rear cockpit. At age 15 while attending Classen High School in Oklahoma City she took on a new flying instructor, Coach J.H. Conger, and flew Congers Aeronca solo. She worked a variety of odd jobs to earn an hour or more flying time on the weekend at a grass field airport in Moore where Congers kept his plane.

On her 17th birthday March 5, 1948 she received her pilot's license. She couldn't let go of her dream to fly even though her parents and several others told her "flying held no future for women."

After high school graduation she enrolled at Oklahoma College for Women in Chickasha where she stayed for two semesters. She purchased a Fairchild P.T. 23 for $500. It was the Fairchild that helped her land a professional job in the fall of 1950 patrolling pipelines in Oklahoma, Kansas and Missouri. The pay barely kept fuel in the plane. To pay for ground school in Wichita three nights a week she worked at the Ponca City Airport.

For a short time she had a full-time job in Duncan teaching flight and ground operations to middle aged oil workers. Then the Oklahoma City downtown air park hired her as a flight instructor, pilot for hire and restaurant waitress.

Jerrie liked flying any place and any time. The Sky Lady Derby from Dallas to Topeka provided her with a challenge in which she placed first in a 500 mile dash race and received $125.

After several other races she took a secretarial job at Miami International Airport while waiting for a pilot slot. While there she met Jack Ford who introduced himself as the founder and president of Fleetway Inc., a company which delivered American surplus planes purchased by other countries. Jerrie introduced herself as a pilot waiting for a job. At first, Ford didn't take her seriously. But a week later he hired her to fly military fighter planes to South America over jungles, mountains and clouds to exotic named cities and countries.

In the summer of 1954 while flying formation over South America, Ford declared his love for Jerrie over the radio. In 1955 Jerrie left her Fleetway job to become a test pilot. She and Ford talked about marriage but she soon realized her love for him was too deep to tie him down to a lifestyle that included a wife and children. She knew his true love would always be the sky. Jerrie left Florida and became chief pilot for Kansas City Flying Service. Two years later Ford died in an airplane explosion.

In 1960 after setting four World Aviation records, Jerrie began NASA testing at the Lovelace Foundation in Albuquerque, New Mexico. She endured the same 75 grueling tests that were administered to the men trying for a position on the Mercury Capsule. Lovelace measured Jerrie's results against the men. Her scores set a standard for future training of other women. Lovelace announced in August 1960 at the Space Naval Congress in Stockholm, Sweden that Jerrie was America's first woman space pilot candidate.

The State of Oklahoma and Oklahoma City planned a hero's welcome home. As Jerrie neared the Tulakes Airport runway she gave the 50 officials and her family an aerial salute by streaking over the field at an altitude of only 50 feet before landing her plane. When she climbed out of the plane and her feet touched the ground, Lieutenant Governor George Nigh presented her with a large bouquet of roses and called her Oklahoma Ambassador to the Moon.

She told reporters the first manned space flight would be in the fall of 1961. In October 1960 Jerrie passed NASA's sensory deprivation test. The test involved being placed into a round pool of tepid water in a completely darkened and sound-proof room in an environment that few people tolerate. After nine hours and 40 minutes Jerrie emerged as calm as when she started, setting a new record.

Following her tests NASA swore her in as a consultant. she worked with the medical team to pick 12 other women for training and she pleaded to let an American woman beat a Russian woman into space. Jerrie traveled to Pensacola, Florida for more testing, then Lovelace notified Jerrie that the Navy had canceled the test for the other 12 women. On July 16, 1963 NASA announced it would pick the next 10 to 15 astronauts from a list of 200 applicants. Jerrie Cobb was one of three women on the list. But NASA chose no women. Jerrie resigned her position as a consultant because the space program was not ready to accept women as astronauts. In June 1963 Valentina Tereshkova of the Soviet Union became the first woman astronaut. Jerrie realized if she couldn't advance human understanding of women's place within the universe, she needed to find another way to serve human kind. She flew off to the jungles of South America to serve the primitive tribal people. She learned the dialects of 15 of the 40 tribes she served. Friends of Jerrie formed the Jerrie Cobb Foundation to support her missions.

The Columbian Air Force awarded her pilot captain wings as the first North American ever to receive an honorary rank. Equador honored her with an airline transport jet pilot license because she found a new route through the Andes to the jungles. In 1976 the Oklahoma Hall of Fame inducted her as the most outstanding aviatrix of the United States. President Nixon honored Jerrie with the Harman Trophy as the top aviatrix in the world. In 1981 an Oklahoma representative nominated Jerrie for the Nobel Peace Prize.

Today at the age of 69 she still flies in Amazonian. She returns to the Foundations home base in Moore Haven, Florida on rare occasions. The 99 International Headquarters Building at the Will Rogers Airport displays a view of Jerrie's awards and a variety of gifts from Amazon natives. Universal Studios plans to present Jerrie's life in a movie.

On June 18, 1983, 20 years after Jerrie left NASA a 32 year old physicist named Sally K. Ride became the first American woman to go into space. She and four colleagues participated in a six-day space shuttle mission, Whether they knew it or not, the ground work for their achievement began in the Oklahoma skies decades earlier.

Vaya con Dios
Jerrie Cobb

Tom Coburn - Physician

My interview with Tom Coburn took place at the Muskogee hospital. It's not often that I meet a doctor/politician, so I found it to be an interesting combination. As a matter of fact, he was one of my most favorite interviews. What intrigued me about him was not just his political views, but the way in which his honesty rang true in his concern for mankind.

Tom was born in Casper, Wyoming but moved to Muskogee, Oklahoma with his family as a small child. He graduated from Muskogee high school in 1966. His father had gone into business for himself in Virginia and wanted Tom to work along side of him. So Tom spent 4 years at Oklahoma State University in Stillwater and received a B.S. degree in accounting. He was one of the top ten Seniors in the School of Business and served as the President of the College of Business Student Council.

From 1970 to 1978 he joined his father's company and was the manufacturing manager at the Ophthalmic Division of Coburn Optical Industries in Colonial Heights, Virginia. Under his leadership, the Virginia division of Coburn Optical grew from 13 employees to more than 350 and captured 35 percent of the U.S. market.

After the family business was sold he changed the course of his life by returning to school to become a physician a career he had always dreamed of pursuing even before going into business with his father. He attended the University of Oklahoma Medical School where he graduated in 1983. He then did his internship in general surgery at Saint Anthony's Hospital in Oklahoma City and family practice residency at the University of Arkansas in Fort Smith.

He returned to Muskogee where he specializes in family medicine and obstetrics. Dr. Coburn and his associates serve more than 10,000 patients and has personally delivered more than 3,000 babies.

As a doctor, Tom has the opportunity to see and feel the concerns many people have as he comes in contact with them on a daily basis. I know all doctors are not what we would categorize as caring, compassionate individuals. Yet Tom seemed to fit easily into that category .

When the opportunity came along for him to run for public office he decided it would be another way he could help people. As a doctor his days were spent hearing and seeing the needs of individuals both young and old. He felt in being a part of Congress he would have the ability to make those needs known and lend a hand in passing bills that would alleviate some of the problems.

He explained the regulations he had to fight against in order to be part of Congress, as well as retain his status as a physician. Having never been a part of the political scene, I can't begin to totally understand the process. However, I do understand what it is like to be one small drop of water in an ocean full of waves. Therefore it is refreshing to know that someone who is feeling the heartbeat of his community daily also has the opportunity to speak on be half of those who so often go unheard.

Tom was first elected to represent Oklahoma's 2nd Congressional District in the U.S. House of Representatives in 1994. He was re-elected in 1996 and 1998, becoming the first Republican to hold the seat for three consecutive terms. He is a member of the Committee on Commerce where he serves as the Vice-Chairman of the subcommittee on Health & Environment. He also serves on the Commerce Committee's subcommittee on Energy & Power.

Tom has made balancing the budget a top priority. He has played a central role in Medicare and health care debates. He founded and serves as co-chairman of the Congressional Family Caucas, a group of about 60 members of the House dedicated to family issues.

He is an avid supporter of congressional reform. He has declined his government pension and health care benefits and has supported legislation to limit perks to all members of Congress.

Tom has written and passed a bill in Congress encouraging the testing of infants for HIV. He has also introduced legislation that would provide senior citizens more health care choices, while also seeking to crack down on Medicare fraud and abuse.

It makes perfect sense to have a man in Congress who understands the needs of the people. Who could be more knowledgeable about health issues than a physician?

I was also impressed with Tom Coburn's strong faith and his unashamed, outspoken approach to his relationship with God. I learned a spiritual lesson during our interview that gave me an understanding I hadn't quite known before. I would like to share Tom's view.

If two good men are in competition against the same high goal and believe they are where they should be in life, then how can one man win while the other loses? To Tom it is very simple. The idea is to be obedient, not necessarily to win. *Whether you win or lose, you have still entered a learning process which ultimately leads to winning.*

I thought back to some earlier interviews. I remembered several who had set their sights on a particular goal only to see that phase of the goal become unattainable. Yet Instead of being defeated, they soon realized the path to their intended destination had taken a very needed turn and they were so thankful in retrospect that it had.

By the time this book is published Tom Coburn may or may not still be in the political arena. I have always had the attitude that I care more about the character of the person running for office than I do the party they run for. I know that because we all carry the title of "human" that automatically means we have different views and ideas about almost everything.

I wouldn't even begin to believe that Tom Coburn would make every decision just as I would like him to. However, during our interview, I witnessed a man that to the best of his ability is trying and has tried to put the welfare of Oklahoma people foremost in his mind. I was honored to have had the opportunity to meet him.

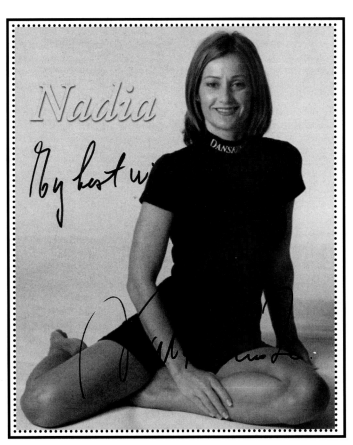

Nadia Comaneci

Gymnast

What a thrill it was to walk into Nadia's office in Norman, Oklahoma and meet her in person for the first time! I guess with her small frame and delicate features she will always be thought of as "cute," no matter what the year says on the calendar of life.

Nadia said as a small child she could always be found jumping around the room in a constant state of movement. She had so much energy that her mother knew she had to find some way of harnessing it. When she was six and a half years old, her mother found a gymnastics school close to their home in Romania. She enrolled Nadia, hoping to give her an outlet for all that energy.

Of course, Nadia was a natural at gymnastics and before long her talents began to draw attention her way. She was always competing and when she turned 12-years old the serious competition began.

The importance of competing is very different in Romania than it is in the United States. Instead of going to the gymnastics school, the gymnastics school comes to you. That way, there is not any time lost in commuting back and forth.

Even though Nadia was obviously talented she said she never realized how special she was in the sport. She didn't know that the whole world had their eyes on Nadia Comaneci. She just enjoyed the traveling and the opportunity to meet other people. There was one difficult aspect to all of her traveling. Her parents weren't allowed to go with her so her coaches had to become surrogate parents as well.

Nadia always loved going shopping when she traveled to the U.S. because in those days, there were so many things to buy here that she couldn't get in Romania, like pink socks instead of the proverbial white.

At the 1976 Olympics in Montreal, Canada 14-year old Nadia captured the hearts of the whole world with her perfect score of 10. At the time the scoreboards in Montreal weren't even designed to accommodate perfection. Therefore, Nadia was the first woman to ever score a perfect 10. By the time the Olympics ended, Nadia had earned seven perfect 10's, three gold medals, one silver, and one bronze. She appeared on the covers of Time, Newsweek and Sports Illustrated all in the same week.

Staying focused and disciplined she says is the key to realizing success in any area of your life.

"Great stuff doesn't come easy," she said. I asked Nadia how she keeps a positive outlook. Her answer was simple. "Knowing that you won't accomplish anything with a negative outlook."

In 1980 at the Moscow Olympics, which had been boycotted by America, Nadia earned two more gold medals and two silver medals. She retired from gymnastics in 1984 and was awarded the prestigious Olympic Order from the President of the International Olympic Committee, Juan Antonio Samaranch.

After retirement, since Romania was still under communist rule, Nadia was forbidden to travel. So she settled into life as a gymnastics coach. In November of 1989 she was no longer able to stand the repressive regime that ruled her country and she fled across the border. Escaping from Romania was risky. She knew there was a possibility she could be shot but she chose to defect for a chance to be free. It was hard leaving her family behind but she knew she had to do it.

These days life is somewhat better in Romania. Nadia has been able to visit her family many times and they have come to America, on occasion, to see her as well.

In 1996 Nadia married Olympic Champion, Bart Conner in a lavish wedding held in Romania. They are hoping some day to have children. In the meantime, Nadia divides her time between performing in exhibitions, commercial endorsements for major companies, speaking engagements and charity events.

Nadia and Bart currently live in Norman and are partners with their manager, Paul Ziert, in the Bart Conner Gymnastics Academy, and the gymnastics manufacturing company, Grips, Etc. Nadia is a contributing editor of the International Gymnast Magazine and is a commentator at major gymnastics competitions for several television networks.

She was inducted into the International Gymnastics Hall of Fame in 1996 and is currently working on a line of cosmetics appropriately called, "NADIA."

Nadia has such a good outlook and feels like life is how you make it. *She believes you create your own destiny. By listening to others you glean from their ideas and create new opportunities. She strongly believes when you are having difficult times, instead of spending time feeling down about it you should step back, take a deep breath and rethink the situation. Then you will make good decisions.*

Nadia took me over to see the gym before I left that day and I could easily visualize other future Olympic winners being groomed once again for a shot at "perfection."

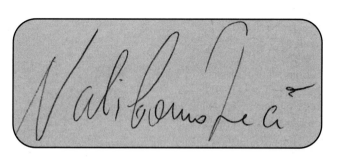

Robert Jackson Conley
Author

Robert was born in Cushing, Oklahoma but his journey in life took him full circle back to the land of the Cherokees and the birthplace of his grandmother. Tahlequah, Oklahoma is what Robert has called home for over 13 years.

The flavor of Indian Territory with its occasional glimpses of the past gives Robert inspiration to write some of his well known and sought after books depicting adventures of the Old West.

With his father, Robert Parris Conley, mother, Peggy Marie Jackson and three siblings Robert spent the majority of his growing up years relocating from one area of the country to the next. His father periodically sold oil field supplies but spent a great deal of time in the Armed Services which kept the family in a constant mode of geographical change.

It wasn't until he was in high school in Wichita Falls, Texas that they finally settled long enough for Robert to finish high school and go on to college at Midwestern University. It was there that he received his bachelor's degree in drama and art in 1966 and his master's degree in English in 1968.

Robert wasn't totally clear about what he wanted to do with his life when he first enrolled in college. He thought he was going to be an artist because his talent for drawing seemed to be an obvious niche. But when he applied a paint brush to the same creation he felt it brought devastation to his masterpiece. Therefore, he decided to pursue another creative desire.

He changed his major to drama and began focusing all of his attention on becoming a bonified actor. He consumed himself with acting roles in the local community theatre and school plays. He also became part of a ballet theatre as a character dancer. Yet when the time came to depart from campus life and pursue acting on a broader scale Robert wasn't prepared for what that pursuit entailed.

At the time the only two places to showcase your talents with any magnitude were Los Angeles, California and New York City and Robert just didn't have a desire to go in either one of those directions. Because he had a lot of English electives from taking so many Shakespeare classes the chairman of the English department suggested he get his master's degree in English and prepare to teach. Robert took the chairman's advice and once again his career choice changed.

His first job was as an English instructor at Northern Illinois University where he intended to work for a few years and then return to his studies to receive his Ph.D. However, his goals were quickly diminished when the miserableness of his situation warranted him taking another look at his life. He didn't like anything about Illinois.

One day while daydreaming about his home state of Oklahoma he began to put some ideas together that he had no idea would eventually take him down an entirely different road. He thought about Indian Territory and the birthplace of his grandmother. He remembered all the stories that had been told to him about Indian outlaws and epic stories of the Old West. He had grown up hearing so much about outlaw Jesse James and began wondering about some of the Indian outlaws that at one time roamed the plains of his homeland.

In pursuit of where his curiosity was leading him he started researching the life of Ned Christie. Ned was a full blooded Cherokee Indian known for being one of the most dangerous and ruthless outlaws of Indian Territory. Yet all the written accounts that Robert could find at the time never seemed to go into any detailed descriptions about Ned Christie's pursuits.

Out of desperation for his own insatiable curiosity about the Old West Robert began penning his own ideas. As a result his first book was titled *Back To Malachi*. Even though it took 15 years to sell his first book he knew he had tapped into an area that allowed his artistic abilities to be parlayed into a paintbrush of color through the written word.

After three years at Northern Illinois University Robert went on to teach at Southwest Missouri State University. Later he was director of Indian Studies at Eastern Montana College, Bacone College and Morningside College as well as Associate Professor of English at Morningside College. In addition he spent a year as Assistant Programs Manager for the Cherokee Nation of Oklahoma.

During his tenure with the Cherokee Nation he met and married his wife Evelyn who was a divorcee with two children, Cheryl and Eddie. This immediately allowed Robert to step into fatherhood.

By the time Robert completed and sold his first four books he decided it was time to say goodbye to his teaching profession and step into the next phase of his life. He had truly become an author. He felt his contributions to the field of writing would continue to lend themselves to even more creative tales. So he moved to Tahlequah, the capitol city of the Cherokee Nation. Since then what started out as a history lesson on the life of Ned Christie turned into the accumulation of 52 published books to Robert's credit.

He wrote the novelization of the Columbia Pictures screenplay, "Geronimo: An American Legend," which was published in the United States by Pocket Books and reprinted in Italy in an Italian translation. His story, *Yellow Bird:* An Imaginary Autobiography, received the Spur Award from Western Writers of America for the Best Short Story of 1988. Nickajack received the Spur for Best Western Novel in 1992 and *The Dark Island* won in 1995. In 1997 Robert was inducted into the Oklahoma Professional Writers Hall of Fame.

I asked Robert to give me some "food for thought" when it comes to success in life and he took me back to the basics. He said reading and writing is of utmost importance no matter what your pursuits are. He credited his grandfather who only had a fourth grade education as being one of the smartest men he ever knew because he read everything he could get his hands on. He taught Robert that anything he wanted to learn could be found in books. *Education, he said, is the key to anyone's future. If you get a good education you will be ready for whatever opportunity happens to come your way.*

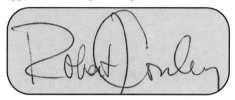

Bart Conner – Gymnast

Even though Bart grew up in Illinois, he had roots to Oklahoma in a round about way since his father was born in Locust Grove.

Illinois is a sports minded state with skating, hockey, football, soccer, and of course, gymnastics. At the age of 10, Bart found himself constantly walking around the house on his hands. So when the suggestion was made to join the YMCA, Bart thought the most logical sport for him to pursue with intensity was gymnastics.

By the time he was 14 years old he had won the U.S. Junior National Championship. Three years later at age 17, he was on his way to the 1976 World Olympics where he became the youngest gymnast ever to win the U.S. Gymnastics Federation All-Around Championship. Bart is America's most decorated male gymnast and the first American to win medals at every level of national and international competition.

Bart met Coach Paul Ziert while in Chicago at a gymnastics meet. When it came time to go to college, Bart decided on Oklahoma University since that was where Ziert was coaching. At Oklahoma University, Bart received a degree in journalism/public relations. While there he trained for the 1980 Olympics in Moscow, but was unable to attend because of the boycott. However, he did make it in to the 1984 Olympics, winning one gold medal with the U.S. team and one gold medal on the parallel bars.

From then on his life took another turn as he was constantly on the road with numerous speaking engagements. He became a television commentator for ABC, CBS, NBC, ESPN and the Turner Broadcasting Network. He has dabbled in films and television roles as an actor on "Highway to Heaven", "Touched by an Angel", and the movie "RAD." Recently he started his own television production company called "Perfect Ten Productions."

Bart has had an interesting life, but he would tell you that the highlight of it all was when he met the "Perfect Ten" gymnast, Nadia Comaneci. Although Nadia doesn't remember meeting Bart in 1976 at a gymnastics meet, he very clearly remembers kissing her on the cheek after they had both won the American Cup. A few months later, Nadia went on to score a perfect 10 at the 1976 Olympics. They became reacquainted in the early 1980's.

In 1989 with coaxing from Coach Paul Ziert they began touring together. By this time Nadia had escaped from what was then communist Romania and was living in Canada. They were spending a lot of time together and when they weren't together they were talking daily on the telephone. In 1991 Bart convinced Nadia to move to Norman, Oklahoma. Then on April 27,1996 they tied the knot and became husband and wife in a State wedding in Bucharest, Romania, which by then had dropped its communist ties.

Bart and Nadia remain very active in the sports world. Along with their production company, Bart is co-owner with his former coach Paul Ziert in The Bart Conner Gymnastics Academy in Norman as well as the International Gymnast Magazine and Grips, Etc. a gymnastics supply company.

Over the years, Bart has learned what it takes to be successful and he attributes it to what he calls having FOCUS.

F - *Find your talent.*
O - *Observe your role models*
C - *Challenge yourself.*
U - *Utilize your resources*
S - *Strive to make a difference.*

Since I was one of the thousands of people that had heard the name Bart Conner over the years, I was thrilled to meet him and Nadia. The two of them together make a "perfect 10" and they tell me that someday they would like to add at least one more to their happy abode. Who knows? Maybe there is another Olympic champion in the making.

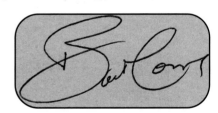

Donald Cooper - Physician

Dr. Cooper and President George Bush

Dr. Cooper was born in Columbus, Kansas on August 11, 1928. The first 14 years of his life were spent there before his family moved to Pittsburg, Kansas.

From age four Donald knew he wanted to become a doctor. In his neighborhood in Columbus a doctor lived next door, one lived down the street and another lived on the street behind him. Donald constantly saw the doctors carrying their black bags into their homes and he thought it would be cool to be a doctor, a desire he never quite forgot.

At age 13 he was too small in stature to be on the football team so they designated him as the team water boy. At 5'1" and 105 pounds he wasn't much of a threat on the football field or basketball court. Eventually he did get to play and lettered in junior high basketball, but by the time he reached high school he decided to take up golf instead.

He played on the high school golf team for two years during which time he also became the athletic trainer. At Pittsburg State University where he received his BA degree, he was also on the golf team and continued his position as athletic trainer. He was in charge of taping ankles and applying analgesic balm to sore and aching muscles which was about the only remedies they had at the time. It's no wonder with such an early start in the sports arena that he would lean toward sports medicine.

During our interview I was privileged to meet Dr. Cooper's wife, Dona. It appears as if the courtship days are still active around the Cooper household. Dr. Cooper's face lit up when he mentioned meeting Dona for the first time at Pittsburg State University. Their first date was January 9, 1948. They were engaged May 16, 1949 and married June 4, 1950. Nine months and two days later their first son Donald L. Jr., "Chip", was born. Cathy and Cheri arrived in 1953 and 1955, and Tad in 1961. Those four children are now married and have given their parents nine grandchildren and two great-grandchildren.

He attended The University of Kansas medical school and graduated in 1953 before being drafted during the Korean War into the U.S. Air Force for two years with the rank of captain. After his military discharge he went into private practice in Manhattan, Kansas where he stayed for two years. He was then recruited as the team physician and Assistant Director of

Student Health Services at Kansas State University, a position he held from 1957 to 1960.

Some of Dr. Cooper's colleagues tried to persuade him from leaving private practice, saying he wouldn't make any money as a team physician. However, even though the pay didn't match up to what he may have been able to make had he stayed in private practice, he believes the rewards far outweighed any monetary value.

In 1960 Dr. Cooper became the Director at the Oklahoma State University Student Health Center and team physician for O.S.U. in Stillwater, Oklahoma where he remained until June 1998. He and Dona still live in the same house they moved into on their 10th wedding anniversary June 4, 1960. So many good things have transpired over those 38 years.

In June 1974, Dr. Cooper was honored as the first recipient of the National Athletic Trainers Association's President's Challenge Sports Medicine Award. The award is given to the top team physician in the country active in sports medicine. He has held numerous offices in the American College Health Association including the presidency in 1967-68.

It is obvious to see how genuine Dr. Cooper is in his relationship with others. He feels extremely honored to have had the opportunity to meet so many well thought of individuals over the years and at times been able to help them by way of his medical expertise. He said he put the first stitches in George Foreman during a boxing match and also took care of Cathy Rigby when he was one of four U.S. Olympic Team physicians during the 1968 Olympics in Mexico City.

Dr. Cooper has had numerous opportunities come his way. He feels like he is one of the luckiest men alive. 'The Lord has blessed me from the day I was born," he said unashamedly.

He was an active member of the President's Council on Physical Fitness and Sports since his appointment in 1981 by President Ronald Reagan with George Allen as chairman. He was also appointed to this Council in 1988 by President Bush to serve four more years with Arnold Schwarzenegger as chairman. For several years from 1969-1976 he was the sports medicine consultant to the National Collegiate Athletic Association Football Rules Committee. In 1979 he concluded nine years of service as a member of the N.C.A.A. Committee on Drug Education, as well as an active member of the Oklahoma State Medical Association's Committee on Alcoholism and Drug Abuse.

Dr. Cooper's five national television appearances include "Good Morning America," in November 1976 when he discussed the safety of helmets in football with David Hartman. In 1980 he appeared on P.B.S. with author James Michener on two one hour shows -"Children in Sports" and "Women in Sports." Then in April 1985 he appeared on the "Today Show" with Bryant Gumbel and Connie Chung discussing Fitness of Youth in America.

He has authored more than 36 articles which appeared in a variety of publications ranging from medical journals to the Sunday sports section of the New York Times.

I don't know how one man can possibly accomplish all Dr. Cooper has. Believe me, the list is far longer than I had room to print. Dr. Cooper is partially retired now although he still maintains an emeritus office at the university. He still works every month as a volunteer physician at the Stillwater Community Health Center, which opened eight years ago. He still practices some for the OSU Athletic Department when needed. He is still on the board of directors for the National Operating Committee on Athletic Equipment and on the Governor's council on Physical Fitness and Sports.

I asked Dr. Cooper how a couple stays married for 50 years and does so in such a harmonious, loving manner like he and Dona apparently do. He said, "Every morning we both say This is the day that the Lord has made. We will rejoice and be glad in it." Dr. Cooper also said he views marriage as a couple climbing a mountain together. When you start out it is easy and then as you go up the mountain you hit rocks and jagged areas but you keep climbing. Sometimes one person falls but the other one helps him get back up. Either way, as time goes on, the couple reaches a new plateau where they have a better view as well as a better understanding.

I was so impressed with Donald and Dona Cooper. Their names alone seem to signify a closeness, a two peas in a pod, twinkie sort of togetherness that can only be admired. Everyone should be as fortunate to have found a love like the two of them share. I end their profile with a poem taken from Dona's *Family Ties* book of poetry which she wrote and accumulated over the years.

TEA FOR TWO
We had lots of tea parties and at one of these, I asked my granddaughter, "Tell me, please,
When you grow up what will you be?" "A teacher," she answered, sipping daintily. Then she added after a second, or two,
"No, I'll just be a plain person like you."

Jack Counts - Business Executive

Jack was a college student majoring in marketing at Oklahoma University. One year he wanted to raise enough money to take a trip to the Bahamas during spring break. So he got some of his fraternity brothers together to take pictures of a school event. What is amazing is Jack wasn't a photographer and had never aspired to be one. He simply liked attending parties and thought why shouldn't he make some money while he's there.

He bought several cameras and put them in the hands of his buddies and the shooting spree began. His father, Jack Counts, Sr. owned and operated nursing homes in the area and saw Jack's venture as nothing more than a pastime and told him to get a real job. He went to work for his father in one of his nursing homes as an assistant administrator. For Jack that subdued type of work was quite a stretch from the liveliness of groups of people who wanted to capture their images on film. After a year he left the nursing home to continue to pursue his picture taking. He began to realize how great the need was to capture lasting memories and his idea was turning into a full fledged business. At the time there were basically no photos being taken at university graduations. Jack decided to seize the opportunity and fill an obvious need. In 1973 he started his own company called "Candid Color Systems," the umbrella of "Party Pic" photos and expanded to other major universities.

Just as he had enlisted his buddies to help with the earlier photos, as he expanded the business, he designated a principle person to partner along with him at each location. The idea caught on like wild fire.

Since taking pictures at college events was obviously a seasonal concept, Jack wanted to find something to fill in the gap between events. Have you ever heard of Moto Photo? Jack started that company along with his first wife. It of course became a major success but has since been sold. For Jack it made perfect sense to find something to take its place.

On a trip to Hawaii an idea was conceived of giving a person (usually a woman) a complete makeover and wardrobe to create a special look and then take what they would call a "Glamour Shot." So in 1989 his new concept was put into motion. Since then, more than six million women worldwide have been photographed at the 140 or so Glamour Shot locations located in forty states and six foreign countries. The company is consistently ranked as one of the top franchises nationally and internationally.

Jack says he feels like a session at Glamour Shots is somewhat of an esteem builder for anyone, and I have to agree with him. I challenge you to find any woman who has indulged in the experience and walked away feeling anything less than glamourous.

As time goes on, Jack and his wife Laurie have continued to stay abreast of the changes that have occurred in our society. For one thing, he knows our style of dress has become more casual, so he has brought in a phase of the business called, "Attitudes." (Don't we all have one?") The idea is to catch people in more candid, casual shots that reveal their own personalities.

Another phase called "Legacies" is geared toward group family shots. Then there is the "Pip Squeak," which introduces the youngest generation. With this type of versatility, Jack feels sure they can meet everyone's own personal needs.

Jack and Laurie are very dedicated to the continued success of Candid Color Systems. With what I see, there is no doubt that their photographic creations will be satisfying customers for decades to come.

Jack has created quite an empire. It's funny how something as simple as an idea to make a few bucks for a college trip could turn into a future of repeated success.

In the beginning Candid Color Systems used other labs to process their photographs. However, with success came their own laboratory which gives them the opportunity to not only process their own work but photographers outside the umbrella of Candid Color Systems as well. The company covers about 40 states. Of course over the years the photographs have expanded to not only graduation pictures but school groups, sports, racing events, weddings, proms and portraits.

Jack Counts, Sr. is working for his son now. A turn of events that leaves them both with an incredible amount of satisfaction.

There is a Bible interpretation that says "What you help create for someone else, God will help create for you." I thought Jack's business clearly defines that scripture. In producing his own success he has opened doors for other photographers to perfect their own talents. He provides help in marketing, research and development, customer service support and so much more.

Eastman Curtis - Pastor/Evangelist

Sumner - Pastor Eastman - Angel - Nicole

Eastman was born in Lakewales, Florida. Years ago, there were only three tourist attractions in Central Florida and Eastman's family owned one of them. Working along side his father at their Florida tourist attraction was what a lot of young people could have easily envied.

However, with those luxuries came the confusion of his growing up years. Some preachers are known for having untarnished lives where every decision they make from the day they are born happens to be socially acceptable. But Eastman seemed to align himself with negative behavior that had him headed in the wrong direction.

By the time he was 11 years old he had already been dismissed from school for drinking in the boy's bathroom. Somehow that didn't seem to make a difference. His rebellious attitude continued for the next several years and led him to get more involved in drinking. This progressed to his usage of illegal drugs. His father took him out of public schools and enrolled him in a military school but still to no avail.

On weekends Eastman performed in a rock and roll band which at the time only added to his rebellious nature. He was a leader and capable of influencing many of his peers to follow his example of booze and drugs. If Eastman could get the good guy to act a little wild and crazy it helped ease the guilt of his bad behavior.

It appeared as if Eastman's choices were going to get him into a heap of trouble when his father told him he was about to spend a few days in jail. Eastman pleaded with his father to give him one last chance. Reluctantly, he agreed and enrolled him in a private school named Howie Academy.

Eastman remembered the times his grandmother had taken him to church and how good he felt when he was there. He had read his Bible occasionally but only saw it as a good book to read and nothing he thought could make a great difference in his life. He prayed whenever he got in trouble but they were "I want something prayers," not anything that required a long-term commitment on his part. However, he was ready now to begin searching for that deeper meaning his grandmother had always told him about.

One day he went to a Baptist church and after the service a little old grandmother told him he could be anything he wanted to be if he would trust God. He decided to make a commitment and on January 15, 1978 he gave his life to the Lord. With great exuberance he began to involve himself with activities he thought would be pleasing to God.

Out of 326 boarding students at Howie Academy Eastman was the only person who professed to be a Christian. He was going to take the necessary steps to change that. He began to hold Bible studies and over half of the students made a commitment to Jesus. Eastman began to see the same influential power he had over his friends in negative ways as being just as strong if used in a positive way. His father saw such a drastic change in him that two weeks later he also made a commitment to Jesus. The rest of the family, which included sisters Kathy and Connie and his mother Jewel followed his lead later.

Eastman graduated from Howie Academy with honors. He spent a year at Brevard College in North Carolina and then transferred to Florida Southern College in Lakeland. He thought he was going to spend his career as a musician because other than the theme park, music was all he had ever known.

While he was attending an Assembly of God church in Lakeland a gospel band called "Living Sound" under the direction of Terry Law came to perform. Eastman had the opportunity to travel with them and be a part of the band for two years. It changed his life forever. He realized he was going to be in full-time ministry.

He enrolled in Southeastern Bible College in Lakeland. While there he met his wife Angel. They were married in 1983 after only knowing each other for 3 months. His first full-time church position was as a youth pastor at the Church of the Open Bible in Spokane, Washington.

Eastman was becoming well acquainted with many pastors as they traveled the country, so when it came time for him to start out on his own he was better equipped for the task. In 1986 he and Angel started Eastman Curtis Ministries. They traveled throughout the nation preaching in numerous churches.

In 1992 he felt the Lord speak to him saying He had called him into the ministry so he could help people. On a second occasion he felt the Lord telling him there was going to be a revival amongst teenagers like there had never been before and Eastman would be part of it. His excitement mounted and he began writing on a legal pad all of his thoughts concerning what he thought his part would be in bringing teenagers closer to God.

He shared with Angel the possibilities of being on radio and television and holding revivals in huge convention centers.

God revealed to him that his promotion was one relationship away. That relationship happened to be with a pastor in Tulsa, Oklahoma who asked Eastman to come and work with him at his church. The pastor taught Eastman about televisions, crusades and conventions for one year. It was an incredible learning time and yet it too, had to come to an end in order for Eastman's destiny to really be fulfilled. *Now it was up to Eastman to figure out how to make all those experiences come together to form the vision God had given him.*

In the beginning it wasn't easy. *Each day he took one step at a time, believing God to bring him through or over each hurdle. He had to keep focused and believe in the vision God gave him or his drive to complete it would vanish. He realized the bigger the vision the bigger the promotion and the harder the struggle would be to get there. Yet God was building character in Eastman that only the struggles could provide. He realized his faith grew, stronger as he conquered each hurdle.* Then one day he was able to believe God for his first congregation. In 1998 he became pastor of Destiny Church located on 145th Street in Tulsa. It started as a Bible Study on Thursday night and has grown to include a Saturday night service and two Sunday morning services. In the past two years the congregation has grown so quickly they are now in a huge building program to provide facilities to accommodate the spiritually hungry people who pass through the doors every week.

The church's name says it all DESTINY. The vision of the church is to fulfill the call God put on Eastman's life many years ago. He is to help people see and fulfill their own destiny with the dreams and visions God has given each one.

"Can a person miss their destiny?" I asked Eastman. "Yes" he said as he quoted Galatians 6:9 - "If you don't grow weary in well doing, you will reap if you faint not." *If you want all that God has prepared for you in this life, don't throw in the towel too early. Never stop dreaming because your next promotion may be linked to the very next person you meet.*

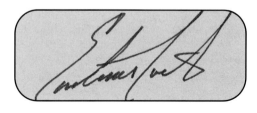

John Denver
Singer/Songwriter

The ties to Oklahoma go way back for the Deutschendorf family. John's grandfather was originally from Germany. Before World War I his family made their way to the states and settled in Bessie, Oklahoma. He was only 18 years old at the time. His plans were to eventually go back to Germany, but he soon met the woman who was to be his wife, so America became his permanent home.

After they married they moved to Corn, Oklahoma on a rented farm, which belonged to Mrs. Deutschendorfs father. They remained there until the farm was sold in 1936 and had to move to a farm managed by the Bureau of Indian Affairs. In 1942 Grandpa Deutschendorf was able to buy his own farm in Cordell, but unfortunately died a year later.

The Deutschendorfs had 11 children. John Denver's father, Henry John, was the second oldest child. The family was very poor, so for entertainment they sat around and told stories or played instruments.

When Henry John was of age he joined the Army Air Corps and was sent to Tulsa to study at Spartan School of Aeronautics. One night he dropped by a nightclub located by the Tulsa Airport. Inside was a beautiful young lady by the name of Erma. Her parents Peter and Mattie Swope owned the nightclub and Erma along with her sister were waitresses. It was pretty much a whirlwind romance because six months later they were married.

Since Henry John was a Army Air Corps pilot it meant they would be traveling a lot. For a while it was difficult for Erma to leave her family in Tulsa in order to follow along with her husband. Many times those homesick feelings would be so overwhelming she would pack her bags and head back to Tulsa for a visit.

At the end of 1943 while living in Roswell, New Mexico their oldest son John was born. Henry John's career took him away from home so often that Erma and John had ample time to visit relatives, making frequent visits to Tulsa.

During a tour of duty in Japan the Deutschendorfs second son Ron was born. John was five years old and having a brother certainly made life a lot more interesting. John was a very shy child who found it difficult at times to feel a part of his surroundings, because the family moved so often. He needed something that would cause him to feel more confident about himself.

His Grandmother Swope from Tulsa bought him his first guitar, a 1910 Gibson acoustic, at age 11 and his mother found a teacher to give him guitar lessons. Obviously their decision was a good one, because John never put that guitar down. Before long he was learning to write songs.

When John was a teenager his father thought it would be a good idea for him to experience what it was like growing up in Bessie, Oklahoma. So he sent him there during the summer to work the wheat harvest. It was a perfect setting for John perched on the seat of a tractor in the middle of a wheat field. All he could see was row after row of wheat and all he could hear was the sound of his own voice putting melody to his newly penned songs.

He dreaded the end of summer and looked forward to the coming year when he could once again feel the solitude and blissfulness of an Oklahoma wheat field. Those summers continued until he enrolled at Texas Tech University.

He was trying to do what was expected of him and go to college, but his heart wasn't in it. John wanted to pursue his music career full time. He left college before the end of his first year and headed for Los Angeles, California. Immediately he began singing in nightclubs and honing his talents as a songwriter. He changed his last name to Denver after acquiring a manager who thought Deutschendorf was not a suitable stage name. He spent three years from 1965 to 1968 traveling around the country as part of a trio, before financial problems caused the group to disband.

It was during those touring days that he met Annie Marten, the young college girl who a year and a half later on June 9, 1967 became his wife. The years that followed brought John a tremendous amount of success.

His first big hit was *Leaving On A Jet Plane*, but his first million seller was *Take Me Home, Country Roads.* Of course a song that immediately comes to mind is *Rocky Mountain High*, a song influenced by the exquisite beauty of Colorado, a place John and Annie decided to make their home in 1970. *Sunshine On My Shoulders* and *Annie's Song* soon followed. John Denver was a household name and his songs were being heard worldwide.

John and Annie adopted two children in the midst of all his success. In 1974 their first child, two-month old Zak enlarged the family circle. Then in the late 1970's, Anna Kate, a Japanese American, brought happiness to their home as well.

In 1977 John was cast in the motion picture "Oh,God", co-starring with George Burns. At first I refused to see the movie thinking it might be sacrilegious in some way. I finally relented and I have to admit I thoroughly enjoyed every minute of it. There are very few movies I have the patience to watch for a second and third time, but "Oh, God" is one I could watch with ease.

You always wish that good things would never come to an end, but John and Annie were divorced in 1982 after 15 years of marriage. John remarried in 1988 to a woman 20 years younger than himself, Cassandra Delaney. They had a beautiful daughter together Jesse Belle, but the marriage was short lived and they were divorced in 1993.

That same year he was the recipient of the prestigious Albert Schweitzer Music Award for his lifelong contribution of music.

Tragically John died on October 12, 1997 when his airplane suddenly crashed, killing him instantly. The whole world seemed to be in mourning for a man who had become a part of everyone's life.

I received a lot of help in compiling this profile by individuals who were kind enough to correspond with me over the internet. Emily@sky.net, Dottie at Honer@erols.com and Aspen Kate were willing to add their input and Carol Blevins at blevins@epix.net sent pictures she had personally taken of John. Even in his passing John has remained an icon in the music business and his loyal fans take every opportunity to acknowledge his amazing talents.

Marion Briscoe Devore

The Arts

Marion Briscoe Devore was born in Chickasha, Oklahoma on April 12, 1922. One might think coming from a wealthy family with such a prominent father as oilman Powel Briscoe and a gracious refined mother like Emma, Marion would be a little delicate flower, but not Marion.

As the youngest of three children she was always ready to go hunting and fishing with her dad. Baseball games and athletic sports were a priority in her everyday life. She said if she had been a boy she probably would have joined her father in the oil business.

After graduating from Classen High School in Oklahoma City Marion attended Smith College. It was then that she met and married Peter Hoffman who was attending Yale University. World War II interrupted their marriage for awhile when Peter was sent overseas. By the time he returned their first child was 2 years old. Together she and Peter had four children.

Marion recalls the days of the polio epidemic when three of her children suffered from that horrible disease, but Marion nursed them all back to health, refusing to let them be affected long term.

Her family was very important to her but she also found time to submit herself to endless hours of auxiliary roles. Women traditionally always filled those positions while men were the ones allowed to conduct all the business. Yet with Marion's strong sense of fearlessness to the world around her she began to assert herself in areas that had always been taboo to women.

She became the first woman president of three organizations normally headed by the most distinguished men of the community. She started the Arts Council of Oklahoma in 1967, becoming its first president. She also became president of the Festival of Arts, president of the Oklahoma Art Center and president and campaign chairman of the Allied Arts Foundation.

Amazingly with all her ties and obvious dedication to the arts, Marion said she is not an artistic person. However, with her current husband of 28 years Dr. John DeVore, she has encouraged him to cultivate his artistic talents.

In addition Marion has served her church, her school, the Red Cross, the United Way, the Junior League and many other organizations. She was one of the recipients of the Fourth Annual Governor's Arts Awards in 1979. Then in 1980 she was inducted into the Oklahoma Hall of Fame for her tireless support, time and leadership in cultural organizations.

She has always been active in her church affairs, being president of All Souls Episcopal Church Auxiliary and on the State Board of Episcopal Church Women. Marion told me she has gone to the healing service held on Wednesdays at her church for over 40 years.

Another great interest of Marions' is her love for plants. She is very conscious of the beauty that surrounds her home because of the lovely flowers adorned there. For health reasons she decided to not only grow plants and flowers but herbs as well. She and John have learned how to eat their meals by adding an herb or two to sweeten or enhance the taste of most foods, finding that salt has been almost entirely removed from their diet.

Exercise has not been lacking around the DeVore home either. Tennis use to be part of her active lifestyle and even though she can no longer participate in that activity, she still walks two miles everyday.

With John still practicing medicine at age 83 and Marion just passing the 79 mark I would say herbs and exercise has served them both well.

Marion's latest project has been her involvement in the Oklahoma City Museum of Arts, which will open its doors in early 2002. It appears as if there is no stopping her love of the arts and her dedication to seeing it flourish in every way possible.

I asked Marion for some tips of wisdom and she quickly stated, *"Don't ever be afraid, even in failure, you learn a valuable lesson. Enjoy life and watch with open eyes for areas in which you can involve yourself. Look for a need and fill it."*

Marion B DeVore

Joe Diffie – Singer/Songwriter

If you would have asked Joe Diffie 25 years ago what he thought he would be doing at the turn of the century, I doubt if he would have described his life as successfully as it is today.

Born in the metropolitan city of Tulsa, Oklahoma to Joe and Flora Diffie his life with his two sisters Monica and Meg seemed pretty normal by most standards. How would he have ever guessed that 25 years later he would be topping the charts with some of the best country music songs around?

Even though success didn't come overnight, as he looks back he sees the steps were being nicely laid in preparation for what was to come.

Joe's dad was a self-taught musician who first introduced him to "the sound of music." He played the piano, guitar and banjo and probably could have made his own success in the music industry had he pursued it. Other family members also contributed to Joe's enlightenment so it was inevitable he would at least attempt to follow their lead.

Joe and his family traveled outside the state for a few years as he was growing up before finally settling in Velma, Oklahoma right outside of Duncan. With Joe's muscular build it was probably a sure bet he would become a high school athlete and make the young girls swoon as they watched him perform in his high school rock and roll band called "Blitz." He also joined a gospel group appropriately named "Genesis II" and they traveled to various churches singing before enthusiastic congregations. Like a lot of young people, Joe never considered the possibilities of making a career out of his singing. He was just trying to have fun.

He had, however, considered going to college to be a chiropractic doctor an interest he formed after a sports injury. So after high school he enrolled in Cameron University in Lawton, hoping to someday graduate with a degree in the medical field. Yet life took a different turn. Joe married soon after starting college and made the decision to leave school in order to work full-time at the nearby foundry.

While still at the foundry he and some other guys at the local church he attended formed a singing group called "Higher Purpose." Without realizing it Joe was continuing to hone his singing talent which would eventually take him to heights he had never let himself imagine.

As the group traveled from church to church many requests were made for them to produce an album, which they eventually did. Joe later sang for a few years with a blue grass band called "Special Addition" and yet he still never considered the possibility of singing as a full-time career. The responsibilities of being a husband and father to his first two children, Parker and Kara, were all he could focus on and music would just have to remain a fun thing to do.

The mid 1980's brought havoc to a lot of lives as the oil crisis put the whole country in a financial crunch. The foundry Joe had been faithfully working in for nine years was suddenly shut down and Joe was out of a job. His marriage ended not too long before and Joe had some decisions to make about what to do with his future.

He was drawing $192 a week on unemployment without any real possibilities for another job when he began to seriously think about moving to Nashville, Tennessee. One of his bluegrass buddies, Charlie Derington, was working at the Gibson Guitar Factory in Nashville and Joe called to see if he could help him get a job.

The first week after working at a steady pace Joe received his check of $176 which was less than he was making drawing unemployment. He was discouraged to say the least and took a trip back to Oklahoma for Christmas, half way expecting not to return. His parents encouraged him to try a little while longer and see if some doors would open for him. This was a bit of advice he is glad he took.

He moved in with his co-worker John Seay to help cut down on living expenses. With his small paycheck from the guitar factory it was hard to make ends meet and pay his monthly child support. Yet there were times when he would go to the mailbox and a check for $20 would be there from his parents to help him along the way.

It just so happened that Johnny Neal, a Nashville songwriter lived next door to Joe. Even though Joe had asked him on several occasions to let him co-write a song with him, Johnny continued to refuse. Being sight impaired and not really knowing Joe, Johnny was a little apprehensive about involving someone else. But as the days unfolded there came a time when Johnny needed transportation to get back home and Joe was there to help.

On the ride home Johnny and Joe wrote a song together which was Joe's first open door into the Nashville music industry. He began writing demo songs for many of the artists and one song led to the next. He became friends with Wayne Perry and Lonnie Wilson. Lonnie is now his producer and plays drums on all of Joe's records. Together the three of them wrote the song *There Goes My Heart Again,* which was sung by Holly Dunn and went to fourth on the charts with Joe singing harmony.

He still remembers going to the mailbox and getting his first royalty check for $16,000 and thinking, "I've got to write some more songs. " As they say, "success begets success" and Joe Diffie was on his way to stardom.

Along the journey he married for the second time and two sons, Tyler and Drew, were born. Yet divorce would once again find its way to Joe. Life continued to open and shut doors which have brought Joe to where he is today. With great hits like *New Way To Light Up An Old Flame* and *Ships That Don't Come In*, Joe found his niche in the music industry.

Awards and accolades have served as a reminder to Joe that he made the right decision when he left Oklahoma to pursue a talent he had been perfecting all his life. He has sold millions of records over the past 10 years with number one hits too numerous to mention. He is a member of the Grand Ole Opry, yet he still remains a down-to-earth guy with "Oklahoma charm."

He married Theresa on March 11, 2000 and the two of them are inseparable. It is hard to imagine what the future holds for Joe. He has had a wonderful career and there is no reason for it to stop anytime soon.

Joe believes *"If you want to accomplish anything in life you have to take steps toward reaching your goal. Do a little bit every day to help further your desire then before long you will begin to reach levels of accomplishment toward your desired goal."* That reminded me of a Bible scripture that says ..."line upon line, precept upon precept"... Isn't it amazing how it takes some of us (present company included) years to find out the answer to success when it was there in black and white all the time.

Ernestine Dillard - Singer

The way life began for Ernestine should have made the little black girl from Nesbitt, Mississippi very bitter but it didn't. Her parents divorced when she was only two-years old. Her mother, being very young and unable to care for all the children financially, split the family up between their father, grandmother and herself. At first, Ernestine stayed with her mother. Her tears and cries of longing were too frequent to have it any other way. But before long, Ernestine also began to spend time with her Aunt in order to give her mother a chance to find her direction in life. Ernestine recalls living in what she called "shot gun houses," old wooden houses that all looked the same, lined up in a row.

Also, at an early age, Ernestine had to endure the pain of a prejudiced world. As a black person she was only allowed to drink from certain public water fountains. Of course there were designated public restrooms as well. She could ride public transportation buses if she paid the driver at the front of the bus, walked back down the steps and entered through the back to find a seat. Black skin wasn't allowed to touch the skin of a white person's hand when money was being exchanged, as if the color of skin could contaminate. I can't imagine living under those kinds of conditions and yet Ernestine experienced it on a constant basis.

Surprisingly, even though she was painfully aware of what was happening around her, she never allowed it to effect her in a negative way. Instead, she was taught to rise above it. Her teachers and family reinforced the fact that she could be a strong person, capable of becoming anything she wanted. In some instances prejudice caused her to try harder to prove to herself and the white people around her that she could do it. An added strength was her family's spiritual ties to the church.

At an early age, Ernestine was aware of how important music was to her life. The first song she learned to sing was an old spiritual, *C'ain't No Grave Hold My Body Down*. Ernestine recalls times she spent singing with her sister and becoming so overwhelmed with the feeling of God's presence she would collapse on the floor, leaving her sister standing along side of her hoping no one else noticed. Ernestine had no idea that some day God would use her to sing before thousands of people in audiences that spanned the world.

When Ernestine turned 6 years old, her mother remarried and had seven more children. Her father also remarried and eventually, 17 children made up the combined households. Ernestine's mother became a strict disciplinarian. Because of it, Ernestine became somewhat insecure about her role as a child in such a large family. She wanted so badly to be a "good girl" and to please her mother .

Those thoughts carried over into her relationship with God. She felt compelled to do all the right things so God would love her and be pleased with her performance. It took years before she realized God loved her unconditionally, no matter how badly she failed in certain areas.

She graduated among the top 25% in high school. Somehow she knew she had a purpose to fulfill in life and was determined to find out what that purpose was. There were some hills to climb along the way and some unwise decisions that would have to be undone. She enrolled in Memphis State University even though she didn't know how she would make it through financially. At the time, Memphis State limited the number of black people that could attend.

Ernestine was one of two black people that was given entry into the nursing school, sort of like a "token" for a trial basis. Along with her schooling, she was the co-founder of a choir that sang at different locations in and around Memphis. She proved to be an asset to Memphis State as well as to the community. She eventually graduated with a nursing degree and a desire to help others in need.

Her first marriage ended in divorce when her husband left her with a four-year old, a two-year old and one child on the way. Four years later, she married again to a man 22 years her senior. She assumed that marriage took place because she was still searching for the father figure she lost when she was two-years old. That marriage lasted nine years and out of it another child was born. So there she was once again alone, only this time with four children to raise.

Ernestine's determination and independence caused her to press on. She still believed there was a purpose for her life and nothing was going to defeat her. It didn't take long before she was enjoying her freedom as a strong, independent, single woman who didn't need a man to validate her existence. To make a clean start, she moved to Indiana and bought a home there, expecting to continue her nursing career, as well as any singing engagements that would arise.

In 1978 she attended a denominational conference in Indiana where she was the featured soloist. While there, she met who was soon to be her future husband and lifelong mate, Loomus Dillard, a pastor from Alexandria, Virginia. During the short time at the conference, Loomus felt quite sure God had spoken to his heart and Ernestine was to some day be his wife. Of course, as you can imagine, when he told Ernestine of his revelation, she thought he must have been hallucinating.

Loomus, however, was very matter of fact about the matter. His slow and deliberate assurance of what he knew would eventually become a reality was mind boggling to Ernestine. She had already experienced two bad marriages and was determined God would have to make it crystal clear if she was ever going to take the plunge again. Loomus returned to Virginia, but continued to call and write Ernestine. With every encounter his request remained the same. Finally, Ernestine prayed and asked God to answer her in a way that seemed impossible for Him to do. She said, "God, if you want me to marry Loomus, you will have to move him to Indiana because I am not moving to Virginia."

As it turns out, that is exactly what God did. The Bishop who was head of the denomination transferred Loomus to Indiana. By September of 1978 they were married and moved to Evansville, Indiana where Loomus pastored in a Methodist Church. He pastored there for several years before relocating to Arizona, California, Washington State and then finally Oklahoma in 1990. By now, Ernestine was traveling all over the United States singing in a variety of locations. God was opening doors for her that she found easy to walk through.

In 1994 Ernestine was informed about a singing contest being held in Savannah, Georgia of which a friend encouraged her to enter. Some of the entrants were very talented and well polished in their singing careers. Since she didn't have any formal training, she didn't think she had the slightest chance to win. The famous Della Reese was one of the adjudicators critiquing the performances of 145 applicants.

Ernestine Dillard won first place and was presented with $10,000. It was an unbelievable night as Della Reese placed the ribbon around Ernestine's neck and reminded her of God's faithfulness. That was a turning point in Ernestine's life. She made preparations to resign her nursing job to devote the rest of her life to singing.

She was honored when she was given the opportunity to sing at the inaugural ball for Governor and Mrs. Frank Keating. We should all remember her magnificent voice when she sang at the memorial for Oklahoma City bombing victims in 1995. Her song "God Bless America" rang out with the presence of God. Ernestine continues to sing all over the world. She sees herself in a continual pursuit to relay the message of Love, Unity and Peace.

My interview with Ernestine started with the two of us sitting on the couch, but it ended with both of us sitting on the floor like a couple of teenagers bearing our souls to each other. Ernestine has come a long way from a wooden "shot gun" shack in Nesbitt, Mississippi

Ernestine Dillard

Jack Dobbins *Coach/Educator*

Jack Dobbins was born in Coweta, Oklahoma in the Dobbins family home on Ben Lumpkin Road on December 6, 1929. Sixteen children were to eventually grace the Dobbins home. Five siblings passed away early on with two of those five living a short while after Jack's birth. Jack was the third youngest child.

What amazing parents whom Jack gives a tremendous amount of credit for his upbringing. His mother Cleo, a pioneer woman, not only nurtured 16 children, but she worked in the fields of their family farm as well. Jack's father Deed worked on the farm in addition to the oil fields in the surrounding area. There was always work to do around the Dobbins acreage and plenty of family to see to it that each task was completed.

Jack said with a large family a designated place of his own was unheard of. In fact, he never slept in a bed without two or three siblings playing tug of war with the covers. Each day was well planned. With no electricity or running water daily chores took on a bit more of a challenge than those of us in the 21st Century have had to endure.

Fortunately the farm had natural gas from seven oil wells located on the land. Royalties coming from the producing oil wells helped tremendously to sustain the family during the depression era.

Jack's parents moved to Oklahoma from Missouri before Oklahoma statehood, traveling in a covered wagon. It was also before public education had come into existence and they were very aware of the importance of a good education. Education was as much a part of the family upbringing as the incredible lessons of hard work and perseverance.

By 5 o'clock every morning you'd find the Dobbins children milking 25 to 30 head of cows and feeding the cattle. Then, with a worked up appetite, they would all file into the kitchen where their mother had prepared a huge breakfast consisting of homemade biscuits and gravy, sausage and, of course, fresh eggs that had recently been gathered from the hen house. I can vividly picture in my mind a troop of anxiously awaiting hungry kids passing a heaping platter of biscuits that quickly dwindled down to a few crumbs.

For years horses and mule teams were the work force that plowed the fields on the Dobbins Farm, but there came a day when Dad Dobbins reluctantly decided to buy a tractor. Coming from the old school he wasn't quite sure if tractors were a passing fancy or the start of a dynamic future.

During Jack's first year of school there were no school buses in Coweta. So he and his brothers and sisters walked about two miles to and from school. On cold snowy days his father would hitch up the horse drawn wagon, fill it with hay and inform the children to bundle up well for their ride to the school house. School attendance was not an option, it was a necessity.

The original two-story brick school house no longer remains. It was torn down and rebuilt in 1939. However, with a little imagination, if you drive by North Broadway in downtown Coweta you can see signs of past generations that must have frolicked around the courtyard.

Sports activities were also an important part of the Dobbins family, yet they were never allowed to get in the way of the chores that had to be accomplished on a daily basis. Even though being on the school athletic team required some after school participation, the Dobbins children had to make sure they were home by 5 o'clock so they could once again milk the cows and take care of the cattle herd. After supper, if any team games were being played, they would make their way back to the school yard.

It seems to me that the Dobbins children were taught not only the importance of education and hard work, but also the need for family loyalty and respect for all those concerned.

In the 1944-45 school year because of the war many supplies and staples were rationed. The school board decided they could not provide athletic transportation for out of town games. They contacted a gentleman who was willing to transport the entire girls and boys teams in the back of his cattle truck to all of the out of town games during those lean years. I'm sure on those cold winter nights 30 young people piled into the back of a cattle truck must have been a sight to see.

Jack grew up with not only a strong emphasis on education from his parents, but he was also extremely influenced by some great teachers in Coweta. Because of the combined efforts of those strong adults Jack was compelled to pursue a teaching degree along with becoming a coach. He graduated from Coweta High School with a class of 28 students in 1947.

Over 50 years has passed since then. What was once a school that taught all grades simultaneously has now been confined to only elementary grades. A new high school now proudly stands on Ben Lumpkin Road right off of Highway 51 headed out of Coweta.

The graduating classes, although not quite as massive as some of the neighboring towns such as Broken Arrow or Tulsa, have continued to produce their fair share of productive individuals who have gone on to reach great heights in their chosen careers.

After graduation in 1947 Jack immediately enrolled the following year at Northeastern State University in Tahlequah, Oklahoma. He didn't have any grandeur ideas of winning the world or becoming the greatest coach that ever lived. But he did want to make a difference in the lives of the students he knew he would have the opportunity to eventually influence.

Coach Tom Rousey at Northeastern was a good role model for Jack's impending career. Coach Rousey was a WWII Marine veteran who had exchanged his military commander status to that of a college athletic coach a position he held for 14 successful years.

Upon college graduation Jack spent two years teaching in Haskell, Oklahoma, one year in Shidler, Oklahoma and five years at Tahlequah High School before going back to his alma mater as the head basketball coach. Up until then Coach Rousey had filled the role of football, baseball and basketball coach.

Not everyone spends his or her whole career at one school, but Jack completed 35 years at Northeastern State University. He couldn't rest with a limited degree so he went on to complete his masters degree as well as his Ph.D. in education.

Jack has received many honors and awards over the years. Just to mention a few, he is a member of the Oklahoma Coaches

Hall of Fame and has been nominated for the 2002 Oklahoma Educators Hall of Fame.

Jack credits a great deal of his success to his wife of 49 years, Zula Belle. Along with being a talented musician and a source of inspiration to Jack, together they raised three children, Michael, Mark and Jack Jr. who have also become productive individuals. Jack lost his wife to illness in 2001 but the memories she left him create an everlasting peace.

Occasionally Jack is reminded of the old homestead on Ben Lumpkin Road and his loving parents who dedicated their lives to their family. Both parents lived to be 86 and remained on the family farm until their deaths.

Phil's life began the 9th of November, 1947 in Seattle, Washington where his father, Reverend James Allen Driscoll was pastor of a small full-gospel church. The first memories he has are of being in church under the piano while his mother played for the song service and his father preached the sermon. They stayed in Seattle for two years and then moved to Spokane, where his dad became pastor of another church called Life Line Church.

He remembers standing on street corners and in convalescent homes playing a little yellow and red plastic trumpet his grandmother gave him while his mother played the accordion and his dad led the service. Two years later they moved to Dallas where they bought some land on credit and built two churches over a period of five years.

At the end of this time his father became building superintendent of the Lancaster, Texas Public School System. He was approaching 60 years of age and had built some 14 churches. Phil's father had an old rusty, silver trumpet he used to play and Phil convinced him to let him have it. By the time he was in the sixth grade, he had already been promoted to the high school band.

It was then that his dad decided to build one last church in the Midwest and picked Tulsa, Oklahoma. The family moved to Tulsa in 1961 and Phil enrolled in Alexander Graham Bell Junior High School. When he was in the seventh grade he became first chair trumpet in the Tulsa All City Band. During the end of his junior high days he was principal trumpet and soloist in the Tulsa Youth Symphony.

In 1964 he began Tulsa Central High School, played a lot of basketball and joined the band. During the next three years he was first trumpet in the concert band, marching band, orchestra and stage band, acquiring some 49 medals and trophies. In his senior year, Phil helped found and organize an all-city touring band which he called the "Young Tulsans." They raised over $30,000 and did a European tour, ending up in Amsterdam, Holland for the World Music Festival. Their band received first place honors and their trumpet section was voted the best out of 53 different bands from 47 different countries.

The Young Tulsans are still in existence today and have done at least one tour per year since 1966. When Phil graduated from high school he had received over 66 full scholarships to American universities for his musical ability.

In 1967 he decided to wait a year on college and went on tour with a jazz band called "Thurlow Spurr and the Spurrlows." For one year they averaged three high school assemblies each day and a religious concert each night. They traveled in every state in the union except Alaska, and Phil became an apprentice to the life of the road musician.

In 1968 he decided to enroll at Baylor University which he attended in the fall. He became first trumpet in the concert band, marching band and symphonic orchestra. He studied under an absolute genius by the name of Daniel Sternberg, who was from Russia. Sternberg had a photographic memory, spoke 10 different languages and was highly renowned as a harpsichordist and symphonic conductor in Europe. Phil purposed in his heart to become like Daniel Sternberg.

While Phil was a freshman at Baylor he started the first jazz band in the history of the college. Jazz band eventually became an accredited course because of its outstanding excellence. Phil became the instructor as a freshman and taught the course for the four years he remained at Baylor. The Baylor Lab Band is still alive today. As a sophomore Phil was offered a contract by Word Records, the largest religious recording company in the world. Shortly thereafter, he flew to Stockholm, Sweden and recorded his first gospel album.

After meeting a gentleman by the name of Jerry Brown who was a judge on the CBS "All American College Show," Phil was whisked off to Hollywood to do his first national television show. Phil won the grand prize and received $5,000. During the entire contest he was judged by Cliff Robertson, Rose Marie, Fabian, Glenn Ford, Henry Fonda, Dean Martin, Walter Matthau and Milton Burle. Wendell Niles, executive producer and owner of the show, decided he wanted to manage Phil.

Within six months Phil was booked on his own USO show touring Japan, the Philippines, Korea, Hawaii, Okinawa and Guam. He traveled with the full rank of a colonel.

Shortly thereafter, he began to do quite a few national television shows including "The Steve Allen Show," "The Della Reese Show," "The Merv Griffin Show" and "The Ed Sullivan Show." At the same time he was offered a contract by A&R Records of New York.

After "The Ed Sullivan Show" the record company that signed Phil went out of business and his songs were tied up in court for five years. Phil went back out on the road to start recovering from that tail spin and played mostly in the mid west. During that time he met a very wealthy man by the name of Harold Koplar who owned the chase Park Plaza Hotel in Saint Louis, Missouri and who took a liking to him and his music. He bought Phil's contract from Wendell Niles and opened a room in the basement of the hotel for Phil to play in.

St. Louis became Phil's home. Yet no matter how hard Mr. Koplar and Phil tried, his dreams just weren't being fulfilled. By this time Phil had. been married. and was fortunate to have a son whom they named Shawn Alexander Driscoll. Phil had been in the same place six nights a week for four years and he felt he was getting stale. He took on a new manager and went on the road again. His marriage went sour and ended in divorce, but he somehow managed to keep a close relationship with his son, Shawn.

Phil ended up in Jacksonville, Florida where he met some people who financially backed him in a night club they called "Driscoll's." The club did well for the next two years. The club became famous as the place to go for consistent entertainment. Phil was a performer whose music affected people positively.

Phil decided to join a couple of guys and start their own recording studio. Phil worked at night and recorded during the day. Within a year he had sold a song to Blood Sweat and Tears which they recorded on their next album. Soon, the recording studio was signed over to Phil and the other two guys went in another direction.

During this time Phil fell in love with Lynne, whom he later married. They were blessed with two children, son Jamie and daughter Danielle. He finally left his partnership at the club and for a short time had another small club. Eventually, as he continued to plug away writing songs and recording them on cassettes, he finally found someone else who took a great liking to his music. CBS wanted him to build a studio facility and find whatever talent he believed in, produce them as well as himself, and co-publish with CBS.

For a period of time life became a little dismembered. Phil was drawn into a cocaine drug habit, busted for it and yet miraculously found new hope. On December 25, 1977 he experienced what he described as an in-filling of the Holy Spirit which is almost impossible to understand unless you have experienced it. Since that day he has never had the faintest desire to see cocaine, be around it or to use it in any way.

76

Phil has a distinguished list of awards which include four Dove Awards, one Grammy Award, one Grammy nomination, one Reader's Choice Award and one CCMA Award.

I don't remember when I personally started listening to Phil Driscoll's amazing trumpet playing, but I do know that once I heard it I never forgot it. If I want to be placed in an incredible shield of worship toward God, all I have to do is put on Phil's music and it catapult's me to higher ground.

Tim DuBois - Executive

Tim is originally from the beautiful town of Grove, Oklahoma, one of my favorite places. Tim's parents, Everett and Jessie DuBois, have passed away but his younger brother Randy still lives there. Tim grew up living on the farm in the same house his mother was born in. His parents were both teachers. Even though they were strong supporters in just about every thing Tim decided to do, they didn't totally understand his interest in music. Tim started playing guitars and performing in bands while in high school. At the time he was just having a lot of fun and hadn't really considered it as being a career. However, in college at Oklahoma State University, he continued to play in rock-n-roll and folk bands and his interest continued to grow.

He spent six years at OSU and earned his bachelor's and master's degrees in accounting. He left there in 1972 and went to work for a large public accounting firm in Dallas called Arthur Anderson. He worked there for a year before going to work for the Federal Reserve System as the Senior Financial Analyst. In the fall of 1974 he moved back to Oklahoma and taught at Tulsa University while traveling back and forth to OSU to acquire his Ph.D. in accounting. His parents, who were both academically inclined, must have really been proud of their son who had gone so far with his education.

While Tim was in Dallas he became interested in country music for the first time. His white collar business friends were really into the Texas version of country music which involved artists such as Waylon Jennings, Willie Nelson and Michael Martin Murphy. In fact, Tim's curiosity was so peaked he went to the Dallas library and read every book he could that had anything to do with the music industry. One of those books was *Quiet Inside The Record Business* by Clyde Davis the guru of country music who later became Tim's boss.

Tim began writing country music because it was fun and he could relate to it since he had been raised on a farm in Oklahoma. Of course any songwriter, even though he might be writing for a hobby, secretly wishes someday his songs would be heard over the airwaves.

While Tim was completing his studies for his Ph.D. at OSU he met Scott Hendricks, a young first or second year student. They began to write songs together along with their brothers, Randy and Mark, and a few other friends. Scott's intentions had always been to be involved in the music industry so his enthusiasm became contagious to Tim.

In the winter of 1975 Tim and Scott took their first trip to Nashville to pitch some songs they had written. With all of Tim's research he knew the proper channels they needed to take to get their foot in the door in Nashville. He wrote professional letters to certain publishers and asked for appointments. He received six or seven favorable replies so they scheduled the trip and took off for Tennessee. Fortunately one of the publishers bought a song Tim and his brother had written. It was a small deal yet it was somehow validation of the fact they were at least in the ballpark. More importantly, Tim met a man named John Ragsdale who became his mentor and great friend. Tim continued to visit Nashville as often as he could, bringing back new songs he had written and networking with people in the music industry.

On one trip back in 1976 he and John re-wrote a song Tim had written called *A Good Old Fashion Saturday Night Honky*

Tonk Bar Room Brawl and it ended up being the first record Tim recorded. It was on RCA Records sung by Vernon Oxford and went to number 37 on the charts.

In 1977 Tim decided it was time to take the real plunge and move to Nashville permanently. He was 29 years old with a wife and two children and a dream he couldn't seem to let go of. He loaded all of their belongings in the back of a Hertz rental truck with a trailer hitch attached to pull their Vega station wagon and they moved to Nashville. He promised to give himself two years to accomplish his goals.

He went to work immediately as a professor at the University of Tennessee in Nashville to keep bread on the table while he pursued his interest in song writing. At the end of two years he still wasn't where he wanted to be, but a friend told him he was the one who set the time limit so he could also change it. He encouraged Tim to give it a while longer.

A few months later Tim got his first real writer's contract at House of Gold Publishing Company for $75 a week. He was being paid as an exclusive songwriter. Within a year he had written three number one hit records. He co-wrote the first song *Midnight Holler* by Razzy Bailey. Then he co-wrote *Love In The First Degree* by Alabama and thirdly he single-handedly wrote *She Got The Gold Mine, I Got The Shaft.* Those three songs launched his career as a songwriter.

In 1984 he put together a group of musicians we now know as Restless Heart. His friend Scott got involved doing the engineering. The first Restless Heart album did very well. On the second album that went gold they had four number one singles. They had four gold albums in a row which was a rarity.

That got Tim involved in production and later in artist management with the west coast company Fitzgerald Hartley. Tim convinced Fitzgerald Hartley, who had always been strictly pop and rock-n-roll, to let him open a country division in Nashville. It is now one of the biggest management companies in town.

In 1988 Tim had just turned 40 years old. After three years of management he resigned his position thinking he wanted to get back into writing. He was in the process of putting together a publishing company when he got a phone call from Clyde Davis who was wanting to start a country division of Arista Records in Nashville. In his wildest dreams Tim never expected to be working for a record company, but even more amazing was Clyde Davis who he had admired for years was contacting him.

He met with Clyde and in March of 1989 he became president of Arista Records of Nashville. The first album Arista produced was Alan Jackson's first album. It went platinum. Within three years Arista Records of Nashville had gone from nothing to gold. Out of the first six albums they put out four of them were gold or platinum.

In 1991 Arista had Brooks and Dunn, Pam Tillis and Diamond Rio who all went gold or platinum.

Tim has had a wonderful career since his first trip to Nashville in 1975. He said if he has a God-given talent it is being able to attract talented people and then stay out of their way so they can do what they do best.

On the spiritual side, Tim feels very humbled by where his life has taken him. He knows he has been given tremendous opportunities. He believes Christianity is all about those little encounters you have everyday that allow you to either deposit positive or negative responses into someone else's life. If you are constantly lifting people up and making them feel better about themselves then you certainly have to be on the right page with God.

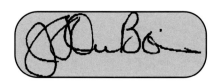

David Duncan

Physician

David pointed out he isn't a native Oklahoman, but he got here as quick as he could and has loved it ever since.

Many years ago as you drove over the Arkansas River into the town of Jenks, Oklahoma it was like stepping into a slower pace of life where serenity was a daily comfort. When Dr. Duncan realized he didn't want to raise his family in Miami, Florida he tacked a Rand McNally Map on the wall, threw a dart at it to see where it would land and decided that was where he would move his family.

As it turns out the chosen state was Oklahoma where he finished his residency and began his search for a small town that would welcome a doctor with big ideas. David located what used to be an old house on main street in Jenks. The house had previously been used for an architectural firm, so David needed to make some changes to prepare it for a doctor's office.

He replaced some of the beams with basic tree trunks that still had their bark, which gave a very interesting look to the decor. In the pediatrics room he mounted part of a fake horse with a saddle on it in one corner so children could sit on it while they were being examined. Outside they turned the detached garage into a small barn for his horse, Tammy that would be pulling Dr. Duncan's buggy. He was determined to become the proverbial country doctor for the town of " Jenks America."

He had his loyal, healthier patients that would come into his office. His patients in the nursing home and 20 or so patients who were pretty much home bound would wait for his visit with Tammy. Even though getting the precise number of milligrams of penicillin is important, David felt there was more to the practice of medicine. Often he gave his patients a ride in the buggy. It thrilled him to see how excited children were when they saw Tammy.

Over the years, many tourists came by to take pictures of this modern day horse and buggy team. David said one of his fondest memories was on a spring day when he pulled up to Riverside Nursing Home and parked his buggy outside Al's room. Al had been his patient for about five years and would never communicate with anyone. The nurses would help him from his bed to his chair everyday where he would sit in front of the television speechless until it was time to be put back in bed.

This particular day when Al saw Dr. Duncan pull up with the horse and buggy outside his window he began trying to get out of his chair. They helped him get up and walk outside and he stared at the horse and buggy without saying a word. Then he tried to climb up into the buggy, but he was too weak. Dr. Duncan said he gave Al a boost up into the buggy and gave him a ride around the courtyard. After they had made about one loop around the nursing home Al began singing *Amazing Grace* at the top of his lungs.

From that moment on, Al never stopped singing during every waking moment of the day, until he passed away a year later. He knew an unbelievable number of hymns and could go all day without repeating one hymn. David said he didn't know what switched in Al's mind, but it was really something to watch.

David said the horse and buggy were symbols for him of what he wanted the field of medicine to represent, almost the opposite of managed care. He wanted to be known as a sincere doctor who genuinely cared about his patients. To be able to take on the suffering of someone else and hopefully have the skills to alleviate their suffering.

David said as he practices medicine he feels like he is one of the luckiest men alive who happened to have gotten "the brass ring." David's horse and buggy days ended after about 10 years due to different changes in the area. His office was moved to Tulsa and his faithful horse Tammy moved on to bigger and better things.

If you drive by Dr. Duncan's home you might still see his retired buggy sitting in amongst the trees. If you look real hard, you might be able to imagine Tammy there as well.

Archie W. Dunham

Business Executive

(Archie on Right)

I interviewed Archie Dunham in 1999 and found him to be an extremely honest and caring Christian man whose strong values still remain one of his highest priorities. After listing Archie's rise to success in the business world, I felt his own speech given during a lecture at the University of Oklahoma spoke more clearly about the heart of Archie Dunham than I could express. Therefore, I chose to include a portion of that speech so everyone could enjoy its contents as much as I did.

Archie is Chairman of the Board and President and Chief Executive Officer of Conoco Inc., the 4th largest energy company in the United States with revenues in excess of $39 billion. He was born in 1938 in Durant, Oklahoma, but grew up in Ada, Oklahoma where he attended school. He served in the U .S. Marine Corps from 1960 to 1964, reaching the rank of captain. After graduating from the University of Oklahoma with a bachelor's degree in geological engineering and a master's degree in business administration, he joined Conoco in 1966 as an associate engineer in Houston.

For seven years he worked in various positions within the natural gas and gas products department and the corporate new project development group traveling extensively in the Middle East, his favorite region in the world. In 1973, he became manager of the gas products division, followed by an appointment to Harvard University's Management Development Program.

Archie was elected executive vice-president of Douglas Oil Company, a Conoco subsidiary in California, in 1976. He became president of the subsidiary in 1979. He returned to Houston in 1981 as vice president of logistics and downstream planning. In 1983, he was named vice-president of transportation, natural gas and gas products.

After participating in Stanford University's Senior Executive Management Program, he became executive vice president of petroleum products, North America in 1985 and was elected to the Conoco board of directors.

In 1987, Archie became senior vice president of DuPont's chemicals and pigments sector at DuPont headquarters in Wilmington, Delaware. He assumed the same position for polymer products in 1989. He returned to Houston in 1992 as Conoco's executive vice president, exploration production. He held that position until becoming president and CEO in January 1996, and then Chairman of the Board in 1999.

Archie continues to remain associated with the University of Oklahoma through service on various boards and fund-raising efforts. He has been honored by both the College of Business Administration and the College of Engineering as a distinguished graduate. In 1994 he was recognized by the Oklahoma Board of Regents for his dedicated service and demonstrated leadership to the University of Oklahoma. He was inducted into the Oklahoma Hall of Fame in 1998.

Archie's lecture dated April 14, 1999: This morning I'd like to share with you some thoughts about what it takes to win in the tough global marketplace of today and ...more importantly what it takes to succeed in the global marketplace of tomorrow. It's growth that I want to talk about. How do you grow...how do you win against tough competition? What will it take for businesses to succeed in the 21st century? I usually answer those questions by discussing the attributes of great companies...and great people.

The first attribute is FOCUS. You can't go everywhere and do everything if you want to perform well. Being effective doesn't depend on how much effort you expend or how hard you work. Effectiveness is achieved when you focus on the right opportunities. The best companies and the most successful leaders have the ability to focus their energies like a laser on the few really important opportunities and problems.

The second attribute of successful people, and companies, is LEADERSHIP. If you are going to succeed, you must have extraordinary leadership. Leaders must constantly challenge their organizations to change. They must look to the future...visualize where their organizations need to be in the future...and then lead their organizations to that future.

A strong leader starts with a compelling vision of where he or she wants to go. Leaders must also be problem solvers. To solve problems, you need to be willing to confront conflict, make difficult decisions and resolve problems. For me, success and peace of mind come from confronting my most difficult problems at the beginning of the day. When I do this, I find myself better able to concentrate on the easier problems that may arise later. When I don't address the difficult problems early, I waste mental and physical energy worrying about them during the day.

Another important trait of effective leaders is judgment, which is probably the most difficult trait to develop. You must learn to be a good listener...gather information from many sources...not react too quickly to what you hear, and above all, don't become angry. Anger stifles communication and impairs your ability to make good decisions. As the Bible states in (James 1:19) Be quick to hear, slow to speak and slow to anger.

The third attribute is BALANCE. Keeping a balance between work and family is very important. Also, balance is important in pursuing long-term versus short-term objectives. In controlling costs versus spending. In strengthening existing businesses versus creating new ones. Leaders must decide how and where to strike those balances.

The fourth attribute, and possibly the most important, is CHARACTER. Some of you might be thinking that in the real world, the only thing that really matters is the bottom line...that the leader's character doesn't matter. *Yet, it is impossible to lead people if you are deficient in character.*

When times are hard, people follow leaders they can trust...leaders who have the moral courage and strength of character to do what they know in their hearts is right. Subordinates will decide whether or not they will follow you long before hard times hit. They watch you every day. You can stumble and make a bad business decision and still recover. But if you show yourself to be a man or woman of poor character, they will never trust you. And if they don't trust you, they won't follow you.

"Watch your thoughts, they become words. Watch your words, they become actions. Watch your actions, they become habits. Watch your habits, they become character. Watch your character...it becomes your destiny."

The final attribute is FLEXIBILITY. In a fast moving, highly competitive world, targets have a way of changing, often without warning. "Flexibility" means being able to refocus resources and still get the job done...being nimble and quick. Your people must be free to act quickly and decisively when opportunities or challenges arise.

In the numerous interviews I have been fortunate to conduct I continue to be amazed at the magnitude of wisdom I gain from each individual. I hope, along with myself, each person who reads this book will lay it aside upon completion feeling they have gained insight that will carry them through to their appointed destination.

Ronnie Dunn

Country Music Star

Ronnie is such a nice guy and one of my favorite performers. He deserves all the success that has come to him and realizes how fortunate he is to have made it so far in the music industry.

He was born in Coleman, Texas on June 1, 1953 to Jessie and Gladys Dunn. He is one of four children including Denise, Renee and Johnny. I had the privilege of meeting Denise and Renee and they, too, carry on the same Okie friendliness that flows so easily from Ronnie.

Ronnie's father Jessie had at one time been a ranch foreman. He grew up as an orphan and was a rugged sort of guy that had dreams of his own to play country music. He became the lead singer and guitar player of a band called Fox Four Five. They played every weekend in different locations around the area and even made a few 78 RPM records. He traveled to Nashville a few times trying to pursue a career in music and took Ronnie right along with him. But it was never meant to be.

The family eventually moved to Tulsa where Ronnie spent his junior year at Skiatook High before Jessie's job took them back to South Texas. After graduating from high school in Tulsa, Ronnie went to college in Abilene while his family moved back to Oklahoma where Jessie began working for Arrow Trucking.

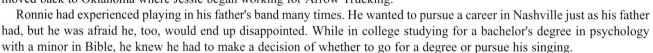

Ronnie had experienced playing in his father's band many times. He wanted to pursue a career in Nashville just as his father had, but he was afraid he, too, would end up disappointed. While in college studying for a bachelor's degree in psychology with a minor in Bible, he knew he had to make a decision of whether to go for a degree or pursue his singing.

His mother sent him a newspaper clipping about Jim Halsey who is a well-known figure in the music industry. Since Halsey had business ties in Tulsa she thought it might be easier for Ronnie to come back to Tulsa and hopefully meet up with him. She thought Ronnie would make a bigger splash in Tulsa before he went on to Nashville. Guess what? It took a while, but Mom was right.

After moving back to Tulsa he worked several odd jobs over the years, just sort of letting life happen while he played his music in clubs on weekends. He had given up on getting a Psychology degree and was beginning to think he was getting too old to get a Nashville recording contract. His band had become the house band for a local dance club in Tulsa called Duke's Country a place all the two-steppers hung out in their spare time.

Eventually Ronnie moved to Grove, a small town just a short drive from Tulsa. He got a job at a liquor store once again just letting life happen. One year later in 1988 the Marboro Company held a singing contest. Jamie Aldecker a friend of Ronnie's who was a drummer for Eric Clapton, was in a convenience store and saw the entry forms and signed one for Ronnie.

About a month later he remembered to tell Ronnie what he had done. Shortly after that, Ronnie received a phone call saying his band had qualified. They didn't have a name for the band at the time, but they became who we now know as "The Tractors" minus Steve Ripley: Ripley was at the time, the engineer and owned the studio they were rehearsing in. He later became part of the band.

Nearly 20 bands competed in Tulsa and Ronnie's band won. From there they went to Nashville where bands from all over the U.S. were competing. They won the contest and part of their winnings was $30,000. Of course after it was split in several directions and taxed, they only received a couple of thousand dollars a piece. They also received a recording session with producer Barry Beckett and Scott Hendricks who now run Capitol and Virgin Records.

At the time, though Scott was producing Restless Heart with Tim DuBois. Ronnie's band cut three songs at a demo session. Those songs were *Boot Scootin' Boogie, You Don't Know Me* and *The Dean Dillion Song.* Eventually Scott put the songs in the hands of Tim DuBois who was just beginning the country side of Arista Records in Nashville. He liked the songs so well he flew to Tulsa some time later to watch the band perform at Joey's Bar.

Tim didn't sign a contract with Ronnie that night, but he took him outside and strongly advised him to move to Nashville. Ronnie pondered what Tim said for almost two years. He remembered the heartache and disappointment his father had experienced and just wasn't sure if he wanted to put himself through it. His father had died two years earlier without ever becoming a musical success so Ronnie still needed time to think about it. I guess if Tim would have offered Ronnie a contract that night it would have been an easier decision but as it stood, Ronnie had some thinking to do.

Two years passed and Ronnie had married his second wife, Janine. He thought Tim DuBois had probably forgotten him by then but he picked up the phone and called him anyway. Surprisingly Tim was in the process of calling him at the same time. He wanted to get the okay from Ronnie to cut *Boot Scootin' Boogie* as a single for the group Asleep At The Wheel.

Ronnie agreed and he and Janine drove to Nashville to meet with Tim DuBois. Tim again encouraged Ronnie to move to Nashville. Still reluctant, Janine finally convinced him he needed to at least give it a try or he would always be wondering. They moved to Nashville and for a few months nothing was happening. They were just praying for a break. Tim was slow about offering Ronnie anything solid because he had just begun Arista Records in Nashville with Alan Jackson as his first solo. He didn't want to mess that up with another solo act too soon.

It just so happened that Kix Brooks was working on a duo act but it didn't work out so Scott mentioned teaming Ronnie up with Kix. At first Tim didn't like the idea but decided to give it a try. Ronnie and Kix started hanging out together writing songs and trying to harmonize their voices. From then on everything happened very fast.

Boot Scootin' Boogie hadn't done too well as a hit for Asleep at the Wheel, but for Brooks and Dunn it went number one. They immediately had four number one hits in a row and took off on a road tour to meet their fans and see exactly how far they could take this ride they were on. In 1992 they won the Duo category at the Annual country Music Awards and have won every year since.

Looking back Ronnie knows his success didn't just happen by chance. He believes it was the plan of God for his life. He remembers the day Tim DuBois called him and encouraged him to come to Nashville. He walked out into a field in Welch, Oklahoma and got down on his knees to pray for God's guidance. On his way back to the house he saw Janine driving down the road toward him with the exciting news that Tim had just called. Ronnie still knew how to pray. It was something he had learned many years ago.

He has learned over the years that persistence and perseverance payoff. Everything has a time and a season and if you are willing to sacrifice hours of hard work then success will come.

I'm still amazed at how many Oklahoma musicians there are in Nashville and how God orchestrated at least two of those Oklahomans (Tim and Scott) to make themselves available when the new kid on the block (Ronnie) came along. It sounds like a "God Thing" to me.

Ralph Ellison ~ Author

I guess the reason I love writing profiles is I am so amazed at the inner workings of an individual's life. I don't think we realize sometimes just how remarkable the scripture is that says, "The steps of a righteous man are ordered by the Lord."

I recently heard a series of video tapes by one of my favorite preachers T.D. Jakes titled, "Nothing Just Happens." He pointed out if our lives are dedicated to God and we want our will to be His will, then nothing either good or bad just happens. That is a hard pill to swallow at times, because some hideous things can happen in our lives. But God promised that "All things work together for the good for those who love God and are called according to His purpose."

Lewis and Ida Ellison's first son, Ralph's brother, died as an infant. When Ralph came along on March 1, 1914 in Oklahoma City, Oklahoma his father wanted to prepare him for the future by giving him a name that portrayed significance. He named him after the 19th century philosopher and writer Ralph Waldo Emerson.

I looked up the name "Ralph" and it means advisor or counselor and "Waldo" means ruler. How remarkable that his name would so easily translate into a leader of men and a well-spring of wisdom. I know the Bible declares names as being very important. Obviously Lewis Ellison saw the importance as well.

Three years after Ralph's birth another son was born, Herbert Ellison. Sadly that same year Ralph's father was killed in an accident, so he was never around to see just how significant his son Ralph would become.

Even though Ralph's mother only had an eighth grade education she was determined to take care of her children. She worked as a maid in Oklahoma City and eventually became involved in politics and became superintendent of several apartment houses. Life was sometimes a struggle, however she continued to reinforce to her children that hard work would eventually create success.

When he was old enough Ralph started helping his mother financially by delivering newspapers and pharmacy items after school. He attended Douglass High School in Oklahoma City, began studying classical music and learned to play several instruments, predominately the trumpet. His goal was to write a symphony by the time he was 26 years old.

I never realized how important setting goals were until I set some and saw what happened because of it. *It makes perfect sense if you don't know where you are going that chances are you will never get there.*

When Ralph graduated from high school in 1933 he was awarded a scholarship to attend Tuskegee Institute, a prestigious black college in Alabama. He had experienced racial segregation in Oklahoma, but nothing compared to the alienation he felt in Alabama. However, as T.D. Jakes stated, "Nothing Just Happens."

Later Ralph used those experiences as a basis to form his highly acclaimed novel *Invisible Man.* He had learned how to outsmart the seemingly witty people who mistook his self-control as fear and his silence as submission.

Ralph's emphasis had mainly been on accomplishing his goals musically until one day, while working in the college library, he ran across a series of books which opened his eyes to other artistic avenues. He began learning photography, sculpture, acting and poetry writing.

In 1936 at age 22 he left Tuskegee headed for New York with the same dream of composing a symphony by the age of 26. He also added to his goals the thought of being an artist.

Have you ever started in a direction and found yourself headed down another road you didn't know was there? A set of circumstances caused Ralph to question his musical career and consider becoming a writer instead. Just as that thought process was developing he got word that his mother had fallen and was injured. He left New York to be by his mother's side. Unfortunately complications developed and she died, so Ralph returned to New York.

On his return to New York he gave more thought to becoming a writer and landed a job in 1938 with the Federal Writers Project. This project was a government program sponsored by the Works Progress Administration to employ hundreds of writers throughout the country. Ralph worked for $22 a week as a researcher. The job required him to interview countless numbers of individuals. Those interviews taught him that the character of a person is revealed in their speech. What an interesting observation and one that we so often overlook. You know the old saying, "Don't judge a book by its cover?" The next line should be, "Judge it by the pages that you read."

At age 25 Ralph had published his first set of short stories titled *Slick Gonna Learn*, followed by *The Birthmark* and *Afternoon.* He also married during that time, but was divorced soon after .

In his early 30's through a mutual friend he met and married Fanny McConnell in 1946. A year earlier he had started the novel *Invisible Man,* having no idea what incredible success the book would bring him. It took seven years to finish the story and get it published. It was such an amazing story about a young man's struggle to understand himself that in 1953 the book won the National Book Award, recognized as being the best novel written in 1952.

Ralph continued to write short stories. In 1967 after working on his second novel their house burned down, destroying all evidence of a year's hard work. He never finished the second novel but continued to write short stories. He published his second collection of short stories in 1986.

In 1975 Ralph was honored by his hometown when a branch library was named after him and a large sculpture was erected in his likeness. President Johnson as well as President Reagan presented him with medals Johnson with the Medal of Freedom in 1969 and Reagan with the National Medal of Arts in 1985.

Ralph Waldo Ellison passed away in 1994, but the insights revealed in his award winning novel will continue to open pathways in the minds of individuals who dare to take a chance and believe in themselves.

Gary England

Meteorologist

Okay, here is another Oklahoman who had the overwhelming fortune to know what he wanted to do with his life at an early age and went for it.

I love this sentence Gary put in his book, *Weathering the Storm.* "Beginning with my boyhood dream of being a television meteorologist, this is the chronicle of my bumpy journey toward my personal perception of success in weather broadcasting."

"My personal perception of success" is what caught my eye. We all have a definition of what success means and yet the word so often scares us to the point we don't pursue it to the ultimate end. Gary realized that finding success isn't always an easy road to travel on, but it is a rewarding one. No matter where life leads you, success is always right around the corner if you don't turn off too early onto the proverbial "dead end" road.

Gary is originally from Seiling in western Oklahoma where he grew up focusing much of his attention on the fickled weather of his fine state. However, with almost non-existent radio coverage in that area, his family relied mainly on weather tips that had been verbally passed down over the years. Some of the tips were: When flies gather on the screen door it's going to rain. The thickness of animals' coats is a good indicator of the intensity of the coming winter. Spring and summer southwest winds suggest hot, dry conditions and a possible drought. East winds usually mean rain within twenty-four hours. Aches and pains foretell a change in the weather for the worse. When horses run and kick across the fields, thunderstorms soon develop. When birds cease to sing, a storm is near. A ring around the sun or moon means a change in the weather. Smoke from a campfire that rises and then moves away in a flat plane means fair weather. Dews and frost usually suggest nice weather.

I would imagine if you had those kinds of conversations floating around the atmosphere on a continual basis you might tend to become an enthusiast on the subject of weather.

With the advent of television entering our world in the late 1940's it became apparent that eventually weather forecasts would become an essential part of television programming. However, it wasn't until spring of 1952 that Harry Volkman broadcast the first televised tornado forecast on WKY -TV, the only television station in Oklahoma City. It was Volkman who was the spark that lit an unquenchable fire in Gary to become a television meteorologist.

After high school graduation Gary thought his next step toward preparing himself for the "weather world" would be a degree from what was then Oklahoma A&M in Stillwater. But before he could actually begin his college career he was sidetracked. The Navy promised him he could attend the Navy Aerographer's Mate Weather School in Lakehurst, New Jersey.

His stint in the military proved to be very educational. After returning home he enrolled at Southwestern State University in Weatherford, Oklahoma. It was during that time in the summer of 1960 he met his wife, Mary Helen Carlisle. Not long after that he enrolled at the University of Oklahoma in Norman.

In reading Gary's book he tells of his own personal fears of stepping into the reality of his chosen career. *It is one thing to talk about what you want to accomplish, but quite another thing to actually step into the unknown arena and cause those dreams to come true.* At times Gary found himself in situations that didn't always appear to be relevant to his endeavors, only to find that *things of great value frequently appear in disguise.*

Sometimes in our quest for a fulfilling career we don't realize how many steps there are in reaching those intended goals. Gary found out there were different roads to travel before arriving at his destination. But during each facet of his journey he learned many lessons along the way.

It was 1973 before he realized the beginning of a career as a television meteorologist. After a short time at KTOK radio in Oklahoma City he was approached by KWTV in Oklahoma City. They had heard him on the radio and thought he would be perfect in television. Almost immediately Gary's talents began to surface. With the help of several ham radio operators, he launched a major effort to organize and train a large number of volunteer storm spotters.

His new ideas which at all times were meant to create safety for the public weren't always well received from his peers. He quickly realized *when you're on the cutting edge you have to expect an avalanche of criticism.* But as we all know, only risk takers make it to the cutting edge.

In early 1976 Gary felt two more items needed to be added to keep KWTV on the forefront. One was a weather satellite machine and the other was a powerful color radar system. With grit and tenacity Gary once again walked the proverbial tightrope to convince others the need was crucial. It would take too much paper to explain the immediate obstacles to his futuristic ideas. The bottom line is in early 1977 KWTV had their new StarCom9 satellite. Then in 1981 the first Doppler radar in the world dedicated to public warnings was also put in place.

In spite of the obstacles, Gary's ideas prevailed. Not only were his ideas developed but from them other pertinent systems were either put into existence or updated. In 1990 First Warning alerts were displayed on our television screens. Then in 1991 a computer program dubbed Storm Tracker to alert the viewing audience of severe weather was put in place. An upgrade of the Dopper radar system renamed Doppler 9000 made its debut in 1992, as well as the Storm Action Video developed by Roger Cooper.

Needless to say a vast majority of movie goers had the opportunity to see Gary in action when Warner Brothers and Steven Speilberg requested his talents in a segment of the spell-bounding film "Twister."

We never know where our lives will take us. But as I've learned from the hundreds of interviews I've conducted over the years, *nothing of any significance happens without taking risks*. Risks may mean not everyone will agree with you or stand behind your decisions. Do you believe enough in your dream to take some risks? Gary did.

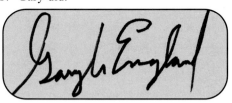

Charles Faudree – *Interior Designer*

I had never met Charles until the afternoon of our interview. In fact, I have never knowingly seen any of his work. Yet as I drove down 15th Street in Tulsa one day and passed his office as I have numerous times over the years, I felt compelled to add him to my list of "Distinguished Oklahomans," having no idea the heights in his career he had actually reached.

I found Charles to be an interesting, warm and talented gentleman. He describes himself as one of those Okies from Muskogee. He was raised in a Catholic home with one sister, Francie and two devoted parents. His father worked for the Katy Railroad and his mother was a homemaker. Neither parents had gone to college, but they wanted more for their son who they had named Charles Hamlet Faudree. The name alone has a ring of distinction to it.

As early as two years old, Charles became fascinated with color and had artistic views that seemed more defined than the average child would have. In the passing of time, Charles knew he wanted to be involved in some form of art. So he set out to find where he would be most suited.

It was interesting to hear Charles say he knew his parents wanted the best for him, but they didn't know how to guide him there. He had to find his own way and discover the niche that was right for him.

As an observation, I've found in some cases if a parent has not experienced tremendous success in their own life it is difficult to intelligently guide his or her child to success. Therefore, the child ends up taking a longer route to get where he was going, if he in fact finds success himself. On the other hand, a parent who knows the keys to success develops those instincts into a child almost without trying, and the child takes the shortest route to success.

Charles entered Northeastern State University after high school and enrolled in a basic art class. The only art degree offered at Northeastern at the time was in teaching, so that is the direction he took.

College days were memorable for Charles. He was known as a creative, fun loving and loyal friend to all of his classmates. He was involved in clubs and organizations and was the manager and then editor of the yearbook. He was also named to Who's Who in American Colleges and Universities his senior year. He successfully graduated in 1960 with a B.A. in Art.

As he walked away from the campus where he spent some incredible years, his emotions were high. He was embarking on a brand new phase of his life, but he was saddened he had to leave so many valuable friends behind.

He accepted his first teaching job in Kansas City so he could go to the Kansas City Art Institute at night and study design. After a year he was increasingly more homesick. His father had passed away during his sophomore year at Northeastern and he felt he needed to be closer to home. So he took a job at Herbert Hoover Jr. High in Oklahoma City. He still wasn't totally content. He liked to teach, but there seemed to be an urging inside of him that made him feel like there was so much more he needed to be doing.

One evening during a conversation at a party he was attending, he was describing the desires he had to design and decorate with antiques. A couple recognized his unique talent and offered to financially back him in an antique venture in Oklahoma City. Charles worked long, hard hours in his first shop they had established in a shopping mall. That venture was a good stepping stone, but it still wasn't where Charles wanted to be in his career.

Three years later in a conversation with a sales representative from Faroy, one of his suppliers, he decided to make another career move. Faroy offered him a job in Dallas, Texas. He was to be the art and display director, decorating showrooms for the company in places like Los Angeles and San Francisco. During that time he found himself making sales pitches for the company. After two years he opted to become a traveling salesman for the company, which would net him a larger salary.

Eight years passed and even though Charles was making a lot of money and enjoyed the travel, he was still frustrated because there was no real creative outlet for him. He was 38 years old and 40 was just around the corner. He needed to make some changes if he was ever going to see his dreams become a reality.

He had designed his sister's home and she was married to a banker in Muskogee. He also designed the home of one who served on the Board of Directors at the same bank. Word of mouth caused other people to contact Charles for his expertise. He started realizing he did in fact have a talent that could bring him a great deal of success both financially and emotionally with peace of mind that he was fulfilling his dream.

He sold his house in Dallas, moved back to Muskogee and opened an antique shop, offering his services as a designer an antique salesman. He intended to have a quiet life in Muskogee selling and decorating a few homes occasionally. Before long the occasionally became frequent and clients were keeping Charles busy and expanding his creative talents.

Eventually his client base grew so much in Tulsa that it made better business sense to relocate. He rented a space in Utica Square where he stayed for 15 years until he bought the building on 15th Street where he has remained to this day.

Charles may have taken a longer route by way of teaching and sales jobs to get to where he is today. But he established a niche in interior design that only he can fill. His work has been featured in almost every publication known in the interior designers' market. He travels to France and England every year to visit antique shops and bring back items that would gorgeously in any home. Among his favorite pit stops while in Paris is the local flea markets, which seem to have valuables that others don't always see. Most of his clients become his friends because designing someone's home becomes a very intimate experience.

Charles has never married but he does enjoy the company of his two lively dogs, Nicolas and Chelsea.

On a spiritual note, Charles gives all the credit to God for his talent and is extremely thankful he is allowed to make his living doing something that is so incredibly rewarding to him. He has had the privilege of experiencing a lot of financial pleasures and yet he has learned it isn't things that make you happy, you have to he happy within yourself and feel secure with who you are.

I asked Charles how you become secure with yourself. His answer, " I think it is a God Deal - an inside job that only a close relationship with God can fix. *To have a good life you have to do the footwork, but God gives the direction. If you make a bad decision then every day you have an opportunity to start all over again."*

Charles Faudree

Lane Frost

Rodeo Champion

I watched the movie "8 seconds" like everyone else did when it was released in 1994 and have never forgotten the story. I spoke with Lane's mother, Elsie, and she was thrilled to have the opportunity to have Lane's profile put in a book such as this. I also contacted Sharon Mahrley who has created Lane's web site at www.lanefrost.com. She consented to let me use the information she has compiled for this profile along with Elsie's comments.

July 30, 2000 was the 11th anniversary of Lane Frost's death. He was only 25 years old at the time of his death and had so many dreams and plans for his future. His memory is alive today in all the young bull riders who strive to be like him. But to be like Lane isn't only riding bulls like he did, but talking to people like he did.

Lane wasn't always the World Champion Bull Rider. But no matter where life took him or what life gave and took from him, he was always a World Champion of a man.

Lane was born on October 12, 1963. At that time, his parents lived in Lapoint, Utah. However, Lane's father Clyde was on the rodeo circuit and his mother Elsie went to stay with her parents in Kim, Colorado while she waited for Lane to arrive. He was born in the hospital at La Junta, Colorado, the closest hospital to Kim.

Lane's full name is Lane Clyde Frost. Clyde was after his father, of course. He has an older sister, Robin, and a younger brother, Cody. When Lane was 25 he was 5' 11" and weighed 145 lbs. He spent his first 14 years in Utah doing chores on the dairy farm which his parents owned and competing in various rodeo events. His mom made his first pair of chaps. She admits to hoping he would out-grow this rodeo thing.

In 1978 the Frost family moved from Vernal, Utah to Lane, Oklahoma, mostly to escape the harsh Utah winters. The name of the town was coincidence, but wasn't it great? Also by moving to Oklahoma, Lane would be closer to the rodeo circuits. He began his freshman year at Atoka High School and his sister Robin began her senior year there. In Oklahoma Lane continued his rodeo learnings and ridings.

Lane's mom says while they did not encourage Lane to ride bulls, they did support him in his decision. In addition to his father's help, he had the help of his father's good friend, Freckles Brown, the 1962 PRCA Bull Riding Champion. Freckles became a very important person in Lane's life. Lane spent hours watching tapes of Freckles' rides.

During his high school years while competing at the National High School Rodeo Association Finals, Lane met two people who affected the rest of his life, Tuff Hedeman in 1980 and Kellie Kyle in 1981. In 1982 Lane graduated from Atoka High School in Atoka, Oklahoma. In 1983 at the age of 19 Lane attained full membership in the Professional Rodeo Cowboys Association. He was offered rodeo scholarships, but decided to pursue a professional rodeo career.

On January 5, 1985 he married Kellie Kyle at the United Methodist Church in Quanah, Texas. In 1985 he also taught his first bull riding class, a class of 10. He not only loved to ride bulls, he loved to help others who wanted to learn to ride. The next year, Lane built a bull riding arena on the family's ranch. He and his father designed the area to be both an arena and a place to work cattle. He didn't have to talk his father into letting him build the arena because they needed new corrals real bad.

He moved to Quanah, Texas (Kellie's home town) although for a while he continued to use Lane, Oklahoma as his "official" home address. His parents still lived there and he was working with his dad there. At the time of his death, Lane was working on building his own ranch with Kellie. They had picked out a piece of property near Marietta, Oklahoma almost halfway between Lane's parents and Kellie's parents. It was important to Lane to continue helping his father with their ranch.

In December of 1987 Lane achieved a goal he worked for all his life. He became the 1987 PRCA Bull Riding Champion of the World. Lane was the last one to ride in the 10th Round of the Finals. If he stayed on for the 8 seconds, he would win the Championship. He won the World Championship, (a season-long "contest" between riders) despite being off for three weeks in August, 1987 when he broke his collarbone on August 20th at the Elks PRCA rodeo in Seminole, Oklahoma. Though he slightly re-injured the collarbone several times near the end of the season, he felt he couldn't take anymore time off without hurting his chances for the Championship.

The year 1988 was a busy one for Lane. In February he competed with the U .S. Rodeo Team at the only exhibition rodeo ever held at the Olympics. At the Winter Olympics in Calgary, Alberta, Canada he won the bronze bull riding medal and the U .S. Team won the gold. From April through June of 1988 he participated in the "Challenge of the Champions" with the bull Red Rock and won. Red Rock had never had a rider stay on the full eight seconds in 309 attempts. Lane rode Red Rock 4 out of 7 tries.

On March 8, 1988 Lane accepted Jesus Christ as his personal savior. His mother Elsie said she wanted the movie "8 seconds" to expound on Lane's relationship with Jesus because it was such an important part of his life. But she couldn't get the movie producers to honor her wishes.

On July 30, 1989 25-year-old Lane Frost was looking forward to this day. It was the last day of Cheyenne Frontier Days and he was in a good position to win this prestigious rodeo. He was currently in second place. He and Kellie were making plans to build their ranch and start raising bulls and a family. At 3:30 p.m. with his bull rope firmly in his hand, Lane nodded his head and gave his familiar "OK boys, OK boys!" In less than 15 seconds Lane Frost was gone from this earthly realm forever.

Before his death Lane had been quoted as saying, "Don't be afraid to go after what you want to do, and what you want to be. Don't be afraid to be willing to pay the price." Lane paid the price throughout his career by the many hours of dedication he invested in the sport, as well as the time with his family he so often had to sacrifice.

On August 2, 1989 Lane was laid to rest at Mount Olivet Cemetery in Hugo, Oklahoma. Clem McSpadden, who was general manager of the National Finals Rodeo for 18 years, gave the eulogy.

In 1993, Kellie remarried. She now lives in Texas with her new husband and their two children.

While the movie "8 Seconds" was about Lane, it was not a documentary. It was part fact, part fiction. Lane. was too good to be true and the producer felt the movie would not be "realistic" unless some things were changed, added or left out. But...if you ever have a chance to view the movie, do it! At the end of the movie there are seven minutes of great footage of the real Lane Frost.

I. J. Ganem

Entertainer

Mr. Showbiz. Sometimes you just look at a person and can tell what they do for a living. At first glance its apparent I.J. is accustomed to stepping onto a theatrical stage of some sort. But when you get past all the glitter, he is the guy next door with the white picket fence and the Jeep parked in the driveway.

I.J. was born in Arizona but his family moved to Sand Springs, Oklahoma when he was two years old. His father Joseph has since passed away but his mother Maxine and his two brothers, Joe III and Tom still remain a vital part of his life. From an early age I.J. became interested in music. He and a couple of his buddies, Randy Ess and Brett Sanders, formed a band called the "Esquires" and were featured on Channel 8 singing *Go Tell It On The*

Mountain. They thought the appearance was quite an exciting opportunity. Brett was the first one to get a guitar and soon Randy was able to buy one but I.J.'s parents just couldn't afford it. His first instrument consisted of carefully drawn guitar strings on a sheet of white paper he held close to him, while he pretended to strum chords and imagine what they sounded like. I.J. realizes now he was building determination into his character, which caused him to eventually mow enough yards to purchase a guitar out of the Alden Catalog.

Eventually the "Esquires" disbanded and I.J., Randy, David Hicks, Phillip Wilson and Terry Burcham developed a rock and roll band called "The Rogues Five." They looked up the word in the dictionary and found out it meant a debonair, dashing kind of guy and they thought that sounded cool.

It was the early 1960's and rock and roll was "hot stuff." Since they were getting in on the ground floor of the craze they were able to open for some top rock and rolls bands like Jim Morrison and the Doors, The Dave Clark Five, Paul Revere and the Raiders and Shadows of Night. They became the house band for Lee Bailey's Dance Party on Channel 6 and played for benefit concerts and school assemblies. Life was good and I.J. was determined to live life to its fullest.

Even though I.J. had performed in a band since he was 13 years old he chose to go to college and pursue his love of art, thinking that would be his future. However, after a couple of years he decided the field of commercial art wasn't right for him and he still needed to find his life's profession.

Through a progression of introductions I.J. met a guy named Ansley and Frank Wheatly who convinced him he should perform at the Cognito Inn, a familiar hot spot for local up and coming businessmen, lawyers, entrepreneurs etc. At first I.J. was opposed to the idea, thinking he couldn't perform a solo act. But the two men were able to persuade him. What started out to be a two week gig, turned into a two year stint and opened many doors for the future. One thing led to another and I.J. was becoming one of the most sought after social entertainers in Tulsa. This eventually escalated him to other cities as well.

I.J. attributes much of his success to his longtime friend, Mike Murphy. Murf as I.J. calls him, became friends with I.J. at the Cognito Inn and they have worked together on three record albums, two music videos and many other music endeavors through the years. He has been a continuous source of inspiration to I.J.

In 1981 I.J. married his childhood sweetheart Tammy Morgan. She is actually a few years younger than I.J. When he was playing with "The Rogues Five" she was one of the young girls looking out her back window wishing she was old enough to be at the dance where I.J. was performing.

For the next few years I.J. continued to work on his music and perfect his stage presence. He also met Jim Thomas who owned the former Celebrity Theatre in Branson, Missouri (now known as the Roy Clark Celebrity Theatre) who helped him make some connections in Nashville.

Then the unthinkable happened. On February 9, 1985 as he was preparing to make a decision to become a star headliner at the Celebrity Theatre in Branson, Tammy had a massive brain hemorrhage. I.J. put his career on hold. For over two years they struggled to get Tammy's health back to normal. The good news is she recovered and they both give God the credit for healing Tammy's body. Not only did she get her health back, but after several years of trying to conceive a child their son Morgan was born in 1986. Morgan now 14 is pursuing a career in music.

I.J.'s career continued to progress with hundreds of performances in and out of the state. By 1996 Jim Thomas had called him for the third time to come and be a star headliner at one of his Branson theatres. This time, I.J. was available.

The theatre had originally been the showplace for the legendary Wayne Newton. In a short time, Branson City Lights grew to be a $5 million major production. It was the largest production ever brought to Branson. The auditorium seated 3,000 people and I.J.'s dressing room which of course was formerly Wayne Newton's, was 2,500 square feet. The marquee in front of the building stood 30 feet tall with I.J.'s smiling face appropriately displayed. I.J. said not to worry, his wife and son kept his ego in check if he for one instant began to believe his own publicity.

After a couple of years Jim Thomas sold the theatre. The new owners made changes I.J. wasn't totally comfortable with so he decided to move on. However, along the way he learned what it took to put on a production as elaborate as Branson City Lights had been. His goal for the future was to once again produce an unforgettable show.

I.J. also learned *"You have to be tenacious to receive what you want out of life.* America is a wonderful place to live and the opportunities are never ending. You can be a kid growing up across from Pee Wee Park in Sand Springs, Oklahoma and excel to anything in life you can dream of doing. *The only thing that can stop you is you."* He also believes if he loses his integrity on the way up the ladder to success then he really has nothing at all.

Family is extremely important to I.J. He remembers an unforgettable moment as his family stood around his father's hospital bed in 1984 giving their last goodbyes. Even though his father had never reached what the world knows as "monetary success," he had a family that thought his worth couldn't be measured in dollars and cents. I.J. realized the most important things in life are the relationships you have with your loved ones. Being surrounded with people who care about "who you are" is far more important than the sometimes "fair weather friends who only care "what you are."

James Garner

Actor

James Garner has forever been one of my favorite actors. My mother, among many others, said it just wouldn't be a completed Distinguished Oklahomans book if James wasn't included.

James has long been regarded as one of America's foremost and distinguished actors. Coming from a background with no ties to show business, James was born April 7, 1928 in the mid-sized city of Norman, Oklahoma. His father, Weldon Bumgarner, was of European ancestry and his mother, Mildred, was one-half Cherokee.

When James was five his mother died and he and his brothers, Jack and Charles, went to live with relatives. At 14 he left home, did odd jobs and at 16 signed on for a short stint in the Merchant Marines. In the meantime his father had moved to Los Angeles. James followed, helping his father in the carpet-laying business while attending Hollywood High School.

He eventually got a job modeling swimsuits. But before his career got started, he found himself in the Army with the distinction of being called Oklahoma's first draftee to the Korean conflict, during which he was awarded a Purple Heart.

After the war he returned stateside and eventually moved back to Los Angeles. When a friend offered him a small part in a Broadway production of "The Caine Mutiny Court Martial," he took it. As he says, "I did it for the money. I had done about 70 different jobs and didn't like any of them."

Thus, James learned his craft from practical experience, and it led to a $150 a week contract with Warner Bros. His first on-camera appearance was with Clint Walker on the TV series "Cheyenne." His feature film debut came in "Toward the Unknown." Next, he gave an acclaimed performance as Marlon Brando's friend in the hit film, "Sayonara," which led to his big break a starring role in the television series "Maverick." "They hired me because I had a cheap contract," says James. Maverick became a hit series and with it James became a star.

Since then, the six foot, three inch actor has starred in roughly 40 films, including "The Children's Hour," "The Great Escape," "The Americanization of Emily (his personal favorite)," "Grand Prix," "Cash McCall," "Move Over, Darling," "Support Your Local Sheriff," "The Skin Game," "Victor/Victoria" and "Murphy's Romance."

One common misconception about James is he always plays himself. Before he was an actor, he was extremely introverted, and the easygoing manner of many of his characters is something he works hard to achieve.

"People are always saying how I seem to go through the paces easily," he says. "They go by what they see on the screen. I always try to make my dialogue sound like it is the first time I've ever said it. Therefore, they think that's me naturally. Actually, it's the writer's dialogue, with the director's direction, and then I have to bring it to the screen as if it's brand new. I've evidently done a good job. I've fooled a lot of people because they think it's just ole Jim saying the words that come to him."

On television he played one of the world's most famous private detectives, Jim Rockford in "The Rockford Files," for which he won an Emmy Award in 1977. "It has to be my favorite television character," he says. "There were so many wonderful elements to that series."

His other television roles include his portrayal of the ailing doctor opposite Mary Tyler Moore in "Heartsounds." He also starred in the miniseries "Space" and in the HBO presentation, "Glitterdome." He went on to star with James Woods in "Promise," the first film to be produced by James' own company, Garner-Duchow Productions, which he formed in 1983 with friend Peter Duchow. "In Promise," James played "Bob," a very likable and sympathetic character.

James again starred with James Woods in "My Name is Bill W." as the character Dr. Bob, who was co-founder of the Alcoholics Anonymous movement. In 1990 he starred in the Hallmark Hall of Fame Presentation "Decoration Day" for which he received an Emmy nomination and a Golden Globe Award for Best Actor in a Mini-Series or Special.

One of James' most touching performances to date came in the Hallmark Hall of Fame Presentation "Breathing Lessons," the highest rated made-for-television movie of the 1993-94 season. Also in 1994, James brought to the big screen another of his unforgettable characters, co-starring with Mel Gibson and Jodie Foster in "Maverick."

In 2002 he co-starred in the last four episodes of "Chicago Hope" for CBS-TV. He also starred in "Space Cowboys" opposite Tommy Lee Jones and Donald Sutherland for director Clint Eastwood.

Away from acting James is passionately involved with auto racing. From 1967-69, he owned a racing team called American International Racing. Its members drove at such sites as Daytona and Sebring and in off-road races like Baja. He has driven the pace car at the Indianapolis 500 on three occasions in 1975, 1977 and 1985.

James is involved with a multitude of humanistic causes. He helped organize Martin Luther King's march on Washington D.C. for civil rights in 1963 and went to Vietnam in 1967 to visit troops. He is also a member of the National Support Committee of the Native American Rights Fund and the National Advisory Board of the United States High School Golf Association. He has been involved with the "Save the Coast" movement to stop offshore drilling in California and is most recently involved with "Save the Children."

All told, James has received one Academy Award nomination, 15 Emmy nominations (two wins), 13 Golden Globe nominations (four wins), two People's Choice Awards and three Screen Actors Guild Award nominations. He was also the recipient of a Clio Award for his Polaroid commercials.

In 1986 James was inducted into the Oklahoma Hall of Fame. He was made Ambassador of Cultural Arts for the State of Oklahoma in November of 1989 and he won the Most Valuable Amateur Trophy at the AT&T Golf Tournament in February 1990. He was inducted into the Cowboy Hall of Fame in Oklahoma City, Oklahoma in March 1990 and in 1993 he received the Western Heritage Award for Lifetime Achievement in Film and Television from the Gene Autry Museum. In 1995 he received a Honorary Doctorate of Humane Letters degree at the University of Oklahoma.

People magazine saluted James with the cover headline, "The Last Real Man." Anyone familiar with his modest nature and supreme talent would agree with that designation.

A gifted and ardent golfer he plays whenever possible. James lives in Los Angeles with his wife, Lois. They have two daughters, Kim and Gigi.

So with all of his displayed talent you can understand why a book dedicated to Distinguished Okahomans had to include the beloved James Garner.

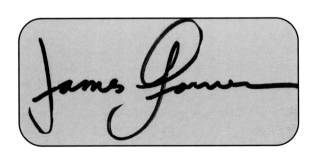

Vince Gill

Singer/Songwriter

    With the help of Alison Auerbach P.R., I waited patiently for two years to get an interview with Vince Gill. I even traveled all the way to Nashville hoping his schedule would be slack enough to fit me in when this project was first underway.

    My persistence wasn't because I'm a star gazed fanatic I believe I have passed that stage in my life. But merely because Vince epitomizes what it means to be from the heartland of America. When he talks and sings you feel the spirit of a man who truly has love in his heart for others.

    Vince is originally from Norman, Oklahoma where he was born April 12, 1957. As the youngest of three, Bob being the oldest followed by Gina, Vince was indoctrinated into the music styles of all his family members. Even though his father Stan was an attorney he was also a great lover of country music along with Vince's mother, Jerene.

    On many occasions their home would be the meeting place for family friends to congregate and hear the sounds of Merle Haggard, Jim Reeves or Bob Wills. His brother Bob, on the other hand, loved the sound of blues while Gina was drawn more to folk music.

    By the time Vince was in junior high school he had made up his mind he was going to become a professional musician. To get his feet wet he played in some garage bands. They had a few performances for school dances but nothing of any great magnitude. Then he aligned himself with a band of musicians called the Bluegrass Review. The band performed at various bluegrass festivals and for the first time Vince got paid for something he loved to do.

    The next performing group he joined was called Mountain Smoke. They were great musicians, but not as serious about becoming professionals because they all except for 17-year-old Vince had day jobs. All he could think about was music and what the next step up the melodious ladder would be.

    After graduating from Northwest Classen High School in 1975, Vince debated which direction his life would take him since he hadn't prepared for college. Then out of the blue he received a phone call from a friend in Kentucky. One of their band members in Bluegrass Alliance had recently quit and they needed someone to take his place. Vince was immediately on his way to Kentucky.

    His next big move was when he joined with Ricky Skaggs' band Boone Creek in Louisville, Kentucky. But his biggest break up to that point was in 1976 when he was hired by master fiddler Byron Berline and moved to Los Angeles, California. Country-rock was booming out there, and acoustic music was doing very well. That is when Vince first began writing songs.

I met Byron Berline a couple of years ago when I interviewed him for this book. I was surprised when he took me upstairs in his fiddle shop and showed me pictures of Vince hanging on the wall. His extremely youthful appearance gave evidence of his innocent progression toward his musical goals.

In 1979 Vince switched gears again when he teamed up with Pure Prairie League as their lead singer, performing hits like *Let Me Love You Tonight* and *Still Right Here In My Heart.*

A greater event occurred in 1982 while he was working with the Cherry Bombs, backing Rodney Crowell and Rosanne Cash. He and his former wife, Janis, who sings with The Sweethearts of the Rodeo brought his beautiful daughter Jenny into the world. From then on the whole world saw, if it is possible, an even softer side of Vince Gill as he on numerous occasions and with great depth of feeling spoke of Jenny.

A move to Nashville in 1984 coincided with his first country recording contract. He really started making a splash when he joined with MCA Nashville in 1989 and started putting out hits like *When I Call Your Name, Liza Jane, Don't Let Our Love Start Slippin' Away, Never Knew Lonely* and *I Still Believe In You.*

I asked Vince what his favorite recording is of songs he has written and he said it would be hard to beat "Go Rest High On That Mountain." He said it so reflects his own personal feelings about the loss of his brother, Bob. He said there have been certain times during his career where particular songs have been pivotal times in his life. He sees those times as part of his journey.

As he looks back over 25 years in the music business he said he isn't as enamored with where he wound up as he is with how much life he experienced along the way.

Vince's ability to play the guitar, dobro (his mother's favorite), mandolin, fiddle and banjo have brought him incredible success. But what stands out the most with Vince is his melodious voice that brings truth to every song he sings.

With the passing of his father in 1997 his reflections went back to his childhood days when great country songs bellowed out through the walls of their home. Remembering his father's words *"Your success is all for nothing if you don't stay the same"* have become nuggets of wisdom that obviously took root inside Vince. His charm and ever enduring graciousness has remained his undeniable trademarks.

Since I believe as many others do that "good things happen to good people," Vince married Amy Grant (another one of America's sweethearts) on March 10, 2000. Equally as wonderful was the birth of their child, Corrina Grant Gill on March 12, 2001.

The music awards Vince has received over the years have been numerous. The list is far too long to even begin to list them all. They range from Billboard pop Hits, Country Music Association Awards, Grammy Awards, TNN Music City News Awards, Academy of Country Music Awards, American Music Awards, Nashville Music Awards and BMI Songwriter Awards. He has been inducted into the Oklahoma Hall of Fame as well as the Oklahoma Cowboy Hall of Fame.

Vince is a wonderful person and indeed worthy of being titled a "Distinguished Oklahoman."

Les Gilliam - Balladeer

In 1999, the Kennedy Center in Washington, D.C. decided to pay tribute to the 50 states in the union, with each state having a specific day to be honored and to present entertainment from the state. The person chosen to represent Oklahoma was none other than Les Gilliam from Ponca City. His performance at the Kennedy Center was broadcast worldwide on the Internet.

This native Oklahoman has entertained all over America and has made five trips to Europe to present his style of American country and western music. He has also been named one of the top five western singers in America by the Western Music Association. He currently does over 150 performances each year.

Being a storyteller is a talent that comes quite easy for Les. Even during our interview, at times the dialog sounded like storytelling. It seemed appropriate for a man who has been named "The Oklahoma Balladeer."

Les was born in the small town of Berwyn, Oklahoma which was renamed Gene Autry, Oklahoma in 1941. When he was seven months old his father Don was killed in a car wreck, so his mother Corinne, at age 28, had the task of raising five children in the back of the grocery store that she and Don owned. It was difficult and the only thing Corinne knew to do was split up the family for a while until she felt capable of handling all five children.

Les's mother and two older sisters lived in the back of the store, which had no heat and no running water. But somehow they managed to keep their spirits high. The other three children were sent to their grandfather's farm west of Berwyn where Les lived from age 4 to10. As it turns out, the famed Gene Autry bought a ranch that backed up to Les's grandfather's farm. Gene Autry didn't live there, but he visited occasionally to check on his rodeo stock. Each time he would visit he tried to convince Les's grandfather to sell him his farm, but the answer was always no.

Les said even though it took years to come into effect, he still believes in some way he was influenced by Gene Autry's presence. Maybe it was because his family always listened to Gene Autry's radio programs.

When Les turned 10 years old his mother was able to rent a house and bring all the children back together, which I'm sure was a happy moment for all of them. Two years before Les finished high school they moved to Ardmore so his mother could go to work for the post office. By this time, his sisters were married and one brother was in college.

One Saturday morning one sister and her husband, who had been living in Odessa, Texas, showed up at Les's house. They brought him a guitar they had rescued from a neighbor before it was thrown out with the daily trash. The guitar had a noticeable split going down the back, but his sister just knew Les could fix it up and use it somehow. Les excitedly took the guitar and went to the music store where he bought a book for 35 cents that he felt would teach him how to play. The sound wasn't very good on the damaged guitar, but it was a guitar and that was all that mattered to Les. He already had a lot of experience singing at church and in school programs, but a guitar was an added bonus.

The next year Les was singing on the radio in Ardmore. He also entered a singing contest sponsored by Jim Reeves and won the contest. That eventually led to other radio and television performances.

After high school graduation, Les entered Murray Junior College and formed a band called "The Arbuckle Mountain Boys." The school started paying the band to go out and represent the college in high schools all over Southeastern Oklahoma. Later, Les transferred to Oklahoma A&M and kept playing in the band. They changed the name of the band to "The Western Rhythm Kings" because they were playing a lot of swing music at various dances.

During college days, Les would often travel to Dallas to appear as a special guest on the Big D Jamboree, a Saturday Night stage and radio show, similar to the Grand Ole Opry. One summer, he lived in Dallas and performed as a regular cast member of the Saturday Night Shindig, a radio and stage show originating from the Band Shell at Fair Park.

During his final year in college, Les met a beautiful young lady from Coffeyville, Kansas. He and Martha were married and moved to the Dallas area where Les' degree in Mathematics won him a computer programmer position with Chance

Vought Aircraft. During the five years they lived in Texas, Les performed on KRLD-TV and radio as a member of the Big D Jamboree cast. Also during this period, Dan, Julie and Cindy were born to the family. But when Conoco started their Computer Department in Ponca City, they convinced Les he should move back to his native state of Oklahoma.

Les stayed at Conoco for 20 years. He took an early retirement and started his own computer consulting business, which he kept for over 15 years. Martha was a home economics teacher at West Jr. High in Ponca City, so between the two of them they were comfortable financially. Certainly a far cry from the lifestyle Les had experienced as a small child.

While Les still had his consulting business some local Ponca City residents began talking about reopening the Ponca City Theater. It had been shut down for many years, and they wanted to see it revitalized and used as a performing arts center. Les agreed to put on a production with a variety of different talent and see if the town would be receptive. They had a Dixieland Band, a Barber Shop Quartet and a Cowboy Show featuring Les, his son and two other guys. They had two sell out performances a week apart.

It created just enough excitement to once again stir up the passion Les had for music and entertaining. One thing led to another and Les decided to go to Oklahoma City and have an album produced. The guy at the studio told him about the Oklahoma Arts Council that is responsible for providing entertainment all over the state of Oklahoma. Les immediately contacted them and auditioned. Of course they loved Les and added him to their list of performers.

Les was at one time selected as the Outstanding Entertainer at the biggest country music festival in Michigan. On April 29, 1998 the Oklahoma State Legislature officially designated Les Gilliam to be "The Oklahoma Balladeer" because he has been a prominent Good Will Ambassador for the State of Oklahoma.

In his shows Les promotes the great state of Oklahoma and its outstanding citizens that have brought honor to the state in their chosen fields. He has performed country & western music to audiences of all ages, from the Oklahoma Governor's Mansion to Austria to Branson and all over the nation

The wonder of it all still amazes him. The way his life has all come together is thrilling for him. He has come full circle from the 15 year old boy in Ardmore who had a broken guitar with which to sound out his first tune. It sounds like a "God Thing" to me the way the life of this Baptist Deacon has unfolded for him.

Sylvan N. Goldman

Inventor

Did you ever stop to think how the cart you pile high with groceries in the supermarket happened to come into being? Usually items like that are pretty much taken for granted with not much thought as to the creative genius behind the idea.

When young Michael Goldman first came to the United States from the Baltic state of Latvia he didn't know that in a few years he would father a son whose inventive ideas would change a part of the world.

In Gainesville, Texas Michael went to work for a wholesale groceries, produce and dry goods company and eventually he married the owner's niece, Hortense. Michael was an asset to the family business. He was enlisted to take over the management of a failing store in Davis, Oklahoma and eventually a store in Ardmore. During this time two sons were born, Alfred Dreyfus Goldman on June 7, 1895 and Sylvan Nathan Goldman on November 15, 1898.

Sylvan didn't really like the dry goods business, but he still had to help out around his father's store after school each day. That's why he was glad when his father sold the store and moved the family to Tulsa in 1913. By this time Sylvan had completed the 8th grade, and his school days were soon to be a thing of the past. His mother's five brothers were operating a wholesale grocery and produce business in Tulsa and owned a branch store in Sapulpa where they put young Sylvan to work. He quickly found the grocery and produce business much more suited to his liking and would soon prove to be his future.

A two year stint in the military interrupted his apprenticeship in the grocery business. When he was released he and his brother teamed up with his Uncle Dreyfus to open a chain of retail grocery stores. On April 3, 1926 the brothers opened their first grocery store, Sun Grocery at 1403 E. 15th Street in Tulsa. Within a year 21 stores would bear the same name and in less than three years 50 stores opened their doors to satisfied customers.

I've always heard that a brilliant man builds a strong company, sells it at a profit and sets out to repeat his brilliance. The Goldman's had been so successful in their chain of stores that they were given the opportunity to trade in their hardworking grocery executive hard hats for the prestige of being stockholders of one of the nation's largest grocery chains, Skaggs-Safeway Stores.

In 1931 Sylvan gave up his bachelorhood and married Margaret Katz of Stillwater, who happened to be the sister of his brother's wife Helen Katz. Sylvan and Margaret raised two sons, Monte and Alfred, both born in the late 1930s.

Due to the stock market crash in 1929 the Goldman Brothers and the Dreyfus family moved to Oklahoma City to start another group of retail stores which they named the Standard Food Markets. Along with those stores in 1934 they bought out five failing Humpty Dumpty grocery stores which had been their major competitor.

Tragedy struck both families in the late 1930s when Uncle Dreyfus died of a sudden blood clot and two years later Sylvan's brother Alfred died of pneumonia. This left Sylvan as the person solely responsible for the families' business interest.

In Sylvan's pursuit to enhance the viability of his stores he stumbled upon a concept that would forever put his name in the history books. Up until that time customers who frequented stores of any type were usually given a wire or wicker basket to carry their items in before purchasing them at the check out counter. Of course, unless the customer was a body builder with excessive strength, a wire basket with a few items in it could become cumbersome and heavy very quickly. Therefore, purchases were limited which meant sales were too.

One day as Sylvan glanced down at a folding chair he visualized what it would be like if one of the wire baskets was mounted on the seat of the chair and wheels attached to the legs. With just a little imagination and a fair amount of creativity he could envision a pushable cart that would provide his customers with a means in which to transport their purchasable items in a less laborious manner. Thus began the invention of what we all know as the "shopping cart."

Of course there were a few cliches that had to be worked out, but Sylvan had indeed created a way to make life easier for customers worldwide. Now every time I go into a grocery store or any other kind of establishment that provides shopping carts I can't help but think of Sylvan Goldman and the huge contribution he made to the shopping experience.

Interestingly, after the introduction of the shopping cart, Sylvan's inventive mind continued to produce creative ideas. The "grocery sacker," a device to hold grocery sacks while the worker checked out each item, was soon implemented. Following his second invention came the inter-office basket carrier and then the luggage cart which is used in airports all over the world.

During Sylvan's inventive days he was still increasing his chain of Humpty Dumpty grocery stores, which by the mid 50's totaled 33 stores.

In 1959 at the age of 61 Sylvan finally retired from the grocery business, but was never idle. He was inducted into the Oklahoma Hall of Fame in 1971. Then in 1972 his first folding shopping cart with its removable baskets was placed in the Smithsonian Institute.

What a worthwhile individual Sylvan Goldman must have been. As an entrepreneur, inventor and philanthropist he managed to contribute a great deal to making life a little easier for us all.

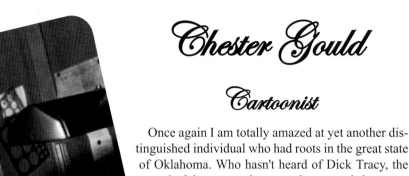

Chester Gould

Cartoonist

Once again I am totally amazed at yet another distinguished individual who had roots in the great state of Oklahoma. Who hasn't heard of Dick Tracy, the wonderful cartoon character that graced the pages of newspapers all over the world? But how did that character come to be a welcomed guest in millions of homes?

Chester, the son of Alice and Gilbert Gould, was born on November 20, 1900 in Pawnee, Oklahoma. His father owned the Pawnee Courier Dispatch, the local community newspaper. At a very early age Chester began sketching characters that gained a great deal of approval from his father. At age seven his father encouraged him to display his work in the newspaper office window so the townspeople could enjoy his work as well. Even though his drawings were still very primitive it was obvious Chester had a talent that astounded those around him.

In the early 1900's Pawnee was a small town that had no postal carrier system. Everyone had to retrieve their mail at the Post Office which happened to be next to the newspaper office. Therefore it was pretty likely that most of the townspeople had an opportunity to view Chester's unique drawings. The recognition and comments he received about his youthful sketches planted a seed of wonder in the young boy's heart. Surely cartooning was for him?

As a young boy Chester did odd jobs around town; sign painting and occasional art pieces in the newspaper. He also worked as a soda jerk at Jay's Drug Store which earned him $15 for a 12 hour day.

His first cartoon to receive national attention was at the age of 16 when he won a contest by The American Boy magazine for a patriotic cartoon.

After high school Chester enrolled at Oklahoma A&M in Stillwater which is now called Oklahoma State University. He studied commerce and marketing and continued to draw cartoons and solicit places for his drawings whenever he could. He began having cartoons published by the Tulsa Democrat and the Daily Oklahoman which stirred his creativity even more.

After two years at Oklahoma A&M a sense of restlessness began to take over in Chester and he knew his sights were set on being a famous cartoonist. The Chicago Tribune Syndicate was by far on the cutting edge of the cartoon world and Chester wanted to be amongst the hoopla of it all.

He arrived in Chicago on August 30, 1921 with $50 in his pocket and a display case full of his published work from the Oklahoma newspapers. Within three months he would turn 21 years old, but he had no idea that many years of struggle still laid before him. The sophisticated Chicago crowd quickly gave Chester a dose of reality when the five local newspapers informed him that his small town sketches lacked maturity for the bright lights of Chicago.

However, a week after arriving in town, being at the right place at the right time proved profitable for Chester. One of the cartoonist at the Chicago Journal was having surgery and needed someone to handle his job for 30 days. Chester was quick to oblige. At the end of the month he was out of a job, but his resume certainly portrayed a more polished look.

In 1924 the Hearst Syndicate offered Chester his first comic strip with the inception of "Fillum Fables." Several other strips were introduced by Chester until he stumbled upon the one strip that would forever link him as a successful cartoonist.

At the time, mobsters were very prevalent in Chicago. Al Capone was a very constant presence in the newspaper headlines nationwide. Chester felt a need to diminish the idolization of Capone and present the world with a respected hero. Publisher Joseph Patterson of the Chicago Tribune gave Chester that opportunity and the much loved detective Dick Tracy was born. Not only did Chester's creative idea bring newness to comic strips, but his artistic style was adopted by many over the years. Chester's ploy to fight evil with good moral comic strip messages won the hearts of the world. By the 1930's the Dick Tracy character was appearing in movies and toys were being produced reflecting the world's interest.

In 1947, Chester introduced Crime Stoppers in the Dick Tracy comic strip. In the strip, Junior, Dick Tracy's adopted son, thought he and his friends could form a detective club to help kids stay out of trouble. Dick Tracy was so impressed with their idea that he took Junior and his friends to the police crime laboratory once a week and taught them about investigation and crime detection.

Two years later as an outgrowth of Crime Stoppers Club, Gould created the Crime Stopper Textbook tips. Each week these tips appeared at the top of the Sunday comic. In 1960, Chester expanded the Crime Stoppers tips to encompass crime prevention.

For 45 years the comic strip was Chester's prime motivation. He had truly become the successful cartoonist he had dreamed of being as a small child. He retired on December 25, 1977 at the age of 77, having written and drawn Dick Tracy for over half of his life. Eight years later on May 11, 1985 Chester Gould passed away. The drawing board and taboret he purchased when he first arrived in Chicago have been placed in a permanent location in the Chester Gould-Dick Tracy Museum in Woodstock, Illinois.

In Pawnee, Oklahoma a mural painted on the side of a building on 6th Street and Harrison Avenue is the world's largest Dick Tracy cartoon rendered by Tulsa artist, Ed Melberg.

My thanks go out to Beth Vargo at the Dick Tracy Museum in Woodstock, Illinois for sending the picture of Chester Gould and the information included in his profile.

Alan C. Greenberg – Business Executive

Alan was born September 3, 1927 in Wichita, Kansas but he was raised along with his brother and sister in Oklahoma City, Oklahoma. By Oklahoma standards his family was considered affluent since his father owned some retail stores.

In high school Alan was known for his athletic ability which landed him a football scholarship to Oklahoma University. He was injured in the second game, ending his dreams of being a football star.

He had always been fascinated with the stock market so after his football injury he decided to focus on the possibility of working on Wall Street. He transferred to the University of Missouri and received a Bachelor of Science degree in business.

After graduation he went to work for Bear, Stearns in 1949 as a clerk. At the time, he had no idea the heights he would eventually reach. He started making money during his first year on Wall Street and from then on he was on a charted path of continued success. He had his share of big wins and big losses, but he won more than he lost.

It wasn't easy to become a partner with Bear, Stearns but Alan's performance in the first 10 years was such that it justified him in becoming a partner in 1958. He became chief executive officer in 1978.

Thirty years ago Alan started a program with senior executives that required them to give at least four percent of their income to charity. There was no stipulation as to what charity a person chose to give their money to. The belief was the concept would be good for the giver, good for the firm and good for the charity.

Obviously the concept proved to work successfully for Alan. The company grew from $46 million in capital to $26.3 billion since the initial concept began.

On a personal level in 1988 Alan gave $1.1 million to the United Jewish Appeal and chaired and supported significantly the New York Police and Fire Widows' and Children's Benefit Fund. He provided $250,000 in scholarships for students at Oklahoma University, established a fund at Oklahoma University's Health Sciences Center to study Parkinson's disease and established a chair in biomedical research at the Oklahoma Medical Research Fund. He was named Philanthropist of the Year by the National Society of Fund Raising Executives in 1989.

Among his awards and honors are: Lehman Award, American Jewish Committee, 1986; Man of the Year, National Conference of Christians and Jews, 1974; trustee, Federation of Jewish Philanthropy; Man of the Year, B'Nai B'rith Youth Services, 1980; knighted by Queen Margrethe II of Denmark into the Knights of the Order of Dannebrog, 1984; former chairman, Raoul Wallenberg Committee of the United States; Golden Plate Award, American Academy of Achievement, 1988; and honorary doctor of Humane Letters degree, Brandeis University, 1989.

Alan is married to Kathryn Olson. He has two children, Lynne and Ted from a previous marriage. When his daughter Lynne graduated from college 23 years ago she asked her father for advice about what she should do. He said, "Why don't you become the first woman member of the American Stock Exchange." she did. It wasn't taboo, but it had never been none before until Lynne took her father's advice. She remained in that position for quite some time until she decided to relinquish her post to focus on her duties as a wife and mother.

Alan is no longer the CEO of Bear, Stearns & Co. Inc., he is Chairman of the Board, which he says doesn't change his role too drastically. He said he will retire some day but has no idea when.

He is a champion bridge player, a world class amateur magician, an excellent archer, and a champion dog trainer .

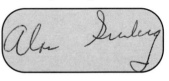

Molly Levite Griffis

Proprietor / Author

Some people are just born with the "gift of gab" and Molly must be one of them. If she wanted to, she could carry on a two way conversation and the only person who needed to be present would be herself.

I say that with all due respect. She is such a wonderful conversationalist! Her exuberance and enthusiasm gets everyone around her excited about whatever area of interest she is talking about at the time. I guess being a former school teacher certainly helps her convey her ideas along to others. Also, her obvious love for people and life seems to overflow with every bit of verbiage.

I first heard about Molly through a newspaper clipping someone sent to me. After setting up an interview appointment I traveled to Norman, Oklahoma to meet Molly at her book/Indian artifacts store. Right away I felt at home as if I had known Molly for years. I'm sure she makes everyone she meets feel the same way. I like to contribute part of that to the friendliness of "Okies." Molly is very proud of her Oklahoma heritage and loves to tell the story of how it all began.

Her grandmother and grandfather, Molly and Peter Levite were Jewish immigrants who started the original Levite's General Store in Apache, Oklahoma in April of 1903.

Grandmother Molly, being from Poland, was so proud to be an American that she named all but one of her seven sons after American presidents such as Abraham Lincoln Levite, William McKinley Levite, Woodrow Wilson Levite and George Washington Levite.

Peter Levite became very well known for his trade with the Indians because of his fairness in dealing with them. He was often quoted as saying the blanket trading he did with the Indians kept his family from starving on many occasions.

George Washington Levite took over the store when his father, Peter passed away in 1939. George and his wife, Lily had two daughters, one was named Georgann and the other they named after George's mother, Molly, who later became Molly Levite Griffis.

George Levite was also a sign painter and a self taught writer. Lily, his wife, was on the main street of Apache one day in the early 1930s when she heard a reporter from the Daily Oklahoman soliciting for a person to write the oil field news for the local area. No one seemed to want the job, so Lily volunteered. She was not a writer, but she knew her husband George was more than capable of writing the articles for her. So George wrote for the Daily Oklahoman under the byline of Mrs.George Levite and no one knew the difference. Then Lily went to the Anadarko and Lawton newspapers and they hired her when they heard of her new found exposure in the Oklahoma City paper.

As the years went by, George and his stories made quite an impact on the community. People began to feel a kinship toward him after reading so much of his work. In the twilight of his years, Molly and Georgann who Molly affectionately calls "sister" decided to give their father a very special Christmas gift. They put together a simple saddle stitched book of some of George's stories. They only had 500 books printed, assuming that would take care of the majority of townspeople in the small community of Apache. They had a book signing in which their father, George Washington Levite, personally signed all 500 books. Within the close of the day all 500 books had been sold.

George was elated by the response of so many people who were interested in his work. So he set out to write more stories, hoping to have another book printed. Sadly, George died of a heart attack at the age of 83 before he was able to see that dream come true. However, Molly and Sister vowed to finish the project for their father some day.

We all know how quickly time passes, and before they knew it, 10 years had already come and gone. Their mother, Lily passed away that Christmas Eve and the sisters were once again reminded of the promise they had made to both of their parents. So they set out to make the promise good. Their deadline was scheduled for the following Christmas. This time they would name the book, *By George For Lily* in memory of their mother.

Instead of the previous 500 books printed they would have 1,000 printed, because they knew they could sell them all. The 1,000 sold turned into 2,000 sold and then 3,000 sold. Before they knew it they had sold 10,000 books right out of Molly's kitchen. It occurred to Molly that people really liked what she was doing and maybe they should expand their horizons. Before long, Molly established a small publishing company to accommodate the many letters she was receiving from other people who wanted her to publish their work.

She had to move out of her kitchen and rent some office space, which she quickly grew out of. She then moved to a bigger place. She contacted the Pendleton Blanket Company who her grandfather had dealt with for so many years. Her blanket sales did so well they were able to cover the printing cost of her books.

In eight years Molly had to move what had now become the Levite Store eight times to provide the needed space. Molly was having a great time with her new found success and was making a lot of people happy along the way.

In the beginning, Molly never set out to have a publishing company. She was merely trying to honor her mother and father. Yet in the midst of it all, she found herself with a remake of her grandfather's 1903 Levite Store. A lot of book signings have been held there in the unique style only Molly can create.

She no longer publishes books, but you can still find an assortment of Oklahoma memorabilia lining her shelves. If you need a good Pendleton blanket, Molly's is the place to go. I'm not sure if she would recognize a stranger, so if you walk into her store, be prepared to make a friend.

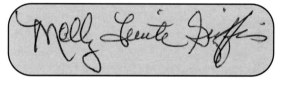

Woody Guthrie
Singer/Songwriter

As I am preparing this profile others are gearing up in Okemah, Oklahoma for the annual Woody Guthrie Festival held each year in July. It's pretty amazing how a simple man could make such an impact that people would organize a yearly celebration to honor him. But even more amazing are the hundreds of individuals who travel from all over the country to join in the outside festivities during one of the hottest months of the year. It would make one wonder just what it was about this man that would draw such attention to his memory.

It was a hot summer day on July 14, 1912 in Okemah when Nora gave birth to she and Charley's second child Woodrow Wilson Guthrie. Charley Guthrie was a land speculator whose quality of living was dictated by the success of the oil industry. Nora was the kind of mother that sang lullabys as she rocked her babies to sleep and taught them cheerful songs to make them laugh. There were three other children in the Guthrie home. Clara was the oldest and Roy and George were the last to come along.

Tragedy seemed to always follow the Guthrie family. Their house in Okemah was destroyed by fire which put the family in a financial crisis. Clara, who was spunky and fun to be around, died when she was 14 years old after the dress she was wearing caught on fire.

For many years Nora's state of mind was unpredictable. At one point she poured kerosene on her husband Charley and set him on fire. Charley survived but the family realized how seriously ill Nora had become. She eventually was sent to a mental hospital where she was deemed insane and spent the rest of her life. Later they found out she was not insane but had been suffering from a mind-crippling disease called Huntington's Chorea.

Woody was about 11 years old when his mother was institutionalized. His father eventually decided to move to Pampa, Texas where another oil boom would provide him with work. After Nora's death Charley married Bettie Jean McPherson. Woody stayed behind in Okemah and began living with another family, but he never felt comfortable so he decided to live on his own.

In spite of the tragedies Woody had already witnessed he found strength within himself to do what needed to be done. His mother had left him with a desire to sing and his father had given him the tenacity it took to be a survivor in a world that would present many obstacles along the way.

Charley eventually convinced Woody to move to Pampa. For a while he attended school there but he let his musical abilities woo him away. He formed a band called the Corncob Trio with his friends Matt Jennings and Cluster Baker. They played and sang for just about anyone that would listen.

Woody fell in love and married Matt's sister Mary in 1933. Together, Woody and Mary had three children, Gwen, Sue and Bill.

The Great Dust Storm hit the Texas, Arkansas and Oklahoma region, sending many wishful thinking people in pursuit of the "gold at the end of the rainbow" which they were told would be found in California. Woody was deeply touched by the hundreds of people he saw as he traveled on his way to that same pot of gold. People whose lives had been turned upside down by the depression gave Woody a platform by which to create many of his most memorable songs.

He wrote hundreds of songs about the migrants like *Do Re Mi,* but he also wrote about the love he had developed for a land we call America in the song *This Land Is Your Land.*

In 1937 Woody landed his own radio show on KFVD in Los Angeles, California. He was becoming a very popular entertainer, but Woody didn't feel comfortable with fame or with money. He eventually made his way to New York with the urging of his friend Will Geer (Will played Grandpa Walton on the TV series "The Waltons"). Woody was in New York when he became highly involved in political issues about the rights of Americans and what they could do to alleviate some of their problems.

With Woody's many travels and constant uprooting of his family Mary became disenchanted with their lives. She wanted to provide a more stable environment for their children so she left Woody and eventually moved back to Texas. It is reported that later in life their son Bill died in a car accident and Sue and Gwen died with Huntington's Disease.

Woody met Marjorie Mazia and they fell in love. They were both still married to other people so marriage was put on hold for a while. Together Woody and Marjorie had four children. Cathy was the oldest child born February 6, 1943 but she died at age four in a tragic house fire. Their son Arlo was born July 10,1947 followed by Joady Ben and Nora.

During World War 11, Woody served in both the Merchant Marines and the Army. Being out to sea in no way quenched his ability to create songs that expressed his every mood.

In the late 1940's Woody's health began to deteriorate and he became increasingly erratic, creating tensions in his personal and professional life. He left Marjorie and met a woman named Anneke Van Kirk. He obtained a Mexican divorce from Marjorie so he could marry Anneke and they had a child named Lorina Lynn.

However, as Woody's health continued to worsen, he returned to New York where Majorie consented to take care of him. It wasn't long before Anneke left and their marriage was dissolved. Woody was mistakenly diagnosed several times as suffering with alcoholism and schizophrenia, but in fact he was another victim of the horrible disease of Huntington Chorea.

Woody spent 13 years in and out of hospitals. He died October 3, 1967 at Creedmoor State Hospital in Queens, New York.

His prolific writing has left a legacy that captured the thoughts and feelings of historic moments in the 1930's, '40's, and '50's. He has been inducted into The Songwriters' Hall of Fame (1971), the Nashville Songwriters' Hall of Fame (1977), and The Rock and Roll Hall of Fame and Museum (1988).

James Halligan – *University President*

Sometimes you meet people for the first time and think, "what a wonderful human being." That is what I thought when I met Dr. James Halligan, president of Oklahoma State University.

He had just returned from having lunch with his wife, Ann, who he has been married to for over 40 years. If I hadn't have known better, I would have thought they were newlyweds. There was as much excitement in his voice over his luncheon date with her that day as I'm sure there was on their first date together. Somehow the integrity of a man seems to ring true to me when I hear someone hold his wife in such high esteem.

Even though Dr. Halligan's life began in relatively meager surroundings, he never saw himself as being deprived of anything. He had three brothers and a sister, a huge vegetable garden and two loving, devoted parents. What more could a child want?

He grew up in a small community in Iowa which had a population of 125 people. Needless to say, his high school class was quite honored with their 16 graduates. His schooling was a wonderful experience because with so few people he had the opportunity to get involved with every activity offered. He played sports as well as performed in plays, which made him feel like a more rounded person.

The most influential person in his life, was his high school English teacher, Mildred Parr, who never failed to remind him on numerous occasions the importance of going to college.

When it came time to go to college, he didn't have the money to enroll. Instead, he enlisted in the Air Force. Ironically, they sent him to Indiana University so he could become a Bulgarian Interpreter for the Air Force Intelligence. I'd say one way or the other, Mildred Parr's wishes were being fulfilled.

In 1957 after four years of military service, Dr. Halligan went back home and married Ann, one of his high school classmates. After finishing another year in the Air Force he got out and decided to go back to college and become a chemical engineer, since that seemed to be a high paying profession and children were beginning to fill the Halligan home. He graduated second in his class and immediately went to work for the Exxon Refinery.

It wasn't long before he once again entered the academic world, this time to receive his doctorate in chemical engineering. By then their family had grown to include three children, Michael, Patrick and Christopher.

During their years with Exxon, they lived in Washington, D.C. and Houston, Texas. Looking for a change of pace and a less hectic lifestyle, Dr. Halligan decided to take a position with the faculty of Texas Tech in Lubbock, Texas. Exxon was very persuasive in trying to get him to continue with their company by assuring him that someday they would probably promote him to vice president.

After thinking it over and talking to his wife, his mind began to wander back to the small town they both grew up in. He realized the "fast track" living didn't seem appealing anymore.

He spent nine years at Texas Tech before moving on to the University of Missouri to become their Dean of Engineering. From there he went to the University of Arkansas as Vice Chancellor, then to New Mexico State University as President for 10 years. He came to Oklahoma State University in 1994.

University life has been extremely rewarding for Dr. Halligan. When he sees the impact the faculty and staff have on the lives of young people on campus, it makes him very proud to know he is a part of it. When he and his wife were first married, they had no idea they would spend the majority of their lives in the field of higher education.

Looking back, Dr. Halligan views life as this wonderful thing that unfolds for every person. Some planning is involved, yet some things are just God given. Dr. Halligan tries to live life intensely, correcting mistakes if possible along the way. He feels lucky to be alive and therefore wants to celebrate life. "Gather ye rosebuds, while ye may."

Listening to a man like Dr. James Halligan will bring encouragement into your life. It's amazing to me how much we miss when we don't heed the advice of others who have traveled life's path a little longer. I wonder how many mistakes could be avoided if we did.

To date, I haven't met Mrs. Halligan, but I have an angelic picture of her in my mind which Dr. Halligan painted for me.

Every morning the two of them start their day by doing exercises. Then he runs two and a half miles followed by their walk together. During their walk they quote a familiar scripture "This is the day that the Lord has made, we will rejoice and be glad in it." That continues to be a daily ritual in their lives because they sincerely believe whether rain or shine, life still begins and ends with a beautiful day.

The decision they make every day to be happy has charted a wonderful path throughout their life together. Happiness, Dr. Halligan says, is really an "inside job."

We decide whether or not we are going to be happy. It's true that some days start out better than others, but you still have a choice of whether or not to be happy. No excuses, no whining, no alibis, just discipline and performance.

An employer wants someone who sees the "glass of life" half full, and is looking diligently for the water fountain to fill it up the rest of the way. It is said that 90% of life is controlled by our attitude and 10% of life is controlled by things that befall us. When the 10% comes, the first thing we need to do is remember the scripture Dr. Halligan and his wife quote every day. "This is the day that the Lord has made, I will rejoice and be glad in it." That is the only way to find your way back to happiness.

Jim Halsey
Music Artist Promoter

Jim Halsey and The Oak Ridge Boys

Jim Halsey's name is synonymous with the term "music industry." For over 50 years he has managed and promoted some of the top artists in the music business.

Jim was born and grew up in Independence, Kansas. His family owned the Halsey Brothers Department Store, which could have been an easy occupation for Jim to get involved in. But the pace was too slow to keep him interested. He did, however, learn a valuable lesson. He remembers his grandfather always talking about the importance of keeping the customer happy and looking out for their needs. He also learned that a successful business was one that put integrity on its list of priorities. Over the years, Jim has tried to carry those same bits of wisdom into his own career.

As a teenager, Jim had a deep desire to be a musician so he played the saxophone in the high school band. In his senior year he wrote a book report on Sol Hurok, one of the great Impresarios of all time. An Impresario is a person that presents shows, manages artists and takes organizations on tour. After reading the book, Jim was fascinated with the lifestyle that Sol Hurok was able to lead: the glamour of opening night, the promotion, sales and marketing of a particular show and the travel from city to city and around the world. It all seemed like the most exciting life anyone could have.

The summer after high school graduation Jim traveled around for a while and had the opportunity to see Duke Ellington, Count Basie and the Woody Herman Band. From the first note they hit, Jim realized even more he could not compete with the big guys when it came to musical ability. However, he was still so enamored with the music industry that he knew he had to find a way to somehow be involved.

He enrolled in Independence Community College. There were no music or entertainment classes offered, so he took some business courses including marketing, accounting and business law. Then, remembering the book he read on Sol Hurok, he set out to become the Impresario of Southeastern Kansas.

The first show he promoted was a swing dance featuring Leon McAuliffe. Jim was only 18 years old when he contacted Leon and asked him if he could book him at the Independence Auditorium that seated 2,400 people. Leon agreed, thinking this unidentifiable voice on the other end of the phone line was a well established promoter, when in fact he had only just begun. Jim rented the auditorium for $15 and charged an admission of $1.50 per person. Remember, that was back in 1949. The show was a complete success and all Jim could think about was how soon he could book the next big show. He promoted a variety of different acts from country music performers to ice shows to classical concerts. Some shows were total sell outs, while others left his pockets a little empty. But with each performance he gained a wealth of experience.

One of his most successful performances was when he booked Hank Thompson in May of 1950. Hank was from Dallas, Texas but toured nationally. Jim would schedule him sometimes at eight or nine locations per booking and have successful turnouts each time.

In December of 1951, when Jim had just turned 21 years old, Hank Thompson called him and said his agent had left to take another job. He wanted to know if Jim would be willing to take his place. It was a dream come true for Jim. Before long, he was no longer the Impresario of Southeastern Kansas. Now he would be known nationally.

Hank Thompson eventually introduced Jim to a young high school girl from Oklahoma City named Wanda Jackson. Jim became her agent and was able to develop her into an enormous star. In 1960 he booked her in Las Vegas for 29 straight weeks. Since that was such an important engagement, Wanda decided to hire an excellent guitar player she had seen at a night club in Washington, D.C.. The young man hadn't made a name for himself yet, but he was on his way to stardom. That great guitar player was Roy Clark. Roy and Jim's lifelong friendship began then and within a year and a half, Jim was promoting Roy and moving him toward his celebrity status. From then on, Jim Halsey became a household name around country music.

Jim opened an office in Los Angeles, then Tulsa and London. Tulsa had been his second home as he was growing up, because he would always go there to listen to bands. In the early 1980s he opened an office in New York and then in the mid-80s he opened one in Nashville.

Jim understood the sales and marketing of the business. He knew if you had a good product and a person that wanted your product, then all you had to do was put the two of them together to create success for everyone. That knowledge, along with Jim's talents and the staff of people he successfully put together, caused the Jim Halsey Company to grow into the largest music agency in the world.

Jim believes there will never be an agency quite like his because they were solely trained and orchestrated in sales and marketing as though they had the philosophy of a manager. A manager looks after his people. The artist is always the most important person. Jim had 41 stars that his company represented, such as Roy Clark, The Oak Ridge Boys, The Judds, Clint Black, Dwight Yoakam and more.

Jim sold his company a few years ago to the William Morris Agency, for no other reason than he had other avenues he wanted desperately to pursue. He started a program with a vision to provide accelerated learning for individuals interested in entering the music and entertainment business. The program was first created and used at Oklahoma City University, where it was acclaimed with the Governor's Award for Excellence in Arts and Education. Jim recently moved the program to Tulsa and opened the Halsey Institute.

Jim's expertise will allow people of all ages to grasp his years of experience at an accelerated pace. Then, students will be prepared to enter all areas of the music industry, With the Halsey Institute Certificate and the Halsey signature, it will open doors and provide job interviews that otherwise may have remained closed.

I know there are not enough years in my lifetime to experience all the career choices I learn about during my interviews. But the Halsey Institute is certainly one I wish I had time to attend.

As one might expect, Jim was inducted into the Oklahoma Music Hall of Fame in October 2000.

Jim is married to Minisa, the daughter of the late world renown artist, Woody Crumbo. She is also an artist in her own right as well as a talented author. Jim and Minissa share four children together. Sherman is a television producer and promoter, Gina is an acupuncturist, Crissy is a ski instructor and Woody is a pilot for United Airlines.

Jim has already had an extremely full life, but there seems to be no end to his entrepreneurial spirit. He has several books slated to come out in the future, the first one being, *How To Make It In The Music Business.*

Jim tries to encourage everyone to follow their dreams as he did. He has never been afraid to step into an area that others said couldn't be done, because he found out on many occasions it was easier than he thought. Being the first one to accomplish something in a particular area is sometimes more important than anything else. Someone may come behind you and do it even better, but you did it first and that only happens once.

"In order to truly be successful, you have to believe in your dream, Jim said. That means even when the hard times come you" don't give up. If you give up, somebody will be right behind you and pick up where you left off and finish your dream for you and you will be standing back wishing, what if ."

Minisa Halsey – Artist/Author

I met Minisa on the day she came to an interview I was having with her husband, Jim Halsey. She gave me a different way of looking at the world, uniquely through the eyes of a woman.

Minisa was born in Tulsa, Oklahoma. She is the daughter of Woody and Lillian Rogue Crumbo. Her father was a very well known Native American artist. He began passing his talent on to Minisa at a very early age when he sat her down beside him with a pencil and piece of paper. Minisa began drawing and realized later that was the beginning of her creativity and self-expression.

When Minisa was a young child her parents, along with herself and her brother Woody, moved to New Mexico. She believes one of the most important experiences of her life happened there. Her father was thrown from his horse and received a dislocated shoulder and a broken arm. Instead of going to the hospital he called on his friend the "medicine man." He reset Crumbo's shoulder and set his broken arm. He placed herbs on his skin around the broken area of his arm and wrapped the arm with a piece of a brown paper bag tied with a string.

Three weeks later Crumbo's arm was totally healed without the use of a cast. It was later reported by a bone specialist that the medicine man's ability to reset the arm was the best he had ever seen.

This experience taught Minisa a person could become so close to the "Creator" and mother earth that his relationship with God would give him an internal vision to know exactly what needs to be done. So Minisa decided she wanted to live her life in a way that she too, would have a true relationship with the Creator.

Over the years she has learned each person has his own path to travel and we each have many teachers along the way. It is interesting that she pointed out the fact we all have many teachers and everyone we come in contact with can teach us something. This "Distinguished Oklahomans" book I feel will teach a lot of people as they read through the events of each person's life.

Minisa also shared a portion of her teaching on the "traditional women's way." Her philosophy, while very complex, is also very simple. However, because the women of our society are not normally taught in this fashion, we have to take a deep breath and like Joyce Hifler would say "Think On These Things" in order to truly understand Minisa's Native American teaching.

She describes how the mother earth takes 12 months to complete her rotation and she doesn't do anything twice. Everything is new and fresh every day. That reminded me of the scripture which says, "God's mercies are new every morning."

Minisa said we all have a charge from God to maintain a relationship with Him. Secondly, we are to live a life of compassion, respect and gratitude for ourselves and for others. Thirdly, neither believe ourselves to be superior or inferior to anyone.

Minisa pointed out the reason for unrest that is so prevalent in our relationships with others. When disagreements arise it is always somebody's fault. If the problem is your fault then self hate and self doubt set in. If the problem is the other person's fault then you either fight with him or quietly blame him for your unhappiness. The real root of the problem, however, is your relationship with God not being in place and in order.

A book written by Minisa will be coming out in the future titled *Moon Circle -The Traditional Women's Way*, which goes into more depth on the part women play in the creation and evolution of life.

After spending time with Minisa and discussing her spiritual beliefs I felt more positive about my own role as a woman. I look forward to reading her book and learning more about the process we all go through in creating our place on Earth.

In conjunction with Minisa's spiritual journey her artistic talents have won her international exposure. In the late 1970's she became the first American Indian artist to have a show of her works in the former Soviet Union. The works she took to the Soviet Union were a series of portraits of American Indians. The portraits were accompanied by poems Minisa wrote.

Minisa's marriage to W.R. Carter took place while she was still in college. Out of that marriage came two children, Woody and Crissy. The two of them are grown and married and parents themselves. She and Carter are no longer married but she describes him as a wonderful man and a good father to their children.

Her journey through life brought her into the presence of her current husband, Jim Halsey, who has become her lifelong mate. His two grow children, Sherman and Gina, add a further dimension to their lives together. Minisa counts herself as being very blessed to have lived her life and had the experiences afforded her.

Minisa Crumbo Halsey

Argus Hamilton – Comedian

If you've been around Oklahoma City for any length of time you've most likely heard of Argus Hamilton. He is the well-known comedian who writes a weekly column in the Daily Oklahoman. But that's not all there is to this nice looking Oklahoma-bred professional who very proudly admits he was born in Poteau, Oklahoma.

Argus James Hamilton III is the son, grandson and great-grandson of Methodist ministers. With that kind of background, how could you even consider him doing anything else with his life other than stand before an audience and entertain or inform in some sort of manner.

At the age of three Argus had already begun to give the church audience a taste of his humor. He was supposed to stand on stage and very politely sing *Away In A Manger,* but instead the words *Hot Diggety Dog Ziggety Boom What You Do To Me* filled the atmosphere of the sanctuary. Well needless to say he invoked laughter throughout the room.

In spite of the fact Argus was so naturally funny he sincerely planned to pursue politics as a chosen career. Obviously, he thought his humor was strictly a pass time for others when in fact it would soon open up an entirely different world for him. He remembers his parents allowed him to stay up late on school nights so he could watch the famous Johnny Carson present his monologue on "The Tonight Show." Then every morning Argus would repeat Johnny's jokes to his high school peers, pretending they were his own creations.

He enrolled at The University of Oklahoma, prepared to study hard and graduate with a major in British History. Of course he was called on to speak from time to time because it was such a natural venue for him. However, one day after performing a monologue at a chapter meeting for Alpha Tau Omega, his friend Greg Hall who now owns the Dyne Exploration Company came up to him and very matter of factly told him "Argus you aren't going to be a lawyer or politician, you are going to be a stand-up comedian." Somewhere deep within Argus he felt that measure of truth was a defining moment. He knew what Greg had just voiced was what he was really cut out to do.

Argus realized that being a stand-up comic was not something he did, it was who he was. He knew that everything he had been doing up to that point was leading him in that direction. So from then on every night became a quest to learn all he could about Will Rogers. Will was a friend of his grandfather, who performed Will's funeral in 1935 in Chelsea, Oklahoma. Argus also studied Bob Hope, Mark Twain and others who he felt would enhance his knowledge of comedy.

He became good friends with Danny Williams who had a talk show called "Danny's Day" on Channel 4 in Oklahoma City. Danny let Argus make guest appearances which were a great help as he continued to prepare for the future.

One night in 1974 he was sitting around with some of his friends at the ATO House watching Freddie Prince perform his debut comedy act on "The Tonight Show." Freddie mentioned a new place in Hollywood called The Comedy Store that had recently opened to showcase new comics. The Comedy Store was where comedians like Jay Leno, David Letterman and Gallager had honed their craft. Immediately, Argus began making plans to leave Oklahoma and head for California.

I asked Argus if it ever occurred to him that he would fail and that maybe he would make the long trip to California for nothing. But he said definitely not. Instead he could hardly wait to get out there amongst everyone else so he could compete.

The Comedy Store at one time was the most famous nightclub in Hollywood called "Ciro's." In 1972 Mitzi Shore bought the club and turned it into a tremendous three stage nightclub showroom as a tribute to the art of stand-up comedy.

The club was well on it's way by the time Argus showed up in 1976. In fact his timing was perfect. He was amongst some of the "greats" just coming up in the business like Robin Williams, Michael Keaton, Louie Anderson, Arsenial Hall and Bob Sagett. Each person would start out with three minutes of material and continue to add to it as their talents and abilities developed.

Then in 1980, only four years from when he first arrived in Los Angeles, he debuted on "The Tonight Show" with Johnny Carson, the man he had been emulating and admiring for over 10 years. Argus began his comedy monologue by discussing the woes of an Oklahoman adjusting to sunny California and then trailing off into talk about the news of the day. He must have made a great hit with Johnny. Instead of staying at his seat behind his desk Johnny greeted Argus on stage and complimented his excellent performance.

That one stint on "The Tonight Show" eventually grew to over 35 appearances and a career that couldn't be stopped. Argus began to tour with Helen Reddy, who's husband Jeff Wald became his manager.

Unfortunately, with all of his success there came a downside. With late nights required in his career and the high energy it took for his performances he soon found he needed the "high" to last long past the walk off the stage. Performing on stage was like being at the most sought after party, which became a thrill that Argus found hard to put to rest at the end of the night. Booze and drugs seemed to be the only way to keep the endorphins flowing and the party in full rage.

Finally in the mid 80's Argus realized he had to do something so he checked himself into The Betty Ford Center and turned his life around. He was so influenced by the Center that he continues to do fund raisers for them and is very active in their alumni association.

Since those early days Argus has continued to increase his talents and ability to make people laugh. For several years he has produced a comic newspaper column which has grown to over 109 daily newspapers throughout the nation. He gives credit for the success of his column to Ed Kelley and Edward L. Gaylord at the Dally Oklahoman who believed in him enough to give him his first newspaper column. Then in 1991 Argus was named Oklahoma's Ambassador of Good Will by the Oklahoma Hall Of Fame.

Argus hasn't forgotten his early days at The Comedy Store. He continues to perform there nightly as well as make occasional appearances on "The Tonight Show. The Los Angeles news continues to highlight reports about him and Paul Harvey quotes him at least two or three times a week. He is also a sought after performer at corporate engagements and conventions.

At the present time he is waiting for the next highlight of his career to come to fruition. He has completed the pilot for a talk show called "From The Hip." The program will begin with Argus doing an opening monologue and then sitting down with three other comedians who review the news of the day in, of course, their comedic fashion.

As always I ask my interviewees for a nugget of wisdom and Argus certainly had one. *He said, I have learned in life that I don't get what I want, I get what I am. If I improve what I am then I improve what I get."* Now that is a nugget of truth.

Angus Hamilton

Marilyn Harris

Author

Being a writer myself, I found Marilyn to be extremely interesting to talk to. I hope some day I have at least as many published books on my list of accomplishments as she does.

Marilyn was born in Oklahoma City, Oklahoma on June 4,1931. When she was 6 years old, the untimely death of her pet cat, Lone Wolf, motivated her to write *Love Poem to Cat,* which unknowingly was her entrance into the literary world.

She has always loved words and her life was sprinkled with episodes of writing events long before she realized she was to become a highly regarded literary figure. She wrote for the school paper, had inclusions in the Thanksgiving pageant script and was constantly jotting down entries in her personal diary. She loved plays and acting and caught herself reverting into those areas of reflection when she wanted to escape to another world. Freud said, "Reality leaves most of us starving."

Her first college days were spent at a small school in Missouri called Cottey, before transferring to Oklahoma University where she received her Bachelor's and Master's degrees in Fine Arts and English. At that point, she still wasn't thinking about becoming a professional writer. It was the 1950's and most women followed the traditional road of marriage and family.

Being a writer was something she loved to do, but she never let herself drift into what seemed to be an unrealistic dream. For her to think she could get paid for something she thoroughly loved doing was just too inconceivable for her to even think about.

In 1953 she married her husband, E.V. Springer, who was pursuing graduate studies at Boston University. Before long two children, John and Karen had graced their home and Marilyn's hands were full with the duties of a devoted wife and mother. Since they lived in the suburbs, her husband had to travel downtown to the university. Because of the long New England winters, Marilyn found herself alone with the children for many hours at a time.

Her domestic chores and solitude began making her feel dull and immensely bored. It was then that she started writing with a vengeance. At first she wrote what she called "bad poetry." When the children were sleeping or playing in their downstairs basement, Marilyn would wander off into a secluded corner and write for a couple of hours. When she resurfaced, so to speak, she felt rejuvenated and more capable of taking on the rest of the day.

Her husband's first teaching job was in New Hampshire. By then, their children were in the first and second grades. Each day, after the children had gone off to school, Marilyn would devote her whole day to writing. It was then that she progressed from poetry to short stories.

A little at a time, she began sending her stories to various publishers. With 265 written short stories, she received 265 rejection slips. How does one continue in a field of endeavor when so many obstacles seem to stand in her way? As I asked that question, I remembered what Paul Harvey said to me during our interview. "We all fall from time to time, but those who deserve even a modicum of what the world calls success, gets up again and sometimes again and again and dusts themselves off."

Marilyn said although she didn't like the rejection slips, she didn't look at them as an indicator of her ability, only as a misjudgment on the part of her critics.

In the mid 1960's in the midst of all the rejection slips, Marilyn and her family moved back to Oklahoma. During a short course at Oklahoma University, she met who was at the time the editor-in-chief of Doubleday. She took that opportunity to present him with 14 of those previously rejected short stories she had accumulated into a collection titled *Kings EX.*

Within two months, Doubleday had given Marilyn a two book contract for the collection of short stories and for one unwritten novel, which was later titled, *In the Midst of Earth.* One of the short stories was selected for inclusion in the 1969 0-Henry collection of the best short stories of 1969. Marilyn knew then she was off and running with a career that stimulated an enormous flow of Marilyn Harris creativity .

In the beginning she had an absolute conviction that what she said in her books could possibly change the world. She felt a great responsibility to get her words out as fast as she could, because she just knew the world needed them.

I knew that self help books would be a source of medicine for a struggling world, but since I had never written a novel, I didn't understand the correlation she was trying to convey. So I asked her, "How does fiction translate into helping someone, since it is a fictitious story?"

Marilyn explained that truth is truth whether it is in a fictitious story or not. Her story of *Hatter Fox* revealed the importance of accepting people for who they are and just because a person is different, it doesn't mean they are inferior.

Marilyn doesn't feel like she has ever written a book that doesn't have some positive philosophy supporting her story.

Next, Marilyn set out to write two juvenile books for young readers -*The Peppersalt Land* and *The Runaway's Diary*, which won the Lewis Carroll Shelf Award in 1973. On the heels of those books came *Hatter Fox*, which was a Literary Guild selection and became a television Movie of the Week for CBS.

Marilyn's career has spanned over a 30 year period, She has successfully written 22 published books. Her last book published was in 1993 titled *Lost and Found.* Virtually all of her novels have been big sellers. Her work has been published in England, France, Germany, Spain, Portugal, Japan, Poland, Italy and Sweden. She has received numerous awards and has been inducted into three prestigious Halls of Fame.

In previous years, she taught the art of creative writing at both Oklahoma University as well as Central State University. During that time she met many students who had varying degrees of completeness in their quest for literary acceptance. Some chose not to pay the price for success while others felt too inadequate within themselves to get there.

Marilyn strongly advocates that people should "be aware of their own personal worth. If only everyone could believe in themselves, the world would be a much better place."

Marilyn feels very fortunate to have been given such an incredible life. She has a great husband, two beautiful, productive children and six grandchildren that know exactly where grandma keeps the candy jar.

Marilyn spends a lot of time in her garden. She believes gardens are a source of peace, because they are basically a mindless activity and yet they yield so much beauty. She doesn't know if there will be another Marilyn Harris book, even though her agent continues to call for an update. Right now, she is enjoying life's quiet moments and her reflections of an incredible journey.

Sam Harris

Singer / Performer

I am so impressed with the wisdom and knowledge Sam Harris has acquired. He always knows what he wants to do and is never afraid to go for it. Sam is a singer, songwriter, actor on Broadway, film and television star and director and producer, but his first love is singing.

Sam was born in Cushing, Oklahoma and raised in Sand Springs. He sang for the first time at the age of 2 and was in his first play at age 5. When he was 15 years old he left home to pursue his dreams of singing and acting. Since he quit school he took correspondence courses to finish.

He used to sing in every joint or dive that would allow him to perform. His big break came when a talent scout spotted him and placed him on the premiere show of "Star Search." Sam exploded into the public eye as the grand champion of "Star Search" with his bellowing voice and charismatic charm. I remember watching him on the broadcast and rooting for the Oklahoma boy who was obviously on his way to stardom.

From there record companies began calling immediately. He chose to go with Motown for his first record label. He sold over, a million copies of *Sam Harris* and *Sam-I-Am,* which he produced. His recordings also include the critically acclaimed *Standard Time* and *Different Stages* both produced, arranged and conducted by the legendary Peter Matz.

Sam has toured the country in concert and has played to sold-out audiences at Carnegie Hall, Los Angeles Universal Amphitheatre and London's West End. He has made appearances on numerous television shows and specials and in countless live productions, working with everyone from Stevie Wonder and George Michael to Liza Minnelli, Madonna and Elizabeth Taylor to name a few.

He has been seen on virtually every talk show from Leno to Oprah to Rosie to Geraldo to Barbara Walters. In the theatre, he has starred in such musicals as *Jesus Christ Superstar, Cabaret, Hard Copy,* and the extensive national tour of Andrew Lloyd Webber's Broadway production of *Joseph and the Amazing Technicolor Dreamcoat.* On Broadway, Sam received a Drama Desk nomination for his role in Tommy Tune's, *Grease* and most recently received a Drama-League Award as well as Tony, Outer Critic's Circle and Drama Desk nominations for his work in Cy Coleman's *The Life.*

He released his newest compact disc, entitled *Revival* in October 1999 and mounted a concert of the same name in the summer of 2000. In addition, he completed the feature film, "In the Weeds." He is developing his musical "Hurry! Hurry! Hollywood" with the prestigious Manhattan Theatre Club.

Sam says life isn't always easy, but he is just pushy enough to cause some things good to happen in his life. I asked how he could go out into the world at such an early age. He said he realized people are basically the same everywhere you go, so why should you fear being around them? If fear keeps you from stretching yourself and trying something unfamiliar, then just realize people are the same and they are in a progression of trying to find themselves as well. *If you are afraid to leave your familiar surroundings you may never reach where you need to be.*

Surround yourself with people who will encourage you in what you want to do with your life. Maybe you are artistic, but you find out as you go further in your search that you aren't going to draw pictures but that you are an architect. Or maybe you like movies and think you would like to be an actor when really what you want to do is produce the shows.

You will never know what you are really supposed to do unless you forget your fears and head in a direction. Eventually, with persistence and weeding through the ideas and obstacles, you find out what you are best suited for.

In the days of "Star Search" Sam was also in the process of writing a sit-com called Down to Earth. The show was very successful and lasted for four years. Sam played in it the first season.

Marques Haynes

Basketball Star

Not everyone remembers the trolley cars that ran down the Sand Springs line headed for downtown Tulsa. Yet Marques would pay his nickel and climb aboard, hoping to be dropped off safely at the Dreamland Theatre on Greenwood Avenue just in time to see his favorite afternoon movie.

In those days, segregation was the key word and the black community was ever mindful of the part it played in their every day lives. However, it was so common place for Marques that it was just like breathing. It was something that was expected and you never spent time worrying about it, or at least that was how Marques handled it. His father

Lemanuel was a common laborer and his mother Hattie was a domestic worker. With four children to raise there wasn't a lot of extra money laying around, so basketball became an activity that occupied many hours for the Haynes family.

As Marques was growing up the only black basketball teams that existed were either church leagues, YMCA leagues, city or All Star teams. Professional black teams were not known until a few years later. So Marques simply played basketball for the enjoyment of the game.

When he entered his high school years, things began to change. He attended Booker T. Washington High School and continued to polish his skills. His church tried to be supportive of his efforts, so when it was time to go off to college they awarded him a $25 scholarship, the first one the church had ever given. In order to redeem the scholarship, he had to report to Langston University, which was 84 miles away.

Marques didn't have a car or the money to ride the bus, so he proceeded to hitchhike. With thirty cents in his pocket, he bought two Mr. Goodbars and one Snickers, which cost a nickel a piece. To go along with the candy bars he bought two bottles of pop, leaving one nickel to spare when he arrived at the university. Immediately the next day he started looking for a job and was hired as part of the campus yard crew. After a couple of years had passed he was able to get an athletic scholarship which helped him the rest of the way through.

The first professional basketball team he was ever on was called the Oklahoma Stars. The team was comprised of Langston players. They would play exhibition games throughout the Oklahoma area. For consecutive years at Langston, Marques was a member of the starting five and was chosen as an All Conference guard. During his senior year at college the Langston team played against the Harlem Globetrotters and won the game. The Globetrotters approached Marques and wanted him to join their organization and travel with them to Dallas, Texas, their next stop. As tempting as the offer was, Marques didn't want to quit school. So he waited until after graduation and joined the organization in the Fall of 1946. Within the organization was a team called the Kansas City Stars that Marques played on for the first two months before joining with the Harlem Globetrotters full time.

Some people may not know that the Harlem Globetrotters' name had no connection to Harlem in New York. The gentleman that put the all black team together chose the name because he wanted the team to be identified as a black team. Harlem was always thought of as being a black area. The team didn't actually appear in Harlem until the late 1970's.

Marques played with the Harlem Globetrotters two different times. The first time was from 1946 until the end of 1953. During that time he was always a member of the starting five. For five of those years he acted as a coach as well as a player. In 1950 he won the Most Valuable Player award against the College All Americans. He also appeared in the "Harlem Globetrotters Story" in 1950 and then in "Go Man Go" about the Harlem Globetrotters in 1953.

In those first few years, traveling with the team wasn't as easy as it is nowadays. There weren't all the major highways and turnpikes, so of course their time on the road was much longer. Also as black people, all accommodations were not available to them. They had to choose carefully when they were going to a particular city. The lines were clearly drawn in some places and in other cities they weren't quite sure.

The absurdity of those kinds of actions seem so ridiculous to the majority of our civilized society now. It's hard to believe the same people we flock to arenas to see in the 21st. Century, could have been so disrespected not so very long ago. I was so appreciative of Marques and his outlook. He said since prejudice had been such common place in a black person's life, they never really thought much about it. They had a job to do as a Globetrotter and so they did it.

They went to the cities that would receive them and the ones that wouldn't they passed on by. The best part about it was Marques and the Harlem Globetrotters loved what they were doing. The audiences that welcomed them made it worth all the effort. Even though the Harlem Globetrotters have always been known for their showmanship and antics performed on the court, it took trained professionals to play the game and win.

At the end of 1953, Marques formed another basketball team called the Harlem Magicians, which he was a part of until 1972. Then he went back to the Harlem Globetrotters for another seven years before ending his career with his own team, the Harlem Magicians.

Marques has lived his whole professional life as a basketball player. He has played in more than 12,000 games over a period of 49 years. He has traveled throughout 103 different countries and has been known as one of the greatest defensive players and dribbler of all time.

So far, he has been inducted into seven Halls of Fame, including the N.A.I.A. Hall of Fame, Sand Springs Hall of Fame, E. Hartford Hall of Fame, Jim Thorpe Hall of Fame, Langston University Athletic Hall of Fame, Texas Black Sports Hall of Fame and Naismith Basketball Hall of Fame.

Marques has come a long ways from the young man who hitchhiked to college with thirty cents in his pocket. Forty-nine years is long enough to play any kind of sport or for that matter, it is a long enough to do just about anything. Yet Marques looks like he could play 49 more years.

Marques devotes his time now to a filter business that he and his wife own in Texas. He occasionally accepts some speaking engagements and offers his expertise as a basketball consultant from time to time. Other than that, his basketball years are a thing of the past.

I can assure you, when Marques travels through cities now, he is welcomed with open arms. His many years on the court have earned him the respect he really deserved all along. Thanks Marques for the many years you dedicated to the sport of basketball.

Marques Haynes

Gerald Heller - Proprietor

I'm sure most of us have seen and heard Kathryn Zaremba sing the theme song for Mays and Drug Warehouse -*Get The Best of Us Every Day*. But, we probably didn't know how it all began.

Gerald was born in St. Louis, Missouri in 1937 to Ida Mae and Isadore Heller. That same year after graduating from pharmacy school his Uncle Harry Ludmeyer opened his first drug store in Joplin, Missouri.

During his training he was told that store names should be chosen with as few letters as possible in order to cut down on the cost of signs. Since the name Ludmeyer didn't fit into the three or four letter limit he decided to copy the name of another successful store. A fellow pharmacy student had opened a store named May's in Iowa and had been experiencing great success. Harry hoped if he used the same name in Joplin his friend's success would be contagious.

One year later Isadore and Harry formed a partnership in the business. The years that followed continued to prove successful and the vision of a small drug store empire began.

Through Gerald's childhood years all he knew about was the drug store business. His father worked long hard hours and at first his mother worked right along side him as the company bookkeeper. It only made sense that Gerald would have a flair for the business as well, so when the time came he attended pharmacy school at The University of Oklahoma.

After graduation, since his father and uncle's stores weren't large enough yet to carry Gerald financially, he decided to go to work for the Katz Drug Store chain in Kansas City.

One Sunday afternoon while Isadore and Ida Mae were on their way to dinner with a couple of their friends in Tulsa they drove by a department store named Oertles. To their amazement people were lined up outside trying to get into the store. Isadore asked if the friends would mind stopping so they could canvas the store and see what all the excitement was about.

Upon returning to Joplin Isadore informed Harry of the small drug department inside of Oertles. He thought it would be a great opportunity for them to take their expertise and share in the department store's success. After discussing the possibility with Max Oertle they convinced Gerald to move to Tulsa and run the leased drug department. This was the beginning of Gerald's own personal journey which would eventually lead him into great personal success.

In August 1960 Gerald moved to Tulsa where he successfully ran the Oertles Drug Department. Oertles eventually was bought out by David's Department Store before going out of business in 1980. By then Gerald had already opened other drug stores under the banner of May's Drug. With the close of David's he decided to start a new venture into the discount drug business and opened his first Drug Warehouse in the same location as David's.

In 1972 Gerald bought out his uncle and father's stores in Joplin and was now well on his way to making Drug Warehouse a household name. The reason for the name change to Drug Warehouse was an attempt to compete in the deep discount drug store market against their own stores, therefore keeping other chains from wanting to come into the area. Of course it worked for a while, but eventually they had to find their way amongst the Wal-Marts and Walgreens of the country. Fortunately, they were able to do that and quite successfully.

Gerald still contributes a great deal of his success to the lessons his uncle and father taught him. He believes a price can't be put on the training they gave him and the time they spent nurturing him in the retail business. As hard task masters they taught him the meaning of hard work and learning his trade through and through.

His uncle once told him "everyone in life has successes and failures, but what really makes you successful is the order in which they fall." To Gerald's credit any failures seemed to come after his successes and by then he already knew "he could."

Gerald was also taught the importance of surrounding himself with good people who were talented in areas where he may be lacking. Success is not a one man show, it takes a team working together to create success in anyone's life.

In the 1970's Gerald joined The National Association of Chain Drug Stores. In 1980 they asked him to be on the Board of Directors and in 1989 he became chairman of the organization and then again in 1996. The organization includes every major chain drug store and most supermarkets and mass merchandizers. Being a part of the organization has been a great help to Gerald and his company in expanding his horizons and knowledge of the industry.

Gerald is married to Sherry whom he met while attending Oklahoma University. Together they have raised three children. Gregg works in the buying department of May's. Tracey is a pharmaceutical representative and her husband Scott also works in the buying department of May's. Then there is Devin who is still single and living in Florida for the time being.

It of course gives Gerald a great deal of pleasure to work alongside his children and share with them the experiences of success in the family business. He said he has tried to pass on to them the advice his father and uncle shared with him. He hopes they will always remember that making a good deal with a person requires the belief that both parties should walk away feeling it was a good experience for all concerned.

At the present time Gerald has 39 May's and Drug Warehouse locations which still include the Missouri stores. The future includes continued expansion into Missouri and eventually Arkansas as well. Who knows what other states may be included in the future?

Gerald has proven he has the key to success in the retail business. I know I love to shop in his store-especially at Christmas time-when I feel a need to see all the unique items he brings to the public. He admits he and his buyers travel all over the world looking for products that will make his stores stand out among others. Doing so has helped place him as one of two independent drug chains in the top 100 markets.

So the next time you walk into a May's or Drug Warehouse and you hear the little jingle ringing in your head *Get The Best of Us Everyday* you'll know you're experiencing the truth.

Mark Hendricks – *Business Professional*

Mark was born and raised in Clinton, Oklahoma along with his brother Scott. After graduating from high school he attended Oklahoma State University. He really had no idea what direction he should go with his life until his accounting instructor, Tim DuBois, encouraged him to become an accountant.

Tim was more than an instructor to Mark. He became a close friend as well and Mark respected his opinion. Along with being a teacher, Tim loved to write songs. Every so often he would have Mark and Scott, both guitar players, over to his house to record demonstration tapes of the songs he wrote. These tapes were then sent to Nashville in hopes of getting them recorded by country artists. After a few successes, Tim eventually moved to Nashville to become a full time songwriter.

Scott and some of the other guys followed some time later. Mark, being the logical business minded person, felt more confident sticking to the traditional way of living as opposed to the throwing caution to the wind and being a "take a risk" kind of guy.

After graduating from college, Mark went to work for a large CPA firm in Tulsa. The accounting profession was experiencing unprecedented growth at the time and Mark, along with other CPA's, were making a lot of money.

After three years the Williams Company approached Mark about coming to work for them. At first he wasn't interested but they offered him a salary he just couldn't turn down. He worked for Williams for nine years, eventually becoming a manager.

Mark thought he was living the American dream. He got married at age 21, built a new home and was rocking along thinking life was great. After 10 years of marriage and no children, he and his wife got a divorce. It was a devastating time for Mark and he had to re-evaluate where his life was headed.

Scott contacted him and said "Now what is your excuse for not moving to Nashville?" By that time, Scott had become very successful himself, but Mark was still leery about giving up the security in business he had acquired over the years. Yet with Scott's insistence that Mark have fun for the first time in his life, he finally relented and headed for Nashville to carry through on the job interviews Scott had set up for him.

Mark went from one company to the next talking to producers and record company presidents but nothing seemed to click for him until he ran across O'Neil Hagaman, a music industry business management and consulting company. They offered him a ridiculous low salary compared to what he had been making at the Williams Company, but for some inexplicable reason he couldn't turn it down. Top executives at Williams assured him success if he stayed. Something, however, was pulling him to Nashville.

It was one of those defining moments. He didn't want to look back some day and regret that he had never given the more creative side of himself a chance. This was his opportunity to be involved in something wildly different and much more creative than what he had ever done. His co-workers told him he was crazy to give up his position at the Williams Company, yet at the same time they seemed a bit envious of his willingness to take such a career risk.

Mark began with O'Neil Hagaman as a business manager in 1991. He had superior skills in computers and high end accounting. In two years and nine months he became the firm's fourth partner.

O'Neil Hagaman is the largest business management and consulting firm in Nashville that is solely dedicated to the entertainment industry. Their clients are music touring artists, song writers, publishers and music industry executives. This group focuses on music royalties, compliance audits, valuations of intellectual properties and litigation matters.

About eight years ago, Mark started a different division within the firm called The Consulting Group. It takes care of all the recording and publishing royalties and performs record royalty audits on behalf of their clients.

Mark has never been sorry for his decision to move to Nashville. Not only has he become very successful but he grew close to his brother Scott, who had one time only represented sibling rivalry.

Mark and Scott developed their work ethics from working on the family farm. While their friends took the summer off, they worked long hours in the fields, seven days a week. They both site the long hours, and the family, that worked along side them as significant character builders.

Together they have created a publishing company called Big Tractor a name chosen as reminiscent of their childhood days. The writers are the ones who run the company which is a very different concept. Since Mark and Scott feel so fortunate to have their own successful careers, they felt an obligation to provide a creative outlet for writers allowing them the opportunity to create their own success. Writers demo their songs in the studio and the staff takes the songs around to Nashville producers and artists who listen and decide if they want to record the songs. If they do, it is a win win situation for everyone.

Mark has learned over the years to come up with his own definition of success before pursuing it. Using money as the yardstick for success, the decision to jump off the corporate ladder and start all over in the music business made no sense. Pursuing what he thought would be fun and make him happy did make sense. *Mark now believes that money is merely a byproduct of success. Success is loving what you do every day. Because you love what you do, you do it well. Because you do it well, the money follows.*

I interviewed Mark at his office in Nashville in 1999. After I came home he sent me a letter along with his picture that was to be included with his profile. I was so touched by his letter I wanted to share it with others.

He said, "After we talked, I realized how self absorbed my comments were. It amazed me that I didn't attribute what success I've enjoyed to the one who gave it to me, God! You absolutely can succeed without God, but it will be meaningless without Him. I went on and on about taking risks in life. Sounds brave, one man taking his chances. Truth is, my courage comes from knowing that in every step I take, God is by my side. I know that all I am and all I will ever be, comes from His grace. Best Regards, Mark Hendricks."

Just for the record, I never felt for one minute Mark was tooting a singular horn. Yet I was impressed he took the extra effort to give God credit.

Scott Hendricks - Country Music Executive

Clinton, Oklahoma should be very proud of their native son, Scott. As early as 13 years old he knew the direction he wanted to go with his life. He was raised on a farm with his brother Mark and learned quickly the meaning of hard work. His parents, Inez and Howard, never gave Scott and his brother the opportunity to be slack in their duties around the farm. They were taught to finish their chores before playing with their friends and honesty and integrity were goals that were never to be compromised.

Scott began writing songs and performing in bands as far back as he can remember. As each year passed it further confirmed to him how desperately he wanted to be involved in the music industry.

After high school with the desire to make records still burning inside of him, he went to see a counselor at Oklahoma State University. The counselor informed him the only class they had that was anywhere close to what he was looking for was a class called architectural acoustics and electro acoustics. With the help of three counselors they put together a program for Scott that would get him at least somewhat closer to his goal. When he graduated he would be able to design music studios. That wasn't his ultimate goal, but at least it would get him involved with music studios and possibly open other doors that would come available.

Scott became acquainted with one of the college instructors, Tim DuBois, who also had a lifelong dream of involvement in the music industry. Many days were spent at Tim's house playing guitars and writing and singing songs along with Scott's brother Mark and a few other musicians.

In 1975 Scott and Tim decided to take a chance and visit Nashville a few times to try and market songs they had written. They weren't setting the world on fire, but at least they were in pursuit of what they thought was a worthwhile goal.

In 1977 Tim left his job at the university and moved to Nashville. He believed if he was ever going to be as involved with music as he wanted to be he needed to live there.

When 1978 rolled around Scott had finished college, packed up everything he owned and moved to Nashville also. He was as determined as Tim to give himself every opportunity to break into the industry. He was willing to make sacrifices if that was what it took to see his dream come to pass.

When Scott first arrived in Nashville he lived in the basement of Tim's house for a while. He went to the local college,

Belmont, and convinced them they needed to offer a class in recording and architectural acoustics. They usually required a master's degree for a person to teach at their college, but they made an exception with Scott since there had never been a course like that at the school. Scott was more or less a pioneer.

He got another job with a company that implemented studios with sound equipment. Even though Scott had never designed a studio yet because he was fresh out of college, they felt his degree qualified him to do a better job at setting up the acoustics than what they could do. His job got him in the door of a lot of music studios and gave him the opportunity to show his talents and make lasting friendships along the way.

One particular studio he worked at was called Glaser Brothers Studio. There was an engineer working there named Ron Treat who was also from Oklahoma. Every night after Scott finished his day job he would hang out with Ron at Glaser Studio and help with anything that needed to be done. After about a year Ron moved away and the studio was looking for someone to replace him. Of course Scott came to mind because he was always there and they knew he was dedicated to the music industry.

That was a great step for Scott but in the back of his mind he still remained focused on his real goal-making records (whatever that meant, he still wasn't quite sure). He just knew he wanted to be in the studio more than he wanted to design studios and he knew some day that door would open for him as well.

As an engineer, he worked unbelievable hours and was able to help with a lot of number one records. Artists began hiring Scott to mix their records. After a while his skills became very much in demand.

Tim and Scott continued to remain great friends. Tim was having equal success in writing songs while Scott was helping make records. One day they decided to put together a group of musicians singing the songs that Tim had written. The group eventually became who we know today as Restless Heart.

By then, Tim and Scott were getting a reputation for being producers and other doors began to open to them as well. Scott produced the song for Monday Night Football- *Are You Ready For Some Football.*

Tim eventually became president of Arista Records and Scott produced almost all of their music for artists like Alan Jackson, Brooks and Dunn, Steve Wariner and others.

Finally, in 1995, Scott became so well known for his quality work and his ever increasing expertise that Capitol Records asked him to come and manage their company. Other changes began to happen over a period of time. It was decided that Virgin Records, who had been around for over 25 years producing pop music with artists like Janet Jackson, The Spice Girls and The Rolling Stones, would start a country division with Scott at the helm. Virgin Records had started in London by a man named Richard Branson who owned Virgin Airlines. They were eventually bought by EMI who owns Capitol records and a lot of other record companies.

Along with his duties at Virgin, Scott and his brother Mark (who had moved to Nashville in 1991) decided to put a publishing company together called Big Tractor, a name reminiscent of their days on the farm, The publishing company is very unique as it is run by the writers. Scott and Mark have created an atmosphere for a group of writers to create songs and then pitch them to artists and producers who in turn hopefully record them on their albums. It has become yet another way for Scott to make records.

As he told me earlier, in the beginning he didn't know what "making records" really entailed for him. He just knew he wanted to be involved in the music industry. When he was younger and playing his guitar in bands around Clinton, Oklahoma he was known as a pretty good musician and probably one of the best Clinton had to offer. When he arrived in Nashville he realized there were some real guitar players there and he could practice 24 hours a day for 10 years and never be as could as they were.

As a songwriter he thought he could write good songs but there was always someone who could do it better. As he began to weed through obstacles he saw where he really fit into the music industry and it was there where he found his success.

Scott said there are hundreds of people who move to Nashville every year hoping to make it big and realizing it is harder than they thought and the competition is fierce. Yet you will never know if you don't give it a try. You can't sit back and dream about it and say I'm better than the other guy. You have to go out there, take a chance and see if you really are. By doing that you also weed through obstacles, just as Scott did, which eventually lead you to what is right for you.

In February 2000 Scott was inducted into the Oklahoma State University Hall of Fame. With the number of Oklahomans who have made their mark successfully in Nashville, you have to wonder what Nashville would be like with out them.

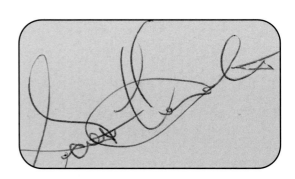

Joyce Hifler

Author

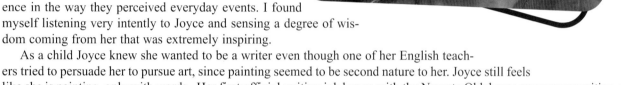

I had an immediate liking for Joyce the first minute I met her. I could then understand why her writing talent was enjoyed by so many for so long. If you have never read any of Joyce Hifler's books, or her daily syndicated newspaper column titled, *Think On These Things,* then you have been deprived. Joyce speaks directly from her heart to yours, not just in print, but in person as well.

During my interviews, Joyce was the second woman of Indian heritage, (Joyce being Cherokee) that has told me how they live close to the earth in their thoughts and perceptions. I had never heard that term before, and yet I realized in both of these women that there was a difference in the way they perceived everyday events. I found myself listening very intently to Joyce and sensing a degree of wisdom coming from her that was extremely inspiring.

As a child Joyce knew she wanted to be a writer even though one of her English teachers tried to persuade her to pursue art, since painting seemed to be second nature to her. Joyce still feels like she is painting, only with words. Her first official writing job began with the Nowata Oklahoma newspaper writing essays about circumstances that everyone could relate to. She simply writes what she is thinking. She reaches into her own spirit and pulls it out. Joyce said she took to heart something that the well known writer Emerson once said, "Write to yourself, and you write to an eternal audience."

When Joyce's column first began, it went by another name, until a Cherokee friend of hers read the column and suggested she read the fourth chapter of Phillipians in the Bible which in his opinion described her column. It reads, "Whatsoever is pure, whatsoever is lovely, whatsoever is of good report, think on these things." Thus Joyce's column became THINK ON THESE THINGS.

Before long one of the editors of the newspaper, Tulsa World suggested she get her column syndicated. Without any further ado, she went straight to New York, and the rest is history.

It's been forty-five years plus since Joyce started writing her column. It has never failed to bring encouragement to others in allowing them to read thoughts that they themselves have felt.

Her first book was published by Doubleday when a salesman from the company was approached about people requesting her work. Her first four books were *Think On These Things,To Everything A Season, All Rivers Run To The Sea,* and *Pathways.* They are all titles that come from Bible references. Her latest book, *When The Night Bird Sings*, is one I'm looking forward to reading. Joyce says when the night bird sings you are due a miracle when you hear it. We could all use a miracle now and then. Joyce has eight books to her credit so far, and says she thinks her greatest book has yet to be written.

Joyce mentioned four people that had influenced her early in life. Her Papa taught her how to shoot, Uncle Carl taught her how to cuss, her grandmother taught her how to gather herbs, and her mother taught her how to pray. She proclaims that it was and is prayer that has saved her and brought her through every circumstance of life.

Joyce lives with her husband Charlie in Bartlesville, Oklahoma, in a deep wooded area which she says keeps her in touch with the earth and nature and no doubt keeps her creative thoughts flowing.

I could have spent the rest of the day talking to Joyce. Her warm, caring spirit brings comfort to those around. I'd like to leave you with some quotes from one of her books and hope you will take advantage of her other great work.

"Opportunity has been known to pound on the door and go unnoticed, and it has been known to whisper and be heard." "We attract a great many of our problems simply by dwelling on them in our thoughts." "Good ideas are the flower of the mind, waiting to bloom for the benefit of the thinker." "Everything we see was first an idea in someone's mind." "Ideas are fleeting messages that pass rapidly through the mind." "Self respect is a necessity in order to keep on good terms with oneself." "It is

said that a great deal of talent is lost in this world for the want of a little courage." "Give without thought of return. For while we are giving with loving selflessness, life shapes for us our heart's desire." "There comes a time when we have to turn a firm and deaf ear to those people who have no other intention than to disturb our peace of mind." "Who are the people who are free of fears? They are the individuals who govern themselves in such a manner as to have thought out their own ideas enough to be able to speak freely for themselves." "All the world listens for the voice that speaks with its heart."

Socrates, being asked the way to honest fame, said, "Study to be what you wish to seem." *Success takes time and moral discipline, but our successes will be as human beings first, and then the crown of success in business will sit easily and firmly.*

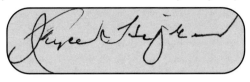

Andy Hillenburg ~ Race Car Driver

Surely we all have enjoyed watching the excitement of a good racing event at least once in our life. I thought it only appropriate to profile one of our Oklahoma boys who has spent his life making at least a portion of those events possible.

Andy was born to Marilyn and Harold Hillenburg on December 14, 1965 in Broken Arrow, Oklahoma. Marilyn's father was the city attorney in Broken Arrow for over 50 years. Harold's father originally had a dairy farm before going into the pipe business with his two sons. They built the business into quite a lucrative company bearing the Hillenburg name.

Andy grew up with a lot of the niceties of life due to the hard work and perseverance of his father, uncle and grandfather in the family business. There was plenty of land for Andy and his sister Kimberly to roam around on and enjoy while straddled on a horse or in Andy's case racing over a hill on his loud motorcycle.

In 1974 Harold bought a super modified race car and sponsored his best friend Ray Crawford, who he had known since the fifth grade, as the driver. Later a second car was purchased and Ray's son Donald began racing it along with his father at the Tulsa Speedway.

At age 14 Andy joined the fun by entering his first race in Muskogee driving a modified midget race car. When Ray Crawford retired from racing Andy took over his position in 1984 and began racing super modified as well as midget cars. Andy graduated from Broken Arrow High School. Unlike some of his other friends he had no desire to go on to college. He just wanted to continue racing.

His father, in an effort to expand his horizons, made Andy quit racing for one year so he could teach him about the pipe business. Yet after the year was up the only thing Andy wanted to do was go back to racing. His father decided to help further his career in racing since he could see it was so much a part of him. Harold made it possible for Andy to join the racing circuit by financially sponsoring him for two years while he honed his talent with the pros of the sport.

In 1986 he not only began driving sprint cars but he married his high school sweetheart DeAnn Daniel. In 1987 Andy joined the Sprint Car World of Outlaws which is currently the number five venue in professional motorsports.

Andy continued to do so well that J & J Enterprises owned by Jack Elam decided to sponsor him. They were the company that built the sprint car Andy was driving. Before long Jack introduced Andy to an independent businessman in Memphis, Tennessee whose name was Howard Blankenship and he began financially sponsoring Andy. The arrangement was good for everyone. It gave Andy the opportunity to continue doing what he loved most.

Andy feels indebted to his father, Jack Elam and Howard Blankenship for believing in him enough to give him the chance to prove his abilities. Howard has since given up his participation, feeling a need to focus on other areas. Jack Elam is still involved. When he first began sponsoring Andy he was selling 48 of his racing cars a year. Now he sells over 180, so his belief in Andy paid off for him as well.

As I drove up to the Hillenburg property I noticed a big purple bus which is Andy's transportation as he travels the racing circuit. Andy was busily hosing down his pickup when I drove into the driveway of his race shop located across the street from his home.

When we walked inside the building I was amazed to see a huge 76 foot semi truck and trailer parked inside with the names John Christner Trucking and Luxaire Heating and Air Conditioning displayed on the side. Other sponsors include Rush Truck Centers, MAC Tools, J&J Chassis, Hoosier Tires and Sander Engineering.

Andy took me inside the semi through the rear entrance tailgate. It was incredible to see this neatly laid out truck full of parts and accessories needed as Andy travels the racing circuit. The floor was shiny hardwood that looked better than some people have in their homes. Against one side lined up neatly on a shelf were several Hoosier Tires ready for instant mounting. There were large built in tool boxes and equipment of every sort that could possibly be needed.

I was surprised to see all the parts of a race car laying on shelves ready to be removed and mounted together like a picture puzzle. Andy said while they are on the road, one car is ready at all times. If need be they can change an engine in about 13 minutes. If they have to build a car from scratch from parts out of the trailer they can do it in five or six hours. It really was quite an impressive set up.

Of course Andy said it wasn't always that way, he had to work his way up to the fine rig he has today. His first transportation was a pickup with a trailer attached to the back. Then he progressed to a dooley truck with a double box open trailer. From there he had an enclosed trailer with a lounge and a lot of spare parts inside. Eventually the semi and trailer were added along with two race cars, spare parts and one full-time employee.

Today, along with the impressive semi and trailer, he has eight to 10 race cars, three full-time employees, one touring bus, a dooley, two pickups and who knows what else. The young guy from Broken Arrow, Oklahoma has done well for himself, but as he stated earlier he couldn't have done it alone. It took several people who believed in him to allow his dream to become a reality.

Andy is known as the "Iron Man" of the Pennzoil World of Outlaws series. His record of 540 consecutive "A-Main" starts is not likely to be broken. Some of the highlights of his career are: first sub 10 second lap in sprint car history; 1988 "Rookie of the Year"; -24 Career "A Main Feature" wins, two time Gold Cup Champion; -finishing third in World of Outlaw points in 1994; -1998 U.S. Dirt Nationals Champion and 1998 winner of the "Springfield Mile."

In our interview I found Andy to be much more than a race car dnver. He is an extremely nice guy who has an incredible love for his family. He is a father of three which include his 10 year old daughter Sawyer (adorable name), his 7 year old son Drew and his 4 year old son Hayden.

The only downside of his racing he says is when he has to be away from his family. He doesn't know how long he will continue to travel the race circuit. He realizes his children are growing up quickly and he refuses to miss out on those cherished moments. He knows they will only be around for a few short years as they, too, find their own way into adulthood.

Becky Hobbs *Singer/Songwriter*

How does a 16 year old girl from Bartlesville, Oklahoma end up a few years later traveling all over the world writing and performing hit songs?

Becky Hobbs has often been referred to as a female Jerry Lee Lewis with her ability to tickle those ivorys. Jerry Lee Lewis had inspired Becky when she was nine years old during one of his concerts in Bartlesville. Years later she became part of one of his concerts as the opening act.

Coming from a small town like Bartlesville, it was almost unheard of for Becky to form an all girl band called the "Four Faces of Eve" when she was 15 years old. Her love of music had drawn her to take piano lessons and learn to play the guitar. At the same time, Becky had a flair for the world of art. However, after a year of college her musical abilities won out over academics and art.

She hit the road with the all girl band who by then had changed its name to " The Sir Prize Package." Night clubs and honky tonk bars became her classrooms as she continued to hone her talents. Eventually the all girl band parted ways, but Becky was still in pursuit of a performing career.

After a brief time in Baton Rouge, Louisiana with a male band called "Swampfox," Becky moved to Los Angeles where she lived for nine years. During that time she and her friend Lewis Anderson co-wrote her first recorded song sung by Helen Reddy. The song was *I'll Be Your Audience* and from there she went on to later write three more songs recorded by Helen Reddy. Becky knew she was finally on her way to a bonified song writing career.

She began writing songs for Al Gallico who was at the time the number one country music independent song publisher. Al was convinced that Becky had great talent as a performer and songwriter. So he introduced her to Jerry Kennedy in Nashville who signed her with Mercury Records. Becky wrote and performed her first single in 1978 called, *I Can't Say Goodbye To You,* which won the American Song Festival Award.

In 1980, she decided rather than fly back and forth from Los Angeles to Nashville she would just relocate to Nashville the town known for songwriters. She began recording songs with Capitol Records and before long she performed a duet with Moe Bandy called, *Let's Get Over Them Together*, which went Top 10 in Billboard Magazine. The whole time, Becky continued to write songs for other performers and became fairly good at developing hits for people like Alabama, Conway Twitty, George Jones, Glen Campbell and John Anderson to name a few.

Her song, *I Want To Know You Before We Make Love,* co-written with Candy Parton went number one when sung by Conway Twitty. Yet the song she says has been her biggest blessing was one she co-wrote with Don Goodman called, *Angels Among Us,* sung by Alabama. The song was inspired by Becky's own experience and has also been part of a television show hosted by Patty Duke several years ago called, "Angels, The Mysterious Messengers."

This year, TNN aired a show called "Angels" which featured Becky singing *Angels Among Us.*

Becky's career as a recording artist has brought her 19 chart singles. She was named Cashbox Magazine's Independent Country Music's Female Artist of the Year in 1994. Becky loves performing internationally, something many artists won't do because you take a cut in pay. Yet in 1992, Becky had the privilege of performing in nine countries in Africa and all over

Europe.

In 1996, Becky married Duane Sciacqua, a talented guitarist/songwriter. Duane plays guitar with Glenn Frey (of the "EAGLES") and has played with Paul McCartney, Joe Walsh, Bruce Willis and Don Johnson. He has also composed and played on numerous television and movie tracks, including "Hotshots" and "Cobra." Becky and Duane are currently writing and recording together. They have a web site that may be interesting to click onto-songs.com/beckyhobbs.

Becky prides herself in always trying to put on a high energy show. She plays the accordion, guitar and piano, which makes the show quite versatile. Just recently Becky once again sang with an all girl band and recorded a few songs with the help of another well known Nashville songwriter, Jim Lauderdale.

I listened to Becky's CD's she sent to me and was extremely impressed with her talent. She is adorable with a fun filled, bubbly spirit. I cried through the love song she wrote about her parents called, *She Broke Her Promise*, which is a tribute to the love her parents shared before her father's death in 1982.

It's impossible to sit still when Becky begins pounding those piano keys with such speed you wonder if the keys are still intact. We were having a phone interview and she put the phone down while she played a wild and crazy piano song.

Becky has had a wonderful career. She truly believes there is a force from which we all come that allows her to create and sing songs. To Becky, that force is God. Becky believes she was born to write and says when she is digging in the dirt she has written some of her best songs.

Darla Hood

Actress

Any adult would almost have to be living on another planet to have never heard of "The Little Rascals." It still amazes me how films like "The Little Rascals" were so well liked in their heyday, yet for some reason society feels they have evolved with such maturity that the wholesome, moral scripts of the past no longer interest us.

Darla Jean Hood was the cute little four year old who replaced Jackie Lynn Taylor when she had grown too tall for the part.

Darla was born on November 4, 1930 in Leedey, Oklahoma, a small town with a population less than 400. Her mother, like so many mothers, saw "star quality" in her little darlin' and enrolled her at the Duffy Dance Studio in Oklahoma City. Her singing and dancing abilities seemed extraordinary for such a small child. Her teacher at the studio was so impressed with her talents that she took her on a trip to New York City.

While staying at the Edison Hotel in Times Square they had the opportunity to attend a performance by the hotel band. After seeing the cute little dark haired child in the audience, the band leader invited her to sing and conduct the orchestra just for fun. Of course the audience loved her. At that moment Darla began experiencing what we all know as a defining moment

in her life. It just so happened that Joe Rivkin, casting director for the Hal Roach Studios in Hollywood, was in the audience. He didn't waste any time setting up a screen test for Darla with Hal Roach. Needless to say, Hal was thoroughly impressed with the little cutie and signed her to a seven year contract with a salary of $75 per week.

Her father, J.C. Hood was a bank officer in Leedey who wasn't particularly thrilled about Darla entering show business, but finally consented to give it a try. Within the first year not only was Darla performing quite well on "The Little Rascals," but other jobs became available for her as well.

Her life seemed incapable of disappointments until 1942 when "The Little Rascals" series came to an end. Darla was stunned. She was 11 years old and the past seven years had been spent with only a few children surrounded by a maze of adults. All of a sudden she found herself having to adjust to being a "normal" kid that was no longer being fussed over for being so adorable. Instead of being tutored on the set she was enrolled in a public school like the millions of other youngsters that were normally glued to their television sets engaged in the antics of "The Little Rascals."

In spite of the shows demise, Darla managed to continue working in the entertainment business, but with less acclaim than what she had once experienced. She formed a singing group called "Darla Hood and the Enchanters." Their backup singing for 1940's films kept Darla's talents active and began opening other doors for her in the business. She wrote songs and cut over a dozen recordings. She later performed nightclub acts at the Copacabana in New York, the Coconut Grove in Hollywood and the Sahara in Las Vegas.

Jose Granson, her manager and a music publisher, became Darla's husband in 1957. Together they shared two children, son Brett and daughter Darla Jo. Marriage to Jose opened other doors for Darla. She began doing voice-overs and television commercials for some of the leading products companies like Campbell Soup and Chicken-of-the-Sea.

As a resident of North Hollywood Darla was looked upon as a nice person and a quality woman. She was only 49 years old when she entered the Parkwood Hospital and died on June 13, 1979. Some reports say she had hepatitis while others say she had a heart attack. Either way she will always be remembered as the dark haired cutie with the baby doll smile who captured the hearts of millions, especially "Alfalfa."

Darla's childhood home still remains in the small town of Leedey, which sets halfway between Elk City and Woodward.

Cluff Hopla – Scientist

It was a blessing meeting with Dr. Cluff Hopla in November 1999. His demeanor was that of a humble man who was by every evidence very qualified for his position and yet graciously accepting it with thanksgiving. It was a pleasure to visit with him during the short time of our interview and be reminded that quality men do sit in high places.

Cluff Hopla was born on December 28, 1917 in Mapleton, Utah a small town at the base of what he describes as a very beautiful mountain in the Wasatch range. Mapleton had a grade school through the eight grade and then students were transported to Springville for junior high and high school.

As a youngster Cluff was very close to his mother Lilly, his four sisters and his older brother. He never knew his biological father other than the fact he had some Chiricahua Apache ancestry. I'm sure that is why Cluff always dreamed of completing an authentic biography of Cochise, the Chiricahua Apache Leader.

His mother married a man by the name of David, but a father and son relationship never developed. Cluff was cruelly informed early on by David that he did not consider him as his son. Some years later when Cluff reached a level of success he remembered those words and realized it was one of the greatest reliefs he had ever incurred.

Pain when it is being inflicted always hurts, but I have found it also makes you strong. In so many of the interviews I have been privileged to conduct I have found time and time again that hardships and pain have most generally been a part of a successful person's life.

At the age of 10 Cluff had the opportunity to read a book by Sir Ronald Ross on the discovery of malaria parasites and the history of it. It made such an impact on him that he decided right then he wanted to be a malariologist. He wanted to find out how diseases like tularemia, brucellosis and rocky mountain spotted fever were transmitted and how they were maintained in nature. From then on he oriented himself in that direction, making sure that his education prepared him for that eventual outcome.

When he was in high school he worked with Mr. Joseph Bagley in a bee and honey business to earn money to help prepare himself for his future. He learned to rear queen bees which obviously was quite an experience.

Even though he hated leaving his mother behind, he was anxious when the time came to enroll in college and continue his medical pursuits. As an undergraduate at Brigham Young University he took a lot of courses in what they then called bacteriology and immunology, thinking it would help him in the direction he wanted to pursue. He learned to bleed lizards and other reptiles in order to take blood smears for diagnosis of different species of malaria parasites.

Cluff received his bachelor of science degree from Brigham Young University in 1941. He then entered the United States Navy as a Pharmacist's Mate, 2nd Class. Just by chance he says, but I believe it was destiny. Cluff was assigned to the field of malariology. The Navy thought he was too inexperienced to really contribute much, but Cluff was able to set up a clinical lab in Del Monte. His abilities were so advanced that he was quickly recognized by his superiors and offered a commission. He served as a malariologist in the Navy from 1942 to 1946.

The Navy sent him to New Guinea and for a while he thought there was a possibility that his work would be in the far reaches of the world. His wife Moyra was a registered nurse and there were thoughts of the two of them making a team in the foreign fields. However, Moyra found that her interests lie more in raising a family then in the primitive regions of New Guinea. Cluff separated from the Naval Reserve in 1958 with the rank of Lt. Commander.

In 1946 he returned to Brigham Young University where he received his masters of Science degree in 1947. After visiting several graduate programs at various universities, he selected the University of Kansas where he worked with Professor Cora Downs in Microbiology and Professor Charles Michener in Eutomology, both imminent scientists in their respective fields. There Dr. Hopla had the freedom to explore tick transmission of tularemia and other pathogenic organisms. He then went on to receive his Ph.D. from the University of Kansas in 1950.

Dr. Cluff Hopla arrived at the University of Oklahoma in 1951 as an assistant professor of zoology and public health, when the School of Public Health was just being developed on the Norman Campus.

From 1955 to 1972 he was involved in the study of the ecology of tularemia in Alaska. He studied the feeding habits of subarctic and arctic mosquitoes to understand their possible relationship in transmission of virus and tularemia organisms. He was awarded a George Lynn Cross Research Professorship in 1970, a title he still holds in emeritus status.

At the time of our interview Dr. Hopla was already creeping up on the 50 year mark of his tenure with the University of Oklahoma. Even though he has already retired as an active professor his emeritus position still keeps him very active. In fact, he had just returned from the research field the week prior to our interview.

After 56 devoted years to his lifelong wife and companion Moyra, he lost her to lung cancer. Together he and Moyra raised three obviously talented and gifted children. Rick, born May 8, 1944 is a biochemist, head of the bio-medical research unit, at Olin Research Laboratory in Providence, Rhode Island.   Dan Michael, born October 24, 1952 is a head and neck surgeon in Florence, South Carolina and Anna Kristine, born May 18, 1954 is a doctor of internal medicine and nephrology and has a dialysis clinic in Martin, Tennessee.

Dr. Hopla's credentials are so impressive and lengthy that there is not room in this short profile to expand on them properly. As a renowned scientist he has probably far surpassed the scope of vision he had as a small boy reading a book by Sir Ronald Ross. Dr. Hopla's dedication to his work has no doubt been overlooked by those who have no knowledge of his field of endeavor. Yet his peers and numerous students who have walked alongside him have had the opportunity to experience the integrity of a man whose depth of commitment has left a mark on this world.

I questioned Dr. Hopla on his quiet and soft spoken demeanor, wondering if he had always been that way. *I ask him to explain to me the meaning of humility which I felt radiated from him and asked how he thought a person could establish a humble spirit within themselves. "By being teachable and willing to share with others the knowledge that you've learned."*

I left Dr. Hopla's office that afternoon knowing I was richer for having met him and quite sure the rest of the world would be too.

John Houchin

Business Executive

John was born in Jackson, Mississippi. When he was 3 years old the family moved to Dallas, Texas and when he was 10 they moved to Muskogee, Oklahoma. His father was a highway paving contractor who found himself spending so much time working in Oklahoma while he was living in Dallas that he decided to make Oklahoma his home. At the time Muskogee was a thriving city while Tulsa was just a flag stop on the Midland Valley Railroad.

There were six children in John's family and yet all of them had the opportunity to attend college. After graduating from Muskogee High School, John wanted to become a lawyer. But his father quickly talked him out of that and encouraged him to become a business man instead.

After spending one year in college the stock market crashed and bankrupted his father, so he and John's mother moved to Newton, Illinois which had been his father's hometown. John was left behind and had to quit college and get a job. The following year he married the love of his life, Louise.

After being out of college for three years he decided to return to OU and get a degree in petroleum engineering. Louise had a secretarial job in Muskogee so John made arrangements for her to stay with her parents for a while so he could go to school in Norman. He roomed with some of his fraternity brothers and they gave him a job as the house manager.

After three semesters of being separated from his wife he was determined to make some changes so she could join him in Norman. He noticed the Logan Apartments, a brand new apartment house that had 24 apartments. He thought if he could talk the owner into letting him manage the apartments he would probably be allotted one to live in as well.

The owner happened to be a state senator from Okmulgee named Dave Logan. John knew his friend George Lynde, a banker in Okmulgee, was friends with Senator Logan. So one weekend he hitched a ride to Muskogee and met with the banker, asking him if he would recommend him as a possible manager for Senator Logan's apartments. The banker agreed and immediately got on the telephone and called Senator Logan. He said, " I have a young man in my office who is of sterling quality and he would like a few minutes of your time." John got on the phone and introduced himself and requested a meeting with the Senator Logan to talk about managing his apartments.

The Senator immediately informed John he had a manager and it would be a waste of time to meet. However, John was persistent saying at some point Senator Logan's situation might change and he would like to meet him just in case. The appointment was arranged and he and Louise met with the Senator. Ironically, two weeks later, John got a phone call from Senator Logan saying indeed there was a change in management and he would be needing John after all. They would receive an apartment to live in plus $30.00 a month salary.

John said, "I have lived a long time and I have a lot of memories. Looking back over the years, the times my wife and I cherished the most were the times we sacrificed for what we received."

That following summer Senator Logan was instrumental in John being hired at Phillips Petroleum as a roustabout making $100 a month. During that period of time John and Louise still needed $25 more a month to cover their expenses. John went to George Lynde, the banker that had helped him contact Senator Logan, and asked if he could get a loan that would deposit $25 dollars a month into his account. Mr. Lynde quickly agreed.

When the money arrived every month it was coming from a private account Mr. Lynde had set up just for John. It had nothing to do with an actual bank loan. John soon figured it out and when the school year was over, he and Louise met with Mr. Lynde and his wife to give them the total amount he had borrowed plus interest. Mr. Lynde refused to take the money, saying he did it because he knew John was struggling and he wanted to be part of the struggle. It was a blessing for him to help John and if he gave back the money it would be robbing him of that blessing. He said, " John, just promise me one thing. Some day I want you to do the same thing for somebody else."

John kept that promise. He established the John Houchin Loan Foundation at Oklahoma University. The Foundation is for any student who needs temporary assistance. They can borrow the money at 1% interest.

When John's senior year in college began he went to his roustabout boss and told him he was giving up his summer job to go back to school. His boss informed him some changes had been made and asked him if he would like to stay on and work the 6 p.m. to midnight shift and still make $100 a month. John agreed even though he knew his days would be full and his sleep would be limited.

He needed to find a car since he would be traveling back and forth from OU to the oil fields in Oklahoma City. During the summer there were plenty of opportunities to hitch a ride with someone else, but now that he would be working the late shift, he would have to find his own transportation.

By the following Saturday he had scraped together $75 and took the interurban from Norman to Oklahoma City. He walked up and down the streets looking for a car he could purchase. The place he tried was a Chrysler dealer who at first told him he didn't have a thing. He then remembered a 1928 Ford Model A that had just been traded in. He offered it to John "as is" with no repairs and no shiny wash job. John took it and was grateful.

From 8 a.m. until 5 p.m. he attended classes and from 6 p.m. to midnight he worked the oil fields. That schedule continued throughout his entire senior year in college.

After graduation, Phillips gave John an engineering assignment as a field engineer for the development of the area around the capitol building. He was eventually transferred to Bartlesville. Months turned into years and John continued to be an asset to Phillips Petroleum. He successfully served as Executive Vice President, Chairman of the Executive Committee and President before he was elected Chairman of the Board in 1971. He never set out to become the Chairman of the Board, but with hard work, loyalty and dedication the door was opened for him.

John has been retired for over 25 years. He and his wife Louise raised three successful children, John Jr., Larry and Jane, who credit their father for teaching them at an early age they could have the confidence to become anything they wanted to be if they wanted it bad enough and were willing to sacrifice to get it.

My interview seemed to go by quickly with Mr. Houchin, I guess because I was so interested in his outlook on life. His beloved Louise has gone on to be with the Lord. I know at times that brings him great pain. Yet I'm sure those precious memories fill his heart with comfort with just the mention of her name.

John M Houchin

Jack Hough - Physician

Jack Van Doren Rough was born in 1920 at Lone Wolf, Oklahoma. Before he was 10 his family, consisting of two sisters and his mother and father, moved to Headrick, Oklahoma. At an early age he became a Christian during a revival meeting. I had never heard it put quite this way, but it rings true for many of us. Jack said the night he made his first commitment to God he was actually committing his soul, not his life.

After hearing the preacher say heaven was the ultimate goal, Jack wanted to make sure he was allowed to go there. However, it took him several years later before he realized God wanted more than his soul. He wanted his heart.

Later the family moved to Cameron, Oklahoma where at the age of 16 Jack graduated from high school. He wrestled with the idea of whether to become a lawyer or a doctor until his father made a few comments that encouraged him to lean toward medicine.

In 1936 he enrolled at Southeastern State College in Durant, Oklahoma and majored in pre-medicine. He graduated summa cum laude in chemistry in 1939. By 1940 he had been admitted to the University of Oklahoma School of Medicine. By then, he seldom went to church because his beliefs were changing. He believed more in science than he did in God. At the time it seemed " never the twain, shall meet." He enjoyed the rounds he made at the hospital except when it came time for otolaryngology. He thought that was boring. But he soon found out his likes and dislikes were about to change.

In 1943 toward the end of his medical school training, Jack met his wife Jodie at a dance held at the local Civic Center. A few months later, they were married and Jack was making preparations to leave for a year's internship at the U.S. Navy Hospital in Farragut, Idaho. He was given an officer's commission and after his internship, he was given orders to join the Fourth Marine Division on Maui.

It was 1945 and Jack was assigned as the doctor to an assault battalion of about 1,200 men. The battalion made an amphibious landing on the shores of Iwo Jima. The soldiers were to liberate the island from the Japanese so Iwo Jima could be used as an Allied way station for long-range bombing missions against the Japanese mainland. Mortars and rockets were landing all around them.

Lieutenant Jack Rough continually risked his own safety to administer medical aid to wounded men lying in open areas of the combat zone. Jack was aware that he was being divinely protected, so he recommitted himself to God. Only this time, he committed his whole being, not just his soul. He knew God was protecting him and there was a divine purpose for his life.

In August of 1945 the U.S. dropped atomic bombs on Hiroshima and Nagasaki and Japan surrendered. The war was over. Because of Jack's bravery and dedication on Iwo Jima, he was later awarded the Bronze Star.

After the war, Jack joined the staff of the Oklahoma City Clinic and the Wesley Hospital in 1946. He practiced head and neck surgery, an area of medicine he at one time thought was boring, but now found to be very challenging. He continued to take advanced courses and performed many pioneering surgeries in that field.

In 1954 he was given the opportunity to observe Dr. Samuel Rosen during a surgical procedure that restored the hearing of a patient while on the operating table. The procedure came about by chance while preparing for another type of surgery. Dr. Rosen accidentally shook the stirrup of the ear loose and the patient's hearing improved on the spot.

Jack was so excited he could hardly wait to get back home and begin practicing the technique himself. Jack practiced the procedure on cadavers at the OU medical school. Then one day he performed the surgery on three patients. Within a few weeks, there were an overwhelming number of phone calls being made to Jack's office from hard-of-hearing people asking for appointments. The response was so overwhelming Jack decided to limit his practice to otology, the care of the ears.

Even though this new type of surgery was astounding, it eventually began to diminish in value because 80% of the stirrups were refixing themselves since the disease was still present. Further research was needed.

By 1958 Jack had moved his practice, the Otologic Medical Clinic, next to the new Baptist Medical Center. Since the 1950's Jack had been interested in the pioneering work of Dr. William House in Los Angeles. Dr. House had developed an experimental approach that would allow the profoundly deaf to hear sounds. Their deafness was due to the destruction of hair cells in the cochlea, located in the inner ear.

The nerve for hearing is the nerve that comes from the brain stem. On its end it has little hair cells that produce the electrical energy. When sound waves hit these little hair cells they vibrate and produce electrical energy that goes to the brain. This is what allows a person to hear.

Dr. House had been bypassing the defective hair cells with a cochlear implant and received some results. In 1978 Jack formed his own coclear implant team to help further explore the possibilities. In 1979 he performed his first cochlear implant operation.

Jack's added improvements to the cochlear implant have continued to enhance the lives of thousands of hearing impaired people. The contributions he and his team have made far exceed the boundaries of the United States. They have extended into third world nations where the need is so great.

Jack is now in his 80's. He remembers times during his career when he was always the youngest. Nowadays, he is seen as the elderly one. Inside he doesn't feel any older because his spirit never ages. We all know that to be true, but it never seems to be a factor until the steps seem a little steeper.

Jack's spiritual commitment has never wavered over the years. He and his wife Jodie founded the non-denominational Covenant Community Church in 1980. For the first two years Jack gave most of the sermons until they recruited a dynamic minister to take over.

As I was working on Jack's profile, I was reminded of a story I once heard. A lady who professed to be a strong Christian and admired for her faithful church attendance and Godly ways suddenly became a very rich woman. Almost immediately she quit attending church and signs of her abundance became evident through her array of material possessions. Even her Christian attitude seemed to wane.

When asked whether this woman would have been better off if she had never received such financial gain, the answer came back that it wouldn't have mattered. Money only revealed what was in the heart of the woman anyway.

In Jack Hough's case his financial gain and prestigious advancement only proved to enhance his spiritual enlightenment as his thankful heart brought him closer and closer to God.

Jimmy Houston
Champion Fisherman

Even though Jimmy was born in Texas he grew up in Oklahoma City until his senior year in high school when his family moved to Lake Tenkiller. He graduated from Tahlequah High School and spent four years at Northeastern State University where he graduated in 1966 with degrees in economics and political science. He intended to become a lawyer. However, during his college days, the demands for making a living sort of got him sidetracked. By the time he graduated his life had already begun to take a different turn.

To meet his financial obligations during college Jimmy did everything he could to make money. He worked at the Elk Creek Marina, was a guide on Lake Tenkiller, was a diver, sold fish and just anything he could to make ends meet. Not only was he trying to supply his own needs, but during that time he became a husband to Chris and father to his first child, Sherri.

He said he can't remember when he wasn't involved in fishing. From the time he could walk or hold a fishing pole he was throwing a line into the mystical waters.

In 1966 when he was a senior in college bass tournaments were just beginning. Jimmy won the Oklahoma State Championship that year. The following year BASS, the largest fishing organization in the world, was formed.

Following graduation Jimmy and his wife Chris started an insurance agency which became very successful after the initial struggles of creating a customer base. The agency allowed him the financial stability to pursue what was soon to become a rewarding career for Jimmy.

Until 1975 he was only entering one or two national fishing tournaments a year. But after winning his first title in 1976 as Bass Angler of the Year he began entering all the tournaments and was becoming quite well known.

Because he was busy fishing in tournaments, holding seminars and making speaking appearances Chris was pretty much running the insurance agency herself. Along with managing the agency she also was left with most of the responsibilities of taking care of the children, which now included son Jamie and nephew Richard who had come to live with them when he was three weeks old.

In 1977 Jimmy contracted with ESPN to produce a fishing show called "Jimmy Houston Outdoors." The show has proven to be very successful over the past 24 years. Five years ago he began filming an additional show called "Jimmy's Outdoor World." It's amazing to see how life allows you to progress in knowledge which leads to such tremendous success.

When Jimmy first began working with ESPN he hired a Tulsa production company and signed a contract for $110,000 that would pay for the program's production, music composition, syndication, shooting and editing. Now, 24 years later, he spends half a million dollars just for television time. He formed his own production company in 1981.

To keep those cameras rolling, in addition to his own programming Jimmy Houston Productions produces several outside programs such as "The Tim Hartman Show," "Primetime Outdoors," "Spur of the Moment" and "Outdoors America" among others.

With all Jimmy's many ventures he doesn't have as much time to fish all the tournaments as he used to. Although in 1998, after staying in the top five the whole year, he finished ninth in the nation which is still considered very good.

Chris no longer operates the insurance agency. They sold it after 13 years. The fruits of her labor have allowed her to pick and choose where she wants to spend her time nowadays. Daughter Sherri runs the family travel agency, Jimmy Houston Travel, as well as the scheduling for her Daddy's personal itinerary.

With six Jimmy Houston Marine dealerships and a retail store he has created opportunities for Jamie and Richard. Jamie runs the dealership on Lake Tenkiller and Richard runs the retail store. Jimmy also has locations in Broken Arrow, McAlester and Oklahoma City as well as in Bentonville and Little Rock, Arkansas. Sherri's husband, Dower, is the manager of the group of stores. In the future he plans to expand to other states if it continues to be a wise decision.

In 1983 Jimmy and some of his fellow fisherman realized they were missing a lot of church services due to their heavy travel schedules. They got together and formed an organization called FOCAS which stands for Fellowship of Christian Anglers Society. It started out as a Bible study conducted on fishing tournament camp grounds. As it has evolved it has become a ministry with local chapters located throughout the country.

Besides the Bible studies each chapter organizes different events throughout the year to help other individuals. Lake Tenkiller holds a Pastor's Day where they bring in over 40 pastors and treat them to an overnight camping adventure of fishing, feasting and fellowship. They also have a Kids Day once a year where 500 pre-registered children are given a hat, shirt, rod and reel and an exciting time they won't soon forget. All sorts of other events are scheduled throughout the year which allows FOCAS to truly be an outreach and extension of bass fishermen all over the nation.

As if that weren't enough, Jimmy has had the opportunity to have three books published bearing his name. The first book titled *Wit and Wisdom* with Jimmy Houston is an instructional storybook which has become a collector's item. The second, *Caught Me A Big 'Un*, is also instructional as well as humorous. Thirdly, *Hooked on Life*, which I found to be an incredible little book, I would recommend as a gift for any fisherman.

Jimmy believes without a doubt God planned his life. He said if he had prayed for God to do something wonderful with his life, he wouldn't have come close to requesting the incredible opportunities God has given him. He has never been satisfied with status quo, he has to push the limits and see exactly how far God will take him.

It is amazing how those who stretch their faith out far enough to grasp the unattainable actually find out it wasn't that far away after all.

Jimmy Houston

Ralph Uriah Blane Hunsecker

Composer

Ha--ve Your--self a Mer--ry Lit--tle Christ--mas. Who hasn't sung the lines to that all time favorite Christmas song?

Ralph Uriah Hunsecker was the first child of businessman Tracy Mark Hunsecker and his wife, Florence Hazel Wilborn Hunsecker. The Hunsecker's second son, Tracy Mark Hunsecker, Jr., was born August 15, 1921.

Broken Arrow, Oklahoma was the place Ralph grew up knowing as his home and even though success took him many miles away he never forgot his roots. After retirement he moved back to Broken Arrow which became his final resting place on November 13, 1995 at the age of 81.

Ralph's father was the owner of three dry goods stores in Broken Arrow, Bixby and Coweta. Ralph often spent his summers working in one of his

father's stores, but his goal was to create music.

His early school days were spent in Broken Arrow, a suburb of Tulsa. His high school days, however, were the beginning of his journey into stardom. Central High School, which at the time was located in the middle of downtown Tulsa at 6th and Cincinnati, became a hallmark for individuals who would go on to create great success.

When Ralph was 17 his parents took him to New York City to see a Broadway show. That event not only gave him great enjoyment but it hooked him into show business from that very moment. It reminded me of the same type of statement Rue McClanahan made during our interview. *Those are called defining moments, when something that seems so insignificant at the time becomes life changing.*

Ralph's talents became quite obvious very early. During the 1932 Tulsa Central High School Daze Talent Show he wrote, sang and danced with the brilliance of a seasoned scholar. After high school he attended Northwestern University to further enhance his creative abilities.

It wasn't long before he made his way to New York City to put his unique talents to work. Although he was proud of his heritage and the name Hunsecker, he decided a New York marquee could more easily display a shorter name. So he changed his name to Ralph Blane.

He studied music in New York City with Estell Liebling and made friends quickly with other talented students. One of those students was Harry Warren. He and Harry began writing songs together and created Buckle Down Winsocki, a song he completed while riding on a New York train.

Ralph's first job on Broadway was in a singing chorus with a man named Hugh Martin from Birmingham, Alabama in "Hooray for What." They soon formed a partnership, realizing they made a good team. Together they wrote many vocal arrangements for a number of individuals. They worked with Irving Berlin, Van Johnson, Cole Porter, Ethel Merman, Betty Grable and many others.

In 1941 he and Hugh formed a quartet called the Martins that was featured on Fred Allen's radio program. Before long success was meeting them at every corner. They signed a contract with MGM where they wrote and arranged scores for many musical films of the 1940's and 1950's. They wrote the 1941 Broadway hit "Best Foot Forward" which was made into an MGM musical in 1943. Other musical films followed such as "My Dream Is Yours," "My Blue Heaven," "One Sunday Afternoon" and "Meet Me In St. Louis" among others.

Ralph and Hugh were nominated in 1944 for *The Trolley Song* from the movie "Meet Me In St.Louis."

On October 5, 1947 Ralph made his way back to Oklahoma to marry Emma Jo Stage at the home of his brother, Tracy Mark. Then the two of them drove to Beverly Hills, California where they lived for several years. They were the proud parents of one son, George Hunsecker who resides in Broken Arrow.

In 1983 Ralph and Hugh were inducted into the Songwriters Hall of Fame by the National Academy of Popular Music.

Ralph and Emma Jo were married for 45 years before Emma Jo passed away November 13, 1992 at age 75.

I thought it was interesting that Emma Jo was three years younger than Ralph and they both passed away three years apart on the same day, November 13.

Ralph's father, Tracy Mark, Sr. preceded his wife's death Florence who passed away in 1987 at the age of 92.

Ralph's brother Tracy Jr., married Doris Josephine Randolph of Bixby, Oklahoma and they had one daughter, Loulie Jean Hunsecker. Tracy Jr. unfortunately died before his 33rd birthday. Loulie was kind enough to send me a photograph of her Uncle Ralph and offer any help she could in compiling his profile.

Ralph was the recipient of numerous awards including The Richard Rodgers Award, an annual program of the ASCAP Foundation funded by the Richard and Dorothy Rodgers Foundation and ASCAP. The ASCAP Richard Rodgers Award was conceived by the late Dorothy Rodgers as a way to recognize veteran composers and lyricists of the American Musical Theatre.

Todd Huston

Mountain Climber

Life never ceases to amaze me. I whine and cry about most things that don't go my way and then I meet someone like Todd and have to remind myself how incredibly shallow I can be.

Courage is defined in Webster's Dictionary as mental or moral strength to persevere and withstand danger, fear or difficulty. Todd has certainly gained the right to wear that badge proudly.

At age 14 Todd endured what most of us only read about in books. A boating accident which injured his legs soon changed the course of his life forever. Yet Todd had the courage to turn his obstacles into mountaintop experiences that leave us all awestruck by his tremendous tenacity.

The well-known Lake Tenkiller in Tahlequah, Oklahoma was a place Todd and his family had enjoyed often as a get-away vacation spot. But on this particular day it was anything but enjoyable. It was Todd's turn to show the family once again what a great time he could have being swept along the rippled waters as his skis took flight. But without warning what was meant to be a fun-filled afternoon turned into a real life nightmare.

Todd's family and friends were oblivious to the struggle he was enduring as they sat laughing and talking inside the boat. Somehow the engine had slipped into reverse and the boat was drifting backwards toward Todd. Tangled in the tow rope, he began helplessly fighting against the threat of the propellers that were coming closer and closer toward him.

Then it happened. The propellers struck his legs and began pulling him into the force. By the time his father was able to pull him into the boat both legs had been severely damaged. Miraculously, a doctor and a nurse happened to be at the lake that day. Without their quick thinking and excellent care, Todd might not be alive today.

After emergency surgery doctors commented Todd had lost three-fourths of his blood, had 40 stitches in his left leg and not enough skin on his right leg to close the wound completely. During the eight weeks he was hospitalized he endured 28 additional surgeries. Only time would tell the future outcome of his injuries.

As Todd's 9th grade of school began it was hard for him to sit on the wooden bleachers and watch his buddies catch football passes and tackle quarterbacks. But his parents kept reminding him of how lucky he was to be alive. At the time, it was hard for Todd to grasp the reality of that statement, but over the course of the next few years he found out they were right.

In his junior year of high school he went through several operations to get skin grafts to take on the back of his right leg, but it was never quite good enough. His right leg remained paralyzed below the knee because the propeller had cut the sciatic nerve. He was constantly trying to fight infections and by the time he was a sophomore in college the problems with his leg were only intensifying. With much regret Todd realized the only thing he could do was go along with the suggestion of doctors and have his leg partially amputated.

At 21 years old he was fitted for an artificial leg. Now he would have the challenge of not only learning how to walk on the artificial leg, but how to deal with his emotions as well. He had been through so much in the past eight years, none of which was easy. But he was finding out with the help of God just how strong and courageous he could be.

He went back to college, eventually became a psychotherapist and began using his professional skill and personal experience to help other amputees and their families. He also trained health care professionals to work with individuals coping with loss.

In 1994 Todd decided to take his message of courage and overcoming obstacles to a different level. As an amputee he set a world record by climbing the highest elevations in each of the 50 states in only 67 days, shattering the original record by 35 days.

Todd has written a book titled *More Than Mountains* which gives an account of his boating accident and his incredible feat of climbing 50 mountains. I guess either because I am a female or because I am very much opposed to causing myself any undue pain, I find it hard to understand why Todd would put himself through such an excruciating ordeal of climbing those mountains. Yet in doing so he has become an example for all of us that with faith in God it is possible to overcome our disabilities and obstacles.

Todd shares candidly in his book about his relationship with God and how grateful he is that God has brought him through so many trials.

Todd's story has appeared in thousands of newspapers throughout the world, on major television networks and numerous radio programs. He has been featured in *Sports Illustrated,* on the CBS special "Year in Sports" and has been a guest on Dr. Robert Schuller's program. He has been honored with several distinguished awards including the Henry Iba Award for Outstanding Citizen Athlete, the Class Act Award and one of the U.S. Jaycees Ten Outstanding Young Americans for 1999.

He is a positive, dynamic, inspirational speaker who is highly sought after for his upbeat approach to overcoming challenges in life.

Most recently Todd entered the political arena when he was elected to serve on Tulsa's City Council. No doubt Todd will be able to make his presence known in a favorable way during his tenure in office. It is hard to be around Todd and not feel a sense of wanting to better yourself or stretch your limits.

Todd and his wife Cindy also share a sweet little son they named Joshua. I had the privilege of meeting Joshua when he was only a few months old. The immense pride of his father could only be overshadowed by the cute little smile on Joshua's face.

If you have a chance to meet Todd or attend one of his speaking engagements you will indeed be inspired. He is one of a kind and definitely worthy to be called a "Distinguished Oklahoman."

Wanda Jackson

Country Music Legend

God doesn't make them any better than the legendary Queen of Rockabilly, Wanda Jackson. I had the privilege of seeing Wanda in concert and interviewing her at her home in March, 2001. What a beautiful lady she is inside and out.

Wanda's entrance into the music world began at an early age. Her cousin Betty Lou Ledbetter, who was five years older than her, began teaching her yodel songs when she was nine years old. The small town of Maud, Oklahoma where Wanda was born on October 20, 1937 had no idea that in a few short years Wanda would introduce the world to a whole new way of experiencing the sound of country music.

A departure from Oklahoma for a few short years gave the Jackson family, comprised of Tom, Nellie and Wanda, an opportunity to experience another part of the United States.

The work situation in Oklahoma had forced Tom to find another way to provide for his family, so he took a job in California working for North American Aviation, Inc.

Tom's continued love for country music soon led the family to attend country and western dances in local Los Angeles ballrooms. In those days many couples took their children along with them while they danced the night away to music by Tex Williams or Bob Wills and the Texas Playboys.

Wanda's love for music increased as she sat wide-eyed next to the stage watching bands perform while her mother and father glided across the ballroom floor. Before long she was voicing her desire to someday be a country singer like the girls she saw performing in the bands. Since Tom was a fiddle player he loved the interest Wanda was showing in country music. He bought her a small Stella guitar when she was 6 years old, but it was hard for her to play because her fingers were still too short to reach around the neck of the guitar to play the frets. But that didn't keep her from singing and spending many hours of enjoyment with her father in their weekly family jam session.

When the war came to an end Tom left the Aviation company and completed schooling to become a barber and a very good one at that. With some of his earnings as a barber he purchased an upright piano so Wanda could start taking lessons. With the long tiring hours Tom spent on his feet cutting other people's hair, he was too tired at the end of the day to engage in the excitement of the dances the family had grown to love.

After a few years Tom's feet became increasingly more sensitive to the long hours of standing and he was forced to make another career change. In 1948 they loaded up their 1946 Pontiac and headed down the highway back to their home state of Oklahoma. This time they set up housekeeping in Oklahoma City which was 65 miles from Maud. Tom got a job as a taxicab driver and Nellie hired on as a seamstress for a local interior designer.

By now Wanda had lost interest in the piano. She was ready to see if her fingers had grown enough to make the guitar an easier instrument to play. Nellie began entering Wanda in talent contests whenever one was made available and of course Wanda could outshine anyone who was competing.

In 1951 the local radio station KLPR sponsored a talent contest. Anyone who could carry a tune was encouraged to participate. Wanda's rendition of Jimmie Rodger's *Blue Yodel #6* won her a 15-rninute on-air spot. The radio station liked her singing so well they put her on "Cousin Jay's Mountain Jamboree" as well as "Uncle Willie's Country Show." Before Wanda was out of high school she was learning first hand what it meant to be in the music business.

In the ninth grade she wrote her first song titled *If You Knew What I Know*, followed by *You'd Be The First One To Know.*

One afternoon when she was closing her guitar case preparing to leave the radio station, she was informed she had an important phone call. On the other end of the line was the number one country recording artist of the nation, Hank Thompson. Wanda stood in amazement as Hank complemented her on her radio performance. But nothing was more exciting than when he invited her to sing with him and the Brazos Valley Boys at the Trianon Ballroom that Saturday night.

Bob Wills had established the Trianon Ballroom as his southwest headquarters in the early 1950's and it was one of the hottest spots around. Wanda was a smashing hit that night and from then on she played occasionally with Hank Thompson. Other doors began opening for Wanda as well. She was beginning to be known as the young, dark headed girl singer that could bellow out notes that rang powerfully through the atmosphere of the night.

Before long, she was invited to perform each week on KWTV Channel 9 with a live audience that gathered around to hear Wanda's unique style of singing. This young high school girl was catching Oklahoma by surprise and there was no stopping point in sight. While her father escorted her to her nightspot performances her mother diligently used her seamstress skills to design dresses for Wanda that would wow the crowds.

In early March 1954 an additional highlight was added to Wanda's quickly rising fame. Hank Thompson helped her secure a recording contract with Decca Records where she remained for two years before signing with Capitol Records for the next 18. The songs *You Can't Have My Love* and *Lovin' Country Style* set Wanda on the road to continued success.

Those early years put Wanda Jackson on an escalating musical career that has spanned over 47 years. She fondly recalls her first meeting with Elvis Presley, the up and coming 20 year old good looking rock and roll singer who would soon become a legend in his own time. Their paths crossing led to a two year relationship which included a ring given to Wanda by Elvis (which she still has today) signifying his affection for her. He also influenced Wanda to add a little rock and roll to her country style. This opened the door for her to become the Queen of Rockabilly music.

Eventually their careers took them in opposite directions. A few years later Wanda fell in love and married Wendell Goodman who not only proved to be the love of her life, but took on the role as her manager and booking agent as well.

In 1971 after Wanda and Wendell had shared 10 years of their life together, another event occurred that would forever change the course of their lives. While back in Oklahoma for a few days, before returning to their busy touring schedule, they were asked by their young children Gina and Greg to join them in church that morning along with Wanda's mother. Even though Wanda and Wendell were members of the church their thoughts had not always included acknowledgment of God in their everyday lives. But on that particular morning God obviously had set a plan in motion. As they both sat together in the church pew Wanda felt God's presence wooing her to begin acknowledging Him and walking in His presence. She turned to Wendell and said, "Honey, there is something I have to do."

Well, in keeping with the scripture "He doeth all things well," God had simultaneously been dealing with Wendell as well. Wendell's reply back to Wanda was, "Me too." Together they gave their hearts to the Lord and their lives have never been the same. As a testament to the validity of their commitment, I can tell you first hand that Wanda and Wendell have a presence about them that only the Lord has the ability to reveal.

Over the years Wanda has continued to share with audiences in the states and abroad songs that will forever link her as a country music legend. When you hear songs like *Right or Wrong* (which she penned), *Stupid Cupid, Let's Have A Party* and *A Little Bitty Tear*, you know you've been plugged into an era that produced the entrance of greatness into country music history.

Wanda is not only a legend, she is an icon for country music. She has been nominated for the Grammy Award twice as the best performing female singer. She has been inducted into The Oklahoma Country Music Hall of Fame, The Rockabilly Hall of Fame, The International Gospel Music Hall of Fame, The Oklahoma Music Hall of Fame and has been awarded The Oklahoma Native Daughter Award. Her biography is scheduled to be out in the future which will only enhance the visions of grandeur Wanda has been privileged to attain.

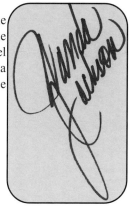

Jane Jayroe

Miss America / T.V. Personality

The small town of Hammon in western Oklahoma awakened one morning to the gentle cries of Jane Jayroe as she made her entrance into this world. Who could have known that several years later she would be crowned Miss America? Her family life growing up must have been extremely comforting. As Jane describes her parents, Pete and Helene, and her sister, Judy she does so with a great sense of pride.

Since her sister was five years older she was often off doing other things which gave Jane a lot of time to herself. It was then that her imagination kept her busy. In spite of the fact she was a shy child, she always felt as if some day she would be performing and entertaining people. Yet for a while the only audience consisted of birds perched high among the trees that seemed somewhat interested as she acted out fantasies in her mind.

The summer before her freshman year of high school the family moved to Laverne. Jane's father was a coach and her mother a teacher so she was always surrounded by an academic atmosphere. Therefore, it was never a question whether or not she would go to college.

She was active on a girl's basketball team which happened to be one of the best teams in the state. Jane believes the stress and pressure of the competitive environment helped form her for the years to come. Realizing that losing was part of winning and she would have to work hard for her rewards prepared her for the road that lay ahead.

Jane's family was active in the Methodist Church and believed it was important to use the talents God has given you. For Jane, those talents were singing and playing the piano. So Jane was naturally expected to sing in the church choir. It was really no effort on her part because she loved to sing. She also sang at almost every event in Laverne along with another classmate and good friend, the now well known singer, writer and composer Jimmy Webb.

One of the highlights of the year for many young girls growing up, including Jane, was the Miss America pageant shown on television. Each year she would sit up close to the television in her living room and attentively watch the pageant. Every time they crowned the new Miss America Jane would cry. She was amazed that some young girl in some little town would be chosen amongst many to live out what seemed to be a Cinderella story.

During Jane's senior year in high school she entered the Miss Laverne Pageant along with several of her classmates. They were judged according to their talent, interview and evening gown. Of course Jane won. She attributes her winning mainly to the fact she was more familiar with performing on stage than most of the other girls. She then entered the Miss Cinderella pageant representing Laverne at Northwestern State College in Alva and won. The winner was to receive a scholarship to Northwestern but Jane wanted to go to Oklahoma City University because it is a Methodist school and its reputation for music have always been so tremendous. She went to OCU and majored in music education. She worked part-time in the journalism department but never really thought about a career in journalism.

In her freshman year at OCU Jane's sorority nominated her for the All College Basketball Queen and she won. In her sophomore year she was asked to enter the Miss Oklahoma City Pageant. She hadn't intended to enter until her junior or senior year, but one of the officials encouraged her to get the experience so she could go on to the Miss Oklahoma Pageant. She won again.

Every title seemed to come so quickly and easily. In June of the same year she won Miss Oklahoma and the following September she became the reigning Miss America of 1967. Suddenly she was an immediate nationwide celebrity. No longer were her queenly duties limited to the confines of the state of Oklahoma. They were far reaching and ever demanding.

Jane said she always cringed during her reign as Miss America when she was introduced as the most beautiful girl in America because she didn't feel like she was. She believes what is inside of a person, how you feel about the people around you and what you think about yourself is so much more important. As Miss America, every girl has the opportunity to create her own identity. One girl's contribution may be different than another girl but each is important. Each girl in some way has had the opportunity to contribute something to the Miss America title.

Jane pointed out the most interesting aspect of winning all her different titles was she never expected to win any of them. She won because she wasn't obsessed with winning. She just loved the opportunity to perform and the excitement of competition. Her enthusiasm would overflow into her performance and the judges would declare her the winner. The shy little girl had finally begun to see the fantasies of her mind turn into reality and she was enjoying every minute of it.

During her reign as Miss American she had to drop out of college for one year, but her time was well spent and life changing. The travel, education, talking under pressure and experience of living under such unique situations prepared her for the next phase of her life.

She resumed her classes after her reign and remained at OCU for the next two years. During college she married Paul Peterson and they eventually moved to Tulsa where Jane received a master's degree in humanities from the University of Tulsa. She spent the rest of her time performing in musical theater and assuming roles in commercials.

On July 4, 1976 her son Tyler was born, but by the end of the year her marriage had ended in divorce and she and her son moved to Oklahoma City.

After a year working for the state Department of Education Jane was offered a position as news anchor for Channel 5 in Oklahoma City. It was an incredible time for her. She loved her on-air responsibilities. Two years later she was offered another news anchor position in Dallas, Texas where she stayed for four years. By 1984 she was growing increasingly homesick for Oklahoma so she moved back and took a position as news anchor for Channel 4 and eventually for Channel 5 once again.

By the time Tyler was a senior in high school, Jane had married Gerald Gamble and she resigned her television anchor position. Even though she loved television she was enjoying the normalcy of not having to work until 11 o'clock at night.

She became the first spokesperson for the Oklahoma Health Center and vice president of the Presbyterian Health Foundation. She also became co-host of the weekly "Discover Oklahoma" statewide television show promoting Oklahoma's tourism attractions and travel opportunities.

In 1999 she received a call from Governor Keating's office asking if she would like to become the cabinet secretary for tourism and recreation and executive director of the Oklahoma Tourism and Recreation Department, an appointed position. She, of course, accepted and holds that position to date.

Jane has had an interesting and rewarding life thusfar. However, she said she has also had her share of trials and disappointments like we all have. She said her faith in God and His ability to carry her through every situation has made all the difference.

I thought it was inspiring that she saw disappointments and trials as gifts. She quoted the scripture "...all things work together for the good..." *She saw her trials as tempering her fear of failure and altering her sense of self pride, not self confidence. When she went through the fire (somewhat fearful) and came out without being singed she became stronger and more confident because of it.*

I thoroughly enjoyed my interview with Jane. Even though it has been several years since she was crowned Miss America, she has never lost the grace and poise we find synonymous with the title.

Dennis Jernigan
Singer/Songwriter

I first learned about Dennis while listening to a radio interview between he and David Warren Ingles on KNYD. I was so impressed with his spiritual outlook and his desire to share his intimate life conflicts with others that I decided his story had to be included.

Dennis was born in Sapulpa, Oklahoma. Soon after his birth his parents Robert and Peggy Jernigan moved to the farm where Robert's parents, Samuel and Myrtle had raised him. They lived three miles from the small town of Boynton, Oklahoma where Dennis and his brothers attended school.

At a very early age Dennis realized he was gifted to play the piano. By the time he was nine years old he was regularly playing for the worship service at First Baptist Church. This was also the church his grandfather, Herman Everett Johnson, had pastored and the church his father, Robert, had led singing in and presently does today.

When Dennis was six or seven years old, his Grandmother Jernigan moved back to the farm in a trailer next to the old farmhouse where Dennis lived. Each day after school Dennis could be found at his grandmother's house practicing piano. It was through his Grandmother Jernigan that the Lord taught him to play the piano. Since they lived so far from any town with a music teacher, he learned to play by ear.

After high school graduation Dennis enrolled at Oklahoma Baptist University. Because of his lack of musical training while growing up, his musical studies at OBU were like learning a whole new language. To be able to actually read and write the music he could see or hear was like a whole new world opening up to him. It would prove to be valuable later in life as he began to express his heart and feelings in song. Upon graduation from OBU in 1981, Dennis spent the summer traveling with a promotional team for the university. While making plans to continue his education by attending a seminary in Louisville, Kentucky a former friend from OBU called and invited him to come and live with them in their family home in Del City, Oklahoma. Since Dennis was not real sure of his decision to go to Louisville, he decided to take his friend's offer in preparation for the next step God was leading him on. When he arrived in Del City his first order of business was to find a job. After spending four years to attain a degree, the only job he could get was driving a school bus. He was soon to find out that even in that God had a plan. He had an early morning route and an afternoon route with several hours to kill in between. He decided to use those hours wisely. He put his Bible on the piano during those in between hours, opened it to Psalms and did what David did. He simply got honest with God. This is where he learned to be a song receiver. He learned to wait on God and sing what he felt or sensed from God.

Dennis kept a journal in which he wrote his deepest, darkest and most intimate thoughts-about anything-out in the open before God. He wrote of hurts, disillusionments, failures, emotions and anything else he felt needed to come out. What he discovered in the process was that God really was concerned about his feelings, whatever they might be, and however dark they might seem.

Soon Dennis began to realize God's love for him was not based upon how well he performed in this life but upon his recognition of God's abiding presence in his life. Dennis realized there was nothing he could do to earn God's love because He loved him no matter what.

Dennis realized his job was simply to seek God's heart. As he became more and more free in his expression to God, others seemed to be drawn to God as well. Dennis formed a trio and for two years they sang and traveled statewide.

In 1983 Dennis fell in love and married Melinda Marie Hewitt. Soon after they were married the babies started coming until nine were joyously filling their home.

Dennis has a unique ministry as a Psalmist. He has endured many emotional conflicts in his spiritual journey toward finding where he truly fits in the plan of God. His insights to who God really is and his own relationship with the Creator has brought healing to himself as well as numerous others who take time to listen with their heart to what Dennis has to say.

In this short profile I didn't think I would do him or God justice by revealing those conflicts that were so heart wrenching for Dennis. Yet I believe with all my heart Dennis has a message to convey to people everywhere of the tender mercies and unwavering love that God has for each one of us. Therefore, I encourage everyone to read Dennis' books *This Is My Destiny* and *A Mystery of Majesty* which reveals an in-depth look at the struggles he has endured and the victories he has won. In doing so, I believe his heart will reveal to you the knowledge of a loving God that you may not have experienced before.

A quote out of one of his books says "*I personally believe that if we find our identity, we will find our destiny. And if we know our identity and our destiny, then we have powerful tools at our disposal for tearing down old habits and for shattering sin's hiding places in our hearts.*"

So often we fear what other people think of us so much that we tie God's hands and keep Him from revealing His plan for our lives. Dennis had a destiny that God had ordained and yet the enemy of his soul set out to stop him. I would like to conclude Dennis' profile with a few quotes that appear on the back of his book *This Is My Destiny.*

Dennis Jernigan has been called the "psalmist of the century" by James Robinson. Jack Hayford called him "one of the purest voices being raised today."

"Two of the strongest evidences of the deity of Christ are the empty tomb and changed lives. Dennis Jernigan is a changed life. Fortunately for us, Dennis has chosen to share his experiences, feelings and insights through music and writings. The expressions of his heart, his vision, and his joy spill over on us and saturate us with the love of God." Dave Rader, Former Head Football Coach, University of Tulsa.

"Dennis displays a thirsting and hunger for God that is not often seen in Christendom today. God has touched him, and he has responded. God has blessed Dennis with gifts that help bring me to worship and praise of the Almighty." Tom A. Coburn, M.D. and former Member of Congress.

Ben Johnson Jr.

Actor

I contacted Ben's sister Helen Johnson Christenson and she was kind enough to include a story about her brother along with a picture.

In 1946, legendary director John Ford and his crew were filming "Fort Apache" in a location Ford was known for using - Monument Valley. Ben Johnson Jr. was acting as a stunt double for Henry Fonda.

One day on the set, "Son" (a nickname given to Ben) was sitting on a horse watching filming of a scene involving a speeding wagon. Things were fine until the wagon turned over, which spooked the team of horses. The wagon headed toward a stonewall. Johnson saw what was happening, rode his horse to the wagon and stopped the runaway team. Not only did he save the team and director riding in the wagon, but also he was awarded a seven year movie contract from Ford's Argosy Pictures at a weekly salary of $5,000. This beat the $50 per month wages he had been making as a ranch hand in the Osage.

Ben Johnson Jr. went to Hollywood as a horse wrangler in 1937 when Howard Hughes hired him to care for 4,000 horses used in the movie, "The Outlaw." Ben spent his first few years as a stuntman and wrangler, doubling for famous actors such as John Wayne, Gary Cooper, Henry Fonda, Jimmy Stewart, Alan Ladd, and Joel McCrea. He also taught many of those same actors how to ride a horse because, after all, he had practically been born on a horse. In fact, he was described as "poetry in motion" when he was astride a horse.

Ben Johnson Jr. was born in 1918 to Ben Johnson Sr. and Ollie in Foraker, Oklahoma. Ben's father, Ben Sr. was foreman of the legendary Chapman-Barnard Ranch in Osage County (now Tallgrass Prairie Preserve), which consisted of approximately 100,000 acres of deeded and leased land. Life on the ranch was not easy; but perhaps this life had a great deal to do with the molding of young Ben's character. Ben had a younger sister, Mary Ann Johnson Miller, who was three years younger, and a half sister, Helen Lee Johnson Christenson.

Ben Jr's, parents were divorced and Ben Jr. did not "take a liking" to school and book learning. He once said the time he spent in school was more time than he wanted to spend there. He did, however, have a great deal of respect for those who received an education and advocated an education for all the young people he came in contact with.

Ben met his wife upon his arrival in California. The horses he was caring for came to the Fat Jones Stables, who supplied livestock, stagecoaches, etc., for the movies. Watching the unloading of horses was Fat's daughter, Carol. Carol asked someone, 'Who is that big jerk?" referencing Ben Jr. And, as it turned out, they were destined to become husband and wife. They celebrated their 50th wedding anniversary just prior to their deaths; Carol in 1994 and Ben in 1996.

Ben's father was world champion steer roper four or five times, so Ben wanted to be. After Ben Sr's death in 1952, Son hit the road. In 1953, he won the world championship in team roping but stated he didn't have $3.00. All he had was a worn-out automobile and a mad wife. He stated many times he was the only cowboy that ever won an Oscar in the movies (for his portrayal of Sam the Lion in "The Last Picture Show") and a world championship in rodeoing. And, he was more proud of the world championship in rodeoing than he was of the Oscar.

Ben and his wife did not have children but they were committed to helping raise money for sick or deprived children. He appeared at many pro-celebrity rodeos in major cities throughout the country and raised millions of dollars on behalf of children.

Ben had roles in over 300 movies, most of them westerns. But he did not receive acclaim until his role in "The Wild Bunch" starring William Holden in 1969. Sam Peckinpah directed the film and Ben described him as a "near lunatic."

"The first time I met him was in 1965 when he asked me to appear in "Major Dundee" with Charlton Heston. I went to his office to meet him, and I was sitting across the desk from Sam when a stuntman came in. Well, Sam abused him something terrible, yelling at him. He did it there, in front of me, and when the man walked out, I just said, "I can't work for you." He said, "Why not?"

I said, ""If you did to me what you did to that man there, I'd hit you right in the d--n nose and you'd run me out of the business, and I'm not that ready to leave." "Well", Sam said,"I'm not that bad. I was just trying to scare him a little." Ben described Peckinpah as a pretty talented guy but he didn't care much about life.

"Some of what he did, showed that he didn't care much about the outcome as long as the movie had blood and guts and thunder. He was pretty nuts. I saved his life about a dozen times, I guess. He would start drinking whiskey and taking pills, and he'd go crazy. He'd go into a bar, walk through the place, find the biggest guy there, and pick a fight with him. He was crazy."

Ben was, on the other hand, eminently sane, which is why, some say, he never became a big celebrity in Hollywood. He was never known as a phony and his ego never got in the way of his being "just Ben Johnson." He always said he didn't have to act; he just played Ben Johnson. He considered his Dad his hero and, as such, he could not have had a more real, bigger-than-life image to model his life after.

His roots in Osage County went deep. He always wanted to come home but said he didn't know how he would make a living. Funny, because he never did buy into the Hollywood scene and never really had a desire to be an actor. He said he could always make a living working on a ranch or in a rodeo but, perhaps his life proves there is a plan for each of us. And, we are not in charge of that plan.

Jennifer Jones

Actress

Phylis Lee Isley was born March 2, 1919 in Tulsa, Oklahoma. Her parents, Phil and Flora Mae, owned and operated a small acting troop called the Isley Stock Company. They would tour small towns outside of Tulsa and perform plays for 10 cents a patron. It was in this environment that young Phylis decided she wanted to be an actress.

The Isleys moved to Oklahoma City in September 1925. Phylis enrolled in the Edgemere Public School and made her acting debut as a peppermint candy cane in a school play.

The Isleys made good money during that time and in 1929, when the stock market crashed, Phil Isley used the money he had made to buy up several independent movie theaters and equip them with sound. It was a smart investment and Isley's chain of theaters paid off nicely. Phylis spent many hours in the movie theaters and was determined as ever to become an actress.

After she graduated from Edgemere High School she enrolled in Monte Cassino, a junior college for girls in Tulsa which was run by Benedictine sisters. (Monte Cassino is no longer a college. It holds classes from pre-school through the eighth grade.) However, Monte Cassino has always been considered one of Tulsa's leading educational institutions. Phylis was unlike most of the other girls in that she was more interested in a career than dating boys.

Phil Isley was impressed with his daughter's enthusiasm and suggested she go to Hollywood where his connections might land her a movie contract. Phylis was more interested in Broadway. Her curiosity had been peaked at the age of nine when her parents took her on a trip to New York.

In 1936 she enrolled at Northwestern University in Evanston, Illinois, a college well known for its drama department. She was disappointed, however, with Northwestern. Her courses were not challenging and she felt as though she was wasting her time there. So she decided to attend the American Academy of Dramatic Arts in New York.

To be admitted Phylis had to audition and she chose one scene from Romeo and Juliet and another from Wingless Victory. Her audition went very well and she was admitted as a student in the fall of 1937. Phylis was much happier at the Academy than she had been at Northwestern and her first semester went well. Following Christmas break and a trip back home to Tulsa, Phylis returned for the winter semester in January of 1938. She was about to meet someone who would take her mind off of acting.

When Phylis resumed her classes at the American Academy of Dramatic Arts on January 2, 1938, she met a fellow student from Utah named Robert Walker. They immediately became very close friends. They both shared a passion for acting. As the semester progressed, Robert and Phylis were inseparable. They spent most of their spare time together discussing acting and the theater as well as taking long walks around New York. They shared a common dream to make a living in the craft that they loved best. It was not long before they were in love.

Phylis returned to Tulsa for the summer and Robert stayed in New York to look for work. He was not very successful and in a spur of the moment decision decided to work on a banana boat. It was a subtle indication of Robert's restless nature and unpredictability. Phylis overlooked his odd career move but was surprised when they reunited in the fall and Robert told her he had decided to quit the Academy. He felt it was a waste of his time and thought he could find work on his own. Phylis agreed with him, and much to the dismay of her parents, she quit the school also.

Phil Isley, worried over his daughter's situation, lured her back to Tulsa with a $25 a week radio job. Phylis told him she would accept only if Robert ,was offered the same deal. Isley agreed and the young couple moved to Tulsa. The new job would be a 13 week stint radio program called "The Phylis Isley Radio Theater."

Robert and Phylis were married on January 2, 1939. Phil Isley urged the couple to go to Hollywood. However, even with her father's letters of recommendation, work was hard to find. Phylis eventually found work at the low budget Republic Studios. She was immediately assigned her first film role in a John Wayne "Three Mesquiteer" western called New Frontier. Robert couldn't find work so they soon moved back to New York.

Robert found steady radio work in New York but Phylis could only find a job modeling hats. She also found out she was pregnant. Their first child, Robert Walker, Jr. was born on April 15, 1940. She was soon pregnant again and a second son, Michael Ross was born on March 13, 1941.

One night the couple saw a new play called Claudia. Phylis learned that a search was being conducted for an actress to play the role for the Chicago production. She secured an audition through Robert Walker's agent but was unable to secure the part.

However, David 0. Selznick was searching for someone for the film version. After an upsetting first audition Phylis was offered a seven year contract. Selznick was one of Hollywood's most brilliant independent producers and his resume included such films as King Kong, Dinner At Eight, A Star is Born and Gone With The Wind. Phylis was soon to become his obsession even though he had been married to Irene Mayer (Louis B. Mayer's daughter) since 1930. Selznick was pleased with everything but the name "Phylis Walker." In late January 1942 Phylis became "Jennifer Jones."

Selznick decided not to cast her in the role of Claudia, but she debuted in "The Song of Bernadette" in December of 1943. It was during the filming of that movie that her and Robert's marriage began to fall apart and they divorced in March 1944. Robert didn't cope with the divorce very well. After a lot of problems he died suddenly in 1951 when doctors gave him sedatives following an emotional outburst.

David Selznick's chief concern was the career of Jennifer Jones. Their relationship intensified over the years and they were married July 13, 1949. On August 12, 1954 Jennifer gave birth to their daughter, Mary Jennifer.

In the mid 1950's Jennifer was popular with the public when she did films like "Love Is A Many Splendored Thing" and "Good Morning, Miss Dove." David's health began to deteriorate because of a bad heart and he died on June 22, 1965. Jennifer was devastated, but after a long period of adjustment she finally began to focus on life again.

She met Norton Simon, multi-millionaire art collector one night when she was attending a party. They had a whirlwind romance and were married on May 29, 1971. Unfortunately her daughter Mary Jennifer never quite got over the death of her father and committed suicide at an early age. Norton was diagnosed with Guillain Barre syndrome in 1986 and died on June 1, 1993. Today Jennifer remains active on the Norton Simon Foundation but is not active in the film community.

This information comes from Phillip Oliver's website, who was kind enough to allow me to take advantage of his research.

Kenneth Jones - Old West Memorabilia

I don't remember how I stumbled onto Kenneth Jones and his Butterfield stagecoach, but I'm sure glad I did. Right in the heart of Chouteau, Oklahoma is a little taste of the wild west that a lot of people haven't been privileged to see.

Kenneth is quite an interesting and talented man. He is a native Oklahoman born in Muskogee and raised in Turley. He went to high school in Tulsa and has lived in the house he built in Chouteau for over 10 years.

He is one of those friendly Oklahoma guys that you could talk to all day and still not run out of things to say. Growing up, he worked alongside his father designing fiberglass boats sold by the Sears Company. Still working part time with his father, in 1951 he went to work for American Airlines, continuing with his creative abilities.

On several occasions American Airlines sent him to trade schools where he learned painting, woodworking and electrical skills. He was a natural at creating something from an idea, a picture or a blueprint. After 35 years at American Airlines he decided to end his tenure and take up a deserved retirement.

His first task was to build a retirement home in Colorado. Then, looking for something else to create, he made a visit to the Cowboy Hall of Fame in Oklahoma City. He set his sights on making a stagecoach like the one displayed there from the 1850's. They say the only difference in Kenneth's stagecoach and the original Butterfield coach on display at the Cowboy Hall of Fame are the scars from where Indian arrows struck it during Butterfield's many tangles with the Plains Indians.

Butterfield's stagecoach carried U.S. mail for three years from Tipton, Missouri through Arkansas and Texas and westward to El Paso, Tucson, San Diego and clear up to San Francisco a route he was known for completing in 23 days.

Kenneth's coach has no plans as of yet to carry mail, but it has on occasion offered a few rides to admiring onlookers.

When I first arrived at Kenneth's home in Chouteau, he took me out to his oversized garage that held his authentic replica of the John Butterfield U.S. Mail Stagecoach. In a limited, uneducated way, I too am interested in things from the past. I guess most of us are to some extent. I was in awe when I saw the stagecoach, knowing that Kenneth had built it himself. It took him 13 1/2 months to finish the project in his spare time.

The coach is made out of oak and is a burnt red and yellow color. He has upholstered the seats with fine leather that puts a great finishing touch on the inside. Both door panels inside and out have mountain scenes that were painted by a talented oil artist. It is reported that the mountain scenes were John Butterfield's trademark, so in keeping with the authenticity of his replica, Kenneth added the scenes as well.

The iron pieces used were all heated and formed by Kenneth. The coach is suspended on two bull hide leather straps that are three inches wide. They were made by Bif Davis, a saddle maker in Salina, Oklahoma. The huge wheels were made by a group of Amish people in Ohio with the front wheels weighing 110 pounds and the back wheels weighing 135 pounds.

Just standing by the stagecoach I could imagine myself in a full length, cinched at the waist dress. I imagined my hair done up in a very stylish French twist, arrayed with a feathered hat and, of course, holding my parasol in one hand as I ever so slightly lifted the hem of my dress to climb into the coach.

Well, so much for that fantasy. The truth is, I have never been too good at roughing it, so it's really better that I am a part of the motorized century instead. However, it was exciting to see all the talent and work that Kenneth put into his stagecoach.

As I looked around the garage, I saw a lifesize wooden Indian that Kenneth had carved by using a chainsaw. Inside his home that he constructed himself, I saw beautiful items he handcarved such as clocks, chandeliers and chairs. Kenneth definitely has a creative mind that has been constantly put to use.

I left Chouteau that afternoon with a little bit of history trivia. The next time I go to a parade, I'm going to watch for the Butterfield Stagecoach and recall once again the story Kenneth told me about the wild west, the U.S. mail and, of course, John Butterfield.

Kenneth Jones

Larry Jones - Child Advocate

I've heard about Larry Jones and "Feed the Children" for more years than I can remember. After talking to Larry, I was able to gain so much more insight into the inner workings of the broadcast I had watched on television.

So often you hear about the sufferings of others and it seems so much easier to turn a deaf ear rather than lend a helping hand to those in need. Larry is originally from Southern Kentucky, but received a basketball scholarship to Oklahoma City University, a Methodist college, in the fall of 1958. At the same time, he decided to enter the field of Christian ministry. Two months before graduating from college, on March 4, 1962 he married Frances, who he calls his Storybook Romance Queen.

Following graduation he toured the Far East playing basketball for a Christian team called Venture for Victory in locations like Japan, Taiwan, Hong Kong and the Philippines. When he returned to the states he began pastoring his first church and did so for two and a half years in Oklahoma City before beginning his in-depth mission work as a revival preacher in 1965.

In 1979 Larry took 13 pastors to Haiti, the poorest country in this hemisphere. Their intentions were to stay a week ministering to the different churches and come back home to resume their same schedules. One night a young boy which they called a street urchin walked up to Larry and asked him for a nickel. Larry asked him why he wanted the money and the boy said he hadn't eaten all day and the nickel would buy him a roll. As Larry reached into his pocket the boy said if you could give me 3 pennies I could cut the roll in half and put butter on it. Then Larry asked, "How much would it cost to buy a coke to wash it down?" "Twelve cents," he said. So all together Larry had given this boy twenty cents to be fed.

Larry realized while this small boy was begging for

Larry Jones and The Oak Ridge Boys

bread, the United States had 35 million metric tons of wheat stored in a grain elevator. He knew he had to tell somebody what he had just witnessed that night. When he returned to the states he appeared on television and told the same story about the little urchin boy.

Within 60 days, over 50 truckloads of wheat were enroute to Larry Jones. He didn't have a clue as to what to do with the wheat, he was simply telling the world about a need. Larry wasn't a farmer and he only owned a house with a two car garage. He had no idea of knowing the broadcast would awaken the hearts of American people in the way it did.

Before long shipments of wheat, black-eyed peas and corn were being shipped to Larry as well. Then a doctor by the name of Larry Biehler offered his medical services and put together a team of doctors that would provide care for these overseas children. Larry was astonished, this wasn't something he had planned. He had no way of transporting the food or a way to distribute it once it got there, but he knew there must be a way.

He went back on television to do another broadcast and asked for help to transport and distribute the food. Two years later in 1981 his overseas efforts were still in full force. Yet he had no idea this was meant to be a lifetime commitment. At the time he was still preaching in crusades all over America. Then one day, one of his fellow workers said, "Larry, we do more of this food distribution than anything else. We need to give it a name." They thought, "well we are feeding children so why don't we just call it "Feed The Children."

Over the years the organization's outreach program has stretched into 85 countries and all 50 states, covering every possible area where there are starving children. I asked Larry how he is able to emotionally handle all the devastation and turmoil that he witnesses on a daily basis. He said there are times that he can't control his emotions, but he has come to realize he can only take one day at a time. In that day he can only do so much, so he chooses to have no regrets, but continues to do the very best he can.

There is not enough room in this profile to expound on all the many facets of the organization. Over the past 20 years a lot of hungry children would have continued to go hungry without the help and compassion of Larry Jones and his team of dedicated workers.

Larry Jones

Kim Josephson

Opera Singer

I don't know much about the opera or opera singers, but I was sent a newspaper article about Kim Josephson and thought he certainly warranted being called a "Distinguished Oklahoman."

Although he was born in Ohio and grew up mostly in Houston, Texas, his early years began, attending Sidney Lanier Elementary school in Tulsa, Oklahoma.

His interest in music and band started early in life. By the time he was in the fifth grade in Houston, Texas, his band director Robert Linder introduced him to the tuba. He excelled greatly with the instrument and began to visualize himself shaping music and becoming an orchestra conductor. He attended the University of Houston, so he could watch and learn from great conductors. He studied tuba with Bill Rose who had been a protege of the great tuba player Bill Bell. While performing as a soloist in the University of Houston band, he signed up for singing lessons as an elective course. His voice teacher Jean Preston was so impressed with his singing ability that she strongly persuaded him to focus more of his attention on singing than on playing the tuba. He eventually took her advice and changed his major. He began singing while still in college with the Houston Opera

Chorus and toured with them and the Texas Opera Theater. Still in the back of his mind he had a dream of becoming a conductor. Kim was becoming so successful with his singing and operatic roles that it all began to go to his head. What had once been a humble, young tuba player had turned into a haughty, young opera singer.

Looking back Kim realized that when he was small in his own eyes God blessed him, but when he became big in his own eyes he lost sight of God. By a set of circumstances, he met a lady by the name of Aileen Vale who wrote the Christian song, *The Joy of the Lord is my Strength..* Before she was finished counseling with him he had a new perspective on life and what his music talents meant in the whole scheme of things. For five years Kim gave up his operatic career in order to get a clearer direction of where his life was headed. When it was time to pick up the reigns again, he was married to Sherri, and they had a family. He was somewhat nervous about taking the plunge again. Yet, they packed up their belongings and moved to New York, determined to give themselves the opportunity for Kim to become an Opera singer. In the beginning it was very hard being in a strange city amongst so many unfamiliar faces. However, within a few months the doors began to open. Kim caught the attention of many of the "greats" in the opera world as he began to win prestigious competitions. His teacher Michael Trimble, helped him through the maze of dizzying decisions. One thing led to another until Kim was performing all over the world. They had arrived in New York in 1986, and by October 10, 1991, he was making his debut with the New York Metropolitan Opera. He progressed quickly from 90 seconds to the leading baritone roles with great reviews in the New York Times and New York Post. After accomplishing an amazing amount of success for several years performing in such operas as La Traviata, Pagliacci, Carmen, Rigoletto and Madam Butterfly, Kim says there was still something missing. He wanted his children to find a sense of value that he believed could only be found in a small town. He wanted them to be able to ride horses, play with their dogs, go to church with their friends and smell the fresh air from an Oklahoma breeze. To make that dream come true, Kim and Sherri bought a farm in the late 1990's in the little town of Vinita, Oklahoma. Their land is overflowing with plum, pear, apple, pecan and cherry trees, three ponds, and a huge landscape to look out upon. The children have their horses, dogs, and friends, and Sherri and Kim have the peace of mind that their children are growing up with the same set of small town values that they experienced not so many years ago.

Kim is indeed quite busy with his career. He is still singing leading roles at the Metropolitan and the Lyric Opera of Chicago. On his occasional trips back to his farm in Vinita he resumes his role as Kim, the regular guy. He stands out in front of his house and can see for miles. When the moon comes out and the coyotes howl it is like music to his ears.

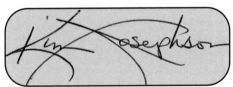

Robert Kamm

University President

What a privilege it was to meet Dr. Robert Kamm and his gracious wife Maxine. It took three years to actually have the interview. Since so much time

had passed, I conceded to conducting a phone interview but Dr. Kamm insisted on a personal chat and I am so glad he did.

Over the years I'm sure if anyone was acquainted with Dr. Kamm they probably knew Mrs. Kamm as well. They appear to be a couple that is inseparable, which is a state in which we all should aspire. I know I was impressed to see the two of them interact with love and respect that has remained over 58 years of marriage. Mrs. Kamm quoted the poem *I Needed the Quiet* by Alice H. Moftensen as she sat across the table. The way in which she delivered the words left me in awe.

Dr. Kamm proudly admits he is a first generation American born in West Union, Iowa on January 22, 1919. It was quite refreshing to hear him speak of his deep spiritual faith and of his desire to help others understand the true meaning of "loving our fellow man." Of course after he described his childhood and his Christian parents Balthasar (a tenant farmer from Switzerland who spoke five languages) and Amelia, it was apparent his Christian roots were deeply grounded.

Education was an important part of his life. His mother taught school for 12 years before she married Balthasar and her emphasis on education remained as she reared her children. Dr. Kamm's observance of her, as well as other fine teachers along the way, made quite an impression on him.

Dr. Kamm attended the University of Northern Iowa in an effort to follow in the steps of educators he had grown to admire. After teaching school for two years his career was sidetracked by a four year tour of duty in the United States Navy during WWII.

During college he met Maxine and they married on July 10, 1943. As a Naval radar student he had the opportunity to attend a three month training program at what was then Oklahoma A&M. He and Maxine had been married only a year when they visited Oklahoma and the two of them became quite enamored with the state and the people they came in contact with. They both remember making the statement "wouldn't it be fun to come back again?," never knowing someday they would do just that.

After being discharged from the Navy Dr. Kamm earned a Ph.D. in psychology and higher education from the University of Minnesota in 1948. He spent the next seven years as the Dean of Students at Drake University before relocating to Texas A&M in a dual capacity as Dean of Students and Dean of the Basic Division.

Two children were added to the Kamm family during this time. Susan was born in 1948 and Steve in 1953.

Almost 15 years had passed since their visit to Oklahoma A&M (now Oklahoma State University) where they had made the comment "wouldn't it be fun to come back again?" Dr. Kamm was offered the position as Dean of the College of Arts and Sciences at Oklahoma State University, a position he held for the next six years. He was appointed as Vice President for Academic Affairs for one year before accepting the role as the 13th President of Oklahoma State University.

During his inaugural speech he spoke of the land grant mission for the university, as well as its academic vision, freedom and sense of community spirit. Lastly, he emphasized the importance of the students, faculty and staffs responsibility to themselves, to others and to God.

"If we measure up to the highest and best within ourselves; if we are committed to serving the needs of fellowmen and of alleviating the problems of society; and if we truly seek to honor God-a God of love and goodness and justice-we will indeed experience freedom in its fullest, richest and most productive sense. And what is most important, we will preserve freedom for generations to follow!"

That speech was made on October 21, 1966 and now 35 years later, in light of the tragic events that occurred on September 11, 2001, Dr. Kamm's words still reverberate a sense of responsibility to not only associates of OSU, but to all of America.

During Dr. Kamm's tenure at OSU he instituted a program called People Emphasis to counteract the upheaval and negative influences of the Vietnam War. That program, which is still in existence at OSU, gave birth to a sense of stability on campus that has remained to this day.

Dr. Kamm's influence over the years has repeatedly been felt throughout OSU, Oklahoma and the world. He has been listed in "Who's Who in America" since 1954. During his presidency at OSU he led in securing the National Wrestling Hall of Fame Museum, as well as the establishment of the Oklahoma Higher Education Museum on the OSU campus. In addition, he played a major role in securing the Mercury Marine factory for Stillwater.

Dr. Kamm was inducted into the Oklahoma Hall of Fame in 1972. In 1995 he was named to the Stillwater Hall of Fame and Maxine was given the same honor in 2000 for their continued contributions.

Dr. Kamm has traveled in 42 nations and has worked with people from 150 different countries. He was appointed as the U.S. ambassador for United Nations Educational, Scientific and Cultural Organization (UNESCO) for 17 months during 1977-78.

After 11 years as the president of Oklahoma State University Dr. Kamm resigned his position to run as the Republican candidate for the U.S. Senate. He lost the election to Senator David Boren who was Oklahoma's governor at the time, yet he didn't view his defeat as a bitter disappointment, rather an educational experience.

Of course he didn't miss a beat and immediately rejoined the faculty at OSU teaching administration education courses and advising graduate students until his retirement on December 31, 1987. But even then he had to remain a doer and headed the Centennial Histories Project, a 25-volume history of the university.

He has written and released three books *It Helps To Laugh, They're Number One!, Leadership for Leadership,* and his fourth book recently released titled *The Best of Mind and Spirit.*

Dr. Kamm was selected to be a torch bearer for the 1996 Olympic games as the procession briefly paused in Stillwater at the National Wrestling Hall of Fame.

As I reflected back to the day of our interview I quickly visualized two white haired individuals bound together by mutual love, trust and respect and remembered the wisdom that radiated and announced their years. Many events and experiences have transpired during their life together. No doubt there are countless individuals who have profited from their tireless efforts to teach and inform. I truly was inspired by them and grateful for the example they set as "a gentleman and a lady."

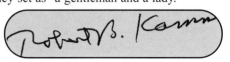

Moe Karimian

Instructor

I met Moe several years ago when I was writing stories for a neighborhood newspaper and was impressed with the level of caring he seemed to have for his fellow man. Knowing he was born and raised in a foreign country that was so unfamiliar to me I was interested in the way in which he grew up.

Moe was born in 1942 in the country of Iran, located next to the Persian Gulf. Born to Akbar and Gohar he is the second oldest of nine children. I've had the privilege of also meeting his youngest brother Tony who I kiddingly refer to as "Antonio." Their father passed away, but their mother Gohar has permanently moved to Oklahoma from Iran. In fact she was highlighted in a Time magazine titled Grandma's Kitchen several years ago because of her exquisite cooking.

Moe told me his childhood was a very pleasant one. His father was in the Persian rug import/export business and therefore the family's income was certainly adequate to meet all their needs. The Iranian language that Moe grew up with is called Farsi. Yet when he entered the 7th grade he was required to learn the English language. In fact, he said Iranians are not allowed to graduate from high school until they have passed the English course. Moe said understanding the English language came fairly easy for him, but he couldn't speak it until he moved to the States.

I asked Moe if everyday life was similar to what we know here in the States. He said during his childhood it was good. They went on walks, frequented movie houses, partied in night clubs and celebrated with friends and family. But now during this turbulent era if a religious government official thinks you're playing music he can confiscate your audio tapes.

Moe wanted me to know that the people of Iran are the kindest, nicest and most giving people you would ever want to meet. He said if you take the religious government with all its bureaucracy out of the country the loving people would be Iran's greatest asset.

Islam is the religion of Iran. Moe said in the original religion Muslims were required to do three things everyday. They were to say something good, do something good and show some good attitude or good habit to someone. It's amazing how we as human beings can take something so pure and good and corrupt it to the point of destruction.

Always in his heart Moe had nurtured a dream to come to the United States. At the time college opportunities were very limited in Iran. There were two universities with about 5,000 people wanting to attend and only 700 being accepted. Everyone else had nowhere else to go.

When Moe graduated from high school he left his country with $400 in his pocket and an invitation from two American colleges. He intended to enroll at Tampa University, but his cousin who was attending Northeastern State College in Tahlequah, Oklahoma persuaded him to go there. A pleasant surprise was awaiting him there. As he was enrolling he looked up and saw a beautiful woman who was applying for a job. He thought she was an Iranian and he just had to meet her. He found out Sylvia was not Iranian, but a Cherokee. Nevertheless he was smitten with her.

I asked Moe how his parents felt about their young boy leaving his home country and moving to the United States. "Oh" he said. "They were proud. When an Iranian child goes to America it is like they won the lottery. My parents would brag to everyone about their son being in college in the United States of America."

The university put Moe to work in the printing office in exchange for room and board. Then, in the summer months, he worked in a restaurant to save money for the following school year. After four years at Northeastern with a degree in Math and Economics he, along with his wife Sylvia, transferred to Oklahoma University in Norman. Two years later they moved to Tulsa.

Moe was supposed to go to work for Amoco, but instead he received a phone call from a Shah representative in Iran. They wanted Moe to come back to Iran and be in charge of a university medical program in Mushhad formatted like that of Georgetown University in Washington, D.C. Moe accepted the position and Sylvia was employed as well because of her degree in sociology and psychology. Moe was excited about the opportunity. Not only would he get to visit his home country but it would allow him to introduce his family to his lovely wife as well. It was 1973 and for four years Moe diligently worked to enhance the university program. Then, as promised, he was sent to Georgetown University in Washington, D.C. to work on his doctorate degree for two years.

Then things began to change. The Shah of Iran was forced to leave the country and Homeni came to power. It was a horrible time and Moe had to break ties with the university in Iran and make other plans for himself and his family.

In 1979 he went to work for Spartan School of Aeronautics in Tulsa. He taught aviation for 18 years and felt it was time to move on and find another area of endeavor. At Spartan he helped thousands of students master the basic subjects in Math and Physics to complete their certification or associate degree. One day while he was driving down a historical stretch of road called Route 66 a terrific idea came to him. There was an isolated strip a few miles long on what Tulsans know as "Eleventh Street." It gained the reputation over the years as a slightly promiscuous arena of night time activities. Scenes ranging from staggering wine-o's to dope pushers and ladies of the night had been known to put everyone in a state of bewilderment from time to time.

Moe felt a real need to help eradicate some of those reoccurring scenes and help clean up at least a portion of that strip of road. One section had been used as an unsolicited "junkyard." Anything from old tires to broken down appliances and an array of unsightly discards were inappropriately setting the scene for that stretch of land.

Moe knew if he took on the challenge he would definitely have his work cut out for him. Located next to the junkyard was another well used building that conveniently housed leftover used syringes and an occasional overnight visitor, which sometimes entertained a "lady of the night."

After purchasing the property Moe hired some less fortunate unemployed workers to help renovate the land. Now as you pass that section on Eleventh Street no longer do you see an unwanted junkyard. In its place you'll find a brand new several hundred square foot building with a nicely paved parking lot upon which several cars are displayed. Moe proudly calls it "Autoplex."

As in most of our lives a little rain sometimes falls. Moe and Sylvia were blessed to have raised two great sons, Cyrus and David. A few years ago they lost their beloved Cyrus at the age of 17. Moe said the tragedy broke his heart and changed his life forever. There was a time when he felt he would never be able to function as a productive person again. It was as if he had been traveling on a highway and had taken the wrong exit, couldn't find his way back and further more didn't want to.

But then one day he was reminded of the beauty that still surrounds him. He realized that his beautiful wife and his dedicated son deserved to have a husband and father that valued their worth as well. In doing so he found that their love helped ease his pain.

Spring welcomes the Iranian New Year. For 12 days people visit friends and family. On the 13th day a prayer goes up to God. In that prayer they dedicate themselves back to God, determined to leave all hate, anger and bitterness behind and go forward with only good thoughts. Moe is proud to be an American. But he never wants to lose sight of his Iranian heritage which has helped create the man he has become.

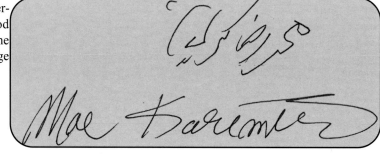

Cathy Keating
First Lady

As a native Oklahoman, Cathy Keating has roots that run deep. She is a descendent of land run pioneers. One of her grandfathers was a co-founder of the Skelly Oil Company. Yet never in her wildest dreams did she think she would some day become the First Lady of Oklahoma.

When I hear the words "First Lady" they seem synonymous with words like elegant, gracious, excellence and poise. Cathy Keating exemplifies all of those attributes. You can't help liking her because she moves in and out of a room like she is everybody's best friend. The good part about it is, she's totally sincere.

She and Governor Keating married after she graduated from Oklahoma University. Even though she had a degree in Elementary Education, her life took on a whole different direction. Seven months after they met they were married and two months later she was on her way to becoming a new mother as well as a legislator's wife.

Cathy said she always knew that Governor Keating was destined for something great because he always did everything with "greatness." Of course in the beginning of his legislative days, she never saw herself as being a part of the political arena. Her hands were full raising their three children and keeping their home a safe haven for all of them. As time went on and the children needed her less she began to play a more active role in her husband's political career.

As in my interview with Governor Keating, Cathy Keating also spoke so highly of their relationship together as a couple. Of course, you would expect that sort of response. However, in my opinion, their admiration for each other far outweighed the typical husband and wife team. Cathy said she had been approached before for a comment on what a perfect marriage relationship they had. Cathy's response was that their marriage was far from being perfect, but they worked toward perfection every day.

Since they both are interested in improving themselves personally, it makes it easier to listen to each other's grievances and be willing to accept responsibility for their behavior that may not always be up to par.

I loved the fact that Cathy was so open and honest. Surely God must place women such as Cathy Keating in key positions to be role models for future generations. I've been told that First Lady Cathy Keating is the most publicly active First Lady in Oklahoma history.

She was instrumental in coordinating the internationally broadcast prayer service after the 1995 Oklahoma City bombing. She believes the prayer service was a direct inspiration from God. The memories are still very clear of how the presence of God hovered over the bombing site and the entire downtown Oklahoma City area.

It was also Cathy Keating who birthed the idea of the book *In Their Name* to honor bombing victims. The book became #10 on the New York Times' best sellers list. One hundred percent of the proceeds from the book went to Project Recovery of Oklahoma City. Because of Cathy Keating's efforts I'm sure the bombing victims and their families received enormous support during such a devastating time in their lives.

Cathy also put out a book, *The Governor's Mansion*, the concept was in the works before the Oklahoma City bombing. She later resumed the project which covered all Governor's Mansions throughout the United States. The idea came to her while she was preparing to renovate the Oklahoma City Governor's Mansion. All proceeds from that book went to the preservation of the Oklahoma City Mansion.

Cathy decided when her husband was running for the office of Governor that if he won, her number one personal mission would be to help instill inside every individual a sense of pride in being an Oklahoman. She knows she is in a position to help people in a great way. Being First Lady opens a lot of doors for her, but with that comes a huge amount of responsibility which she takes very seriously.

I asked the First Lady what her plans are after their term in office ends. She clearly stated, "The truth is, we just want life to be fulfilling. We know we are responsible for making that happen. Happiness comes from within your heart and the more you give, the more you get."

Cathy Keating

Frank Keating
Governor

Governor Keating's whole life has revolved around service to mankind. As a young boy, his parents instilled in him the value of public service and encouraged him to always give back to his community. Although he had never planned on being the Governor of Oklahoma, the path was being systematically laid out for him.

He held class offices from the 7th grade clear through college. He said it wasn't because he was particularly capable, it was simply part of his culture to be involved. As a young person, he was active on several civic boards. He said there are literally a thousand civic groups doing 10,000 good deeds that anyone could get involved in. Whether your resources are great or small, there is room to be involved if you want to be.

Directly out of law school Frank became an FBI agent on the East and West coast. He later served as a U .S. Attorney and as a member of the Oklahoma Legislature, where he gained the position of Senate Minority Leader. Now, as the 25th Governor of Oklahoma for his second term, he has once again proven he knows the value of public service.

Upon re-election he became the second Governor in Oklahoma history to win a second consecutive term. He is the first Republican Governor in state history to win re-election.

His list of accomplishments as Governor are too numerous to list in their entirety, yet here are a few.

His administration is nationally recognized for historic achievements, steady economic growth, tax cuts and wide-ranging reform.

He is the first Governor in 50 years to propose, advocate and achieve a cut in the state income tax rate.

In 5 years of his term, nearly 150,000 new jobs have been created.

In February 2000, he signed the largest teacher pay raise in Oklahoma history.

In March 2000, he made history by appointing the highest ranking African American Judge in Oklahoma history.

The First Lady describes Governor Keating as a statesman rather than a politician. She defines a statesman as being a person who stands up for what he believes is right and doesn't make a decision on whether or not it will get him elected. A statesman makes a decision on what will keep a country or state strong and make it a better place for people to live.

In interviewing Governor Keating as well as the First Lady, I was so impressed with how highly they both spoke of each other. I was under the impression that Governor Keating could have talked all afternoon about how talented and successful his wife is. He said their lives have been blessed with many opportunities and yet true success for him is knowing his wife and family love him and see him as a man of character who is capable of doing the right thing without having to think about it.

   Governor Keating takes his responsibility as a parent very seriously. He said he views his children as unique creatures of God that are placed on this earth for a specific purpose. He doesn't see them as just mirrors of himself or his wife, but as their own person with their own personal destinies.

   Governor Keating has certainly stretched his abilities over the years and believes that everyone should broaden their horizons in areas they never considered before. He feels some people are afraid of opportunities because they are afraid of failure. Yet *if you never reach for goals that seem to be out of your grasp, you may be missing out on some golden opportunities.*

   I was somewhat disappointed when Governor Keating was not picked as Governor George Bush's running mate for the presidential election. Yet Governor Keating's life has always proven to be right on course. There is no reason to believe any mistake was made.

   Who knows what the future will hold politically for Governor Keating? In the meantime, he will remain as the capable Governor of the state of Oklahoma, for which he proudly and honorably holds the title.

Karen Keith - T.V. Personality

   When they say "friendly Okie," they have to be talking about Karen Keith. After talking with her and hearing how she grew up, it was easy to see how she could be such a fun-loving person.

   Family means a great deal to Karen. She fondly recalls growing up in Muskogee, Oklahoma with three brothers, a younger sister and a mom and dad who never took vacations without all five of their children. A cabin at Trails End in Tahlequah became the family's summer getaway. Karen remembers swimming in the Illinois River and hiking along wooded trails. The closeness she felt with her family gave her a sense of stability and set Karen on a charted path to be successful in anything she decided to do.

   In high school a neighbor encouraged her to get involved with the 4-H Club. At times she would travel with the club to places like Kansas City, Washington D.C. and Chicago. While in Chicago Karen was introduced to Boston Pops Conductor Arthur Fiedler, she liked being on that stage and in the lights perhaps this was a rehearsal for what would become her lifes work.

   One of her work study programs in college was with the journalism and broadcasting department. It didn't take long for her to realize that telling stories, reporting news and that sort of thing was what she wanted to do with her life. From then on Karen was determined to do what it took to accomplish her goal. At one point she was working three jobs to put herself through college at Oklahoma State University.

   While in college she spent one semester going abroad with World Campus Afloat. She traveled to places like Africa, India and the Orient. It was a pivotal point in her life because it gave her a greater sense and depth about people of other cultures and nationalities. It gave her a greater understanding and tolerance for other religions and beliefs.

   She feels like she has seen the good, the bad and the ugly, and when all is said and done, people from all races and backgrounds are basically the same. Everyone is striving to be happy and loved by their fellow man.

During Karen's senior year in college she worked for Channel 8 as a weekend reporter. Then she transferred to Joplin, Missouri for eight months as an anchor person doing news and sports. Just by chance, on a vacation trip to Colorado while she was still employed in Joplin, she dropped off a video tape of herself to a CBS affiliate in Colorado Springs, not really expecting anything to become of it. However, they hired her on the spot.

She couldn't pass it up because it was experience that was vital to the continued success of her career. A year later Channel 8 called her back. She bounced around to a few other stations for a while before finally being hired at Channel 2 in 1981.

Karen said she experienced every news cast shift that Channel 2 had to offer. Her whole career up to that point had been weekend work and she was beginning to think that was all she would ever be allowed to do. It was frustrating because it meant every Christmas, holiday and weekend family event was normally unattended by her.

Finally the day came when she was given the opportunity to do the early morning and mid-day slot. Eventually, it was mid-day and five, six and ten anchor. Throughout it all, Karen said there was never a time that she wished she wasn't doing what she was doing. Night or day, weekend or not, Karen knew she was right where she belonged.

Now the icing has been put on the cake and Karen is doing a job tailor-made for her. She is the executive producer and host of "Oklahoma Living" for Channel 2. She says she is having a blast doing the show because she gets to see and do all the stories she pigeonholed over the years. Karen says she has met some amazing people and visited remote corners of our state to find interesting tidbits to share with her viewers. She is determined to always leave positive petals wherever she goes and is thankful for the wonderful people of Oklahoma who allow her to share in their lives.

Karen feels very strongly about everyone *staying focused on their common goals rather than their differences*-a tip we should carry throughout all of our relationships. She has proven with her own life that hard work and perseverance leads to success. Things don't just fall into place by chance. *We have to take charge of our lives, decide what we want to do and go after it.*

Karen, in my opinion, is one of Oklahoma's "Greats." I doubt if she ever meets a stranger and she never sees a blue, white or no collar worker.

John Kilpatrick

Business Executive

With as many different entrepreneurial hats John has worn, you would think he would be totally out of ideas. Yet somehow I don't think he ever will be.

John was born in Oklahoma City, Oklahoma where he has spent his entire life. Even the building he works out of holds the key to the family legacy. The building was built in 1927 as part of the Kilpatrick Lumber Company which encompassed two

full blocks. They also had branches in Tulsa, Topeka, Lubbock and Little Rock.

Even though growing up he never thought about being a part of the family business, he found himself right there when the time was right. Even though he stepped into his father's beginnings, he still had to have the fortitude and wherewithal to continue its success.

When he and his brother joined the family business they began to branch out into other areas as well. Since family owned lumber businesses have almost entirely phased out due to places like Lowes, Home Depot and other chains, their decision to diversify was a wise one.

Some of John's endeavors have been owning a Ford agency, a construction company, an outdoor advertising company, a travel agency and a dairy company. While in the construction business he built shopping centers, motels, a city hall and senior citizen homes. He built Taco Bell restaurants, Texaco stations, McDonald's restaurants and Safeway stores. He learned how to build to suit a tenant who in return would sign a long term lease.

For John, his timing was usually right and he had a flair for seeing something and realizing its potential which brought him much success. However, he does admit he has managed to have a few failures as well. He quoted Alfred sloan, founder of General Motors, who said, "Success is the ability to make one more right decision than you made wrong."

John reminded me even large corporations make mistakes which is all part of doing business. Coke came out with "New Coke" and it was a failure. Ford built the Edsel and it was a failure. New products don't always spell success, but you keep on trying. When you get into something that isn't working you sell it or close it down.

John and his partner built the first McDonalds that came to Oklahoma City. At the time no one was familiar with McDonald's. They had originated in Chicago and had only been in business for two years. Their financial situation was still a little shaky being the new kid on the block, so they required them to pay a year's rent in advance before he would build the building.

When John first got involved with California based Taco Bell, they only had 300 restaurants and were struggling. They were trying to expand and needed wise counsel. John flew to California and met with the company president who took his advice. John began building Taco Bell restaurants all over the country. He became their landlord for many years while they were establishing themselves. He also was appointed to their corporate board of directors.

Of course success begets success. Taco Bell eventually sold out to Pepsico for $35 million. How wonderful it must be for John to drive past a Taco Bell restaurant and know in some part he was a key to its success.

John believes strongly about people getting involved with their community. When he was in his 30's he was the youngest member of the board of directors for the 1st National Bank in Oklahoma City. He was also the 2nd youngest president of the Oklahoma City Chamber of Commerce. He was friends with Howard Edmondson and with Harold Stuart in Tulsa and was co-finance chairman of Edmondson's campaign to help him become the youngest governor in Oklahoma.

Opportunities just continued to fall in John's lap because he kept himself involved. When Howard Edmondson became governor he appointed John to be vice chairman of the Turnpike Authority. There is no pay involved, but John loved the job. It is a governing board in which a staff is hired. The board meets once a month but John was involved in the day to day operations of the turnpike.

Even though governors have changed over the years, John remained on the Turnpike Authority board for 32 years serving under 8 governors. Obviously, each governor knew quality when he saw it. When Governor Henry Bellmon, governor for the second time, suggested one of the turnpikes be named the John Kilpatrick Turnpike, it came as quite a shock to John.

John humbly remarked he guessed he received that honor because he had given himself in service to the Turnpike Authority through eight governors and 32 years. My goodness, I would say so!! Some people can't make it through two years as a paid employee and yet John served the position 32 years with no monetary compensation.

Amazingly after all this time and his tremendous efforts, he still doesn't consider himself a successful man in the eyes of the world -a statement I still don't understand.

John is currently on the board or trustee of six institutions. In the past the list consisted of over 50 positions as president, chairman or director. John has certainly made his mark on this world and particularly in Oklahoma City. He loves to take on challenges that seem impossible to accomplish. Who knows what giant leap of faith he will undertake next?

He took me on a tour of one of his office rooms full of memorabilia. I could see the uniqueness in John simply by the treasures he holds so dear.

Maybe some day he will consider himself successful. For those of us still climbing the ladder, the rung John is on has gone completely out of view.

Roberta Knie
Singer

Cordell, Oklahoma must be very proud of Roberta Knie. She started playing the clarinet when she was 9 years old and continued playing through high school. Since she advanced so quickly with her instrument, it never occurred to her she had another talent she could excel in as well. She was noted for being a bookworm, but her extremely shy nature seemed to concern her sister Rosemary.

When Roberta was a sophomore in high school Rosemary's friend Pattie Boothe, now Pattie Boothe Arnold, whom they had known for years, came to teach vocal music. Rosemary suggested she listen to Roberta's voice and encourage her to sing. She hoped if Roberta began singing it would bring her out of her shyness and cause her to be more outgoing with interests that encompassed more than what could be found inside the pages of a book.

Roberta was raised in the Baptist Church and the only songs she was familiar with were sung from hymnals on Sunday morning. So Pattie took Roberta to the church, opened a hymnal and began playing a familiar song on the piano while Roberta sang along. Pattie was amazed at the big voice that resonated from 16 year old Roberta. Surprisingly, it was Roberta's first realization that she had such an alluring voice.

At the time, Cordell High School had an abundance of singers and musicians. Four of Roberta's classmates decided to further their education in music and solicited Pattie for additional training to groom them to be music majors.

Roberta began entering competitions and continued to score high marks as she pursued her God-given talent.

In her junior year at the University of Oklahoma, two famous opera singers were part of the faculty staff. Although Roberta didn't study with them they encouraged her to change her major from vocal music education to a performance degree which she did and graduated with in 1960.

After graduation she went to England and furthered her studies in London at the Royal Academy of Music, studying with Dame Eva Turner before being hired as Cherubino in Mozart's The Marriage of Figaro with a small opera company in Germany.

From 1964 until 1974 she was carefully nurtured in the opera houses of Graz, Freiburg and Hagen by musicians with direct links to the musical past. She studied the music, language and style of Ricard Strauss with Gustav Cerny, assistant to Clemens Krauss. She learned and restudied the roles of Elsa, Elisabeth-Tannhauser, Isolde, Senta and the Ring Cycle Brunnhildes with Maximillian Kojetinsky, Studienleiter in Bayreuth for 35 years beginning under Siegfried Wagner.

She emphatically stated she doesn't think anything in life is coincidental. Even though her singing career seemed to come together quite easily, she feels confident it wasn't by chance but indeed a path she was being led down. She believes when one is raised with a firm belief in a higher power that power guides everything in your life not just your career.

Roberta's extensive operatic repertoire included Mozart's Donna Anna, Fiordiligi, the Countess and Elektra in Idomeneo, Verdi's Lady Macbeth, Leonora in Il Trovatore, Leonora in La Forza del Destino, Elisabetta in Don Carlos, and Desdemona. She has been a frequent guest with major international orchestras including the Philadelphia Orchestra under Zubin Mehta, the Cleveland Orchestra under Lorin Maazel and Erich Leinsdorf and the Paris Radio Orchestra under Giuseppe Patane.

Roberta is keenly aware she was nurtured and taught by some very fine conductors and coaches who encouraged her along the way. It is extremely important to Roberta that she give an outstanding performance every time she stands before an audience. She feels that if she touches even one listener she has fulfilled her goal.

In 1976 Roberta made her Metropolitan Opera debut as Chrysotemis in Elektra. The New York Post wrote she is a "healthy, expressive soprano." She has sung Isolde over 60 times and it is in this role that she made her debut with both Dallas Civic Opera and at Covent Garden.

In 1978 The Washington Post wrote, "Roberta Knie may be the foremost soprano for the large Wagner roles. She is the most impressive artist to appear in this repertoire for years."

Roberta never forgot her Oklahoma heritage and represented her state with distinction as "Oklahoma's Ambassador of Goodwill" in 1980.

In 1982 she was further honored by being inducted into the Oklahoma Hall of Fame.

In 1987 Roberta took some time off from her singing career and began devoting some of her time to teaching, coaching and counseling singers. She was enjoying this time of her life but when the 1990s rolled around she began studying again to perform the role of Strauss Elektra. She had moved back to Austria and was preparing herself for her role when she began having a health crisis she couldn't ignore. She was diagnosed with a weakened retina in one eye and a detaching retina in the other. Surgery was performed to correct the condition, but her doctor advised her of risks she would be taking with her eye sight if she continued singing.

The choice to retire from singing to save her sight was an easy decision for Roberta. She had experienced a rewarding career for many years and she was now content in focusing all of her time on her students.

From 1992 until 1995 she was guest professor at the Hochscule-fur-Musik and Darstellende Kunst in Graz, Austria. In 1995 she returned to the United States where she maintains a private teaching studio, frequently judges vocal competitions, counsels professional singers and conducts master classes in the U.S. and Europe.

Roberta's European students and her current students continue to be hired in major European houses, Canada, the New York City Opera and the Metropolitan Opera.

Roberta knows her experience as a singer provides invaluable information for her students. From the business aspect she has an intimate knowledge of managers, opera houses, the demands of traveling in all situations. In teaching she understands the demands of conductors and the reality of singing with an orchestra. She knows what it is to be completely concentrated, to stress musical accuracy and to sing stylistic phrasing.

Video Artists International recently produced a video of the Canadian Opera production of extended excerpts from Tristan and Isolde with Roberta Knie and Jon Vickers in the title roles.

It was quite interesting to talk with Roberta. She has traveled all over the world, met interesting people and experienced some incredible roles as an operatic performer. Life has been so full and busy that there was no time to devote to marriage and children, a choice Roberta said leaves her with no regrets.

It is hard for me to relate to Roberta's life since our experiences are worlds apart from each other. But I would like to have experienced just a tenth of the excitement she has been so blessed to have encountered.

Meyer and Manya Korenblit

Holocaust Survivors

I never expected to ever meet anyone who had survived the horrible events of the Holocaust. Yet one of my most rewarding interviews took place in Ponca City, Oklahoma when I had the privilege to meet Meyer and Manya Korenblit. To hear their story and yet witness two people who have such a love for mankind is almost too amazing to be true.

Meyer was 17 years old and Manya was 16 when the fear and torment of the Nazi invasion began its final stages to take over their lives. During the three previous years Jewish families were ordered by the Germans not to leave their homes after 6 P. M. Now it was October 27, 1942 in the town of Hrubieszow, Poland. Up until the German invasion Meyer's father Avrum had successfully operated his own flour mill. Many of the townspeople would bring their wheat to Avrum to have it processed.

But life as they knew it was once again about to make a drastic change. There was word on the streets that the Jews were going to be taken captive and Avrum and his wife Malka made plans to hide their family. Manya was Meyer's true love and she, too, was preparing with her family to take refuge in their own secret hiding place. However Meyer desperately wanted Manya by his side. He made his way through the town streets to Manya's house, trying to avoid being caught by the Nazi's. When he arrived to Manya's surprise he asked her to come with him and hide out with his family. Manya was torn with the decision to go with the man she loved or hide with her own family.

Her parents, Shlomo and Mincha, saw the struggle Manya was having within herself. Even though Shlomo was a brick layer by trade and had built a strong wall within their home in which to hide his family safely he wasn't at all sure the Nazi's wouldn't find them. The one drawback was their home was located in town, which made it even more vulnerable to enemy attack. With much agonizing Shlomo and Mincha told Manya to go with Meyer and take her young brother Chaim who was pleading to go with them as well. I think in their hearts Shlomo and Mincha knew their chance of survival was slim, but maybe Manya and Chaim would have a chance with Meyer.

Manya took one last look at her parents and her other siblings and clung to Meyer as the three of them made their way through the darkness of the night. Their hiding place was to be an underground tunnel covered by a huge haystack. A Polish friend of the family had dug out the tunnel in the field behind his barn. That was the beginning of their run for freedom.

After my interview with Meyer and Manya they presented me with a book their son Michael had written titled, *Until We Meet Again,* which documented their lives during the horrible Holocaust days. There are many stories that can be told and have been told about that horrific time. But what makes the telling of their story so unique is the waging war of two young people determined to survive the horrors in order to seal their love forever.

The book is an incredible love story not only between Meyer and Manya, but their undying love and devotion for their parents and siblings. Of the 8,000 Jews from their home place in Hrubieszow, Poland fewer than 200 people survived. Among those were Meyer, Manya and Chaim.

Chaim was their unexpected miracle. As desperately as they had tried to stay together Meyer, Manya and Chaim had to separate from Avrum and the rest of the family. As the situation continued to worsen the three were separated from each other as well, transported from one concentration camp to the other, always wondering, always praying that the other one would remain strong. The fears that haunted them day and night about the families they left behind were finally realized when they heard rumors that Avrum and the rest of Meyer's family had been killed. Later they were told Manya's family had not survived either. From all reports it appeared as if Chaim's life had ended in the fiery furnace at one of the hellacious concentration camps.

Meyer and Manya made a pact with each other that if they ever made it out alive they would return to Hrubiezow and wait for the other one to return. Manya did just that. But Meyer, feeling the devastation of his own torturous years in the concentration camps, felt almost assured that Manya would not have been able to survive the whole ordeal. Unable to emotionally face that fact, Meyer decided not to return to Hrubiezow. He felt too fragile at the time to enter a town where he and Manya had shared so many dreams, only to be faced with the realization that those dreams were lost forever.

However, what seemed by chance but was really divinely appointed, Meyer was approached by a young man who revealed to him that Manya was alive and waiting for him in Hrubiezow. What a reunion that must have been the first time they set eyes on each other. I'm sure it must have taken a while to realize they weren't dreaming. They really were together at last. Bitter-sweet thoughts must have played a major role that day knowing the rest of the family could not join their jubilant reunion. However, almost three years later, Meyer was reunited with his brother Motl and 40 years later they screamed with delight when they were put in touch once again with Manya's younger brother Chaim. He had survived after all.

As I left Ponca City that day I remember hugging and kissing them both and feeling as if I had known them forever. Even though Manya is old enough to be my mother, there were times as I watched her recall those memories that she still resembled that young, frightened teenage girl who had to desperately hold on to life. As she talked with me her eyes occasionally filled up with tears yet she would shake off the emotions just before the first teardrop fell.

It has been over 50 years since they endured such torture and yet in many ways it felt like yesterday. She showed me the letters and numbers that were tattooed into her skin on both arms and remarked how much it had hurt. As I sat listening I found it so hard to believe what they were describing could actually happen to civilized human beings. How could anyone ever survive? I could understand those events occurring in a novel or a fairy tale of some sort, but to two beautiful people that sat before me?

My thoughts when I first saw Meyer were "oh what a character he must be." He likes to throw you off guard with his bits of humor that leave you wondering if he was just kidding or not. He said his humor helped keep him alive along with his deep desire to be with Manya. It was amazing to hear the emotional strength Meyer had at such an early age, but he gives most of the credit for that to his father Avrum. He was taught to trust God, honor, love and respect his family and be strong and confident in the face of adversity. Meyer proved he had learned his lessons well.

As we said our goodbyes that day I promised I would finish reading their book by the end of the week. I kept my promise. It was an easy promise to keep, because I found it hard to put the book down even long enough to sleep. Meyer told me I better not cry when I read the book, because I had already shed a few tears at his home. But I couldn't keep my end of the bargain that time. I found myself late one evening crying as if part of my own family had been so unjustly brutalized. For a moment I felt a huge wave of depression go all over me. I literally had to talk to myself in order to change the atmosphere that seemed to fill the room.

Why do bad things happen to good people? I guess that's a question only God can answer. I do know this, only the love of God could make two people who survived such an ordeal continue to radiate His presence. Since those horrific days God blessed them with two sons, Sammy born in 1941, Michael in 1951 and five grandchildren. Shalom.

Paul Lambert - Executive

Paul's family was living in Sapulpa, Oklahoma when he was born at a Tulsa hospital in 1946. His father Floyd was working for the Texaco Pipeline but by the time Paul turned 5 years old his father wanted to go into business for himself. The family moved to Tishomingo where Floyd became a wholesale gasoline distributor and later opened a Goodyear Service store. His mother was a stay-at-home mom and homemaker.

With two brothers, Jim and Delmer, who were quite a lot older than Paul, he almost feels like he grew up as an only child. Education was a priority. By the time Paul was in junior high school he knew he would go to college and there was no question about it. He was taught a good education would enable him to have a better start in life. Even though he knew education was the key, he didn't quite know what direction to go as a chosen career.

He spent two years at Murray Junior College in Tishomingo, taking a wide range of subjects hoping something would trigger his interest. He had a history professor named Lloyd Goss who had a unique way of teaching and caused Paul to develop an interest for history. Paul later went to East Central College in Ada and received a bachelor's degree in social studies education with an emphasis on history. His professors were very instrumental in encouraging him to go even further with his education and at least receive his master's degree. Still thinking he would probably teach on the college level, he was accepted at Oklahoma State University and not only received his master's degree but his Ph.D., as well.

One day one of the college department heads informed Paul there was a position that needed to be filled at the Oklahoma Heritage Association in Oklahoma City. The school wanted to send a few students down to interview for the opening and asked if Paul would like to apply. He was interviewed and offered the job and took the position in February of 1973.

The Oklahoma Heritage Association was started in 1927 by Anna B. Korn. It's original name was Oklahoma Memorial Association. Up until 1960 its primary function was to conduct the annual Oklahoma Hall of Fame induction ceremony and to promote Oklahoma Statehood Day every year on November 16th.

When Ms. Korn passed away, members of the board convinced Stanley Draper, Sr., a long time civic leader and former president of Oklahoma City Chamber of Commerce, to become a full-time volunteer. He led the organization's re-birth and was instrumental in having the name changed to Oklahoma Heritage Association. By 1973 they had acquired the donated mansion of Judge and Mrs. Robert A. Hefner Sr.. Restorations were made to the mansion as well as the building of an additional wing.

When Paul took his position in 1973 the library and gardens had just been completed and the center was preparing to have it's first garden party. A garden party has occurred every year since.

Stanley Draper spent the next three years before his death in 1976 doing all he could to help Paul run the organization. After Stanley's death, Paul became the executive director of the center. His responsibilities are for the overall administration of programs as well as the budget. He now holds the title of president.

His marriage to Judy in 1969 made them the typical "yuppie couple." Judy was a secretary at an engineering company and decided she wanted to get her MBA degree. This allowed her to have an interesting career as well. They soon realized they were missing a vital part of life so they gave birth to their son, Matthew. Paul said he looks forward to helping him grow into adulthood. I thought that was a loving way of describing the transition.

Many other accomplishments have come about during Paul's tenure at the Association. In 1976 the first book was published in their Trackmaker biography series with a book on the life of Judge Hefner. Since then over 60 books have been published about Oklahoma. The organization now has five different series of books they publish.

Trackmaker biographies are of Oklahomans who are either members of the Hall of Fame or that caliber. Horizon deals with institutions, organizations or movements of history. County History is fairly new. Oklahoma Statesman focuses on people in public service who are now deceased. Lastly the Oklahoma Voices Series features stories that are autobiographical and written by the person. Although they aren't a huge fund raiser, the books do generate some income for the Heritage Center.

A few years ago a magazine was started called Oklahoma Magazine of the Oklahoma Heritage Association. It focuses on historical subjects of interest in the state. The center awards college scholarships to high school students and would like those scholarships to expand and include outstanding Oklahoma history students in each Oklahoma county. Along with those awards they also recognize outstanding Oklahoma History Teachers.

Of course the biggest event of the year is the induction of distinguished individuals into the Oklahoma Hall of Fame. The public nominates people they think qualify for the title and those names are brought before a selection committee which recommends who should be inducted to the associations Board of Directors. It is a very difficult job to narrow the selection down to six or seven individuals each year. As we all know, Oklahoma has an overwhelming number of people who easily fit into that category and every year more possibilities seem to be added.

The Induction ceremony is a black tie affair held in November and televised statewide. Not only are inductees distinguished but the people who come to introduce the inductee is normally of high status. They have had presenters such as Ronald Reagan, Henry Kissinger, George Bush and Bill Clinton to name a few.

Paul has been so pleased with his position at the center. It has not only given him a greater appreciation for Oklahoma, but it has allowed him to meet individuals he would have never had the opportunity to be in contact with.

Paul has co-authored some of the books in the Oklahoma series. He would love the opportunity to research and write more but time is a factor. He does, however, feel somewhat comforted by the fact he is helping others accomplish goals in their writing careers.

As I was making preparations to begin this book it was suggested to me by Dr. Eugene Swearingen that I should go to the Heritage Center and meet Paul. Up to that point I really had never known anything about the association or its many functions. Paul was very helpful to me as he has been to many over the years. That has remained one of the continuous threads which runs through the lives of distinguished individuals, the desire and ability to help others.

Paul's function as executive director and president of the Oklahoma Heritage Association for the past 27 years has allowed the state of Oklahoma as well as others to realize the magnitude of individuals who help make up our great state. Without his increasing efforts, the association would not be what it is today.

Paul F. Lambert

Louis L'Amour – Author

Sometimes don't you wish everyone could live forever. There are so many incredible people who touch our lives in some way every day. The talented individuals who fill this universe keep us all in a constant progression to reveal the very best that lies within us.

Louis L'Amour is one of those individuals whose life portrayed significance and fortitude. Even in his passing he has remained a person whose name is synonymous with the Wild West and storytellers of all times. In corresponding with his son Beau, I'm pleased to be able to profile Louis L'Amour as being part of Oklahoma's history. I've taken the information Beau has compiled on his website to present to our readers.

The man who would become Louis L'Amour grew up in the fading days of the American frontier. He was born Louis Dearborn LaMoore on March 22, 1908, the last of seven children in the family of Dr. Louis Charles LaMoore and Emily Dearborn LaMoore. His home, for the first 15 years of his life, was Jamestown, North Dakota, a medium sized farming community situated in the valley where Pipestem Creek flows into the James River.

Dr. LaMoore was a large animal veterinarian who came to Dakota Territory in 1882. As times changed he also sold farm machinery, bossed harvesting crews and held several positions in city and state government.

Though the land around Jamestown was mostly given to farming, Louis and his older brothers often met cowboys as they came through on the Northern Pacific Railroad, traveling to market with stock cars full of cattle or returning to their ranches in the western part of North Dakota or Montana.

When Louis was very young his grandfather, Abraham Truman Dearborn, came to live in a little house just in back of the LaMoore's. He told Louis of the great battles in history and of his own experiences as a soldier in both the Civil and Indian wars. Two of Louis' uncles worked on ranches for many years. It was in the company of men such as these that Louis was first exposed to the history and adventure of the American Frontier.

Though the LaMoore household had a modest collection of books, it was at the nearby Alfred Dickey Free Library where his eldest sister Edna was a librarian that Louis spent many long hours exploring indepth subjects only touched on by the schools.

By the beginning of the 1920's Louis and his adopted brother John were the only children left in the LaMoore household. Edna had moved away to pursue a career as a schoolteacher. His eldest brother Parker was on his way to becoming a successful newspaperman and political aide. Second brother Yale managed a grocery store where John and Louis occasionally worked. The twins, Clara and Clarice, died while infants and his beloved sister Emmy Lou succumbed to the 1918 epidemic of Spanish influenza.

Jamestown, North Dakota provided Louis with an idyllic childhood, but hard times finally uprooted the family and set them on a course that would forever alter Louis life. Dr. LaMoore, his wife Emily, and their sons Louis and John took their fortunes on the road. They traveled across the country in an often-desperate seven-year odyssey. It was in these various places and while working odd jobs that young Louis met the wide variety of characters that would later become the inspiration for his writing.

In the years after leaving Jamestown Louis had a sporadic career as a professional boxer. Louis ended his fighting career by coaching several successful Golden Glove teams; the first few in Oklahoma. On his own, Louis hoboed across the country, hopping freight trains with men who had been riding the rails for half a century. Traveling around the country and working in various remote locations gave Louis an intimate first-hand knowledge of the territory and landscape where the majority of his stories would be set.

Though he left school in the 10th grade Louis had a thirst for knowledge. Often he went without meals in order to afford to buy books. He sometimes worked long and hard so he could quit working temporarily and afford to study full time.

After several years in the Pacific Northwest, Louis' parents moved to a little farm that their eldest son, Parker, had purchased in Oklahoma. They had a house, animals, occasional crops, and their lives returned to normal. Slowly the LaMoore family began to put down roots.

I talked to Al Hester from Choctaw who had been a friend to Louis. He said the LaMoore family moved to Choctaw around 1932. Even though Louis eventually began traveling quite often, he still considered Choctaw his home until he moved to Los Angeles after his stint in the Army. Louis used to be Al's trainer when he was making his mark as a Golden Glove competitor. Occasionally Louis traveled with Al during his competitions. One time when Al broke his leg during a boxing match Louis was there to carry him half a mile to the streetcar which would transport them home. Al remembers Louis as a man without wheels, walking everywhere he went in Choctaw. They lived two miles from the downtown portion of Choctaw so Louis must have gotten his exercise on a daily basis.

I asked Al if he had read any of Louis' books and of course his reply was "every one of them." Al says he unfortunately wasn't smart enough at the time to keep some of the books Louis had given him in the early days of his writing.

Louis' son Beau came to visit Al in 1998 and wanted Al to show him where his Dad lived in Choctaw. The only evidence remaining on the property was the lean-to barn behind where the house once set. Al at one time lived only a block from the LaMoore house in the home where he was raised. Some citizens in Choctaw are now in the process of trying to get the town library to be named the Louis L'Amour Library.

Louis always wanted to be a writer, but in his early days he thought his writing would take the form of poetry. But poetry wasn't bringing him any money. For years he struggled to learn his craft. Finally he sold a short story called *Anything for a Pal* to a pulp magazine called *True Gang Life*. He made less than $8, but he took it as a sign and committed his attention to writing for the pulps. The hoped for breakthrough took almost two years to come. In 1937 he sold a short story called *Gloves for a Tiger* to Thrilling Adventures Magazine and, this time, other sales followed quickly.

Louis was inducted into the U.S. Army late in the summer of 1942. Before he returned home he was promoted to 1st Lieutenant and was briefly a company commander. He returned to Choctaw for a brief time in 1946 and tried to convince his friend Al to participate in professional boxing. But Al was no longer inclined to pursue boxing.

Louis, on the other hand, took the advice of a friend in the publishing business who encouraged him to move to Los Angeles and begin writing western stories. In one year he sold almost a story a week. From then on it was one novel after another which later began to produce into lucrative film adaptations.

In 1956 Louis married Katherine Elizabeth Adams, an aspiring actress. Together they traveled all over the west searching out locations and doing research for Louis' books. In 1961 their son Beau was born and in 1964 they had a daughter, Angelique.

In 1960 Louis developed his famous Sackett family series. He traveled extensively to promote books and movies and, for the first time in his life, bought a house. By 1973 his new found wealth allowed him to move into a better neighborhood in West Los Angeles. Louis finally felt independent and secure for the first time in his adult life. He was 65 years old. Louis won the Western Writers of America's Golden Spur Award, North Dakota's Theodore Roosevelt Rough Rider Award and later the Western Writer's of America's Golden Saddleman Award. In 1983 U.S. Congress awarded him the National Gold Medal and a year later the Medal of Freedom. His books have been translated into over 15 foreign languages and are sold in English in almost a dozen countries.

In the summer of 1987 Louis caught pneumonia. In a few weeks he threw it off, but that fall he caught it again. A biopsy revealed a thin veil of cancerous material running throughout his lungs. Surgery was impossible. He began his long postponed memoir, *Education of a Wandering Man.* He was editing the book the afternoon he died. In June 1988, a few days before he passed away, Louis was notified that sales of his books had topped two hundred million.

Since his death Bantam Books has continued to release the work of Louis L'Amour. His son Beau is working hard to continue the legacy his father left. Beau's talents are being recognized as he pursues his own creative abilities. Hopefully, generations to come will continue to enjoy the insightful look of the old west through the eyes of Louis L'Amour.

Patience Sewell Latting - *Mayor*

What a blessing it was to meet Patience, a woman whose name fits her perfectly. She was born in Texhoma, Oklahoma which she pointed out is not Lake Texoma. Texhoma is a city located in the Panhandle. There is a railroad track that runs through the middle of town which is the dividing line between Texhoma, Oklahoma and Texhoma, Texas.

Patience's father, Frank A. Sewell, Sr., was the president of a small bank in Texhoma. Her mother was a stay-at-home mom who kept busy with the care of Patience and her younger brother Frank, Jr. Except for a few years when her family lived in Colorado and California, she was raised and attended school in Texhoma. At the time there were only about 850 residents in Texhoma. Patience loved growing up there because her family knew a lot of people. In a small community people tend to look out for each other.

Patience had an enjoyable childhood and a comfortable life. Her parents taught her very early how important education was to her future. She remembers at a young age visiting the public library every Sunday afternoon which helped her explore the possibilities the world had to offer.

Patience brought out a very good point which causes a lot of deserving people to miss out on opportunities in life. *"Talents and abilities may not be developed in a person's life if someone doesn't encourage them in a particular direction."* It is especially important in the formative years. Those years go by so quickly. They are often known as the "Que Sera Sera whatever will be, will be" years. However, the outcome is not always what we intend our lives to be if they aren't directed in the proper way.

Patience was fortunate. Her parents taught her to study, do her best in school and be an avid reader. There is an old saying "Readers are Leaders." Patience proved the statement to be true. With her strong family background she wasn't afraid to step out and take on challenges.

She went to college for four years at Oklahoma University majoring in mathematics and minoring in English and achieving the award of Phi Beta Kappa in her junior year. Afterwards she went to Columbia University in New York and studied economics and statistics. While in New York she and a few of her friends took time to enjoy the many pleasures of New York. They went to the opera, the symphony and plays off and on broadway. She remembers what a terrific time she had being young and experiencing life in a city that was so different from where she grew up. But Oklahoma was still her home.

After graduate school she spent a year working for Chase National Bank, which at the time was one of the largest banks in the world. She worked in the library and research department as a researcher. If bank officers needed information in a particular area the research department was well equipped with materials to provide the needed data.

It was an interesting time in her life but she knew even though New York was a beautiful and exciting city, she still wanted to marry and raise a family in Oklahoma. After working at the bank she moved to Oklahoma City. She became re-acquainted with Trimble Latting whom she met at Oklahoma University and dated for a short while after college. They were married August 23, 1941 and spent their honeymoon driving to Washington D.C. where he was going to be stationed for a while as part of the Army Air Force.

Patience and Trimble were married 55 years before Trimble passed away in October 1996. The adjustment of living alone after so many years together has taken some getting used to but her memories of their life together carry her through.

I asked Patience how two people stay together for 55 years. She said most importantly you have to want it to work bad enough to stay committed. Fortunately, she and Trimble had a lot in common. They were wise enough to realize they were two separate individuals who had independent interests. They were determined not to smother each other, but to allow the other person to live his or her life freely.

She encouraged him and he likewise encouraged her to fulfill her dreams, to live life to its fullest on their own terms and to give each other breathing room so when they came back together it was a pleasurable time. They also tried to make sure they both weren't angry at the same time. They learned that counting to 10 before speaking really does work. They also understood there would be times when one person is not feeling up to par and may not be carrying his load, but the other person willingly picks up the slack until the other can get back into the swing of things.

Oh how I wish everyone would take heed to those remarks. Obviously after 55 years Patience and Trimble have proven their formula for how a long-lasting marriage works.

In reference to God, Patience believes there is a power greater than ourselves. She always tries to think what would God want her to do when she goes through a trial in her life. If she waits patiently, she feels assured He has led her in the right direction. Even though some people may not believe in God's presence, they would be amazed at how lonely they would feel if His presence really was taken from them.

Patience's grooming for a political career began early. She was elected as the Outstanding Woman Student while at Oklahoma University. Her services as a member and leader of the League of Women Voters helped single her out for one of the more difficult assignments in state government. She was appointed by the Federal Court to help with the historic reapportionment of the Oklahoma legislature in 1964.

In 1967 she was elected to the Oklahoma City Council, the first woman to ever sit on the city's council. In 1971 she was elected mayor, once again, the first woman to hold that office. In fact, when she was elected Mayor, Oklahoma City became the first major city in the U.S. to elect a woman mayor. She held the mayor's post for three consecutive terms.

Patience said she is often asked "Why a woman mayor?" Her reply is "Why not?" Some would ask "Isn't politics too dirty for a woman?" Patience again would reply "If that is true, then that is even more reason to elect a woman to help clean it up."

After her term as mayor ended in 1983, she was appointed to serve on the board of the Oklahoma City Branch of the Federal Reserve Bank of Kansas City where she remained for six years.

Patience is fully retired from the political arena. She enjoys visiting her grown children who are scattered in different areas of the world. Her daughter Nancy lives in Singapore. Her son James lives in Palm Desert, California. The oldest daughter Francelia lives in Oklahoma City and her youngest daughter Cynthia lives in Atlanta, Georgia.

In June of 1998 the Edgemere Park Historical Preservation Society dedicated a park bench to Trimble and Patience. It sits in the park across the street from the home they shared together from 1961 to 1996. The bench is a continued remembrance of a love that never failed.

Patience Latting

James Leake

Businessman

James' grandfather was a law clerk who originally came from Illinois, but moved to Guthrie, Oklahoma to homestead 16 lots. In a tent on one of those lots is where James' father was born in 1891. His grandfather knew some of the engineers who had surveyed Oklahoma before the run in 1889. He asked them where to go to have good farming land and they said up by Chandler. So he hitched a ride for a dollar on a wagon from Guthrie to eight miles south of Chandler and proceeded to walk the rest of the way. Now remember, this was way back in the 1800's. Traveling was hard and resources were limited.

On the way he met a preacher that was also homesteading around the Chandler area. They talked while they walked a mile further down the road to draw water just so they could sit around a campfire and drink a hot cup of coffee. Later the grandfather located the lot of land he wanted to homestead, so after looking it over he made his way back to Guthrie and went to the land office to secure the lot he had found. It was in the Fall of the year.

James' father was still a small child when his father packed up their belongings and moved his family to Chandler. There were a lot of improvements that had to be made to the land in order to make it livable. Everywhere

Jimmy Leake with the 1911 Rolls-Royce Silver Ghost he purchased in London for $26,000 in 1965.

they looked the grass was belly high to a horse. He had his work cut out for him. He built a one room house on the land and James still has pictures of the house in different stages of development.

The biggest fear they had at the time was the prairie fires. The grass was so heavy that if a fire started it was very hard to put out. Later, both of James' grandfathers built a log church and a cemetery in the area. The first person buried in the cemetery was a person who was burned in a prairie fire. James' grandfather eventually built the Stone School and that is where James' father met his mother when she came there to teach.

James' grandfather was a visionary. He started building ponds because there was no water near his house. His ponds were the largest bodies of water in the area and when the Magnolia Oil Company needed water while drilling their wells they came to James' grandfather. He made a deal with them if they would put his son to work he would sell them the water.

So in 1923 James' father went to work for the Magnolia Oil Company. He was a pumper working part-time and hoping to advance to full-time. He set up a 10 horsepower pump on the pond and pumped a two inch stream of water three miles to fill up the tanks where the oil drilling was taking place. James remembers the day when his father came home excited because he had been promoted to full time and was making $50 a month, which was a lot of money back then.

He also remembers the day they started drilling using a one cylinder engine. It stood out in James' mind so vividly that in later years he placed an oil rig on the Channel 8 transmitter site as remembrance of those childhood days.

James' father worked for the oil company from 1923 until 1956. He was a lease superintendent in Chandler by the time he retired.

James had a wonderful childhood growing up in Chandler. He graduated from Chandler High School where he was selected as the best citizen in the school and received a scholarship to Oklahoma Baptist University. However, instead of going there he entered Oklahoma University in the Fall of 1935 as a pre-med student. He was at Oklahoma University five years before he decided he didn't want to be a medical doctor. During his college days he operated several businesses and it was looking as if that was where his talents were.

In September of 1940 he married Marjory Griffin from Muskogee whose father owned the Griffin Grocery Company and several radio stations. James went to work for Marjory's father as a salesman a few months before they were married. James had heard how Mr. Griffin had acquired his first radio station and was hoping that some day he would be a part of that business as well.

James was doing so well in his job that a year later his father-in-law transferred him to the Dallas, Texas office so he could become the manager. He was there until 1945 when his father-in-law passed away. James and his family then moved back to Muskogee to help manage that office as well as the peanut company and the radio stations.

As was told to James, the Oklahoma College for Women had the KOCW Radio Station in Chickasha and was wanting to sell it because it wasn't making any money. Mr. Griffin bought the station for $1,000 and was going to move it to Muskogee.

After some further thought, he decided if he could somehow hook up with a major station like CBS he could really make the station profitable. He went to New York and met with a gentleman who agreed to be affiliated with Mr. Griffin's station, but only if he would move it to Tulsa instead of the smaller town of Muskogee. Mr. Griffin agreed and KTUL Channel 8 became the second radio station behind KVOO and began airing in January of 1934.

Of course the next step in later years became the development and ownership of several television stations. James described the evolution of inventions as first starting with a vision. *A vision is wisdom, and wisdom comes during the development of an idea or invention by actually doing something first and that one step leads to another until you have created what you had envisioned all along.* Working in a field with a team of horses makes you dream of having a tractor. You have to be doing something in order for the pieces to begin falling into place.

One of the greatest incentives of all time, is to be dirt poor, because that gives you the desire to do better. *Some people only go so far and quit because they have no vision. Others can see far past what the natural eye can see and dream dreams that don't even seem possible. James believes strongly in the guidance of God in a person's life and has learned over the years how to tap into that guidance. He describes it as needing to be in communication with the source of divine guidance.*

"If you aren't in communication with the source then it is like hanging up the telephone without leaving a message, he said. *If you keep your mind open and ready to receive the direction, it will come.* The guy with vision remembers all that he has learned and fits it into the rest of the puzzle. The guy without vision says, I'm done for anyway, so I'm not going to do anything to try and save myself."

"Most people who have faith don't always know how the divine direction works, they just know that it does, he continued. *You have to have faith in yourself and faith that there is someone else at the other end of your faith. You have to believe if you keep going you are going to reach that faith. If you don't have faith, it's because you aren't opening yourself up to believe. If you have the patience to give and then wait to get, it will come to you.*

When you see the tremendous success that Mr. James Leake has experienced over the years, you have to believe there are some huge nuggets of truth in what he says. In the twilight of his years, Mr. Leake remains a wealth of inspiration and information and surely a man that anyone could call a friend.

I was told that at one time he had the world's largest Rolls Royce collection of approximately 500 cars. Of course The Leake Car Auction is still an annual event that displays cars we would all like to have parked in our driveways.

I feel honored to have met James C. Leake. I planned on having other informative talks with him. However he passed away July 3, 2001. He will be missed, but his legacy will continue.

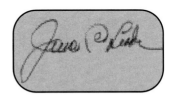

Andrew Moses Lester - Sculptor

On a bitter cold November 14th day in 1914, a boy was born in his grandfathers old dugout sod house near Cheyenne, Oklahoma within sight of the location of the 1868 battle of the Washita.

In the years that followed Oklahoma would find this great-great-grandson of Davy Crockett had become a well-known and respected sculptor.

At age four the family moved to Oklahoma City. His mother, Della and father, William were hard working people who struggled to provide for their family of seven. Eventually it took a toll on the marriage and William deserted the family, an event Andrew spent years trying to recover from but finally found the courage to forgive his father.

Andrew had a wise comment to make," He said, "When you have trials and difficulties life gives you a balance so you can handle the more important issues."

As a young boy Andrew took on part of the responsibility to provide for the family after his father left. He was a caddy for the golf course and had a newspaper route which he ran whether sleet, snow, rain or shine. They raised chickens and grew vegetables in their garden. Somehow, in spite of the hardships, Andrew knew he was meant for greatness.

Andrew discovered he had a talent for sculpture at the age of 14. He was fishing with some friends and they were carving their initials in the rocks. He picked up a piece of sandstone, curious as to whether he could carve something out of it. He took it home and with his pocket knife carved a buffalo being attacked by wolves. The item is now displayed in the Oklahoma Historical Museum in Oklahoma City.

As a Boy Scout he sculpted a bust of Abraham Lincoln which his Scout Master and math teacher took to the Oklahoma County Fair. It won first place. Then they took it to the Oklahoma State Fair and it won first place again. At the time Andrew had never had any art lessons or previous training of any kind. To his surprise, he was featured on the front page of the newspaper. This was the beginning of his quest for perfection in the art world.

While a student at Putnam City High School, Andrew sculpted a bust of Davy Crockett, his great-great-grandfather. It was dedicated at the Alamo August 17, 1933.

Andrew is famous for his western bronzes and portrait memorials of the men who made America and carved the virgin lands of the Oklahoma Territory. He feels portrait memorials are links in the human chain of Oklahoma memories of those who made history, changed it or lived it for those who choose to remember and wish to be.

The exterior signature of a person's soul. That is what Andrew enjoys recreating in all of his sculpture work.

Andrew studied ceramics at the University of Oklahoma under John Frank, founder of Frankhoma Pottery, and completed his bachelor of arts degree at Oklahoma A&M in 1940. He was National Youth Administration California state supervisor of ceramics and taught art in Palm Springs, San Bernardino and Pittsburg, California high schools (1940-1970): at Los Angeles State College from (1959-1961) and at University of California, Riverside (1957-1970).

Andrew specialized in portrait bust memorials since 1972, creating more than 100, including busts of notables such as OSU basketball coach Eddie Sutton, Dallas Cowboy quarterback Troy Aikman, Olympic Gold Medal winner, Jim Thorpe, former coach Hank Iba and James Saied of Saied Music who was known as the reincarnate of John Philip Sousa.

In 1970 he was listed in the edition Top U.S. Educators of Secondary Schools. In 1978-79 he was listed in Who's Who in the West and in 1979 he made International Biographies. In 1981-82 he was listed in Who's Who in California.

In 1993, on the occasion of the 135th Anniversary of the Battle of the Washita in Cheyenne, Oklahoma, Andrew's bust of Chief Black Kettle was dedicated. Andrew had been recognized by the Cheyenne Tribe and was given the name White

Buffalo, the name he chose for his Art Gallery located for several years in Guthrie, Oklahoma and briefly in Cheyenne.

Andrew received a citation in 1999 from the state legislature for his artwork promoting cultural harmony and diversity. He urged lawmakers to provide money for the arts so that the state centennial celebration in 2007 could inspire generations of Oklahomans.

In January 2000, Andrew's bust of Olympian Jim Thorpe was dedicated and put on display at the U.S. Olympic Committee headquarters in Colorado Springs, Colorado.

I had the opportunity to view some of Andrew's work during our interview and was quite impressed with the detail shown in each sculpture. He is such a gentle loving man that we immediately struck up a warm conversation laced with a few tears as he shared his heart with me on many issues.

Andrew's first wife has since passed away but he remarried and shares his life with Jeanne, his wife of 8 years who he met in the Jordan River Temple in Sandy, Utah. He is the father of five children which include his son, David and four daughters, Lillian, Andrea, Judy and Lorraine. They are all very proud of the accomplishments their father has made throughout his lifetime.

Over the years numerous articles have been written about Andrew Lester's incredible contributions. I know the Bible says " A man is worth his hire," which simply means it is all right and even honorable to receive payment for your talents and gifts. Yet Andrew will probably go down in history as being the famous sculptor who thought it more blessed to give than to receive.

I was honored to have spent a few hours with Andrew and Jeanne. I hope in some small way his inclusion in this Distinguished Oklahomans book will at least capture his greatness in word if not in monetary gain.

I was saddened to hear that Andrew passed away at his home October 21, 2000. He was so excited about having his life profiled in this book. I wish he could have lived long enough to see it. He will be missed. Details are being worked out to have Andrew's art collection permanently displayed in a gallery-probably in Cheyenne, Oklahoma.

Andrew M. Lester

Billie Letts

Author

Billie was born in Tulsa, Oklahoma in 1938. She was an only child to Bill and Virginia Gipson, who had wanted a boy so they named her Billie Dean. They had both come from a poor family and neither of them had finished high school. Yet some years later, after returning from military service and holding down a couple of different jobs, Billie's father started his own company called Arctic Air Conditioning.

Both parents worked very hard in the business and taught Billie the importance of hard work as well. They were quite proud of her when she graduated from Union High School in 1956 and then went on to Northeastern State in Tahlequah for two years. By then their business was flourishing and they were able to pay Billie's way through college.

At the age of 12 Billie entered a writing contest sponsored by a radio station. In 100 words or less she was to write an essay on why she listened to that radio station. She won a watch in the contest and right away thought she must definitely be a writer. The funny thing about it is, everything she said in the essay was all made up. There wasn't a shred of truth in it. But she realized there was profit to be made in telling stories.

She continued to write throughout her school days and into her married life, but she never really tried to have anything published. Her husband Dennis was continuing his education as an English teacher and eventually received his Ph.D. In his pursuit of higher education, it stirred Billie up to do the same, so she decided to become an English teacher as well.

After Dennis finished his course work at the University of Illinois, they moved back to Oklahoma to the town of Durant. Billie began attending Southeastern University to receive her master's degree. In 1975 after the fall of Saigon, one of the college administrators went to Fort Chaffee and brought 150 Vietnamese refugees back to Durant. Since Billie had a background in English as a second language she volunteered to teach a night class to the Vietnamese. In doing so she got very involved with their lives. Unknowingly, her connection to them would someday aid her as characters in a book.

Billie continued to occasionally write short stories. she sent some to her friends as gifts and periodically would send a story to a publisher, but nothing seemed to come of it. As her time to start thinking about retirement began to draw near, she started thinking more about her writing. By then, her youngest son Tracy was living in Chicago, acting in some good theater and turning out some powerful writing for the stage. Her son Shawn was living in Singapore doing the work he loved-playing, composing and arranging music. Dennis already retired from teaching, had started acting in films and as of now has accumulated over 40 feature films and television movies.

Billie bought books on screenwriting and taught herself about format and structure. She was still teaching and had a creative writing course she instructed at the college, and many of her students were wanting to write screenplays as well. It was a lot of fun for Billie and she continued to write screenplays for about eight years with no real outlet for them except one that was used as a play for a community theater. So she went back to writing short stories.

At age 55 she started attending writer's conferences in Tulsa and Oklahoma City and eventually attended one in New Orleans. At the New Orleans conference there were 12 New York agents who allowed writers 15 minutes of their time if they had signed up. Billie, of course, took advantage of the opportunity and gave agent Elaine Markson, one of her screenplays. She explained how she had previously been writing screenplays, and was back to writing short stories which her husband called *Tales From Wal-Mart.*

Elaine took the screenplay and four days later Billie received a phone call from her saying she thought she could sell the play, called "Verritas the Prince of Truth," a story about a comic book super hero who comes to life. Elaine then told Billie to send her the short stories she had written about Wal-Mart.

One of the stories was called *Where the Heart Is.* When the agent called back she encouraged Billie to produce that short story into a full fledged book. Two years later Billie had the finished product. In May of 1994 she gave the story to Elaine and by June of 1994 the story had been bought by Jamie Raab at Warner Books. The next month the film rights were sold to 20th Century Fox and then foreign sales started pouring in.

By 1995 the book was published and Billie was on her way to an extensive book signing tour. Billie retired as a teacher. She loved the classroom but there wasn't enough time to do both, and she had wanted to be a writer for as long as she could remember. When she walked into the first bookstore and saw her name on the front of her book she felt like she was finally ready to say "now I am a real writer," but she realized she had really been a writer for almost 50 years.

Doors were beginning to open wide for Billie. She traveled to Denmark, Finland, Norway and London. The invitations just never seemed to stop. Then Billie decided to send five chapters of her second book, *Honk and Holler,* to her agent and it was bought the following week. Billie had 14 months to finish the entire book. She moved to Tulsa and lived secretly for six months in a high rise condo where no one but her husband, agent and editor could reach her. Of course she finished the book and during the time of our interview she was working on her third. Who knows how many manuscripts will come from Billie's creative storehouse.

Billie's book *Where The Heart Is* was featured on one of Oprah's Book of the Month Club shows. The television crew shot Oprah and Billie dining at a Wal-Mart snack bar. I'm sure that was a great thrill for Billie. Yet what must have been one of her greatest thrills so far was when the movie came out on the big screen. I had not had the chance to read Billie's book, but I did go see the movie. I thought it was wonderful. Too close for comfort in some areas, but nevertheless a movie I was glad I attended.

Billie has certainly learned a lot over the years about life and the ways in which we can enhance our destiny. *She said there is an energy that somehow makes its way to us. If everyone would open themselves up to the energy they would have a greater chance of experiencing all life has to offer. You have to be willing to expose who you are and how you think. Be willing to be vulnerable. Take a risk and find out for your own self who you really are. Your talents are very important, but discipline is the key to success. Without talent you can't start, but without discipline you can't finish.*

Guy Logsdon
Professor / Writer / Musician

Guy is an internationally recognized authority on western and cowboy music, poetry and musicians as well as on the life, times and music of Woody Guthrie. Other research interests include Will Rogers, the Dust Bowl and its migrants, western swing music including Bob and Johnnie Lee Wills, Native American history, arts and crafts and Southwestern history, literature and folklife.

He is a native Oklahoman who has been fortunate to work with the tools his parents instilled in him. His father Guy, a native Texan, taught him to play and love old-time western music. His mother Mattie, a lady of Native American descent, endowed him with a love and passion for books and knowledge. He is a scholar, a writer, an entertainer, a teacher, a librarian and a collector of traditional lore and books.

Guy was born in Ada, Oklahoma, a town he said he dearly loves. Being one of five children with numerous aunts, uncles and cousins he felt like the majority of Ada must have been populated by the Logsdon clan. His father Guy Sr. owned a furniture store in Ada, but at one time had envisioned being a well-known entertainer. He was once offered a vaudeville contract, however his mother with a somewhat rigid view of entertainers, believed them to be lacking in moral stability. She refused to allow her son to follow in those footsteps. So Guy Sr. limited his music to his own pleasure and taught each of his children how to play an instrument.

Guy, the youngest of his sons, played the bass fiddle in their family band called The Western Seven. Then when he was a junior in high school he joined with four other boys to form a band called The Diamond D Boys. Music was a major part of his youthful years and has continued to play a huge role in his life.

When it was time for college he enrolled at East Central University in Ada. He desired to be one of the world's greatest photographers, a talent he used to work his way through college. He became an English teacher and taught school in California, Arizona and Oklahoma. He was the reference librarian at Oklahoma State University before becoming Director of Libraries at the University of Tulsa in 1967. For many years he served the University of Tulsa as Director of Libraries and Professor of Education and American Folklife.

In 1970-71 Guy wrote and narrated 16 television shows titled "Folklore of the Southwest" for the Oklahoma Education Television Authority. The shows were so popular that five additional shows were produced in 1973-74. He served as a consultant for the United Artist movie, "Bound for Glory" and for the Ginger Productions television documentary, "Woody Guthrie: Hard Travelin'." He performed on Michael Feldman's "Whad' Ya Know?" radio show, "Bill Kurtis' The Real Cowboy: Portrait of an American Icon" television documentary and numerous other radio and television shows.

He has performed for a wide variety of audiences throughout the nation including featured appearances at the Smithsonian Institution's Annual Festival of American Folklife; the National Museum of American Art, Washington, D.C., Central Park, New York City; the annual Cowboy Poetry Gathering and the Cowboy Music Gathering, Elko, Nevada; the National Cowboy & Western Heritage Museum, Oklahoma City; the Lincoln County Cowboy Symposium, Ruidoso Downs, New Mexico; the "Tribute to the Singing Cowboys," Autry Western Heritage Museum, Los Angeles, California; the stage show "Revels on the Range," Hanover, New Hampshire and hundreds of other communities and gatherings across the nation.

Guy's book *The Whorehouse Bells Were Ringing* and *Other Songs Cowboys Sing* (University of Illinois Press, 1989) is a classic study of cowboy songs, and his compilation Cowboy Songs on Folkways for Smithsonian/Folkways Recordings received numerous reviews declaring it to be one of the most important cowboy song anthologies ever produced. He co-authored an almanac of cowboy/western singers, *Saddle Serenaders* (Gibbs Smith Publisher, 1994), and his latest co-authored book is about his hometown, *Ada, Oklahoma: Queen City of the Chickasaw Nation* (Donning Company, 1999).

Guy has published the highly acclaimed *Coolin' Down: An Anthology of Contemporary Cowboy Poetry* and has written over 100 articles, essays and encyclopedia entries.

In 1990-91 his scholarly work about Woody Guthrie earned Guy a Senior Post-Doctoral Fellowship at the Smithsonian

Institution to compile a biblio-discography of the songs of Woody Guthrie. In 1993 the National Endowment for the Humanities awarded him a major independent scholar grant to continue his Guthrie project, and as a Smithsonian Research Associate he compiled and annotated four compact disc collections for Smithsonian/Folkways Recordings.

He and Jeff Place, Smithsonian/Folkways Archivist, have co-compiled and annotated six compact discs including Woody Guthrie: The Asch Recordings Vol. 1-4 which was reviewed as "...one of the indispensable documents of 20th century American music." Guy was a contributing writer for the Smithsonian Institution Traveling Exhibition Service (SITES) exhibit This Land Is Your Land: The Life and Legacy of Woody Guthrie, and also has annotated six recording collections of Jack Guthrie, Tex Ritter and Marty Robbins for the German company, Bear Family Records.

In early 2000 Guy released his own collection of songs titled *Traditional Cowboy Songs* featuring him singing most of the cowboy songs unaccompanied-the traditional cowboy way.

Guy has received awards for his efforts from the Oklahoma Heritage Association, the University of Oklahoma and Westerners International. In 1993 the Governor of Oklahoma awarded him "Special Recognition" for contributions to the arts and culture of Oklahoma. The National Cowboy Symposium, Lubbock, Texas, in 1997 awarded him for "Contributions to Western Music" and in 1998 the "All-Around Cowboy Culture" award. The Academy of Western Artists in 1997 awarded him with the "Will Rogers' Memorial Award for Outstanding Achievement in the Performance Arts." He also has served on a wide variety of civic boards and academic committees including the Board of Directors of the Oklahoma Historical Society.

The day I went to Guy's house to interview him I was amazed at the number of books lining his walls. I thought I had a lot of books that I can never part with, but he had me beat hands down. I had been told by a mutual friend, Ray Bingham that Guy was a very interesting person and worthy to be included in this book. Ray was certainly right.

Of course it was impossible to miss the array of Hop-Along-Cassidy memorabilia that Guy so proudly displays. He still intends to publish a book some day which he says will be a three part book encompassing Clarence Mulford, creator of the character, William Boyd and Hop-Along Cassidy. I'll look forward to reading that book.

Guy was kind enough to play his guitar for me and sing part of a cowboy song. At the end of our interview he didn't let me leave empty handed. He gave me a copy of his latest C.D. on *Traditional Cowboy Songs* as well as the book he co-authored titled *Saddle Serenaders*. I was so impressed with the content of his book and the way in which each person was profiled. Guy Logsdon certainly has been living a full and productive life and his talents never seem to wane.

William Polk Longmire, Jr. - Physician

Bill's profile was written from his book *Life is Short, The Art is Long* by Sherman M. Mellinkoff, M.D.
Bill's father, William Polk Longmire, Sr. grew up in Tennessee. He always longed to be a physician and learn the powers

of medicine and the practice of healing. At the Louisville Hospital College of Medicine, Polk was a conscientious student. It is possible both he and his instructors discovered that he had the gift of dexterity. Dexterity alone does not make a great surgeon-much learning is also required. But without this gift a medical student is probably well advised and usually inclined to enter one of the many medical specialties apart from surgical ones.

After graduating from medical school at the age of 23, Polk returned to Tennessee. For a short time he thought about establishing his practice in LaFollette, a town not far from the Longmire farm, but he was restless. He packed a few belongings, including his stethoscope and set out for Colorado on the Frisco Railroad. The railroad had only recently been extended into the Indian Territory of Oklahoma.

By the time the train stopped in St. Louis, he had changed his mind about Colorado. Some men he met on the train had fired his imagination about the Oklahoma frontier. He changed his ticket in St. Louis and went to the end of the new line in the little village of Sapulpa. When Polk arrived in Sapulpa an older physician, Dr. Lyford, was already looking for an associate. A partnership was formed: Lyford and Longmire, Physicians and Surgeons.

Not long after Polk's arrival in Sapulpa he met a young school teacher, Grace May Weeks, whom he courted and married a year or so later. Grace's father was Judge Samuel Weeks who served simultaneously as the local postmaster, United States Marshal and a mayor of Sapulpa.

The Longmires, Grace and Polk, had four children. The first two died in infancy. The third child, Mildred, died of a malignant melanoma in 1953. The fourth child, a year and a half younger than Mildred, was named William Polk, Jr.

Bill Longmire as a child attended Sunday School where his mother was a teacher. In the public grade school he was identified as a superior student and skipped a year, thus entering the four-year Sapulpa High School at the age of 13.

Mrs. Ellinghausen was the study hall teacher during Bill's senior year. She gave Bill the feeling that education should be exciting and boundless, and if he wanted to be a doctor he should become one of his country's best.

In 1930 Bill went to the University of Oklahoma where two professors made a lasting impression upon him. One was the president of the university, William Bennett Bizzell. President Bizzell selected about 20 of the best senior students, of whom Bill was one, for monthly dinners at the President's house. Discussions were informal, stimulating and culturally far ranging, widening the horizons of these young Oklahomans.

The other influential Oklahoma University teacher in Bill's life was Professor Aute Richards, chairman of the Department of Zoology. Both Dr. Richards and his wife Mildred were Johns Hopkins University Ph.D.'s. Dr. Richards advised Bill near the end of his first year what courses he should taken to prepare himself for the study of medicine.

In Bill's senior year he was asked by Dr. Richards where he hoped to attend medical school. Bill mentioned Oklahoma, Vanderbilt and Tulane as possibilities he had been thinking about. "Oh, no," Dr. Richards replied. "There is only one school for you-Johns Hopkins." Dr. Richards assured Bill he would be accepted on his recommendation.

In the fall of 1934 at the age of 21, Bill left Sapulpa by rail one evening and changed trains in St. Louis the next morning. After a full day and another night's travel he arrived in Baltimore at Johns Hopkins University.

It wasn't long before Bill became certain he wanted to be a neurosurgeon. In the summer of his third year, Bill, with the recommendation of Professor Bard, secured a fellowship at the new Montreal Neurological Institute, founded and directed by Wilder Penfield.

In his senior year at Hopkins Bill hoped to secure an internship in surgery, the first step towards becoming a general surgeon or specialist in any branch of surgery, such as neurosurgery. Bill received a letter of appointment as surgical intern on the Halsted Service of the John Hopkins Hospital from July 1, 1938 to June 30, 1939.

In October of 1939 Bill married Jane Jarvis Cornelius, born and reared in Baltimore. She worked as a receptionist and librarian in the Wilmer Eye Institute of the Johns Hopkins Hospital.

In the fall of 1940 Bill's academic training as a surgeon was suddenly interrupted when his father suffered a stroke. Bill asked Dr. Warfield Firor, acting chairman of surgery, if he could have an indefinite leave of absence to move back to Sapulpa and take care of his father's medical practice until his health resumed. His request was granted.

He returned to Sapulpa with his wife Jane and helped his father with his practice until July of 1942. For a time he lost his position at Johns Hopkins but later, through a set of circumstances, regained it and was known as one of the brightest young stars on the Hopkins surgical faculty.

Following his chief residency, Bill was asked to remain on the Hopkins full-time faculty. He rose from instructor to associate professor by 1948. Bill was asked to direct the Plastic Surgery Service.

In 1948 Bill was invited by Dr. Blalock to meet three visitors from Los Angeles. The three professors had been asked by Dr. Stafford L. Warren, founding dean of the UCLA School of Medicine, to conduct a nationwide search for UCLA's first Professor of Surgery. Not long afterward Bill was invited by Dean Warren to visit UCLA for on-site consideration to become the founding chairman of the Department of Surgery. Bill was named to the post and served for 28 years.

The one part of Dr. Warren's description that Bill found most appealing was the idea of building a whole medical school from scratch. Between November of 1948 and the following July Bill recruited to UCLA a small cadre of surgeons. The first medical students-28 of them-were to arrive in 1951. The medical school and hospital buildings, delayed in part by unforeseeable domestic consequences of the Korean War, opened in July of 1955.

Under Bill Longmire's chairmanship, the Department of Surgery on the UCLA campus, began from ground zero and grew into nine exceedingly active divisions -Cardiothoracic Surgery, General Surgery, Head and Neck Surgery, Neurosurgery, Orthopedic Surgery, Pediatric Surgery, Plastic Surgery, Surgical Oncology and Urology.

Bob Losure – *Journalist / Newscaster / Author*

Bob is another success story in life, as well as in journalism. Born and raised in Tulsa, Oklahoma, Bob as an only child knew the direction he wanted to go with his life. He had always been an avid reader and describes himself as a "book worm." During his sophomore year in high school his English teacher, Sheila Parr encouraged him to enroll in her journalism class for the following year, because she saw such potential in him.

The seed she planted took root. Not only did Bob take her journalism class, but he became the editor of the school newspaper. Before long he found himself engulfed in the desire to write. He wrote for the Tulsa World, Tulsa School Life, the Southside Times and the West Tulsa County News. He didn't care if he ever got paid, he just wanted to write.

His first professional job after college was at KTOW in Sand Springs where he played records all night from Midnight to 5 A.M. for $1.60 per hour. He originally applied there for a position in their news department only to find out that there wasn't a news department. Instead, he became Country Bob Curtis, KTOW's local disc jockey. He was there for eight months before the late hours got the best of him and he had to find another way to follow his dream.

He went to KAKC Radio to audition as a disc jockey for Lee Bayley, the program director. Lee thought Bob was terrible. However, Bob left his resume anyway and a week later Bayley called and said there was a news position available so Bob snapped it up immediately. That was the position he had wanted in the first place. He went from a big-time salary of $1.60 an hour at KTOW to $2.25 at KAKC. Along with reporting the news the job included spinning hit songs by The Doors, Jefferson Airplane and The Beach Boys. He had more fun than he ever expected. Being a serious broadcaster would just have to wait

In May of 1969 Bob graduated from Tulsa University after having already spent two years at Oklahoma University. He was now ready to get serious about his career. He left Tulsa in July of 1969 to go to Detroit and work at a powerful 50,000-watt rock-and-roll station, CKLW, again doing the 20/20 news format that he had done at KAKC. After a couple of other stints the lure of coming back to his hometown of Tulsa was too much, and in mid-1971 he returned and began working for KRMG as "Bob In The Traffic" a reporter and anchor. His first real chance at being a radio reporter. He stayed there until October 18, 1976 when he became a reporter for the CBS television affiliate KOTV Channel 6. Within two years he was anchoring the weekend news. Eventually, he became co-anchor with Clayton Vaughn for five years.

In April 1985, something we think will never happen to us, happened to Bob. He found out he had a form of cancer that had possibly spread into his lymph nodes in his stomach and chest. Within days he was in surgery. Two of the 70 lymph nodes removed were cancerous, indicating the cancer was on the move to his lungs and brain. Chemo treatments were inevitable. Bob was going to have to endure as much of it as his body could stand.

In the meantime, KOTV had found a replacement for Bob which left him fighting for his life as well as his career. The best part is Bob knew he wasn't going to die. He just felt in his heart that his time on earth wasn't finished. Fortunately, his agent Conrad Shadlen called him with news that CNN Headline News had an opening. Bob was going to have to go to Atlanta for an audition between his first and second chemo sessions.

With his hair beginning to fall out and a body that wasn't as strong as it normally was, he flew to Atlanta. Even knowing about his condition CNN hired him believing if he had enough courage to audition for the job under those conditions he was certainly worthy of the position.

Bob stayed at CNN from 1985 to 1997 when he had just turned 50 years old. He had been given the opportunity to reach a plateau of success that had been very rewarding to him. He covered stories at CNN that would have put a feather in any-one's cap, but now he felt it was time to move on.

His bout with cancer is a distant memory and since he is still a young man he opted to become a freelance speaker and emcee. He enjoys producing corporate videos for companies like Home Depot, IBM, Bell South and others.

In 1998 he published his first book titled, *Five Seconds to Air.* The book tells stories about his years with CNN, his victory over his fight with cancer, the pros and cons of broadcast journalism and advice to the masses. It's the advice from Bob's book that I found so inspiring, so I would like to pass some of his tips along to others. If anyone wants the full impact I'm sure he would love to make one of his books available.

Know what you want out of life. *Change your goals, as you change your needs.* Accept the fact that you will have ups and downs in life and some people will help you through them while others will not. *Always have a positive frame of mind. Adversity will either make you bitter and weak or challenged and strong.* If all we do is blame our childhood on our parents, misery will follow us around like a junkyard dog. Your life experiences makes you one of a kind. *There are some wonderful hidden qualities inside you, that if you let them come out, will make you feel that you are an important part of this world.* People will respond to the way you care about them. The good in being alive every day makes all the negative things in life seem insignificant in comparison. If you are sitting there saying you'd like to change your life, but the timing is just not right, I've got this late breaking bulletin for you: take a chance. W*hatever happens, embrace a positive meaning from it, knowing it has helped mold you into a new and improved version of who you really want to be.* The time may never be perfectly right, but the clock is ticking on your time on this earth. The only risks that you'll never regret are the ones you didn't take.

Susie Luchsinger

Singer/Songwriter

For Susie's profile I'm using quotes from her book she sent me *A Tender Road Home*, which I'm sure everyone will find quite interesting and enlightening.

Along with three siblings, Susie grew up on a ranch in southeastern Oklahoma, 30 miles south of McAlester and 15 miles north of Atoka. She is the youngest of the four McEntire kids. Alice Lynn is the oldest. Del Stanley (nicknamed Pake) is next in line followed by Reba McEntire and lastly Susie. Susie's parents, Clark Vincent and Jacqueline Smith McEntire, instilled into all four of their children traits and talents conducive of their own personalities.

Clark was a rodeo champion and Jacqueline was a dedicated mother and homemaker who Susie said must have had a hidden desire to become a professional singer. While Jacqueline kept the family singing harmony either at the supper table, in the car or traveling to a rodeo, Clark introduced them to the rodeo circuit.

Unlike her sister Reba, Susie was quite a loner as a child. She was happy just to go off by herself and let her imagination run free. She sucked her thumb until she was in the third grade. She had a lisp when she spoke and stuttered too. *She said her insecurities accompanied her up through her college years and into marriage. Along the way, insecurity picked up a partner- fear of failure.*

Even though the McEntires were a musical family, other than singing around the house or in the car Susie didn't sing publicly until she was in the second grade when she performed in the Thanksgiving Play.

After Susie graduated from college in 1980 with a degree in personnel management and a minor in accounting she went to work at J.D. Simmons, Inc. in Oklahoma City. Reba had just signed a record contract and was appearing as a solo act. In late 1980, the National Finals Rodeo was held in Oklahoma City. Reba was scheduled to sing the national anthem each night and since Susie was living in the city, she attended the rodeo with her.

On Friday and Saturday nights after the rodeo, Reba and her band provided a dance at the Myriad Convention Center. It was at the dance Susie first met rodeo cowboy Paul Luchsinger who would soon become her husband.

The first time Susie remembers singing on stage with Reba was in a concert in June 1980. Among other great hits they performed *I Don't Want to Be a One Night Stand,* which was Reba's first single. Besides the performances, Susie accompanied Reba on many of her promotional trips to radio stations or wherever her record company was promoting her latest single or album. Unknowingly, God was preparing Susie for the day she would be going into those radio stations to promote her own albums.

Susie performed on stage with Reba for nearly two years during which time she married Paul Luchsinger on November 27, 1981 at the First Baptist Church in Stringtown. They had never truly discussed their expectations of each other or what they considered to be normal in a relationship. They were just in a hurry to get married and start living together. Paul continued to travel the rodeo circuit while Susie kept singing with Reba. When they both returned home they would fall into each other's arms and relish their time together.

Several months into their marriage Paul began finding it more difficult to allow Susie to travel with Reba. He disliked the fact they sometimes sang in honky tonk bars and clubs. He also hated the fact she was traveling in a tour bus with Reba and six male band members. Before long Paul was constantly struggling with bouts of jealousy that never seemed to get resolved. By the time they had been married a year, Paul's jealousy had caused him to begin knocking doors off their hinges. His anger quickly progressed to verbal and physical abuse as well. It would not stop for the next 12 years.

In June 1982, married only six months, Susie found out she was pregnant. For the first three months of her pregnancy she continued to perform with Reba on the road. By August it was becoming harder for her to travel so Reba gave Susie the opportunity to work in her office. Paul and Susie's first child, Eldon Paul (E.P.) Luchsinger, was born on March 4, 1983. Susie continued to work for Reba until E.P. was six months old. She then began singing in bars and clubs on the weekends with her brother Pake.

Paul would still have occasional outbursts of anger which led to some type of violence for no apparent reason. Yet after every incident he would plead for Susie's forgiveness and swear he would never let it happen again.

Years later, Paul and Susie finally went to professional marriage counseling. One of the things they learned was in homes where domestic violence exists, abusive relationships often start by the abusive partner interrogating his or her partner, and by not allowing that person freedom to go anywhere or to have platonic relationships with other women or men. The abuser is perpetually suspicious. Although Paul was good looking, strong, well built and intelligent he was extremely insecure. Consequently it was difficult for him to have confidence in Susie.

In mid-1984 Susie discontinued her singing with Pake and began traveling with Paul. She had re-dedicated her life to the Lord and to singing Christian music. Paul was having a tremendous year rodeoing. At the National Finals Rodeo Susie was asked to sing several songs for the main meeting of the Cowboy Christian Fellowship, the organization that sponsors Cowboy Churches at rodeos around the world.

Susie completed her first solo album in 1985. She selected ten songs that sounded as country as she could find, yet still had strong Christian messages. Susie was no stranger to the "Christian" world. She grew up with the strong influence of her Grandmother Smith teaching her about Jesus. Paul was no newcomer either. He was raised Catholic and his Christian roots ran deep. Yet, in spite of their spiritual upbringing they couldn't seem to get control of the blazing horror of violence that seemed to invade their home.

In mid-1985 Paul was ranked the number one steer wrestler in the world. That same year Susie and Paul established Psalms Ministries which caused them to change their focus more on ministry than on rodeoing. People began inviting them to speak at rodeos as well as churches. Susie would sing songs and Paul would give a testimony or speak briefly from the Bible.

In 1986 Susie's second album was produced. For the next 10 years she recorded a new album every year. Also in 1986 their second child, daughter Lucchese was born. But during this whole time of ministry Paul was still having out bursts of anger and more domestic violence. Paul felt his violence was a permissible vent for his anger. He discovered he could control Susie by his anger. Yet that control was not allowing Susie to be the unique person God had created her to be. At the time Susie didn't realize it was not her place to control Paul's anger by what she said or did differently.

On July 17, 1989 their third child, son Samuel was born. In 1991 Susie did her first music video, *God's Kept Me*. By 1992 she was receiving airplay nationwide on both country and gospel radio stations. She was named "Country Gospel Artist of the Year" by Nashville's Gospel Voice magazine. That same year she received the "Female Vocalist of the Year award" from the International Country Gospel Music Association, as well as the "Video of the Year" award for her *So It Goes* video. In 1993, Cashbox magazine named her "Top Female Vocalist" in the country field. In 1994 numerous awards continued to follow Susie's dynamic career. At the same time, she and Paul were still ministering around the country with Paul's abusive behavior still very much an issue.

In 1996 Paul and Susie took a sabbatical in Seattle, Washington. Ken Hutcherson, a former defensive linebacker for the Dallas Cowboys and Seattle Seahawks was instrumental in helping the two of them turn their lives around. Ken agreed to counsel with them if Paul would agree to be accountable to Ken for his behavior. Because of the great respect Paul had for Ken, he accepted his terms. They spent a great deal of time in Bible study. Paul began to see how very selfish he was. *The root of his anger really stemmed from "wanting what he wanted when he wanted it." He realized it wasn't Susie that made him angry. He had an angry, bitter heart. The circumstances or the events of life, or the people around him, did not make him the way he was. They revealed the way he was. He realized if he had anger or bitterness in his heart, it was going to come out when the pressure was on.*

Paul and Susie have continued their ministry only now they are better equipped to minister to hurt individuals who have suffered through similar situations. Paul said he still gets angry from time to time like we all do, but now the violent responses are only a distant memory.

Carl Magee

Inventor

Can you imagine what it was like the first time people drove down the streets of Oklahoma City, pulled into a parking spot and found a parking meter ready for them to deposit coins in which indicated their arrival? I'm sure it felt pretty much like it did the first time we drove through a toll gate and had to forfeit money to continue driving to our final destination.

Carl C. Magee had been appointed as part of the Oklahoma City Chamber of Commerce traffic committee. It seems with the growing population people were parking their cars in front of shops or businesses where they remained all day, leaving nowhere for others who

came along later to park. His task was to remedy the problems of parking in the downtown area. Of course Carl's solution was to install a device that would charge a person for parking, thereby reducing their desire for an extended stay. But how was he to accomplish that task?

After two attempts with professional machinists to no avail, Carl decided to discuss his idea with his friend, Dean Phillip S. Donnell of the Oklahoma State University College of Engineering. Dean Donnell gathered the engineering department faculty together for a luncheon to discuss Carl's idea. At that meeting Carl was introduced to Professor H.G. Thuesen who would become a great help to the project.

Carl came up with an idea to sponsor a contest for OSU engineering students to develop a parking meter. The opening of the competition began January 4, 1933 and the deadline for constructed models was May 4, 1933. Unfortunately none of the models could totally assure them of a smooth operational system. Professor Thuesen teamed up with one of his former engineering students, Gerald A. Hale. They took Carl Magee's idea and designed and constructed the first complete and operable parking meter.

On July 16, 1935 Oklahoma City residents woke up to a new device on their downtown streets. Good ideas are sometimes laced with some opposition. Some residents ridiculed and made light of the need for such devices. Often change is hard for some people, especially those who had grown up hitching their horse and buggy up to a "free standing post" along "anywhere you'd like" lane. However, the parking meter proved to not only eliminate at least part of the parking problem but also brought additional revenue into the city. Now in the United States alone there are an estimated five million parking meters in use.

The Magee-Hale Park-O-Meter Company was the first manufacturer of the parking meter with factories in Oklahoma City and Tulsa. In 1963 Rockwell moved the facilities to Russellville, Arkansas. Then in 1976 POM Incorporated was organized to purchase Rockwell International's parking meter business.

Mickey (Charles) Mantle

Baseball Star

Since I didn't have the privilege of meeting Mickey Mantle his profile was accumulated from the book *A Hero All His Life -A Memoir* by the Mantle Family, as well as *Mickey Mantle Mini-Biography* by Lewis Early.

This photo, from the cover of Mickey's video autobiography titled Mickey Mantle: *The American Dream Comes to Life,* shows Mickey at Boston's Fenway Park in 1956. (For information about the program call 1-800-THE MICK.) Learn more about Mickey at the Official Mickey Mantle website: http:/ /www.themick.com.

Nobody had a more devoted father than Elvin (Mutt) Mantle. My dad started teaching me to switch-hit when I was four years old. He and Grandpa Charlie Mantle both worked in the zinc mines and on weekends pitched in the local semi-pro leagues. There were usually three hours of daylight left in the summer when my dad got home, and we spent them playing ball. He pitched to me right-handed and my grandpa pitched to me left-handed, and the two of them taught me to switch-hit before I reached the second grade.

Mutt Mantle's boy was going to be a big league baseball player, and that was it. He named me after Mickey Cochrane, one of his favorites, a catcher who hit .349 for the Philadelphia Athletics the year I was born -1931. My full name is Mickey Charles Mantle.

My father never told me he loved me, but he showed it by all the hours he spent with me, all the hopes he invested in me. He saw his role as pushing me, always keeping my mind on getting better. I worked hard at doing that because I wanted to please him.

I was the oldest of five kids: the twins, Ray and Roy, my sister, Barbara and Larry, all four to nine years younger. My mother Lovell didn't lavish affection on us either, but she was more vocal and emotional than dad. Mom made every baseball uniform I wore up to the time I was 16.

Until I signed with the Yankees I had spent my whole life in a small corner where three States, Oklahoma, Kansas and Missouri come together. I was born in Spavinaw, Oklahoma but moved to Commerce just a few years later and lived at 319 South Quincy.

When I was 13 Grandpa died of Hodgkin's Disease. That disease would eventually take my father, two uncles and later my son.

I adored my dad and was just like him in many ways. I was shy and found it hard to show my emotions. I couldn't open up to people and they mistook my shyness for rudeness.

By the time I was 15 I was playing town ball against grown ups and working in the mines with my father. I developed tremendous strength working at the lead mines. One job in particular, that of "screen ape," was responsible for giving me incredibly strong wrists, shoulders, arms and forearms. A "screen ape" smashed large rocks into small stones with a sledge-hammer. The strength I developed from this work and other farm chores later helped me hit some of the longest home runs in the history of the game.

By the time I reached high school my ability was well beyond that of my contemporaries. I played not only baseball but also football and basketball. It was during practice for a high school football game that I was accidentally kicked on the left shin. The wound developed into the bone disease osteomyelitis. It became so serious doctors wanted to amputate my leg, but my mother wouldn't hear of it and my dad drove me 175 miles to the Crippled Children's Hospital in Oklahoma City. There I was treated with a new wonder drug called penicillin, receiving doses every three hours around the clock. Miraculously my leg was saved although it kept me from entering the military a few years later .

At age 16 I played with a local semi-pro team, the Baxter Springs Whiz Kids. Players usually weren't considered for the Whiz Kids until after they had turned 18.

In 1948 Yankees scout Tom Greenwade came to Baxter Springs to watch my teammate, third baseman Billy Johnson, in a Whiz Kids game. During the game I hit two homers, one righty and one lefty, into a river well past the ballpark's fences. Greenwade wanted to sign me on the spot but couldn't when he found out I was only 16 and still in high school. But he promised he would come back and sign me on my graduation day in 1949.

Good to his word, Greenwade was there right on schedule and signed me to a minor league contract with the Yankees' Class D team in Independence, Kansas. I signed for $400 to play the remainder of the season with an $1,100 signing bonus.

After finishing the summer at Independence where the team won the Kansas-Oklahoma-Missouri Championship, I went on to play with the Yankees' Class C team in Joplin, Missouri. The following year, 1951, I was invited to spring training with the Yankees in Arizona. By the time the Yankees reached New York for their exhibition series with the Brooklyn Dodgers, Yankees manager Casey Stengel talked Yankees two owners, Del Webb and Dan Topping and General Manager George Weiss into bringing me up to the Yankees for the season. It was the first time any player jumped from Class C directly to the Yankees.

That fall the Yankees played the New York Giants in my first World Series.

During my career with the Yankees I played more games as a Yankee than any other player (2,401), won three Most Valuable Player awards and won baseball's Triple Crown in 1956. I appeared in 12 World Series during my first 14 years with the Yankees, winning seven World Championships.

I met my wife Meryln in 1949 when I was playing ball for the Yankees farm team and Meryln was a senior in high school. My dad's wish after he got sick was that I would marry Meryln. We were married December 23, 1951 and Dad died May 6, 1952 at the age of 39.

Of the 18 seasons I played with the Yankees I got through a total of three without a serious injury. After an interview with Howard Cosell in the spring of 1956, I opened up to him about my fear of dying young and from then on I carried that with me. "The doomed Yankees slugger, playing out his career in the valley of death." What I didn't realize was the kind of effect this story would have on my sons. We all went through the years thinking I was going to live to be 40 and then die of a horrible death.

Meryln and I had four sons. Mickey Jr. was born in 1953, David in 1955, Billy in 1958 and Danny in 1960.

I was 24 when I had my breakout year in 1956, leading the league in hitting (.353), home runs (52) and runs batted in (130). I was the first Yankee to hit more than 50 home runs since Babe Ruth and the first to win the Triple Crown since Lou Gehrig in 1934. I also received the Most Valuable Player award. The next year I won the MVP trophy again, hitting (.65) with 34 homers, even though I reinjured my left leg in September and missed several games. I tore up my left shoulder in the 1958 World Series against Milwaukee in a collision with Red Schoendienst. I was never quite the hitter I had been from the left side of the plate.

No matter which way the breaks went, I was always lucky. I had been issued a jersey with Number 6 on the back my rookie year -a kind of subtle way of priming the publicity pump. Ruth had worn Number 3, Gehrig was Number 4, and DiMaggio, whose last year was my first, had Number 5. But when I hit a slump in the middle of my rookie season and was sent to the minors, Andy Carey, a young third baseman, wound up with Number 6. When I came back I inherited the number that became part of my identity -Number 7.

I played 18 years with the Yankees and appeared in more games than any player in the history of the franchise. We made it to the World Series in 12 of my first 14 years I was there.

Mickey retired after the 1968 season. In 1974 he was inducted into the Baseball Hall of Fame. He was only the seventh player to make it on his first try. In the late eighties the memorabilia business exploded. His name and signature were suddenly very valuable. In 1988 his name was used on a newly opened eatery called Mickey Mantle's Sports Bar and Restaurant located in Central Park South.

Prior to his death on August 13, 1995 he formed the Mickey Mantle Foundation and dedicated much of the last weeks of his life to reviewing and approving the plans and mission of the foundation which was to promote organ donor awareness. Mickey is laid to rest in a crypt next to his son Billy at the Sparkman- Hillcrest Cemetery in Texas.

Barbara McAlister

Opera Singer / Artist

Barbara is originally from Muskogee, Oklahoma. She describes her childhood as being wonderful and considers herself one of the luckiest children in the world to have the family she was blessed with. Her parents, Clara and Lawrence McAlister, along with her two older brothers, John and Lawrence Jr., saw to it that Barbara was well taken care of and exposed to as many opportunities as possible.

Barbara's mother was German and was born in Maryland in 1905. She passed away in 1996. She was the editor for "Fine Arts Philatelist," a magazine she created and its circulation covered places all over the world including Russia and China.

Barbara's father was born in 1905 in Indian territory and was orphaned at an early age. He practiced radiology for 58 years in Muskogee. He was also trained as a classical singer and was part of a barbershop quartet. He passed away in 1994 at the age of 89.

Barbara remembers always being around music. Musicians with classical voices frequently visited her parents and gathered around the room as her mother helped accompany on the piano.

Barbara loved listening to classical and country western records. Because of the early musical influences she dedicated her life to music. However her second love is painting in the Native American Traditional style. Her grandfather influenced her by teaching her how to draw.

At age 13 Barbara decided she wanted to be an opera singer, but had no idea the number of years of studying her desire would entail. She graduated from Oklahoma City University with a degree in voice. She had the opportunity to be part of summer stock theatre every summer while she was in college.

One summer she met some Hollywood actors at Theaterland in North Carolina, a summer stock rep. theatre run by Oklahoma actor Clu Gulager, who invited her to come to Hollywood and continue her pursuit of singing and performing. As soon as she graduated from college she packed up her Ford Mustang and headed west. She lived in the Hollywood area nine years and continued to study voice with voice teacher Lee Sweetland.

After nine years Barbara won the Loren Zachary competition and was awarded a trip to Europe to audition for a European Opera. Her career actually began while she was in Germany. She spent 10 years performing for the German Repertory Theatre. In those 10 years out of 100 performances a year she probably set a record by only missing two performances.

Each month she was required to learn a new opera which would last two to three hours in duration. For the entire 10 years she sang only German during performances. It's no wonder she is known for singing excellent German.

In 1987 her parents, who were in their later years, encouraged her to come back to the states. She moved to New York to pursue the Opera and sing in English and Italian, hoping to perform in America as she had in Germany. She was awarded a grant from the New York Wagner Society.

She loves singing Opera in English and wishes they were more available. Barbara continues to travel and perform in different theaters. I was surprised to hear there are so many opera houses throughout the U.S. other than the New York Metropolitan. Barbara considers herself very fortunate to have been successfully performing for over 25 years.

Being an Oklahoman she is very interested in becoming more involved with the Cherokee Nation and promoting the arts in Oklahoma. Her paintings are on display at the Five Civilized Tribes Museum in Muskogee, Oklahoma and in private collections in the United States and Europe. She would love to see Mountain Windsong produced annually in Tahlequah, Oklahoma.

As an internationally known opera singer many doors have opened for Barbara. She wants to continue to gain status in her field because she feels it gives her a greater opportunity to help others promote themselves as well. She has recently performed in Menotti's Opera "The Consul" in Kennedy Center-Washington, D.C. This was the Washington Opera's 50th anniversary production of "The Consul." Barbara was hired by Ed Purrington, former director of the Tulsa Opera. The opera was staged by 89 year old Menotti himself -fulfilling one of Barbara's career dreams-working with Menotti. On opening night Barbara produced small drawings of Indian children for various visitors. Menotti kindly wrote Barbara a note thanking her.

Barbara had one of her paintings displayed for a period of time in The Lincoln Center Family Art Show which she considered a great honor.

Barbara is one of the recipients of the First Cherokee Medal of Honor from the Cherokee Nation of Oklahoma. This yearly event has included celebrities like Rita Coolidge who is known for her contribution to Native American Heritage.

Though Barbara lives primarily in New York she divides her time between New York and Oklahoma. She performs quite often through the Oklahoma State Arts Council and was quite thrilled to be part of Tahlequah's musical drama "Mountain Windsong," taken from the book written by Robert Conley. Barbara played "Qualla" a role she created.

I had the opportunity to meet her during one of her trips back home to Oklahoma. She gave me one of her C.D.'s titled *Soul Journey* and I had the privilege of hearing her beautiful operatic voice. I enjoyed it so much more since I had met the person behind the voice. The cover of her C.D. displays a sampling of her art which also left me with a great sense of pride and appreciation for her. I'm sure the future will continue to open doors for Barbara to share her exceptional talents.

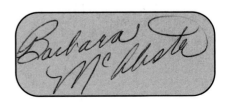

Rue McClanahan

Actress

I've probably seen every episode of "The Golden Girls" that has ever been televised and watched numerous reruns over the years. Even though I never had the opportunity, I used to think how fun it would be to room with two or three other women and share all of my life experiences.

"The Golden Girls" certainly left me feeling enthusiastic about life and what could be expected during the middle years. They probably didn't set out to make any earth- shattering statements, but occasionally one would slip through that would cause you to think for a minute or two. Mostly though, "The Golden Girls" kept you laughing and relaxing for 30 minutes before you really had to take on the cares of the day.

I never realized until just a couple of years ago that Rue McClanahan, who played the part of Blanche Devereaux, was raised right in my own home state. Her character on the show is the one most women secretly would like to imitate at certain times in their lives. Blanche is the carefree, exuber-

ant, feisty middle-aged woman who isn't afraid of her own sexuality and flaunts her femininity as if it is a badge of courage.

In talking with Rue she mentioned how playing the part of Blanche gave her confidence and enabled her to feel more comfortable around other people. I was thoroughly thrilled to have the opportunity to talk with Rue and confirm in my own mind how truly genuine and warm she really is.

She was born Eddi-Rue in Healdton, Oklahoma. Her parents, Rheua-Nell and William Edwin, must have been somewhat delighted when a family member came up with the idea of combining both of their names as the signature of their first child. When she was grown she relinquished the first half of her name, feeling a little more comfortable simply being called "Rue."

Rheua-Nell and William eventually made their home in Ardmore and by this time another child had come along, a sister for Rue who they called Melinda.

Even as a small child in Healdton, Rue was destined to be in the spotlight. Her mother was mesmerized with the world of acting and began taking Rue to movies before she was old enough to talk. Tap dancing lessons were soon to follow, but Rue quickly found a dislike for those routines and opted for ballet instead.

During a family move to Houston, Texas, Rue was introduced to ballet and practiced diligently for a year. However, when they returned to Oklahoma there were no dancing instructors, so Rue had to put those talents on hold for several years. A gentleman by the name of Neucomb Rice, who had been the corps de ballet on Broadway, opened The Oklahoma Dancing Academy.

Rue had a natural ability for ballet and dance so she became the star of the class. At first her interest had simply been out of the quest for fun, but then she began to realize she was really good at this stuff. She came to realize that all the talented actresses she saw on the movie screens weren't all born in Hollywood, but had relocated from places just like where she lived.

A dream began to develop inside of her that she secretly kept to herself. She was unsure that people would believe her if she told them she was going to become an actress someday. When she was a junior in high school Neucomb Rice decided to move to Borger, Texas and offered Rue the opportunity to own his dance academy if she would faithfully run it for a year. Rue jumped at the chance, yet still remembering her dream to become an actress.

After high school graduation she enrolled at The University of Tulsa and majored in drama. Her parents still had no idea how serious Rue was about an acting career. At the age of 15 they had taken a family vacation to New York. Rue never forgot the feeling of belonging she felt when she first stepped foot on New York soil. It was that intuitive knowing that kept her focused on her dream back in Oklahoma, a place that to her seemed far removed from the "bright lights of the theatrical world."

Immediately after college graduation Rue headed for New York. I asked her if she was fearful moving to a big city, but she said she was more afraid of not going than actually being there. It was something she had wanted for a long time and fear of any sort was not going to keep her from realizing her dreams.

She enrolled at the Herbert Berghof Studios and began studies at the Metropolitan School of Ballet. Her first acting experience was at the Erie Playhouse where she performed for a year and gained a tremendous amount of experience in the arts. They paid her $40 a week before taxes, an amount that was more than enough to keep her housed in her one room apartment with the pull-out sofa located across the street from the playhouse.

While at the playhouse she met Tom Bish and married him five months later, but the marriage only lasted a year. During that time she found out she was pregnant, but Tom didn't turn out to be the solid kind of guy that could take on the responsibility of a child. Rue found herself back in Ardmore with her family, awaiting the birth of her son, Mark. She reopened the Oklahoma Dancing Academy and operated it until Mark was six months old.

Falling into the proverbial trap of "you must have a man in your life" caused her to once again marry. Norman Hartweg had been a good friend for a long time. It seemed natural that their friendship would evolve into marriage. But that union also dissolved after four years of diligent effort.

By 1964 Rue was back in New York determined to pick up where she left off in her acting career. She thought it would be best for the time being if she left her son Mark in Oklahoma under the care of her mother, not realizing just how hard the separation from him would be. She landed a role in "The Secret Life of Walter Mitty." Unfortunately, that wasn't the only role she landed. She once again married "Mr. Wrong," who wore the name of Peter DeMaio. She also brought Mark to New York City to set up family life.

The next few years brought repeated success in her career as she took on acting roles that continued to expand her abilities. She was cast in the broadway show "Jimmy Shine" in 1967 and spent 14 months as a homicidal character on the top-rated soap opera "Another World." One role followed after the other. Norman Lear, who saw her in an off- Broadway show, contacted her to play a role in "All In The Family," as well as "Maude," which meant she would be moving to Hollywood, California.

Her marriage to Peter ended after many futile attempts to provide Mark with a home environment, only to realize they were both better off alone rather than under such conditions.

Rue surprisingly endured two more failed marriages, with Gus Fisher in 1976 and then Tom Keel in the early 80's. Each marriage for Rue was meant to last a lifetime, but her good intentions always seemed to rapidly turn into a nightmare.

In spite of her successful acting career, which includes Broadway, theatre and films too numerous to even list, she still hadn't found the mate that could satisfy the longing in her soul. In 1987 she was awarded an Emmy for her outstanding portrayal of Blanche in "The Golden Girls." She has been nominated for four Golden Globes and received a Golden Apple, as well as an Obie.

For a while she worked with and created a line of clothing for women rightly called "A Touch of Rue." She has the beginning outline of a book comically titled, *My First Five Husbands* and has successfully completed several short stories, as well as a couple of musicals and screenplays. Rue has definitely left fingerprints in a variety of places and her enthusiasm for life continues to invade the atmosphere around her.

After many years of unrequited love Rue finally took a deep breath and fell into the arms of a man who truly deserves her unwavering devotion. She met Morrow Wilson in May of 1997 just as she was diagnosed with breast cancer and by Christmas they were married. Even through a trying time of sickness Morrow stood faithfully by her side. I spoke to Morrow briefly and felt a need to jump up and shout to the world "she finally made it."

Mark is a successful guitarist in Austin, and Rue and Morrow make their home in New York, where she will appear on Broadway in the 2001-2002 season in "The Women."

Reba McEntire

Entertainer

What a fascinating career Reba has had thus far and there seems to be no end in sight. If you tune into her latest endeavor her television sitcom rightly titled "Reba," you'll see yet another element of her incredible talent. Not only has she wowed the nation with her incredible voice for over two decades, but now she is entertaining us with her on camera humor as well. It seems that this multi-talented young lady keeps bringing her audience a wider range of her many attributes and we just keep giving her award after award for her efforts.

Reba was born on March 28, 1955 in the great state of Oklahoma. With older sister Alice, brother Pake and younger sister Christian recording artist Susie Luchsinger the McEntire household rarely experienced a quiet moment. Reba's father Clark Vincent is a former three time world champion tie down steer roper. It was his love of rodeoing and ranching that kept the McEntire children on horses from the time they were old enough to straddle one. Reba's mother, Jacqueline taught school until the birth of her first child. From then on her life was filled with motherly duties that left very little room for outside activities.

Reba was competing in rodeos by the time she was eleven years old and ran barrels until she was 21. Her singing career began as a small child in the first grade when she sang *A Way In a Manager* during the Christmas program. From then on having a microphone in her hand seemed natural for Reba and the future events proved it to be true. By the time she was in the 11th grade at Kiowa High School Pake, Susie and Reba were singing alot together and eventually formed what they called the Singing McEntires. The bands occasional performances gave Reba the needed experience singing before crowds even though at the time she had no idea what the future was about to unveil for her.

After high school graduation she went to college in Durant at Southeastern Oklahoma State University where she majored in elementary education with a minor in music. While in college she became a member of the Chorvettes a singing and dancing group that performed on campus and in neighboring towns. Of course this was another opportunity for Reba to hone her talent and prepare herself for a successful singing career that she had no idea was coming her way.

In 1974 during the summer of her sophomore year she was given the opportunity by Clem McSpadden to sing the National Anthem at a National Finals Rodeo. It was there that she had the opportunity to meet country music legend Red Steagall. Right away he wanted her to go to Nashville and pitch her singing talent to some of the record companies. In March of 1975 Reba and her mama headed for Nashville. Reba made her first demonstration recording in a studio owned by Fred Carter and took the demo to Jim Fogelsong president of ABC Records who gently rejected her believing there wasn't room for another girl singer. But they didn't give up. On November 11, 1975 Reba was signed by Glenn Keener of Phonogram-Mercury Records. On January 22, 1976 she did her first recording session with Glenn Keener when they recorded the 1950's Roger Miller/Ray Price song *Invitation to the Blues*.

The year 1976 would also bring wedding bells when Reba married Charlie Battles on June 21st at Stringtown Baptist Church in Stringtown,

Oklahoma.

Even though success has been tremendous for Reba she did have her days of playing VFW Halls, Rodeos and honky tonks and any place else that would allow her to showcase her talent. It was during those early years that Red Steagall introduced her to his good friend and country music promoter Ray Bingham. He and his wife Kathy became great friends and supporters of Reba's career. They booked her in every venue possible and on many occasions went with out their commissions just to get Reba's name out there.

In 1983 Reba had her first number one song with *Can't Even Get The Blues.* She recorded seventy songs with Mercury Records before changing over to MCA Records. In 1984 she was named Female Vocalist of the Year by the Country Music Association. In 1986 she was named Entertainer of the Year and by 1987 she had won Female Vocalist of the Year for the fourth time. Needless to say we have seen her continue to accumulate many more awards over the years.

In 1987 Reba and Charlie ended their marriage. Reba relinquished their 214 acre Oklahoma ranch to Charlie and she moved permanently to Nashville.

Narvel who had been part of Reba's band and a great friend also began helping her run her career. Eventually they realized there was much more to their togetherness than just business. On June 3, 1989 they became husband and wife.

I had the pleasure of meeting Reba and Narvel several years ago when Reba was being inducted into the Oklahoma Hall of Fame. They certainly make a great couple and success sure looks good on them both. Of course their son Shelby has become the center of their world. I wonder if he is another entertainer in the making.

Reba's spiritual roots go deep. She isn't ashamed to tell you that God is an understood connection to her every day life. Her grandmother was the person who introduced her to Jesus Christ. She grew up watching her grandmother on her knees praying and expecting God to answer her prayers. Even though her busy schedule doesn't permit her to attend church on a regular basis Reba is quite confident that God is in control of her life. Her grandmother who has since passed on would be proud of all God has helped her to accomplish.

Maybe that spiritual connection is what caused Reba to be given the 2002 Humanitarian Award from the Country Music Association. Reba makes it a habit to give back to the community and to the world because of all that has been given to her.

So many wonderful opportunities have been given to Reba. From music to stage, films and television what more could one human being accomplish. But I assure you if there are more avenues to travel Reba will drive down them in a blaze of glory. *She knows if she goes with her heart and doesn't follow the beat of another drummer she'll do just fine.* You know, I really think she knows what she's talking about.

Gene McFall

Entertainer

Gene must be good at what he does. As I went over my interview notes to write his story, the lines seemed to reverberate with the voice of Will Rogers. I thought, wait a minute, keep in mind this is Gene McFall.

Gene was born and raised in South Central Kentucky, His father, Lloyd McFall, owned a machine shop and had hoped when he retired Gene would take over the business. But Gene had no desire to pursue that line of work and only agreed to help his father occasionally, if he really needed him.

In the third grade, Gene got his first taste of acting when his teacher asked him to play the part of Tom Sawyer in their school play. From then on, every time there was a play, Gene had a part in it.

After high school, acting began to be a desire that Gene wanted very much to pursue. However, in Nancy, Kentucky, very few people went to college and if they did it was unheard of for someone to major in drama. So Gene decided to go the expected route and took a factory job at General Electric in Louisville, Kentucky. Soon after, he married and had a child and life was status quo.

After 19 months working in the factory, Gene realized he didn't want to spend the rest of his life on an assembly line, so he better get into college. He majored in Physical Education, Health and Recreation and became a head basketball coach for a school in Kentucky.

You would think that Gene would have been content, but he wasn't. In the back of his mind he had never forgotten his desire to act. He just couldn't make himself believe that it was alright to follow his dream.

To appease his restlessness, he quit his coaching job and began to work for the state in public health. The day came when once again he thought, I don't like where I am and what I am doing with my life. He auditioned for some outdoor dramas and got the part of Daniel Boone's brother in "The Legend of Daniel Boone." He took a 70% pay cut to go into show business, yet he was more content than he had ever been in his life.

After the first couple of years performing in "The Legend of Daniel Boone," he became part of the management team as well as one of the actors. During that time, comments were being made that he looked and sounded like Will Rogers.

In 1970 he saw actor James Whitmore in a television special portraying Will Rogers. He was so impressed that he video taped the show, declaring someday he would play the part of Will Rogers.

Out of his desire to perform, Gene put together a production company where he traveled to dinner theaters and country clubs performing short skits, A few years had passed when he decided to go to Hollywood and see where that would lead him.

He got a few small parts in television shows like "All In The Family" and "Archie Bunker's Place," but didn't really feel like he was getting anywhere. So he moved back to Kentucky and continued touring the country with his theater productions.

While performing in Tulsa, Oklahoma, he took a sight seeing trip to the Will Rogers Memorial in Claremore, Oklahoma. He saw film clips and listened to the radio broadcast of Will Rogers and knew right then he could play the part of Will Rogers. Gene looked enough like Will that he felt sure he could pull it off as soon as he learned the techniques to sounding like Will. Gene's rural upbringing and high morals and values seem to mesh easily with what people remember of Will Rogers.

Gene contacted James Whitmore's staff and they gave him the opportunity to meet with them and consider the possibilities, even though they had always been reluctant to allow anyone to play the role of Will Rogers other than James Whitmore.

After flying to Hollywood and meeting the staff, they overwhelmingly agreed that Gene was indeed capable of portraying Will Rogers with dignity and style. For seven years Gene traveled the same circuits he had previously with his touring production, but this time it was under the leadership of James Whitmore's staff.

Eventually, Gene decided to develop his own program. After doing some further research at the Will Rogers Memorial, Gene put together "The Witty World of Will Rogers."

It has been 18 years since Gene first began to portray Will Rogers and his shows are still just as fresh as the day he started. What Gene loves most about portraying Will Rogers is knowing that he makes people laugh with his humor, and gives them food for thought.

The Will Rogers Memorial and the Will Rogers family think Gene does the most authentic show of Will that they have ever seen. That is verified by their willingness to allow Gene full reign at the Memorial in Claremore.

Since I hadn't seen Gene's performance, he began to describe to me how it all begins. As I listened, I could clearly see Will Rogers and even commented to Gene how amazing it was that he could make Will come alive like that.

Gene starts his performance before an audience with a coat and tie on and begins to tell about Will Rogers. As he talks, he begins to slowly take his coat and tie off. He puts a stick of chewing gum in his mouth and turns his back to the audience while he pulls a lock of hair down on his forehead. Then, he puts his cowboy hat on and turns around to the crowd, while spinning a rope.

From that point, he becomes the image of Will Rogers. He uses Will's words that were once heard on his radio broadcasts and his newspaper articles back in the 1920's and 30's. At the end of the show, he comes back out of character and once again, standing before the crowd, he becomes Gene McFall.

The first Rogers family member that Gene performed in front of was Will Rogers, Jr. at a country club in Arizona back in 1984. Since he knew Will was in the audience he was somewhat intimidated. Gene knew if he was going to convince Will Jr., it better be the best performance he had ever done.

After the show, Gene called Will Jr. onto the stage for an introduction. Will Jr.'s comments about Gene were inspiring, as well as encouraging. He told the audience that Gene had truly captured the spirit of his father.

Gene would rather not be thought of as an imitator of Will Rogers, but rather be known as one who captures the essence of the man. Gene said he may not look or even sound just like Will, but hopefully what he has to say, the way he says it and his ability to convey the way Will must have felt, is what people want to see.

One of the biggest compliments Gene has ever received is when someone walked up to him after a performance and told him they felt like they had just spent the evening with Will Rogers.

I knew exactly what that person must have felt like, because during our interview I had to keep reminding myself that the man I heard talking was really Gene McFall.

Gene is honored to be nationally recognized as portraying Will Rogers and says it feels great never having to apologize for playing the role of a man that was so highly respected.

Gene still has one unfinished dream. Along with writing some screen plays, he feels like the icing on the cake for him would be to play the lead role in a movie about Will Rogers. We will all be rooting for you Gene, because "Dreams Do Come True."

Gene McFall

J. W. McLean

Business

This profile has been written from excerpts taken from Bill's book The Persuader written by Odie B. Faulk. I couldn't have told the story better and I didn't want anyone to miss out on the wealth of learning contained in those pages.

There are 10 keys Bill has listed as being links to success in anyone's life. Hopefully, each reader will apply them to their own life.

Bill was born to Margaret and L.W. McLean on April 2, 1922 in Okmulgee, Oklahoma but grew up in Muskogee. He had one brother George McLean.

Bill was already showing leadership skills in high school as he became junior class president. In his senior year he was elected president of the band and president of the student body. Bill learned firsthand the enormous value of warmth in communicating effectively with others. *His first key to becoming a persuader was creative warmth.*

Bill graduated from high school in 1939 and was on his way the following September to Oklahoma University. He enrolled in the School of Business Administration pursuing a dual major, finance and accounting. It was a requirement that he enroll for two years in the ROTC program. At the end of that time, he either had to sign up for another two years of ROTC or sign up for the draft.

On December 7, 1941 the war broke out -Pearl Harbor. Bill was determined to achieve military excellence. His mental preparation for his final year of ROTC really did wonders. Because of his high academic work and consistent leadership among his fellow cadets, he was selected as the Cadet Colonel for the closing spring semester. He would lead his class to Fort Sill the following summer for Officer Candidate School, where they would finally earn their commission. *(People notice hard work and God rewards it).*

Bill realized because of the wartime situation they were facing his very life may well depend on how prepared he was as a soldier. *His second key to becoming a persuader was self-preservation.*

During Bill's tour of duty in the military he began conducting a voluntary class for enlisted men at Fort Jackson on "How to Read a Financial Statement." He became good friends with the office manager at a brokerage firm who allowed him to use information taken from their brochures to teach his class.

The office manager was so impressed with Bill's continual dedication to his volunteer class that he checked into Bill enrolling in their Account Executive Training School in New York. He believed Bill was just the kind of person Merrill Lynch needed working for them. *His perseverance was the key to his introduction into investment banking.*

After his training in New York Bill was assigned to the office in Tulsa. Almost daily he made office calls to prospects selling them on the idea of opening an account with Merrill Lynch. After two and a half years with Merrill Lynch he found himself in the office of one of his customers who had been a close friend of his father. His name was Elmo Thompson, executive vice-president of the First National Bank & Trust Company of Tulsa.

In less than a month Bill was working as an assistant cashier for the bank. Within a few weeks he became active as a correspondent banker. He was one of four bank officers to travel a six-state region to visit their other bank customers. Bill was determined to bring in new accounts and he brought back five. Needless to say, at the next board meeting Bill was elected as an assistant vice-president. *His key to success with the far away bankers was the overwhelming excitement he conveyed to them about what he had to offer.*

Bill remained in Tulsa for 12 years. During that time a daughter and two sons were born to Bill and his wife Eleanor, Margo, Lawrence and Scott.

In 1958 Bill met the CEO of Texas National Bank of Houston, who invited Bill to discuss succeeding him in three to five years. He really had no desire to leave Tulsa, yet wondered if he should look into it. After visiting Houston with his wife they finally concluded to accept the position. In September of 1958 they moved to Houston. By January of 1959 at the Texas National Bank's annual meeting it was announced that J .W. McLean, who joined the bank as a senior vice president only four months earlier, was named president and chief executive officer. His predecessor resigned for reasons of failing health. The three to five years lead had evaporated quickly.

From the beginning when Bill contemplated coming to the Texas bank he had wondered about the possibility of a merger between the city's big four national banks. He soon found out the complexity of that challenge was mind-boggling to everyone and *the key was simplification.* Bill was able to convince negotiators to take a "ball park" approach which would prove profitable for everyone concerned. In the end, the merger resulted in what became known as Texas Commerce Bank.

A year after the merger, Bill was to find himself again in a transition. That transition led him to Bank of America in San Francisco, California where he became the bank's first director of marketing. By far the most significant contribution Bill made to Bank of America was pioneering the national acceptance of what we know today as the Visa Credit Card.

His idea was to get banks from across the entire U.S. to begin using what Bank of America called the BankAmericard, but why use another bank's card when they had local cards coming from their own bank? Bill had to convince other banks that they needed to use his nationwide card. A card that would allow people to use it anywhere in the U.S., not just in their local area.

After a survey, objective research that took several weeks to accomplish, Bill had the ammunition to convince banks throughout the U.S. to use the BankAmericard. However, he knew it would be much easier if another name perhaps a short one-could be found that would through instant recognition convey both confidence and understanding of the service immediately.

Not long after Bill's departure to continue his personal destiny, a committee he appointed came up with a name to replace BankAmericard -VISA. How gratifying it was to have had an early role in the evolution of the first nation-wide bank credit card.

When Bill turned 40 he was approached about being the new CEO for Oklahoma City's Liberty National Bank & Trust Company. Even though his future with Bank of America could hold some potentially great blessings, at Liberty National not only would he be CEO, but he would have stock options. In time those options would rank him among the bank's largest owner, plus a significant number of shares would go at quite a reasonable price. The choice was made and they moved back to Oklahoma.

On his first bank meeting with 90 officers he asked them to give a written opinion about certain issues. Bill knew one of the bank's main problems was a lack of space. The question was, do they go through extensive remodeling or do they build a new facility? *The key was getting an independent expert opinion.* The man who developed the New York City Pan-Am building was brought in to survey the possibilities. His opinion clinched the deal.

The groundbreaking ceremony for a new 36 story home was scheduled for Liberty's 50th birthday, September 3, 1968, less than nine months following Bill's first day as CEO on December 18, 1967. Some 30 months later in 1972 Bill dedicated the new Liberty Tower, the crown of Oklahoma City's skyline. At the time Liberty was Oklahoma's fourth largest bank, but Bill wanted it to be number one. It happened three years later.

Bill knew the key to growth was superior customer service. But how do you make that happen? *The key was Growth sharing seeking ways of enhancing growth both professionally and personally of everyone you supervise.* That is caused by goal planning (what an individual can do to become better at their job) and incentive bonus programs.

In the 1980's the U.S. went through a tremendous upheaval due to volatile crude oil prices. In mid-1982 Bill alerted himself to any opportunities for a major acquisition of any troubled banks in Tulsa. He felt Liberty needed to have an extended location in Tulsa.

The most feasible candidate was First of Tulsa. The answer would be to have a huge corporate umbrella that would allow First of Tulsa and Liberty all the room each could ever need in which to retain their complete and separate ongoing identities. The merger became effective July 17, 1984.

Just letting it happen is overcoming the obstacle of an absence of incentives or defeating retirement. The only acceptable definition of the word "retirement" would be a complete rejection of the notion of "just taking it easy." Bill felt he would rather substitute other productive activities for his professional career. For Bill, it was writing more books and numerous consulting and speaking engagements.

Bill retired at age 65 on April 2, 1987 with nearly 20 years at Liberty and 40 years in the banking business. Life has never been better for the McLeans, spending summers in Colorado. But wherever they are, they read their Daily Word each morning-a habit Bill formed back in 1950 as one of his Mother's last requests and his greatest key to success.

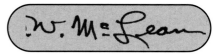

Leonard McMurry

Sculptor

Since I'm from Tulsa, it would be impossible not to have seen the 65 foot bronze casting of the praying hands at Oral Roberts University. And of course I have driven along the highway in Oklahoma City and seen the massive, over sized monument of Buffalo Bill Cody at the Cowboy Hall of Fame. Yet I had never met the man or put a face to the name of the person who created such masterpieces until the day of our interview.

There before me sat a humble, soft spoken individual who had no need to boast of his incredible work, because it undeniably spoke for itself.

Leonard McMurry was born on a cotton farm near Memphis, Texas. From as early as he can remember his desire had always been to be an artist. He loved to draw comics, especially the characters" Jiggs" and "Maggie." He drew them so often from memory that eventually people from around his part of the country nicknamed him "Jiggs."

There were no art teachers in his town so what he learned was by his own trial and error. He thought he would like to paint so he began copying pictures of calendars and photographs using oils and pastels. He then decided to try and sculpture something but the only substance he had to work with was clay dirt from his backyard and gip rock that was almost impossible to carve.

Leonard's insatiable desire to create was of such magnitude he was in constant search of a way to increase his knowledge of the art.

Throughout his teen years he became very proficient at copying images of interest to him. All the while he tried to increase his natural talents.

In 1934 after graduating from high school he entered West Texas State Teachers College, but the art department didn't offer any classes in sculpture After a semester he became discouraged and left the college. He wanted desperately to go away to an art college but his parents were still not quite ready to let their young son venture off to some big city far away from home.

In an effort to head in some challenging direction, Leonard decided he would try to become a mechanical engineer in the Army. He enrolled at Texas A&M. Trying to fit a square peg into a round hole just wasn't working either. He was constantly finding himself drawn to his artistic side, which wasn't particularly relevant to the engineering field.

After a year he left Texas A&M. By this time his parents were more understanding of his needs and felt better about letting him go out of state to a college that could offer him the training he needed.

Anyone who has experienced parenthood knows the struggles a person goes through trying to make the transition from nurturing parent to available friend. In time, it happens as it did with Leonard's parents.

In 1937 Leonard enrolled at Washington University in St. Louis, Missouri to dedicate himself to learning the art of sculpture. He longed for the day when he could receive instruction from someone whose passion for the art was as strong as his had always been.

His instructor, Carl C. Mose, was more than a teacher. He became like a father to Leonard. He made Leonard his classroom assistant and began to steer him toward realistic subjects rather than focusing on abstract objects. Mr. Mose allowed Leonard to work with him on some of his own commissioned monumental projects. This further increased Leonard's love of sculpture.

He finished his schooling in St. Louis in 1941 and spent three years in the Army before being discharged in 1945.

In 1949 he was accepted as a student of Professor Ivan Mestrovic, a famous sculptor at Syracuse University. He studied with the professor for three years. Afterwards, he hoped to get a teaching job at some university. He sent inquiries to 65 different universities, but not one of them responded favorably.

After contacting his sister in Oklahoma and telling her of his disappointing responses, Leonard's brother-in-law tried to encourage him to give up art and come to Oklahoma. They promised to help him find a farm which would hopefully fill the void and make Leonard happy. He did as they requested and moved to Stilwell, Oklahoma but his desire to create beautiful art couldn't be disposed of that easily.

Leonard's cousin from Texas eventually contacted him and told him about her friend Nan Sheets, an art director in Oklahoma City. His cousin Mildred sent some photographs of his work to Ms. Sheets hoping the Chamber of Commerce would have some interest in using Leonard's talents. The Chamber and Ms. Sheets loved Leonard's work and persuaded him to move to Oklahoma City in 1955.

It was then that the windows of heaven seemed to open for Leonard McMurry. He was given a one-man show by the Art Center and from there many admirers began to commission him for his outstanding talent.

His list of sculptures are amazing. I would love to view every single one of his incredible pieces of art. I say that because the few I had the opportunity to see at his home left me wanting to see more. Two of my favorites were the "The Cotton Picker" statue and "The Temptation of Christ" portraying Jesus and the devil. His characters seem to come alive. As I studied their intricate features, I knew each sculpture had a story to tell.

Mr. McMurry told me if a sculpture doesn't have a soul then it is worthless. When he creates he first captures the soul of the creation in his own mind. Then the character, proportion, composition and technique take over from there. He said no matter how large or small a piece of art is, if it doesn't have monumental quality it is a very poor piece of art. I knew exactly what he meant as I viewed his art.

As I was preparing to leave Mr. McMurry's home he left me with a nugget of truth. *Even though his accomplishments have been great and numerous he still doesn't feel totally accomplished.*

"Why?" I asked.

"Because I always know there is so much more for me to learn," he replied.

187

Dale McNamara

Golf Coach

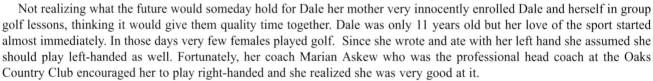

The closest I've ever been to playing golf is at the local putt-putt golf course, but somehow I don't think that counts as being the "real thing."

I'd been looking for a golfer I could include in my book. I asked a few people and had looked up individuals on the internet, but I wasn't sure what direction to go. Then I received a call from my brother, Jerry who said he had just met the retired Tulsa University golf coach. Luckily, he took it upon himself to talk with her about my project. The rest is history.

Sometimes you meet people whose silver spoon never seems to tarnish. Life for Dale McNamara has unfolded in a very precise way. As an only child born in Tulsa, Oklahoma to Lloyd and Rae Fleming, the doorway to her destiny was opened at a very early age. Her parents knew the importance of exposing Dale to a variety of opportunities and then letting her choose the direction of her life.

She witnessed a lot of football games since her father had been an Oklahoma University football player. He had a lifetime membership to the O Club so before each football game the Club would be their first stop. She rode horses and played tennis like most girls, but her most favorite sport was golf.

Not realizing what the future would someday hold for Dale her mother very innocently enrolled Dale and herself in group golf lessons, thinking it would give them quality time together. Dale was only 11 years old but her love of the sport started almost immediately. In those days very few females played golf. Since she wrote and ate with her left hand she assumed she should play left-handed as well. Fortunately, her coach Marian Askew who was the professional head coach at the Oaks Country Club encouraged her to play right-handed and she realized she was very good at it.

Even during recreational times her parents thought it was important to instill values. She remembers her father telling her not to waste time playing the game. In other words, if she was going to play he wanted her to be serious about it. Whether she was practicing or actually playing it cost him a quarter every time she picked up a ball. It's amazing how some bits of parental influence last us a lifetime. Her father also planted a seed for the future when he told her golf was a sport she could play for the rest of her life.

At age 13 Dale had the opportunity to play her first junior golf tournament. One of her girlfriends who also played golf invited her to travel to Chicago where a tournament was being played. Not only did Dale enjoy the tournament but she realized how much fun she could have traveling as well. Being so young she wasn't thinking about golf as a career choice. She just knew she was having a terrific time. However, as one year turned into the next, her competitive spirit began to be enhanced.

She played golf up through high school and attended many tournaments over the years. After high school graduation she attended both Oklahoma University and Tulsa University and continued to hone her talent. Then she was given an opportunity to play a four month tour from January to April that began in Florida. Toward the end of the tour, a major turning point occurred in her life.

It was April and they were in Pinehurst, North Carolina. The qualifying round was canceled because bad weather had turned into sleeting. Dale was sitting around a table playing a game of bridge when a tall, good looking guy came walking into the room. His name was Jim McNamara and he was from Erie, Pennsylvania. He and seven other guys were on spring break and came to Pinehurst to play golf to get away from the Pennsylvania snow. Jim struck up a conversation with Dale and asked her where she was from. Obviously he didn't know much about Oklahoma because when she told him she was from Tulsa his comment was "that's in the sticks isn't it?"

I guess the comment didn't offend Dale too much because two years later she married Jim. If you count up the years since 1959 it sounds like one of those "happily ever after" marriages.

Up until they married Dale continued to play tournaments and was offered the opportunity to turn professional and be sponsored by Wilson Sporting Goods. When she thought about the commitment and what it would entail she decided to turn it down. She felt like she had met the man of her dreams and she didn't want to miss a minute of their time together. Sounds like a " hopeless romantic" to me.

As soon as they were married they moved to Erie. It was a definite weather adventure for Dale. She had never seen that much snow in her entire life. Relief came when they would visit family in Tulsa during the Christmas holidays and the weather would be gorgeous. The saying is "if you don't like the weather in Oklahoma just wait a few minutes and it will change."

After four and a half years and the birth of their first daughter Cathy they decided to leave Erie and move to Tulsa. At first it was hard for Jim, but for those who have grown to know him, he has adjusted quite well.

Dale's life besides being a devoted wife consisted of motherly duties that doubled after the birth of Melissa who was born in Tulsa. She became well acquainted through her volunteer work and her role as chairman of the Junior League of Tulsa Fore Tulsa Charity Golf Tournament. She was happy with her life and didn't expect any great changes until Tulsa University called her out of the blue with a proposal. They needed to start a women's golf program and they wanted Dale to be the coach.

Her first response was "I appreciate the offer, but I don't think so." However, she did mention it to Jim and his response was somewhat different. He encouraged her to accept the position. Because of a lack of funds the job would begin in a volunteer capacity, but he felt it would be something she would enjoy tremendously. Dale reminded him of how unqualified she was to be a coach since she had never trained for such a position. But Jim's retort convinced her of how qualified she was as a player to become a coach.

She accepted the position thinking it would probably only entail a few hours a week. Boy, was she wrong! It just goes to show you how important volunteer work can be. All volunteer jobs don't turn into full time careers, but many of them open up doors you never thought existed.

It was 1974 and Dale had no idea that 26 years later she would retire as Tulsa University's first well seasoned women's golf coach. Their first tournament was played in Albuquerque, New Mexico and right away Dale saw something that didn't set very well with her. The men's teams looked like a million dollars while all the women's teams where dressed in "come as you are" attire. She made up her mind their team was going to make a dress statement. The Tulsa University Women's Golf Team became the first women's team in the nation to have matching uniforms and golf bags.

After Dale's second year as a volunteer coach the position became financially attractive. The second year Nancy Lopez joined the team and they became an instant tradition. The team went from unknowns to national champions. Dale is especially proud of her 1988 season when the team won the national championship, she became the National Coach of the Year and her daughter Melissa won an individual medal. She said it was a script that couldn't have been written. Melissa went on to play in the LPGA for the next 12 years. Upon her mother's retirement she has picked up the baton and has become TU's second women's golf coach.

I asked Dale what it took to be a Nancy Lopez? She said a love for the game, a lot of dedication and a tremendous amount of ATTITUDE. *Dale has a theory called "The Three A's" -Attitude, Atmosphere and Ability. If the attitude is good then the atmosphere is going to be good and that allows the ability to come through.* Also she said she believes in what she calls the IC Approach (inner conceit). When you get up in the morning and look in the mirror you need to say some positive statements to yourself, things like, "I'm so good looking," "I'm qualified to be successful in an my pursuits"and "what a wonderful prosperous day this is going to be." Even if you don't particularly feel that way everyday you still make the positive statements.

She said a lot of " academy awards " are made by those kinds of performances. *But the truth is positive statements turn into positive results if you've done what it takes to prepare yourself.* Dale also advised that you keep your conceited statements to yourself, because the aura of confidence needs no verbal communication.

Since retirement The Williams Company has recruited her to be the tournament consultant for the Williams LPGA Championship and Mayor Susan Savage enlisted her to be on the park board to help keep our public golf courses up to par. No pun intended. Just recently she was made the Honorary Chairman for the "Susan B. Coleman" race for the cure for cancer as well as Honorary Chairman of the American Cancer Society Golf Tournament. Lastly, she has been elected as a board member of the YWCA. Did I say she was in retirement?

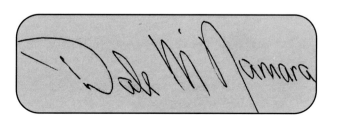

Frank H. McPherson – Business

Frank was born April 29, 1933 in Stilwell, Oklahoma. His father was a farmer but wanted Frank to experience life beyond what farming had to offer.

In Frank's junior year of high school he began spending summers with his aunt and uncle in Houston, Texas. He was exposed to a variety of work experiences including working on a derrick barge in Galveston Bay, a riverboat on the Mississippi, "roughnecking" on barge drilling rigs in the Louisiana Gulf Coast and "roustabouting" in a Texas oil field. With each experience his resolve to become an engineer strengthened.

In 1957 he graduated from Oklahoma State University in mechanical and petroleum engineering. Upon graduation he joined Kerr-McGee Corporation, leaving shortly thereafter to serve as an officer in the United States Air Force. He was instrumental in Kerr-McGee increasing support to public and higher education

In 1960 he rejoined Kerr-McGee as a petroleum engineer and began his rise through the ranks. He became manager of the Gulf Coast off-shore and on-shore operations in 1969.

In 1973 he was named president of Kerr-McGee's newly formed coal unit, with responsibility for uranium operations added in 1976 and chemical and refining units in 1978. He was named president of Kerr-McGee in 1980 and was elected as chairman of the board and chief executive officer in 1983.

Frank is an ardent supporter of education. The company was one of the first to establish endowed chairs at the two comprehensive universities, two at Oklahoma State University and two at the University of Oklahoma. His involvement in education includes serving as chairman of the Oklahoma City Public School Foundation, the Foundation for Excellence and he led Kerr-McGee Corporation to form the first partnership with a local elementary school in which employees were encouraged and given time off to tutor a child once a week. He and his wife Nadine have continued to tutor since he retired.

Frank retired in 1997 after 40 years of service. He said he had enjoyed a very interesting and satisfying career. He has many good memories of the wonderful people with whom he had in his numerous and varied assignments. Looking back he recalls many situations that presented difficult challenges, but proved to be valuable learning experiences.

Frank believes every young man would benefit greatly from being required to work in "hard, sweaty" manual labor jobs in his teenage years. It teaches valuable aspects of life that are otherwise missed and it is one of the best motivators for encouraging young people to obtain a good education.

Frank said success usually is the result of hard work, initiative, willingness to learn from others and being in the right place at the right time.

Frank said he would like to be remembered as a good husband and father, and individual who stood for Christian principals and as a person of highest integrity. He became a Christian as a young person and has read the Bible and prayed on a regular basis over the years. He gives God the credit for whatever business and professional success he has achieved.

Frank married his high school sweetheart, Nadine in 1955. He considers her to be his best friend and his constant supporter. Together they have raised three sons and one daughter and now have 14 grandchildren. He has always believed strongly in his obligation as a parent and felt if he failed as a father, he gets an "F" in life.

Frank A. McPherson

Clem McSpadden

Legislator / Rodeo Announcer / Rancher

One of my most favorite people. A real Okie. A friend to all. A cowboy through and through.

Will Rogers' father was Clem Rogers. Will's oldest sister, Sally married Tom McSpadden who was Clem McSpadden's grandfather. When Clem McSpadden was born on November 9, 1925 in Bushyhead, Oklahoma he was named after his grandfather, Clem Rogers which also made him the grand-nephew of Will Rogers. In the summer of 1927 before Clem turned two years old his parents Herb and Madalyn moved to Oolagah to live on Will Rogers' ranch. Will was no longer living there as he had moved away in 1901 at the age of 22.

Clem Rogers had come to Oklahoma in the 1850's. He owned a trading post between Oolagah and Talala on the west side of Highway 169. They named a creek there Rabs Creek after Rab, one of Clem's two slaves. The other slave's name was Huse.

Tom and Sally Rogers McSpadden settled on a ranch five miles southwest of Chelsea in 1885. The ranch has remained in the McSpadden family for over 100 years. When Clem's father passed away he bought out his brothers claim to the land except for the old house and forty acres.

Clem McSpadden grew up on Will Rogers' ranch and graduated from Oolagah High School. Even after Clem moved away his parents continued to live on the ranch a total of 30 years.

Upon his graduation, Clem joined the Navy for two and a half years. He was a Naval Officer in World War II. He then came back to Oklahoma and graduated from Oklahoma A&M which is now referred to as Oklahoma State University.

Since Clem was raised on a ranch, cattle and cowboys were all he knew. In 1947 when he was still in college he went with friends to some rodeos in Missouri and Iowa. In Story City, Iowa a rodeo had been rained out and yet a few die hards decided to stick around and compete in the mud. There wasn't an announcer so Clem volunteered. That was his first experience as an announcer. The following week in Davenport, Iowa the announcer, failed to show up and once again Clem was allowed to fill in. After the first performance he began receiving $25 per performance and there were four performances. In addition, he won the calf roping contest and won $286. So for a day's work $386 seemed rather inviting for a young cowboy from a small town in Oklahoma.

After a few years it became increasingly harder for Clem to compete as well as announce, so he chose to focus on the announcing. In the beginning he was announcing 10 to 12 rodeos a year and later it increased to 30 or 40 per year. Around the same time he quit competing he decided to run for public office.

He was elected to the State Senate in 1954. At the time, he was the youngest member of the Senate. Twelve years later he was elected President Pro-tem of the Senate. He was also the youngest person ever elected in that position. He served the State Senate from 1955 to 1972. One of his greatest accomplishments in the Legislature was the Rural Water Bill which established Rural Water Districts in Oklahoma.

In 1973 and 1974 Clem was elected to the United States House of Representatives and became the first first-year Freshman to serve on the Rules Committee. He received the appointment from Speaker of the House Carl Albert who received some flack for selecting a freshman. Obviously he saw potential in Clem and of course Clem's excellent service spoke for itself as to Carl Albert's right decision.

After two years in Congress Clem and his wife Donna opted to leave Washington and move back to Chelsea, Oklahoma. He thought he had a pretty good chance of becoming Governor of Oklahoma. However, David Boren ran against him and won.

Before long Clem was approached by some strip miners to help with their organization. That led Clem to become a lobbyist which he has continued to this day. He now represents 15 different companies and organizations. A lobbyist is a person who represents a company or organization to the government.

During all these years through the State Senate, Congress and his lobbying, Clem has continued to serve as a rodeo announcer. He was the first to announce rodeos on horseback using a wireless microphone. He was the first American to announce the Calgary Stampede in Calgary, Canada. He has presented more nationwide telecasts of rodeos than any other announcer, appearing on ABC's Wide World of Sports and other televised specials.

Clem has been inducted into four Halls of Fame; Oklahoma Hall of Fame, Pro Rodeo Hall of Fame, Colorado Springs, Cowboy Hall of Fame, Oklahoma City and Oklahoma State University Hall of Fame, Stillwater. He was also named "Rodeo Man of the Year."

Clem was General Manager of the National Finals Rodeo for 18 years: He brought pasture roping to Oklahoma at his Bushyhead Ranch. He also produced "World's Richest Roping and Western Art Show" at his Busyhead Ranch, which funded a portion of the Chelsea Public Library and provided scholarships for youth. In addition, the "Clem McSpadden Youth Rodeo" is in its 4th year at the Tulsa Expo Center. Clem is the author of the popular and often requested *Cowboys Prayer* and patriotic tribute *If Our Flag Could Talk*.

Clem is in his 70's and still announces rodeos although he admits he is drawing near the end of his tenure.

As you drive into Chelsea you will see a sign on a stretch of road appropriately named "Clem McSpadden Highway." He loves living in Chelsea. He said 1,500 people lived there 30 years ago, and 1,500 people still live there today. Clem can go anywhere he wants in this world, but he always comes back home to Chelsea.

I asked Clem for a tidbit of wisdom and he said, *"It's not what happens, it's what you keep from happening that's important. In other words, know your subject matter well enough you can anticipate the unexpected. Sense the pitfalls before they happen. Be prepared."*

Walter Merrick - Horse Breeder

I had the pleasure of traveling to Sayre, Oklahoma to meet with Walter and his wife Christien. They were kind enough to show me around their ranch and try to inform me about the wonderful world of horse breeding and racing. What a remark-

able couple the two of them are. Christien (no, I haven't misspelled her name) is quite a character herself. I'm sure a best selling novel could be written based on her antics and lively personality traits.

Walter was born October 5, 1911 on the Figure 2 Ranch in Wheeler County, Texas, whose eastern border touches Oklahoma. With those many years to his credit you would think he would be propped up reading a book somewhere waiting for his next meal to be served. But not Walter. When I arrived at his ranch he was like any cowboy 50 years younger taking on the events of the day with robust anticipation.

When Walter was a young child an influenza epidemic left his father an invalid. At age 8 Walter, the youngest of five children, began taking odd jobs to help supplement the family income.

In 1921 Walter's two brothers, who had both fought in and were wounded during World War I, moved to southern Colorado. Hoping the climate might benefit their patriarch the rest of the family also relocated to the area.

When Walter was 14 years old and in the eighth grade he met a rancher who offered him a job as a "rough string" rider. He quit school two weeks before the end of the year to take the job, fearing it may not be available if he waited. The job consisted of 12 to 15 spirited horses that needed to be convinced they would make good ranch horses. For this bone-jarring work Walter was paid $55 a month. He worked on the ranch for four years and sent most of the money he earned to his parents, who had moved to Oklahoma.

In 1928 Walter's mother wrote to him asking him to come home. His father's health had worsened. Walter returned and went to work on the Figure 2 Ranch. He was hired by ranch manager Champ Davis to break 75 broncs. The job paid $10 for each horse he broke and included room and board. Later that year he became a full-time ranch hand and received $45 a month.

In 1929 on the Figure 2 Ranch Walter met his wife to be Christien Shinn. They were married the following year and spent their first winter together "calving" some of the Figure 2 cows. Part of their pay for that winter was 14 calves. When the time came for him to brand his stock, he enlisted the help of a fellow ranch hand. The man asked what the brand was going to be and Walter said "I don't know I hadn't thought about it. How many calves are there?" He was told 14. "Put 14 on them," he said.

Although his 14 brand was inspired by cattle, it would become far better known for being placed on the left hip of some of the fastest horses in the history of short-distance racing.

Walter and Christien lived on the Figure 2 Ranch during the Great Depression of the early 1930's. At one point, their wages were reduced to $20 a month. To supplement their income Walter began entering rodeos on the weekends. He competed in saddle bronc and roping events. To further sustain themselves financially during that time, both Walter and Christien milked cows, picked cotton and worked cattle.

In 1936 Walter became foreman of the Figure 2 Ranch which just goes to show you what faithfulness and commitment will do for you. His salary increased to $75 a month. It was during this time he decided to raise a few fast cow ponies. He began by purchasing a stallion and several mares. The stallion's name was Midnight Jr.

When the American Quarter Horse Association was founded in 1940, Walter had Midnight Jr. and the mares inspected for possible registration with the association. But after thinking about it a little longer Walter decided not to sell them at that time. During the next few years Walter competed with Midnight Jr. at rodeos and in match races.

In 1941 many of Walter's horses sported Midnight Jr. bloodlines. That year he sold the black stallion to H.S. Bissell of Las Cruces, New Mexico. His next stallion was Grey Badger II, a son of Midnight Jr. In time Grey Badger II and Walter became one of the most noted match-racing duos in the Southwest. In western Oklahoma stories of the pair's success are legendary.

In 1945 Walter joined with Leonard Milligan to hold the first registered Quarter Horse sale in history. With proceeds from the sale, Walter purchased his first ranch in western Oklahoma.

By 1950 when Quarter Horse racing was becoming more lucrative, Walter began concentrating on getting more speed from his herd of horses. He decided to add thoroughbred blood to his breeding program. In 1951 he leased a young stallion by the name of Three Bars. Walter got a considerable amount of criticism for his decision to infuse his herd with Thoroughbred blood, but he felt he was making the right decision. Later, when his bred horses such as Bob's Folly began burning up the quarter mile tracks in the late 1950's and early 1960's, horsemen rushed to jump on the Three Bars band wagon.

In 1967, Lena's Bar, a Thoroughbred daughter of Three Bars, foaled Easy Jet, who was sired by a Quarterhorse named Jet Deck.

With the breeding of Jet Smooth in 1965 and Easy Jet in 1967 Walter completed the requirements for an AQHA Championship. Jet Smooth proved himself on the track and in the showing. The stallion earned almost $80,000 in racing. As a sire, Jet Smooth sired Quarter Horses that earned 348 racing ROMs. He also sired 23 halter-point earners.

Easy Jet was one of the most successful racing horses in history. He earned over $7,206,478 on the track and won the All-American Futurity in 1969.

In 1979 Walter was inducted into the Western Heritage Hall of Fame in Elk City and recognized by Oklahoma State University with the Masters Breeder's Award in Genetics. In 1981 he was inducted into the Oklahoma Hall of Fame. Walter is internationally known as the master of Quarterhorse racing and breeding. His genius has repeatedly brought forth golden steeds by the score whose gifts to Quarterhorse racing are legendary.

In October 2000 Walter was honored by the AQHA and presented a beautiful trophy for being the only breeder who had registered horses in 1940 and every year since for the past 50 years.

Walter and his family still all work on their ranch in Sayre, Oklahoma. Their oldest son Jimmy managed the ranch until he passed away a few years ago. His daughter Sherry Lynn is responsible for running the ranch's office and their youngest son Joe is in charge of the ranch's cattle operation.

Jack Merritt
U.S. Army General

Jack was born October 23, 1930 in Lawton, Oklahoma to Theodore and Queenie Wood. In 1932 when he was almost 2 years old, his father was killed in a car accident. It was during the depression and his mother was having a hard time financially.

For a while Jack spent most of his time staying with other relatives, mostly his aunt and uncle. His uncle was the Chief of Police in Lawton and at one time was hoping to adopt Jack.

However, Jack's mother met Earl Merritt who had grown up in Fletcher, Oklahoma. They were married in 1935 and lived in a couple of different towns before finally settling down for a few years in Enid. It wasn't long before his new brother John was born and sister Barbara followed.

Jack didn't want to be the only member of the family with a different name so he took on his stepfather's name. Earl became Jack's father in every sense of the word. Jack's mother was convinced the best thing she could do for him was have him take speech lessons to develop self-confidence. He was feeling anything but confident because Earl was a traveling salesman. Every time they settled down for a while in one place and Jack would begin to make friends, they would have to move again. From Enid they moved several times before finally settling in Oklahoma City where by this time Jack was in the second half of his sophomore year.

Classen had a top notch speech and debate class which helped Jack tremendously. The spring of his senior year he won the state oratorical championship in Norman and went on to Canton, Ohio to compete. He didn't win oratory there but he did take first place in men's radio speaking. Fortunately, the family didn't move again until Jack was able to graduate from Classen High School in 1948.

Robert S. Kerr was running for office and Jack applied for a job with his campaign staff. He was teamed up with a journalism student from Oklahoma University. They were given a car with speaker horns on top and a turn table in the back and they cruised around town playing country music and soliciting people to come to the courthouse square and listen to them speak on behalf of Robert Kerr. (This may have been one of the last of the old-time campaigns)

That fall Jack enrolled at Oklahoma University thinking he was going to be a lawyer and perhaps go into politics some day. On the weekends to make some needed money he gave speeches for the Democratic Party.

In the spring of 1950 Jack asked his friend to get him a blind date. It turned out to be his future wife Rosemary, who had also been born in Lawton and graduated from Oklahoma University that year.

Jack remained at Oklahoma University until 1951 when he left school to work for his father's company, Merritt Wholesale Company in Oklahoma City. He was notified late in 1951 that he was to be drafted and entered the military service in March of 1952, going directly from Oklahoma City to Fort Sill.

At Fort Sill he took basic training and entered Officer Candidate School in September 1952. He graduated in March of 1953 and was commissioned as a second lieutenant of Field Artillery. He remained at OCS as a tactical officer until being assigned to Korea in September 1955.

In October of 1953 Jack married Rosemary Ralston. They both agreed the Army would be a good opportunity for them.

In 1955 he went to airborne training at Fort Benning, Georgia. During his brief assignment he had the opportunity to be in the presence of numerous high-ranking dignitaries including President Sygman Rhee, the President of Korea.

In 1957 the Merritts moved to Fort Meade, Maryland where Jack continued his duties as aide-de-camp to General C.P. Bixell.

In the summer of 1957 General Bixell retired and the Merritts moved back to Fort Sill where Jack entered the 10 month long Field Artillery Battery Officer Course. He graduated in 1958 and immediately went off to finish his bachelor's degree at the University of Nebraska at Omaha. After returning from Nebraska in 1959 he was assigned to the Lacrosse Missile Gunnery Department until 1960 when he entered the Advanced Officers Course and graduated in May of 1961.

He then was assigned to Stuttgart, Germany, first as Assistant Operations and Plans Officer and then on to Ansbach, Germany as a battery commander, operations officer and battalion executive officer.

In the early spring of 1963 the Merritts transferred back to Stuttgart where he served as the Corps War Plans Officer until 1964. They moved to Maxwell Air Force Base, Alabama where Jack attended the Air Force Command and Staff College. While there he simultaneously pursued a master's degree in Business Administration from George Washington University. He graduated in 1965 and was assigned to the Pentagon where he served successively on the Army Staff and then on the Staff of the Secretary of Defense in the Systems Analysis Office.

In 1968 Jack was assigned to Vietnam where he assumed command of the 3rd Battalion of the 34th Artillery. It was a battalion of light howitzers which were mounted on barges and used landing craft to tow the barges on the canals of the Mekong River delta. Using these barges as platforms, these guns would be employed as conventional artillery.

With this unique form of transportation, coupled also with helicopter-borne operations, Merritt and his battalion traversed the entire delta in support of the operations of the joint Army-Navy Riverine Brigade, going from Saigon across the delta to the Cambodian Gulf. After a year in command of this battalion, Merritt was reassigned back to the states. During that year he had been awarded the Silver Star, the Bronze Star, the Air Medal, the Distinguished Flying Cross, the Legion of Merit and the Soldier's Medal.

In 1970 he was made Deputy Director of the Program Analysis Division under Henry Kissinger. In May of 1974 Merritt was assigned to Fort Hood and promoted to Brigadier General.

In 1982 as a Lieutenant General he was assigned to Fort Leavenworth, Kansas as Commander of the Combined Arms Center and Deputy Commanding General of the Training and Doctrine Command. However, he was shortly called to the Pentagon as Director of Joint Staff.

In 1985 with the rank of General, he went to Belgium as the United States Representative to the North Atlantic Council Military Committee. He remained there until his retirement in 1987 after 35 years of military service.

General Merritt's only regret was he didn't have as much time to spend with his wife and three sons, Steven, Grover and Roger as he would have liked.

Of course I couldn't leave our interview without asking the General for some tips of wisdom. First he said he never felt like he had a sense of destiny, only a sense of *doing well enough today that he would be qualified for tomorrow.* Everyone needs a high tolerance of ambiguity. You can't always expect to have finite answers. Sometimes you have to make decisions when you have data that is competing with equal weight and then you have to decide how do I live with ambiguity. *How do you not make mistakes? By making mistakes.* Whatever happens between you and another person you need to give them the "presumption of good intent." Maybe they are doing as well as they can. If you are feeling I just can't tolerate anymore from them then wait a while -you can do better.

Jody Miller

Singer

Pretty little Jody Miller, she may have matured somewhat since she recorded her first hit song *He Walks Like A Man* in the early 1960's, but she's never lost that alluring personality, her funny wit or her attractive looks.

As I headed toward her home in Blanchard, Oklahoma one Saturday afternoon I was pleasantly surprised when she greeted me with a warm handshake and a smile that lit up her cozy little office. With two album covers in tow that dated back over 30 years ago I asked if she would be kind enough to autograph them and of course she did.

Jody's parents, John and Fay, must have been two proud individuals the day Jody made her entrance into this world via Phoenix, Arizona. I can only speculate, but I imagine with Jody's strong personality and adorable looks the whole hospital probably knew she was around.

Jody was the youngest child out of five girls. She spent the first eight years of her life in Oakland, California. Unfortunately her parents had a mutual parting of the ways and Jody was sent to Blanchard, Oklahoma to live with her Grandmother Miller.

The move brought with it a totally different style of living than what Jody in her few short years had become accustomed to, but children have a way of adjusting and Jody was certainly not an exception to the rule.

In California Jody was surrounded with music and instruments and people who craved the magical expression of lyrics mixed with high and low notes. Her parents had exposed her and her sisters to the world of music at an early age. If they weren't mingling amongst the musicians at one club or the other, they were sitting around the house providing their own musical jam sessions that lasted for hours.

Jody's dad played the fiddle and her mother loved to sing while Jody and her sisters joined right in. Jody had what she said was a "big voice," meaning she could bellow out those words, a trait that still remains her trademark.

In Blanchard, a small little town in the Midwest, Jody found living at grandma's to be quite different from the hustle and bustle of Oakland. Grandma's house didn't even have the luxury of running water, and the age gap between the two of them seemed like centuries apart. But in spite of the cultural differences Jody had a spark of musical destiny that didn't have a chance of laying dormant for long.

Eventually her dad moved back to Blanchard but her mother remained in California. Jody's school years were never dull or void of a musical outlet. She joined the choir and in high school she participated in an all girl trio singing songs like *Lets Sip A Soda at The Sweetshop* and *Sincerely.*

Jody has never dubbed herself as a songwriter, but the title of "entertainer" just came natural for her. She felt she needed some accompaniment while riding along in the school buses headed for a ball game, so she purchased a ukulele which served the purpose just fine.

Shortly after high school graduation Jody married Monty Brooks, who has become her lifelong companion. I met Monty. His firm handshake and friendly Oklahoma smile quickly assured me Jody made a quality decision 40 years ago.

In the early 1960's while singing in a local coffee house in Norman (the college town that highly supports the University of Oklahoma) Jody's young, alluring voice caught the ear of a group called "The Limelighters." Their immediate comment was "Our agent would love to see you." Of course Jody didn't have to be told twice. She thought "Los Angeles, here I come."

She and Monty packed their bags and off they went to sunny California. One of the first people she contacted was a fellow Oklahoman and famed actor Dale Robertson. Jody sang for Dale and after hearing her dynamite voice, he immediately called one of his friends at Capitol Records. The friend was equally impressed after hearing her perform at the famous Troubadour in Los Angeles and Jody was on her way to a coveted recording contract. Within six months she had her first chart record, *He Walks Like A Man*, which was an instant success.

Then Jody was invited to the San Remo Song Festival in Europe where famed Italian songwriter Gino Demaggio wrote the song *You Don't Have To Say You Love Me* for Jody to sing at the festival. Jody Miller became an instant hit in Italy during her three months stay.

Before she left for Italy she found out she was pregnant but she wasn't about to tell the people in charge for fear they would cancel her trip. As it turned out everything went well and nine months later Monty and Jody welcomed their bright-eyed little baby girl Robin into the world. Jody had a picture of Robin sitting in her office the day of our interview. You could certainly tell to whom she belonged.

After returning from the San Remo Festival in 1965 there was a lot of fan-fare going on about a young singer named Roger Miller (no relation) who had just put out a song called *King Of The Road* that was tearing up the charts. Mary Taylor, a songwriter who was under contract with Capitol Records, jumped on the idea and wrote a song called *Queen Of The House* using the same melody as Roger's hit. Of course it was Jody Miller who they chose to take it to the top.

The record headed playlists on pop, easy listening and country stations all over the nation and launched a series of records and awards, television shows, stage, Vegas and rodeo circuit engagements for Jody. As a result, she won a prestigious Grammy award and her career was off and running.

Jody cut eight albums with Capitol Records before her contract expired. About that time Robin had turned 8 years old and Monty and Jody decided to move back to Blanchard so Robin could grow up in an area they had grown to appreciate as a good place to raise children. About the time they got settled Jody signed another contract. This time it was with Billy Sherrill and Columbia Records in Nashville, launching a brand new sound on country stations across the nation with songs like *He's So Fine* that won her a Grammy nomination. After eight more years of musical success Jody decided to hang it up for a while and spend some quality time focusing on her family in Blanchard. So for seven years Jody just played wife and mother and let her music career fade away. By 1987 she was itching to sing again but she knew the name Jody Miller would have to be dusted off and resurfaced with a brand new style.

"Why not try some patriotic songs" she thought, which eventually opened doors for her to perform alongside George Bush's Presidential campaign. Then, in 1993, she added yet another phase to the already versatile Jody Miller. She became "born again" in 1993 and opened herself up to a whole array of gospel music.

As you can well imagine, Jody has done it all. Her career has brought her before numerous celebrities like Bob Hope, Red Skeleton, Roy Clark and many others. She has appeared on "Hee Haw," "The Tonight Show," and "American Bandstand" to name a few. Yet, she's still not ready to hang up her guitar or muffle her "big voice."

I had the opportunity to watch Jody perform in March 2001 and see first hand what a great entertainer she really is.

Jody had two bits of wisdom to share with me. First she said *"listen to that still small voice, it will guide you if you will let it."* Secondly, *"Align yourself with the right kind of people that will move you toward your destiny, not away from it."*

Roger Miller
Singer/Songwriter

My thanks go to Mary for allowing me to use the information compiled on her husband, Roger Miller's website. She was also gracious to send me a picture to go along with the story. I doubt if there is a handful of people who haven't heard the incredible talents of Roger Miller. I count it a privilege to include him in this book.

Songwriter, singer, guitarist, fiddler, drummer, TV star, humorist, honky-tonk man, Broadway composer, and perhaps above all else, an awesome wit - Roger was all of these and more. Roger was always on my list of participants for this book, but after talking to his very good friend and former relative, Sheb Wooley it stirred me up even more to get his profile written.

Roger Dean Miller was born January 2, 1936 in Fort Worth, Texas, the youngest of three boys. His father, Jean Miller, died at the age of 26 from spinal meningitis. Roger was only a year old. It was during the depression and Roger's mother, Laudene Holt Miller, was in her early 20's. She was just not able to provide for the boys. So each of Jean's three brothers came and took one of the boys to live with them. Roger moved in with Amelia and Elmer Miller on a farm outside Erick, Oklahoma.

Roger had a difficult childhood. Most days were spent in the cotton fields picking cotton or working the land. He never really accepted the separation of his family. He was lonely and unhappy but his mind took him to places he could only dream about. Walking three miles to his one-room school each day, he started composing songs.

"It's really a good thing that he made it in the music business cause he would have starved to death as a farmer," says entertainer Sheb Wooley, an Erick native who at one time was married to Roger's cousin, Melva Laure Miller.

Fifteen years older than Roger, Sheb's career led him to Hollywood and the movies. In those days, Sheb and Roger would ride out "fixin fences, chasing steers and talking about stardom," Sheb recalls. The two would listen to the Grand Ole Opry on Saturday nights and the Light Crust Doughboys on Fort Worth radio by day. Roger came to idolize Bob Wills and Hank Williams, but it was Sheb who taught Roger his first chords on guitar, bought him his first fiddle and who represented the very real world of show business that Roger wanted so much for himself.

Eager to follow in Sheb's long tall footsteps while he was still in high school, Roger started running away, knocking around from town to town through Texas and Oklahoma. He took whatever work he could find by day and haunted the honky-tonks by night.

His drifting came to an abrupt halt when he stole a guitar in Texas and crossed the state line back into Oklahoma. He so desperately wanted a guitar to write songs on and this seemed the only way to get one, since pulling cotton bowles would never earn him the kind of money he needed for a guitar.

Roger turned himself in the next day and rather than put him in jail they offered to let him join the Army. Although he was only 17, he chose to go into the service. He was eager to go someplace else and before long he was shipped to Korea. Roger was terribly homesick, but his world was growing larger.

Toward the end of his tour with the Army, he was sent to Fort McPherson in Atlanta. Assigned to Special Services, he played fiddle in the Circle A Wranglers, a well known service outfit previously started by PFC Faron Young.

After Roger's discharge from the Army, he headed directly for Nashville to see Chet Atkins. He told Chet he was a songwriter and Chet asked him to play something. Seeing Roger didn't have a guitar, Chet offered his to him. Roger just couldn't believe he was sitting in front of Chet Atkins and playing his guitar. Roger proceeded to sing in one key and play in another. Chet was kind about it but suggested he work on his songs a little more and come back.

Needing to work while he pursued his dream, Roger took a job as a bellhop at the Andrew Jackson Hotel. Situated right in the thick of Nashville's downtown music district, the Andrew Jackson gave him proximity to the small but vibrant country scene. Roger soon became known as the "Singing Bellhop." He would sing a song to anyone who would listen on the way up or down the elevator.

His first break finally came when he was hired to play fiddle in Minnie Pearl's road band. His second break came when he met George Jones at the WSM radio station one night and played him some of his songs. Jones then introduced Roger to Don Pierce and Pappy Daily of Mercury-Starday Records and asked them to listen to some of the new kid's material. Roger impressed the Starday brass enough to be granted a session in Houston.

George and Roger rode to Texas together and wrote some songs along the way. They co-authored *Tall, Tall Trees,* which George recorded in the spring of 1957 and *Happy Child* which Jimmy Dean recorded that same spring. Meanwhile, Roger cut some of his own songs including *My Pillow*, and *Poor Little John.* That October they were paired on the first single of Roger Miller's career.

Married and with his first child, Alan, on the way, Roger considered getting out of the business entirely. He decided to move to Amarillo and join the fire department. He would work all night and then go to clubs and sing after work. At a show in Amarillo, Roger met Ray Price and several months later, the superstar singer hired him to replace tour singer Van Howard in the Cherokee Cowboys.

With his wife Barbara, Roger moved back to Nashville, bringing with him a new song called *Invitation to the Blues.* He somehow got the song to movie cowboy Rex Allen, who recorded it for Decca in early 1958. Before the Price record gave him full-fledged hit writer's credentials, Roger had already signed a songwriting deal with Tree Publishing for an unprecedented $50 a week. Roger started to score hits for other artists like Ernest Tubb, Faron Young and Jim Reeves.

In 1958 he landed a deal with Decca Records to record his own songs. He had already parted ways with the Cherokee Cowboys, but remained great friends with Ray Price. For a year and and a half Roger began playing drums for Faron Young. During this time he signed a deal with RCA's Nashville office, which was run by guitar legend Chet Atkins.

It had been many years since Roger's first meeting with Chet. At the time, RCA's biggest country act was Jim Reeves, and his success with Roger's songs probably had a lot to do with making the deal. On August 10, 1960 Roger recorded what was to become *In the Summertime* at his first RCA session.

Less than a year later, Roger broke into the Top Ten for the first time with *When Two Worlds Collide,* which he and Bill Anderson wrote by the light of the moon in the back seat of Roger's Rambler station wagon. However, financially Roger was experiencing a great amount of difficulty. His first marriage, which had given him three children, was falling apart and by November 1963 he was dropped from RCA.

Roger was beginning to doubt that country music could make him a living. Then Jimmy Dean, who was guest hosting on "The Tonight Show," invited Roger on the program. He was a smash hit. Appearances on other shows soon followed. Then Mercury Records in Nashville signed him on. It was during this time he wrote *Chug-a-lug, chug-a-lug* and Roger's first smash hit *Dang Me.* The day *Dang Me* was released Roger was playing in a club in northern California for $75, but in about a week the phone started ringing. By the summer of 1965 Roger's career was made. The first royalty check he received from Tree Publishing was for $168,000.

Needless to say, Roger's success was phenomenal. His songs still live on today in the hearts of so many people. His life on this Earth ended way too soon when he contracted a form of lung cancer. After a year of treatment and one remission, Roger died at the Century City Hospital on October 25, 1992, at the young age of 56.

Roger and Mary were blessed to share two children together, Taylor and Adam. In 1995, Roger was post-humously inducted into the Country Music Hall of Fame. "This would have been his ultimate dream come true," says Mary.

When asked how Roger wanted to be remembered, he replied, "I just don't want to be forgotten." I hope at least in part, this profile adds to his wish.

Shannon Miller - Gymnast

Shannon was born in Rolla, Missouri on March 10, 1977. When she was six months old her father, Ron Miller accepted a job as a professor at the University of Central Oklahoma in Edmond. So her family, which also consisted of her mother, Claudia and sister, Tessa, moved to Edmond.

At age four, Shannon decided she wanted to start ballet and jazz dancing like her sister Tessa who was two years older. That lasted for a while until Shannon decided she would like to have a trampoline. When the backyard trampoline and the living room furniture were about to cry out for help, her parents decided to enroll her at the local gymnastics center called "Adventures in Gymnastics."

It was obvious Shannon had a talent. Her father began taking her back and forth to the gym every day on his lunch hour. Within a year Shannon was doing so well they promoted her to the junior elite team. The team didn't compete, but members went to clinics and camps to improve their skills so one day when they were old enough they could represent the U.S. in international competitions.

Shannon and her mother took a trip to Russia as part of the junior elite program. It was there that she met gymnastics coach Steve Nunno, another Oklahoman. When Shannon returned from Moscow she began attending Steve's gym and became a part of his team, the "Dynamos."

Shannon's abilities were so obvious that her coach advanced her quickly. Her first national competition was the 1987 USAIGC National Gymnastics Championship at the University of Delaware in Newark. This was her first television appearance and already she was capturing the hearts of the American people.

In 1988 she traveled to Athens, Georgia for the U.S. Classic. There she was named as the best gymnast in the country in the children's division.

In 1990 Shannon was doing so well and achieving at such a high speed that she decided to enter the U.S. Championships as a senior, even though she was only 13. She was the youngest competitor ever to make the senior national team. Her coach Steve Nunno has always commented on what a meticulous worker Shannon has always been. Everything she does she does to perfection.

Before the 1992 Olympic Games Shannon had become the best in the gym. She practiced roughly 35 hours a week. Setting goals were an important part of her training. She knew she had to be aiming at something to accomplish it. She wanted to win the 1992 U.S. Championships and the Olympic Trials. She wanted to make the Olympic team and possibly win an Olympic medal.

It is said that one of her greatest attributes is her ability to push past the hard stuff instead of watering down her routine. She is determined to overcome her problems and force herself to do the skill correctly. When I heard that I wondered how many of us flake out when the going gets rough. Yet even at such a young age, *Shannon was determined to push past the obstacles, knowing that was the only way she would ever become a champion.*

In March of 1992 Shannon was invited to Los Angeles as part of Milton's Superstars of Gymnastics. Included in the group were people like Nadia Comaneci, Olga Korbut and Mary Lou Retton.

Shannon finished first in the Olympic Trials and soon she would be on her way to the 1992 Olympics as part of the U.S. team. The team consisted of Shannon Miller, Kim Zmeskal, Kerri Strug, Betty Okino, Dominique Dawes, Michelle Campi and Wendy Bruce.

At age 15 Shannon was one of the youngest athletes in Barcelona. On the second day of the Olympics she was awarded a 9.95, the highest score of the U.S. team. In individual standings Shannon was in first place.

Her total medal count from the 1992 Summer Olympics was five: two silver and three bronze. She won the most medals of any U.S. athlete in Barcelona to become the most decorated American at the 1992 Olympics, both summer and winter games. She also tied Mary Lou Retton's record for the most medals ever won by an American woman at a non boycotted Olympics. The only thing she had left to do now was focus on the 1996 Olympics where she wanted to go for the gold.

By now her whole life had changed. She was bombarded with fan mail, phone calls and interviews. Her hometown erected a road sign at the city line reading "City of Edmond, Home of Shannon Miller, Winner of Five Olympic Medals, Barcelona 1992."

Of course we all know Shannon went to the 1996 Olympic Games as part of the "Magnificent Seven" and came back with two gold medals -one team gold and one gold on the balance beam. The first American ever to win Gold on the beam.

Shannon's career has been phenomenal. She has earned seven Olympic medals and nine World Championship medals since 1992. She has won 58 International and 49 National competition medals and over 50% of each have been gold.

In June of 1999, Shannon married another Oklahoma native, Chris Phillips, a medical student, before an Olympic size crowd of 900 guests. Shannon's bridesmaids included her six Olympic gold medal teammates. The wedding received so much public attention that it was covered on Extra and People Magazine.

Shannon's future is probably whatever she wants it to be. Her academic studies at the University of Oklahoma will add to her accomplishments. She is an excellent student in every aspect of her life. She contributes an enormous amount of her time to charities and believes that anything is possible with hard work, determination and professionalism.

Shannon has made Oklahoma proud which is another reason why a statue by Shan Gray was erected in what is know as Shannon Miller Park. Whatever Shannon chooses to do in the future I'm sure it will continue to be with excellence.

Teresa Miller

Author / T.V. Personality

Teresa, I believe, is one of those people who has a lot of hidden treasures within her that you aren't aware of unless you take the time to investigate. Her subdued manner doesn't begin to reveal the depth of her intuitive nature.

She was born in the relatively small town of Tahlequah, Oklahoma and raised by her grandmother. Her father was an attorney who was very active in the community. Her mother, however, died when Teresa was only two years old, leaving a void that has been hard to fill. Yet, at the same time the emptiness has caused her to reach inside of herself and pull out strength she may have not otherwise recognized she had.

It is interesting how a person's life turns out in spite of their adversities. In my many interviews, I have been astounded by the number of successful individuals who lost a parent as a young child yet have gone on

to become strong, influential people.

In Teresa's life, even though her mother hasn't been with her in the flesh, she has always been with her in spirit. Teresa feels honored that she resembles" her mother in looks and demeanor. In some ways she feels like she is allowing people to know her mother through herself. What a beautiful tribute!

Teresa credits her ability to use her imagination to create characters for her novels, to the loss of her mother. As a child, because of her loss, she learned how to create in her mind a person she thought her mother would be like. That creative ability later turned into a technique she used to create the characters in her books. Of course even that revelation didn't come over night. Teresa had to struggle in those early years to find direction for her life and rid herself of some temporary confusion.

She began writing as a teenager after reading a series of the well loved Nancy Drew books. Teresa felt a need to write the ending to the stories, as if somehow that gave closure for her own life.

Veering off for a while, she contemplated becoming an actress and was accepted into the American Academy of Dramatic Arts in New York. After high school graduation she took off for the big city in hopes of making a splash in the world of drama. It wasn't long before the young, naive girl from Tahlequah with the Oklahoma accent realized she just didn't fit into that world. She headed back home and enrolled at Northeastern State University, determined to find the direction for her life.

During that time she wrote two books which could never get past the rejection desk at every publishing house she sent them to. She was feeling rather humiliated each time her manuscript was sent back with a refusal to publish. She felt sure the whole post office was aware of her so called defeat. She didn't let that stop her though.

Teresa continued with her education and received her bachelor's and master's degrees. She was finishing graduate school when she sent off her third book to a New York agent. The manuscript titled *Remnants of Glory* was published a few months later. Twenty-eight year old Teresa was finally going to receive some recognition for all her efforts. She enjoyed the success of her book for a few years and was settling down to write another novel when her elderly grandmother who had raised her became terminally ill.

The decision wasn't negotiable, Teresa would dedicate herself to her grandmother for as long as she was needed. After a few years as a full-time nursemaid her grandmother passed away. In the midst of her loss she realized she hadn't even had time to write and felt like there was no creativity left in her. However, she had to make a living and establish herself in the professional world. It appeared as if her dream to continue writing was lost. But she so longed for the feeling of being connected to the world of words and the company of other writers.

She accepted a job as an English teacher at Rogers State College in Claremore, Oklahoma. Eventually, out of Teresa s longing to be involved in the field of writing, she began a television program called "Writing Out Loud" which features interviews with writers from all over the country. In addition, a short time later she developed The Oklahoma Center for Poets and Writers which holds an annual event honoring amazingly talented writers. Both of those developments came about because of Teresa's unquenched longing to be involved with writing. She felt compelled to help other writers, even if it meant she herself would never again write a successful novel.

However, Teresa has now come full circle. Her years of being an advocate for others has opened doors of creativity for herself. Her previous book *Remnants of Glory* has been re-published. She also has another novel out titled *Family Correspondence*. Who knows what books will arise from Teresa's rekindled creative mind in the future.

Teresa is happy with life, and even though it took longer to get where she wanted to be in terms of her talent, she learned a lesson that can ring true for all of us.

" *Find ways to make what you feel you have lost, work to your advantage.* " *When she had given up on her own dream, she helped promote someone else's. In return, she found what she only imagined she had lost.*

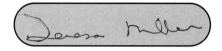

Melvin Moran

Business

I had never been to Seminole, Oklahoma until the day of my interview with Mr. Moran. I had already experienced a full day of interviewing in Oklahoma City, and Seminole was the last stop on my way back to Tulsa. The directions given to me were quite good, and I arrived in Seminole sometime around 7 p.m. As I turned into Moran's neighborhood, I immediately saw a lady who was busily grooming her lawn. The "Doubting Thomas" in me just had to stop and inquire as to whether I was headed in the right direction.

"Oh yes," she said. "The Moran house is just ahead as you make the curve to the right. You can't miss it. It's the big two-story house."

Sure enough, it was located right where Mr. Moran told me it would be. The nice lady was a "ray of sunshine," so I was glad I stopped to talk to her anyway. Mr. Moran greeted me at the door with a very warm and inviting smile, which immediately put me at ease.

To my great surprise, he informed me that as soon as we finished our interview he and his wife, Jasmine wanted to take me out to dinner. Those were the right words to say to me, because I already felt like the road had beaten every bit of energy out of me, and I hadn't taken the time to have a good meal in the last couple of days.

As we sat down to begin our interview, I suddenly had a cat in my lap. He was curious to see who this unexpected visitor might be. I love animals, so his presence just put me more at ease.

Mr. Moran was so casual, easy-going, and laid back with a touch of humor in his voice. As he began to share his story, I saw the added dimension to his personality that made him that way. He was born in St. Joseph, Missouri, and soon after his birth his family moved to Maud, Oklahoma where he spent the first four years of his life. They moved on to Seminole, Oklahoma for a few years.

Eventually the family comprised of Melvin, his brother and sister, his devoted stay-at-home mom and his father, who owned Moran Pipe and Supply company, moved to Tulsa, Oklahoma. Melvin graduated from high school in Tulsa and went to college at the University of Missouri. While in college Melvin was just sure that the talents he had acquired during his high school years, writing a comedy column for the Central High School newspaper was the direction his life would be going.

The University of Missouri had a good journalism school, and Melvin thought he would like to be a comedy/television writer. However, during his sophomore year in college, one of his professors told him that beginning writers in comedy only made $25.00 a week starting out. So right away Melvin thought there must be a better way to make a living. He changed his major to business and graduated with no regrets.

My first thought was, "Oh no, he gave up his dream," but Mr. Moran assured me he didn't make a mistake. After college he spent two years in the Air Force and met his beautiful wife, Jasmine, during his tour in England. Then in 1953 he joined his father in the family business.

Jasmine had been a professional actress and singer in London and yet her love for Melvin was too strong to allow him to return to Oklahoma without her. Melvin assured her that even though her acting career would possibly come to a halt, he was willing to provide her with an exciting life to replace what she was giving up! They moved to Seminole and Melvin commuted back and forth to their Tulsa business, as needed. There's something about the little city of Seminole, Melvin said, that just always fascinated him, and Jasmine readily agrees. Melvin's father wanted to make sure his son was well equipped in every area of the business, so he made him start at the bottom and work his way up. In 1981 they sold the supply part of the business and yet continued to run the oil business. Surely, after all of these years, Melvin would want to retire, but he said he still goes to work at Moran Oil at least a few hours each day.

After work he heads off to check on his newest project which he started in 1993. The Jasmine Moran Children's Museum is appropriately named after the "love of his life." The museum is located where else, but in Seminole. On our way to dinner that evening, they drove me through the parking lot of the museum since it was already closed for the day. The idea for the museum came about after a trip to Michigan in 1988 that the Morans took with two of their grandchildren. They visited a children's museum there and were so fascinated that they decided to bring the concept back to Oklahoma.

I could see that the Morans were very happy with what they had accomplished in life, and there was no sign of any slowing down in sight. In spite of the fact that Mr. Moran had been in the oil business for forty-five years, his appearance, as well as his energy level, was no indicator of that. His involvement on several company boards was no surprise, and politics of course was something Mr. Moran naturally found himself involved

He thinks everyone should take an active interest in the community. With his undying love for Seminole, which he so unashamedly speaks of, I wasn't a bit surprised when he told me he had at one time served as the mayor. The list just continues to go on and on with all the activities and accomplishments that Mr. Moran has been involved with over the years and yet he still had time to be a father to two daughters Marilyn and Elisa and a son David.

My curiosity was still peaked and I had to find out if he ever missed his talent as a comedian/writer.

"Why no," he said. "How can I miss something that I've continued to make a part of my life?"

Then he proceeded to show me a video clip of him performing some stand-up comedy. He certainly was a natural, and the script flowed from him with ease. He proceeded to tell me of all the many comedy shows he had produced and skits he has performed in. I was amazed. So I asked him, "How does one man fit so much into one lifetime?" Again, I wasn't surprised with the answer he gave.

"I was raised in a very religious Jewish home and my mother always told me many times that I might be the only Jewish kid in the school," he said. "How I interact with people and what I do with my life will be an immediate reflection on what people think of Jewish people, so I must be the best that I can be. Along with those remarks my parents instilled in me that hard work was one of the ingredients to doing my best, and I've always tried to remember that."

When the evening came to a close, I assured the Morans I would be back some day to tour their museum and once again visit the quaint little city of Seminole. As I returned to my car and proceeded down their driveway, I was so glad I had been privileged to meet the two of them. Somehow the hour and a half drive back home that night at 10 p.m. didn't seem as bad with the remembrance of an excellent Mexican dinner, the laughter of Mr. Moran's Comedy clip and thoughts of the many interesting facets of his life.

I also realized that the decision to induct Mr. Moran into the Oklahoma Hall of Fame in 1997 was certainly a wise one.

Joshua Morrow

Actor

I just had to include Joshua as one of the Distinguished Oklahomans. To begin with he deserves it. Secondly, he is a terrific guy and thirdly the soap opera he plays on has been part of our family viewing since I was in grade school. Granted I don't get to see it as often as I would like, but I still feel a sense of loyalty to it.

Joshua was born February 8, 1974 in Juneau, Alaska where his father, Kem was stationed in the Coast Guard. When Joshua was two years old his parents divorced. His mother Rebecca moved to California and married David Nichols. His father settled in Sapulpa, Oklahoma with Joshua and his daughter, Jamie. Some time later, love found its way once again to Kem and he married Elizabeth.

Joshua spent most of his growing up years in a constant state of transition. His father was a high school soccer coach, who now also coaches football and basketball. His job required a great deal of transferring from one town or state to another which kept Joshua changing schools on a frequent basis. Fortunately, even though it was rough being the new kid on the block, Joshua was blessed with having the ability to make friends quickly.

When he was in the fifth grade the family moved to Guthrie, Oklahoma. When he reached junior high they transferred again, but this time out of state to Alamogordo, New Mexico. In the ninth grade he attended five schools in one year before the family moved back to Oklahoma and settled in Skiatook.

In spite of all the re-locations Joshua carried a 3.8 grade point average and played in all most every sport imaginable. In Skiatook he made the All-State football and soccer teams. He would have made baseball too had he not transferred to Westlake School his senior year to live with his mom and her family which included two sisters, Tracey and Alexis.

Joshua had been spending the summers with his mother in California for several years. On a whim in the middle of his senior year he decided he might like to go to law school in California. If so, he needed to establish residency early so his tuition would be cheaper.

A few months after moving to California Joshua responded to an ad he saw in the local newspaper, asking for actors to audition for a local theatre company, The Young Artists Ensemble in Thousand Oaks. The company director, Preston Sparks cast Joshua in the leading role of the father in "Ordinary People." Then he won the lead in the company's production of "Picnic."

In 1992 Joshua entered Moorpark College majoring in communications with a minor in theatre. Of course by then acting was in his blood and the thought of being a lawyer was a distant memory.

In April, 1994 Joshua was performing in "Dark of the Moon" when a talent scout saw him and introduced him to the casting director for "The Bold and the Beautiful." While he didn't get the role, Joshua was excited enough just to get the audition. Two months later in June he was cast as Nick Newman on the ever popular day time soap opera "The Young and the Restless."

Joshua is one of the main characters who plays the married son of one of the key families. He describes his character as "likable, confident, borderline cocky and a very determined young man." It's amazing how closely his character parallels his own self.

Joshua has won the "Outstanding Younger Lead Actor" award at the "Soap Opera Awards" and is also a multiple and current Emmy nominee. He landed the title role in his first TV movie, the USA Network telefilm, "My Stepson, My Lover." He would still like to do some other acting projects outside the "Young and the Restless" set, but right now he is too crucial to the show to spend much time elsewhere.

Joshua has remained very close to his parents. He refers to his Dad as his best friend and a true gentleman. His mother, he remarks, is the the one who taught him how to treat a women with respect. No doubt that is why one of Joshua's main goals in life is to be the best father, best brother, best son and best husband the world has ever seen.

He considers himself a very confident person who likes who he has turned out to be. He readily gives the credit for who he is to his parents who instilled in him high morals and manners conducive to a gentleman.

Joshua has been steadily dating Tobe Keeney (short for October) for almost five years. She is a school teacher and someone Joshua highly admires and respects. On December 22, 2000 the romantic side of Joshua couldn't hold back any longer. He went a step further and presented Tobe with a 3.1 carat diamond ring symbolic of his lifetime commitment to her. The two plan to be married in September, 2001. Even though they only live a few blocks from each other they have continued to maintain separate households, until the two, truly do become one.

He vividly remembers his childhood days growing up in Oklahoma and would love to see his children experience the same sort of upbringing he feels he was blessed with. Hollywood has a much different set of standards than Oklahoma does. But Joshua has a good head on his shoulders and says there is no chance he will succumb to any lesser standards than what were instilled in him as a child. He has every intention of making sure his own children are raised with the same moral guidelines that gave him a good start in life.

Besides being extremely athletic, Joshua loves collecting sports memorabilia. His goal is to collect enough souvenirs to build the ultimate "dream room." His signed goodies already include multiple Michael Jordan, Wayne Gretsky and Charles Barkley items. Plus, he has a Brett Favre autographed football, a Rollie Fingers baseball and a David Robinson basketball. He is well on his way to a terrific display.

In case acting and memorabilia collecting is not enough to keep this young man's mind totally activated at all times, Joshua has become the lead singer in a band called 3deep. If interested, you can check out his music by going to www.3deep.com on the worldwide web.

I had the opportunity to see Joshua live and in action at the Tulsa Women's Show over a year ago. Other than being gorgeous and a heartthrob for all the young women who attended, he didn't carry the typical air of a Hollywood star. While in Oklahoma Joshua was an Okie with Oklahoma charm. The OU tattoo he wears proudly on his arm signified his undying love for Oklahoma and the Sooner team.

I talked to his father Kem who stood off to the side watching with great admiration as his son interacted with the audience. I commented how very proud he must be of Joshua. He replied, "I was proud of him long before he became an actor."

Joshua feels so extremely lucky to have this lot in life that he almost feels guilty for having it so good. For me I would like to think "Good Things Happen To Good People."

Joshua encourages everyone if they have a goal they want to see fulfilled, they must continue to believe in themselves. A lot of people may tell you it can't be done but you have to believe there is a spot for you. With faith, hard work and persistence you will meet your goals and often surpass them.

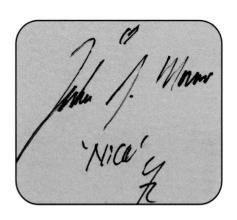

George Nigh

Governor

George was born on June 9, 1927 in McAlester, Oklahoma to Wilbur and Irene Nigh. Growing up seemed to be an enjoyable experience for George. He was the youngest of four boys with the fifth child, a girl, coming along 15 years later.

Uniquely his family had a creative way of solving disputes in their home, they played games. George said a card table was part of their living room decor. Instead of complaining to their parents to solve an issue they were instructed to play a game of pitch or dominoes and the winner's choice stood firm.

George learned at an early age the meaning of work. His father owned a grocery store and all the Nigh boys were given the opportunity to participate in everyday transactions.

As far back as he can remember George always wanted to be governor of Oklahoma. His hero was Franklin Roosevelt. George remembers sitting beside the family radio listening and being inspired by Roosevelt's fireside chats.

His first political event was when he was in junior high school. Attorney Tom G. Hale was campaigning to become the county judge. George organized 30 kids on bikes to ride through a four block area of town yelling "Vote for Tom G. Hale." George was always active in school elections to the point his classmates nicknamed him "Governor" because his leadership abilities always showed through.

Since the ninth grade in 1942 when he was in a vocation's class and announced his desire to be governor, he never waned even though at times he wondered if it was ever going to happen.

George attended college at Eastern State College in Wilburton for two years and was active in the Young Democrats. He was the first college student ever elected as an officer of the Young Democrats of Oklahoma. He was active in managing Senator Robert Kerr's campaign for the U.S. Senate in 1948 and loved the opportunity which was just another stepping stone toward his climb to the governorship.

When he was a senior at East Central University in Ada he filed to be in the legislature in Pittsburg County and won. At the time, at age 22 he became the youngest member in the legislature. He served for eight years, all the time still wanting to be governor. He always told everyone that someday it would happen.

During that period of time the legislature only met every other year so you had to have another occupation. He became a high school history teacher in McAlester. In 1958 after being a teacher for seven years and in the legislature for eight the superintendent and the principal of the school where he taught suggested he choose between education and politics.

He was offered a couple of opportunities to become a principal, which would move him up the ladder in education. However, George knew if he made that kind of commitment he would eventually give up his dream to become governor and he didn't want that to happen.

He didn't feel he was known well enough to run for governor yet, so he ran for lieutenant governor and won when Howard Edmondson was elected governor. George was 31 years old and the youngest lieutenant governor in the nation. Howard was 33 and the youngest governor. At the time the lieutenant governor's position had no real meaning other than they would take over as governor if something critical should occur. George set out to change that and give the lieutenant governor responsibilities he had never had before.

He became an active part of boards and commissions that had never been available to the lieutenant governor before. He became chairman of the Department of Commerce. He convinced the legislature to create the Tourism and Recreation Commission of which he became chairman. He went to the Legislature and convinced them the lieutenant governor needed to be on enough boards and commissions that in case anything happened to the governor, the lieutenant governor would know what to do.

The position of lieutenant governor runs for a four-year term. George held the elected office for 16 years. After his first term in 1962 he ran for governor and lost, but he never gave up on his dream. You can't run for two offices at the same time, so for a while he was out of a job, $100,000 in debt, with no car and no home. But even then his dream to become governor still remained fixed in his mind.

During that year he was introduced to his wife to be, Donna, a divorcee with an 11 year old son, Mike. She was a successful career woman and really wasn't looking for a commitment, but George won her heart. They married on October 19, 1963, making George a father for the first time at the age of 36. In 1965 daughter Georgeann was born.

George made a quality decision not to run against the governor he was serving under. Through the administrations of Dewey Bartlett, David Hall and David Boren he kept his position as lieutenant governor. When Boren was up for re-election he decided instead to run for U.S. Senate and won. George was then free to run for governor and won. It took 30 years to see his dream become a reality, but it finally happened.

George loved being the governor of Oklahoma. In 1982 he ran for re-election and became the first governor in Oklahoma to ever be consecutively re-elected. He has always been a cheerleader for Oklahoma (so to speak). While he was in the legislature he was a promoter for the Oklahoma Today Magazine. He altered the bill that made the legal abbreviation of Oklahoma - OK, which he says is the image of our state. George reminded me the song "Oklahoma" and the broadway production Oklahoma is the number one public relations tool for our state.

After George's eight years as governor he then became the Distinguished Statesman in Residence at the University of Central Oklahoma in Edmond. He lectured, taught classes etc. When the university president unexpectedly retired George, became president of UCO. After all those years of being the youngest in every position he held, he was now the oldest president ever hired as president of an Oklahoma university. He pledged to stay with the university for five years, which he did. After taking off a year to hang around the house, trim trees, pull weeds and clean the garage he decided to find another area to display his talents.

He is currently director of community relations and member of the Board of Directors for Local Oklahoma Bank in Oklahoma City.

A book has been recently written by Bob Burke on the life of George Nigh entitled *Good Guys Wear White Hats*. The inception of the book has stirred up some ideas for other books George would like to see published.

George believes the secret for life is Living for Tomorrow not Yesterday. You lose the future when you live in the past. Don't waste your time watering last year's crop.

Steve Owens - Athlete

Steve had no choice when it came to being born in Gore, Oklahoma on December 9, 1947. But he did have a choice as to whether he wanted to dedicate and discipline himself to become a Heisman Trophy Winner.

With seven boys and two girls the Owens household must have had a conversation of some kind going on pretty much all the time. No doubt their home was probably a boiling pot of information relating to a variety of subjects. Naturally, one subject would have had to be sports.

Anyone who has ever been down around Gore knows what a beautiful part of Oklahoma it is. The first six years of Steve's life were spent there before his father, Olen was hired by a trucking company in Miami, Oklahoma. Gore was a happy place to live, but Steve remembers how financially poor they were during that time. All the boys had to share a bedroom and their bathroom facilities were located out back somewhere. Steve said when they sold their house in Gore the total sum of $250 enabled the new owners to take possession immediately with the receipt stamped "paid in full."

Miami was a bigger town and more conducive to a sports minded individual. Steve knew at a very early age that athletics was an important part of his life. Fortunately, Steve had some great coaches encouraging him along the way. His father supported him in his efforts even though he had never played sports. His mother Cherry, on the other hand, played basketball in school, so no doubt she probably had some pointers to give him every now and then.

It wasn't long before Steve was dreaming of playing football for Oklahoma University and then going on to play professionally. His parents were both strong believers in their children getting a good education and establishing a good work ethic. Steve was taught if he set his goals high enough and dedicated himself to the pursuit of his goal he would eventually succeed.

His first step was to acquire a scholarship, which he did in his senior year of high school. In fact 70 different colleges offered Steve the opportunity he was looking for, but his heart remained with OU.

In 1966 Steve stepped onto the Oklahoma University campus feeling very confident that his goals were going to be met. Everything would have been wonderful except for one major hitch. His high school sweetheart Barbara was still in Miami. After a while the miles that separated them left Steve feeling so homesick it was all he could think about most of the time.

One afternoon he called home and talked briefly to his father about his loneliness. He certainly expected his father to be sympathetic and suggest he come home immediately. However, his father's response was not at all what Steve expected. "Where are you going to live if you come home Son?" "Well, at home of course, Dad." "I'm sorry Steve, but your space has already been taken over by someone else."

Steve probably felt a huge twinge of pain accompanied with a severe sense of disappointment. But he later realized his father was showing him some "tough love," the kind he really needed. He managed somehow to make it through his freshman year, but when summer came he and Barbara married and she moved to Norman with him. From then on Steve felt like everything was beginning to go his way.

The year 1969 will always remain a defining moment in Steve's life. He had been an All-American halfback for two years. He had played in the Big Eight conference in 1967, 1968 and 1969. He was Big 8 player of the year in 1968 and 1969 which led him to be a Heisman Trophy winner his senior year.

He was drafted in the first round by the Detroit Lions and became the first Detroit Lion to gain over 1,000 yards in a season. He was an All-Pro selection in 1971. Steve's dreams as a young boy had come true. His commitment and dedication had paid off and he was reaping the rewards.

In 1976 due to a serious knee injury Steve retired from football. Being a die-hard Oklahoman he said the day after he retired he had a moving company load all of their belongings and they were headed back to Norman.

From the start of his football career he had been wisely advised by his attorney to make plans for retirement. Even as a strong 6 foot 2 and a half inch "mean machine," human bodies are subject to fail when least expected. Steve received good counsel from his attorney, so when he retired he was financially prepared to pursue other avenues of interest.

He has been involved in several successful business ventures over the years, three of which he still maintains. He is CEO of Steve Owens Associates which is a financial services company. He is President of Owens-Powell & Associates, a full line property and casualty agency, and he has interest in four restaurants.

In 1991 Steve was honored by being named to the Oklahoma Sports Hall of Fame and The National Football Foundation College Hall of Fame. In addition, he was named The Walter Camp Foundation Alumnus of the Year. Then in 1992 he was inducted into the Orange Bowl Hall of Fame. Steve has served on numerous boards in the community and is still involved in his hometown of Miami through the Steve Owens Foundation.

One very special honor came a couple of years ago when Gore, Oklahoma developed a sports complex for baseball, soccer and football and named it the Steve Owens Sports Complex. Steve's father passed away several years ago, so he never had a chance to see the sports complex. But you can imagine how proud it would make him feel knowing he left Gore with virtually $250 his pocket in 1953 and now the town has honored one of his own children.

I was impressed with Steve's thoughts about life and the importance he puts on relationships. Memories of wonderful times spent with his wife Barbara and sons Blake and Mike continually fill his thoughts.

There is never an appropriate time for loss, yet on September 6, 1997 he and Barbara began the journey of trying to understand and cope with the death of their son Blake. It has been a trying time in all of their lives. Steve admits his faith in God and a multitude of caring friends and family have helped bring them through this devastating time.

Steve doesn't know what his next venture will be. He's a talented man who has succeeded in many areas and yet feels there may still be some stones unturned. In the meantime, he plans on spending some time traveling with Barbara and creating some lasting memories with his son Michael and his new daughter-in-law Cory.

Eva Phillips

Songwriter

Eva was born in Parks, Arkansas to Melvin and Dovie Carter. Serving God and living a Christian life is all she has ever known. Her father was one of the early pioneers of the Assembly of God Church that was formed in 1914 in Hot Springs, Arkansas. He pastored in Mena, Arkansas for 33 years until he passed away in 1960 at the age of 68.

There were eight siblings in the Carter family who were taught from the time they were two years of age to sing. They traveled through western Arkansas and parts of Oklahoma ministering in churches and praying for the needs of people.

When Eva was an infant her mother and father were standing by the side of the road when a car driving by hit Dovie and ran over her leg, crushing her ankle. The injury was so bad that gangrene set into her leg and doctors thought they might have to amputate. But Eva's father wouldn't give up that easy. For three days and nights he paced up and down the floor praying for her healing. His tenacity paid off and the surgery was canceled.

Trusting God and seeing Him perform miracles in people's lives was something Eva experienced with her family on a regular basis. She didn't know what it was like to stay home from church on a Sunday morning. To Eva and the Carter family, worshipping God was all a part of life.

Of course Eva has had her share of disappointments and sadness like we all have. Her first husband passed away at an early age and left her feeling quite depressed for a long period of time. She had always been so quick to bounce back when hardships occurred, but she had already buried her mother and father and now her husband was gone as well.

In 1982 she moved to Tulsa, Oklahoma and met Bob Phillips through a mutual friend. Within two months, in spite of others cautioning her it was too soon, she and Bob married. Of course they have proven everyone wrong for the past 18 years.

Several years ago after Eva had reconciled her feelings of loss from the deaths of her loved ones she began once again to write songs and sing. She became friends with four ladies who were songwriters who wanted to get together to learn the basics of songwriting. They began meeting at Martin East Library, then they were invited to the Charity Baptist Church. Eventually they began meeting in their own church Faith and Inspiration Center and the group continued to grow.

What had started as a small group of ladies wanting to meet together for support and encouragement, turned into Christian Songwriters Association, Inc. founded by Eva Phillips. It is an inter-denominational association of all faiths, working together in unity and love to lift up Jesus in word and song. Participants learned the basics of songwriting, how to copyright their work and submit it to publishers. They learned the difference between writing country, traditional, contemporary or southern gospel music. Their songs were critiqued by other songwriters in the group to give everyone a better understanding of the impact their songs would have on an audience. Currently the association has over 75 active members.

In 1996 Eva met Billy Hale founder and president of the Country Gospel Music Association in Pulaski, Virginia, an organization which extends throughout the United States. Billy was in Tulsa trying to find someone to lead the Association around a six state area including Oklahoma, Kansas, Texas, Arkansas, Louisiana and Mississippi.

At first Eva wasn't interested because she was perfectly content with her leadership role in her organization. However, Billy insisted she would be perfect for the job and encouraged her by pointing out how many people she would be able to help promote. One of the main goals of the association was to discover new talent and help promote them to the public.

Eva agreed to take the position and the first year when she attended the annual convention in Topeka, Kansas she was nominated to win three awards -Songwriter of the Year, Promoter of the Year and Female Vocalist of the Year for the Country Gospel Music Association of the six state area. Eva was surprised to hear so many people were aware of her contributions. She then went on to the National Convention in Knoxville, Tennessee and was selected as Promoter Nationwide.

In order to be nominated you had to sing a song and give a testimony. Eva gave a testimony about helping a young girl get a song she had written played on the radio. Eva describes the next few minutes that transpired as a "wave of the Holy Spirit" going through the room. The more of the story she relayed the more tearful she became until many people in the room were crying as well. When she completed the story she was supposed to sing, but had difficulty getting the words to go past the lump in her throat. Her very thoughtful husband Bob quietly appeared on stage just at the right moment and began singing for her until Eva's voice slowly began flowing in the background.

After the lure of the moment had ended and the evening was over Eva and Bob returned to their hotel room. Eva was tormented thinking she had made a complete fool of herself and wondered if she would be able to face everyone at the conclusion of the convention the next day.

Surprisingly, when she and Bob arrived the next morning and took their seats, gospel recording star Todd Hervey came and knelt at their feet. As he held their hands he said, "You all were worth the whole trip." Then one by one other people came up and relayed heartwarming remarks as well. As a result, Eva overwhelmingly received the award.

Since that time Eva has continued to be recognized and rewarded for her continuous help and support of other songwriters as well as her own personal songs. One of her special triumphs was when LuLu Roman, well-known for her appearances on the hit show "Hee Haw," recorded her song *Please Lord Take Over My Life.*

Eva is such a good example of God's faithfulness to reward his children in due time at the appropriate season of their lives.

In 1999 Eva and Bob gave everything else up to become Pastors of an inter-denominational church at 21385 E. 44th Street in Broken Arrow.

No doubt there are other dreams and goals left to be fulfilled. Yet I'm sure she is confident God has it all in control and the chorus of her life will be sung as it should.

Eva J. Phillips

Mary Kay Place - Actress

Mary Kay Place is an interesting, likable, talented person and on top of that she is a native Oklahoman. By the time we finished our phone interview, I felt like I had been having a chat with one of my high school classmates. Mary Kay is a warm lady who hasn't let the bright lights of Hollywood dim her vision of what it means to be a caring and thoughtful individual. Undoubtedly, she was meant to be part of the Hollywood scene since life has unfolded so incredibly well for her.

She was born in Tulsa, Oklahoma on September 23,1947. She describes her family made up of her parents, Brad and Gwen, and her two brothers, Phil and Ken, as having a sense of humor that keeps life quite interesting.

Her father is a retired art professor from the University of Tulsa. Even though he never pursued an acting career Mary Kay views him as having a natural theatrical flair with his storytelling abilities combined with his humorous insights. Right by his side is Mary Kay's mother Gwen who is a retired teacher also. Not only have the two of them taught their children the importance of humor in their daily life but they instilled a tremendous sense of family loyalty which has remained solid over the years.

As a young child Mary Kay was the typical 3 year-old who was summoned to perform and sing in front of family and friends. However, to Mary Kay those performances became a natural part of life and began to develop a growing sense of creativity within her. As early as elementary school she began performing in class plays and continued on through high school. She remembers writing a school paper in junior high describing her desire to have a career

in acting, long before the thought had a chance to become a reality.

When she attended the University of Tulsa, Mary Kay studied radio and television production. In those days the department was in it's infancy and geared to local production. Since then, TU has developed an impressive department with a Film Studies Major among the programs offered. In terms of preparation for her career, Mary Kay says she now realizes an emphasis in literature and history would have been helpful as well. Of course Mary Kay had her sights set on Hollywood.

Mary Kay feels extremely fortunate with the way her career began. While attending TU she met John Ashley, an actor who had come to the university to speak to her class. He was kind enough to give her the name of a person to contact at CBS Television City that could direct her to personnel. Mary Kay didn't care what she had to do, she just wanted her foot in the door at CBS so she could earn her way into an acting career. She was confident she would someday become an actress if she kept her eyes open and learned what was needed along the way.

I'm sure excitement was in the air as she drove down the highway headed for Hollywood. Here she was a young college graduate with a dream in her heart and the tenacity it took to fulfill that dream.

CBS hired her as a clerk typist in the music clearance department and later as part of the production staff. She admits some of her jobs weren't ideal, she was a "dog"/assoc. producer for a local children's show -"it was like a sauna bath inside the dog costume!" but she learned a lot on each job. And she was at least at the right place waiting for her break to come.

She received her first on-camera role as an "extra" while working as a secretary for comedian Tim Conway on his CBS Comedy Hour. Next, she worked for Norman Lear's company and gained a lot of experience with comedy script writing while working for the head writer's of "Maude."

One day while walking across the CBS parking lot with a friend, she began singing a funny song she had written called *If Communism Comes Knocking At Your Door, Don't Answer It.* She was overheard by a couple of writers from the comedy show "All In The Family" who were so intrigued they immediately contacted producer Norman Lear. Mary Kay was given the opportunity to act in an episode of "All In The Family" and sing her humorous little song which began to open other doors for her as well.

Mary Kay began co-writing with Linda Boodworth for numerous TV series, including "M* A *S*H", The Mary Tyler Moore Show and Phyllis.

In January 1976 she was given the incredible opportunity to portray Loretta Haggers in the critically acclaimed comedy series, "Mary Hartman, Mary Hartman." In this role she won the EMMY for Best Supporting Actress in a comedy.

As a result of singing on episodes of "Mary Hartman, Mary Hartman" where she wrote over 75 songs for the character, she began receiving offers to produce an album. She wasn't interested in doing a joke album and since she wasn't in pursuit of a singing career she turned every offer down until Emmy Lou Harris approached her. Her knowledge of Emmy Lou's professionalism created a desire to see an album come to fruition.

Mary Kay was signed with Columbia Records where she was nominated for a Grammy in what she described as a thrilling and amazing time.

Mary Kay's talents didn't stop with television and music albums. She has appeared in numerous feature films some of which are "Bound For Glory," "Private Benjamin," "Starting Over," "The Big Chill" and "Manny and Lo," (for which she received a Best Supporting Female award nomination from the Independent Spirit Awards). If I listed all of her accomplishments there wouldn't be room enough to enlighten readers about other facets of Mary Kay's life.

I was intrigued with the fact that such a beautiful and talented woman had never chosen to marry and have children. It's quite obvious by looking at her she has been approached with the subject on different occasions, however, she opted to stay single.

We discussed the importance of a person listening to their "whole being" and following what their gut instincts are. Everything that looks right for you isn't necessarily the right thing to do. *She pointed out how survival in life is all about consciousness, which I realized was a thought provoking statement. So often we go through life letting the "river of decisions" be made by others whereas if we kept control of our lives we would come closer to being on the right track.*

As an actress Mary Kay enjoys the opportunity to portray human emotions such as joy and sadness which teaches all of us how closely knit together we really are. If in her acting roles she can show humanity in its fullest, she feels assured she has done the best job she could ever do.

I was so impressed with Mary Kay Place and quite convinced her "pursuit of purpose" in life had unfolded as it should. Whatever the future holds Mary Kay is prepared to embrace it with strength of character and the tenacity of a seasoned actress.

Wm. R. Pogue

U.S.A.F. Colonel / Astronaut

The next time someone asks, "What is so special about Okemah, Oklahoma?," you will be able to tell them it is where the distinguished and well thought of William R. Pogue was born on January 23, 1930.

I'm sure his parents Alex and Margaret Pogue, had no idea that 43 years later their son would be orbiting the Earth for 84 days during the final manned flight of the Skylab space station.

Bill's adolescent years were spent in Central, Oklahoma where both of his parents taught in rural schools. Then in 1943 the family moved to Sand Springs, Oklahoma where his father accepted a position as principal of Lake Station School. He retired in 1969.

Because of the obvious good example his parents had set for him, Bill enrolled at Oklahoma Baptist University to prepare himself for a teaching career. However, after graduating in 1951 with a Bachelor of Science degree, rumors led him to believe he might be drafted into the Army due to the Korean War.

To sidetrack someone else's choice for his life he decided to enlist in the Air Force. Out of five children in the Pogue family, Bill was the only one who decided to go into the military.

He enlisted in January 1951 and went through tech school. He was going to be a B-29 gunner, but they called him to flight school in September before going on to gunnery school. He had a one year combat tour in Korea while serving with the Fifth Air Force and had logged in 43 missions when the war finally ended.

After returning to Luke Air Force Base in Phoenix, Arizona he spent the next year or so as a gunnery instructor. He still thought however, he would someday return home and begin his teaching career. The following two years were to be the most fun he had experienced thus far. From 1955 to 1957 he was a member of the USAF precision aerobatic flying team, the Thunderbirds. "What a wonderful experience." Bill said they had some close calls occasionally while in flight, but never lost anyone on their team.

In 1958 Bill made his way back to Oklahoma and enrolled at Oklahoma State University where he received his master's degree in mathematics. He then became an assistant professor in the mathematics department at the Air Force Academy but relinquished that position early in order to participate in Test Pilot School, hoping to make the astronaut selection which finally occurred in 1965.

It was a long and involved selection process with extensive psychological and physical tests. After the selection was made they were then required to interview with certain individuals at the Johnson Space Center.

Bill was selected in the fifth group of astronauts in 1966 and was on the support crews for Apollos 7, 11 and 14. He was scheduled to fly on Apollo 19, but Apollo 17 was the last Apollo to launch and Apollo 18 and 19 were cancelled. So Bill was given the opportunity to fly on the final Earth orbiting manned flight of the Skylab Space Station which launched on November 16, 1973.

They orbited at a nominal altitude of approximately 270 miles, between 50 degrees north and south latitude. Bill's 84-day space flight aboard the Skylab Space Station with astronauts Jerry Carr and Ed Gibson set eight endurance and distance records. They were able to see 80 percent of the Earth's land surface.

Jerry and Bill busied themselves with cameras, sensors and metals processing experiments. Ed, a solar physicist, was in charge of pointing six camera telescopes at the sun and comet Kohoutek. Daily medical experiments took the most time as they evaluated how their bodies adapted to their weightless environment.

The astronauts took four spacewalks. Bill made two of the space walks (one for a new record-over seven hours) and conducted numerous experiments related to studies of the Earth, the sun and the long-term effects of zero-gravity on crew members. Both of Bill's walks totaled 13 hours and 31 minutes outside the craft.

I asked Bill on a spiritual level what it was like to be in outer space. He said it was quite inspiring to look back at planet Earth and know you are far from it. You would have to be a real insensitive clod not to be impressed with the awe of it all. He remarked how tremendous it was to be outside the Skylab moving at five miles a second while attached to a 60 foot umbilical line that carries oxygen and water for their water cooled long johns. He said you can actually see "motion."

After 84 days in space Jerry Carr, Bill Pogue and Ed Gibson returned to Earth on February 8, 1974. They had circled the globe 1,214 times and brought back 1,718 pounds of film, data and biomedical specimens for scientific studies.

Bill sent me a video tape he produced called "We're Go For Launch to ZERO-G," which in layman's terms means (absolutely no gravity). After watching the video I realized it certainly takes a unique individual to become an astronaut. I understand more about the extensive psychological and physical tests they have to endure in order to make the rank.

Being an astronaut does put a person on a prestigious level, but it appears to be a level that requires an extreme dedication to that field of endeavor. My hat is off to you, Astronaut Bill Pogue. Without the determination and dedication of individuals like Bill, so many important discoveries would still be left undone.

Bill retired from NASA and from the Air Force as a colonel in 1977 and worked as an independent technical contractor for several aerospace and energy firms. From 1984 to 1998 he provided contract technical support to the Boeing Company for the Space Station Freedom program which was later modified into the International Space Station project.

In 1996 he was named Director of Advanced Technologies for Lost & Found International, a Scottsdale, Arizona company providing products and services that enable finders of lost items to contact the owner for quick return.

In October 1997 Bill was inducted into the U.S. Astronaut Hall of Fame at Titusville, Florida. Currently Bill spends most of his time speaking or writing. He has revised for the second time a paperback book he wrote in 1985 titled, *How Do You Go To The Bathroom In Space,* a book he was kind enough to send to me. He also has finished another book titled *Space Trivia,* which will be out soon. who knows how many other creative works are waiting to be unveiled.

I asked Bill to indulge me with some of life's lessons he has learned over the years and he promptly obliged. "Take advantage of opportunities and don't be afraid to fail." Bill pointed out he was one of eight people who was offered the opportunity to try out for the Thunderbirds. Out of those eight, only three people accepted the offer because some of them were afraid to fail. *If you aren't willing to take risk you'll miss out on a lot life has to offer .*

Wiley Post - Aviator

So much has been said and written about Wiley Post. He was indeed a remarkable man and one who deserves to be remembered. He was given the name of Wiley Hardeman Post on the day of his birth, November 22, 1898 in Grand Saline, Texas.

Wiley's Oklahoma days began in 1907 when his parents bought 160 acres six miles west of Rush Springs, Oklahoma. They only spent three years in Rush Springs and decided to move to Burns, Oklahoma. Wiley never enjoyed farm life, but he also didn't enjoy the ritual of attending school everyday. So by the time he was 11 years old he checked himself out of school and never returned.

With five brothers and one sister there was never a dull moment around the Post house. Wiley became quite a handyman learning to repair items that needed fixing for other people around the area. He quickly began acquiring a little savings that came in handy when it was time to purchase his very own bicycle at age 13.

A visit to the Lawton, Oklahoma State Fair revealed a defining moment in Wiley's life, yet at the time he didn't really know it. He saw an airplane and listened to the pilot describe his exciting adventures. Wiley began visualizing his own exploits and planning how he could make them a reality in his life.

By the time he turned 17 he decided to leave home and begin the path toward his dream. He went to work for a construction company in Lawton who was building an airport at Fort Sill. Wiley spent every minute he could at the airport trying to find a way to learn about flying.

His dream was put on hold for a few years because a bad decision landed him in the State Reformatory at Granite. Fortunately, what was meant to be a 10 year sentence was miraculously reduced to less than a year with a 12 year parole sentence. However, the stigma attached to his incarceration was like a dark cloud that loomed over him for quite some time.

He eventually signed on with a flying circus act in Wewoka, Burrell Tibbs and his "Texas Topnotch Fliers." To his surprise the only position available was a parachute jumper, something he knew absolutely nothing about. Luckily he succeeded and became a top notch jumper. In addition some of the pilots were giving him flying lessons and he could see his dream beginning to fall into place.

The next step was to try and purchase his own plane. He went to work for a drilling company with the intentions of saving as much money as possible to purchase a plane. Everything was going along as planned until the day a roughneck struck an iron bolt with a sledgehammer and a chip off of the bolt flew off and imbedded itself in Wiley's left eye. Infection quickly set in and doctors were forced to remove his left eye.

It appeared as if his dream to become a pilot with his own airplane would now become an impossible task. He was 28 years old with one eye, a prison record and an elementary education. But Wiley's spirit of tenacity wouldn't allow him to lay down and quit. He was more determined than ever to accomplish his goals.

He was awarded $1,800 for the loss of his eye. A black patch worn over his eye became his trademark. He purchased a used Canuck airplane for $240, spent $300 on repairs and was ready to fly. He solicited himself for hire to flying circuses and to businessmen who needed speedy transportation.

In 1927 he married a 17 year old girl named Mae Laine. He was forced to sell his airplane because of costly repair bills and began flying a plane called the Winnie Mae for a couple of oilmen in Chickasha, Oklahoma. It was quite interesting in that his mother's name was Mae, his wife's name was Mae and he was flying a plane named Winnie Mae.

As Wiley continued to dream and fantasize about his adventures in flying he began thinking about the possibility of flying around the world. His fantasy came true on June 23, 1931 when he took off from Roosevelt Field in New York. Eight days, 15 hours and 51 minutes later he arrived back in New York, setting a new world record. He had flown along with his navigator Harold Gatty 15,474 miles in just under 208 hours.

In a few short years Wiley had made a name for himself as the world's most famous pilot. His next goal was to complete the flight once again, only this time as a solo pilot.

Two years later on July 15, 1933 Wiley began his solo flight, once again starting from New York. On July 22, 1933 Wiley broke his previous record by flying around the world in seven days, 18 hours, 49 and a half minutes with a total of 115 hours, 36 and a half minutes. Wiley set records that had never been set before. He was the first person to fly around the world twice and the first person to make the flight alone.

Success begets success and experience spurs innovative ideas. Wiley eventually invented the first pressurized flying suit to solve the problem of altitude flying. By 1935 he had become president of the Wiley Post Aircraft Corporation in Oklahoma City. The company built 13 open-cockpit biplanes.

Wiley became good friends with Will Rogers (the famous newspaper columnist, radio personality and trick roper) after his first around the world flight in 1931. In 1935 Wiley asked Will to finance a flying trip to Siberia to convince the world about the possibilities of paid passenger flights.

On August 6, 1935 Wiley and Will began their flight from Seattle, Washington. They continually experienced delays along the way because of bad weather, but Wiley had battled through such things before without much trouble. This time, however, was different. On August 12th they landed in Fairbanks, Alaska and planned to go on to Point Barrow, but the weather delayed them. Three days later Wiley decided to try again to get to Point Barrow, assuming the weather would soon clear up.

After refueling at Harding Lake 40 miles from their takeoff in Fairbanks, Wiley was supposed to contact Point Barrow for a weather check. Disappointedly there were no phones to call out on so Wiley prepared himself for flight.

If the phone call had been made, Wiley would have known it was extremely unsafe to fly. After flying several hours from Harding Lake with poor visibility Wiley lost his way and landed at an Eskimo camp on the lagoon beside the river. They got out of the plane and asked the Eskimos to direct them to Point Barrow, which apparently was only 10 minutes away.

They were so close and yet they never made their final destination. As Wiley took off from the lagoon the engine started sputtering and quit. Within an instant the plane made a nosedive into the shallow lagoon. Wiley and Will were instantly killed.

Wiley's life ended way too soon, but so many of his dreams had been fulfilled in the space of a few short years. Wiley was buried in Oklahoma City and his wife Mae, who passed away almost 50 years later, was laid to rest beside him.

Dave Rader

Coach

What a Gentleman! What a Godly man!

Dave Rader was born in Wichita, Kansas but moved to Tulsa, Oklahoma in 1961. He spoke very highly of his parents J.R. and Janice, as he recalled how attentive they were to him and his brother growing up.

Like most children there are so many things our parents do for us when we are young that shape our lives and yet we don't recognize it until we are older. Dave was always athletic and fondly remembers how faithful his father was at attending all of his games. That carried over into the lives of his own children as he created those same types of memories for them. His mother on the other hand was the one who encouraged him that he could do anything he wanted to do.

"It wasn't the mere words," he said. "It was her belief that I could and for whatever reason, it sunk in."

As Dave looks back, it was inevitable that he would be involved in sports. He lettered three times in three years of high school. After graduation from Will Rogers High School in Tulsa, he enrolled at Tulsa University where he played football there as well. His dream was to be a professional football player.

Just before he graduated from college in 1979 he was drafted by the San Diego Chargers, but was cut that same August. He came back to Tulsa University, completed his degree and graduated that May. By Memorial weekend he and his new wife Janet were on their way to New Jersey to once again be a part of the New York Giants. But by August he had been cut from the team.

I think most of us would have tucked our tails and ran by then, but Dave didn't feel like a failure. He simply felt like the team had made a wrong decision. However, for a short while he was entertained by his own private pity party. At the time he probably didn't fully understand the lesson he was learning but he later saw it very clearly.

"Your plans may not be what someone else's plans are for you, but sometimes you have to make adjustments because you are under their authority, he said. "Did I like it? NO! Am I better for going through it? SURE! It was a great learning time, what you would call a chance to mature."

As I have heard so many times in my interviews, people start out in one area of their dream and end up in another area, which is still linked to the original dream, but they become more successful there. Dave knew his life would be involved with sports because it was a burning fire inside of him. Yet his position was not as a player, but as a coach.

After being cut by the Giants, Dave took a job at the World Trade Center with a company who built nuclear power plants. A few months later on a short trip back to Tulsa for his brother's wedding he went on a few interviews which landed him a job with a company called Oil Dynamics. In spite of his new job he still couldn't forget his dream.

Once again he went for a tryout. This time it was with the New England Patriots, which resulted in one more cut. The realization finally hit him. This was not the route for him to take. He was trying to be content at his job with Oil Dynamics, while he and Janet played the typical role of "yuppies" in a college town.

Fortunately, Dave had retained his relationship with Giants Head Coach Ray Perkins who had cut him from the team. Even though Dave had not agreed with the coach's decision, he did highly admire the man. Occasionally, Coach Perkins would alert Dave when different positions would become available. In December of 1982 Coach Perkins took a job with the University of Alabama and asked Dave to be his assistant coach, which he accepted in January of 1983. His career had finally began in a field he had dreamed of most of his life. In December of 1986 he was asked to come to his alma mater, Tulsa University, to become their assistant coach this led to him becoming their head coach in May of 1988.

There were a lot of highlights during Dave's tenure at Tulsa University from 1988 to 1999. He had the privilege of guiding young men through their college football years. He spoke of different players he had watched endure hardships and then come back even stronger than before.

From what I've heard, Dave was a man that was highly respected by his players as well as his co-workers. I could easily understand that as I sat and talked with him and saw the sincerity of his heart. I was particularly impressed with his dedication to his family and the high standards he set for himself as a father. How many men do we know that read books authored by Godly men to help guide them in raising their children or influencing lives? That's the kind of man I would want to have in authority over my athletic son or my team of employees.

I was saddened when Dave's coaching career ended at Tulsa University. However, I remember him saying that God was in control of his life and the road that lay before him was surely paved with more of God's blessings for himself and his family.

Debra Ramirez – Singer/Songwriter

What a beautiful lady inside and out!

Debra was born in Buffalo, Oklahoma but was raised in Guymon. She's never experienced life without God being the main focus. Her parents Martin and Dora were strong Christians who felt it was their privilege to raise their son, Eddie and daughter Debra to know God.

Debra described two incidents during the time of her birth which she refers to as "miracles." Her right foot was crooked and the doctors said she would have to have surgery or walk with a limp. Yet her mother believed God had something more in store for Debra. When the family pastor prayed for Debra, her foot was miraculously healed and she never had the surgery.

Secondly, within a few days after Debra was born, her mother had a bleeding ulcer and was hemorrhaging. Doctors were

terribly concerned because they couldn't seem to get the bleeding stopped. Dora prayed and told God she had always wanted a boy and a girl and now she had them. She pleaded with God to spare her life because at the time, her husband was not a Christian and Dora had to know her children would be raised to know God.

To make a long story short, God healed her. Because of the tremendous demonstration of faith, Dora's husband saw in her during the time of her illness, he accepted God into his life a few months later.

Debra grew up with her parents teaching her how to trust and lean on God: *Even during times of discouragement, her parents would remind her of the many times God had intervened on her behalf. They constantly taught her to count her many blessings and rehearse her past victories.* Debra grew into adulthood as a strong, independent woman yet with an earthly father who she leaned on heavily as her protector.

Unfortunately, Debra's father passed on in 1995 and she had to come to the realization he was no longer there to lean on. Now the only father she could rely on was her Heavenly Father. Amazingly the transition was smoother than it is for some people because her father had taught her all her life to trust God. Now without her father's help she was forced to take some of those lessons and put them to the test. You need only to talk to Debra to realize having a good earthly father makes trusting your Heavenly Father so much easier.

When Debra was a senior in high school, she entered her first pageant and won Guymon's Ideal Miss. After high school graduation, she attended Panhandle State University for two years. She won her third pageant at Panhandle State and competed for the title of Miss Oklahoma for the first time. Debra transferred to Oral Roberts University in 1981, where she majored in Business Management.

Debra always desired to fulfill God's plan, and believed that Father God always had the best plan for her life. After prayerful consideration, she felt the desire to continue competing in the Miss America Pageant System.

Debra had always been involved in music, either playing the piano, singing, coronet or baritone. Her musical abilities played a key role in her ultimately winning six Miss America Preliminary titles.

It wasn't until 1983 that Debra would compete on the Miss Oklahoma Stage again. It had taken three years and seven preliminary pageants to capture the crown of Miss Queen of the West. Debra's goal was to become Miss America. She placed in the Top Ten in the Miss Oklahoma Pageant that year.

In 1984 Debra won the title of Miss Wheatland. She had just graduated from college and was on her way to seeing her dream fulfilled. But to her disappointment, she did not make the Top Ten finalist.

Debra took some time to search her heart and to receive God's guidance. She had believed that God had led her thus far. But after not winning again, had she missed His plan? During this time her voice teacher encouraged her to move to Tempe, AZ and work on her Master's Degree in Music Theatre. Following the peace in her heart, she made the move to Arizona.

Her dream to become Miss America remained in her heart. After much prayer and encouragement she entered a local pageant and won the title of Miss Maricopa County. But instead of winning Miss America, she was the First runner-up and the Grand Talent Winner. Disappointed but not ready to quit, the next year she entered the Miss Phoenix Pageant. But again she was the Talent winner and First runner-up.

Debra believed the dream in her heart was from God. So why wasn't she winning? After praying and seeking God's guidance, she believed she was to move back to Oklahoma. Within a few weeks of being back, she won the title of Miss Lake Eufaula. But again at the State finals she was First runner-up and the Grand Talent Winner.

Now Debra had only one year of eligibility to compete. During this season of refinement, she recognized the call of God on her life, and began attending Rhema Bible Training Center to better prepare her for the ministry. Continuing to follow her dream, she entered again and won the title of Miss Grand Lake. And in the 1988 Miss Oklahoma Pageant, Debra again was First runner-up.

The truth of Proverbs 3:5,6 rang in her heart, that if you will trust in the Lord with all your heart and not lean on your own understanding, acknowledge Him in all your ways, He promised He would direct your paths. She made the choice to believe and trust Him that His plan was the best. Now, she realizes that those years of training and perseverance have prepared her for today.

Debra has followed the direction of God for her life and is in the full time ministry. As a licensed and ordained minister, she shares the uncompromising Word of God through her music and teaching. Her ministry bridges the gap of age and denomination.

She has completed a variety of teaching tapes, as well as being in demand as a motivational and inspirational speaker for both Christian and secular groups. Having seventeen years of vocal training in classical and contemporary music, she also sings America's favorite patriotic songs. She travels throughout the United States speaking and singing to thousands in congregations, women's groups, youth and singles groups and national conferences.

Debra's desire is to be a minister of God's grace and love. Her gifts have given her opportunity to speak and sing in some of the largest churches in the United States. In addition to Missions work in Mexico and Guatemala, she has frequently appeared on a wide variety of Television Programs including the TBN Christian Network, Lesea Broadcasting, "Richard Roberts Live," etc. She has released four music recordings with others scheduled for release in the future.

As she reflects on her life's experience, she sees how the hand of God has woven the tapestry of her life. Sure there have been times of disappointment, but there have also been great times of celebration, and she can clearly see that God has and will continue to direct her path.

She said often people tell her they can't hear God speaking to them and directing their lives. Yet Debra knows God talks to everyone and if there is a problem hearing Him we need to find out why. She has a simple solution. *She said the voice of direction is the same voice of correction. If a person closes his ears to God's correction then when it is time for direction you won't recognize His voice. Therefore, go back to the time you knew you were supposed to do something and complete the task. Then you will be able to hear the voice of God clearly.*

Tony Randall

Actor

Leonard Rosenberg always knew he wanted to be an actor. Even though life began for him in the midwestern town of Tulsa, Oklahoma on February 26, 1920 his sights were focused on New York at a very early age.

The 1920's and 30's must have been so different for Tony Randall. As he witnessed the theatrical roadshows that came through Tulsa he probably fantasized about a world that was far removed from his limited existence. He must have visualized a place full of excitement and adventure that only existed for a privileged few.

He remembers the night when a European Ballet Company came through Tulsa performing Swan Lake and Sheherezade. Most of the audience had never seen a performance like that before. Tony recalls his first experience with a celebrity was at the age of 14 when Katherine Cornell came to Tulsa to perform in Romeo and Juliet and gave him her autograph for twenty five cents. Without a doubt those and other incidents left an image in Tony's mind that was to carry him all the way to his destiny.

Tony graduated from Central High School which at the time was located in the middle of downtown Tulsa. The building with its concrete steps that led upward to the front entrance where young teenagers use to gather each morning before school, still remains. However the hallways no longer ring out the exuberant sounds of young people scurrying along before the last bell ushers them into their classrooms.

Instead, you'll find a generation of hard working employees who have become part of one of Tulsa's leading businesses. I must say the building has a cleaner more exquisite outward appearance than it did when it was a schoolhouse. But it will always be viewed with memories of outstanding young adults who have gone on to do great things.

After high school graduation Tony enrolled in Northwestern University where he majored in speech and drama. He then went to New York and studied at Columbia University and the Neighborhood Playhouse with the renowned Sanford Meisner.

In my adventures of interviewing, and I do consider it an adventure, I have found that a person's hometown is sort of an incubator for its community of adults. It usually happens one of two ways, either the wholesomeness of the town carries through to other areas of endeavor in a person's life or the lack of certain facets causes them to look harder and deeper for their dreams and aspirations. Either way the town launches a great multitude of people who owe their success at least in part to earlier phases of their upbringing.

Tony married for the first time at a young age to his wife of 54 years, Florence, who passed away after a long illness in 1992.

Tony's Broadway debut was in 1941 in "A Circle of Chalk." He appeared in a few more plays before being selected to join another honorable profession, as a member of the United States Army. He served four years in the Signal Corps, being discharged as a Lieutenant.

It was interesting to note that Katherine Cornell, who he cited as his first celebrity exposure, later became his peer in the theatrical performance of "Anthony and Cleopatra." When television came along Tony was quickly chosen as one of the top actors of the day. From panel shows and hilarious comedies to dramatic character roles the name Tony Randall became a household word.

Most of us fondly remember Tony's role as "Felix" on the long running comedy "The Odd Couple" where he co-starred with Jack Klugman. No two people could have been more suited for roles opposite each other than those two talented performers.

Tony has acted alongside some of the most talented women in the business. As the desperate, pathetic husband opposite Joanne Woodward in "No Down Payment," "Let's Make Love" opposite Marilyn Monroe; "The Mating Game" with Debbie Reynolds; and the trilogy of his Doris Day-Rock Hudson movies, "Pillow Talk," "Send Me No Flowers" and "Lover Come Back." His versatility has been proven time and time again and he remains one of the most well-known figures in the acting world.

In 1991 Tony achieved a lifelong dream when he launched his National Actors Theatre. The Theatre is a not-for-profit subscription based company formed to bring the great classical repertoire of the world, with the finest actors, to a theatre that is within reach of all. As a gala black tie benefit for his theatre, Tony brought "The Odd Couple" back to Broadway. He was reunited with Jack Klugman along with an all-star cast that put on a brilliant performance. That ignited continuing performances with Jack Klugman as they toured with "The Odd Couple" in Palm Beach, Los Angeles and across the U.S.

Tony no doubt has proven to be successful in every area he has set out to accomplish. The world has become far more enriched by his contributions not only in theatre, television and film, but also in his efforts to speak out concerning causes that mean a great deal to him.

I'm sure his audience of fans cheered when he found love again in 1995 and married Heather Harlan. Equally inspiring was the announcement of his first child Julia Laurette on April 11, 1997 and then Jefferson Salvini on June 15, 1998.

Life has certainly brought a great deal of rewarding paths for Tony Randall to walk along. I'm sure all were marked with complete dedication and perseverance.

Oklahoma is proud of their native son and the many accomplishments he has achieved over the years. He along with many other talented people have made Oklahoma a place that can always be named as a boiling pot for individuals who have gone on and successfully created their destinies.

Dennis J. Reimer

U.S. Army General

I spoke to General Reimer on a phone interview. I found him to be very interesting and the kind of gentleman you would expect to hold such a high ranking position in our country.

Born on July 12, 1939 he is a native of Medford, Oklahoma. Coming from a small town he said everyone had a tenancy to watch out for each other. That caused everyone to keep their values in check and place a high priority on living a productive life.

None of his family had a military background so there was no prodding by any of them for him to enter the service. It just so happened that one day while in high school he began reading about West Point and it planted a seed of interest he had to pursue.

He knew he would need congressional influence in order to be accepted so he sent a letter to Oklahoma Congressman Page Belcher. Belcher's return letter informed Dennis he would not be able to help him because enrollment was too full at the time. Thinking that door was closed to him he enrolled in college at Alva. Surprisingly, during his first year, Belcher contacted him and said things had changed and he could go take the entrance exam.

Being at West Point meant committing himself to four years of academics whereby he would then be required to serve five years in the military. He graduated with a Bachelor of Science degree from the U.S. Military Academy in 1962 and began his career as a Field Artillery Officer. Obviously he was a natural and military life suited him fine. His promotion came so easy that he never thought about discontinuing his career.

He later went on to receive a Master of Science degree from Shippensburg State University. General Reimer's military experience spans command positions from company to division level, and service on staffs up to Headquarters, Department of the Army.

His commands include an infantry company at Fort Benning, Georgia, an artillery battalion at Fort Carson, Colorado, the division artillery for the 8th Infantry Division in Germany, the corps artillery at Fort Sill, Oklahoma and the 4th Infantry Division at Fort Carson. He has served in a variety of joint and combined assignments.

General Reimer served two combat tours in Vietnam, one as an advisor to a battalion of the South Vietnamese Army and the other as an executive officer for an artillery battalion in the 9th Infantry Division.

He also served in Korea as the Chief of Staff, Combined Field Army and Assistant Chief of Staff for Operations and Training, Republic of Korea/United States Combined Forces Command.

He served three other tours at the Pentagon as aide-de-camp to Army Chief of Staff General Creighton Abrams, as the Deputy Chief of Staff for Operations and Plans for the Army during Desert Storm and as Army Vice Chief of Staff.

General Reimer's awards for peacetime and combat service include the Defense Distinguished Service Medal, the Distinguished Service Medal, two Legions of Merit, the Distinguished Flying Cross (his helicopter went down during combat), six awards of the Bronze Star Medal (one with "V" device for valor), the Purple Heart (for being wounded in battle) and the Combat Infantryman Badge. He also wears the Parachutist Badge, the Aircraft Crewman Badge, and the Ranger Tab.

I asked the General if it ever crossed his mind during combat that he wouldn't survive. He said there is always some concern, but soldiers are trained to survive under the worst of conditions so concerns are usually minimal.

He believes every young man should experience military life for some length of time. It makes for strong leadership skills and discipline in all areas of his life.

General Reimer retired in June 1999 after 37 years in the Army. He said it is hard after all those years to wake up in the morning and no longer be a part of the every day routine. He feels he still has a lot to offer though, and intends to contribute all he can for the next several years until he decides to fully retire.

He remarked how fortunate he was to have spent some incredible years doing what he loved to do. The knowledge and skills he learned definitely formed his life.

General Reimer is married to the former Mary Jo Powers. They have a son, Michael and a daughter, Ann Marie.

Gary Richardson

Attorney

I'm not sure I had an iron clad reason to believe all attorneys were crooks. But I know I've spent most of my life believing as some others have that the statement was probably true. I'm so glad I had the opportunity to meet an attorney who has the ability to change that perspective for a lot of individuals.

I had been told by I. J. Ganem for over a year about this well-deserving friend of his I should interview for this book. Almost without exception, when I.J. and I would talk he would ask again if I had contacted his friend Gary Richardson and without fail, I would have to say no. Then one day, my friend John Venturella mentioned his admiration for Gary as well.

I've learned over the years that usually if a person or thing is continually brought to your attention that there comes a time when you should take heed. Boy, am I glad I finally did. I told I.J. and John to give Gary my phone number and we would set up and interview, but Gary graciously refused to make the call. Instead, he waited to see if I would call him. I guess my opinion had always been that attorneys were too arrogant not to toot their own horns, but I found that statement to be untrue with Gary.

On the day of our interview I arrived early, which gave me time to view many of the newspaper articles exhibited on Gary's outer office walls. Before I began reading the articles however, I first stood in awe at the beautiful layout of his office waiting area. Success was certainly evident with the handsome decor of cherrywood paneling and the beautiful chandelier that hung over the stairway. I certainly thought to myself this would be a great look for which to make a statement.

When Gary arrived through the elevator doors which opened into his upstairs domain, the image I had of his persona was not misguided. The 6'2" trial lawyer described to me proved to be a gentleman from the moment he stepped into the room. The minutes that followed solidified my assumptions.

Gary was born in Caddo, Oklahoma but at the age of nine the family moved to South Texas where Gary remained until 1959. His father William (Bill), a tenant farmer/lay minister, once dreamed of being a judge, but instead looked on with pride when his son eventually entered the law arena.

Gary learned responsibility at an early age growing up on a farm with his twin sister Rheda Joy. By the time he was 14 years old he was driving a truck helping his father on the farm. Often he was referred to as "Bill's little man" because you could always catch him working diligently alongside his father.

Both of his parents were responsible for teaching their children the spiritual side of life. Even though Bill wasn't really knowledgeable about such things until he married Madeline, it didn't take him long to see the importance of God in their everyday affairs.

After graduating from Rio Rondo High School Gary attended Bethany Nazarene College. After completion of his college years he went to work as an insurance adjustor which put him in contact with a lot of attorneys. Gary experienced a very successful career, but it was during that time he realized just how important it was to become a lawyer himself.

He knew it wouldn't be easy to acquire a law degree because by this time he was married and had three children Chuck, Chad and Chandra to support. But he was determined to see his dream come to pass. With five insurance agencies to oversee, a full-time college curriculum and a song leader position at the local Baptist Church, Gary's hands were full. In spite of the heavy load he finished law school in 1972, but for the next two years he continued to keep his position with the insurance company.

In 1974 he was contacted by an individual requesting he come to Oklahoma and take the position as assistant insurance commissioner. At first Gary refused to even consider the idea. He was making $60,000 a year in Texas with an expense account and a company car. The commissioner's position only paid $12,000 a year. It seemed ludicrous to even consider the possibility since he had a wife and three children to support.

Somehow he was convinced to go to Oklahoma City and discuss becoming the assistant insurance commissioner as well as part of the legal staff. To his surprise, when he entered the room he intuitively knew he was where he was supposed to be. He kept the position for a year and a half until Commissioner Joe B. Hunt passed away.

He was then offered the position as Assistant District Attorney in Muskogee where he remained for the next two years. I excitedly thought his salary probably went up quite a bit with that position, but Gary said only $500 more a year. Once again Gary knew he was in the right position inspite of the lack of the "greenback dollar."

The next few years found him in his own private law practice with 76 year old Douglas Garrett. The work was interesting, but Gary found it hard to try cases in a small town. To be in court during the week and then sit alongside the defendant that Sunday morning in church was just not a happy feeling. During his tenure at the law firm he was enticed to run for Congress twice. Both times he lost yet he knew he would some day run for an elected office again.

From May 1981 to 1984 Gary became the U.S. Attorney for the Eastern District of Oklahoma where he prosecuted several high profile cases, and won. His next career move was to take on a task others said he couldn't accomplish. Gary had become well acquainted with the needs of people and their struggles to be heard and exonerated. He wanted to start his own law firm which solely protected the rights of the people. In other words he would become strictly a plaintiff lawyer, unwilling to solicit defense work.

His colleagues said it would be too hard to keep the firm afloat by putting such limitations on his work, but Gary remained unyielding. He wanted to be a voice for the people. It took five years of stick-to-it-ness to totally secure his position, but Gary never wavered in his convictions. Now 17 years later he is known as "A Champion of the Underdog" or "Oklahomans Legal Topgun," signifying his quest to represent the little people against the power structure and winning.

As we continued our interview Gary cited a couple of cases he had won and pointed out the importance of selling "truth" when he is in the courtroom. Truth seems to work for Gary which reminds me of the scripture "...and the truth shall set you free." Obviously, God thought it was of great importance as well.

Even though Gary's ego doesn't need any further stroking and his millionaire pockets are fuller than any individual's need be, he has his sights set on one more goal. He wants to be the next Governor of Oklahoma, as an Independent, so once again he can represent the little people and win.

With his deep abiding faith in God's sovereignty, the support of his second wife Sandy, his two step children Austin and Ryan as well as Chuck, Chad and Chandra he is sure to have continued success in all areas of his life.

Gary Richardson

Lynn Riggs
Playwright

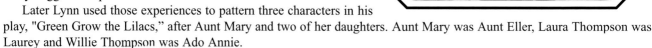

I was thrilled when I went looking for information on Lynn Riggs and stumbled upon his nephew Leo living right here amongst us. I've driven to Claremore on many occasions, traveled down Lynn Riggs Boulevard and wondered for a moment just who this individual was. Having the opportunity to speak with Leo made it possible to feel a connection to Lynn I wouldn't have otherwise felt. Leo provided the majority of information for Lynn's profile from a write-up that had been done on his uncle many years ago.

Lynn Riggs was born August 31, 1899 in the Cooweescoowee District about three miles southwest of Claremore. His parents were William Grant and Rose Ella Duncan Riggs. Unfortunately, his mother died when he was 2 years old. His father remarried six months later, but Lynn, his sister Mattie (Leo's mother) and brother Edgar couldn't quite adjust to their stepmother. So the children moved in with their Aunt Mary Riggs Thompson Brice.

Later Lynn used those experiences to pattern three characters in his play, "Green Grow the Lilacs," after Aunt Mary and two of her daughters. Aunt Mary was Aunt Eller, Laura Thompson was Laurey and Willie Thompson was Ado Annie.

Lynn graduated from high school in 1917 at Eastern University Preparatory School in Claremore. Soon afterwards he moved to Chicago and worked in the claims department at the Adams Express Company.

If one focused on just the beginning of a person's life it would be hard to image anything extraordinary coming from it. However, if you manage to hang in for the long haul you begin to see a life unfolding that is sprinkled with grandeur and excitement in every turn.

After leaving Chicago Lynn moved to New York City. He was a proof reader for the Wall Street Journal, an extra in movies shot in Astoria and the Bronx, and then a clerk in Macy's Bookstore.

Lynn returned to Claremore in 1919 and eventually enrolled in the School of Fine Arts and Sciences at the University of Oklahoma in September of 1920. At the end of his first year he was hired as a student assistant in English. He soon fell in love with a student named Eileen Yost, but he later lost her when a young man with a Stutz Bearcat automobile enrolled in school.

In 1922 Lynn's first play "Cuckoo" was performed at the University of Oklahoma. That summer he toured 11 states with the Chautauqua group. He sang second tenor in the quartet headed by first tenor Joe Benton. Joe later became Joseph Bentoneli of Italian opera fame.

In the spring of 1923 Lynn was on the editorial staff of the Oklahoma Whirlwinds Life of Sooner-Land, a gossip and humor magazine. Late in 1923 he was confined to a sanitarium with a severe case of pulmonary tuberculosis.

In 1925 Lynn wrote "Knives from Syria," a one-act play; "Big Lake," a full-length play which was published in 1927; and he finished "Sump'n Like Wings" which was about the people in Claremore.

He returned to New York in 1926 and it was there he wrote "A Lantern to See By," "Reckless," and "Borned In Texas." After returning to Oklahoma for a short while and becoming the first Oklahoma recipient of the John Guggenheim Fellowship award, he sailed for France in July of 1928. He resided at 12 Rue Kepler in Paris and began writing "Green Grow the Lilacs" in the Café Les Deux Magots. He didn't like the climate there, so early in 1929 he moved to the South of France where he lived at 12 Rue du Piolet in Cagnes Sur Mer. There he completed "Green Grow the Lilacs."

He returned to New York in the fall of 1929. The Theatre Guild presented "Green Grow the Lilacs" in Boston on December 8, 1930 and in New York City on January 26, 1931. Lynn went on to write several more plays including "The Cherokee Night" and" Russet Mantle." Lionel Barrymore once said, "The Cherokee Night is one of the best plays I have read in 20 years."

Lynn also worked as a script writer for Paramount, Metro-Goldwyn-Mayer and Universal Studios.

During a time when the Theatre Guild was going through a financial crisis, Theresa Helbrun, a director of the Guild who was a great admirer of Lynn's work, thought his play "Green Grow the Lilacs" contained the perfect elements for a musical. She called composer Richard Rodgers to see if he was interested. He told her if she could get Oscar Hammerstein II to join the project as the lyricist, he would sign on.

Hammerstein was familiar with Lynn's play and shared Theresa's view that it would make a great musical. With a great deal of effort and a strong force of faith guiding them the show debuted on Broadway in 1943 as OKLAHOMA!

Oscar Hammerstein II, went on record as saying, "Mr. Riggs' play is the wellspring of almost all that is good in Oklahoma. I kept many of the lines of the original play without making any changes in them at all for the simple reason they could not be improved on - at any rate, not by me. Lynn Riggs and "Green Grow the Lilacs" are the very soul of Oklahoma. I had been impressed by Lynn Riggs' description at the start of his play. ("It is a radiant summer morning --the kind of morning which, enveloping the shapes of earth --men, cattle in the meadow, blades of the young corn, streams --makes them seem to exist now for the first time, their images giving off a visible golden emanation that is partly true and partly a trick of imagination, focusing to keep alive a loveliness that may pass away.")

On first reading these words, I had thought what a pity to waste them on stage directions. Only readers could enjoy them. An audience would never hear them. Yet, if they did, how quickly they would slip into the wood of the story. Remembering this reaction, I reread the description and determined to put it into song. *Oh What a Beautiful Mornin'* opens the play and creates an atmosphere of relaxation and peace and tenderness. My indebtedness to Mr. Riggs' description is obvious. The cattle and the corn and the golden haze on the meadow are all there."

In 1946 when the play premiered in Oklahoma the state declared the day a legal holiday.

Lynn died of cancer in New York City on June 30, 1954. Around 1965 his sister, Mattie Cundiff, gave many of his books and personal memorabilia to found the Lynn Riggs Memorial in his honor at Claremore.

However, there came a time when space to house the memorabilia was needed. So Leo and his wife Gladys moved the museum to 121 N. Weenonah and once again opened it to the public on July 19, 1997. Along with an array of historical memorabilia sits the original surrey with the fringe on top from the movie, "Oklahoma."

Leo is 84 years old and lives in Tulsa with Gladys, but he continues to keep a close watch on the museum. He still believes as we all should that Lynn Riggs deserves credit for instilling within us a sense of great pride when we hear the words, *Oh, what a beautiful mornin', oh, what a beautiful day, I've got a wonderful feeling, everything is going my way.* Of course if you have never seen the play Oklahoma you may not be able to grasp the meaning behind the song. May I suggest you do what it takes to avail yourself of the opportunity .

Lynn Riggs

Dale Robertson - Actor

His voice has often been referred to as one of America's most recognized.

Probably one of my very favorite interviews was with Dale Robertson, since I grew up watching the television series, "The Tales of Wells Fargo." I never knew that the tall, good looking gentleman with the strong, robust voice who appeared on my television set every week was from my own home state of Oklahoma. Knowing that made our interview even that much more appealing.

Some people never seem to change. Even though Dale's hair is a little lesser shade of color than in previous years, he is still as charming and handsome as he ever was.

Dale was born in Harrah, Oklahoma, which is 22 miles from Oklahoma City on July 14, 1923. In 1927 his parents, Varvel and Melvin and his two brothers, Roxy and Chet moved from the farm to Oklahoma City. Dale's father had a dream of becoming a professional baseball player and was known by greats like Dizzy Dean as being a very talented player-one of the best Dizzy had ever seen.

On many occasions there were family discussions about Melvin pursuing his dream, but Varvel continued to protest. She wasn't about to be left alone on a farm with three boys to raise. She threatened Melvin that she would move into town if he left. Melvin wouldn't hear of that, because he was adamant about his boys being raised on the farm. So he gave up on his dream.

In return, Melvin became an alcoholic, which in the long run separated him from his family anyway. It was a sad turn of events. Who knows what the right choice should have been? Dale didn't blame his mother for not wanting to raise her boys alone. Ultimately the task was supposed to be a shared effort.

Dale speaks very highly of his mother and credits her for instilling strengths in he and his brothers that made them capable of enduring many hardships in life.

As a teenager, Dale became involved in what they called "Match Fights" throughout Kansas, Missouri, Illinois, Texas and Oklahoma. Unlike the way fights are operated today, there were no promoters involved. Any money accumulated for the match was given directly to the fighters. Dale used his earnings to help support the family and raise horses on their farm.

One night after a fight in Wichita, Kansas, a gentleman approached Dale about performing in a picture called "Golden Boy." He felt the part would be perfect for Dale. Dale was only 15 years old and had no desire to act, so he turned down the offer.

One year was spent in college at the Oklahoma Military Academy before Dale enlisted in the Army along with his brothers and other family members. Pearl Harbor had just been bombed and Dale and his brothers didn't want to wait to be drafted. They enlisted feeling it was their duty to help fight for their country. Dale went to Officer Candidate School, where he was commissioned as a Second Lieutenant.

Toward the end of his tour during a brief time in California, he contacted his mother to say he probably wouldn't get to come home for Christmas. He wanted to know what she would like him to send her as a present. Her request was a portrait of him that would take the place of old snapshots and newspaper clippings. So he and 13 other guys went to the corner of Hollywood and Wilcox to the Amos Carr Studios, which ironically is located catty corner from where Dale's Hollywood Star is now displayed. Dale and the rest of the guys had their pictures taken and asked Mary Parsons, who ran the studio, to send the pictures to their parents if they shipped out and couldn't make it back to the Studio.

As it turned out, they didn't make it back. Dale was sent overseas for what he thought was going to be a three month stay, but ended up only being 72 hours. He was a tank commander and had been peering out of the top of a military tank when it hit a mine. It blew Dale out of the tank, injuring him and killing everyone else in the tank. After spending time in a hospital in Ft. Bragg, North Carolina, Dale was medically discharged and sent back to Oklahoma. He commented that his experiences during war time did more to form his life than anything before or after.

In the meantime, after sending the portraits to the different parents, Mary Parsons took one of the pictures she had held back of Dale and had it enlarged. Then she placed it in the front display window of the studio so all the pedestrians walking past could see it. Before long, Dale was receiving letters from agents and other people connected with the movie industry offering him the opportunity to do some screen testing. He saved the letters and when he returned home after his discharge he pulled them out and re-read them, pondering the possibilities.

Since the war had ended, jobs were scarce. He knew he couldn't go back to fighting because of his leg injuries. He wasn't really pursuing a long time acting career, he just saw it as a means to make enough money to buy some horses and get the farm running again.

On February 18, 1946 when Dale was 23 years old, he left Oklahoma for Hollywood, California to locate one of the agents who had sent him a letter. He didn't know it, but since the war was over, many of the more established actors had returned to Hollywood and the need wasn't as great for newcomers like Dale. After going through four agents, he eventually found one suited for him.

Years later, Dale was reading through some of those old letters and ran across one he hadn't pursued. It was a letter from David O' Selsnick, who had been one of the top movie producers. He was known for producing quality movies and had at one time been married to actress Jennifer Jones. If Dale had acknowledged O'Selsnick's letter first, his career would have gotten a better start.

Even though he loves the idea of making pictures, Dale said he never did enjoy being an actor. I was shocked to hear that, especially since he was so good at what he did. Some things we don't particularly like though, can become great stepping stones.

Dale's first motion picture was "Flamingo Road" in 1947, when he was just 24 years old. His career includes 63 major motion pictures. He was the second biggest box office draw for three consecutive years.

His television career included well over 430 shows. He starred in and was the owner of the successful "Tales of Wells Fargo" series, which I fondly recall. That show ran from 1957 to 1962, producing 265 episodes. Those of us who saw the series remember the Borax and Buick commercials. They were the only sponsors the entire duration of the show.

Dale finally moved back to Oklahoma in 1976 to the life he always loved. He finds great comfort in the solace of his home he shares with his best friend and wife, Susan. He also enjoys occasional visits with his two daughters Rochelle and Rebel, and his granddaughter, Jade.

Dale has spent much of his career learning every facet of motion picture taking and scoring. He has written numerous scripts for motion pictures and television. His list of accomplishments and awards are too long to list. He is currently working on seven scripts, a task he loves doing. He still has too much to offer to quit, but he has the privilege of completing task at his own pace now.

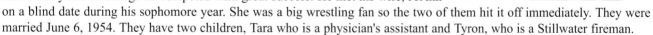

Myron Roderick – Wrestling Coach

Myron is the son of Boyd and Julia Roderick and originally from Kansas. He is one of five children with two brothers and two sisters. His father was a school teacher and coach and eventually became head of student activities at Winfield College in 1949. He passed away at age 89. Myron's mother passed away at age 95.

It was pretty natural for Myron to involve himself in sports. When he was a sophomore in high school, along with playing football and running track, he was encouraged to join the wrestling team because he was so small in stature. While his Winfield team wrestled against Ponca City and Blackwell, Oklahoma, Coach Art Griffith at Oklahoma State University and Port Robertson at The University of Oklahoma approached Myron about coming to compete on their college teams. Myron chose Oklahoma State University, which at the time was called Oklahoma A&M.

At that time you weren't allowed to wrestle during your freshman year but for the next three years of college he competed with great success. He met his wife, JoAnn on a blind date during his sophomore year. She was a big wrestling fan so the two of them hit it off immediately. They were married June 6, 1954. They have two children, Tara who is a physician's assistant and Tyron, who is a Stillwater fireman.

During college Myron won 42 of 44 matches and three NCAA championships as an individual in 1954, 1955 and 1956. He placed fourth in the 1956 Olympic Games at Melbourne, Australia.

Coach Griffith retired. Henry Iba, who was the university's athletic director and became known as one of Oklahoma's greatest basketball coaches, asked Myron if he would like to take Coach Griffith's place after he returned from the olympics. Myron quickly accepted and took over the position as head wrestling coach on January 1, 1957.

During his coaching career Myron's teams won seven NCAA titles, making him the youngest coach ever to win an NCAA team title. Myron was named Coach of the Year three times and was inducted into the OSU Alumni Hall of Fame. He was one of the most successful coaches in collegiate sports history. His Oklahoma State teams dominated wrestling for 13 years, 1957-1969, posting a dual meet record of 140 victories against 10 losses and seven draws. They captured nine of 13 Big Eight Conference titles and seven NCAA championships.

His wrestlers won 20 individual NCAA championships and four gold medals in the Olympic Games. Myron also coached the Cowboys to a National AAU team title in freestyle and another in the Greco-Roman style. He was the USA coach in the 1963 World Championships and assistant coach in the 1964 Olympics.

At the conclusion of his coaching career, he became the first executive director for the U.S.A. Wrestling Federation in 1969. During his five-year tenure, he originated the concept of a Hall of Fame for wrestling and launched a successful campaign along with Dr. Mel Jones to create the national museum. The museum displays and stores the history of the sport as well as plaques to honor inductees.

Because of his outstanding career as an athlete, coach and contributor to the sport of wrestling, Roderick was named the museum's Man of the Year in 1971 and was elected to the charter class of the Hall of Fame in 1976.

In 1974 he left wrestling to become executive director of the International Racquetball Association, the governing body of a sport in which he has won a dozen national singles and doubles championships.

In 1983 he returned to Oklahoma State University as athletic director until 1990 when he took over as president of the National Amateur Wrestling Hall of Fame, located on the OSU campus. As president of the Hall of Fame he has taken the Hall to new heights. He has developed programs to recognize Outstanding Americans, Order of Merit, Medal of Courage, Outstanding Officials, Dave Schultz High School Excellence Awards, Coaches Lifetime Service -the State Chapter Programs.

Myron said he loved coaching and if he had it to do over again he would probably have coached longer. But at the time, he thought he had won many titles and other opportunities were opening to him which he felt he should take.

Coach Roderick said it is important for anyone to set goals higher than what you think you can attain because you never know what you can do until you try. The harder you work and the more focused you become the quicker you see your goals being met.

Myron Roderick

Will Rogers - Entertainer/Actor

There probably isn't anyone in the English-speaking world who hasn't heard of Will Rogers, one of Oklahoma's most favorite sons. He was born on November 4, 1879 as William Penn Adair Rogers in a house located four miles northeast of Oologah. His parents, Clem and Mary Rogers, had seven other children, but Will for some reason was the one that was to become world famous and a friend to everyone.

Will started school at Drumgoole school which was a few miles east of Chelsea across the river from the family ranch. There was something about Will that made it impossible for him to sit still for very long. He was constantly interacting with his classmates which gave him the reputation of being the campus cutup.

Unfortunately, Will's mother died before he turned 11 years old, but his father later married a lady by the name of Mary Bibles. Even though Will loved interacting with his classmates he felt restless and unable to stay focused on his class work for any length of time. After transferring to a few different schools and lastly attending a military school of which his father recommended, Will eventually dropped out after the 10th grade to help his father on their ranch.

In 1893 his father took him to the Chicago World's Fair. Will was only 14 years old at the time and Buffalo Bill and his Wild West Show was one of the attractions. Within the Wild West Show was a Mexican matador by the name of Vincente Oropeza who fascinated Will with his amazing rope tricks. Even though Will had already adapted some rop- ing abilities of his own, he was intrigued by Oropeza's style and was determined to be as good as he was.

In 1902 Will left his father's ranch in Oklahoma in search of a more fulfilling life. He was headed for Argentina, but was sidetracked in New York where he met Florenz Ziegfeld, an acquaintance which would someday add a new dimension to his future. He then teamed up with Texas Jack's Wild West Show and toured throughout Africa for $20.00

a week. Later he became involved with the Wirth Brothers Circus in New Zealand where he was featured as "The Cherokee Kid" with his amazing roping tricks.

By 1904 he was getting a little homesick for his family back in Oklahoma. But a brief stay gave him the spark he needed to continue on with his exploits. The St. Louis World's Fair would prove to be another turning point in Will's life, because it was there that he became reacquainted with a young lady he had met in the fall of 1899.

Betty Blake had already won his heart from their first meeting, but the two of them were still too shy to make any kind of a longlasting commitment. For the time being their frequent letter writing would have to suffice for their lack of bravery.

On April 27, 1905 Will made his first appearance at Madison Square Garden with the Wild West Show and then on to Vaudeville. A year later he had a short visit with his sister Maud in Chelsea where he and Betty had agreed to meet, but there again their shy ways kept them at arms length. However, after another short visit in 1907 they finally put their inhibitions aside and on November 25, 1908 they were married.

At first Betty was not in favor of the career choice Will had made. She didn't think show business was a worthy profession. For a short time Will had considered giving it all up to please Betty, but it soon became obvious he was doing exactly what he was created to do. Before long Will became known not just for his lariat talents, but for his humor and ability to make an audience laugh.

Will's talents eventually landed him a position in the Ziegfeld Follies where his meager starting salary quickly escalated. By the time he left the follies 10 years later his $1,000 a week career choice was creating a great deal of attention. Movies were next on the agenda when Samuel Goldwyn offered Will $150,000 a year to star in his projects.

Will and Betty had four children born between 1911 and 1918: Will Jr., Mary, Jim and Fred. Unfortunately, while Will was filming his first movie in California, his three boys came down with diphtheria and the youngest, Fred died.

Will made 13 pictures for Goldwyn before forming his own independent company, which financially was not a successful venture for Will. Then in 1923 producer Hal Roach offered Will a movie contract for $2,500 a week. Will did 14 comedies for Hal Roach and performed in 50 silent films.

When sound was introduced into the motion picture field Will, of course, was a natural. For over six years he created what was known as his most successful years of fame. With motion pictures also came his weekly syndicated newspaper column of humorous comments which he based on current events. For 13 years he continued his Sunday column until his untimely death.

Aviation became a great love of Will's and even though he never learned to fly himself he was fascinated with those who did. His greatest pilot friend was the one-eyed flyer from Will's home state of Oklahoma, Wiley Post. Wiley held the speed record for flying around the world and also invented the first pressure suit for high altitude flying.

It was while he was on an adventurous flying trip with Wiley Post that his life was snuffed out in a matter of minutes. After visiting with some Eskimos who were fishing on the Walakpa Lagoon on August 15, 1935, Wiley and Will took flight headed for Barrow, Alaska which was only 16 miles further. As they took off their plane engine appeared to be having problems and before they could do anything to solve it the plane began to nose dive into the bay. Will and Wiley were killed instantly.

Will Rogers will forever be synonymous with the phrase "I never met a man I didn't like." His memorable wit and humor has continued to be a topic of many books and articles written about him. He was a man who was truly thought to be a friend to all. Even though many decades have passed since his death he still remains an interesting figure in the halls of the past.

The Will Rogers Museum in Claremore, Oklahoma was kind enough to donate a picture to add to Will's profile. The museum is quite an interesting and informative display of a beloved Oklahoman who became a friend to all.

Betty Rohde - Author

What a treat it was to interview Betty! Not only did she give me a great success story but she took me for a ride on her golf cart to the neighborhood restaurant which happened to be "The Fin and Feather Resort" and bought my lunch as well.

Betty was born and raised in Gore, Oklahoma, which in my opinion happens to be a beautiful area. Betty said she comes from a long line of country people. Her father was a farmer and she remembers him killing hogs and hanging them up in the backyard.

Even though she had no idea she would someday be the author of a successful cookbook she was introduced to cooking at a very early age. When she was six years old her mother, who lay sick in bed, asked her to prepare fried chicken for the

family. Betty brought the chicken to her mother's bedside so she could instruct her on how to cut it up. Betty said the pieces were unidentifiable when she finished but at least they were cut up. She then went into the kitchen and pulled a rickety chair up to the gas stove where the big black iron skillet full of lard was kept.

Betty doesn't remember if she fixed anything to go with the chicken, but the cooking experience has remained a long lasting memory. From then on her mother was very good about letting Betty have full run of the kitchen, of course teaching her some southern cooking tips along the way.

When she graduated from high school she went to business school in Tulsa and got a job as a secretary, but she wasn't totally satisfied with her career. She married and in between the birth of her two children she decided to go to college and pursue a degree in business education and home economics.

Since she had spent most of her life being trained by her mother to be a southern cook, she was quite amused by the way her economics teacher prepared biscuits. The teacher cut the biscuits out and placed them on a cookie sheet. Betty couldn't keep quiet. She had to tell the teacher that was not the way she makes biscuits. Of course the teacher said, "How do you do it?" I cut them out and flip them from front to back, preferably in bacon grease and lay them side by side. Years later that same economics teacher was thrilled when she was able to buy one of Betty's famous cookbooks.

Betty and her first husband were divorced and in 1973 she moved to Tulsa and later married Bob Rohde, a successful mechanical engineer. With his three children and Betty's two they had a houseful when it came time to cook a meal. It easily took three chickens and five pounds of potatoes to feed their family.

By the time the children grew up and moved away from home, Betty had cooked too many southern meals to even begin to count and her body began to round out a little. Betty and Bob moved to Gore so she could take care of her ailing parents. Yet Betty's southern cooking didn't miss a lick. Life revolved around cooking. They entertained a lot and there were always church socials, weddings, funerals or a variety of occasions she could find to cook or prepare something.

Betty began to have health problems and decided to get a checkup. Her doctor said if she didn't go on a low-fat diet she would most likely have a stroke or a heart attack. Those words struck home. Her cholesterol was 279 and her triglycerides were 698. She also found out some of her health problems were hereditary, so she knew she better do something to correct it.

That evening she cooked boiled chicken and stewed potatoes and had a hard time eating it because it just wasn't her southern cooking. But she knew she had to do something to change her lifestyle. This was in 1990 when there wasn't much talk about low-fat meals. So she decided to make a game out of it and see what kinds of meals she could come up with that had little or no fat in them.

She would go to the grocery store and read labels on food and noticed that a majority of them didn't have the fat content listed. At the time, the law that required that disclosure had not been passed. Betty was on a crusade to trim the fat. In the first six months she lost 40 pounds and then began to exercise more and lost 20 more pounds.

Her friends began to tell her she needed to write a cookbook with low fat-healthy recipes. At first she wondered if anyone would buy it, but she soon found out a lot of people would and did.

She began by self-publishing her first book *So Fat-Low Fat- No Fat* through one of the companies churches use for their congregational cookbooks. She had 200 books printed and stacked in her home. Within the first two weeks everyone in her church had bought a book and the Muskogee Phoenix wanted to write an article about Betty and her new low-fat recipes. After much discussion, Bob and one of Betty's friends convinced her she better order 400 more books to get ready for incoming orders that would be triggered by the newspaper article. The full six-page article came out early one morning and by 6:00 p.m. that evening all 400 books were sold.

Betty knew she had a good thing going so she decided to contact other towns and see if she could stir up some interest there as well. Before long Channel 2 news had contacted Betty for an interview and more sales were made. Then Channel 2 offered Betty a chance to appear once a month to share her recipes with the viewers. Betty said you can sell a lot of books with two and a half minutes of air time. She went from ordering 400 books to 800 books and eventually 10,000 at a time.

In 1993 Betty's soft cover cookbook was Oklahoman's best seller in all the bookstores. One day a representative from one of the big publishers was told by a bookstore owner how well Betty's book was doing and felt sure some large publisher would pick it up soon. Well, the representative of Simon and Shuster did just that and before long Betty was getting a call.

She said she felt like Cinderella when photographers and reporters showed up in her living room flashing pictures and taking quotes. The publisher said they were printing 30,000 books and were going to send her on a book tour around the country. Betty was astounded that they were only printing 30,000. She said, " I sold 30,000 out of the back of my car." They soon found out Betty was right. Before she landed in Portland for the beginning of her book tour, all 30,000 books had been sold. They had no books for the first three weeks of the tour. The next printing was 100,000 and Betty said that's more like it. To her surprise she was contacted by the shopping channel QVC just before Christmas that year. All Betty could think to say was "Merry Christmas to Me."

Since then she has written five other cookbooks *More So Fat-Low Fat- No Fat,* the Italian version, Mexican version, Dessert version and *So Fat-Low Fat-No Fat Celebration* with more than a million copies in print. New ideas continue to be developed. One of my favorite Betty Rohde recipes is White Chicken Chili. You need to try it, you'll be glad you did.

Kelvin Sampson

Basketball Coach

When I met with Kelvin Sampson and heard some of his ideas and ways in which he coaches, my thoughts immediately went to the late Oklahoma basketball coach Grady Skillern. He was my first encounter with an athletic icon whom I later wrote about in his biography, *Unforgettable Grady.* The similarities I see in Coach Sampson solidifies my thoughts that he is not only a great coach, but a strong, independent, morally sound human being and worthy of the title Distinguished Oklahoman.

I know so little about basketball or sports of any kind, but I do have a heart for our teams and have an immense desire for them to win. I was spell-bound bouncing from the chair to sitting cross-legged in the floor in front of the television while Oklahoma University battled it out with Indiana University in their last game of the season. They had triumphantly progressed to the Final

Four and were striving for the championship.

My enthusiasm as I yelled, screamed and let out agonizing sighs was causing me a great deal of stress. There was even a point when I thought "why am I doing this to myself?" But never the less I hung in there rooting all the way for the "Sooners." On that particular day Indiana became the victors, but the win had not come easy. Oklahoma played a terrific game! Even though my knowledge of the sport is limited, the excitement of seeing the Sooners battle so strongly for the title was quite memorable.

Coach Sampson's childhood growing up in Pembroke, North Carolina pretty much sealed his future career choice. His father Ned Sampson, who was a high school coach, led Kelvin by example every day of his life. Even though Kelvin's mother Eva wanted him to be a dentist and he had considered pursuing a law degree, the coaching fever had been deeply imbedded and it would soon surface to the point of no return.

Ned's coaching and teaching career never brought him to great financial heights, but Kelvin knew that and was prepared to work extra jobs on the side if need be. He had watched his father take on extra tasks and it taught him a great deal about the value of money and what it means to love what you do.

In high school with his father as his coach he was a three-sport star. In football, he was an option quarterback and outside linebacker. He was a point guard on the basketball team and a catcher and outfielder on the baseball team. Kelvin admits his father was hard on him and didn't let him get slack just because of who he was. Kelvin learned discipline from his father and knowledge of the incredible need for practice. During his junior year of high school he met Karen, his future wife, who would prove to be an asset to his career.

After high school he enrolled at Pembroke State University (now the University of North Carolina at Pembroke) with a major in political science, but college basketball became a very important part of his curriculum. Kelvin was a winner who did many things to help his team win whether it was through leadership or making hustle plays. In his senior year of college he did student teaching at Hoke County High School in Raeford, North Carolina. After college he took the LSAT for law school and received an acceptance letter from Wake Forest University Law School. But he also took the GRE test for graduate school. Among others he received an acceptance letter from Michigan State which happened to be hosting an NCAA Tournament in March of that year. The tournament helped sway his decision.

That year he and Karen became engaged but she stayed in North Carolina and continued to teach first grade while Kelvin moved to East Lansing, Michigan to begin his graduate work. When they married in the summer of 1979 she moved there also.

Jud Heathcote was Michigan State's head basketball coach and Kelvin wanted desperately to be one of his assistants, but his answer kept coming back no. Finally, during the 1979-80 season, he was given the opportunity to be the graduate assistant for the junior varsity team with assistant coach Fred Paulsen. After practices with the junior varsity Kelvin took every opportunity to learn from Coach Heathcote. He would watch Heathcote with the varsity team and then sit in on the coaches meetings. He took a lot of Heathcote's teaching principles to heart. He learned about Heathcote's 2-3 matchup zone defense and how to coach half-court offense. He also learned that Heathcote was hardest on his best players.

By the end of the season Kelvin had a decision to make. He could either continue as a graduate assistant at Michigan State and further his education, take a high school coaching job in North Carolina or go with Fred Paulsen to Montana Tech as an assistant coach with a stipend of only $1,100 a year. After seeking Heathcote's advice the decision was made. Montana Tech was on the college level and he would be an assistant coach, not just a grad assistant. Kelvin knew how hard it was to get into college coaching and here was an opportunity. He wasn't about to let money decide whether he took it or not. He knew he and Karen would find a way to make ends meet (a perfect example of a defining moment).

As it turned out Fred Paulsen stayed less than half a season before he moved on and Kelvin at age 24, was immediately advanced to the position of head coach. The stipend was done away with and he was offered $16,000 a year. He felt like he had won the lottery. Other firsts happened while they were in Montana. Kelvin and Karen welcomed the birth of their daughter Lauren.

By the time Coach Sampson left Montana Tech he had brought the team from obscurity with crowds of 200 to 300 people to filling their home stands with 1,500 fans. They went from a last place team to a first place team in the Frontier League.

After four years it was time for another change when Coach Len Stevens convinced Kelvin to be his assistant coach at Washington State University. Stevens had only been there three years, and even though Coach Sampson would be going from a head coaching position to an assistant coaching position, he thought it would be a good career move.

He soon found out it was hard going backwards with his role as assistant coach and considered making another move after his first season when he heard Stevens after his second season was moving on as well. To his surprise, Coach Sampson was offered the head coaching position at Washington State which he accepted.

His coaching abilities continued to shine at Washington State. In the 1990-91 season he was named Pac-10 Conference Coach of the Year after taking Washington State to a 16-12 overall mark and a fifth-place finish in the Pac-10. Then in 1994 they made it to the NCAA Tournament with triumphs including a win against his mentor, Jud Heathcote of Michigan State.

One more career move was in store for Coach Sampson. A lot of great things transpired while he was at Washington State, including the birth of their son Kellen, but it was time to relocate once again. The University of Oklahoma was aggressively pursuing Coach Sampson. It wasn't an easy decision because he had grown so fond of his Washington State team, but he knew it was the right time and the right decision. Of course the whole nation is aware that it was the right decision. Coach Sampson has been with OU for eight consecutive years and the team has been to eight consecutive NCAA Tournaments. Then of course this year the team won 31 games and the Big 12 Championship, ranking in the top 5 almost the entire season and then getting the chance to go to the Final Four. What a run!!

Coach Sampson said he loves quotes and tries to live by them. A few are: *Don't look at obstacles as problems, see them as opportunities. Adversity makes men out of all of us and sometimes prosperity can create a monster. Don't fear failure because the first step on the ladder of success is failure. You learn courage by battling through adversity. Have enough discipline, character, toughness and resolve about you that when you face adversity it doesn't effect you. Success is having the ability to see where you want to go and how you want to get there. That's your vision.*

Coach Sampson believes we all need to have an identity, not just a vision. We need to be known for something and whatever we are known for it's what we have chosen. *You will be known for either the good or the bad, so choose wisely. Have enough self confidence that you compete in life with a tenacity that is uncommon.*

Coach Sampson's thoughts toward winning the game have changed over the years. Oh sure, he wants to win and he strives to win, but that's not all there is to playing the game. He takes his responsibility of influencing his team for "the game of life" very seriously. He knows these young men have been put at least partially in his care and what he is able to instill in them during those few short years can be life changing. He has witnessed so many of them come to the university as young boys and graduate as strong, competent young men. He truly believes that a good coach is defined by much more than whether he wins or loses a game, but how he has effected lives of those around him.

If a coach makes those kind of statements and he isn't a winning coach then you can assume he has another agenda for making the statement. But coming from a champion like Coach Sampson you know he is speaking from his heart. It reminds me of the sub-title on my *Unforgettable Grady* book that says "a man who changed lives, just by living his own." That sounds like Coach Sampson to me. Like he says, *"Every journey has its end. But in the end, it is the journey that counts."*

Kelvin Sampson

Virginia Austin Schubert

Volunteer

The word privileged has to come to mind when you think of Virginia Austin, a native of Oklahoma born September 16, 1943 in Oklahoma City. I heard a sermon once titled "Favor Ain't Fair." A person would tend to believe that statement when they hear the life that has gently unfolded for Virginia.

As an only child to parents Lewis and Virginia Lee Thomas she learned not only what it meant to be privileged, but also what it meant to give to others. It has been said, "you do what you know," and Virginia was taught at an early age to volunteer her time to make life easier for others.

Virginia's mother, a stay-at-home mom gave her a sense of security knowing she was always just a whisper or a phone call away. Her Dad provided the occasional trips to "Blinn House" (a home for girls), where he instilled in her the attitude of volunteerism. Watching her father give his time, as well as frequent gifts to the young girls, gave Virginia tremendous insight and began to mold her into the person she was meant to be.

During her school years it became very natural for her to volunteer her time. As a pre-teen she was part of a pilot volunteer program at the Oklahoma Medical Research Foundation. As a student at Casady School she was involved in sports and extra-curricular activities. She was the editor of the school newspaper, a cheerleader and involved herself in various other areas. While in high school she was given the opportunity to spend time in western Europe, France and Sweden primarily.

As Virginia looks back she realizes her earlier experiences prepared her for her life's role as a professional volunteer. The days at "Blinn House" taught her not only to give back, but exposed her to people of different backgrounds. Those experiences gave her the desire to learn about people from other areas of the world and how they live and work. Over the years she has traveled extensively, giving of her time and talents wherever the need arose.

Interestingly the "Blinn House" found its way back into Virginia's life. The house was renovated and became the headquarters of the Junior League of Oklahoma City. Virginia not only spearheaded the renovation, but she became one of its first presidents and chief executive officers to occupy the building.

During that time she ensured effective and efficient operations of this volunteer organization which encompasses some 180,000 members in more than 270 local Junior Leagues in the U.S., Canada, Mexico and England. She administered a $5 million annual budget and led a professional staff of 63 members. She established the Association's endowment fund. She developed a highly effective ongoing development program and fundraising campaigns that generated contributions of $18 million.

Under her leadership the League launched new membership recruitment policies and procedures that greatly expanded local Junior League membership. She also initiated and managed major national program trusts including ones for alcohol awareness and adolescent pregnancy prevention.

Virginia states she was a pretty traditional mother and homemaker through much of her life, but her predisposition for volunteering came to a head in 1991 when she took on a paid staff position at the "Points of Light Foundation." The notion was to promote volunteer community service across the country. The foundation had a tag line which said, "Do something good, feel something real." Up until that point Virginia's positions had always been solely volunteer.

I pondered for a few minutes on how blessed she was to have the opportunity to spend the majority of her life "solely volunteering." To be honest, I didn't really understand how a person could make a career out of volunteering. I have donated some of my time on occasion, but life never afforded me the opportunity to not "bring home the bacon" to some degree. I asked Virginia the ignorant question "how" and through the course of our interview it became quite clear.

While some of us volunteer on a "if I don't have anything better to do" basis, Virginia made it a lifestyle. Granted, she had the distinct privilege of having a home life which didn't require her to work at a paying job in order to support the family. But I've got a feeling even if she had been worse off financially she still would have volunteered the majority of her life.

What really makes her special and qualifies her to be named among the "Distinguished" individuals is her tireless efforts to look past her own "advantages in life" and focus on the needs of others.

While obviously very involved in her volunteer work, Virginia also found the time and energy to raise three productive children, Tom, Michael and Elisabeth.

One of the things very close to her heart was the development of the Myriad Gardens complex in Oklahoma City. She worked closely with Dean McGee in helping bring the botanical gardens into fruition and develop the organizational structure. She was also appointed by the mayor of Oklahoma City as a member of the Myriad Gardens Foundation for years.

Virginia served as a principal speaker in communities in Canada and the U.S. from 1986 through 2000 and has been interviewed frequently for radio, television and print media on a national basis.

In 1989 the Oklahoma Heritage Association recognized Virginia's outstanding contributions both locally and internationally and inducted her into the Oklahoma Hall of Fame.

After her 10 year tenure with the Points of Light Foundation Virginia resigned her position, but of course has continued to be an active volunteer. During our interview she was making plans for her next trip to Africa as a volunteer for The International Youth Foundation, the world's largest public foundation focused entirely on children and youth.

In the midst of her active life Virginia is preparing to celebrate her first year anniversary with her new husband Richard Schubert.

Virginia Austin Schubert has more than 20 years of progressively responsible management and leadership experience. She has achieved an extensive record of organizing, developing and managing effective and productive programs for non-profit organizations and businesses. She is a proven public speaker and organizational representative. Virginia has demonstrated the ability to manage multiple projects simultaneously and bring each to a successful completion on schedule and within budget.

Sequoyah
Cherokee Syllabary

Can you imagine not being able to read or write? That is how many Cherokee Indians had to live until a Cherokee silversmith by the name of Sequoyah devised an alphabet whose 85 characters represented every sound in the Cherokee language.

Sequoyah was born in 1776 at the village of Tuskeegee near Vonore, Tennessee. His mother Wut-teh was the daughter of a Cherokee Chief and his father Nathaniel Gist was a Virginia fur trader. It is said that Sequoyah was probably born handicapped since his Cherokee name means "pig's foot."

Sequoyah left Tennessee as a young boy when whites began to enter the territory. At first he moved to Georgia where he began learning the skills of a silversmith. White silversmiths had begun signing their names on their finished products, so a man who purchased one of Sequoyah's works suggested he sign his name also. Sequoyah had no idea how to write his own name, but the seed had been planted in his mind to learn. He visited Charles Hicks, a wealthy farmer, who taught Sequoyah how to spell his name by writing the letters on a piece of paper.

He eventually moved to Willstown, Alabama and enlisted in the Cherokee Regiment, on the United States side under General Andrew Jackson to fight British troops and the Creek Indians in the war of 1812. During the war he and other Cherokees were unable to write letters home, read military orders or record events as they occurred. This experience gave way to even more determination for Sequoyah to develop a writing system to help his people.

The Tsa-La-Gi people whom the whites called Cherokee were known as an industrious race of warriors. Yet not many considered them to be anything other than savages whose intelligence level weakened them.

Sequoyah married a Cherokee and began raising a family, but his thoughts of literacy for the Cherokee people still remained foremost in his mind. After the war he began to make the symbols that could make words. He was able to reduce thousands of Cherokee thoughts to 85 symbols representing sounds. In 1821, after 12 years of working on the new language, he and his daughter Ayoka introduced the new syllabary to the Cherokee people. Of course his efforts forever changed the lives of Cherokee Indians.

In 1824 the National Council at New Echota, Georgia awarded Sequoyah a silver medal, as well as a lifetime literary pension to honor his efforts.

By 1825 not only was a portion of the Bible translated into Cherokee, but numerous hymns were as well. By then there was no stopping the Cherokee and their drive to communicate as the white people had been all along.

In 1828 they began publishing the "Cherokee Phoenix," the first national bi-lingual newspaper, along with religious pamphlets, educational materials and legal documents. Elias Boudinot was the first editor of the "Cherokee Phoenix" and Reverend Samuel Worcester, a missionary, was director.

Sequoyah moved to Arkansas shortly after the first publication of the newspaper and then moved on to Oklahoma where he lived for the next 10 years. The Cherokees were removed from their Georgia and Alabama homes in 1938 to Tahlequah, Oklahoma which is still the capital of the Cherokee nation. In 1939 Sequoyah signed the act of union as president of the Western Cherokees and later in the same year he was signer of the Cherokee constitution.

In the spring of 1842 he traveled to California with some companions and his son Teesce. It is said that the large Sequoia Tree was named after him. On his return trip home Sequoyah died in San Fernando, Texas in 1843. The exact burial place is unknown.

H.A. Scomp, a member of Emory College faculty was quoted as saying, "Sequoyah was perhaps the most remarkable man who ever lived on Georgia soil. He was neither a politician, nor an ecclesiastic, nor a scholar, but merely a Cherokee Indian of mixed blood. And strange to say, this Indian acquired permanent fame, neither expecting it or seeking it."

Ted Shackelford

Actor

Being able to interview Ted for my book was an absolute must and I so appreciate him taking time out to allow me the privilege.

I have to admit it, I was a die hard fan of the "Knots Landing" series where Ted (played as Gary Ewing) held one of the starring roles. When I first became a fan I had no idea he was an Oklahoman, but after finding out it made the show if possible even that much more intriguing to watch. I asked Ted if he was anything like the character he portrayed and he said, "absolutely not."

Ted was born in Oklahoma City and for the most part was raised in Oklahoma. The family spent some time traveling while Ted's father was in the military at places like Guam and Long Island. By 1956 they had moved permanently back to Tulsa.

Ted is one of five children. His brother Mark still lives in Tulsa and is a practicing veterinarian. His sister Kelly lives in Kansas City while brother Patrick lives in Wyoming. Unfortunately their brother Todd passed away in 1999.

While attending Edison High School Ted was the typical athlete. He played football and was part of the wrestling team. He had no idea what he was going to pursue as a career when he graduated in 1964.

He enrolled at Westminster College in Fulton, Missouri where he studied until 1967. He transferred to the University of Denver where he graduated in 1969 with degrees in English and theatre. At the time there was a major community theatre in Denver called Helen Bonfils. Helen was also the owner of the Denver Post. The theatre was known for being as good as most professional theatres.

It was in Denver that Ted first worked professionally in the theatre. This opened doors for him in the world of acting.

Dinner theatres were also very popular in the early 1970's and an actor could do quite well performing in them to establish his needed credentials of an Equity card as well. Ted appeared in such plays as "Night of the Iguana," "Detective Story," "Bus Stop" and "Play it Again Sam" while also holding down a job at an ad agency. He quickly found he could make more money performing in the theatres than he could at the ad agency.

He moved to New York in 1975 and for a time worked as the night manager of the Carlyle Hotel. He was also an understudy for a part in the Broadway play "Murder Among Friends." In 1976 he landed his first major television role as Raymond Gordon in NBC's soap opera, "Another World."

Two months before he turned 30 years old he married his first wife Jan. After a year on "Another World" he was able to save money and he and Jan moved to Los Angeles to continue his quest for fame. He began accumulating an impressive list of prime-time credits including "The Rockford Files," "Soap" and "Hotel."

The character of Gary Ewing began on the popular series "Dallas," which developed into a spin-off, "Knots Landing," offering Ted a showcase for his unique talents and obvious charm. His marriage to Jan ended after 10 years which like for all of us is an adjustment. "Knots Landing" aired for 14 years and ended (much to the disappointment of all its fans) in 1993. Even though Ted said he was nothing like his character he loved playing the part.

In 1995 there was a reunion show of "Knots Landing" but Ted said the script just wasn't up to par and the show didn't do as well in the ratings as they had hoped.

I asked Ted if he would ever consider performing in another television series and he said, "in a heartbeat."

Ted has never had a desire to produce or direct films. He describes those duties as "grown-up work." He has never wanted to be anything but an actor.

In 1991 he married Annett, a successful publicist in Los Angeles whose company represents Shackelford.

I found Ted to be very personable during our interview. He was somewhat modest about all he has accomplished over the years. The list is quite impressive yet Ted's appetite for acting seems to never be quenched. Some of you may remember him in his television guest spots on "The Practice," "Cybill," and "Promised Land" or movies such as "Stolen Women," "Harvest of the Heart" or "Mother of the Bride."

He is currently filming in India on a film called "Panic." I hope I have the chance to see it when it airs.

Ted doubts if he will ever move back to Oklahoma. Los Angeles has become his home and of course his link to the acting world.

I wish the best for Ted and his wife Annett. Oklahoma has and will continue to launch forth individuals who make all of us proud to say we're from the "Heartland of America."

Jean Shepard- Country Music Legend

I had the opportunity to take a trip to Branson, Missouri to view the "Grand Ladies of Country" who were performing at the 76 Music Hall. Jean Shepard, who has been a member of the Grand Ole Opry for 46 years, has put together a group of ladies who have lived their lives singing chart hitting country music. I sat there with a great deal of pride as I watched these ladies woo their audience down a musical memory lane.

Jean Shepard of course is the "Mother" of them all and rightly so. She is very proud of those 67 years that make up her title of "Grand Lady." Her love for traditional country music shows in every song she sings, and her loyalty to the country music roots have no likelihood of waning.

On a personal note, her mannerisms and funny antics reminded me so much of my grandmother who passed away several years ago that I found myself feeling a closeness with Jean from the moment I met her.

This witty lady was born in Pauls Valley, Oklahoma. Her parents, Hoit and Alla Mae, must have been one strong, dedicated couple because they successfully managed to raise 10 children who speak very fondly of their youthful days at home.

After spending several years in Hugo, Oklahoma, Jean's family moved to California so her father could secure a job as a ranch foreman. Obviously the "air of country" took a liking to Jean in more ways than one. When she was a sophomore in high school she and some other girls formed a band called "The Melody Ranch Girls." The name stemmed from a local dance hall called Noble's Melody Ranch owned and operated by Noble.

Jean played the upright bass which was purchased for her with money collected from the sale of the family furniture. Her parents played such a vital part in the lives of their children and they were quick to support Jean in her musical endeavor.

At the time there weren't many country female musicians, but nevertheless Jean had a deep desire to change that in the minds of everyone around her. Hank Williams Sr., Lefty Frizzell, Hank Thompson and Jimmie Rodgers were musical icons to her and she felt quite comfortable singing her female version of their songs.

One night while Hank Thompson was performing at the Melody Ranch, Noble asked Hank if he would allow Jean to sing a song with his band. Hank was so impressed with Jean's ability that he asked her if she would like to have a recording contract. "Of course," she said, thinking it would probably never happen.

But Hank Thompson, being the kind ole soul that he is, saw to it that it did happen. Even though a few months passed before it became a reality there came a day when little Miss Jean Shepard was signing on the dotted line with Capitol Records. Jean was not yet 21 years old, so the California courts had jurisdiction over the approval of the contract.

Her first record was recorded with a fellow Oklahoman, well known steel guitar player Speedy West. Since Jean was so young and a female besides, the record company wouldn't put her name alone on the label. The record was titled *Crying Steel Guitar* featuring Jean Shepard and Speedy West, but Jean didn't care, she was on her way to musical stardom.

Her second record *The Dear John Letter* with Ferlin Husky sold 10 million copies in 1953. She will forever be linked to that timely song which happened to come out at the end of the Korean War. Since she was still under 21 years old and needed to travel outside the state to promote the hit record, Ferlin Husky was appointed as her guardian. To be so young and yet have so much success come her way was an incredible accomplishment for Miss Jean Shepard.

While still reveling in her celebrity status she was asked to join the Ozark Jubilee in Springfield, Missouri, hosted by the famed Red Foley. She fondly remembers those early days and the admiration she felt for Red Foley as she watched his warm-hearted nature put everyone at ease.

Springfield was not to be the last stop on her musical journey. In the early part of 1955 she headed for Nashville, Tennessee, the city known for country music and talented performers. It didn't take long before Jean was a regular on the Grand Ole Opry. On November 21, 1955 Jim who was the manager of the Grand Ole Opry surprised Jean with a birthday present she wasn't expecting. He announced that evening to her delight that she was the newest member of the Grand Ole Opry.

One of her dearest friends and producer of her first record, Ken Nelson, once made the comment to Hank Thompson that he didn't think there was a place for women in country music. Obviously Ken had to eat those words as he helped change his own statement by guiding Jean into her well deserved spot in country music history.

Many people will remember Hawk Shaw Hawkins who died in the plane crash with Patsy Cline. Hawk Shaw, a very respected country music singer, had a number one hit titled *Lonesome 77203* when his life ended on that fatal night. Jean fondly remembers him as her best friend, husband and father of her two sons. Their oldest son was named after Don Gibson and Marty Robbins and he bears the name Don Robbins. Jean was pregnant with their second son at the time of Hawk Shaw's death and she appropriately named him Harold Franklin Hawkins II after his father.

Thankfully, Bennie came into her life and together they share not only their musical abilities but 10 children and 28 grandchildren.

The Opry has always been a very important part of Jean's life and her sense of loyalty for the establishment has never changed. As much as she loves and respects the talents of the newer generation, Jean is and will always be a "diehard traditional music guru." In my opinion, why shouldn't she be? There is always room for change, but we must never forget our roots or the foundation of anything that has allowed distinction, significance and beauty to come into our lives.

Since starting the "Grand Ladies of Country" in Branson in May of 2000, Jean has had to shuffle her schedule between Nashville and Branson, but after all these years I'm sure it comes pretty natural to her. I encourage everyone to take time to visit Jean and her "clan of beauties" at the 76 Music Hall in Branson, Missouri I promise, you won't be disappointed.

Donna Shirley - Aerodynamicist

Donna's life had to have been planned out. When some little girls were playing with their dolls and deciding which tea cup to drink from, Donna was daydreaming about her first trip into space.

Donna was born in Pauls Valley, Oklahoma but spent most of her childhood in Wynnewood except for a short time spent in California. She was a very bright child who was reading at the third grade level before she finished the first grade. Her favorite place to read as a six year old child, was up in a Sycamore tree that was firmly planted in her great aunt and uncle's front yard. She was 10 when she saw an article about a rocket blasting out of the earth's orbit. From then on all she could think about was how she would someday travel into space.

She found school life to be somewhat socially dissatisfying, because she didn't seem to fit in. Her I.Q. tests scored her 30 points higher than everyone else in her class. She was two years younger than her classmates and a tomboy on top of that. So books remained her escape when she was feeling lonely and out of touch with the world.

From her earliest memory, she loved airplanes. Her best present she ever received was the flying lessons her father bought for her when she was 15 years old.

Donna was valedictorian of her senior class and upon graduation she immediately entered the University of Oklahoma as an engineering student. By her sophomore year in college, some of the tomboy image was beginning to fade into a more sophisticated look. She began to wear makeup, picked up some fashion tips and stopped wearing her hair in a frizzy perm. Her looks and demeanor changed so much that she won the title of Miss Wynnewood. Her mother wanted her to go on to win Miss Oklahoma and then Miss America, but it just wasn't meant to be.

At one point she changed her major from engineering to journalism, but found out quickly that a job as a specification writer for McDonnell Aircraft in St. Louis, Missouri was not what she had in mind. So she returned to Oklahoma University and was accepted in the aerospace engineering department. Donna graduated in the spring of 1965 with a Bachelors' in Aerospace/Mechanical Engineering-a field few women ever enter.

I thought it was interesting that she realized her mistake in changing her major and went back to complete it. I wonder how many other people would have just gone on with the mistake and never tried to correct it. I wonder how many people miss opportunities that could have been theirs, because they fail to acknowledge their mistakes.

Donna returned to the McDonnell plant and became an aerodynamicist. She helped develop a proposal for a NASA mission to Mars that would land in 1971. This was her big project, with two orbiters and two landers, and it was supervised by the Jet Propulsion Laboratory in California. Her duties were to study possible shapes for the entry vehicle and analyze incoming trajectories.

As the proposal was nearing completion, Donna was concerned as to whether or not McDonnell would get the contract. She certainly didn't want to miss out on being a part of this extraordinary project. She knew no matter which aerospace contractor got the job, JPL would still be managing the Mars mission. She moved to California so she could go to work for the Jet Propulsion Laboratory.

In 1967, Donna and her colleagues flew from JPL to NASA's Langley research center near Hampton, Virginia with their one-tenth scale models of the blunt sphere-cone shapes they thought had the best chance of surviving a descent through the martian atmosphere. They had calculated a range of entry conditions they thought would make for a successful landing and were planning a full scale program to design and test the vehicle.

Suddenly, Congress cut the funding saying the project was too expensive. Donna was out of a job. She had just finished her master's degree in aerospace engineering, but she was JPL's junior aerodynamicist and thus the most expendable. She spent six months working for a private company in aerodynamics until a job came open in JPL's trajectory analysis section. Trajectory analysts calculate how a spacecraft can fly from earth to other planets, taking into account the gravity of the sun, the planets, and other forces that push on the spacecraft in space.

Donna became quickly bored with that job, because it wasn't preparing her for a current mission. She switched jobs with someone and for two years she designed an automated drug identification system to combat the nation's exploding drug problem. Then through her social contacts, she was hired as the Mariner Venus Mercury 1973 mission analyst. They are the people who look around and see what part of a mission needs fixing and fix it.

On November 3, 1973, Mariner 10 was launched in Florida at Cape Canaveral and was a total success. A few years later, Donna got married and then in 1977 she gave birth to her daughter, Laura. After taking some time off, Donna spent 15 months doing some analysis and mission design, but she wasn't content with that. She wanted another project.

She was given an opportunity to help run a study that would generate ideas for a new space station. NASA wanted a robot that could fly alongside the space station assembling pieces or handing tools to the astronauts. Donna put together a robotics program and managed it from 1985 to 1987.

Even though she already had a wonderful career, her lifelong quest to get to Mars had not yet happened and she was frustrated. It had been 30 years, when was it going to happen?

In 1987 Donna started leading the research into Martian rovers. By 1989 her research team had rover designs and the tools and technology to start implementing them. Their first design was a robot named Robby, that weighed nearly a ton. It was a very smart rover but it was just too expensive to send such a large rover to Mars. In 1992 Donna was appointed head of the microrover project. It looked like the best chance she had to get to Mars. In 1993 Donna came up with the idea of having an essay contest to name the rover and bring some publicity to the project. Out of 3,000 entries, Sojourner Truth was the clear favorite name that had been submitted by a 12 year old girl.

Donna became the Mars Program manager in 1994. Her assignment was to lead the U.S. effort to explore Mars. They were to send robots to sniff out the planet and see if they could find any signs of life. In December of 1996, Pathfinder was launched and on July 4, 1997 it landed with Sojourner on Mars. Pathfinder returned with 26 billion bits of information, including more than 16,000 images from the lander and 550 images from the rover. Included were more than 15 chemical analysis of rocks and extensive data on winds and other weather factors.

All together, Sojourner had traveled over 100 meters on the surface of Mars, far more than the 10 meters they had hoped for. The Sojourner was a success.

Donna's speaking engagements increased. Hundreds of people wanted her autograph and awards came pouring in. Finally, Donna had achieved her passion. She had helped open the door for humans on Mars.

Donna has come full circle. She has returned to her home state of Oklahoma and to her alma mater Oklahoma University to teach the next generation about space. She has been named assistant dean for advanced program development in the University of Oklahoma College of Engineering, where she has helped start a robotics program.

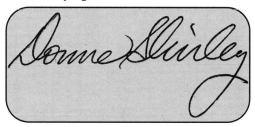

Sky Shivers - Storyteller / Entertainer

I first heard of Sky on the Oasis Network Radio Station (90.5). He was being interviewed by David Warren. Sky is such an interesting character and his countrified, Okie accent just lures you into hearing what he has to say. I wasn't at all disappointed when I went to his home and met him and his family who were just as likeable and charming as Sky.

Sky's parents lived in Prague, Oklahoma but Sky was born in Stroud because the Prague hospital was full to capacity on the day Sky made his entrance. Stratford, Oklahoma ended up being where he grew up because his father is a country preacher and his work took him there. I can only imagine what Sky was like growing up, but I assure you he must have kept his parents entertained just by being there.

His life has been anything but boring. He met his wife Debora while they were both attending the same high school. Later they attended another school together, but this time to learn how to make saddles and cowboy boots. They

made plans to open up a business together but before they had a chance something of greater interest sidetracked them for a while.

In 1976 the national celebration of America's 200th birthday was being recognized by a bicentennial wagon train headed across the United States. The train was going to pass through Henryetta, Oklahoma and was offering anyone interested in joining the train to meet them along the way. Sky and Debora thought it would be a great opportunity to display their goods and at the same time have the adventure of a life time. So they quit school and sold everything they had, which Sky mentioned was only three items because they were pretty much broke.

Before they left on the wagon train Sky's father performed their wedding ceremony inside the wagon circle. The next morning they climbed onto a wagon they purchased with borrowed money and off they were headed for Valley Forge, Pennsylvania.

The wagon train had already been traveling for two months and there was four months left to travel in order to reach their destination by July 4, 1976. It was an incredible journey for the Shivers. They traveled four miles an hour for four months.

Sky said that gives a newly married couple a lot of time to talk, and to tell you the truth not all the conversations were nice ones.

They got weary from time to time and were limited on their resources. They left Oklahoma with $200 dollars in their pocket. They had to feed four horses, one dog and themselves. So intense scrimping was required as well as selling leather items they made when the train set up camp in a town. They look back now and figure the adventure was either a plan of God for them or He just allowed them to do it because it was an episode in their life they will never forget.

At the end of the journey they didn't know what they were going to do with their wagon and four horses and no car or money to get back home. But the most important factor was how were they going to say good-bye to some wonderful strangers they had spent four long months with who had become some of their best friends. Their common goal was to get from one town to the other with no mishaps. They experienced run away horses and broken wagon wheels and a variety of other needs that had to be attended to. Everyone learned to look after the other person and no one was going to be left behind.

Now, four months later, they had to say good-bye to friends they knew they probably would never see again. It took Sky and Debora over a year after returning home to pull themselves emotionally away from the people they had learned to love.

Their college gave them their degrees when they returned, saying they had accomplished more on the wagon train than they could have ever taught them. Sky and Debora both got jobs and began working and saving. Three years later they were able to buy land and start the business they had dreamed of.

In 1980 their first daughter Tracy Lynn was born and following her in 1983 came daughter Karie Lynn. Then in 1984 Sky heard there was going to be another wagon train leaving Texas on January 1, 1986. As Debora sat sipping on a glass of tea, pregnant with their third daughter Kristy Lynn, Sky asked her if she would like to join the train. Of course they both agreed and their plans began to form. This time they were going to get sponsors to help make the trip a little easier, and sell the business they worked hard to build. But for Sky and Debora it was something they just had to do.

With three children ages 6, 3 and 13 months they climbed onto a wagon train in Sulphur Springs, Texas. In the wagon behind them was Sky's brother David and his wife Teresa and their 3 year old daughter Abby. They heard so much about the fascination of the trail they, too, had to come along.

Texas was celebrating its 150 years of freedom from Mexico and the wagon train was part of the celebration. It was to travel the entire perimeter of Texas, taking six months to complete and arrive in Ft. Worth on July 4, 1986.

On this trip the Shivers learned the destination was not the highlight of the trip but the trip itself. They intended to enjoy it all the way. Day by day, minute by minute they wanted to savor every moment. Some of their friends back home thought they were crazy to give up their business to travel with a wagon train, but Sky said they just didn't understand. The adventure of it all was well worth the discomfort or the monetary value that may have been left behind.

Sky said those two wagon train events shaped, changed and absolutely flavored and colored every perspective he and Debora had about life from then on.

I think there are probably many people sitting back reading Sky's story that would love to have been in his shoes. But it takes someone like Sky to be willing to risk it all for a taste of a world unfamiliar to most of us.

Since his wagon train days Sky and his family have been involved in many other facets of life too many to expound on. He has become a well known storyteller who says if you live an interesting life like he has, you will always have something to tell. The microphone has become his friend. Sky said he doesn't understand anybody that is afraid to speak into a microphone. After all, it is your own voice coming through.

Sky uses a lot of humor in his storytelling. He said people remember what you've said a lot longer if you do. Of course for Sky I'm sure humor comes very natural for him. He also said talking about human emotions is what makes a good storyteller because everyone then has an opportunity to relate to what you are saying. Sky has been told he is a cross between Bill Crosby and Jeff Foxworthy and I must agree. Yet Sky has a uniqueness about himself that is all his own.

Sky told me about how he teaches people that words have color. *When we speak our words are like a paint brush that strokes across the pages of one's mind, creating a descriptive story that has the ability to captivate its audience.*

Sky was raised believing in God and *he has kept his faith alive by using God as the glasses he views the world through.*

I was thoroughly impressed with Sky and his family. It would do us all well to spend a little time savoring his humor and tips of wisdom. Sky has a busy schedule traveling and speaking to groups in his storytelling manner. If you have never been a part of one of his audiences you have truly missed out.

Jim Shoulders

Rodeo Champion

When you think of a true cowboy, most people visualize a rugged individual that has gut, determination and an over abundance of courage. That is exactly how you could describe Oklahoma bred, Jim Shoulders.

Born and raised in Tulsa, Oklahoma, Jim never expected that someday he would be a 16 time World Rodeo Champion. With four boys and no girls in the family they were bound to do something daring when all four of them got together, but Jim went above and beyond the call of duty.

At about age 12, Jim started attending rodeos and riding calves in the minor league rodeos in Collinsville, Oklahoma. When he was 14 years old he went to a rodeo in Oilton, Oklahoma, entered the bull riding contest and won $18 on his event.

Since he was use to receiving 25 cents an hour shocking oats and wheat, it didn't take long for him to realize that rodeoing was far more lucrative than what he was accustomed to. In the beginning, rodeoing was just a way for Jim to make money. Before long, it involved more than money, it was the thrill of the ride.

In 1945 he joined the Cowboy Turtles Association, which was later renamed The Rodeo Cowboys Association. By then, he was well on his way to stardom, even though he didn't know it at the time. His parents were both very supportive of his rodeoing and were quick to help with transportation or finances when needed.

He recalled a funny story while he was still going to East Central High School in Tulsa. He had left school at noon three days in a row to attend the Muskogee Fair Rodeo. When he returned to school the following Monday, he was told he couldn't return to class until he had reported to the superintendent. When he told Mr. Gallen, the superintendent, he had an excused absence from his parents to go to the rodeo, Mr. Gallen looking surprised said, "You can't have an excused absence to go to a rodeo. Why did you go anyway?" Jim pulled $500 out of his pocket and laid it on Mr. Gallen's desk.

"That's Why" Jim said. "I won almost $700 in three days rodeoing and I sure haven't made that here and neither have you."

Jim knew that was a disrespectful remark to make, but he knew that Mr. Gallen only made $400 plus a house for his monthly wages. Astounded, Mr. Gallen said, "you make that much rodeoing?"

From then on, Mr. Gallen never questioned Jim's excused absences. If Jim was missing from school, Mr. Gallen would contact him when he returned just to see how much he had made. Mr. Gallen became one of Jim's biggest fans and kept up with him for years after high school.

In 1947 when Jim was 19 years old he married his wife, Sharon. He took her to Madison Square Garden to enter the rodeo. He hoped to make enough money so they could have a nice honeymoon. He surprised even himself when he won both events and won $5,000.

Jim stills views that championship as meaning the most to him, because he was only a year out of high school and already making a name for himself in the world of rodeos.

In later years, Jim became the only cowboy to ever be accepted into the Madison Square Garden Sports Hall of Fame.

In 1949 Jim won his first World Championship. For the next 10 years he accumulated seven world championships in bull riding, four world championships in bareback bronc riding and five world championships as the All-Around Cowboy.

When asked if he had had any injuries, his reply was yes, but not serious ones. I guess that depends on what your definition of serious is. Jim has had his legs shattered and broken, his teeth knocked out, his collarbone severed and his face and cheekbones caved in. Yet he continued to play in a sport in which he excelled.

The last year Jim won a championship was in 1959, but he continued to compete at major rodeos until 1970. In 1960 he also started the Jim Shoulders Rodeo Riding School Inc. to provide stock and produce major league PRCA rodeos and help train young people to become professionals, many of which have been eligible to compete in the Pro Rodeos.

The name Jim Shoulders is synonymous with the word "cowboy." He will probably always be involved in rodeos in some way.

Since 1948 Jim has been an endorsee for the Wrangler Jean Company. No one else has ever been associated that many years with one product. What better person could there be to represent a cowboy jean company than Jim Shoulders?

Jim and Sharon moved to Henryetta in 1950 and raised their four children on a ranch that they still own today.

As you drive into Henryetta you will see an impressive sign which says, "Home of Jim Shoulders and Troy Aikman." Jim is quick to tell you that Troy only agreed to the sign being displayed if Jim's name was going to be first billing. That only seems fitting, I would say. Not that either one is more distinguished than the other, but I've always believed, as Troy obviously does, that with age comes a certain degree of earned respect.

Bob Simmons - Coach

Bob was raised with his two sisters in Cleveland, Ohio. His parents, Fred and Annabelle, are strong Christians who believed it was very important to raise their children in the church. His father worked as a factory supervisor and his mother was a domestic worker.

Bob was the first one in his family to go to college. His father was quick to brag about how proud he was of his athletic son, who acquired a football scholarship to Bowling Green State University. Bob lettered three times as a linebacker and was All-Mid American Conference as a senior when he registered 150 tackles.

After graduating in 1971 with a major in physical education Bob went on to receive his master's degree in college student personnel. He was hired at Bowling Green as their counseling specialist in the counseling and placement office. It was during that time he developed what is called an academic advisory position. Now most colleges have athletic academic advisors, but at the time Bowling was one of the first.

Bob originally wanted to be a professional football player, but since that didn't work out he thought he would probably spend the rest of his career as a counselor and advisor. He began making plans to get his Ph.D. In the Spring of 1976 Head Football Coach Don Nehlen asked him to participate in helping the team coach the receivers and the quarterback in the fall. Bob quickly realized he loved being a coach so he split his duties between coaching, advising and counseling for one and a half football seasons. When the coaching staff changed, Bob didn't think he would get to coach any longer so he went back to his regular duties. But his desire to coach continued to weigh on him.

He decided to go to the National Coaches Conference which was being held in Miami, Florida. He met several coaches, one being Doyt Perry, one of the great head football coaches. He was willing to put in a good word for Bob with Chuck Stobart who was going to be the new head coach at Bowling Green. Don Nehlen also relayed kind remarks about Bob to Chuck and the position to coach outside linebackers at Bowling Green was offered to Bob. He held that position from 1977 until 1980. Then Bob had the opportunity to work again with Don Nehlen who was transferring to the University of West Virginia. He remained there for the next eight years.

Bob talks very highly of his wife Linda, who he married in 1971. She was the one who held the family, consisting of their three children Brandon, Nathan and Lelanna, together while Bob was consumed with honing his talent as a football coach. Bob admits in the beginning he had a hard time balancing family time with his ever increasing desire to succeed as a coach. He credits Linda for being faithful to stand by his side and teach their children that Daddy would be there to participate in family events if he could be. If he couldn't, it didn't mean he loved them any less.

After eight years at the University of Virginia Bob had the opportunity to go to the University of Colorado in Boulder. He worked for seven years with head coach Bill McCartney. McCartney was also the founder of Promise Keepers, a men's organization dedicated to the furtherance of the gospel of Christ. Bob believes God planned for him and Bill to meet, not only for Bill to teach him more about coaching, but to convey a stronger sense of God's purpose for his life.

When Bill quit coaching to go into full-time ministry, Bob wanted to take over the head coach position, but he wasn't selected. Bill convinced Bob he had done all he could do to get the job and from then on it was up to God's plan for his life.

After other offers Bob was finally given the opportunity to become head coach at Oklahoma State University in 1994. He experienced a great deal of success with the football team but his physical body began to show signs of deterioration in the summer of 1997. He developed high blood pressure and some unusual stiffness in his joints and muscles.

Over time his kidneys began to shut down. He was told he would either start routinely on a dialysis machine or a kidney donor would have to be located, which might not be an easy task. Linda once again stepped up to the plate (so to speak). She wanted to be tested as his kidney donor. For the longest time Bob wouldn't even consider putting Linda in that position. But Linda wouldn't have it any other way.

As you might guess, the operation performed on March 10, 1998 was extremely successful and the recovery time for Bob and Linda was incredibly fast. Bob's family took this time of crisis to connect even more strongly with their spiritual beliefs. They learned how to trust God for other things over the years, so they were convinced they could trust him during the crucial time of the kidney transplant.

Bob continued another two seasons with Oklahoma State University. He and Linda are planning on writing a book that details their lives and their ordeal working up to the kidney transplant. The purpose of the book will be geared toward their trust and faith in God's undying faithfulness toward them and His everlasting love on their behalf.

Lee Allan Smith

Executive / Promoter

Here I was on another beautiful sunny day headed for Oklahoma City. Lee Allan Smith was to be my first interview of the day. I found his office quickly since it was located right off of the expressway. I was greeted by a very hospitable staff, one of which was Lee Allan's daughter, Jennifer.

As you enter his office your gaze automatically shifts to the left of the room, where a huge, white stuffed "Steiff"polar bear has taken up residence. Off to the left is a bronze sculpture of none other than one of country music's all-time best entertainers, Vince Gill.

Other memorabilia was displayed in that room as well, but none as cherished as the large portrait of Lee Allan's three daughters that hung on the wall close to his desk. They were displayed as a constant reminder that fatherhood is his

greatest role in life. He proudly told how he used to sing, *You Are My Sunshine* to each one of his girls as they were growing up.

At the time of the interview none of the girls had decided to walk down the marriage aisle. Dad contributes that to the "doting father syndrome."

I am always in awe when I hear a dad take such pride in raising his children. Because of the wonderful example Lee Allan Smith has set, he will someday walk down the aisle with all three of his beautiful, confident daughters and proudly relinquish each one over to the care of some loving, deserving man.

There is an old saying "Behind every successful man is a good woman." Lee Allan certainly feels that way about his wife of 41 years, DeAnn Dudenhoeffer, from Grandfield, Oklahoma. His admiration of her as a wife and mother of his three beautiful daughters is equally apparent from the photos that are displayed in his office.

As we continued our interview, Lee Allan humbly told of his early rearing and was quick to acknowledge his parents as being the people who influenced his life the most. Even though his father died when he was only 12 years old, his fond memories of him still remain strong, while the nurturing of his mother helped establish his own self-worth.

After graduating from Classen High School he attended the University of Oklahoma, followed by two years as a Lieutenant in the United States Air Force. He then returned to Oklahoma City. During that time, unknowingly the steps of his destiny were being laid out before him.

As a Special Service Officer, he was required to organize sporting and show events. His organizational skills had been developed in college, which gave him an edge as he began his duties for the Air Force. His overactive desire to constantly be involved in some kind of activity was proving to be an asset for him and the Air Force as well.

Eventually his obligations to the Air Force came to an end, and for a while he wasn't sure what direction he wanted to go with his life. Most of his friends were going into the oil business, but that really wasn't what he wanted to do. He tried being a stockbroker for a few weeks, but that didn't appeal to him either. So he went to work for a clothing store until he could decide on what the next phase of his life should be.

It's interesting to look back on our lives and see how certain choices so directly affect our successes as well as our failures. One day while he was busily at work at the clothing store he became engaged in conversation with a male customer. As it turned out, the gentleman worked at WKY Radio and Television, owned by The Gaylord Family.

Their conversation was a defining moment in young Lee Allan's life. Soon after, he began working for the station as a salesperson. As time went on he progressed up the ladder from sales manager to general manager. What seemed to be an insignificant decision to work in the clothing store turned into a 31-year career in radio and television from 1956 to 1977. After leaving the television business, Lee Allan began working for Ackerman McQueen advertising agency. He is currently Vice Chairman of Ackerman McQueen and President of Oklahoma Events, which is a subsidiary of the agency.

He has proven to be a vital liaison for Oklahoma, especially in the entertainment world. Some of the events have included the "Stars and Stripes" production, a patriotic show that ran from 1969 through 1976. Guests included stars like Red Skelton, Kate Smith and Bob Hope. The ratings were phenomenal and drew tremendous attention to Oklahoma as it quickly became a syndicated show and was nationally telecast on NBC for four years.

Some of his other accomplishments included hosting many sporting events and broadway shows such as Guys and Dolls and The Will Rogers Follies, but the most significant was serving as president of the local organizing committee for the 1989 U.S. Olympic Festival.

I'm sorry to say I have never been to the Oklahoma City Zoo but I understand Lee Allan was instrumental in the establishment of the aquatic exhibit which features dolphin shows. He has been responsible for so many Oklahoma events that we all have been fortunate to enjoy. He would be the first to tell you that nothing is accomplished without hard work and the contributions from many other people who contributed to the overall team effort.

"Procrastination is the enemy of us all and if you procrastinate too long the window of opportunity will eventually close." Lee Allan said.

When asked what his proudest moments were, he humbly stated that they would be being inducted into the Oklahoma Hall of Fame and into the Association of Broadcasters Hall of Fame as well as the Public School Foundation's Wall of Fame. He admitted even though he was often the man who received the accolades, it took many individuals to complete the task.

245

Shawntel Smith

Miss America

What a ray of sunshine!! When Shawntel walks into a room the atmosphere has to change for the better.

She is originally from Muldrow, Oklahoma and the daughter of Gailen and Karen Smith. With her younger brother and sister, Michael and Carisa, she grew up experiencing strong families ties which probably contributes greatly to her positive, enthusiastic outlook on life. Her parents had the ability to instill into each one of the children a sense of uniqueness which made them feel special.

Because of their Christian faith they taught their children they had God-given talents and skills and helped identify those strengths and support them in whatever they were.

Shawntel never had any interest in being in a beauty pageant. Her plans had always been to attend college and pursue a business degree although she didn't know in what capacity. Her father had always been in the furniture business and owned his own store. Shawntel worked with him on a limited basis and was intrigued with the business side but really didn't know what direction to go.

During her senior year in high school she entered the Muldrow Senior Miss Pageant. All the senior girls usually participated and Shawntel just happened to be one of them. Surprisingly to her, she won. Since she had never considered the pageant seriously she felt that would be the end of her competing.

She entered Westark Community College in Ft. Smith, Arkansas and soon after was approached by the activities director about entering the college pageant. At first Shawntel said no. She had won in Muldrow, but that was a little town. Why should she expect she could win again? Besides, she was trying to focus on her college degree. However, her friend Stephanie wanted to enter the pageant and asked Shawntel if she would participate with her. Even if they didn't win they would receive $250 dollars just for competing.

Obviously $250 dollars could pay for a few school books so Shawntel agreed to compete. She placed second runner-up and received a one year tuition scholarship. She realized competing was not such a futile thing after all. When she checked into it further she found out even more about the opportunities that were out there if she was willing to make the effort. The next year she competed and placed fourth runner-up, not as well as she would have liked, but she was still awarded a tuitional scholarship because she placed.

She began thinking about the Miss Oklahoma and Miss America pageants and realized she could not only pay her college tuitions, but have the opportunity to affect others as well by sharing her own personal beliefs and ideas. Shawntel remembered her Dad saying persistence paid off and she wanted to see if he was right.

She transferred to Northeastern State University in Tahlequah after she finished her first two years of college. She won her first local pageant at NSU which made her eligible for Miss Oklahoma. Through the whole process she remained in school and worked part-time. While still at Northeastern she placed in the Top 10 in the Miss Muskogee Pageant and the following year she was Top 10 in the Miss Stroud Pageant.

By then she had completed her bachelor's degree at Northeastern and had started working as the marketing director at the Northeastern State University Muskogee campus. She gave up on the idea of pursuing the Miss Oklahoma or Miss America titles. She thought since she had only placed in the Top 10 the last couple of pageants, perhaps it wasn't meant for her to hold either of the top titles.

Soon after she started her new job she received a phone call saying the pageant had failed to notify her of a scholarship to Oklahoma City University she had won. Shawntel was about to turn down the scholarship, saying she had already completed her bachelor's degree when they suggested she study for her master's degree. Shawntel quickly agreed and within a week she quit her job in Muskogee and moved to Oklahoma City.

She started working and was content with her job and schooling when a pageant official called once again and encouraged her to enter the Miss Tulsa State Fair Pageant. It would be the last pageant she would be eligible for before aging out. Shawntel gave it some thought and decided to compete.

She won the title of Miss Tulsa State Fair and went on to win Miss Oklahoma and then finally Miss America 1996. It was an incredible journey for Shawntel. She has won over $75,000 dollars in scholarship assistance which certainly made college life much easier. *It also taught her that instant gratification shouldn't be a way of life. In many instances you won't be happy with things that come too quickly.* If your dreams and goals don't happen over night then keep working on them. If it is in your heart then the dream is worth fighting for.

I asked Shawntel besides just being adorable what was it that set her apart from other contestants. She felt it was her ability to be herself and enjoy what she was experiencing rather than be so competitive she beat herself. I thought that was a good point and remembered Jane Jayroe, Miss America 1966 saying practically the same thing. When winning isn't everything then you can relax and just be who you are. Obviously, their philosophy works.

Of course we all know Shawntel's platform for the Miss America pageant was the School to Work program. She is proud of the fact a lot of people joined with her in promoting the program. The participation of states grew from seven at the beginning of her reign to all 50 states by the end of the year.

Doors continue to open for Shawntel. She shares the spotlight with Jim Buratti on the television show "Discover Oklahoma." The two of them make an excellent team. She is also the spokesperson for Crown Auto World commercials in which she does a fine job.

Yet of great importance to her and what she spends the majority of her time on is her motivational speaking as she travels the U.S. She speaks on a variety of topics including leadership, good ethics and setting goals. She said a lot of topics she speaks on are ideas or information she has gained from someone else, which happens to be a key of how we all can grow intellectually.

Shawntel's relationship with God has remained strong through all of her accolades. She is quick to share with people the importance of her faith, and talking with Shawntel it is evident she not only speaks it but acts it out as well. *She believes you need to be focused if you want to achieve a goal and take small steps if you don't know the grand plan. Each step will lead you to the next step and before you know it your goal will become a reality.*

Shawntel had the privilege of meeting General Swartzkoff who told her *"It takes two things to become a good leader. The first is to always do what is right which gives you self dignity. The second is when placed in command, take charge."* Shawntel has taken that bit of advice to heart. She realizes as we all should that we are all placed in command of our own lives and no one can make you a success but yourself. So take charge!

Stephen Robert Smith - Tupper the Clown

Who doesn't like a clown? You can be in the foulest of moods and notice a somewhat peculiar looking character walk into the room and the whole atmosphere begins to change.

It was hard to decide which clown to include in my list of Distinguished Oklahomans. I inquired several times over the course of a year to find just the right person. However the list was so staggeringly long I found myself in a quandary. But I do believe I found the person in which the title is definitely fitting.

Stephen was born in El Paso, Texas but has spent most of his life in Oklahoma. It's not surprising that his career would be focused around an audience. After all, he grew up watching his father Robert W. Smith take center stage as a Methodist preacher. For years the family transferred every couple of years from one church to the other all over Oklahoma.

It was interesting to hear Stephen admit how during his school years he molded his personally to fit whatever group of people he found himself amongst. Unknowingly in the beginning he was creating a theatrical stage, so to speak, in real life that would eventually catapult him into his future career.

After graduating from Bartlesville College High he enrolled in Oklahoma City University. His plans were to finish college and attend a theological seminary in Dayton, Ohio to prepare for a career in religious theater. In spite of the fact his early high school years had been lightly sprinkled with a measure of rebellion, he still had a deep desire to be a "spiritual guy."

While in college Stephen met and married Carol. On weekends they went to a couple of churches they had been asked to pastor. For the most part they believed a typical church setting with Stephen at the pastoral helm would be the course for their life. Yet they soon found out that Stephen's talents were more on the educational side of ministry as opposed to the pulpit.

He was introduced to a gentleman by the name of John Hinkle who at the time was employed by the Oklahoma Libraries Association. Mr. Hinkle taught Stephen the art of ventriloquism. They developed a puppet named Gib and during the summer months Mr. Hinkle would send him to various libraries across the state to perform puppet shows.

In addition Stephen met a lady while still in college who introduced him to the wonderful world of clowning. It was certainly obvious that Stephen's charted path was beginning to be well defined. He took on the clown name of "Tupper" because his older brother had a friend named Tupper. Stephen viewed his brother's friend as the kind of guy who could get by with just about anything, so why not clowning?

I had the opportunity to sit and talk in length to "Tupper." He offered to wear his clown suit during our interview, but since we were meeting at a local Pizza Hut I felt the safest approach would be for him to wear his regular street clothes. I could see me trying to get through an interview with 30 gawking individuals trying to get his attention. However, Tupper did make a couple of stylish balloons while we were there. One was his all famous guitar and the other was a caterpillar emerging from his cocoon and turning into a beautiful butterfly.

Tupper loaned me a personal video which I viewed once I returned home. The video showed Tupper applying his clown makeup, performing his puppet-ventriloquist act and making numerous balloon items. Tupper amazingly can make around 500 different images from his balloon creations. He admitted he has become quite efficient in applying his clown makeup. He has it down to an eight minute all inclusive transformation. Even the red mark on his cheek which signifies the ability for the clown within him to emerge is always applied.

Remember what he said about his school days and how he would allow his personality to be altered depending on what town his family had relocated to? Well, Stephen carried that versatility right into his career. Along with his clown character he also plays the part of Professor B. Looney, Okie Dokie, Samuel Austin Worcester, Peter Cartwright and Ben Franklin.

Stephen is a very dedicated performer who has traveled to several states to share his talents. He was once the National

Chaplain for the American Guild of English Bell Ringers. It has remained very important to Stephen to keep his clowning and performing an example of good, clean entertainment. That is why he has continued to be invited to churches of all denominations. He loves to weave his "clowning around" into a sombering salvation message or an inspiring introduction to a heart-felt communion service.

Whether he is Tupper the Clown, Professor B. Looney or any of the other characters he pulls out of his "talent hat" he remains dedicated to his craft. His audiences are like family and he treats them as such.

Stephen and Carol have raised three children. Jeremy is following in the footsteps of his grandfather's preaching ministry. Matthew is interested in computers and will enter Tulsa University next year and 16 year old Miranda is still in high school.

I asked Stephen how his children react to his clownish ways and he said each day seems to bring a different reaction.

Stephen worked for years as an artist in residence with the State Arts Council. Now he has aligned himself with the State Humanities Council. Children of all ages love his educational programs which have brought a lot of humor into their lives over the years. He especially loves the opportunity to change the way a person views a problem within themselves or others by pointing to the problem through the eyes and heart of a clown.

We all have sad days from time to time, but when Tupper finds himself in front of an audience on those particular days and sees the faces of an adoring crowd, the pain in his soul immediately becomes secondary.

What a wonderful life it must be to be a clown! Not only does Tupper make people laugh but he has the opportunity to change the way they think about a majority of issues.

If anyone would like to take advantage of Tupper's talents, you can contact him through the internet at Tuppertheclown.com or BLooney.com or Christiansanity.com. You won't be sorry that you did.

Tupper the Clown
Stephen Smith

Thomas Stafford - Astronaut

Thomas Patten Stafford was born September 17, 1930 in Weatherford, Oklahoma to Mary Ellen Patten Stafford and Dr. Thomas Sabert Stafford. He is a 1948 graduate from Weatherford High School. He graduated with honors in 1952 from the U.S. Naval Academy, Annapolis, Maryland and was commissioned a second lieutenant in the United States Air Force. His pilot wings were awarded to him at Connally Air Force Base, Texas in September 1953.

After completing advanced interceptor training, he was assigned to the 54th Fighter- Interceptor Squad, Ellsworth Air Force Base, South Dakota. In 1955 he was transferred to the 496th Fighter-Interceptor Squad, Hahn Air Base, Germany where he was a pilot, flight leader and flight test maintenance officer flying the F-86D aircraft.

Tom entered the Air Force Experimental Flight Test Pilot School at Edwards Air Force Base, California in August 1958 and received the A.B. Honts Award as the outstanding graduate in April 1959. He remained with the school as an instructor and later was chief of the performance branch. He is co-author of the

Pilot's Handbook for Performance Flight Testing and the *Aerodynamics Handbook for Performance Flight Testing.*

On his 32nd birthday in 1962 NASA selected him as an astronaut. In December 1965 he was the pilot of Gemini VI, the first rendezvous in space, and helped in the development of techniques to prove the basic theory and practicality of space rendezvous.

The first attempt was canceled when the rendezvous target vehicle and adjoining rocket exploded shortly after launch. The second attempt failed because the astronaut Titan II rocket shut down just after ignition, nearly triggering a launch pad abort. They could have ejected out of the seats and destroyed the Gemini, but they chose not to abort, instead saving the Gemini.

Three days later on December 15, 1965 Mission Commander Wally Schirra and Tom Stafford were again strapped into the Gemini Spacecraft cockpit and launched on an epic space mission. The primary purpose of the Gemini space mission was to achieve the first rendezvous between two manned spacecraft-an important maneuver for a later flight to the moon. The second agena target vehicle had been destroyed and NASA quickly launched the Gemini VII crew of Frank Borman and James Lovell to act as a target for Gemini VI. After nearly six hours of chasing Gemini VII Commander Stafford and Sphirra successfully completed the task.

In June 1966 Tom was commander of Gemini IX and performed three different types of rendezvous, including a demonstration of an early rendezvous that would be the standard used in Apollo, the first optical rendezvous and a lunar-orbit abort rendezvous.

The objectives mission was to rendezvous with the target vehicle, perform a space walk and demonstrate controlled re-entry. However, bad luck continued with Gemini IX. The agena exploded during launch phase. Bad luck continued when the astronauts spied the rendezvous target vehicle. The protective shroud had not completely separated and parts covered the target's docking collar. The astronauts could not dock but they did accomplish the only overhead rendezvous and the first optical rendezvous ever performed.

During the mission Gene Cernan became the second American to walk in space while on a record breaking two hour VA extravehicular activity and the first man to walk in space completely around the world. Commander Stafford had to call Cernan back into the space craft early when the space walker experienced major problems with the environmental control.

When Gemini IX returned to earth with Commander Stafford at the controls he was able to accomplish one of the most accurate atmospheric reentries in history as he brought the spacecraft to within 3/8 mile of its projected impact point in the Atlantic Ocean.

From August 1966 to October 1968 Colonel Stafford headed the mission planning analysis and software development responsibilities for the Project Apollo astronaut group. He was a member of the group which helped formulate the sequence of missions leading to the first lunar-landing mission. He demonstrated and implemented the theory of a pilot manually flying the Saturn booster into orbit and the translunar-injection maneuver.

General Stafford was commander of Apollo 10 in May 1969. It was the first flight of the lunar module to the moon. He performed the first rendezvous around the Moon and descended to within nine miles of the lunar surface, but because the module weighed too much, the mission could not set down on the lunar surface. However, he selected the site of the first lunar landing, which occurred two months later.

During re-entry from this mission, General Stafford achieved the highest speed ever attained by man at 28,547 statute miles per hour. This set the world's all-time speed record and he was cited in the Guinness Book of World Records for the feat. The 10 day flight of Apollo 10 had tested every phase of a lunar landing and short of an actual touch down on the moon Commander Stafford's crew had opened the door for the first landing on the moon.

In June 1969 NASA selected Tom Stafford to succeed legendary astronaut Allen Shepard as the new chief of the astronaut office, one of the space agency's most important and powerful positions. His new responsibilities included crew selection and training, new astronaut selection and support for mission planning and training. The office gave Commander Stafford and increased influence and visibility within the NASA organization.

He logged his fourth space flight as Apollo commander of the Apollo-Soyuz Test Project mission from July 15-24, 1975. This was a joint space flight culminating in the historic first meeting in space between American astronauts and Soviet cosmonauts. The event signaled a major advance in efforts for the conduct of joint experiments and the exchange of mutual assistance in future international space explorations.

General Stafford assumed command of the Air Force Flight Test Center on November 4, 1975. He was promoted to the grade of Major General on August 9, 1975 and on March 15, 1978 he was promoted to Lt. General. On May 1, 1978 he assumed duties as Deputy Chief of Staff, Research Development and Acquisition, Headquarters USAF, Washington, D.C.

It was during this time that he personally initiated the start of the F-117A Stealth Fighter. In a Chicago hotel room in early 1979 he wrote the initial specifications on a piece of hotel stationary and started the advanced technology bomber development. This aircraft is now designated the B-2 "Stealth Bomber."

In 1979 Lt.. General Tom Stafford retired from the Air Force. He co-founded the technical consulting firm of Stafford,

Burke and Hecker, Inc., in Alexandria, Virginia.

In June 1990, Vice President Dan Quayle and the then NASA Administrator, Admiral Richard Truly, asked General Stafford to chair a team to independently advise NASA on how to carry out President Bush's vision of returning to the Moon, this time to stay, and then go on to explore Mars. The completed study, "America at the Threshold," is a road map for the next 30 years of the U .S. Manned Space Flight Program.

In 1992 he received the Congressional Space Medal of Honor as the eighth recipient to have received this award in history.

General Stafford has served as an advisor to the National Aeronautics and Space Administration and the Air Force Systems Command. He has also chaired numerous governmental committees including the Operational Oversight Committee to service and repair the Hubble Telescope the Shuttle-MTR Independent Oversight Review Committee and presently the International Space Station Independent Oversight Review Committee for Safety and Operational Readiness.

General Stafford is currently married to the former Linda Ann Dishman of Chelsea, Oklahoma. He has two daughters from a former marriage, Dionne Kay and Karin Elaine, and two grandsons.

I had the opportunity to visit the museum located in Weatherford to honor General Stafford. After talking with him briefly I realized I wouldn't be able to describe his career any better than the museum had done, so I let their write-up basically say it all.

A.T. Stair

Scientist

Dr. Stair was born in Oklahoma City, but raised on a farm in the town of Canton, located in the Panhandle of Oklahoma. He quickly found out farming was a laborious job that involved an extreme amount of physical exertion. He realized driving a tractor, raising cattle and delivering milk was something he neither had the patience for or the consuming desire to do.

As rewarding as the task is to many of our admired and deserving farmers, Dr. Stair knew it was not the direction he wanted his life to go. In viewing his options he felt sure an academic education was the path more suited for him so he set out after high school to pursue that avenue.

He knew whatever he wanted to accomplish in life would require a lot of commitment and effort on his part. One thing he had learned from farming was that hard work would eventually yield a successful crop.

While attending Oklahoma University he received a degree in mathematics. He was fortunate to be offered a Physics scholarship by a very fine Norwegian professor named Dr. Nielson, who was a student of Bohr (being the equivalent of Einstein).

The Korean War was in progress and many of his friends were sent to battle. However, officials

thought Dr. Stair's abilities would be much more utilized in the ROTC training program studying for his Ph.D. Upon completion of his studies the Korean War was coming to an end and Dr. Stair was on his way to one of the finest military laboratories in Boston, Massachusetts.

Being in Boston was quite a stretch from the fertile plains of Oklahoma. Boston was surrounded by buildings with limited vision of the land around them, something Dr. Stair had always taken for granted. Boston did have its own attributes however. With 70 universities it was overflowing with a tremendous climate for learning.

Dr. Stair knew that he wanted to be involved in research and immediately began testing what was soon to be called, "atomic bombs." At the time they were high-powered explosives. He was assigned to do measurements of the explosives. When the explosives go off in the atmosphere they release tremendous energy. Dr. Stair's task was to measure that energy and determine how much destruction it could cause.

Up to that point, there was no logical understanding as to what was happening. Dr. Stair's research was crucial for the expansion of the world's knowledge in that area.

After his stint in the military, Dr. Stair stayed on as a civilian scientist and set up a major laboratory to continue his study in the fundamentals of chemistry and physics. It took over 10 years before they had a better understanding of the atmosphere which eventually led him into research of the Northern Lights (Aurora).

With his abundance of curiosity, Dr. Stair proceeded to go a step further and became involved in testing aboard the first U.S. Space Shuttle. He devised an instrument box that was attached to the outside of the space shuttle and was to be electronically activated by the push of a button. The day finally came when the shuttle was to go into space and Dr. Stair's invention would be put to the test. The shuttle was in flight and the control button to the instrument box was pressed, but nothing happened. It was pressed again and again, but still nothing.

At the time, the man space walks had not yet begun, so there was no way to actually have a person open the instrument box from outside the shuttle while it was in space. They did, however, have the Canadian Robot Arm. They had the arm swing around and hit the front of the box, hoping it would come open, but that was to no avail. They later found the failure was due to a technician's bad wiring. Eight years later the experiment was tried again with great success.

Dr. Stair noted as a scientist you are constantly in search of a problem to solve and an avenue in which to do it. Dr. Stair also gained a reputation for the technology called the "Fourier," which deals with infra-red lighting. Infra-red is the light beyond where the naked eye can see, but is where all the molecules exist and are identifiable. He helped develop an instrument that was small enough to hold in your hand to measure molecules in the infra-red zone. Up to that time the instrument was so large it filled up a whole room.

Dr. Stair's accomplishments seem to go on and on. In spite of my own personal lack of scientific knowledge, I found myself immersed in the awe of it all. To add to his list of endeavors he also became the chief scientist on a satellite that has been in space for 10 years. He has to monitor the satellite on a continual basis. For the last 5 years he has been communicating with Russians at the request of the defense department to help build trust between the two in order for our satellites to be placed in the universe together.

I asked Dr. Stair how he related his scientific discoveries to the spiritual side of life. Even though he admitted his knowledge in spiritual matters is limited, he said his years of research are very much like a quest to understand nature better. In so many ways there is a very God-like feeling you experience when you realize you have tapped into an area that has never been revealed to society before.

To some extent he felt like he was helping create a sense of immortality by eventually passing on his research findings to the next generation.

Since our interview Dr. Stair has been profiled in Rainbow magazine published by his national college fraternity, Delta Tau Delta, as one of 100 Most Influential Delts of the 20th Century.

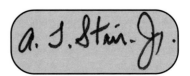

Willard Stone - Sculptor

I looked at Willard's work that is lovingly displayed around the homestead museum in Locust Grove, Oklahoma and marveled at his creativity and obvious thrust toward creation. It's almost hard sometimes not to turn green with envy when you see the talent that so easily flows from a person like Willard. You silently wish some of the gift would somehow transcend to the portion of your brain that could create such magnificent work.

I met his wife, Sophie who was kind enough to grant an interview, since Willard has already taken up residence alongside the masterful Creator who gave him such a talent. I could somehow picture the two of them going through life together and watching it unfold in just the way it should. I commented to Sophie after looking at several pictures tucked away in an album what a nice looking man Willard was and she quickly replied, "I'd have to agree with you." As the mother of 11 children she, too, had a few stories to tell I'm sure, but time didn't allow it.

As a boy, Willard knew the hardships of life as well as the triumphs. His father died when he was two years old and his mother raised the family working as a sharecropper in the cotton fields near Oktaha, Oklahoma. At age 13 Willard lost a portion of two fingers and the thumb on his right hand from a dynamite cap explosion. For a while it left him with a sense of hopelessness, yet he found solace in a talent that was beginning to emerge inside of him.

He loved rainy days and one day as he was walking home from school he picked up a clump of damp red clay from the side of the road and began molding it into shapes of animals he was familiar with. Not only was the molding of the clay therapeutic for his hand, it also provided him with the stepping stones toward his intended pursuit of purpose.

Sophie told the story about Willard, as a teenager, sitting by the side of the road and sculpting small pieces and displaying them on the mailbox in front of his mother's home. On this particular day a car drove by and immediately turned around and came back to where Willard was sitting delicately molding damp clay. At first Willard thought he was in trouble for displaying his work on top of the mailbox, but he soon found out it was curiosity that turned that car around.

One of the men in the car was Grant Foreman, the dean of Oklahoma historians. He was so impressed with Willard's talent he encouraged him to seek formal training. Willard enrolled at Bacone Indian College in 1936 where Acee Blue Eagle and Woody Crumbo attempted to guide him further. However, it wasn't long before they realized that Willard knew much of what they had to teach him. So they set up a studio for him in a storage closet and suggested he let the creative juices flow. Willard began sculpting wood pieces that quickly won him national recognition.

After leaving college he worked at various jobs to make ends meet, since his sculpting didn't quite cover all of his and Sophie's needs. In the 1940's, oil patron and art collector Thomas Gilcrease gave Willard a three-year grant as an artist in residence at the Gilcrease Institute of American History and Art. That opportunity was a huge stepping stone for Willard, however at the end of three years he found himself once again needing to find work to keep a steady flow of income for his wife and their quickly growing family.

He went to work for Ernest Wiemann Ironworks in Tulsa, which I found intriguing since I had interviewed Mr. Wiemann for a previous book. He made clay patterns for Mr. Wiemann to turn into interesting pieces of ironwork. After leaving that job he signed on with Douglas Aircraft in Tulsa as a die finisher.

Sophie recalled stories of Willard car pooling back and forth to work and leaving shavings of wood sprinkled in the floor-board of different buddies' cars. At first it caused quite a stir amongst the wives, until Willard surprised them with a piece of intricately carved wood as a peace offering. Even though Willard's talent was recognized by others as being exquisite and remarkable, he never thought of himself as being anyone special. In fact, in later years he wondered what the hoopla over him was all about.

By 1961 Willard's sculpting had finally reached the point where he could resign his job at the aircraft firm and devote all of his attention to his God-given talent. His sculpture had become so popular with collectors he had a backlog of commissioned pieces.

Willard was creating works of art that left admirers in awe and himself filled with gratitude for the opportunity.

To produce a piece, Willard sketched his idea on paper then selected a seasoned wood that had the right grain and suited the color of the subject. He sketched on the wood, blocked it out with a knife and chisel and then slowly and precisely carved the details with a pocket knife.

I was one of the fortunate ones to see some of Willard's work in his studio, which is still maintained on his property. It was amazing how a block of wood could reach right into my spirit and allow me to feel the message Willard had intended for each piece. Every sculpture had a thought behind its creation and every creation was able to stand alone in its interpretation. One would have to view Willard's art themselves to actually appreciate the words I speak. A few of my favorites were "Something To Believe In," which I ranked number one, then "Help Us Cross Tomorrow's Roads," "Transplant," "Cowboy Baby," and "Adam's Rib."

Willard Stone truly was an amazing artist who gave all the credit for his ability to God, who he believed in and who he knew kept a watch over him.

Willard Stone

Bob Stoops – Coach

The year 2000 will forever be remembered in Oklahoma history as the year Coach Bob Stoops led The University of Oklahoma football team straight to the top in the nation.

Ron and Dee Dee Stoops had their hands full raising a family of six children in Youngstown, Ohio. Yet from the conversation I had with Bob, all the children knew they were a blessing and not a burden.

Bob's father was a high school teacher and coach at a Catholic school in Youngstown for 28 years. After hearing how his father kept the Stoops children so involved in the activities of his coaching career, it was easy to understand Bob's own tolerance level. I was somewhat surprised when I saw his young daughter Mackenzie walk into his office during our interview and then a few minutes later a child of one of the other staff members as well.

Since I had never experienced an office atmosphere that was so laid back and relaxed, at first it seemed a little odd. But then when you hear Coach Stoops relay his philosophy concerning his family and staff at

Oklahoma University it makes you wish you had thought of the idea yourself.

A lot of dedication goes into coaching a first rate football team and it's not without sacrifices. Therefore, when Coach Stoops sees an opportunity to steal away a few precious moments with his children whether at home or at the office-he takes the opportunity. Just like his father, Coach Stoops feels the importance of sharing his whole life with his family, not just the parts that are left over after a tired and stressful day. Whenever possible he allows his children to share in the same experiences that he revels in on a daily basis.

I asked Coach Stoops what he felt this kind of interaction would mean to his children. He sincerely thinks not only will they feel a love and a closeness to their father, but they will be able to learn first hand what it means to interact at a young age in a variety of relationships.

One of the best parts about his philosophy is he allows his staff the same opportunity he gives his own children. That's not to say that The University of Oklahoma is a daycare center, only that the football staff on occasion has the freedom to raise their children with the belief they are every bit as important as the functions that surround their daddies' lives.

I can't tell you how impressed I was with the level of wisdom that seemed to permeate through this Oklahoma coach. It is easy to see how he was able to turn a losing football team into national champions. The same confidence and atmosphere of respect he instills in his children is the same level of commitment he shows to his athletes. *When a person really cares, it shows.*

Bob entered the University of Iowa after graduating from high school, not aware at the time that he would someday become a coach. Even though he had a football scholarship and was enjoying his position on the college team, his major in college was business. Yet as time went on and his mind reflected often to the exhilaration of sports he realized the imprisonment of an office desk just wasn't for him. He needed to continue to experience a competitive spirit in an athletic world. He also needed to feel the excitement of a cheering crowd as the winning team made its way to victory.

Fortunately the coaches at The University of Iowa gave him the opportunity to follow his heart. After graduating with his marketing and business degree he became a graduate assistant for Coach Hayden Fry and Defensive Coordinator Bill Brashier. He knew he wanted to coach on the college level but he didn't start out with any grand ideas of becoming the number one coach in the nation. All he wanted was to do the very best job possible. He trusted if he put his best foot forward more opportunities would present themselves, and they did. Stoops was a graduate student for three years before becoming a volunteer assistant for the next two years. Then he spent nine months as an assistant at Kent State University before becoming a defensive coach, co-defensive coordinator and eventually assistant head coach under Bill Snyder at Kansas State University. Seven years later he was asked to join the staff at The University of Florida with Steve Spurrier where he remained for three years as defensive coordinator and assistant head coach. In 1999 Oklahoma University had the foresight to recruit him as head coach for what would be the winningest team in the nation one year later.

I asked Coach Stoops what makes a successful coach. "Passion," he said. "Not just for the game, but for all the in between stuff like training and preparing the players and coaches." Coach Stoops is a big believer in making sure his people are happy and laughing and smiling alot. He wants to know they are enjoying life, because without the joy it isn't worth doing.

He admits when he first came to Oklahoma getting the team into shape was quite a challenge. But *he knew if he could convince the players how to change their perception of themselves they would become winners.* He had to teach the players how to earn the right to expect the public to see them as winners. He said *so often people talk about being a winner but they don't want to do what it takes to become one. Sometimes that lack of initiative is rooted in a person's own lack of confidence in themselves. If you truly know you have worked hard enough to be the best then you can expect to be rewarded for your efforts. Success comes to those with a prepared mind.*

Another nugget of truth Coach Stoops said was, *"Never accept excuses for not succeeding. When you rely on excuses you are justifying failure.* There is always a reason why something isn't as complete as it should be. Take time to look at yourself in the mirror and ask why? It isn't your children, your spouse, your family, your job, your broken home or the many difficult situations you may find yourself in. It is, however, your attitude about those situations that set the pace for success or failure. *Choose to use your obstacles to motivate you rather than defeat you and you'll be a winner every time.*

Of course Coach Stoops hopes to experience more victories at The University of Oklahoma. However, with his wife Carol and their three children Mackenzie, Drake and Isaac, he already feels like his life is overflowing with triumph.

I must say I walked away from that interview feeling very blessed that I had been given the opportunity to meet Coach Stoops. I believe as I'm sure he does that whatever the future holds for him it will be exactly what God had in store.

Jim Stovall—Author/Executive

I've never met a man quite like Jim Stovall. With incredible obstacles, Jim overcame his challenges and rose to heights many of us only dream of attaining.

I met Jim several years ago and have continued to be amazed at the success he has created in his life. They say with years, if we are lucky, usually comes wisdom, but I found that Jim acquired an extra dose of wisdom way before his time. As a sight-impaired person Jim has maintained the ability to envision the proverbial glass half-full, the distant mile almost there and the mountain yet to climb only a molehill.

A few minutes spent with Jim is all that is required to turn your negative, downtrodden thoughts into workable possibilities. He has encouraged me many times and often I find myself reflecting back to Jim as I plunge into a day that seems to be filled with staggering hardships. I consider Jim a mentor in my own life as well as the multitude of individuals that cross his path on a yearly basis. Jim has proven by example that when life gives you a barrel of lemons make lemonade for everyone around you.

Jim's parents George and Florene Stovall had a huge impact on the way Jim viewed life and the expectations of sought after dreams. He remembers very clearly the pain his parents endured after the death of one son before Jim was born and then a daughter who died of leukemia when she was four years old.

Jim's earliest memories are of his sister Nancy who passed on before Jim ever had a chance to understand the meaning of having an older sister. Fortunately, when Jim was five years old, his brother Bob was born. He remains not only a great brother but an enduring friend.

With the pain his parents had already endured with the loss of two children, Jim was overwhelmingly aware that the battles to come in his own life would once again stretch the limits for both of his parents. Therefore, in spite of his own pain, Jim had to learn at an early age how to turn his obstacles into victories, not only for himself but for the well-being of his most deserving parents.

The first time Jim noticed he had a sight problem was when he was seven years old playing on a little league baseball team. As the sun set and darkness invaded the playing field Jim could no longer distinguish the baseball from other things in his surroundings. His condition they found out several years later was diagnosed as juvenile macular degeneration. The macula lutea is the center part of the retina, the "screen" on which images form. The doctor informed Jim it was just a matter of time until he completely lost his sight.

At the age of 17 Jim had to seriously consider what he was going to do with the rest of his life. His college days were ahead of him, but what was he to do? At a trip to the local state fair he witnessed two events that set his thinking into motion.

He saw an exhibition by the national Olympic weight-lifting team as well as a musical concert in the fairgrounds stadium.

Jim was quite sure a blind guy could accomplish both of those feats and he was determined to do it. Pursuing those two avenues allowed Jim to focus on what he could do versus what his disability kept him from doing.

However, as time loomed on and Jim found his ability to see quickly diminishing, he came face to face with the reality of whether or not he could overcome the devastation and loss that seemed to overwhelm him. Jim said unlike many individuals who find themselves drifting through life with no real focus on their future, he was forced to examine where his life was headed.

Jim admits there was a time when the vast world beyond the four walls of his bedroom was too frightening for him to encounter. Yet with the help and support of his family, along with others including Professor Harold Paul at Oral Roberts University, Jim began to face his fears. He enrolled in the college's courses that would set the tone for his future.

Since his sight had deteriorated so quickly he needed help reading the textbooks and completing his assignments. One of his first readers was Crystal, who later became his wife. Jim graduated from ORU with a combination degree in psychology and sociology, summa cum laude-with highest honors.

I know sometimes we go through life wondering repeatedly when will the big break come and when will our ship truly come in. One afternoon Jim put one of his favorite movies into the VCR assuming he could listen and remember all the visuals he had once experienced. But he found his memory lacking in some crucial areas which left him frustrated and somewhat angry. His disability triggered an idea which quickly became a dream that turned into reality. Jim knew there were a lot of people in the world just like him and something needed to be done to help them enjoy an occasional movie, which is an everyday occurrence for sighted individuals. Jim points out that on many occasions people are given opportunities to rectify situations in the world around them. Yet all too often they set the ideas aside, assuming someone else will take care of the problem when in fact they may be the very one who has the resources to make the accomplishment come to pass.

After doing some research, Jim discovered there was a multitude of blind and visually impaired people in the United States. He called a friend of his who was also sight impaired, Kathy Harper. After hearing Jim's idea of providing a way for sight impaired people to enjoy television programming Kathy gave up her paralegal career to join Jim in his worthwhile endeavor. Thus was born The Narrative Television Network, which makes movies and television accessible for our nation's 13 million blind and visually impaired people and their families.

Jim believes that God has a plan for all of our lives if we will be patient and take the steps necessary to reveal the blueprint. Sometimes it seems as if the plan will never come to pass and yet perseverance reveals success.

Jim's words of encouragement continue to ring through my thoughts as I am so often reminded that *life is not a practice run. It is the World Series, the Olympics and the Super Bowl all rolled up into one. Instead of spending so much time waiting to live and preparing to live, Jim says just live.*

In addition to Jim's successful television network he has become an accomplished author and motivational speaker. His desire to become a weight lifter was realized many years back when he became a national champion Olympic weightlifter. Even his desire to become a musician has not gone lacking. I witnessed Jim's ability to tickle the ivorys at a performance during one of his motivational speeches.

Without a doubt Jim has turned his obstacles into opportunities and made enough lemonade to quench the thirst of millions.

Eddie Sutton

Coach

I met Coach Sutton for the first time in the early 1990's when I was writing my first book, *Unforgettable Grady.* He was kind enough to add a few quotes about the man we both loved and admired, Coach Grady Skillern.

I'll never forget the first thing Coach Sutton asked when I requested a few minutes of his time to get his heartfelt feelings about Coach Skillern. He said, "What qualifies you to write about basketball?" I truthfully had to say, "Absolutely nothing. In fact, I know pretty much zero about sports. But I do know how to write about the heart of a man." He said, "Okay, set up an appointment with my secretary, Mary Lee and I'll give you as much time as you need."

Hopefully he was pleased when the book came out in print and he was able to see the fruits of my labor. I know Coach Skillern was, and the two of us were extremely grateful for Coach Sutton's contribution.

Eddie was born in Dodge City, Kansas but grew up in Bucklin. Being the only child of Orville and Beryl Sutton, he felt privileged by all the attention his parents were able to bestow on him. Eddie's admiration for his dad is evident when he talks about his father's limited education and yet his ability to tackle almost any task.

After World War II Orville began farming 160 acres of rented farmland where the family raised wheat and cattle. Among other chores it was Eddie's obligation to milk the cow twice a day and take care of his horse named Tony. Until he was in the eighth grade his family still lit up their house by kerosene lamps and used the two-holer out back for their private times. What seems primitive for some of us who have never lived the simpler life, Eddie saw as some of his most cherished memories.

Since Bucklin was a small community most children were able to get involved with every event and sport available. Eddie, of course, was very athletic. But he also sang in the Glee Club and mixed chorus and participated in various school plays.

From the time he was in the eighth grade he knew he wanted to be a coach. His physical stature had gotten the jump on a lot of his classmates and his leadership abilities seemed to be quite advanced for his age as well. So it only seemed natural that the other students would look up to him.

In preparation for college Eddie felt fortunate to have four great basketball coaches around the area. He just needed to decide which school would be best suited for him. Coach Phog Allen was at the University of Kansas. Coach Tex Winter was at Kansas State. Coach Ralph Miller was at Wichita State and Coach Henry Iba was at Oklahoma State University. Even though he knew he couldn't go wrong with whatever decision he made, he chose OSU.

After receiving his bachelor's degree at OSU he stayed on for another year as a graduate assistant for Coach Iba and earned his master's degree. Then he was ready to pursue his dream of becoming a coach.

In 1959, Central High School in Tulsa was looking for a head coach for their basketball team. Coach Skillern, one of Central's former head coaches, was then in the administrative position as Tulsa's Athletic Director. Two years earlier he had refused to give Myron Roderick the position as head coach for Edison High School because he had just graduated from college and had not yet been in the coaching system. Coach Skillern had an iron clad rule that he never hired someone as a head coach outside the system. They had to work their way up from assistant coach. As it turned out, a few weeks later Myron was hired at Oklahoma State University as their head wrestling coach, a position he successfully held for the next 13 years.

Eddie remembered that bit of information when he met with Coach Skillern to apply for the head coaching position at Central. Of course Coach Skillern's iron clad rule was still in effect and Eddie knew that, but he went to apply anyway. He said, "Coach Skillern, you made a mistake when you didn't hire Myron Roderick." Knowing Coach Skillern, I can see him quietly pondering Eddie's statement. Of course Eddie admits Coach Skillern could have continued his relentless rule. But, being the wise gentleman he was, he took time to listen to Eddie's argument and re-evaluated his position.

At age 23 Eddie became head coach of Tulsa Central High School. His beginning salary was $4,550 dollars a year. His duties ranged from teaching history class to coaching basketball, football and golf from 1959-1966.

Following his departure from Central, 24 years needed to pass before he was able to step into a position which has continued to bring him nationwide recognition.

From 1966 to 1969 he was given the opportunity to start a junior college program at the College of Southern Idaho in Twin Falls. The campus wasn't built when Coach Sutton stepped into his position. Now, the school is considered one of the great junior colleges in the country.

In 1969 to 1974 he became the athletic director for Creighton University in Omaha, Nebraska. While there he took the basketball team to the NCAA Tournament.

For the next 11 years from 1974-1985 he was head coach of the University of Arkansas where he took his team to the NCAA Tournament as well as the Final Four. Coach Sutton felt he could grow as a person as well as a coach by the variety of experiences he was encountering as he transferred from one institution to another. He left the University of Arkansas to go to the University of Kentucky from 1985-1989. Once again, his team made it to the NCAA Tournament.

Then his career took a surprising detour as he stepped out of coaching for a year to work in public relations for Nike International. It was a change of pace but nevertheless he had a great time doing it.

In 1990 Coach Myron Roderick was the athletic director for Oklahoma State University. When the coaching position became available he contacted Coach Sutton and hired him to be OSU's head basketball coach. Coach Sutton has taken OSU to the NCAA Tournament and to the Final Four in 1995. He has watched at least 23 young men leave college and go into the NBA.

Coach Sutton has had a wonderful career. He has taken his coaching position very seriously over the years. He has tried to be a strong, moral example to his players and teach them the importance of discipline. He said *"It isn't enough just to want to be successful, a person has to be willing to pay his dues to society. If you want to be a champion in any area you have to be willing to pay the price. Set high goals, but remember they are only accomplished through hard work and persistence."*

As our interview was concluding Coach Sutton gave credit to his wife of over 40 years, Patsy. He commented how she has always bolstered his ego and given him the strength needed when an event didn't quite turn out the way he wanted. When he mentioned his sons, Stephen Edward, Sean Patrick and Scott Andrew the pride in his voice was unmistakable.

Eugene Swearingen

Author/Executive

After the completion of my previous book *Movers and Shakers,* Dr. Swearingen complimented my work and suggested I carry the concept further into what has become *Distinguished Oklahomans.* Coming from a professor and businessman of such high caliber as Dr. Swearingen I took it as quite an honor to have his approval. I will always be grateful to him for encouraging me to go a step further and accomplish what I hope everyone will agree is a book worthy to be read by all.

Dr. Swearingen was born in Nebraska, but his parents Ruth and Laurrel, moved to Perry, Oklahoma when he was five years old so his father could pursue a job as an electrical engineer. Dr. Swearingen said his parents were a constant inspiration to he and his two brothers. As a result, they all three became successful adults.

Because of his mother's constant insistence, he always knew he would go to college. In 1937 there were only two colleges in the area from which to pick:Tonkawa Junior College and Oklahoma State University. Tonkawa's full tuition per semester was $7.50 and OSU's tuition was $12.50 per semester. He couldn't raise the extra $5 so he went to Tonkawa for two years and later transferred to OSU.

When he finished college, he spent three years as a Boy Scout Executive in Nashville, Arkansas. Amongst his Scouts was a young egotistical boy by the name of Ross Perot. We all know what happened to him. During that time, Dr. Swearingen married his loving wife Aasalee, with whom he spent 54 incredible years.

In 1943 it appeared as though he might be drafted, so to avoid it he joined the U.S. Navy. At one point he questioned his decision. It was August 2, 1944 in the North Atlantic, 1,000 miles east of the Newfoundland Coast. He was on the U.S.S. Fiske, DE-143, a destroyer escort chasing submarines. They found two instead of one. They were making their run on one German submarine and the other one came around on the other side. Their whole ship blew up.

The bow sunk in 15 minutes. There were no life boats floating in the water. Dr. Swearingen was in the North Atlantic in 50-degree water for five hours waiting to be rescued. His main thought was whether they would be picked up before nightfall. Thankfully it was summertime or he would have frozen to death.

When his tour of duty was completed he returned to OSU and received a Master's Degree in Economics. He had a desire to teach and knew the Dean of Business at OSU was going to retire in four years. If he wanted to obtain his position, he knew he had to have a Ph.D., so he went to Stanford University and received his doctorate in Economics. He stepped into the Dean's position one year after graduation.

From there he became Vice President for University Development, Vice President for Academic Affairs and Vice President for Business and Finance. He wanted to be President of OSU, but instead he was very fortunate to become President of Tulsa University for a year and a half. Then he was drawn away by a proposition too good to pass up.

John Williams approached him about becoming president of the National Bank of Tulsa, which later became the Bank of Oklahoma. In their negotiations Dr. Swearingen had no idea what the salary of a bank president should be, so he asked for considerably more than the amount he had been receiving from Tulsa University. Mr. Williams' immediate response was, "O.K.," so Dr. Swearingen realized he had sold out too cheap. Quickly he said, "also I would like share options." How many shares?" Mr. Williams said. Again, Dr. Swearingen wasn't sure what to say. He asked for 25,000 shares. "O.K.," Mr. Williams said without hesitation.

Dr. Swearingen said he has found in life you get no more than what you think you deserve. If you don't ask, you won't get it. Now if you aren't worth what you think you are, then you have to be willing to get the extra education or training it takes to be worth it. If you only think you're worth $30,000 and you make $30,000 and plop down in your easy chair and drink beer thinking you've finally arrived, then you probably haven't arrived at all.

Dr. Swearingen said he always thought he was worth over $100,000 dollars and guess what? He got it. But he was always willing to do what it took to deserve it.

After he took the position at the bank he found out there were only five college graduates working there, so he started hiring 15 MBA's per year. One of the bank officers came up to him one day and asked, "How many bright people can we afford to have in this bank?" He looked at him rather startled and said, "Well let's see, we have 800 employees, how about 800 bright people?" The bank grew tremendously. By the time Dr. Swearingen left the bank they were employing over 300 graduates.

As editor of a case book on business policy, now in its fourth edition, Dr. Swearingen has published many articles. He has served extensively as a management consultant to business, conducting development programs for many firms. He is past president of the National Council for Small Business Management Development. He was inducted into the Oklahoma Hall of Fame in 1973 and into the OSU Alumni Hall of Fame in 1978.

Having served as a member of the Oklahoma State Regents for Higher Education from 1977-1986, Dr. Swearingen was also chairman and member of the Board of Trustees of the Southwestern Graduate School Foundation for Banking Education from 1977-1983.

Dr. Swearingen is listed in Who's Who in the World, Who's Who in American Education, Who's Who in Finance and Industry, Who's Who in America, Who's Who in Banking, Who's Who Among Authors, and the Dictionary of International Biography.

Dr. Swearingen loves mentoring young people on how to become successful. That is one reason why he continues to devote his time as a teacher at Oral Roberts University. He initially planned on teaching there for a year but the year has expanded to over 19 years. From what I hear, his students rank him at the top as an educational leader.

In 1996 Dr. Swearingen put out a revised edition of his popular book *Success and Beyond* 50 Keys. I have my own copy personally signed by Dr. Eugene Swearingen which I consider to be a treasured book amongst my repertoire of "bound works of knowledge."

Dr. Swearingen's cherished wife Aasalee died March 11, 1996. After much grief and depression, his children and grand-children inspired him to continue on, along with a statement his mother use to say, "If it's going to be, it's up to me."

As the book of Ecclesiastes states in the Bible, "There is a time for everything, a season for every activity under heaven. A time to be born and a time to die. A time to plant and a time to harvest. A time to cry and a time to laugh. A time to grieve and a time to dance. A time to love....."

Dr. Swearingen has experienced all those times in his life. Being a spiritual man he understands those words very clearly. Thankfully, two years ago, a time to love came into season again when he married Jane.

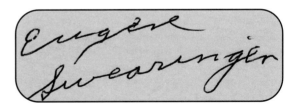

George William Swisher - Business

What a fascinating story Bill told of his childhood years. His grandfather Swisher came to Oklahoma in 1896 as a young lawyer from Illinois following in the career steps of his father. He died at 96 being one of the oldest practicing members of the bar association.

Bill's father was born in 1907. His college years were spent in Danville, Kentucky where he met Bill's mother who was originally from Lexington. They married and moved to Oklahoma City where, like his father he became a lawyer.

Bill was born in 1930. Of course it was expected young Bill would also follow in the steps of the Swisher men before him but the tide was beginning to change.

When Bill was five years old his parents divorced and his mother moved back to Kentucky. Until he was 16 years old he traveled back and forth between homes. His grandfather Robert Tipton was a tobacco and cattle farmer who owned a large tract of land. At one time he was known as one of the largest tobacco producers in the world. He was 7 feet tall and raised in the mountains of Kentucky with only a fifth grade education, but he knew the meaning of hard work.

Every summer Bill had the choice of working on the tobacco farm or being part of his grandmother's country club setting. Bill chose the farm. He was fascinated with the life his grandfather had created and wanted to learn as much about it as he could. There were tractors with rubber tires and electric starters, a bull dozer and a road grater. At an early age Bill was exposed to different types of machinery and he fell in love with the possibilities he saw were available.

His grandfather had his own way of teaching Bill. At age five he was known as the water boy carrying water buckets wherever they were needed. When he turned seven he was taught to drive a team of mules. By the time he was eight he was operating the bull dozer. At the age of 13 he was allowed to go on cattle buying trips with his grandfather and by the age of 16 he was trusted to go on buying trips alone. Bill was learning some incredible lessons from his grandfather that would prove to be stepping stones into his future.

Bill graduated from high school in 1948. After spending a year and a half traveling around the country with a construction crew, he began making plans to go to college. Before he could enroll the Korean War broke out and for two years he found himself assigned to the Navy working in naval construction. Two years later he returned to Oklahoma City and began working as a salesman for Wiley Stewart Machinery Company, an equipment distributor. The first year Bill sold more equipment (dollar wise) than the company had ever sold since it was established in 1901.

In 1953, which was just a year later, Bill bought the 50 year old company. His grandfather Swisher who was financially well off let Bill mortgage one of the buildings he owned. Bill also borrowed $200,000 from Prudential Life Insurance Company when the interest was only four percent. At the time the company was doing a couple of million dollars worth of business and by 1964 they were up to 12 million.

During the early 60s Bill wanted to be more inventive with the machinery and yet manufacturers were reluctant to make changes. So in 1963 Bill decided to become his own manufacturer. He knew there was a niche in the road paving business and he believed he could fill the need. Up to then roads were being paved manually and Bill thought he could build a machine that would automatically cut the final grade for highway and airport runway projects.

With an engineer, a mechanic and a pilot, Bill began to design a piece of equipment to meet the demand. The machine would straddle a road base and clip it off to 1/8th inch tolerance or some predetermined level. They built the prototype and set it behind the Cattleman's Cafe in the stockyards.

Bill wrote a letter to the top 100 paving contractors in the U.S. He provided a picture of the prototype on a grade on a construction sight so they could see exactly the way it looked and functioned. Sixty-nine of those companies solicited sent representatives to Oklahoma City to see the machine and watch it work. Bill's message to the companies was that they lacked productivity and control and he was confident he had the solution.

Bill took each representative and showed him how he could walk alongside the piece of machinery while it did repair work on the road. The people were amazed. Bill and his newly formed company CMI (Construction Machinery Incorporated) took 22 orders thinking that was all they could get built before the end of the year. The machines cost $150,000 and Bill demanded 25% cash down payment.

"Talk about a perfect con game," Bill said. "Here I was meeting people in a cafe showing them a piece of machinery out back and asking for money up front."

However, it was legit. They built the machines and over the next two years they dominated the industry worldwide. The first road they worked on was the turnpike from Henryetta to Hugo.

By 1968 they exported the first machine to Europe and became a public company. Then in 1974 CMI developed the first milling machine. It cuts off the top of an existing pavement and recovers it so you can drive on it immediately. Today there are about 14,000 of those machines around the world.

The whole process was of great interest to me. I see road equipment differently now when I'm driving along a road that seems to be overloaded with one big machine after the other. I think back to a young boy who was groomed as a small child to make a significant contribution to the mechanization of agriculture and construction.

Bill believes in order to be successful you can't be complacent. You have to have curiosity about the world around you. If you aren't able to broaden your horizons then the world will pass right by you.

Bill has been married for over 40 years to his closest and best supporter, Wanda. Together they raised seven children who they consider their best friends as well as their greatest successes, George William III, Thane, Kyle, Ann, Kelly, Scott, and Christopher.

Joseph Taylor
Sculptor/Rancher

One of my favorite interviews was with Professor Joseph Taylor, who to my disappointment passed away December 1, 2000 at the age of 93. Our meeting took place at the professor's home in Ninnekah, Oklahoma where he lived with his caregiver and ranch foreman, Mary Goucher. At first glance, I knew I was going to enjoy my time with this gentle soul whose only concern seemed to be my comfort through his ability to show his charming, hospitable nature.

Joseph was born February 1, 1907 in Wilbur, Washington to Moses Richard and Lula (Killman) Taylor. With four brothers and three sisters I'm sure there wasn't a dull moment around their home. Joseph's father had wanted to homestead in Wilbur but he wasn't happy with the lot of land he had acquired. So he decided to move the family to the Province of Alberta, Canada.

Joseph was only 3 years old at the time but he remembers the trip as the family loaded all its belongings in a covered wagon pulled by a team of horses. One of the horses was a special pet of Joseph. He was there the night the mare gave birth to one of its colts which left a lasting memory on the lad.

Joseph was very young when he first began showing signs of his artistic abilities. At age 7 he entered a drawing contest in the county fair and won first place. He continued to do so for the next three years. At age 10, he entered the adult division and again won top honors. By then he had learned the art of shading by looking at and studying the pictures in a Timothy Eaton catalog.

Because of his love for the outdoors and his lifestyle on the farm Joseph's drawings in the beginning seemed to always depict the horses that he loved. As his talent increased, he began to dabble in the art of sculpture. His first attempt was at wood carving and from there his knowledge continued to increase.

In 1918 the Taylor family returned to Washington and settled on a farm near Chelhalis. There came a time when the hardships of survival became such that Joseph's father mortgaged the farm in order to send some of the brothers to school. The boys were astonished when they found out what their father had been forced to do. Instead of taking a chance of losing the farm the brothers quit school for a time and got jobs until the loan could be repaid. Joseph's love for his family is certainly apparent as he reminisces over the past.

Joseph graduated from high school as an outstanding student in 1927. He attended the University of Washington majoring in painting and sculpture and graduated in 1932 with a Master of Fine Arts Degree. While attending the university he entered the Northwest Art Exhibition, a show of professional artists, and won Best of Show honors. He also was elected Phi Beta Kappa, an honor mostly reserved for philosophers.

Two years earlier on April 19, 1930 he married his high school sweetheart Elsie Viola Rapier. It was a marriage that was to last for the next 62 years.

Upon college graduation, Joseph and Elsie began mailing out resumes to prospective colleges in an attempt to acquire a teaching professor's position. In amongst 125 letters sent out Joseph accepted the invitation to become a professor at the University of Oklahoma in Norman where he spent the next 37 years.

During that time the awards and recognition he received were numerous. While on leave from the University of Oklahoma in 1939 to tour Europe (a trip cut short due to the German bombing of London) he went to New York. While he was there one of his sculptures was displayed in the Metropolitan Museum.

In 1960 he was named to Who's Who in America and was inducted into the Oklahoma Hall of Fame. Following was the David Ross Boyd Professorship in 1963. During a 12 month period in 1964-65 he and Elsie took a leave-of-absence to tour Europe, Asia, and Australia.

In addition to his teaching duties he has created over 500 sculptures of important individuals, ranging from plaques to more than life size. His work is displayed in scores of state buildings and private homes.

Professor Taylor has always worked in clay, stone, bronze, wood and welded metal. He has worked more in clay than in any other medium, however he has been awarded the most recognition from his wood sculptures.

In 1969 he retired from the University of Oklahoma. The last 15 years of his tenure he held the title of Distinguished Professor.

Of course retirement was just a word to Professor Taylor. He continued to accept commissions for various projects as well as occasional speaking engagements.

In addition to his distinguished career at the University of Oklahoma, Professor Taylor began as early as 1935 to pursue his ranching interests, a love he has had from early childhood. He became a very successful rancher and cattle breeder, which he enjoyed the rest of his life. His last few years were spent working with friends on his ranch outside of Alex, Oklahoma.

Even though Professor Taylor had great success as a sculptor, rancher and teacher his greatest love was getting to spend time walking among his cows and hand feeding them. He also loved working the land with his bulldozer. He built over 100 ponds on the ranch. Anyone who visited had to go on his personal tour and would have the opportunity to hand feed the cows.

On July 25, 1999 the Joe Taylor Museum honoring this remarkable man for his lifetime of work in sculpture was opened to the public in Ninnekah, Oklahoma.

At the conclusion of our interview the day was coming to an end and the night skies would soon appear. Professor Taylor was genuinely concerned about my two hour drive back home. He tried very persuasively to offer me a comfortable bed in one of his guest rooms for the night but I assured him I would be fine.

I have mentioned him often to other individuals hoping I would some day get to visit him again. He was one of those people you can never quite forget. I will always remember the quality of man that stood outside his home waving good-bye to a friend he had only met a short time earlier.

Joseph Taylor

Norma Jean Taylor

Singer

Pretty Miss Norma Jean. That's the term that has been used to describe this beautiful woman from the great state of Oklahoma. What a treat it was to meet her and hear about yet another Oklahoman that has made a successful career in country music.

Coming from Wellston, Oklahoma which is 40 miles east of Oklahoma City, Norma Jean had her roots sunk deep in the country lyrics of her day. Since she and her family were poor country people, their only means of entertainment was usually what they could conger up on their own. It's amazing how what seems at the time to be so trivial can become a lifelong pursuit of your destiny.

When Norma Jean was 6 years old she began dreaming of the day she could sing country songs like *Don't Fence Me In* by Cole Porter. Her aunt was the one responsible for teaching her to play an instrument. By the time she was 12 years old she was strumming her guitar and singing, dreaming of the day she would become a country music star.

By then, her family had moved to Oklahoma City and another young girl who eventually made a name in country music became Norma Jean's best friend. Her name was Wanda Jackson. Wanda became a big influence in Norma Jean's life. Since the two of them were pursuing the same career their time spent together was filled with encouragement for the other.

Norma Jean said entering the world of country music in those days was a mixed blessing. On one hand it came easy for her, but since there were only a handful of girls pursuing country music there were obstacles to overcome.

At the age of 14 Norma Jean found an outlet for her enthusiasm when she started performing at the late Merl Lindsay's Lindsay Land Ballroom in Oklahoma City. Merl and his Oklahoma Night Riders was a western swing band that formed in early 1940. His Oklahoma City ballroom became an outlet for many touring bands and eager newcomers such as "Pretty Miss Norma Jean." The ballroom had been an old skating rink above the Farmers Market which proved to be a suitable place to entertain crowds.

All during high school Norma Jean traveled on the weekends performing with western bands and some of her favorite mentors like Merl Lindsay and Leon McAuliffe. Her talents were being honed and the excitement of her musical career stayed in the forefront of her mind.

She also began to perform on a local radio program (KLPR) in Oklahoma City. Her friend Wanda Jackson was also one of the station's performers, so there again they were both able to encourage the other's efforts.

It was Wanda who had the first opportunity to become a part of the ABC-TV Ozark Jubilee operated by the famed Red Foley in Springfield, Missouri. Norma Jean had been turned down when she first solicited a position at the Jubilee, but her longtime friend Wanda wouldn't let that decision stay. She encouraged the Jubilee to welcome Norma Jean which they did in 1958.

For the next year or so Norma Jean eagerly continued her performances around Oklahoma, Missouri and the surrounding areas. It just so happened she met another up and coming country legend, Porter Wagoner, while she was at the Ozark Jubilee. That was soon to become a successful alliance for her.

She moved to Nashville and for a while lived with another Ozark Jubilee acquaintance, Mary Wilkins and her husband. Mary, who had written songs like *One Day At A Time*, became a good friend to Norma Jean and taught her a lot about the music industry.

By the mid 1960's Porter Wagoner had landed his own syndicated television show which was seen by millions of country music fans and wanted Norma Jean to join him on the weekly program. It was, of course, a great match for both of them and certainly created a lot of recognition for Norma Jean. For seven years Norma Jean stood alongside Porter as together they created magic in the country music world.

It wasn't long before other people began to take notice and the world famous "Grand Ole Opry" signed Norma Jean as one of their elite members. Columbia Records as well linked her to a recording contract where she had some great chart hitting records before joining the roster of RCA Victor Records where she enjoyed her greatest recording career. Norma Jean recorded 27 albums for RCA and numerous singles. One of her big hits, *Let's Go All The Way,* was nominated for a "Grammy."

After seven years on the Porter Wagoner show Norma Jean said her goodbyes. Someone else was bidding for her undivided attention and she felt compelled to follow his lead. She fell in love with a fellow entertainer, Jody Taylor, who was part of the duet Jude and Jody. After reveling in his own musical success for a while this Oklahoma boy decided to return to his home state and open a furniture store which is still operating today. Norma Jean put her career on hold and accompanied Jody back to Oklahoma.

Jody had two children from a previous marriage, Randy and Sherrie, and together he and Norma had their daughter Roma. Life became a series of family development and household responsibilities which were too consuming to include a music career as well. For a while Norma Jean continued to travel back and forth to Nashville but as time went on it was inevitable that her family had to take first place in her life.

Unfortunately, in 1982 Norma Jean and Jody's marriage came to an end. She took Roma and the two of them moved back to Nashville. Since she hadn't kept up with her Nashville connections she was somewhat in the position of starting all over again. She really didn't have the intentions of performing, but she wanted to be involved in the music industry in some way.

She and a friend started an agency to help promote young hopefuls in the music industry and she found a measure of success in her efforts. However, she would occasionally run into clients that upon meeting with Norma Jean wanted to book her as an entertainer rather than her clients. Consequently, after about five years, they closed the agency and Norma Jean went on with her renewed musical career. Jean Shepard, who had remained her friend from her days on the Grand Ole Opry, was helpful in stirring up Norma Jean's career once again.

These days are a little different from her earlier years of performing, yet they are none the less rewarding. When Jean Shepard contacted her about being part of the "Grand Ladies of Country" in Branson, Missouri Norma felt it was a great opportunity and took her up on her offer.

I had the privilege of watching Norma Jean perform in Branson and I was thrilled to see the genuine excitement she felt as she stood before an anxious crowd who had come to see one of the "Grand Ladies of Country Music."

Bill Thomas

Actor

Bill is the typical guy who knew what he wanted, he just took the long road to get there.

He was born in Sapulpa, Oklahoma to William and Mary Thomas. His mother, a pediatric nurse, and his father, a railroad worker, were instrumental in guiding Bill through his informative years to get him to where he is today.

By the time Bill was in the 6th grade he knew he wanted to be an actor. He began to involve himself in school plays and felt comfortable when he made the audience laugh or react in some way. When he entered Central High School in Tulsa he not only joined the drama class, but he was on the wrestling team as well. At the time the jocks thought actors were cissys and the actors thought jocks were dumb. Bill, of course, was enjoying both worlds.

Upon graduation in 1970, Bill had 27 wrestling scholarships which he knew would give him a great start in college. Yet he was still unsure of which direction to go. His freshman year was spent at Northern Oklahoma College, but he soon grew tired of the wrestling scene. He switched to Tulsa Junior College which had only recently opened but he still wasn't satisfied. His next move was to Morgan State University in Baltimore on another wrestling scholarship. But once again, he found himself discontented. Bill was wrestling physically as well as mentally trying to figure out what direction he should go with his life.

One more college move to Northeastern in Tahlequah finally landed him a degree in speech and drama. In case he didn't go out and set Hollywood on fire he knew he better have a backup plan, so he had teaching drama as a fall back. He did his student teaching at McLain High School and Monroe Middle School in Tulsa.

Three years out of college he had an opportunity to enter the world of pro wrestling. To Bill, pro wrestling was a lot like drama, so he felt in some way he would still be fulfilling his dream to act. *One thing about Bill, he wasn't afraid to go through doors of opportunity. Some people never do, therefore they miss their chances to find their true niche in life.*

I'm sure as he was going through the different doors he was merely searching for his rightful place in this world. One step continued to lead to the next. Even though each step was not totally satisfying it was leading him down a path which he found later to be increasingly more satisfying.

During his pro wrestling career he became well acquainted with Leroy McQuirk and Bill Watts. Leroy was a well known wrestling promoter and Bill Watts was a pro wrestling star. Together, they took an interest in Bill and wanted to help him in whatever area they could.

Wrestling was still not giving Bill the satisfaction he so desperately needed. He was scheduled to make his television wrestling debut in Amarillo, Texas when he decided he just didn't want to go in that direction.

One day he was watching a newscaster on television and thought "1 can do what he is doing and probably even better." He happened to mention the idea to Leroy who immediately wanted to help him. Since the wrestling matches were being televised in 33 cities, Leroy was in contact with a lot of individuals in the television world.

Between Leroy and Bill Watts they were able to get Thomas a slot in Alexandria, Louisiana. Bill reported news, sports and weather there for a year and a half, as well as a 30 minute talk show called "Concerned." From there he went to Shreveport, Louisiana for a year and a half and then on to New Orleans for two years. All the while Bill was trying to substitute his desire to act with everything else that seemed to come his way. He had even convinced himself his television work was somehow related to acting only on the other side of the set.

Bill said he always heard "actors act not because they want to but because they have to." He was finding that statement to be more and more true.

After leaving New Orleans he came back to Tulsa and for a short time was the recreational supervisor for the Tulsa Housing Authority. That lasted a little over a year. He then went to KRMG radio reporting news. His desire to act still lay dormant.

One day his relationship with a particular person led him to someone who asked him to audition for a play at Theatre North. From then on, even though his life has been sprinkled with various other fields of endeavor, he has continued to pursue his dream of acting which has become his top priority.

Bill has appeared in numerous films, videos, and commercials throughout his home state of Oklahoma as well as around the country and abroad. He has appeared on television and radio talk shows on numerous occasions stressing the need for organization and cultural diversity.

He is a renowned speaker, facilitator, actor and community activist across the nation. At present, he is a faculty member of Tulsa Community College where he teaches several courses in sociology. Along with that he has established his own company "So You Wanna Productions" to assist individuals who are interested in pursuing an acting career. The production company offers Acting on Film Techniques, Tools of the Trade, Training for Video or Public Service Announcement Projects, How to Get an Agent and several more areas.

Bill admits most of his life has been made up of knowing someone who led him to someone else. Of course more exposure leads to more exposure. Bill feels fortunate to have accomplished as much as he has so far, but he definitely has no desire to quit pursuing avenues of opportunity that open for him. With four agents located in different states who continually work for him, he stays busy throughout the year. The next big break is always just around the corner because for Bill there is no quitting in sight. Like he said, "quit for what?" "I'm not here for just a good time, I'm here for a long time." *"I want to speak while my voice is still heard."*

Bill hopes he has helped a lot of people along the way. When he stands before God in Eternity he hopes to hear Him say "Well done, my good and faithful servant."

Bill knows there are times he falls short yet he asks himself, "Did I help somebody, did I extend a hand, did I inspire or motivate someone?" *"Life is a journey. Find someone who does what you would like to be doing and listen and watch them. Don't give up. Persevere. He who endures shall win. Always remember, overnight success is just a myth."*

I enjoyed my interview with Bill. I also was blessed to meet his wife Wanda who is a part of the "Prayz" singers. She has a story to tell and a voice that needs to be heard. After talking with her for a few minutes there is no doubt in my mind she will accomplish whatever she sets out to do.

Along with their children Phil, Kelease and Carmalitta, Bill and Wanda make a good team. Life will continue to unfold as it should for them. Even though Bill has been in the acting business for over 30 years, he still thinks the best is yet to come.

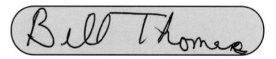

Bill Thomas - Judge

I had never met Judge Thomas before the day of our interview but I had become acquainted with his son, John. Realizing the quality that radiated from him, I felt his father would surely fit into the category of Distinguished Oklahoman. My assumption was correct.

Judge Thomas was born in Miami, Oklahoma on January 27, 1926. He was the son of Judge William Thomas Sr. and Mildred (Wilson) Thomas. Bill attributes his own desire to become a judge to the close relationship he shared with his father. It was touching to hear him speak so highly of his father believing if he could be half the man he was he would have a cause to be proud.

Judge Thomas said he was a sickly child who had an attack of polio

while in the first grade. Fortunately it only lasted for 14 weeks and he didn't suffer any crippling effects. He had diphtheria twice and his doctors were constantly on the lookout to see what that Thomas kid would catch next. He eventually grew out of those sickly years and life went on as it should.

Bill knew what the depression was but it never affected him like it did some of his friends because his family's financial status was somewhat better. However, it was of great importance to Bill's father that he instill in Bill and his brother Robert that even though they were being raised in an affluent home they were still no better than anyone else.

If the other kids wore overalls, Bill was required to wear them also. If the other kids wore cheap tennis shoes, Bill had to wear the same. He was taught to be just one of the gang.

Bill's father was a deacon in their local Baptist church and so of course Bill was raised in a Christian atmosphere. This only enhanced his desire to please his family and be a friend to all.

After attending high school in Miami he graduated from Oklahoma Military Academy in Claremore, Oklahoma. Bill entered the U.S. Navy. He was a radar operator and a fire control man for the Navy Artillery Fire until 1946. He then came back to Oklahoma, enrolled in Northeastern A&M College and later went on to Oklahoma University as a pre-law student.

On August 8, 1948 he married one of his high school classmates, Betty Lou Harper. After graduation they moved to Pryor on March 28, 1952. Bill and Betty were expecting their first child, William M. Thomas III. As a lawyer Bill didn't want to appear in front of his father while trying cases. He felt people would either believe he won a case because of his father or lost because of his father and Bill wanted to stand on his own merit.

In June of that year he hadn't been practicing too long when the county attorney, Jack Burris was assassinated in Locust Grove. Within a couple of hours Bill was appointed to take over his position. Bill served as county attorney in Pryor for five years. During that time their second son, John Philip was born in 1955 and then their daughter, Mary Ann in 1956.

Bill admits he was a strict father. As he progressed in his career he went from being a lawyer to a county attorney then a city judge, municipal judge and lastly an associate district judge. He was constantly aware of the breakdown of families who appeared before the court. Drugs were becoming a troublesome detriment to many young people and Bill was determined to protect his children the best way he could.

Obviously he and his wife Betty did a wonderful job raising their children. They have all become productive citizens and have given their parents every reason to be proud of them. His oldest son William attended Northeastern State University before entering the Marines. He then enrolled at the University of Missouri and received a degree in criminal justice. He is now a surveyor in Miami, Oklahoma. John was also a Marine, a graduate of Oral Roberts University and has a master's degree in psychology from Northeastern State University. He attended Louisville Seminary for a year believing he wanted to be a pastor, but soon found he was more suited to one on one counseling than congregational speaking. Their daughter Mary Ann is a graduate of Northeastern State University and is a History teacher in the Pitcher school system.

Judge Thomas held the position as district judge for 20 years. He primarily handled divorce and domestic cases. He really feels he was able to help a lot of people over the years change their minds about the direction they were taking their families.

He said the majority of divorces are caused from issues over money. Society is driven by the advertising appeal that "more is better." The pressure to attain what they can't afford causes credit cards to reach their maximum limit with interests rates so high they can't climb over the debt. Many young people want to attain immediately what their fathers and grandfathers acquired after many years of labor.

Even the television shows we spend hours watching proclaim to society that "more is better." Actors drive late model cars, wear expensive clothing and eat at the finest restaurants. Then in an attempt to experience what the imaginary world has to offer, people try to imitate the same behavior. In return it only causes destruction.

Judge Thomas believes in giving to his community. At one time he was president of the Junior Chamber of Commerce. He was the Democratic county chairman for 10 years and the National Committeeman for the Young Democrats. He is a member of Odd Fellows lodge #70, Masonic Lodge 100 and has been in the Lions Club for over 35 years with no absences. He is also the president of the Mayes County Historical Society. I would say he is involved in his community.

He said being involved allows you to meet other people who are interested in being successful in life and causes you to want to be better yourself. He also believes if a parent gets involved in the community their children will follow their example. In return it allows them a better opportunity to become a productive citizen. They are less likely to get involved in areas that will lead to destruction in their lives.

W. M Thomas, Jr.

B.J. Thomas

Singer

On June 24, 2000 I had the opportunity to see B.J. in concert for the first time at the Brady Theater in Tulsa, Oklahoma. I had conducted a phone interview the day before, but I was glad to get a chance to see him perform. He was dressed in a black pair of leather pants and a casual looking shirt. A gold chain hung around his neck and a gold wedding band often flashed as he brought his hand to his chest in a heart felt gesture.

B.J.'s voice is unmistakable. The quality and melodious sound still remains his trademark. His smile was contagious and for those of us who have heard his songs for years felt an incredible sense of kinship with him. It was refreshing to hear a song that left you with a warm feeling inside.

As I sat there and watched his performance, the glare of bright lights beat down on him and perspiration eventually began to cover his entire face. Occasionally he took the towel provided for him and lightly patted his face, but really to no avail. He was a real trooper. After an incredible performance in which he sang songs like: *Rain Drops Keep Fallin' On My Head, Hooked On a Feeling, I Just Can't Help Believin',* and *What Ever Happened To Old Fashioned Love,* he quickly changed clothes and came out to the lobby to sign autographs until every last person was satisfied. I was impressed to say the least.

B.J. was born in Hugo, Oklahoma and even though he was raised in Texas, he still has that friendly Oklahoma charm. I will remember his concert for a long time to come. Not because it was a flashy concert, because it wasn't. He didn't run across the stage or do any antics to keep you spellbound. He very simply sang with ease, poise, sincerity and caring of heart with that smile that made you feel right at home.

He is to be complimented for all he has accomplished over the years. B.J. is truly a legend and very worthy of the title "Distinguished Oklahoman."

I guess you would have to say singing is just what B.J. was put on this earth to do. He started singing with some of his teenage buddies when he was 15 years old. They formed a group and called themselves "The Triumphs." At first it was just for fun, never really thinking anything would become of it. There were a lot of "garage bands" in the late 1950's and very few really made careers out of their singing. However, B.J. and the band were having such a good time performing at dances and local gigs they decided to put together a few records using local companies in the Texas area.

Radio stations were kind enough to play some of those records so B.J. continued going down this musical path with still no idea where it would eventually lead him. Several years passed and B.J. was beginning to believe stardom and a Top 10 song was never to be. Then, when he was 23 years old, he recorded an old Hank William's song titled *I'm So Lonesome I Could Cry. It* went number one almost immediately. B.J. was on his way and his musical talent was going to take him there.

Since then, he has sold more than 50 million records and earned two platinum and eleven gold records. He has recorded in the pop, country, adult contemporary and gospel genres. He has won five Grammy and two Dove awards. In 1981, B.J. became the 60th member of the Grand Ole Opry.

B.J. admits he had a long struggle with drug addiction during a portion of his career. Thankfully, he was able to get a handle on it before he became a statistic like so many people during that era. Sometimes unfair judgments were made about B.J. during those drug days. I guess all of us should walk a mile in the other person's shoes before we judge too strongly.

He married his beautiful wife Gloria on December 9, 1968 and together they have raised three great daughters -Paige, Erin and Nora. The love between he and Gloria has carried them through a lot of storms in life. You can tell when B.J. sings a love song he is thinking about someone, and he unashamedly admits it is Gloria who is always on his mind.

B.J. grew up going to a Southern Baptist Church and yet he lacked a great deal of spiritual understanding. In 1976 he and

Gloria established a closer relationship with God in what he calls a "spiritual awakening." They began to realize if they wanted to be truly happy, their happiness had to come from within.

It was natural for B.J. to want to express his feelings through his music since he had been doing that all of his life. He recorded the first platinum album in gospel music history with his song *Home Where I Belong.* He was excited about his new found freedom from drugs and alcohol. He knew freedom had occurred because of his spiritual awakening and he was ready to share his joy with the world.

It was a wonderful time in his career and Christian music meant a great deal to him. He was singing his heart out to audiences of all ages. He gave them a mixture of the old songs that had brought him such success as well as the Christian songs that had opened up a whole new world for him. However, the time came when certain Christians felt it was wrong for him to sing Christian music mingled with secular songs. B.J. had a dilemma. How could he make the Christian world happy yet not turn his back on the music that had brought him to where he was. The answer was, he couldn't.

It was a confusing time for B.J. and his family. He had to re-evaluate where he stood on some issues and determine what was the right path for him to go down. As it turned out, he chose to continue singing what is categorized as secular music along with his gospel songs. Of course that left some people unhappy with his decision. There are some secular songs out on our air waves that shouldn't be sung in front of any audiences. But those aren't the kind of songs that have ever been a part of B.J.'s repertoire.

In my opinion, I think he made the right choice. I'm so glad that God looks on the heart, as opposed to us earthly creatures that look on the outer man.

B.J. feels very blessed to be in a profession he loves so much. He never plans to retire as long as he can continue to make music that people enjoy listening to. He never gets tired of performing. There are days that his body is physically tired and traveling begins to take its toll. But his love of music and the enjoyment he gets out of performing in front of his fans far outweighs any discomfort.

Hank Thompson

Singer/Songwriter

How could you think of the Midwest without visualizing horses galloping across the prairies or climbing the cliffs of a wooded hillside? And how could you think about country music without recalling the legendary brilliance of Hank Thompson?

On September 3, 1925 in Waco, Texas Henry William Thompson became the only child born to Ilda and Jule Thompson. In those days during the depression there was no such thing as the "country music business." There were singers and musicians such as Jimmie Rodgers and later Gene Autry, but they were icons that seemed too unreachable.

It wasn't until the late 1930's and into the 1940's that country music began taking on a more serious note. With the entrance of the Grand Ole Opry stars like Ernest Tubbs, Bill Monroe and Roy Acuff were beginning to emerge.

Hank got his first guitar when he was 10 years old. It was only meant to be played as a means of passing the time. But as time passed he became more and more acquainted with the hillbilly music of the day. By the time country music began forming into a business, Hank was well on his way to presenting some of his own creative tunes.

As a young boy he began honing his skills by performing in various amateur talent shows. His ability to entertain a crowd and display his musical skills began to open a lot of doors for him to sing and perform at numerous local functions. That success eventually landed him a daily sponsored radio program called "Hank The Hired Hand."

Even with all his early success he still viewed his attempts as a hobby, which occasionally brought in a few dollars.

During World War II Hank entered the Navy. Along with singing and picking his guitar for the restless guys in his unit, he also successfully pursued a trade as a radio technician. In officer's training the Navy sent him to various universities to continue his education. After he was discharged he returned to Texas with the intentions of returning to college and completing his degree. However, in the interim he obtained another radio program and began performing once again.

His popularity began to soar and fan mail started pouring in. For the first time Hank took a long look at his talents as a performer and felt compelled to give himself the opportunity to pursue a musical career. He put a band together which he named Brazos Valley Boys. Before long he had a #1 song on the Hit Parade of Hillbilly music with his original *Whoa Sailor* he had penned while entertaining his Navy buddies. Soon Hank was signed to Capitol Records and his hit *Humpty Dumpty Heart* peaked at #2.

In 1951 Hank took his western swing band and moved to Oklahoma where his fame just continued to soar. Hank Thompson and The Brazos Valley Boys were voted #1 Country Western Band for 15 consecutive years by Billboard magazine.

His 1952 hit *The Wild Side of Life* opened the door for Kitty Wells, the first female singer to top the country charts. Her answer to Hank's *The Wild Side Of Life* was put forth in her song *It Wasn't God Who Made Honkytonk Angels,* and marked her as the "First Lady of Country Music."

In the early 1950's while already performing a live television show in front of an excitable audience at WKY in Oklahoma City, The Hank Thompson Show became the first variety show to be viewed on a color broadcast.

Hank was making history, but it was only one of the "firsts" his career would experience. With his electronic knowledge Hank and his band were the first act to tour with a sound and lighting system; first to receive corporate tour sponsorship; first to record a live album HankThompson, *Live At The Golden Nugget In Las Vegas* released on Capitol Records in 1960; first country music show to play in Las Vegas and first to record in Hi-Fi stereo.

In the midst of it all he sold over 60 million records and became the first entertainer to take Western Swing into the domain of fashionable ballrooms such as the Meadowbrook in New York and The Prom in St. Paul.

While Hank was making an incredible name for himself in the world of country music, he was also making sure he continued to help others along the way. Wanda Jackson, Queen of Rockabilly, will forever be indebted to Hank for his willingness to share his spotlight with a young girl eager to set the musical world on fire.

After all these years, Wanda is still quick to acknowledge the role Hank played in her rise to stardom. As I interviewed Wanda she commented on the lasting effect Hank has on her life. Even today his influence is evident in the style and mannerism she puts forth while she's entertaining.

In 1989 Hank was honored when he was elected into the prestigious "Country Music Hall of Fame." Now, at age 75, Hank's life has spanned seven decades and there is no end in sight. His voice is still as clear and strong as it ever was, a fact he contributes to the wisdom of singing in his own voice range and not straining past his own musical realm.

I can't even imagine what it must feel like to be in his shoes and know he has shared in so many history-making moments of country music. He is often referred to as the "King of Western Swing," his brand of music, from it's first introduction in the 1940's was like no others. Hank's music was a magical blend of big band bravura with the fiddle and steel guitar joining in.

My phone interview with Hank was enlightening as well as enjoyable, as I pictured this gentleman of western grandeur entertaining countless individuals over the decades. I've always had a soft spot in my heart for people with the "wisdom of the years" and continually find myself soaking up the knowledge they so easily exude.

After spending almost 40 years in Oklahoma, Hank and his wife, Ann moved back to Texas a few years ago, but he still makes occasional visits to his second home.

Patti Thompson

Singer

I used to watch Patti sing on the Oral Roberts Show many years ago. She was bubbly, energetic and always had a pearly white smile. On the day of our interview she apparently hadn't changed a bit.

Patti was born in Durant, Oklahoma but grew up in Oregon and lived there until she graduated from high school at the age of 18. As a small child coming from a Christian home, Patti had one request that she continually asked God. "Please" she said. "Allow me to do something in my life that will fulfill my destiny." It was a rather wise request for such a young child of 5, but she felt in her heart God had a reason for her life.

When Patti was 11 her father developed crippling rheumatoid arthritis which kept him from functioning in many ways as a father should. However, being the only girl of three children, Patti was well aware of how much her father loved and cherished his little girl. In spite of her father's inability to share activities with Patti, he instilled in her a sense of worth that made her feel like she could accomplish anything she wanted to do.

Her talents of writing and singing began at the age of 15. She became part of a Christian music group called The Continentals. Even though Patti loves varied types of music, she prefers writing and singing gospel music. It helps her stay focused on what is important in her life. It keeps her centered on her hopes and dreams and keeps her faith alive. She said she has often said a song is like a prayer in which all of your inner longings flow out to God. *She believes many of the songs she has written are really conversations acknowledging God's blessings in her life.*

I asked Patti what a person should do if he doesn't know what his destiny is. Her answer was simple. "Intensely ask God over and over."

In 1965 Patti moved to Tulsa, Oklahoma and enrolled at Oral Roberts University. It was ORU's first year of classes. Because of Patti's beautiful voice she became the lead female vocalist for the ORU World Action Singers, while Richard Roberts was the male vocalist. By 1968 Richard and Patti had become not only a team on television, but a couple in life.

Patti's main goal was to fulfill her childhood request to God that He would use her to fulfill His purposes for her life. Marriage to Richard seemed like the natural thing to do. They both loved God and sang so well together it only made sense that they should be married. What neither one of them realized was how much the ministry and the television show would take over their lives. They never had a chance to grow up or grow together. The pressures put upon them were so great while their youth still lacked much in Godly wisdom.

Of course most people know that Richard and Patti's marriage ended in divorce. It was a sad and painful time for everyone involved. Even television viewers felt the pain of such a tremendous loss.

Many years have passed since then and life has gone on as it should. Patti has continued to use her God-given voice and music abilities to worship God and give encouragement to others. She debuted *El Shaddai,* The Musical which she co-wrote and in which she sang the female lead at Carnegie Hall and John F. Kennedy Center as well as many other major halls across America. She has sung before kings and queens and traveled all over the world. *She strongly believes how our lives turn out is a result of what we decide to do in the midst of the painful times.*

Life offers us an opportunity to develop character and wisdom. The secret of life is when pain, humiliation and sorrow appear to have defeated you and yet you pick yourself up and walk in spite of it all. Patti believes that we make life choices not because of what happens to us; or what someone does to us; but life choices are made as a clear reflection of our own inner values. No amount of pain of loss can steal one's destiny. The only thing that can stop one's destiny is disobedience, self imposed guilt, stubbornness or self pity.

I think I could have sat and talked to Patti all day. It was easy to relate to her life and the way she dealt with her relationship with God. That old saying "Don't judge a man, until you have walked a mile in his shoes" seems to fit well for the events that happened in Patti's past. She is a beautiful woman inside and out. There is no doubt God has and will continue to use her in a mighty way, just as she prayed so many years ago.

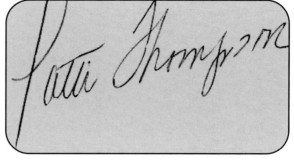

Ralph G. Thompson - Judge

Judge Ralph G. Thompson was born in Oklahoma City in 1934, the son of Lee B. and Elaine Bizzell Thompson and the grandson of Dr. William Bennett Bizzell, fifth president of the University of Oklahoma.

Even though he grew up in Oklahoma City, since his grandfather was president of the University, Norman became like a second home. His first seven Thanksgivings and Christmases were spent at the Boyd House-the Presidential Home.

His school years were spent in the Oklahoma City public schools. In 1952 he enrolled at the University of Oklahoma and in 1956 he received a degree in business administration and a USAF commission. He spent two years in Oklahoma University law school before entering the Air Force where he spent three years on active duty. He was engaged in criminal investigation and counter-intelligence activities as a special agent of the Office of Special Investigations.

After returning home he completed his law degree and graduated from law school in 1961. He continued as an active reservist for the next 24 years. Upon his retirement from the Air Force Reserve in 1987 as a colonel, he was awarded the Legion of Merit.

Judge Thompson said, " In my career, I've worn judicial black and Air Force blue and I've worn them both with equal pride."

For 15 years prior to his appointment to the federal court, Judge Thompson was in the private practice of law in Oklahoma City in partnership with his father, Lee B. Thompson. Lee was president of the Oklahoma Bar Association and a member of the American College of Trial Lawyers.

In 1964 he married Barbara Hencke, an Oklahoma City French teacher. Together they raised three daughters, all of whom are graduates of the University of Oklahoma -Lisa, Elaine and Maria. In 1995 Barbara was selected as both Oklahoma's and America's Mother of the Year.

Judge Thompson's career in public service began in 1966, serving two terms as a member of the Oklahoma House of Representatives. In what he considers one of his most satisfying contributions in public service, he was one of the chief authors of the Oklahoma Judicial Reform Plan. This plan, by constitutional amendment, provided a new and reformed court system for the State of Oklahoma. He also authored Oklahoma's first modern narcotics control act. After his first year in office he was named "Oklahoma City's Outstanding Young Man" and one of three "Outstanding Young Oklahomans" by the Oklahoma State Junior Chamber of Commerce.

During those four years he became closely associated with Dewey Bartlett, Jim Inhofe, Henry Bellmon, David Boren and George Nigh. In 1970 Governor Bartlett was running for re-election and asked Thompson to be his running mate as Lieutenant

Governor. Bartlett and Thompson were both Republicans. George Nigh was running for re-election as Lieutenant Governor and he was a Democrat. He and Thompson were friends even though they were opponents. It was one of the cleanest political races ever fought because they shared mutual friendship and respect. However, neither Bartlett or Thompson were successful. Governor Bartlett lost to David Hall and Thompson lost to George Nigh.

In 1972 Dewey Bartlett was elected to the U.S. Senate. In 1975 with his sponsorship and that of Senator Henry Bellmon, President Gerald Ford appointed Ralph Thompson to the Federal Court for the Western District of Oklahoma. Judge Thompson was 40 years old when he stepped into that position becoming one of the youngest federal judges in the nation.

In 1980 he was named "Outstanding Federal Trial Judge in the State of Oklahoma" by the Oklahoma Trial Lawyers Association. In 1988 was awarded the first Judicial Service Award by the Oklahoma County Bar Association. He was Chief Judge of the Court from 1986 to 1993. From 1992 to 1994 he served as President of the United States District Judges Association of the Tenth Circuit. He is an Oklahoma University alumnus member of Phi Beta Kappa and The Order of the COIF. In 1993 he received O.U.'s Distinguished Service Award, the university's and its alumni association's highest honor.

By appointment of Chief Justice Rehnquist, he served a seven year term on the United States Foreign Intelligence Surveillance Court, a court of seven federal judges empowered to deal with foreign espionage activities.

In 1997 he was elected the Tenth Circuit's U.S. District Judge representative to the Judicial Conference of the United States, the policy making body of the federal judiciary. By appointment of the Chief Justice, in 1998, he became one of the six senior executive members of that body.

He is the co-author, with Bob Burke, of *Bryce Harlow, Mr. Integrity,* for which they were nominated for a Pulitzer Prize in 2000.

Five seconds before the Oklahoma City bombing, Judge Thompson was standing at his office window looking out over the Murrah building giving dictation to his secretary. He finished his dictation, put his microphone down and took the tape out of the dictating machine. He turned and walked to his secretary in the outer office to hand her the tape and the explosion occurred. His office was destroyed and no one would have survived if they had been standing by the window. Five seconds saved his life. Yet many of his close friends lost their lives along with their children.

I can't even imagine what that day was like for Judge Thompson. Obviously his life was spared for a reason. He is very grateful for the way his life and career have unfolded. He believes he has received far more in life than he would have ever had reason to expect.

Jim Thorpe

Athlete

Jim Thorpe will forever be known as a legendary athlete, a man whose athletic abilities far surpassed the norm. In 1950 he was selected as the nation's Most Outstanding Athlete of the first half of the 20th Century and in 2000 he was awarded ABC's Wide World of Sports Athlete of the Century.

Jim was born a twin on May 28, 1887 in a one room cabin in Prague, Oklahoma. His mother Charlotte and father Hiram farmed the land and kept the family fed and clothed, but life was not easy and not all of the Thorpe children survived. Out of 11 children only five grew to adulthood.

Jim had some French and Irish blood but he was mostly Sac and Fox Indian heritage. His Indian name was Wa-Tha-Huck, translated "Bright Path." He was a descendant of Black Hawk, a Sac and Fox warrior. It is reported that Jim was as proud of being a descendant of Black Hawk as he had ever been of his many athletic awards.

Hiram and Charlotte believed in education for their children. They both had attended mission schools in Kansas and realized how important it was for a person to be able to read and write. A Sac and Fox mission school was established in their area in 1872, so when Jim and his twin brother Charlie turned 6 years old in the summer of 1893 they were sent to this manual-labor school. The school placed the children under a regimen of strict discipline, manual labor and part-time study.

When Jim was very young he adapted to the regimen of the school, but as he grew older he began to rebel and ran away on several occasions. His twin brother, Charlie died of pneumonia in 1897 and from then on Jim refused to stay at the mission school. In 1898 after repeatedly punishing Jim for running away, his father Hiram had him transferred to Haskell School located 300 miles from their home in Lawrence, Kansas. The school was run like an Army post with reveille at 5:45 a.m. and taps at 9:00 p.m. Even though Jim began learning a great deal about sports while he was at Haskell he still rebelled about being placed there.

His mother died during childbirth in 1902 at the age of 39 when Jim was only 15 years old. His father remarried three months later to a woman named Julia Mixon and a few months later they had a son. For a couple of years Jim attended a public school at Garden Grove so he could help take care of two of his younger siblings. Unfortunately, Hiram died unexpectedly in 1904, a few weeks after Jim had transferred to a mission school in Carlisle, Pennsylvania.

Jim had been a loner since the death of his twin brother Charlie, but now that both of his parents were gone he needed something to give him purpose in life. He chose to immerse himself in sports.

In 1908 Jim was recognized as a superior athlete when he was selected as a third-team All American halfback. Then in 1909 he won five gold medals and a bronze medal for the Carlisle track team. During the summer of 1909 he went to North Carolina to play minor league baseball for the Rocky Mountain team. He returned to play baseball for Fayetteville, North Carolina in 1910.

During the next two years, 1911 and 1912 Jim played some memorable football for Carlisle. Also in 1912 he went on to try out for the U.S. Olympic team at the Polo Grounds in New York City. At the conclusion of the tryouts he qualified for both the pentathlon and decathlon Olympic events. The American Olympic team won a total of 16 gold medals that year, two of which were Jim Thorpe's.

On February 1, 1913 Jim signed a contract with the New York Giants baseball team and in October of the same year he married Iva Miller who he met at Carlisle School. Their first child, James Jr., was born in 1915 followed by three daughters over the next eight years, Gail, Charlotte and Grace. His first born only lived until the age of three when he died of infantile paralysis.

Jim went on to play with Cincinnati and then the Boston Braves. His last official game was in 1928 at the age of 40. During his baseball career he also played football during the winter months. At the time football wasn't as big a sport as it is now. In 1920 representatives of 11 professional football teams met in Canton, Ohio to form the American Professional Football Association and elected Jim Thorpe as its president. Two years later the organization became the National Football League. The entry fee for a team to join the association back then was $100. Now it is millions of dollars. How do you figure that?

Jim and Iva divorced in 1923 and in 1925 Jim married Freeda Kirkpatrick. They had four sons together, Carl Phillip, William, Richard and John.

After Jim retired from his athletic career he began playing small parts in Hollywood films. He also became quite a sought after lecturer on a nationwide tour of schools promoting athletics. Unfortunately the speaking engagements kept Jim away from home a lot, which must have caused some friction at home. Jim and Freeda divorced in 1941 after 15 years of marriage. He suffered a heart attack in 1942 which caused him to move back to Oklahoma.

On June 2, 1945 he married Patricia Gladys Askew who had been a huge fan of his during his professional football days. She encouraged him with his speaking tours and convinced him to charge more than he had currently been receiving.

Burt Lancaster was cast by Warner Brothers to play the part of Jim Thorpe in a film titled Jim Thorpe-All American in 1949. Warner employed Jim as a technical advisor to help Lancaster learn the basics of kicking a football.

In 1951 Jim had surgery to remove a cancerous spot on his lip and in 1952 he suffered his second non-fatal heart attack. But his third heart attack was fatal on March 28, 1953, two months after celebrating his 65th birthday.

For a while Jim's body was placed in a mausoleum in Shawnee, Oklahoma and was later transferred to Tulsa. Yet his final resting place was chosen by his wife Patricia when she moved him to northeastern Pennsylvania. The town of Mauch Chunk and East Mauch Chunk renamed their town Jim Thorpe, Pennsylvania. The memorial was placed in a small field along route 903 just outside the town's business district.

In 1955 the NFL named its annual Most Valuable Player award the Jim Thorpe Trophy. Also each year a Jim Thorpe award is given to the best collegiate defensive back. Since his death he has been voted to the National College Football Hall of Fame, National Indian Hall of Fame, Pennsylvania Hall of Fame, The National Football Hall of Fame and The National Track and Field Hall of Fame. If you travel through Prague and Yale, Oklahoma you will see that both towns have signs that say "Home of Jim Thorpe." Yale was where he shared his home with his first wife Iva Miller which was later opened to the public.

Wayman Tisdale

Basketball Star

If you know anything about basketball, you have heard about Wayman Tisdale. He is a Tulsa, Oklahoma, Booker T. Washington High School graduate who was a three time All-American and the first freshman ever to be named to the Associated Press All-American Squad. He was a 1984 Olympic Gold Medalist, leading the team in rebounding with a 6.4 boards per game average. He holds Oklahoma University's career record for points, rebounds, field goals, field goal attempts and field goal percentages, and was voted the Most Valuable Player in Big Eight history.

Wayman will tell you his success began as a result of being born into the close knit family of Louis and Debra Tisdale. As one of six children, Wayman still recalls that growing up his best friends were his siblings Brenda, Larry, Weldon, William and Danny. They were who you would usually find him hanging out with.

Wayman's father was a Baptist preacher and his mother, a homemaker. The spiritual influences of his parents were carried through into adulthood with all six of their children. Three of his brothers became ministers and his sister married a minister. Even though Wayman and his brother Danny didn't choose the ministry route, they both have lived their lives with the same spiritual values that their parents instilled in them.

As a child Wayman thought he would spend his entire life playing music. His love for music and playing bass began when he was a young boy and his father gave him a toy guitar. Like most little boys who at the time aren't experienced musicians, it wasn't long before Wayman had broken all but two strings on his toy guitar. But those two strings had an amazing bass sound that Wayman never quite forgot.

He began to play bass when he was in grade school and then for the church choir. By the time he reached junior high his height was beginning to catch everyone's attention. His brothers all played basketball, so it was an assumption that Wayman should play too, even though at the time he wasn't the least bit interested. He just wanted to play music.

In the eighth grade he played basketball simply because people thought he ought to. But by the ninth grade, he played because he wanted to. From the ninth grade through the twelfth grade he was known as the "Man of the Year." ABC, NBC and 60 Minutes came to Tulsa to view Wayman as an exceptional high school athlete. Rolling Stone Magazine did a huge spread on him in their monthly publication.

News of Wayman's young success was everywhere. Colleges across the country were trying to recruit him. Wayman had his choice, but he chose to go to Oklahoma University. His father told him if he made a name playing at OU then every time Oklahoma basketball was mentioned they would have to mention him.

In 1985, after three years at Oklahoma University, he skipped his senior year to play for the Indiana Pacers. He played for three and a half years before he was traded to Sacramento where he spent five and a half years. Then he opted to go to the Phoenix Suns for three years, ending a 12 year career in the NBA.

Wayman brought out an interesting point for what motivates a man to success, and that is "purpose" (a reason for doing something). In basketball or anything else that Wayman has excelled in, success came when he decided to be the best he could be. He had "purpose."

So often people miss out on their dreams because either someone tells them they can't do it or they lack the drive to make it come to pass. Even though Wayman was playing professional basketball he never forgot his love for music. He continued to play bass every chance he could, hoping someday he would be able to play professionally and make a name for himself in music as well. He had "purpose."

Several people tried to tell him he couldn't be an athlete and a musician, but Wayman wouldn't listen. He knew God had given him the talent, but it was up to him to use it. If he wanted to see success he had to do whatever it took to get there. So he hung out with high level musicians and learned from them and continued to hone his talent. At first he wasn't taken seriously. People thought music was just a novelty to him, since all they could see him as was an athlete. But he hung in there and eventually got over the hurdle to become a bonified professional musician.

His first musical contract was with the former Motown Records in 1994 with his first album titled *Power Forward*. Since then he has put out his second album titled *Decisions* produced by Atlantic Records, the oldest record company in the industry and the number one record company in the world.

Wayman moved back to Tulsa in 1997 after retiring from the NBA. Along with his own musical career Wayman has established a company called Tisway Productions which produces music for other jazz, R&B and gospel music artists. Wayman also has set up a scholarship foundation as well as his own line of practice gear that is sold at "Just for Feet" stores across the country.

Wayman is one of those big guys that walks into a room and people can't help but notice. At around 6'8" he of course towers above most everyone. However, to go along with his over extended height, he appears to have a heart large enough to balance him out quite well. Wayman truly is a man that has proven as he himself will tell you, *"Putting God first in your life opens doors that only He can open."*

Doris Eaton Travis - Ziegfeld Follies

As one of seven children born to Charles and Mary Eaton on March 4, 1904 in Norfolk, Virginia, Doris has earned her way into the hearts of many over the course of her life. Her father was a line-a-type operator for the newspaper in Norfolk. To increase his salary, the family moved to Washington, D.C. where the last two of their seven children were born. It was there where Doris's show business career began.

Evelyn, the oldest sibling who was 17 at the time-10 years older than Doris-loved the theatre. One day while she was reading the newspaper she ran across an advertisement telling that the New York Shubert Theatrical Company was coming to town performing the play "The Bluebird" and they needed some local children to play some of the parts. The play was to be performed at the Belasco Theatre in Washington, D.C. Evelyn quickly asked her mother if she would allow her to take Pearl, Mary and Doris to the audition. Their mother agreed. When the Eaton children arrived the director hired all three on the spot. Evelyn didn't dance or perform but she was a great talent agent for her siblings.

Shortly after the appearance in "The Bluebird," Evelyn found another ad placed by the local Poli's Stock Company needing children for one of their plays.

Doris's mother gave consent again for Evelyn to take the children to the director of the local stock company. Not only were the three-Mary, Pearl and Doris hired but also a younger brother and a cousin living with the Eaton family. This play was called "Mrs. Wiggs of the Cabbage

Patch" and needed seven children, five of which were supplied by the Eaton family. From then on the director told his assistant that whenever a child was needed for a play to " Just call Mrs. Eaton for she has them all ages and sizes and sexes."

One December at the close of the season, the company borrowed "The Bluebird" from the Shuberts for the Christmas week production. Mary and Doris were now old enough to play the leading roles. Shortly after this the Shuberts decided to put out another touring company of "The Bluebird" and asked the stock company for the names of the children who had played it for them. Soon came a call from the Shubert office to Mother Eaton to bring the two children -Mary and Doris -to New York for an audition, all expenses paid. The children were hired and at the end of the road tour the family was moved to New York, since it seemed several of them were developing talent that brought lucrative engagements in theatrical circles. It was a bold move for the family but it turned out to be the right one. By this time Doris was 11 years old. The Shuberts recognized sister Mary's talent for ballet dancing and sent her to the outstanding classical ballet school conducted by Theodore Kosloff. The Poli Company continued to call on Mrs. Eaton to supply children for their New England states companies and this kept Doris busy, missing much of the formal education for those years, making it up in summer classes quite often.

In 1918 when Doris was 14 years old, her sister Pearl had become a chorus girl in the Ziegfeld Follies, the most popular show on Broadway. She had become the director's assistant. They were in the process of putting together a group of chorus girls who would go on tour in place of the several New York girls who didn't want to go on the road.

One day Doris asked her mother if she could go with Pearl to the New Amsterdam theatre where the Follies performed and where they were holding the rehearsals. Her mother consented. During a break, Pearl came over and sat on the bench where Doris was sitting. Before long, the director came over to give Pearl some instructions. He kept looking at Doris and finally asked, "Who is this?" Pearl introduced Doris and the director asked if Doris could dance. Pearl said "yes." He then wanted to know if she could dance well enough to understudy Ann Pennington one of the star dancers in the Follies and travel on the road tour all expenses paid accompanied by her mother. Again Pearl said "Yes." After the family discussion it was agreed to accept the offer. The next day Doris went to the rehearsal and became a Ziegfeld Follies Girl. Doris was with the Follies in 1918,1919, and 1920. She described the Follies as being a fantasyland. When she would go through the stage door, put on her make-up, dress in costume and appear on stage, she felt like she had just stepped into another world. The Follies began in 1912. During the stock market crash they were not produced for a couple of years but Ziegfeld re-established the company and remained a few more years with annual productions.

After the three years in the Follies, during the period between productions, a theatrical broadway agent approached Mrs. Eaton to let Doris meet a movie director from London who was looking for a young girl to play the leading role in a silent movie he was developing. It was 1921 and the movie industry in England was still very young in London. Apparently the director felt he had to come to America to find the right person to fill the role. Doris was thrilled with the opportunity. Her mother was to travel with her. The experience was exciting and educational for some of the segments of the story took the company to Egypt for several location scenes.

After returning to the states Doris was offered an opportunity to go to Hollywood as a featured dancer in a musical review at the Cocoanut Grove in the Ambassador Hotel. The dining room which was patronized by many of the movie stars. The engagement ended and she married the producer who died from a heart attack a few months after the marriage.

She then moved back to New York, rejoining her family and continuing her show business career between Broadway and Hollywood. With the financial crash in 1929 the number of plays produced on Broadway or elsewhere was cut drastically which meant actors and actresses had few opportunities to work. By 1936 Doris realized she would have to find another way to make a living. Dancing was all she knew. A friend of hers called one night and told Doris she had taken her son to the Arthur Murray studios of social and tap dancing for tap dancing lessons. The instructor had said that they needed another tap teacher. Doris went to the studio the next day, had an interview with Arthur Murray who was impressed with her theatrical background, and hired her immediately. That was the beginning of a whole new career for Doris. Two years later, with one of the other instructors with whom she had much practice and done many exhibitions, she and her partner Cy Andrews opened the first Arthur Murray studio outside of New York. This was the beginning of the development of branch studios across the country for Arthur Murray, all modeled after the success of Doris and Cy in Detroit, Michigan. In 1964 Doris bought out Cy's interest in the Michigan Franchise and continued on her own. She had remarried during her partnership with Cy. In 1940 she had broken the studio rules and went out with one of her students. For the next eight years Paul H. Travis and Doris had many engagements. In 1949 they decided to make it official and were married in a little church around the corner from the studio. Over the years Paul and Doris had many delightful evenings of dancing together. Paul had continued to take lessons at the studio and had reached a professional level of talent doing many dance exhibitions with Doris on the local television show she produced in Detroit for seven seasons. No doubt it was an activity that kept them both in shape and feeling young.

After buying Cy's interest in the Michigan Arthur Murray franchise, Doris opened several studios throughout the state, finally numbering nineteen. At the time, Paul developed five small specialty mills to manufacture small items the automotive companies needed but did not want to set up machinery in their large factories. The time came when he received a lucrative offer to sell his factories to a large corporation. With this accomplished Paul turned his attention toward looking for a so-called retirement activity. Breeding and racing quarter horses appealed to him so Doris sold her Arthur Murray studios and she and Paul purchased an 880 acre ranch in Norman, Oklahoma. They moved in 1970 and decided to become useful Oklahomans.

I was amazed to find out Doris had received a bachelor's degree in history at the University Oklahoma in 1992 at age 88 with a 3.65 average. It took her 11 years to complete the task but she did it and now wants to pursue a master's degree. She said, *"Life can never grow dull if you keep on learning."*

In 1998 The Oklahoma Heritage Association named her as its Oklahoma Goodwill Ambassador. As if that wasn't enough, Doris was also asked to return to the newly renovated New Amsterdam theatre in New York to appear as a special guest with four other former Ziegfeld Follies girls at Broadway's annual Easter Bonnet Charity Competition. This appearance led to a request by Rosie O'Donnell to appear as a guest on her show. Last but not least came a request from Hollywood to play a small part in the Jim Carrey movie "Man on the Moon."

Doris has had an exciting and fulfilling career. Her family biography *The Days We Danced* will soon be published. There seems to be no slowing down for Doris and why should she? I asked her how she has stayed so vibrant and she said, *"Your body is at the mercy of your mind. So keep your mind active and you will continue to progress."*

Doris Eaton Travis

Frosty Troy
Speaker / Journalist

I've only heard Frosty speak in person once, but it was enough to make a lasting memory. Frosty is from McAlester, Oklahoma. He was sixth in a family of eleven children. He describes himself as being a skinny kid who wasn't into football and sports like the rest of his brothers. He would rather be found tucked away in some quiet place reading a good book. His favorite library was in the home of his grandmother, where he says he spent numerous hours reading every book on the shelves.

He received his education at St. John's Catholic School, and at one time had considered becoming a Priest. Yet, as he began to mature intellectually there was a part of him that seemed to rebel against not being allowed to question authority. Even though his heart leaned in a spiritual direction there was something lacking.

One day Sister Mary Andrew a Benedictine nun, acknowledged his creative abilities and suggested he should become a writer. From that point forward, his life's journey was set.

So, how did Frosty Troy become such a well sought after speaker and acclaimed journalist? His brothers had often teased him for not wanting to pass a football back and forth or swing a punch at an opposing boxer. Given his size, Frosty wasn't cut out for sports. The only thing he could focus on was how to make a difference by filling notebooks into the night--often under a blanket, using a Boy Scout flashlight.

Later in life, his athletic brothers came to realize that even though sports is great, it only last for a while. Frosty on the other hand could write for the rest of his life.

After high school and serving in the Army in Korea with two other brothers, Frosty began his quest to become a writer. With some additional higher education under his belt, he went to work for the McAlester New-Capital, Muskogee Phoenix and Lawton Constitution. By the mid 1950's he was hired by the Tulsa Tribune. He loved the Tribune. He recalls the great staff, award-winning reporters who taught him so much. Publisher Jenkin Lloyd Jones gave Frosty opportunities to expand his journalistic career and hone the talent that he was so eager to display to the world.

Frosty was assigned to the state capitol bureau and then the Washington Bureau. He eventually became associate editor, which put him as the second in command at the paper. Along the way he was writing articles on social issues for the Oklahoma City Diocesan Catholic newspaper. The Sooner Catholic. It was closed when the subsidy was withdrawn due to the paper's fierce opposition to the Vietnam war.

Father John Joyce tried to keep it going as an independent journal, renamed The Oklahoma Observer, but he gave up and offered it to Frosty. With the support of his wife Helen, he jumped at the offer to take the paper. He left the Tribune after 13 successful years, borrowing $18,000 to keep the Observer going. With Helen as publisher, they launched Oklahoma's only "second opinion."

The Observer was and always has been, a journal of commentary on politics, government and social issues. In the early years, Helen refused to leave their two children to fend for themselves or stay with sitters, so she published The Observer in the bedroom of their home until their children graduated from high school.

Frosty remarked how that he and Helen's parenting was to constantly be "in the face" of their children. To be there when they got home from school. To be at all the school functions. To be the homeroom mother, or in Frosty's case, the P.T.A. President. In Frosty's and Helen's opinion "to be or not to be," determines whether or not you raise "good" kids.

At first the paper was partially funded by 22 advertisers. However, when someone else is helping to pay your way they want to contribute in the decision making. That didn't set well with Frosty. For years he had been given ample opportunities to speak around the country. As time went on the speaking engagements became lucrative enough that Helen and Frosty no longer needed advertisers. They decided to rely on his speeches and the good graces of his faithful newspaper subscribers.

The paper has a circulation that covers every zip code in the state. Most of the people who subscribe are socially committed. His goal is to make people think about the issues. He is not concerned about whether he changes minds, he gives reader the opportunity to take a second look, a chance to think.

Frosty said, *"The real gift of a thinking person is to be able to hold opposing opinions in your mind at the same time and weigh them both equally."* We all find that hard to do at times. It seems to go along with the proverbial "ego trip" we sometimes take.

Frosty and Helen have published The Observer for over thirty years and they still believe that education is the key to every problem we have in this country. He hopes in some way The Observer and his numerous speaking engagements have helped to inform people, or at least allowed them to "think" about the different options we have as Americans.

With the recognition and numerous distinguished awards that Frosty has received over the years, I believe he has accomplished what he set out to do. As I said earlier, if you ever hear Frosty speak, whether you agree with his ideas or not, you won't forget his ability to make you stop and think about your own.

Frosty was fortunate to have realized at an early age that he was a gifted writer and speaker. Yet *he feels that everyone has a gift within them, but so few find out what the gift is because they don't really spend the time to look for it. Many people give up too easily assuming that the gift doesn't exist when in fact they haven't really looked. "Be prepared to spend some time* pursuing your gifts."

In closing, I was reminded of Frosty's spiritual interests which began so many years ago. He opted not to become a Catholic Priest, but he never forgot God's guidance in his life. Since this country was built on spiritual values, *Frosty believes that if you show him a person who is successful in his personal life as well as his public life, then they will usually have spiritual values.*

He often tells young people that he would never presume to tell them what to believe, because that would insult their intelligence. *However, he encourages them to launch a spiritual journey, to find something bigger than themselves and their family to believe in, because there will come a time when the valley is too deep and the hill too high and the only way to make it is to cry out for God's help.*

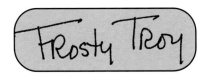

Billy Tubbs - Coach

Coach Billy Tubbs admits that he is probably viewed as not being politically correct in his views and speech. I had heard that about Coach Tubbs, but in spite of it he has managed to create quite a career for himself. Billy was born in St. Louis, Missouri, and lived a few years in Arkansas before moving to Tulsa when he was in the fifth grade. I was saddened when I learned that his father had died when Billy was only two years old and his mother died when he was thirteen. Fortunately, he had a married brother nine years older than he who became his second Dad and took on the responsibility of raising him. Too many young boys with those kinds of obstacles would have been devastated. Yet Billy seemed to adjust remarkably and said he never considered himself as deprived or underprivileged.

He did however learn the value of work at a very young age. While some boys were out playing with their friends, Billy was washing windows and making wire coat hangers at the cleaners where his mother worked. During his free time, when not under the watchful eye of his older brother, Billy was pretty much on his own roaming around the streets of Tulsa checking in with Mom occasionally. Since his brother was athletic, Billy was constantly around older guys playing baseball and basketball and grew to love sports. He thought since he wasn't an academic wizard, sports was probably the hook that kept him enrolled in school when a lot of other boys his age were dropping out and getting jobs.

Billy received a basketball scholarship at Lonmorris College in Jacksonville, Texas, which was a good thing, or he probably wouldn't have pursued a college degree. After two years he transferred to Lamar University in Beaumont, Texas, where he continued to play ball. As it turns out, even though he didn't go to college with the idea of being a coach, somewhere in the process he began to realize that was exactly what he should do. He seemed to be surrounded with coaches and people who encouraged him to excel and helped him make good decisions concerning his career. So for a young guy that started out in life not caring about academics, college, or necessarily a career, he graduated with a Masters Degree in Education.

His first teaching job was as a head coach at a high school in Crockett, Texas, for one year. Then he returned to his Alma Mater, Lamar University where he became the assistant coach and stayed eleven years. He loved Crockett, Texas, and he loved Lamar University, but his dream was to someday be one of the best coaches in America and to climb professionally to a lofty plateau. In order to do that, he had to leave one great school and go to another one. It wasn't about money, he said, it was about opportunity. So he took a head coaching job at Southwestern University in Georgetown, Texas. In order to take the job he had to take a pay cut, but he knew it was a step up the plateau, so he made the move.

I asked Coach Tubbs if climbing the plateau wasn't for money, then what was it for? "I guess ego," he said. "But even more than that you just want to be in the big leagues if you are going to play professional sports. That comes from having a competitive nature."

I could understand that, because unless you have no drive at all, everybody wants to excel in whatever they set out to do.

He stayed at Southwestern for two years and then relocated to two more colleges before finally coming to Oklahoma University as their head coach for fourteen years. It's no secret that Billy Tubbs was known as the "winningest coach" at OU, reaching goals that people projected they could not reach. Billy said that he loves to not only break records, but to set records that can't be broken.

Billy left Oklahoma University in 1994 to become head coach at Texas Christian University for no reason other than he was ready for a change. Who knows, maybe someday he and his wife Patricia will move back to Oklahoma, since they have a grown son and daughter still living here. Until then, he will continue to set high goals for himself and his players on whatever court he may be on.

Since coaching a game is about winning, I asked Coach Tubbs to give me some tips for succeeding in any area of life and he said, *"To be successful you have to be determined and make your goal an obsession. If you don't put a lot of time and energy into it, then you have nothing to lose and will probably give up before the task is completed. Winning or succeeding is nothing more than an ATTITUDE."*

John Venturella - Songwriter

I met John a couple of years ago when he contacted me concerning my previous book, *Movers and Shakers*. He had recently produced a fascinating poster depicting the names of famous Oklahomans. Since unknowingly we had been working on the same informative track he suggested we pool our respective ideas and promote them together occasionally. It became a winning situation for both of us not only financially but in the friendship that grew and continues to grow.

John is an incredible person who I felt deserved to wear the title of "Distinguished Oklahoman" even though by the twist of his tongue you are immediately alerted that he is originally from the big city of Brooklyn, New York.

John's parents are both from Italy, a place I always picture as being the romantic mecca of the world. Of course, how can you think of Italy or Italians without visualizing large family gatherings with members preparing to sit down for a mouth watering "pasta" dinner? Even though New York became the geographical location for their family gatherings, the Italian influence still remained vivid. Food was a great way of expressing love for one another. John remembers quite well the aroma of garlic, onions and parsley that seemed to always seep from his mother's kitchen as she sang out in her operatic voice.

Since John was the only male child in a family with three sisters who watched his every move, he became well acclimated to a woman's point of view. For John, his close knit family gave him the stability he needed to become a strong, caring man. His father, who displayed a dominant personality, also taught John the importance of being a man of integrity. He told him, "Always tell the truth, don't lie because you have to be a man of your word."

John, like most children, didn't always agree with his father and was often admonished when he had done wrong. But in the midst of correction John always knew the gleam in his father's eyes was affirmation that he was loved. Years later the admiration John felt for his father was relayed in a song he wrote titled *My Father and My Friend*.

Music had always been a big part of his life. Although he sang in the Glee Club as a child, he didn't show much interest. The house was filled with music as his Dad played the guitar and harmonica and his mother sang out in her soprano voice. At the time, John couldn't appreciate the importance of it all. He had no idea that many years later it would become a vital part of his very existence.

Even though I have only known John for a short time I can readily see how his parent's teachings run deep into his heart and have made him who he is today.

John attended Catholic schools through his senior year and then enrolled in St. Francis College in Brooklyn. He received degrees in economics and labor relations and began his career in human resources.

As his skills increased he took a position with a company in Massachusetts called Texas Instruments, a job he said he not only liked but thoroughly loved. His job took him to the beautiful country of Spain where he and his wife Carolyn and their three children Mark, Lisa and Michael spent an incredible two years. Their next assignment was in the beautiful city of Nice, France for two years, during which time they traveled to 25 other countries.

John and his family were exposed to people and cultures that greatly expanded their thinking and created some wonderful memories that would last them a lifetime.

John eventually gave up his position with Texas Instruments to become a corporate vice president for Memorex Telex, a worldwide organization. His position with Memorex also took him to live abroad in the wonderful country of Switzerland and England.

Unfortunately, John's marriage ended in 1989. In 1992 he decided to move back to the States in order to spend more time with his children, who were grown and married, and his father who was growing increasingly ill.

In the early 1970's John experienced a spiritual awakening in his life when he went to a 72-hour retreat called Cursillo which is the parent of "The Walk To Emmaus." It was during that time John turned his life over to the Lord and was committed to living a Christian life.

Over the years his desire to serve the Lord never waned but continued to increase. In 1992 after he moved back to the states and resigned his position at Memorex Telex he attended another "Walk to Emmaus" retreat. During one of the nightly sessions the song *Surely the Presence of the Lord is in this Place* was played. Suddenly John felt what seemed like electricity going throughout his body and he began to cry.

Music had never effected John like that before and he stood there wondering why. A couple of days later he sat down to try and write the words he heard as the melody began to play over and over in his mind. But the words that came to him were all his own. That was the beginning of John's songwriting career as he penned the words to *Chosen By A King,* the title song of what was to be his first album.

This was all still very strange to John. He had been part of corporate America for over 25 years and all of a sudden he found himself writing down words to songs that were flowing out of his head. He wasn't a singer so he began to search for the person who he felt God must be preparing for the task.

John said he believes in God-incidents not coincidents. *"If we are trying to live a good Christian life, God will put people in our path to help us through our journey of becoming who we are meant to be."*

Debra Ramirez, a beautiful young woman of Spanish descent was introduced to John. From the moment she sang the first line of his song John knew she must be the one God had prepared.

Eight years have passed since John and Debra first met and began working together. They have published three albums and their songs have been sung in front of countless live audiences as well as over the radio airwaves and television in an effort to worship and glorify God. The Lord has now placed 8 Christian performing artists, authors and speakers in his life whom John represents as their business manager. He also is working on co-producing a TV show involving music.

John is more committed than ever to serve the Lord. He has watched his life unfold in a way that brings him much contentment and joy. He truly believes God has a plan for everyone's life, but it is up to us to spend time finding out what the plan is.

Some helpful hints he gave were *"Begin weeding out the things you don't like and you will eventually see the things you love. Spend time with people to see if their talents are something that interest you. Take a career test. Go to the library and read about various occupations. Finding your position in life is a journey. Enjoy the journey, the experiences along the way will help you grow."*

Jimmy Wallis
Comedian

What I really like is when two people who are virtually strangers can sit down and talk to each other for the first time and feel completely at ease in their conversation. That's how I felt with comedian Jimmy Wallis.

One of my favorite times of the day is when I hear something that causes a smile to beam across my face or the sound of laughter to fill the atmosphere around me. The Bible says, "A merry heart does good like a medicine." I have found that to be a profound statement. Therefore, I just had to include a comedian in my list of Distinguished Oklahomans.

Jimmy Wallis was raised in Broken Bow, Oklahoma, one of the prettiest places in the state. He has fond memories of his childhood with his father Bascom, mother Maxine and older brother Bascom, Jr. It seems his father was a naturally funny man. But even though his humor surely rubbed off on Jimmy to some extent, he really wasn't the reason for Jimmy's

journey into professional comedy.

His mother, on the other hand, was the most disciplined member of the family. She helped Jimmy on several occasions during his school years, prepare for a performance to make others laugh. She had no idea what she thought was a child entertaining a few friends would eventually take him into a lifelong career.

At age 5 Jimmy saw a ventriloquist perform at his grade school and he immediately decided he wanted to learn that skill. He was a chubby kid growing up who always felt like he was in the shadow of his older brother. Jimmy wasn't athletic, he was the guy that was always the last one picked for a team sport. But boy, was he ever funny! If he couldn't out play you he could certainly make you laugh trying. He use to like impersonating voices like Bugs Bunny and cartoon characters. Of course he made the other familiar sounds like most boys do-thunder or airplanes and cars.

Even though he was growing taller in stature as the years progressed he never waned in his yearning to have a doll to perform ventriloquism with. His mother and father owned a five and dime store. For a few years they tried to find a doll for him, but either the dolls were extremely popular or only a few were produced. His parents had a hard time at Christmas each year trying to find him one.

Finally, when Jimmy was 12 years old, his parents anxiously waited to see the look on his face as he opened that long awaited Christmas present. There inside the box was the dummy doll with the moveable mouth. For $6.98 Jimmy was on his way to being a ventriloquist.

While the rest of the family made its way into the kitchen to prepare breakfast, Jimmy prepared his doll to perform. When his parents came back into the room a few minutes later Jimmy had his doll he called "Danny" making a modified voice of Bugs Bunny saying, "Hey, how are you." He remembers how his parent's jaws dropped in amazement. Then in walks his brother, who in Jimmy's eyes had all the looks as well as all the talents. He, too, stood in awe as he heard Jimmy's doll seem to come alive. Jimmy looked at his family and said, "Hey, I think I've got something here." And sure enough he did.

It didn't take long before Jimmy's talent became a household word around school and amongst his teachers and friends. His hours of practice eventually paid off and he began entertaining on a continual basis. Everybody wanted to hear that Wallis kid do his impersonations and hear his Danny doll perform.

Later on Jimmy was able to purchase a second doll, a Jerry Mahonney doll he named Terry. At times he would sit Danny on one knee and Terry on the other and they would converse about all sorts of topics.

In 1955 the Elvis craze began, so of course Jimmy had to have a guitar as well. To his knowledge he put together Oklahoma's first Rock and Roll band called, "The Roadrunners." Playing his guitar and singing like Elvis helped with his college expenses when he entered The University of Oklahoma in 1957. The band's first recordings, "Fallen Dream" and "Sheet Board Down" helped expand the popularity of his group to a several state region.

Jimmy was doing quite well as a performer, appearing on numerous television and radio stations. Then in 1960 he got his first big break when Mark Leddy saw him performing in Boston at a magic convention. Leddy was the booking agent for the Ed Sullivan Show. Mark had Jimmy come to New York to audition for Ed Sullivan and for an appearance at Radio City Music Hall.

Later in 1960, the owner of the "Roaring Twenties" in the St. Louis Gaslight Square District saw Jimmy working at a club near Branson, Missouri and hired him to work that popular nightspot. Record breaking runs at the 'Twenties and growing reviews in VARIETY and the St. Louis papers led to Jimmy's signing with Playboy Clubs International. That relationship lasted over a decade.

Jimmy has had the opportunity to work with some of the funniest guys in the entertainment business. To name a few, Dick Gregory was probably the first black comedian that made us laugh at race problems. Jackie Gale was at one time Playboy's number one comic. Also, Jackie Leonard's style was later emulated by the well known Don Rickles, only with a more vicious approach.

Another highlight of Jimmy's career was when the Oklahoma House of Representatives voted him Oklahoman's Top Comedian and CBS- TV signed him on to appear with Art Linkletter on Hollywood Talent Scouts in 1966.

Even though Jimmy has performed at Disneyland, The Tropicana, The Sahara, The Flamingo, the Riviera and other clubs in Las Vegas his most rewarding stint was during the Vietnam era. With a performing contract that was intended to last 13 weeks Jimmy found a group of soldiers that made the dangers of Vietnam worth it all. It was during the infamous Tet Offensive of 1968 that Jimmy perfected his comedy performance "The Bunker Hunker."

Where some entertainers played it safe and performed at the USO and other safe havens, Jimmy found himself in the boonies. When he performed there were mortars, rockets and gunshots going off all around him. He didn't have to be there, but he remained for three years eager to help keep the spirits of our honored soldiers intact.

After Vietnam Las Vegas became his venue once again with a whole array of guest appearances with people such as Wayne Newton, Lou Rawls, Lola Falana, Ben Vereen, Al Hirt, Ann Murray, Andy Gibb, Suzanne Sommers, Rip Taylor, Debbie Reynolds and others. Over the course of his career, Jimmy has appeared with over 50 stars and internationally known groups.

He has served with General William Westmoreland, Admiral Zumwalt and Michael Quale as an advisor to the American Academy for Entertainment at U.S. Veterans Hospitals. The year 2000 marked 45 years as a professional and 40 years of "being on the road."

Life has also blessed Jimmy with two beautiful daughters, Lori and Shauna, who have every right to be very proud of their "funny" father.

Jimmy Wallis

Michael Wallis - Author

What a treat to meet "Mr. Route 66" Michael Wallis. It was especially enjoyable to view the room in which all of his creations are pruned and polished to perfection.

Distinguished Oklahoman and musical artist Ronnie Dunn was the previous owner of Michael's house. Ronnie wrote music

in the same upstairs hideaway room before he made his way to Nashville.

There were some other interesting individuals who at one time laid claim to the land or occupied the house on Rockford Road. But that is a whole other story of its own. Obviously, the Rockford house, as well as the upstairs room, could tell a lot of stories on its own.

At the time of our interview Michael was making plans to relocate and take up residence at Sophian Plaza in downtown Tulsa. I guess it is time for someone else to fill those rooms with distinction.

Michael was born in 1945 in St. Louis, Missouri, a state he says is called "the mother of all states" and the launching pad for the west. This is the state that produced the Pony Express, Lewis Clark and all the wagon trains. The gateway to the west has become the big archway that came along 20 years later. But most importantly, it produced Oklahoma's beloved Michael Wallis.

Michael describes his family growing up as middle-class. His father Herbert worked as a designer, his mother Ann a homemaker, and two older sisters mothered him as well.

His childhood days yielded many good memories. He reminisces about playing catch with his dad and going on fishing excursions. As a kid he remembers playing games with surplus items brought back from the war-old helmets and tins. He collected turtles and arrowheads and roamed all over the fields outside St. Louis. He mowed lawns, collected lightning bugs, blew up firecrackers and saved baseball cards. In other words, he was the typical neighborhood boy looking for a little adventure.

Michael attended Western Military Academy during his high school years, expecting to go on to West Point and become an engineer. However, after reviewing the situation with the head master, they both came to the conclusion that Michael was suited for a more alluring, romantic lifestyle than one so rigidly set forth by the engineering world. Michael, although not totally convinced, had some writing talents that would later prove to be award winning.

After his freshman year at Central Methodist College where he majored in humanities, he decided to join the U.S. Marines. One week later he found himself in boot camp at Parris Island, South Carolina. For the next few years although most of his time belonged to Uncle Sam, he found ways in which to increase his appetite for adventure. Michael admits he was well into his 30's before he really matured as a man. Until then he was determined to experience life on his own terms and weave a path on what was later to be identified as a literary journey.

In 1968, fresh out of the Marines, Michael enrolled at the University of Missouri. That's where he first met Suzanne in an introductory Spanish class she was teaching. A short time later they moved to New Mexico. Even though their time together brought a close friendship, they parted ways to pursue other interests. Suzanne returned to the University of Missouri, obtaining two master's degrees, while Michael remained in Santa Fe.

It was there in New Mexico where he began honing his writing skills as a newspaper correspondent and paid the bills working as a bartender, social worker, printer, ranch hand, and ski-resort manager. During the mid-70's he was reporter, editor, and bureau chief for a chain of daily newspapers in Texas. Then he signed on as a special correspondent for Time-Life publications and worked out of Miami for Time's Caribbean Bureau. He covered the refugee exodus from Cuba and even traveled with smugglers to report on drug trade in the Caribbean basin.

In the summer of 1980 when the temperature climbed to 110 degrees, Michael went to Tulsa with photographer Terrence Moore to report on a series of stories on the Old West. They stayed at the historic Mayo Hotel and Michael was intrigued by the architectural flavor that seemed to permeate Tulsa. Long story short, he made contact with Suzanne and they decided to relocate and make their home in Tulsa, Oklahoma.

In 1982, Michael and Suzanne moved into their house on Rockford Road. They joined forces with Joyce Gideon and became Wallis Gideon Wallis, a public relations agency which has since become the Wallis Group, a successful public relations -advertising agency with local, regional and national accounts.

Suzanne's brother, Jim Fitzgerald, an editor for Doubleday, came for a visit that same year. Michael had been mentally preparing to write his first book. Ironically, when Jim returned to New York, publisher Bill Barry informed him of some unsolicited material he had received from John Phillips, grandson of Phillips Petroleum founder Frank Phillips. They needed a biographer and of course the rest is history.

Michael said sometimes there are book ideas and authors and occasionally they gently collide. The book was titled *Oil Man* with the forward written by John Phillips.

With Michael's immediate success he acquired his first agent, Carol Mann, and spawned another creation which will forever link people to Michael Wallis -*Route 66*.

Since then Michael has changed agents but his creativity and endless quest for intriguing stories has never changed. He has been nominated on three occasions for the Pulitzer Prize and was also a nominee for the National Book Award.

He has won several other prestigious awards and honors including the 1994 Lynn Riggs Award from Rogers State College in Claremore, Oklahoma. In 1994 he was the first inductee into the Oklahoma Route 66 Hall of Fame. He received the coveted Steinbeck Award in 1996 and was inducted into the Oklahoma Professional Writers Hall of Fame. In 1999 he was inducted into the Missouri Writers Hall of Fame and received the Arrell Gibson Lifetime Achievement Award from the Oklahoma Center for the Book.

Michael said it is important to have a healthy ego, a confidence in yourself and your vision, if you are ever going to accomplish your goals. While you can't always believe your own publicity you can maintain a good measure of self-esteem which will catapult you into success. The ability to look at a glass half full rather than half empty is the mark of a positive person. *When negative situations happen, deal with it head on and you'll come through it.*

As a writer at age 55 he is a long way from retirement, but I asked Michael if he sees any type of retirement in his future. "Retire from what?" he asked. He is having too good of a time to even consider it. He hopes when he passes on he'll be sitting at his word processor pounding out another best seller.

Sam Walton

Business

I wonder what it would be like to know almost everyone in America shops at your store? Talk about contributing to the welfare of others, I'd say Sam Walton did that and much more.

Sam was born in Kingfisher, Oklahoma in 1918. His parents, Tom and Nan Walton, seemed to have been very unique individuals. Even though monetarily their lifestyle was somewhat meager, they were hard workers, always coming up with an idea to enhance the family's provisions.

Their values quickly influenced Sam. At an early age he was performing whatever tasks he could to bring funds into the home, from selling bottled milk his mother had prepared to peddling magazines and throwing newspapers.

We have a world full of talented and inspiring young people in this 21st century. However, it would do us all a great deal of good if we could step back in time and view the families raised in the early part of the 20th century. Almost without exception they had a strong sense of family loyalty, responsibility and knew the value of hard work.

I think too often in today's times we try to shield our children from having to work too hard for fear they might resent us or just stop trying when in fact those traits produce individuals who can build empires like Walmart.

By the time Sam turned 5 years old his family had relocated to Missouri where he attended school up through college. In 1940 he graduated from the University of Missouri with a business degree. Not only had he accumulated a lot of study hours, but he worked hard as well putting himself through college with the varied jobs he continued to hold down.

After graduation and some soul searching about which direction to go with his career he settled on an offer made to him by the J.C. Penney Company in DesMoines, Iowa. He kept that position for 18 months before deciding to check out possibilities in Tulsa. His plans were some what side tracked when he ended up working for a gun powder plant in Pryor, while living in Claremore.

Suddenly it was time for one of those "defining moments" during an evening of recreation at the local bowling alley. It was there that he met Miss Helen Robson who he married February 14,1943.

A two year stint in the Army delayed his next career move, but he never lost sight of his goal to put his degree to good use and own his own business. Helen came from a well-to-do prominent family in Claremore. Her father Leland Robson was an attorney, a rancher and founder of the Rogers County Bank in Claremore. Helen was used to viewing things in a calculated manner. With a business degree in finance she too felt assured that Sam's goals of owning his own business could very well become a reality.

Not wanting to lean too heavily on her father's successes, yet needing his help financially to get started, Sam and Helen took off for Newport, Arkansas. With a small loan from Leland, Sam and Helen were determined to make a success out of their own venture.

On September 1,1945 at the age of 27, Samuel Moore Walton took his partially borrowed $25,000 and opened his first Ben Franklin five-and-dime franchise store. With only 18 months of previous retail experience he was in for some crucial lessons if he was going to be a successful merchant. Needless to say, Sam was a quick study. Within five years the fledgling business he had taken over had become the number one Ben Franklin store in the six state region. However, Sam's landlord refused to renew his lease, forcing him to move from Newport, a town he and Helen and their four children Rob, Jim, John and Alice had grown to love.

Of course his next store location unknowingly was the town that would someday be known to house the Wal-Mart Corporate Offices. In the meantime, he once again started with a fledgling company that needed the "Walton touch." Bentonville, Arkansas became the home of Walton's Five and Dime. Within the next 15 years he had grown with stores in

Fayetteville, Little Rock, Springdale and Siloam Springs and eventually into Kansas. However, Sam knew he needed to grow with the times and that meant expanding from a five and dime to a full blown discount store. Thus was born the first Wal-Mart Discount Store in Rogers, Arkansas on July 2, 1962.

Sam contributes a lot of his success to pure tenacity. There is a lot to be said about never giving up even though it looks as if there is no way to win. Sam was determined to be successful. Even though losing his lease in Newport seemed like a devastating turn of events it caused him to purpose in his heart to find continued success elsewhere.

As he focused on store locations in small towns and rural areas he learned that success was often found in hidden places. Unlike others who may have thought big cities would bring greater success, Sam focused on the small out of the way spots. His goal was to sell brand-name products in high volume at low discount prices. What a novel idea!

Wal-Mart went public in 1970 and by 1991 was the nation's largest retailer, with 1,700 stores. Sam remained president and CEO until 1988 and chairman until his death from bone cancer on April 5, 1992.

What a legacy Sam Walton left to the world! Known as one of the richest men in the country, he proved to himself and others that hard work and goal setting pays off.

On March 17, 1992 in the auditorium of Wal-Mart general offices Sam Walton was presented the Presidential Medal of Freedom, our nation's highest civilian award, by President and Mrs. Bush.

Dennis Weaver

Actor

Even though Dennis was born on June 4, 1924 in Joplin, Missouri the impact he made during the short time he spent at Oklahoma University made it a must to include him as one of the distinguished few.

I introduced myself to Dennis six or seven years ago as he was casually eating in a Tulsa restaurant. No, I couldn't pass up the chance to say something to him. I took the opportunity to invite him to a gathering of business people the following evening.

Dennis has always been one of my favorite actors. Gunsmoke has been off the air for so many years it's hard to count them all. Yet those of us who were fortunate to see it will forever remember the 6' 2" lanky, limping sidekick of Marshall Matt Dillion. In his character role as Chester with his all familiar signature line "Mis-ter Dillion" and his atrocious tasting black coffee, Dennis Weaver brought fame to himself as well as a 1959 Emmy Award.

Of course his list of credits are lengthy to say the least, but another of my favorites was the television series "McCloud." Sam McCloud was the tall marshall (a nice twist) from Taos, New Mexico who found himself amongst the hustle and bustle of New York City -the "fish out of water" so to speak.

We all know that there are "actors" and then there are "ACTORS" and Dennis Weaver without a doubt fits into the latter.

Dennis grew up on a farm in Joplin and was a top notch athlete. He set many football and track and field records and at the time was named one of the Midwest's top high school athletes. But sports wasn't his only love. At a young age he began dreaming of an acting career. Many years ago in an interview Dennis was quoted as saying " I used to go to a Saturday matinee movie, usually a western or a Tarzan picture, where they had obvious heroes and very obvious villains. I'd go home and act out all the parts."

After high school graduation Dennis enrolled in Joplin Junior College, but left after a year and decided to join the Navy where he spent the next 27 months. While in the Navy he set a speed and agility test record as a member of the Navy's track and field squad.

He and Gerry Stowell met in junior high school. Their relationship continued to blossom through their high school years and marriage followed in 1945. They have proven after 56 years of marriage there is such a thing as commitment.

After Dennis's separation from the Navy he decided to resume his college education. He enrolled at Oklahoma University where he had been awarded a football scholarship. Unfortunately, he suffered a knee injury during spring practice and he had to give up football. However he represented Oklahoma University at the olympic tryouts in New York in 1948 and placed sixth in the nation out of 36 entrants.

Oklahoma University was known then as it is today as having one of the top rated drama schools in the country. Dennis was determined to become and actor, so he chose OU to help meet that goal.

We Oklahoma fans would like to believe at least in part that the Sooner State was the launching pad for Dennis Weaver to become such a successful actor. Of course as with any distinguished person, there are people who crossed his path who created defining moments in his life, yet it was Dennis himself who took those moments and molded them into success.

When he and Gerry first moved to Norman they lived in the basement of a radio professor's house. It was just a small one room apartment and "broke" was a term they considered themselves most of the time. Dennis was on the track team and played a very active role in the drama school. Gerry was one of the hard working typists who prepared others students' theses papers for 50 cents a page and juggled the $90 a month GI Bill to help make ends meet.

After graduating from OU Dennis and Gerry headed for New York where he enrolled at the Actors' Studio. He worked odd jobs to help feed the family which had grown with the addition of their son, Rick, born October 29, 1948.

By 1952 he had signed with Universal Studios in his film debut of The Redhead From Wyoming. Their second son Robby was born April 8, 1953 and their son Rusty was born February 19, 1959 completing the Weaver household.

Dennis's acting work continued to increase and in 1955 he was offered the spot on Gunsmoke which catapulted his career. In spite of his endearing character and overwhelming success on "Gunsmoke," Dennis left the show in 1964 to pursue other projects. His diversified talents needed to be expanded and Dennis longed for the opportunity to show the world he didn't need to be pigeon-holed into one type of character.

Of course he showed the world many times over as he starred in television series like "Gentle Ben," "Kentucky Jones," "Stone," "Buck James" and of course, "McCloud," the role that brought him three Emmy nominations.

The silver screen has also had its share of Dennis's talents as he appeared in "Touch Of Evil," "Ten Wanted Men," "Seven Angry Men," "Dragnet" and "A Man Called Sledge."

Dennis has a comedic side which he demonstrated on "The Sonny and Cher Comedy Hour," "The Flip Wilson Show" and "Hee Haw." In addition, Dennis has revealed his love for country music as a singer/songwriter. For a while he recorded for the late Hoyt Axton's Jeremiah Records.

From 1973 to 1975, Dennis served as president of the Screen Actors Guild. He was inducted into the National Cowboy Hall of Fame in Oklahoma City in 1981, then in 1986 he received his star on the Hollywood Walk of Fame.

Remarkably Dennis has too many accomplishments to list them all. In 1993, he founded the Institute of Ecolonomics based on his conviction that a truly sustainable future requires a healthy environment and a prosperous economy. Dennis has long believed that the key to realizing both is mutual cooperation. The mission of the Institute of Ecolonomics is to bring together champions of the environment and leaders in business and industry to open up unprecedented avenues of cooperation. (www.ecolonomics.org)

Dennis is an extremely active man who is continually working on some idea or project. Alice, who has remained his diligent assistant for many years was kind enough to send a picture of Dennis and help with the reviewing of his profile, for which I am most grateful.

Jimmy Webb - Composer

As an Oklahoma-born son of a preacher, Jimmy Webb has received immense critical acclaim during his almost thirty years of success as a musical composer. He is the only artist ever to receive Grammy awards for music, lyrics, and orchestration, he is a member of the National Academy of Popular Music Songwriter's Hall of Fame, the Nashville Songwriter's Hall of Fame and according to BMI, his *By The Time I Get To Phoenix,* has been the third most performed song in the last fifty years, with *Up, Up and Away* on the same list in the top thirty. Jimmy's *Wichita Lineman* has been listed in MOJO Magazine's worldwide survey of the best one hundred singles of all time in the top fifty. The National Academy of Songwriters also named Jimmy as 1993's recipient of their Lifetime Achievement Award, although TIME Magazine was early to acknowledge Jimmy Webb's range and proficiency back in 1968 when it referred to his astonishing string of hits, and commented on " Jimmy's" gift for strong, varied rhythms, inventive structures, and rich, sometimes surprising harmonies" Jimmy was also inducted by actor Michael Douglas in November '99 into the Oklahoma Hall of Fame as one of the State's most celebrated sons, he was inducted onto the Board of Directors for The Songwriters' Hall of Fame in early 2000, and serves on the Board of Directors for ASCAP.

Having five top ten hits within a 20-month period, Jimmy Webb concluded the 1960's with an international name that was bandied around on the musical air currents as a "new genius." In a natural extension of his work, Jimmy began the Seventies intent on launching his own performing career, releasing six albums in eleven years, including *Words And Music* (1970),-and *So:On* (1971), *Land's End* (1974), *El Mirage* (19??), and *Angel Heart* (1982),-while writing hits for other recording stars. Throughout the years, he continued to hone his performance skills, and earned distinguished reviews and praise.

Jimmy has also added his genius to a number of film and television projects. Beginning his scoring career in 1968, he wrote the title song and a mid-summer hit (*Montage*) for the James Garner-Debbie Reynolds comedy, "How Sweet It Is!" followed by an adventurous score for the 1971 classic Western, "Doc." In 1973 he demonstrated his wit, humor and musical breadth with a score for the provocative "Naked Ape," followed by his music for "Voices," which was warmly received in 1979. Jimmy provided a dazzling score for the highly successful animated film, "The Last Unicorn," Germany's second-highest grossing film in 1982, which also included his title song, *That's All I've Got To Say,* later recorded by Art Garfunkel. That success was followed by the score for Cannon Film's Vietnam sage, "The Hanoi Hilton." Although he rarely collaborates, Jimmy and Carly Simon wrote the title track of her album, *Film Noir* and completed *A Dream Worth Keeping,* with Alan Silvestri for Twentieth Century's 1992 release, *Fern Gully: The Last Rainforest,* recorded by Sheena Easton. His solo effort, *Christmas Will Return* was included in Disney's '94 smash hit, 'The Santa Clause." Now contemplating commitments for future film projects, Jimmy Webb continues in his reign as one of the few masters of American music, leading one reviewer to comment, "There is something of a return to 1930' glamour in Jimmy's work, a suggestion of the great era of lush films scoring when velvet-sounding violins appeared seemingly out of nowhere and emotion erupted from the music itself."

Clarifying himself as a romanticist, Jimmy's use of vivid imagery simultaneously captures and involves his listeners' emotions, which should come as no surprise to the songwriter who states, "I like words. I like the way they clash around together and bang up against each other, especially in songs." In a progression of his celebrated talent as a lyricist, Jimmy continued in the 1990's furthering his enormous range of interests by completing a best-selling book, *Tunesmith: Inside The Art of Songwriting,* considered by many to be the "Bible of songwriting."

Jimmy's accomplishments as a composer, arranger, and producer demonstrate beyond question that he remains as important and vital a cultural figure today as he was over thirty years ago. Embraced by his peers, Jimmy has influenced and affected some of the finest musical talents of our time. Frank Sinatra declared *By The Time I Get To Phoenix* as "the greatest torch song ever written," and said he enjoyed singing Jimmy Webb tunes because "he has been blessed with the emotions and artistic talent of the great lyricists." The late Sammy Cahn commented, "I think one of the real, real geniuses is Jimmy Webb. His *MacArthur Park* is a major piece of work, major. I'd almost compare it to Gershwin's *Rhapsody in Blue* in size and scope" Singer Michael Feinstein, who recorded Jimmy's *Time Enough For Love,* for his 1993 album, "Forever," and included another Jimmy Webb track *Wasn't There A Moment* on "Such Sweet Sorrow," his first album for Atlantic, says he's "interested in the work of the great masters from any era, and certainly, Jimmy Webb is a master of this era, of today" Feinstein is also recording an "all-Webb" album for 2001 as is Kenny Rankin for the near future. Billy Joel credits Jimmy as a major influence on his own foray into the music business. "When I was starting out as a songwriter," says Joel, "I looked to Jimmy Webb as one of the most innovative and musically proficient songwriters of our generation." His songs transcend their precedent-setting critical and commercial acclaim to achieve the level of true classics--a permanent part of the American musical landscape, the sound track of an era. In his book about songwriting, Jimmy states, "the paramount joy of the craft is that, however simply it is begun, it can take the songwriter on a lifelong voyage across many distant and wondrous musical seas.

Roger Webb

University President

Little boys in Heavener, Oklahoma, have a special advantage when they run and play in the woods, being soldiers or pioneers or Indian scouts. For the children of Heavener often stand transfixed at the massive and mysterious runestone in their woods, wondering at the meaning of those strange marks that are said to have been chiseled in the massive rock by Viking explorers nearly a thousand years ago.

Perhaps that's why Roger Webb was always curious about the world beyond LeFlore County, wanting to learn and discover new things. For beyond his love of baseball and his beautiful Oklahoma hills and mountains, Roger Webb was always curious about things, and loved to learn. He wanted to be a teacher when he grew up, so that he could share the fascination of discovery with others.

His parents, Grace and E.A. Webb, watched with lots of hometown pride as Roger went off to Stillwater to earn a liberal arts degree, and then to Norman to study law on a Ford Foundation Scholarship. And they smiled to think of their son being selected as a White House Fellow to work for President Johnson, and then be hired to work on the legislative staff in the Office of the Secretary of the U.S. Senate.

It was an exciting world of action and ideas for a young man, but Roger Webb was happy to return to Oklahoma in 1974 and continue a life of public service when he was named Commissioner of Public Safety. Once again, it was a period of discovery and change, but Roger Webb still felt a tie to education.

So, when the presidency of Northeastern State University in Tahlequah became open, Webb felt that it was a chance for him to continue public service to his state in a new way. For the next nineteen years he led NSU on a new path of growth in terms of size, quality and impact on young lives. The campus doubled in size under his leadership, began exciting new programs and established a College of Optometry, which has gained national recognition.

In 1997, with the retirement of former Governor George Nigh from the presidency of the state's third largest university, Roger Webb was tapped by the Regents for Oklahoma Colleges to assume leadership of the University of Central Oklahoma.

As was the case with Tahlequah nineteen years earlier, President Webb took on this new challenge with characteristic enthusiasm and new ideas for the school's future.

Building on a tradition of small classes, personal attention and an excellent faculty which is more interested in teaching than anything else, Webb has established an extraordinary goal for UCO: to make this metropolitan university the premier undergraduate institution in the state of Oklahoma. Coping with scarce resources but relying on the loyalty and dedication of the campus community, the school is already becoming known as a place to experience real world preparation for careers in a fast-changing world of global markets and emerging technologies.

Committed to developing and delivering programs which make sense for the changing markets of a new century, President Webb and his faculty have helped their students make history. Already known as a center for fine and performing arts in Oklahoma, UCO has also emerged as a national leader in preparing students for careers in engineering physics and bio-medical engineering. Scores of other professional programs place graduates throughout the state's commerce and industry.

The College of Business produces top caliber graduates and MBA's and UCO is also recognized for its quality offerings in Liberal Arts, Math and Science and its new College of Arts, Media and Design. An energized Graduate College offers a wide range of Masters' Degree programs and has also made the school a focal point for both graduate and undergraduate research.

An array of new structures and programs are transforming the campus: new apartments and suites which double the residential population; a state-of-art wellness center which serves students, faculty and staff; an exciting new Jazz Lab and a new performing arts venue...all features which enrich both the campus and the metropolitan area surrounding it.

But the university enterprise closest to Roger Webb's heart is the College of Education, helping him realize the vision of his youth to help the young people of our state enjoy and profit by discovery and growth. As the leading provider of teachers for the classrooms of Oklahoma, President Webb has marshaled resources to help the College of Education set new standards for Oklahoma in teacher preparation. Pioneering the Teacher Warranty program in Oklahoma, UCO continues to innovate and enhance the way teachers are trained, equipped and supported as they perform their great service in birthing our state's future through our children.

It's been nearly fifty years since a young Roger Webb first stared at those strange markings on the Heavener runestone, and wondered about the people who had carved them, 500 years before Columbus "discovered" the New World. But one can still see the same sense of wonder and energy as Roger Webb moves through the 200-acre campus in Edmond, among the 14,000 students who come to UCO each year. He remains committed to discovery and ideas, and to sharing and passing along the great traditions which give universities life and purpose.

Joe Webster

Singer

Even though Joe is a true Oklahoman through and through he was born in Charleston, South Carolina. His father Joseph worked for the railroad in Charleston, but when Joe was two years old they were transferred to Savannah, Georgia where they remained until he was ten years old. His father died when he was 10 so his mother Ida, along with his brother Fred and his sister Gloria, moved to Bartlesville, Oklahoma where his grandparents lived.

Up until the move to Bartlesville Joe had created quite a stir in Savannah with his showmanship ability. His mother saw talent in him at an early age and by the time he was 5 years old she was signing him up for every amateur show that came along.

Joe was an eye catcher with his dazzling young voice and his ability to woo the crowd with his adorable dancing routine that would often find him on bended knees at the end of a song like "Sonny Boy." Of course his mother would make sure he was dressed in attire conducive to a talented performer.

By the time he was six years old he was appearing on a local radio show at WTOC in Savannah. His family became quite good friends with Johnny Mercer who picked Joe up on many occasions so he could perform at different functions. Joe even remembers spending nights at Johnny's house, but at the time he had no idea what an influential person Johnny was in the entertainment business. All Joe knew was he was being allowed to sing and perform with a variety of bands that seemed in awe with his young talent.

Art Linkletter and Joe Webster

When they moved to Bartlesville invitations continued to come Joe's way. You would often find him at civic clubs, organizations, parties and major get togethers all over Bartlesville. It appeared as if Joe had his future mapped out and it was going to be an exciting one.

In high school he formed The Joe Webster Band. Even though he could play a little on the drums he decided his real talent was in singing. The band did quite well. For four years during high school he was invited to be part of the talent showcased on KVOO radio in Tulsa which brought him great reviews and allowed him to meet a lot of influential people in the radio and music business.

When he was in the eleventh grade he went to a function at Oklahoma State University which was called Oklahoma A&M at the time. While there he met a man who would become a lifelong friend, Jimmie Baker. Jimmie had a college band rightfully known as The Jimmie Baker Band. Joe was so impressed with his band and wanted very much to be part of it some day. Jimmie told him there might be a possibility after he graduated from high school. However, after high school, World War II was in full swing and Joe willingly became part of the United States Army for the next few years.

After the war with the G.I. Bill in hand he made his way to Oklahoma A&M and once again met his friend Jimmie Baker. It just so happened a beautiful young lady by the name of Shirleen Fuhring was one of Jimmie's band singers. Because of her rather long and difficult to pronounce name Jimmie had her change her stage name to Sheryl Scott. Joe and Shirleen started dating, which has proven to be a good thing and has lasted over 50 years. Since band finances were limited and Jimmie was already paying Shirleen a salary Joe convinced Shirleen to split her pay with him.

Eventually college days came to an end and Joe and Shirleen moved to Oklahoma City where Joe became a staff vocalist on WKY radio. For the next few years he reveled in the opportunity to perform as a variety of singing characters depending on what genre of music was being played.

After Joe and Shirleen married she quit the singing business, but I commented it would be great to watch them perform again some time. If they do, I'd sure like to be there.

Television eventually came on the scene. At first there was no national coverage, so television programming was strictly local and with a live audience. Joe became quite a celebrity in Oklahoma City. It was difficult to go out amongst the public without being approached for an autograph, but Joe was thrilled with the opportunity. I'm sure with his gregarious personality and his talented singing ability the public found it hard to stay away.

For 13 years Oklahoma City music fans could tune into their favorite radio station or flip on their televisions and be entertained by one of the city's finest. Several national celebrities from time to time made appearances with Joe in Oklahoma City which further enhanced his talent resume. Of special interest to Joe was when he was invited with singing partner Helen Wood to appear on the Kate Smith Show in New York City.

There came a day when Joe decided he'd like to further his career and see what California had to offer. He packed up his belongings and he and Shirleen left for Hollywood. Being pretty naive with the protocol of the music business, Joe had no idea that he needed an agent to help promote himself. He later found out that his friend and mentor Johnny Mercer owned Capitol Records in California. But that revelation didn't come until some time later. If it had been known earlier Joe's future may have turned out quite differently.

As it was he met Harry Belafonte, who of course is a major success in the music world. Joe was given the opportunity to travel with him and a group of performers which again would have given him a huge leap in his profession.

However, about that time Shirleen discovered she was expecting a child. She had already miscarried her first child and was very concerned about taking good care of herself during this next pregnancy. Shirleen wanted to go back to Oklahoma, and being the loving husband he was Joe agreed. He realized he was missing a golden opportunity in his life. Although he had a small part in the traveling production he also knew it had the potential of carrying him even farther. But they were homeward bound. They've often looked back over the years and thought "what if," but then "what if" may have changed everything they have grown to cherish in their lives-the birth of their four children, Kirk, Mark, Laurie and Julie and nine beautiful grandchildren.

When they came back to Oklahoma City Joe worked for the television station performing for a few more years and in conjunction went to work for Pittsburgh Corning where he retired after 17 years. Of course when music is that much a part of who you are, you can't let it die on the vine. Joe continued to have his own band and still does to this day. Oh, they may have slowed down a little since their first inception, but Joe is every bit the performer that he once was.

Joe Webster

Max Weitzenhoffer

Theater

It's not hard to imagine Max Weitzenhoffer as a theatrical producer and director. His looks, his demeanor and his speech give him away.

Max was born in Oklahoma City, Oklahoma. His father was successful as the co-owner in the Davon Drilling Company. Max was an only child and describes his family as being financially comfortable. He remembers having a nice childhood that was void of the difficulties that so many children have to endure. Even though he was what we would call a privileged child, he still feels like he learned some valuable lessons from his father who was strict, yet fair. His mother was a "stay at home" Mom who was very well educated and saw to it that Max was generously exposed to the cultural side of life. Trips to the theater was a common occurrence in Oklahoma as well as their second home in La Jolla, California, where Summer Stock Theater was a weekly event. Between the Theater and Max's own fantasy world, he began to develop interest in areas most people aren't exposed to. Even though he was a very quiet person, he was an active drama student in school. He felt like that gave him the opportunity to expand past his own shy personality. Without realizing it, he was drifting toward a career in theater, and his parents and teachers were encouraging him.

When it came time for college Max enrolled at Oklahoma University. He didn't really know what direction he should take academically, since he had never made extremely high grades in school. Fortunately, drama classes were part of the curriculum, so Max signed up and worked hard. Before long, he could see that this was an area he had been groomed for all of his life.

Some times people have preconceived ideas of what they want to attain or become in a certain occupation. They often become exhausted trying to fit into a role that they are not completely suited for, but they are determined to make it work. Max knew he wanted to be connected to the theatrical world having been exposed to it most of his life. He had numerous professional contacts that he had acquired over the years. So, the natural progression would have been to become an actor. However, Max knew he wasn't a good actor, because of his less than aggressive personality. Yet, he was extremely talented as a producer and director. He was able to see beyond his limitations into what his grooming for the theater had really been all about.

As I have been told so often as I interview successful people. "Be prepared to relinquish your own set of ideas in order to truly see what is best suited for you." I'm often reminded of the gentleman whose entire family were singers and yet he could barely carry a note. Instead of wasting his life trying to become a singer, he began promoting singers and success followed him every where he went.

Max has had a very rewarding, successful career in theater. In the beginning he produced many shows that wouldn't have necessarily been considered successful, but he didn't quit trying. His big breakthrough came in 1976 when he produced the play "Dracula," that won a Tony Award. That success began establishing him within the industry, and people started to take notice of his talents.

Max says, "It isn't about money, it's about the thrill of the theater. The magical feeling that goes through you as the lights go down and the curtain rises. At that moment, you know you have to be a part of the magic, whether you get paid or not. You can't always be successful with every show, but hopefully the successes are bigger than the failures."

In 1991, Max produced the "Will Rogers Follies," which also won a Tony Award. It ran three years in New York, and then began a successful road tour.

After the "Will Rogers Follies" Max needed a change and he convinced Oklahoma University to let him start a musical theatre program. The school had been offering a drama degree but they didn't have a program. Since the inception of the program the faculty has grown from one member to five members plus Max as the producer/director. Part of the purpose of the program is to develop new musicals and shows. By the time a student has completed the program he is equipped to audition as a singer, dancer and actor not only on Broadway but as part of touring shows, cruise lines, Branson, Vegas, Disney World and any other entertainment outlet. Max is dedicated to his role at the university in which he receives no remuneration. His satisfaction comes from helping young people to get where they want to be in a business he has enjoyed for so many years.

Max has won the New York Drama Critic Circle Award as a producer. He has also received the Oklahoma Cowboy Hall of Fame Wranglers Award. In 1994 he was inducted into the Oklahoma Hall of Fame and has been honored by the University of Oklahoma with an Honorary Doctorate.

He divides his time now as a producer-director between New York and Norman.

He strongly believes that if you have been extremely successful in life, then it is your obligation to help someone else do the same. I know that success breeds success and if you want to be successful you should learn from successful people. So World, "Get Ready." With the guidance of Max Weinzenhoffer and the Drama Staff of Oklahoma University the theater industry is bound to spring forth with numerous creative people who will give all of the rest of us many hours of entertaining moments. When the lights go down, and the curtain rises on the next theatrical performance, we will all wonder if just maybe, Max Weinzenhoffer had a part to play in its success.

Wesley W. "Speedy" West

Musician

Once again, another great talent living in the state of Oklahoma. Even though Wesley was born in Springfield, Missouri on January 25, 1924 he found Oklahoma the place most suited for the sunset of his years.

His parents, Finley and Sue West, were a great influence in Wesley's life. His father was a linotype operator who worked for a gospel publishing house for 28 years before taking a position at a newspaper company. In his spare time Finley played guitar and sang gospel songs, so it was pretty natural for his son Wesley to inherit the desire to play music as well.

At age 9, Wesley became friends with three Cline brothers who attended his school. Wesley would sometimes go to their house after school to play baseball in their backyard. Usually after a time of play the Clines' mother would yell out to them it was time to practice their music. The three Cline brothers Ralph, Dorrell and Eldon ranged between the ages of 8 and 13 and were already performing on a weekly radio show.

Ralph played the Hawaiian guitar which is now known as the steel guitar. Wesley was in awe with that instrument. It just so happened that Wesley had one of the only bicycles in that area of town. So he made a deal with Ralph that if he would show him how to play a chord or two on his Hawaiian guitar he would let him ride his bike.

Eventually Wesley's father bought him his own $12 Hawaiian guitar and history unknowingly was in the making. Wesley spent every spare minute learning how to play. There

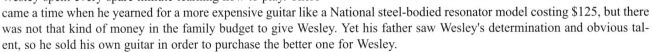

came a time when he yearned for a more expensive guitar like a National steel-bodied resonator model costing $125, but there was not that kind of money in the family budget to give Wesley. Yet his father saw Wesley's determination and obvious talent, so he sold his own guitar in order to purchase the better one for Wesley.

In the 9th grade Wesley won a prize in a school amateur talent contest. By the late 1930's he was spending hours practicing and listening to steel players like Leon McAuliffe and others.

In 1941, at age 17, Wesley married his first wife, Opal Mae. They lived in St. Louis for a year, where Wesley worked at a factory but continued to play music as much as possible. Around 1942 Wesley and Opal moved to Strafford, Missouri near Springfield where they lived and worked on a 200 acre farm owned by Wesley's father.

In 1946 a Grand Ole Opry tent show came to Springfield starring Eddy Arnold and Minnie Pearl. Wesley was so inspired by their talents that he began to think more seriously about pursuing a musical career.

Wesley began to play the steel locally at jam sessions that broadcast over KWTO radio in Springfield. He also played with friends and other local musicians as often as he could. Someone eventually told him about the musical opportunities available in Southern California which would allow him to make as much as $25 a night.

Wesley was playing at a jam session sponsored by KWTO during a pie social event. Slim Wilson, a local country music personality, introduced Wesley to the audience as "Speedy West," a name which has brought him great recognition.

On June 13, 1946 with only $150 in his pocket, Speedy, his wife and their 2-1/2 year old son, Donnie, packed all they could into a 1936 Lincoln Zephyr and headed for Southern California.

During the first few months after arriving in Los Angeles, Speedy worked during the day at a dry cleaners and played steel guitar at night with a group called the Missouri Wranglers. He worked as much as he could at night and on weekends, playing at local bars such as Murphy's and the nearby Fargo Club and the Four Acres.

In 1947 Speedy bought an amp created by Leo Fender, who owned a radio shop in Fullerton, California. In addition to amplifiers, Leo also designed and built steel guitars. This amp was called Fender's Professional Model, which had an all-wood body and handle with chrome trim on the front grille.

Now equipped with a new amp, Speedy felt the necessity of having a more up-to-date steel guitar to replace the homemade electric steel he brought from Missouri. Paul Bigsby from Downey, California a pattern maker, built Speedy a pedal steel. Bigsby had also built a 3-neck non-pedal steel for Joaquin Murphey.

In 1948 Speedy was working at Murphy's Club, located in the skidrow area of Los Angeles when he first met Jimmy Bryant. Jimmy was working down the street from Murphy's at the Fargo Club. One night Jimmy invited Speedy to come and play with him at the Fargo Club and that was the beginning of their long professional and personal relationship.

In the spring of 1948 Spade Cooley, who had a 23-piece western swing band that included a full horn section, hired Speedy. At the time Spade also hosted the Hoffman Hayride TV Variety Show, broadcast by KTLA on Saturday nights in addition to playing various dance jobs. Speedy's job with Spade lasted for five months.

After Spade, Speedy played at the Riverside Rancho in the Shambrock Cowboys Band. It was about that time that friends familiar with Speedy's talents introduced him to Cliffie Stone, assistant A&R man for Capitol Records. Speedy's first recording session was with Eddie Kirk who sang *Candy Kisses.*

Beginning in early 1949 Speedy worked full time doing recording sessions and joined the Hank Penny western swing band. In late 1949 he left Penny when he was hired by Cliffie Stone on his radio program, Dinner Bell Round-Up (later known as the Hometown Jamboree.) Many careers were launched with the help of Cliffie Stone, such as Tennessee Ernie Ford, Merle Travis and others. Eventually Cliffie's show was aired on television which gave Speedy even more exposure.

In 1950 Speedy was given the opportunity to record with Tennessee Ernie Ford and Kay Starr. The songs recorded were *I'll Never Be Free* and *Ain't Nobody's Business But My Own.* Speedy landed a contract with Capitol Records in 1951 with Jimmy Bryant accompanying him.

Between 1950 and 1955 Speedy (with and without Jimmy) played on over 6,000 recordings with 177 different artists.

Also in the early 1950's, Speedy appeared in three Western movies. He began performing on Red Foley's television show "Ozark Jubilee" and had several guests spots on other television specials.

Speedy kept his contract with Capitol Records until 1962. In the meantime he had switched from a Bigsby guitar to a Fender 1000. But country music was beginning to lose its popularity and the opportunities to play were getting scarce. So Speedy made arrangements to work for Fender Musical Instruments as manager of their warehouse in Tulsa, Oklahoma where he moved in September 1960. He continued to play his steel guitar at various functions and had the opportunity to travel all over the country .

In 1974 Speedy, along with fellow musician Sherrill Cummins who owned the Guitar House on Admiral Street in Tulsa, opened what country music lovers know as the "Caravan" on 41st Street. The existing building had at one time been used as a department store called the Caravan and Speedy and Sherrill decided the name fit for their endeavor as well. Speedy's involvement in the Caravan only lasted for about five months. Sherrill eventually purchased the land as well and kept the Caravan for several years before selling it to its current owner.

Speedy's famed guitar playing was showcased as part of the Caravan entertainment along with other musicians in the Speedy West band. He showed me a picture of how the bandstand area looked at that time, which is vastly different from what we see today. Even though the Caravan has continued to be a favorite night spot for country music, Speedy was disappointed when he viewed the establishment several years ago and found the interior lacking the touch of his remembered past.

Speedy had a stroke in 1981 which ended his performing days, but not his vivid memories of all the exciting times. He showed me around his music room which displayed many pictures as well as the huge plaque from his induction into the International Steel Guitar Hall of Fame. Even though he no longer plays his steel guitar professionally, he was kind enough to play a song for me so I could take a glimpse into the musical world of Speedy West. I felt honored as I left the home he shares with his hospitable wife Mary. His son Donnie passed away several years ago, but his youngest son "Speedy West Jr." resides in Oklahoma City and has developed his own style of guitar playing and has become a great picker on both guitar and steel guitar.

Charles Banks Wilson - Artist

Here I am, once again amazed by the talents that can emerge from a single human being. I have viewed many of the sketches created by Charles Banks Wilson and stand in awe of his incredible ability. So often as I work on a profile I find myself wishing I could be like that person and experience the level of expertise they have acquired.

I know nothing happens overnight and along with a talent comes a great deal of dedication and hard work. Charles Banks Wilson has paid the price to be known as one of the most talented artist of our time.

Charles has some interesting family roots. At one time his grandfather, John Joseph Wilson was a circus trapeze performer. While Oklahoma was still considered Indian Territory, he, his wife Carrie and their son Charles Burtrum moved to Miami, Oklahoma. John worked as a house painter and Carrie opened a restaurant.

Charles Burtrum had a flair for playing the trombone and had hoped to be a professional musician. He had a good start toward that goal when the U.S. Army decided they needed a little of his time. By then he had married Bertha Juanita Banks, a grade school teacher from Arkansas. Charles was fortunate to continue his love of music while serving his country by becoming director of a divisional band and a stretcher-bearer in combat. While Charles participated in World War I his wife Bertha went back to her parent's home in Springdale, Arkansas to give birth to their son, Charles Banks Wilson on August 6, 1918.

When the war ended Charles Burtrum and Bertha, along with their new son, returned to Miami and Charles Sr. became a house painter like his father John. Before long he opened his own paint store, which unknowingly began to unveil his son Charles' hidden talents. The younger Charles could be found drawing on just about anything from cardboard inserts found in the paint boxes to pieces of furniture.

In high school his drawing talents improved as he participated in various projects. With some encouragement Charles enrolled in the Art Institute of Chicago in 1936 at the age of 18. Besides his intense classroom studies, Charles spent many hours outside the classroom sketching people and exhibits that would enhance his abilities. Students were encouraged to draw what they knew.

Charles was introduced to the art of lithography which is a drawing executed directly onto a slab of Bavarian limestone. With the correct drawing instruments and the application of ink the drawing is then transferred to paper, making an original magnificent piece of art.

As he reflected back to his home state he realized what better subjects could he choose for his drawings than the Indian tribes which were so prevalent in Oklahoma. At first his instructors didn't seem overly excited about his choice, but his fellow students bought his lithography prints faster than he could produce them.

After three years at the Institute and several awards later he decided to spend the summer of 1939 in Oklahoma, focusing on painting pictures of Indians and learning from his surroundings. He set up a studio above the family paint store which happened to be located across the street from the bus station. Charles solicited people waiting for a bus to pose briefly in his upstairs studio. The majority of the participants were Seneca Indians who Charles paid twenty-five cents an hour to pose. Charles' talents continued to improve and he received opportunities for his work to be published locally and nationally.

In the summer of 1941 Charles married Edna McKibben in Miami's First Presbyterian Church. They immediately left for New York where Charles was commissioned to produce a print for the Associated American Artists. While there Charles became friends with New York's leading lithographer, George Miller who printed Charles' commissioned piece of art. He and Edna also met and made friends with other individuals who were quite well known in the community which made two lonely Okies feel somewhat more at home.

Among his acquaintances was Helen Greenhood, an art editor at Holiday House, a publisher of children's books. She taught Charles a great deal about illustrating and he was given the opportunity to illustrate David Greenhood's book *The Hill* published in 1943. That same year his work also appeared in Jim Kjelgaard's *Rebel Siege*. Over the next 20 years Charles illustrated nearly 30 books. Several of the books were literary classics and a number of them won national awards for book design.

The year 1945 ushered in a new dimension to Charles and Edna's life with the birth of their first child, Geoffrey Banks Wilson.

In 1947 Charles authored his own book, *Quapaw Agency Indians*, which gained such success it was reprinted three times. Charles became so well respected and known for his artistic abilities he was soon asked to teach a class at Northeastern Oklahoma A&M College, even though he had never been educated as a teacher. He continued teaching until 1960 when the demand for his own commissioned projects began to consume his time.

Since leaving New York Charles had not issued any other lithographs until 1947. In 1952 he purchased his own press. George Miller continued printing Charles' work until then. His first mural commission was from John D. Rockefeller, Jr. who asked him to create a mural for the wall behind the bar at the Rockefellers' Jackson Lake Lodge in Wyoming in 1954. That same year his daughter Carrie Vee was born.

The 1950's seemed to bombard Charles with opportunities to display his talents, from history book illustrations to portraits of Will Rogers to lake fishing in Oklahoma for Ford Motor Company.

In 1963 the Oklahoma legislature authorized the creation of works of art in public buildings for the first time in its history. Guess who they commissioned to do the work? Four life-size portraits were created by Charles -one of Will Rogers, Cherokee linguist Sequoyah, U.S. Senator Robert S. Kerr, and Olympic athlete Jim Thorpe. All four portraits are exhibited in the rotunda of the capitol in Oklahoma City.

If I took the time to actually list and elaborate on all of the projects and commissions that Charles has completed over the years there wouldn't be enough space in this book to include the other 199 profiles. His work has been admired and purchased by great men and women everywhere.

In 1977 he was inducted into the Oklahoma Hall of Fame with the Honorable Carl Albert delivering the citation. He truly is a man with an incredible talent who started out drawing in a childlike manner and has escalated to the highest degree of excellence.

Mike Wimmer

Artist

It's hard not to turn green with envy when I see Mike's artistic abilities. It's amazing how he can take a little bit of oil paint, blob it on a canvas and it turns into characters or scenes that appear to come to life.

Born and raised in Muskogee, Oklahoma, Mike's flair for art has been a part of his life since he was two years old drawing a keepsake for his mother.

His first art show net him $1,200 and a 1st, 2nd and 3rd place showing, while he was still in junior high school. Yet his aspirations were to be a professional football player with art being an occasional hobby. He made All State in high school and was preparing to go to college on a football scholarship. With his athletic build, determination and tough guy outlook he thought it was just a matter of time before he was signed to a professional football team. Until he stood beside a 300 pound football player at the All State Camp and found out what the term "tough" really means.

After returning home he humbled himself and asked a few adults he respected what they thought his chances would be in the professional league. Fortunately they were truthful with him. He took their advice, gave up football and put his whole focus toward his talent in art.

Oklahoma University had a great art program, but their techniques just weren't the style of art Mike wanted to pursue. One of his professors, being a wise man and wanting to help guide Mike, set up an apprenticeship for him in Arlington, Texas with the well known and talented artist, Don Punchatz.

For three years Mike did everything he could to learn from Punchatz. He was taught how to think like an artist and how to present his portfolio to potential clients. He learned pricing and copyright laws and the ability to accept rejection as a "not right now" answer rather than a "never ever" answer. He learned techniques and styles and what was really right for him. It was on the job training that prepared him for a career in art that has proven time and time again to have been the right choice.

After his apprenticeship he married Carmelita and they moved back to Norman, Oklahoma where they still live today. Mike began doing freelance work for a textbook company called Economy Publishing. They kept him busy for five years creating textbook covers and page illustrations. He learned to work fast, knowing the paycheck came at the end of the project.

Of course he didn't stop with just one account, he kept himself busy with one client after the other. Most of his jobs came by knocking on doors and showing his portfolio. He got a lot of rejection, but he also got a lot of acceptance. He always remembered what he had learned with Punchatz. *"No" doesn't mean "not ever," it simply means "not right now."*

Mike's second trip to New York landed him his first job with a top notch publisher, Harper Collins as well as Macmillan. He had learned how to present his portfolio properly to publishers and agencies, and realized the quality of his presentation got a lot of attention. He hired his own New York agent who kept his talent constantly in view of potential clients. Mike was beginning to make a name for himself and a position in the world of art.

He has been given so many good opportunities to display his talent. He is the creator of the new "Mr. Clean," which portrays a kinder, gentler man. He has created posters like The Lion King for Disney, C.D. covers and sound track albums. He has clients like American Airlines, Kimberly Clark, Milton Bradley, Readers Digest, Southwestern Bell and more. Yet he says the artwork he enjoys creating the most is what he doesn't get paid for at all. That being portraits of his two beautiful children.

Ever since his two children were born, Mike has dedicated himself to being the best father he could be. Even though he hadn't considered himself as being a spiritual person, when he found out he and his wife were going to have their first child, he felt compelled to make some changes.

Before his first child Elijah (Eli) was born, Mike read the entire Bible through three times, learning more about God than he ever had. The things he didn't understand, he didn't worry about. What he did understand began changing his life forever. He named his son Elijah which means "Yahweh is God," because the birth of Elijah was proof to Mike that Yahweh was God.

His daughter Lauren Alexandria was born four years later. Her name means "Victorious One."

As Mike paints portraits of his children each year, he does it not just to see what they look like, but also to reveal who they are.

In my opinion, it's not by chance that Mike has become such a successful artist. He has first and foremost dedicated himself to being a Godly man. In return as the scripture states, God has given him the ability to acquire wealth -not just in material things, but in every way possible.

Mike Wimmer

Alfre Woodard

Actress

Alfre, the youngest of three children born in Tulsa, Oklahoma on November 8, 1953 was destined to be an actress. As a young girl in high school she was an energetic cheerleader as well a member of the track team. Her parents were amazed at the amount of energy Alfre was constantly exuding, not knowing her exuberance came from an over-active force of creativity. One of her intuitive teachers spoke up one day and encouraged Alfre to channel her energy into acting. From that point on she became focused on a career that would lead her to great heights and fame in the theatrical world.

High school plays such as "The House Of Bernarda Alba" and "Counsel For The Defense" were her beginning, but she quickly realized she needed further training to give her an edge against the competition. She studied drama at Boston University and for a brief time performed in the theatre in "Me And Bessie." After four years at the University when others were continuing their efforts at the theatre Alfre made her way to Los Angeles, California.

In 1978 she appeared with Jeff Goldblum in "Remember My Name." The following year she starred in Altman's "Health" and four years later she was nominated for an Academy Award for her work in "Cross Creek." From there she continued to increase her visibility and hone her talents to become a sought after seasoned actress.

It is unlikely that anyone could have missed seeing a performance of Alfre, if not on television then on the big screen. Most people are familiar with her television roles on "St. Elsewhere," "Hill Street Blues" and "LA Law" all of which she received an Emmy Award.

Alfre received four acting awards for her performance in the HBO New York City production of "Miss Ever's Boys" which aired on HBO in February 1997; she received a Golden Globe Award, Cable ACE Award, a Screen Actors Guild Award and an Emmy Award for Best Actress in a television mini-series or movie. She also starred in the USA Cable tele film "The Member Of The Wedding" which aired in January 1997 and was previously seen on screen with a starring role in the Paramount Pictures production of "Star Trek: First Contact" and in the thriller "Primal Fear" opposite Richard Gere.

Presumably Alfre has had it all including her own family with husband actor-turned writer Roderick Spencer and their two children Mavis and Duncan. It can't be an easy task to put so much effort into a successful career and still have time to raise a family, but Alfre is doing it.

Alfre has starred in the ensemble film "How To Make An American Quilt" and Spike Lee's family drama "Crooklyn." She co-starred in the NBC-TV adaptation of Jonathan Swift's "Gulliver's Travels." Her starring performance in the Hallmark Hall of Fame production of August Wilson's play "The Piano Lesson" earned her a Best Actress Award from the Screen Actors Guild and an Emmy Award nomination.

Most recently Alfre has starred in Lawrence Kasdan's film "Mumford," and the Wesley Snipes' production of "Down In The Delta," directed by Dr. Maya Angelou. She also was seen in New Line's "Love 'N Basketball" and has lent her voice to two animated films from Disney. She provides the voice of a lemur named "Pilo" in "Dinosaur" and she serves as the narrator for "John Henry."

John Wooley
Journalist / Author

I've been hearing the name John Wooley around Tulsa for I don't know how long. He must know half of the city, so I decided I'd add one more person to his list and make an appointment to interview him.

John was born in St. Paul, Minnesota on April 4, 1949. When he was 4 years old his father, John MacFarlane Wooley passed away. So his mother, Ruth moved back to her hometown of Chelsea, Oklahoma. John informed me when his son Jonathan MacFarlane graduated from Chelsea High School in 2002 it was a culmination of three generations at that one school,- Ruth, John and Jonathan. That is something to be proud of.

It's no surprise that John is a writer, it's in his genes. His grandmother Mary M. Wooley who lived to be 100 years old spent her entire life involved in the literary world. Besides writing for the Saturday Evening Post she made her living writing for magazines like *True Confessions* and *True Story.* I don't know if those magazines are still in circulation, but I remember when I was a small child my mother always had one of those magazines laying around somewhere. When I was old enough to read I read my fair share of them as well.

John said he received his first rejection slip for his literary work at age 14, but nevertheless his desire for writing continued to grow. His mother who leaned toward the "school of thought" that he needed to have a backup plan encouraged him to get a degree in something other than writing. John opted for a biology degree from Oklahoma State University. Yet he still wasn't going to forget about writing and sold his first story at age 19. It was an eight page horror story that he sold for $25 to the Eerie Magazine.

After college he wrote and sold a couple more stories while working for The Ralston Purina Company in Edmond as their first plant sanitarian. But despite his biology degree he was elated when he left there 7 months later to go on active duty as a Naval Reservist aboard a helicopter carrier.

After his military discharge as a Vietnam veteran John was eligible for the G.I. Bill. He took advantage of that opportunity and enrolled at Central State College. This time he was determined to follow his dream of writing. Interestingly, his creative writing teacher was none other than Distinguished Oklahoman Marilyn Harris. Her book *Hatter Fox* had just been made into a movie, so obviously he would be taught by the best. He remembers Marilyn signing one of her books for him and commenting, "Someday you're going to be signing one of your books for me."

John has always been a horror story buff. He grew up watching old movies on television like "The Mummy," "Frankenstein," and "Dracula." He also loved the magazine titled *Famous Monsters of Filmland.* So needless to say, he wrote his first novel *Demon Wind* as his master thesis for college. However, even he wasn't thrilled with the outcome and hopes no one ever finds it hidden under the layers of dust in the college library archives.

After receiving his master's degree he took a job at Rose State College in Del City. During that time he collaborated with a few other young writers and established what he named the Robert B. Leslie Foundation. It was named after one of his favorite old-time writers, Robert Leslie Bellem. John's first book, published by Bowling Green State University's Popular Press in 1983, was a collection of Bellem's old pulp-magazine stories.

One gentleman in his foundation was Michael McQuay who has since passed on, but not before he had 50 books to his credit. Another part of the group was Ron Wolfe who wrote for the Tulsa Tribune for many years and is now writing for the Arkansas Democrat Gazette as a feature writer.

In 1979 John married Janis who was originally from Tulsa and they decided to move to Foyil, a little town right outside of Chelsea. John went to work for Rogers State teaching creative writing. On the side he collaborated with Ron Wolfe long distance to create the book *Old Fears.* It is a story about an adult male who returns to his hometown to find that all of his childhood fears were coming to pass. The book sold to Franklin Watts Publishing and John and Ron thought they were off and running. However, they didn't sell another book for nine long years.

In 1981 Ken Jackson who has since passed on was the book editor for the Tulsa World newspaper. He and John had become friends while they were both teaching at Rogers State. He suggested John write some articles for the Sunday World supplement which was then called OK Magazine, sort of like the Spot insertion in the Tulsa World today. John agreed.

The first story he wrote was about the totem pole located between Foyil and Adair. It had been a landmark since the 1950's, but was in horrible disrepair. John had no idea he had created such an interesting story until he pulled up to the totem pole the Sunday his story came out and found difficulty parking. A line of cars filled with curious passengers had accumulated along the side of the road viewing this intriguing piece of history.

Then in 1983 Tom Carter, who was the country music reporter for the Tulsa World, resigned to relocate in Nashville, Tennessee as a celebrity biographer. Ken Jackson suggested John fill his spot. Of course he did and John's writing career has continued to blossom over the years. He has written, co-written or edited 11 books. He has written two movies and three documentaries.

John said he disciplines himself and gets up at 6 a.m. every morning but Tuesday to write for two hours before he leaves for work. Each Tuesday he foregoes writing in order to meet with the famed Billy Parker to tape their collaborated radio show "Swingin Country" which highlights old country music and western swing music. The program airs on Saturday morning from 7 to 9 and Sunday night from 10 to midnight. John said he has learned more about show business from Billy than anyone else he knows.

In addition John works with Studio Tulsa doing a show called "Warped Vinyl." It's a monologue about old vinyl albums and what can be found on those outdated tracks.

John is very proud of his lot in life. Besides being an accomplished author, he takes great pride in being able to review individuals in their chosen fields and highlights their careers through the medium of the Tulsa World. He calls it "Celebrating Their Creativity."

He has learned over the years just how important our words are, whether written or spoken. When they go out into the air ways they carry with them "moral weight." Words have the opportunity to create a force of either good or evil and we take on undeniable responsibility as to which direction they go.

John gave me a copy of his latest book, *Awash In The Blood.* You guessed it, it's a horror story. I read it from cover to cover in one sitting. Even though it's content definitely took an imaginative approach, it took no imagination to distinguish the war between good and evil. Ultimately the good prevailed and I sighed a sigh of relief.

No one knows what still lies unwritten in the corridors of John's creative mind, so be aware. Who knows what lurks around the next corner?

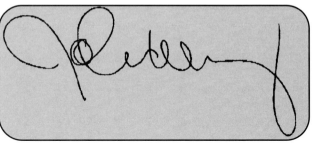

Sheb Wooley

Actor / Singer / Songwriter

I'm sure everyone has heard of the *One Eyed, One Horn, Flying Purple People Eater.* But did you know it was a song created by one of Erick, Oklahoma's most distinguished public figures? So much so, Erick named a street after him, Sheb Wooley Boulevard. I am anxious to meet him in person, but I felt like I knew him after the first few minutes on the phone.

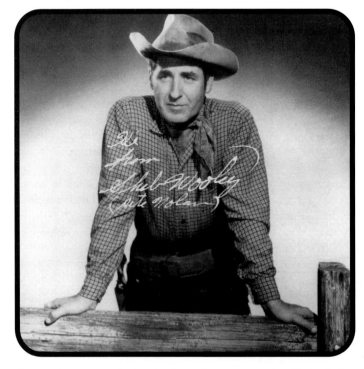

Even though Erick is a small town just across the border from the Texas panhandle it obviously has done something right in order to have raised such quality people as Sheb Wooley. A few years later country music star Roger Miller came along.

Sheb was born April 10, 1921 to William Curtis and Ora Wooley. As a young boy probably around 9 years old Sheb used to go with his parents to the town's country dances. It didn't take long before Sheb found himself sitting on the stage between the guitar and fiddle player dreaming of the day he could fill their shoes. *He found out later if you dream the dream and it becomes strong enough it will put you into motion and become reality.*

By the time he was 15 he had his own band, The Plainview Melody Boys and they had their own show on a radio station in nearby Elk City, Oklahoma. As a teenager Sheb was a skilled rodeo rider and became quite accustomed to sitting on horses --a skill that later served him well in Hollywood. However, because of a rodeo accident while still in his youth, he injured his leg which made him ineligible for the Armed Services.

In 1945, right after World War II, he left for Nashville thinking he wasn't going to wait any longer to begin making his dream come true. He had over 100 songs written and felt like someone needed to hear what they were. He spent a year in Nashville hoping to be recognized for his talents and be given an incredible break into the business. Mainly he just received encouragement from people like Ernest Tubb to continue on.

He eventually did land a spot as a performer on WLAC Radio in Nashville at 4:45 a.m. singing his own originals. Even though the time slot was in the wee hours of the morning it gave him some exposure until another slot came open at 4:45 p.m. He also cut four sides at the WSM Radio studios for the Bullet record label. Though two of them were not released until several years later and the others were never issued, they were none-the-less some of the first records he ever recorded in Music City. Sheb also started making personal appearances and his dream was beginning to step into the light.

An interesting side note to his career which is funny now but at the time must have been an exciting as well as humbling experience. Sheb said during those early days in Nashville he had a picture made of himself with a song printed on the back. He made that available to his fans for 25 cents. He told how excited he was each week when he checked his mail and retrieved the quarters that fell from those most wanted envelopes making (Cherished memories).

During this time Sheb was married to Roger Miller's cousin, Melva Laurie, who was working for famed singer/songwriter Eddy Arnold. Eddy thought it would be a good idea for Sheb to go to Dallas and hook up with a friend of his who had a radio show on one of the local stations there. Sheb took his advice and headed for Dallas.

When Eddy's lead didn't pan out Sheb went on over to WBAP in Ft. Worth and landed a 15 minute radio show sponsored by Calumet Baking Powder. He also put his own band together, the Calumet Indians. His show was broadcast over a dozen or so different 50,000 watt stations throughout the southwestern United States. The exposure soon made Sheb and the band much in demand for personal appearances.

While Sheb was in Nashville he had been told by different individuals he should pursue acting and someday make his way to Hollywood, so in 1950 he headed that way. His first order of business was to find an agent. He laughingly says the agent describes that day somewhat different than what he remembers.

Supposedly Sheb walked into his office wearing a big ole cowboy hat and said "I want to be a movie star." But no matter how the story is told Sheb became just that. At first he was cast in a play which he admits he wasn't very good in, but as a result he was seen by a local talent scout. It seems Warner Brothers was looking for a few young new faces and at the time Sheb laughingly says, "I had one! "

He was cast into his first motion picture, "Rocky Mountain" starring Errol Flynn. Sheb resided in Hollywood from 1950-1979 and appeared in over 70 feature films. His most notable was when he played killer Ben Miller in "High Noon" starring Gary Cooper and Grace Kelly (her first film). Other highly recognizable films he played in were "War Wagon" with John Wayne and Kirk Douglas, "Rio Bravo" with John Wayne, "Distant Drums" with Gary Cooper and "Giant" with James Dean and Elizabeth Taylor.

There were times in those early years in Hollywood when there would be a lull in his acting career and he would write more songs and perform in local honky tonks around the area just to keep food on the table. But in 1954 a song he had written called *Too Young To Tango* became a million seller for the very popular Theresa Brewer. Then heavy hitter Hank Snow recorded Sheb's song *When Mexican Joe Met Jole Blon,* and it sold around 400,000 copies.

Surely everyone has either seen or heard about the extremely popular television show "Rawhide" that aired from 1959-1967. Sheb played the role of "Pete Nolan," Clint Eastwood's faithful scout. In addition, he wrote several scripts for the series in which Clint Eastwood also got his real start in the film business.

During the pilot making of "Rawhide" Sheb wrote his greatest hit song ever called *Purple People Eater*. The song came about during a conversation with one of his songwriter friends. Don Robertson was telling Sheb about his son coming home from school with a joke about purple people. After hearing the joke Sheb suggested the two of them write a song about it, but Don wasn't interested, thinking it wasn't his style. Later Sheb spent an hour or so jotting down a few lines and the rest is musical smash-hit history.

With some reservations MGM Records released the song and within three days it was one of the hottest songs in the world, selling several million copies. Sheb said after all these years there are now two "purple people eater" dolls out on the market that you can probably purchase for around $10 that play that all familiar song.

In 1969 Sheb was one of the original cast members of "Hee Haw," the long-running country comedy series for which he wrote the theme song.

After Sheb left Hollywood in 1979 he moved back to Nashville where he continues to live today with his wife Linda, who is also his best friend and strongest promoter.

I wish I had space to tell you all the other numerous projects Sheb has accomplished over the years. He is truly one of the most unique and talented individuals you would ever want to meet. In compiling this book it has been one of the most painstaking projects I have ever attempted. I have never worked so hard and long in my life. Yet when I meet people like Sheb Wooley, it makes it all worthwhile.

R.A. Young - Business

R.A. Young on the Right

It was quite an honor for me to meet Mr. Young. I grew up going to his variety stores, but I never thought there was a real man behind the third letter in T.G.&Y.

Mr. Young was born in 1904 to C.W. and Phoebie Young. He describes himself as coming from humble beginnings, since his father was a poor farmer and his mother a "stay at home" mom raising eight children.

At the time of our interview, R.A. was 95 years old. As he spoke of his mother it was as if she were still right there, when in fact, she passed away when he was eight years old. His father passed away when he was 20.

R.A. spoke of how he would watch his mother time and time again working in their kitchen, and then all of a sudden she would stop, close her eyes and begin whispering. That whispering, he found out later, was his mother praying. He gives her credit for his spiritual side. After teaching a men's Bible class for 40 years, he is definitely qualified for a spiritual side.

Before his mother died, she made the oldest brother, Kenneth promise he would make sure all the children went through college. That was a promise he swore he would keep, and he did. Kenneth didn't marry until he was 50 years old, and all eight children had been through college at Oklahoma State University.

During R.A.'s college days he worked at five different jobs simultaneously to get himself through school, while the oldest brother made sure he never went hungry. What a wonderful tribute to a praying mother. It is amazing that a mother could have so much impact on the lives of her eight children, even though her time with them was limited.

R.A.'s first job after college was as a principal of a school in Mountainview, Oklahoma. From there he went to Folgerty Junior High in Guthrie, Oklahoma. It was in Guthrie that he met a man by the name of Willis, who was a manager for the Kress Variety Store in Pueblo, Colorado. They struck up a friendship that led to Mr. Willis eventually leaving his position in

Colorado and starting a variety store with R.A. in Pauls Valley, Oklahoma. They called the store The Willis Young Company.

In time, another store was opened in Kingfisher and Mr. Young moved there to run that store. He eventually bought out Mr. Willis's share of the Kingfisher store and renamed it the R.A. Young Company. That one store grew to 18 stores in different cities in Oklahoma.

Eight years later in 1936 he joined forces with R.E. Tomlinson and E.L. Gosselin to form a chain of 25 stores which we all grew to know as T.G.&Y. Tomlinson was the money backer with no active participation. Gosselin was the promoter and public relations person, as well as the buyer. R.A. Young was the guy with the business sense who operated the stores. By the time the men sold out to the Butler Brothers almost 30 years later, they had increased their stores to 500 throughout the United States. The company continued to grow and eventually had 950 stores in 29 states.

R.A. couldn't bring himself to totally stay uninvolved, so he took on the position of a consultant and senior member of the board until he was almost 80 years old. I'm sure it's hard to let go of something you have nurtured from its infancy. There is no longer a chain of T.G.&Y. stores, they have been bought out by Household International of which R.A. Young is still a stockholder.

R.A. has also been married to Verna, his wife of 70 years, which is another example of Mr. Young's loyalty and faithfulness. Together they raised two beautiful daughters, Carolyn and Karita. He proudly told me he has four grandchildren he has had the privilege of putting through college. Each one of them has a very lucrative trust fund because R.A. is a firm believer of helping them now while they need his help.

When I think back to all of his success, it once again leads me to his mother. In eight short, formative years, she was able to instill strength and character in R.A. that could never be erased.

Mr. Young is a true gentleman. In 1967 he was inducted into the Oklahoma Hall of Fame. He served on many company boards over the years and has exemplified qualities that continue to rank him in the category of a Distinguished Oklahoman.

Stanton Young - Business

I had just finished an interesting interview with Lee Allan Smith and my appointment with Stanton Young wasn't until 2:00 in the afternoon, so I had a little time to spare. That was helpful though because it gave me time to gather my thoughts about the previous meeting and prepare me for Mr. Young.

My experience with interviewing people has always been so rewarding. I find myself on a continual learning journey. Everywhere I go and every person I meet seems to teach me something new and different about life. Not only does it give me respect for them, but it helps create in me a desire to become a better person.

When I arrived at Stanton's office I was greeted with a friendly smile from his secretary, Shirley Schritter. She introduced me to Stanton and we proceeded to walk into his impressive office where he offered me a very comfortable spot in his quaint sitting area. Almost immediately I began to feel a gentleness about him that was extremely comforting, which alerted me to the reason for his success.

Stanton was born in McAlester, Oklahoma in 1927 and by 1932 he and his family had moved to Oklahoma City. Because of his father's ties to the oil industry Stanton was introduced early to the oil business. His family influences were of significant benefit to him as his school teacher mother and his entrepreneurial minded father nurtured him. Even though it appeared natural that Stanton would make his career in the oil industry, his first thoughts had been to go into the medical field.

He enrolled in college to pursue medicine but quickly saw that wasn't the direction he should go in. However, a few years later he found himself with ties to the medical community.

At Oklahoma University Stanton majored in accounting with a minor in economics. He went on to receive a master's degree in geology and geography. While in college he became friends with Professor John R. Morris, Ph.D., who influenced him greatly and left him with a sense of gratitude for the importance of education.

Because of his influence, in 1950 Stanton began giving scholarships to deserving black students in the school of business who would agree with him that upon graduation they would live and work in Oklahoma. He continued that program for several years. For the past 18 years he has endowed a Master Teacher Award to the University of Oklahoma's Science Center which is recognized as the most important award the college of medicine offers each year. The award is $15,000.

The obvious question to me was why the College of Medicine? At age 28 Stanton was elected as an Elder in the Westminster Presbyterian Church where he was involved in its Teaching Ministry for seven years. Having already established a desire to help his fellow man, he wanted to reach out into the community beyond the four walls of the church and make a statement to the outside world that the church cared. It just so happened that the health care industry allowed him to become involved in a Ministry of Healing as Chairman of the Presbyterian Hospital.

Since so much had been mentioned about Stanton's church background, I asked him to share his spiritual beliefs with me. Not only does he believe that Christianity is a means to seek personal salvation, but is, also, a means to reach out and seek to improve the human condition of others.

To commit to that idea he became involved in civil rights issues. During the 1960's he observed the unfair treatment put upon so many people of the black community that threatened their rights as American citizens. He recalled prejudice incidents such as the exclusion of African Americans at the drug store food counters or the denying of accommodations at a local downtown hotel. At City Hall there were designated restrooms and drinking fountains for the "Blacks" who were considered to be of lesser importance. They were still required to move to the back of the bus when they entered what was meant to be public transportation.

It was not a happy time in the history of the state. Stanton was given the opportunity to help facilitate some of the changes that needed to be made.

In 1965 the Economic Opportunity Act was voted in under the Johnson Administration. At the time Stanton was the vice president of the Oklahoma City Chamber of Commerce. He was asked to be the first chairman of that program in the community. He developed so much trust with people that he held the position for three terms.

It was apparent that Stanton took his responsibility as a caring person very seriously. "I really believe someday there will be a Kingdom of God established here on earth," he said. "If each one of us could help that happen one second sooner, all of our lives would be so much better."

In 1963 Stanton decided to expand his business ventures so he bought the Journey House Travel Agency which he still owns today. In 1967 he led a group which purchased the Pepsi Cola franchises covering about one-third of Oklahoma which were sold in 1983.

I asked Stanton with all his success has he ever had any failures. "Oh yes," he said. "I've drilled my share of dry holes." Then what is your solution to dealing with failure? "Failure is just a part of living," he said. "If you make decisions on all of the facts available you should not be disappointed. However, any perceived failure should be viewed as an opportunity in disguise."

I thoroughly enjoyed my time with Stanton. Our interview came to a close as we talked about his wife, Barbara and their three children. Lee lives in Oklahoma City and is involved in investments. One daughter, Marie Elise is a CPA and lives in Vermont and their other daughter, Carol unfortunately passed away in 1985. In her memory her brother and sister have established the Carol Elizabeth Foundation that helps fund educational and medical assistance in Central America where she spent most of her career. They have also established the Barbara and Stanton Young Foundation which gives grants in the health care and health research areas.

Lastly Stanton was inducted into the Oklahoma Hall of Fame in 1988. Along with his many accomplishments he has been known as the "Bridge Builder" and "Peacemaker" between people and factions. No one had to sell me on that definition of this man. I realized it from the moment I stepped into his presence.

Kathryn Zaremba

Actress / Singer

What an incredible young lady. I met Kathryn just before her sixteenth birthday. She has more personality than what should be legally allowed for one human being. She makes some of us appear very boring.

I'm sure you've seen Kathryn's local commercials for the Price Mart Grocery Stores or Drug Warehouse. Yet, you may not know that she started her career when she was only seven years old. Innocently wanting to be part of everything her older sister was doing, Kathryn enrolled in the Broken Arrow Academy of Dance owned by Kirstin Jolissant. At the time, Broken Arrow High School was auditioning for parts in the play "Annie." Kathryn was given the role of Molly and her sister played the part of Duffy. Continuing to take classes at the Academy and Theatre Arts they heard about auditions for "Annie" that were taking place in Oklahoma City, so they went there to try out as well. Kathryn again played the part of Molly while her sister took on the role of Tessie. While they were in Oklahoma City, they met the dog trainer for the original broadway production of "Annie," (Bill Berloni). He informed them that there were going to be auditions the following week in Houston for a sequel of "Annie" called "Annie Warbucks." He was just sure that Kathryn was the perfect person for an orphan and she should go to Houston and audition. Kathryn's mother asked the director's opinion, and her comment was more than encouraging. She said, "If you don't want Kathryn to have the part, then don't take her, because if she auditions, she will get it." Sure enough Kathryn went to Houston and was cast immediately as an orphan for the touring company, which resulted in a four month tour. Not long after that, the decision was made to take the production to Broadway. The now 9 year old, 3 foot and 11 inch Kathryn was cast as Annie Warbucks. Her eyes still sparkle when she tells about her numerous experiences during that year on Broadway. She had the opportunity to meet some incredible people. Since she was so young she didn't realize then the caliber of people she was meeting. She just knew she was having a blast doing it. She recalls one event when she sang at the White House for the President. She knew it was a big deal to be there, but not until she got a few years older did she realize not everyone has that kind of opportunity.

When her year on Broadway came to an end she took a short trip back to Oklahoma for a visit before heading off for California. She already had a taste of performing and wanted to see what Hollywood might have in store for her. Within a month she had landed a role on a television pilot as well as a musical called Ruthless. She later did several commercials for corporations like Nike, McDonalds, Kodak and Mattel. Television shows like "Full House," "Sisters," and "Jeff Foxworthy" gave her reoccurring roles that continued to solidify her acting abilities as well as the Disney Movie "Toothless" starring Kirstie Alley.

The summer before she entered the eighth grade she decided she wanted to come back home to Broken Arrow, Oklahoma and just be an ordinary school kid for a while.

Kathryn is working hard trying to finish high school. She keeps up on her acting and singing skills by attending a camp every summer in Florida as well as occasional trips to New York where she has been a part of a few musical C.D.'s performed by Broadway Kids. I had the opportunity to listen to Kathryn's C.D., which highlights songs sung by different young people. Kathryn's voice was unmistakable, she needed no introduction.

When Kathryn graduates from high school she plans to move to New York and submerge herself in her career. She feels so fortunate to be who she is and to have had the opportunities that have come her way.

I was so impressed with this young girl that was growing up to be a beautiful young lady inside and out. Her maturity level far surpassed someone her age. It goes without saying that her mother Terrie and her grandparents Gerry and Bill have done a wonderful job guiding Kathryn into adulthood. Not only is she a talented singer and performer, but she also is a loving, caring individual that sees life in a way that has brought happiness to her whole family. There is no doubt that Kathryn has a wonderful future ahead of her. I'm sure she will continue to make Broken Arrow and the State of Oklahoma very proud of her.

In 1994, Kathryn was awarded Oklahoma's Ambassador of Goodwill by Governor Walters and was presented by Senator David Boren.

I couldn't leave our interview without having Kathryn sing the all-famous song *Tomorrow* from her Broadway hit. I sat there with tears in my eyes, feeling a sense of motherly pride for a child performer that had won my heart.

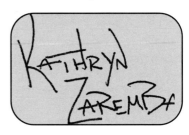

Henry Zarrow - Business

A perfect example of a "True Gentleman."

Henry was born February 12, 1916 in Milwaukee, Wisconsin of poor Russian immigrants. They moved to Tulsa, Oklahoma when Henry was only a few months old. While he was growing up his father, Sam Zarrow had a grocery store on the north side of Tulsa. His mother, Rose always told him there were too many hours involved in running a grocery store and she wanted him to find another means of work.

Henry volunteered to work for his uncle who had a second-hand pipe-yard. He was willing to work for nothing so he could learn the business. One night when his uncle had a rush order to get out, he paid Henry $10 for helping him most of the night.

Henry graduated from Central High School in 1934 and attended Oklahoma University and Tulsa University.

In his quest to be more involved in the pipe business, he became acquainted with a gentleman by the name of Abe Pepis. He told him about a place around the corner from his uncle's pipeyard that he could rent at a very low price and begin his own pipeyard.

He started first with junk pipe and then progressed to second-hand pipe. All the while, he was hoping someday he would be able to sell new pipe to all of the pipeline companies. In order to sell new pipe, you were required to have a store or the pipe mills would not sell to you.

In 1937 when he was 21 years old, his dream came true. He opened his first store in Pawhuska, Oklahoma and named it Sooner Pipe and Supply. At the time Pawhuska was a booming city and a great place to start a new business. A lot of people who bought scrap pipe from Henry eventually became presidents of their own companies and came to Henry to buy their new pipe. As Henry's business grew, his customers' businesses grew as well. They were all on their way to a brighter future.

Before long Henry's father sold his grocery store and went to work for Henry. His younger brother Jack followed 10 years later.

The business grew quickly. They expanded into Kansas, Alabama, Louisiana, California and Texas. The work was so exciting for Henry! He met a lot of wonderful people along the way who helped him become successful.

The same year he opened his first store, he married his wife Anne. She blessed him with two children, Stuart and Judy, who in return have given him seven grandchildren.

In 1953 Henry bought Bigheart Pipe Line Corporation, A-Z Terminal Corporation and TK Valve & Manufacturing, Inc. It wasn't long before Henry's dream had expanded to include sales all over the world.

Over the years Henry has felt it is important to give back to the community that had given so much to him. He has involved himself in numerous charitable organizations, one of which is the "homeless shelter."

In Henry's opinion, there is no excuse for a person not to be able to give to someone if he really wants to. His first opportunity to give was when he had no money at all. He had to borrow $500 in order to give it away. He paid the money back and from then on made giving a lifelong practice. That reminds me of a scripture that says "Give and it shall be given to you, pressed down, shaken together and overflowing will men give unto you." Henry has certainly proven with his abundant wealth and tremendous success the truth of that scripture.

In 1979 Henry was honored with the Brotherhood Award by the National Conference of Christians and Jews. In 1981 he was given the Service to Mankind Award by the Sertoma Club, the highest honor that organization gives. His awards and tributes have been many. He is one of the founders of the American Trauma Society which operates on a national basis. He has been on numerous boards over the years, too many to even begin to mention.

Henry admits how fortunate he has been in life. He has had the chance to meet a number of people, see some beautiful sights and partake in a vast amount of opportunities and experiences.

He is a firm believer in a person having integrity and their word being their bond. He has surrounded himself with people he knew he could trust. He believes they influenced him and he may have influenced them also to some degree.

Henry said his meager beginnings, which he thought would only allow him to make a living, somehow with the help of God developed into so much more. He has had a good life for which he is so very grateful.

I will never forget my interview with Henry Zarrow. His presence speaks volumes. He is the kind of man where a handshake would be all that was needed to seal the deal. No wonder God has blessed him so abundantly.

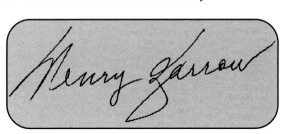

Paul Ziert ~ Coach/Business Executive

Paul was born in Iowa, but grew up just outside of Peoria, Illinois. His father, Hugh worked for the Caterpiller Tractor Company. His mother, Eva was extremely musical. She could play the piano, organ, accordion, clarinet or just about any musical instrument.

Because of her love for music, when Paul was six years old she enrolled him in dance classes. He took tap, jazz and acrobatics. That is where his love for gymnastics first began. To add to that he joined the YMCA and practiced tumbling.

His love of gymnastics continued to grow until he became junior national tumbling champion. He was supposed to go to the University of Illinois on an athletic scholarship when he realized he had a chipped bone in his elbow. Believing doctors when they told him he wouldn't be able to compete anymore, he reluctantly turned down the athletic scholarship. These days, a lot can be done to correct a chipped elbow, but there weren't many options back then. Paul went to Illinois State University instead on an academic scholarship. His degree was in mathematics, so in order to be involved in gymnastics he would have to become a teacher. For Paul, there was no other way, because he still desperately wanted to be a part of gymnastics.

His first teaching job was in the suburbs of Southside Chicago. He taught mathematics and gymnastics there for eight years. Five of those years he spent his summer months at Stanford University getting his masters degree in mathematics.

In 1973, he was offered the job as head gymnastics coach for Oklahoma University where they had a gymnastics team. From 1973 to 1976, Paul was one of three coaches who developed the junior national program for boys in the United States. Because of that, he was able to travel to different gym training camps.

At one of those camps he became acquainted with Bart Conner, who later became the United States most decorated male gymnast. Paul recruited Bart to join the team at Oklahoma University in 1976. A lasting friendship began to form between Paul and Bart. Together they set out to build a million dollar training facility. The athletic department gave $250,000 dollars and the rest was raised in an 18 month period. Paul still thinks the facility is the nicest one in the United States.

After the facility was built, Paul took Bart to the 1984 Olympic Games where he came home with two gold medals. Paul decided to stop coaching at that point, but he still wanted to find avenues to stay involved with gymnastics. He and Bart began tossing a few ideas around. Some of those results can be found in Norman, Oklahoma at the Bart Conner Gymnastics Academy located at 3206 Bart Conner Drive.

There are many facets to their combined efforts in the sport of gymnastics. They have an 18,000 square foot gym on site, which is constantly filled with aspiring young athletes.

Along with the gym, another building is located on the same property. This building houses the offices of Paul Ziert, Bart Conner and Nadia Comaneci. Within those walls, wheels are constantly turning, creating ways to further acknowledge the great sport of gymnastics that Paul, Bart and Nadia have poured their lives into.

They bought the International Gymnast Magazine in 1992 from the original owner who established the magazine in 1957. The accumulated issues contain the complete history of the sport of gymnastics. Although the elderly founder had many offers to buy the publication, he wanted Paul Ziert & Associates to have the magazine because he knew they would keep it current.

Paul Ziert & Associates are the largest manufacturers of grips, the leather hand guards used by a gymnast on the uneven bars, rings and high bar. Paul Ziert & Associates are also the only American manufacturers of gym shoes. The shoes, believe it or not, are made by hand, one shoe at a time.

It is so inspiring when you meet someone that has such a fire inside of them that it continues to burn with more speed and fervency as the years go by. Paul's love for gymnastics have never ceased to exist. He prides himself in being a perennial student, always wanting to be on the cutting edge of some learning experience. He knows it's easy to get lazy with your life and settle for status quo, but he wants to always be learning something that will enhance life and give joy to the next new morning.

Paul F. Ziert

Jerry Zirkle – Minister/Radio

The Christian radio station KNYD out of Broken Arrow, Oklahoma has given me many hours of incredible teaching over the years. One of the preachers who has always encouraged me with his obvious love for the Lord has been Jerry Zirkle. His message has always been very simple yet he has the overwhelming ability to make me understand the Father and Child relationship that can exist between a person and God.

On many occasions I have passed by his office building always telling myself I need to contact him for an interview, yet it took almost three years to get the task accomplished. The day of our interview I was privileged to meet Jerry and see for myself what a gentle, caring man he really is.

As I sat down in front of his desk I immediately glanced down to the name plate that seemed to jump out at me. On the name plate were the words "El Shaddai Jr." My heart leaped, feeling a sense of knowing what was meant by that title. Jerry said the nameplate, given to him by some of his previous Bible students, has been a source of controversy for those who didn't understand his boldness in displaying it. However, I knew from my own spiritual revelations that not only did it show Jerry's reverence of the Lord, but also his confidence in his relationship with God.

Jerry commented, "I am my Father's favorite son, I'm just not the only one." I now know the importance of having that kind of confidence in a relationship with God and yet it took me years of struggling to know it was all right to feel that way. Without a doubt, I believe society as a whole would be so much better off if everyone could experience the kind of relationship with God that enables them to proudly wear the title of El Shaddai Jr., the All Sufficient One's, son.

Jerry was born into a family of eight children on March 15, 1937 in Akron, Ohio. His father was in the carpentry business and taught all of his sons the trade as well. Jerry said by the time he was 14 years old he could pretty much build a house on his own.

Even though Jerry's father didn't become a Christian until the year of his death, his mother saw to it that each of her children had a spiritual walk with God. As a result, all eight children at one point found themselves in Christian ministry. Jerry remembers his mother always reminding him when he walked out the door that he was foremost a Christian, so make sure his actions revealed it.

By the time he was 9 years old Jerry and his brother Bob were featured on the local Akron radio station WADC where they remained for the next 22 years. With guitar in hand and voices that sounded forth the praises of God, the Zirkle Boys as they were called began to establish themselves in the Christian world. On weekends their schedules were usually booked solid with invitations from people who heard them on the radio and wanted them to share their talents and beliefs with their congregations.

Christian ministry was all Jerry really knew. He held down several secular jobs over the years and owning his own business, but ministry was always what he wanted to do. There came a day when he wasn't satisfied with the knowledge he had about the Bible and wanted to increase his learning by more intensive study.

In August of 1978 when Jerry was 42 years old he moved to Oklahoma to enter the Rhema Bible Training Center to further equip himself for the ministry. Being a father of five and a husband to Linda, he wanted to care for them as he always had, yet he had a burning desire to follow a path he had not yet totally given himself to. They packed everything they owned and with trailer in tow left Ohio headed for Oklahoma.

At a time when most men are slowing down in their career pursuit, Jerry was gearing up for a whole new realm of endeavor. At age 44 Jerry became the pastor of Living Water Teaching in Broken Arrow, Oklahoma along with his brother Jim who held the position as president of the organization. For 18 years they worked alongside each other training and sending over 100 young people to the mission fields in Central America. Jerry has preached half way around the world and sat before kings and presidents of other countries telling them about God.

In 1986 when David Ingles launched the Oasis Network he encouraged Jerry to once again let his voice be heard. At first Jerry refused, thinking his days on radio had long passed. But with a little more persuasion he found himself sitting behind a microphone making friends simply by sharing his love for the Lord.

In 1994 Jerry felt a change coming to his life. He resigned his position at the church, determined to see what the Lord was wanting to reveal to him. *With change sometimes comes a season of unknowing, yet Jerry was confident that in time God would show him the direction he needed to go.*

Since a faith walk has been a way of life for Jerry for so many years he was accustomed to the battles that go along with it. He reminded me that *battles in life are a fight of faith, not a fight with the devil or issues that come into our lives.* There is a scripture that says, "The violent take it by force" that seems to sound the opposite of what Christians are supposed to be known for. But if you know the true meaning it makes perfect sense. *The ones with tenacity and inner spiritual strength are the survivors and winners in life. They mean business to the point that they never give up or quit.*

Radio continued to be Jerry's main focus until two years ago when he stepped back into the role of a pastor. He thought his season for pastoring had ended when he resigned from Living Water Teaching Center. Surely he was too old to pick up the reigns once again. But after much prayer, God revealed to him he was more equipped for the position now than he ever had been before. *With age comes wisdom and the ability for God to trust you even further because your track record has been established.*

Jerry feels like this is a great time in his life. He said he never stops learning about God's faithfulness and His desire to bless His children. Of course he understands God's ways more now than he did 40 years ago. His comprehension about what it means to be El Shaddai Jr. gives him comfort and builds a shield of faith around him that can no longer be jeopardized by insecurities or lack of knowledge. With maturity comes the opportunity to finally step into a safe place of knowing and believing as the great hymn of old states, "How Great Thou Art."

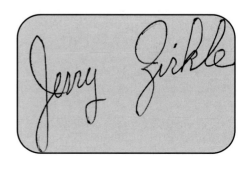

Nazih Zuhdi – Surgeon

I've never met a man quite like Dr. Nazih Zuhdi. Even his name is unique. When I left his office the day of our interview I really felt like I had been in the presence of greatness. Even though Dr. Zuhdi is an American, after spending a couple of hours with him I had a whole new appreciation for people of the Middle East-the land of all the prophets of God.

He states: I am of Semitic lineage and Arabian heritage with Turkish and Tcherkess genes. I am a committed Muslim. I was born to Omar and Lutfiye Zuhdi in Beirut, Lebanon on May 19, 1925. I grew up in the most ancient city of Halab. Beneath my playful feet lay, according to legend, seven levels of cities past, civilizations gone and worlds lost. Very early in my terrestrial walk of life I heard through the emptiness of the heart of a child and later, I read in the sacred holiness of the mosque the glorious flowing verses of The Holy Quran-the words of God. Five words "to God do we submit" embody (consolidate, are) the foundational tenet of the three Abrahamic religions: Judaism, Christianity and Islam. This commonality of the fundamental tenet intertwines and interweaves the seemingly variant peoples. God ordained that there be variant peoples -"So vie one with another in virtuous deeds. To God you will all return, so He will inform you of that wherein you differed." (The Holy Quran, Chapter 5:51)

In a speech Dr. Zuhdi put forth an explanation for the unrest in the world. I was so moved by the depth of his words I had to include them also.

He states: Scenes of horror and displays of terror occur because, not of a delicate world balance to maintain, as they claim, but because of a demonic world balance we tolerate, I assert. We should all be haunted by the words of my preferred poet of all times, the Bedouin Al Maare. Listen to his paraphrased words from more than a thousand years, "Remember, remember to tread lightly when we walk, for under our feet are ourselves, our ashes through the ages." Though blind, Al Maare saw what God wanted. This code of conduct gave form to my thought, molded my philosophy and made me what I am. My uncharted sojourn to Oklahoma, my scientific pursuits and my medical vocation seem to be my anointed pathway to a destined Grand Design, long before my foot was set on the trek-a paradigm beyond a limited Judeo-Christian tradition into the full realization of the complete and final Judeo-Christian-lslamic reality.

He dreams of the day when we no more cower in the darkest corners, shivering from our fear of one another-together our uplifted prayers will chase away the ghosts of our ugly, bloody, and senseless past and present.

Now that I am beyond three scores and ten, I am starting to feel the gentle, tender and warm breeze of my celestial domain. My scientific pursuits and my medical vocation have been established. My uncharted sojourn of the nomad that I am led me to this land and I made it my home. My first marriage was to Lamya Mujahed and together we had two sons, Omar and Nabil as well as two grandson, Christopher and Noah. Later, I married an Oklahoman, Annette McMichael and my family grew to include three more children, Adam, Nazette and Zachariah. Yet for over 40 years in this blessed land I have chanted and hummed and chanted, again paraphrasing poet Al Maare with his words, "Remember, remember to tread lightly when you walk-for under your feet some day will be myself and later my ashes for the ages."

I know at times it is hard for people of other cultures to relate and understand the inner feelings of each other. But one thing I solidified in my own mind after spending time with Dr. Zuhdi is there is no dividing line between the Spirit of God.

He sees no black or white, no bond or free, no Greek or Jew, the only thing that can separate us is our individual rejection of the Spirit of God. After hearing Dr. Zuhdi describe his success as a spiritual journey of which he willingly submitted to God's leadership, the only God, I wasn't at all surprised to hear of his incredible achievements.

After attending the American University in Beirut where he received his medical degree he came to the United States in 1950 to complete his residency in New York and Minnesota. Dr. Zuhdi's studies of heart disease and heart surgery began in 1951 at Columbia University-Presbyterian Hospital Medical Center in New York City with pioneers George Humphrey, Arthur Blakemore and Arthur Voorhees.

After transferring to State University of New York-Kings County Hospital Medical Center he participated as a trainee with others, led by Professor Clarence Dennis in developing Dennis' rotating screen oxygenators. This work culminated in a successful open-heart surgery (one of five worldwide at that time) and in the first use of a heart-lung machine for support in chronic heart failure, both in 1955.

Later in 1956 Dr. Zuhdi worked at the University of Minnesota with Dr. C. Walton Lillehei, who had extensive innovative procedures in heart-lung machines and open-heart surgery. These experiences paved the way later to further designs by Dr. Zuhdi in cardiopulmonary bypass and heart-lung machines.

John Schilling, M.D., then the Chief of Surgery at the University of Oklahoma Medical School, imported Dr. Zuhdi in October of 1957 and Dr. Allen Greer was fundamental in retaining him. Greer, Carey, and Zuhdi, Inc. was formed.

Dr. Zuhdi's most notable contribution occurred late in 1959 at Mercy Hospital Research Laboratory which he had established. After eight years of periodical but persistent research, he developed the double helical reservoir heart-lung machine which simplified total body perfusion for open-heart surgery and was adopted worldwide. It served as the vehicle for his hypothermic techniques and his inventive total intentional hemodilution techniques which revolutionized total and partial cardiopulmonary bypass for clinical open-heart surgery and heart transplantation.

The next wave in the scientific endeavors of Dr. Zuhdi again at Mercy Hospital Research Laboratory was to embark on the development of an artificial heart. He favored the concept of a bypass artificial heart as opposed to a replacement artificial heart. If a bypass artificial heart were to be clinically used and failed, the patient possibly may survive with his own heart. In 1964 he finally inserted the most suitable prototype built by Dow Corning as per Dr. Zuhdi's design, in the chest of a dog as a total left bypass artificial heart and to his delight the dog survived with normal behavior for 96 hours. However, Dr. Zuhdi did not pursue that artificial heart concept any further. Having learned through these studies with Commander Clark Ritchie mechanisms of pulse waves, ejection fractions and rates needed for the artificial heart to optimally perform, he recognized that the problem rested in the unavailability at that time, of a substance compatible with human blood for long periods of time.

Also in 1960 Dr. Zuhdi and Dr. Carey were the first surgeons in the world to have a pregnant mother and her child survive following open heart surgery. Before then either the mother or child died or the child was born disfigured.

In 1970 at the Baptist Medical Center Dr. Zuhdi was the first in the United States to use a porcine aortic valve ala Carpentier in a human. He also placed in humans such stabilized valves, both in the aortic and mitral positions for the first time in the world at Baptist Medical Center of Oklahoma in February, 1970 following the tedious experimental work at the Hancock Laboratories in Anaheim, California.

At the Baptist Medical Center of Oklahoma he performed the first heart-transplant in Oklahoma in March 1985. He performed the first piggy-back heart transplant in Oklahoma in May of 1985 (an additional heart added to the existing heart). He performed the first heart-lung transplant in Oklahoma in June 1987. He performed the first single-lung transplant in Oklahoma in 1990, and the first double-lung transplant in Oklahoma in 1994. He performed the first left ventricle assist device in Oklahoma in 1987. He engineered the Oklahoma Transplantation Institute that he founded in 1984 into the only comprehensive solid-organ transplant facility in Oklahoma. This facility was renamed at Integris Health as Nazih Zuhdi Transplantation Institute in 1999. Previously, he co-founded and became the first chairman of the Oklahoma Cardiovascular Institute and the Oklahoma Heart Center.

Dr. Zudhi is included in Dwight Harken's Founders Group of Heart Surgery. He is also included in the Milestones of Cardiology of the American College of Cardiology. He was inducted into the Oklahoma Hall of Fame in 1994 and is one of 59 Oklahomans etched in the monoliths of the Oklahoma Heritage Gardens at the Fairgrounds in Oklahoma City. To top it off Dr. Zudhi was one of four featured physicians in the Historical Millennium Edition of the Sunday Oklahoman published in late 2000.

As we were finishing our interview Dr. Zuhdi called a young lady into his office and introduced her. She was Amber, the niece of the child Ginger, mentioned earlier who was the first to survive open heart surgery along with her pregnant mother. Dr. Zuhdi said she has been given an irrevocable position at the hospital for as long as she would like.

316

Victoria Lee

Conclusion

What a wonderful opportunity it has been to interview and research the lives of 200 very unique individuals. It was a continual learning process in which I came to further understand the meaning of success and how it comes about in a person's life. Each individual had a different journey with a path laid out specifically for them. Some took detours along the way while others stayed right on course. Yet, ultimately because of their unquenchable tenacity they all made it through the maze of lifes experiences to find their true identity.

I certainly feel honored to have had the privilege of working on this project. It too has become part of my own destiny. Not only will this book honor those who have been chosen to be included, but the wealth of encouragement and obvious tips of wisdom will help others to create their own success in this life.

As they say, success begets success and the quickest way to success is by learning from others. Trying to re-invent the wheel isn't necessary, only improving it's moving parts.

I hope each reader who may still be seeking success will take with them a huge doze of encouragement knowing that they too can be successful. For those who have already created success I pray that you will take the time to freely pass on to others the wisdom of your experiences.

Blessings,

Victoria Lee

Editor, Christy Wheeland lives in Haskell, Oklahoma along with her husband Bob and daughter Victoria. With a degree in Public Relations from Oklahoma State University, Christy is an asset to the community with her bubbly personality and her warmth toward others.